Urban Women in Contemporary India

A Reader

Edited by

Rehana Ghadially

SAGE Publications
Los Angeles ▪ London ▪ New Delhi ▪ Singapore

First published in 2007 by

Sage Publications India Pvt Ltd
B1/I1, Mohan Cooperative Industrial Area
Mathura Road
New Delhi 110 044
www.sagepub.in

Sage Publications Inc
2455 Teller Road
Thousand Oaks, California 91320

Sage Publications Ltd
1 Oliver's Yard, 55 City Road
London EC1Y 1SP

Sage Publications Asia-Pacific Pte Ltd
33 Pekin Street
#02-01 Far East Square
Singapore 048763

Published by Vivek Mehra for Sage Publications India Pvt Ltd, phototypeset in 10/12 pt Aldine401 BT by Star Compugraphics Private Limited, Delhi, and printed at Chaman Enterprises, New Delhi.

Library of Congress Cataloging-in-Publication Data

Urban women in contemporary India : a reader / edited by Rehana Ghadially.
    p.   cm.
  Includes bibliographical references and Index.
  1. Urban women—India—Social conditions. 2. Women's rights—India. 3. Feminism—India. I. Ghadially, Rehana, 1945–

HQ1742.U73	305.420954'091732—dc22	2007	2007001006

ISBN: 978-0-7619-3520-9 (PB)   978-81-7829-675-3 (India-PB)

Sage Production Team: Anamika Mukherjee, Shweta Vachani and Mathew P.J.

*Dedicated to my nieces, Khadija, Mahera, Lamiya and all
girl children in India.*

Contents

List of Tables

As I write this preface, I am stunned by the fact that the women's movement in India has not moved much; and yet I know that many women, including myself, have come a long way. When I was working on my first edited volume, custodial rape (besides dowry deaths) was at the fore of women's consciousness, and as I write this, the newspaper headlines report the rape of minor girls by police in Mumbai city. Violence against women, not to mention the other concerns that diminish women's lives, remains large. Despite the effort of academics, researchers, activists, and private and public organisations, India has yet to shine for its women. Editing this volume is part of the effort to make this happen.

I spent the best part of the late 1970s and 1980s teaching women's studies to undergraduate male engineering students. The experience of teaching, the search for teaching material, the response of the students to the course; the protest marches, meetings and other gatherings I attended; the reading of Simone de Beauvoir's *The Second Sex*, Betty Friedan's *The Feminine Mystique* and poems of Kamala Das—these were the inspirational sources for the first edited volume, titled *Women in Indian Society: A Reader*, published in 1988. At the time of its publication a friend and colleague of mine, Dr U. Kalpagam, mentioned that no work had been done on the women of my community, and that perhaps it was time to move in that direction. I set about doing research on the women of the Ismaili sect of South Asian Muslims known as the Bohras. I spent a little over a decade on this topic, and published more than a dozen articles in national and international journals. At about this time, representatives from Sage Publications, New Delhi, approached me with the request to prepare and edit a second reader. When I set myself to it, I knew I was working under an entirely different set of circumstances, both at the professional and societal levels. First, I was no longer teaching a gender studies course to undergraduate male engineering students. Second, at the time of editing the first reader there was a shortage of published research, but the second time around there was more to choose from. Third, unlike in the case of the first reader, I did not have to physically do the exhausting rounds of libraries in search of material—access to the Internet put me on the information highway this time. Fourth, I was no longer working with paper and pen—I had graduated, thanks to my Institute, to working on a computer. Finally, unlike earlier, this time around the Indian Institute of Technology, Mumbai, where I work, was more than willing to support the book project. While the conditions of my professional life had changed for the better, the social reality outside seemed to have become more complex, unmanageable, uncertain, dynamic—and these were the circumstances in which the Reader had to be placed. The major engines of change in India are dealt with in the Introduction; of which, neo-liberal globalisation is the underlying phenomenon, for the fluidity.

Given the changed circumstances, the two Readers differ—in coverage, content and authors. The earlier Reader had five sections (Context, Stereotypes, Violence, Media and Awareness), while this has six themes or sections (Re-constructing Gender, Media, Violence, Neo-Liberal Globalisation, Information and Communication Technologies, Politics and Political Participation). Media and violence against women figure in both volumes, highlighting the critical nature of these areas for Indian women. The section on Stereotypes, which highlighted stereotyped notions of roles and personality traits, attitudes towards women's roles—including the dimensions of the modern and traditional, which invariably accompanied them—appears in a new avatar in this Reader as Re-constructing Gender. The Context section in the earlier Reader had emphasised the impact of religion, tradition and myths in shaping gender; in this Reader, Neo-Liberal Globalisation zeroes in on the diversity of influences, besides tradition and religion, on gender and gender relations. The section on Awareness, which figured in the earlier Reader, finds no place in the present one. At the time many urban, educated, middle-class women were fired by the ideas generated and involved in the movement, and one of the goals of the movement was to see that these ideas reached the grassroots level. These ideas have indeed percolated far beyond the privileged few with their knowledge of the English language. The emphasis is now on action and solution. This Reader includes two new themes worthy of interest to students and scholars, namely Information and Communication Technologies, and Politics and Political Participation, both aimed at making women complete citizens at the national level as well as enabling them to take their proper place as global citizens.

Besides coverage and content, the new Reader also reflects greater diversity among the contributors. The earlier Reader had 12 Indian authors living in India, eight Indian authors living in the United States, and three North American scholars. This reader has 12 Indian authors (two of whom are organisations), seven Indian scholars living in the West (US, Canada, UK), and nine western scholars (US, UK and Germany). While the contribution of Indian scholars here or abroad is almost the same, there is an increase in the number of western authors, whether writing alone or collaborating with Indians. The diversity of the contributors' origins reflects a somewhat wider spectrum of western scholars with an interest in Indian women's concerns, and also echoes the opening up of the Indian economy, making it easier for westerners to work here. It also brings forward new perspectives and insights and provides new solutions thinking about and looking at Indian women's issues. In the first volume, 69.57 per cent of contributors were women, whereas 89.29 per cent have contributed to the present one. Despite the entry of men, Women's Studies rightly remains women's forte.

When the policies to integrate India into the global market were put in place, women activists rallied against globalisation and a market-driven economy, seeing in it the threat of an increased feminisation of poverty and commodification of women. With the passage of time and the perception of the inevitability of these phenomena, the thrust has shifted to dealing with the impacts of globalisation and a market-driven economy on women and society. Keeping this background in mind, the themes represented in this anthology have a contemporary and universal appeal, and seek to highlight the positions that women are placed in their struggle for gender equality, the issues they face, the challenges before them, and strategies that are needed to meet them.

Given the rich diversity of Indian women (rural, poor, minority women, etc.), it would be false to claim that the anthology addresses the concerns of all women. The selection of articles in this Reader tilt towards the urban, middle-class, educated women. Poor and rural women have been the centre of focus of development experts and international and national governmental organisations. Besides, unlike China, which opened its agricultural sector to economic reforms much earlier (in 1978), India's agricultural sectors still remains highly regulated. Its gradual opening is inevitable, and the full impact of market forces on this sector will materialise in time. It is urban India that has taken the initial benefit and brunt of globalisation, and hence the focus on these women. Minority women have not received their due attention from scholars. To counter this trend of homogenisation, some have taken up the task of making the experiences of marginalised women visible. The recent attempt at historical research on Muslim women in colonial India and the need to profile their socio-economic status, and not just their Personal Law, can be interpreted as an effort to counter the overwhelming visibility of Hindu women and the invisibility of other minority women in India. The question of diversity is also being addressed through regional studies on women, which take into account local history and culture. To the extent that such an inclusion is now visible, a wider understanding of women's condition is possible. These can be topics of anthologies in their own right. Lastly, the anthology also reflects the perspectives of different disciplines and the varied methodological approaches of the authors.

All the actors involved in the improvement of women's lives in India have covered a tremendous amount of ground, and it is difficult to do justice in one volume to all their concerns, strategies, achievements and setbacks. Law, education, employment and health issues all deserve their place in this volume; however, practical considerations make this task a difficult one. Also, this volume keeps in mind the old and new concerns in the women's movement and the academic arena, and tries to do justice to both. Each section here contains three to four articles, and is preceded by an introduction.

The ideas and desire to write and edit a book become a reality due to people around you. I wish to thank Mr Kunjukunju for assisting me in the computer work. I am grateful to Ms Farida Umrani and Ms Shubha Ranganathan for editorial assistance, and wish to express my appreciation to the Indian Institute of Technology (Curriculum Development Programme), Mumbai, for the financial support received to complete the manuscript.

Introduction

Rehana Ghadially

For the purpose of this introduction I have divided the period of the women's movement in India into two time slots—from 1975 to 1989, and from 1990 to the turn of the new millennium. The late 1980s and early 1990s characterised a disjunction in India's economic policies, which was dictated by international funding agencies and followed by neo-liberal globalisation. These factors changed the very parameters under which women and nations functioned, and this is what the introduction focuses primarily on. The chapter begins with a brief review of the happenings in the women's movement in the 1970s and the 1980s, and follows with a more detailed exposition of events since the 1990s.

It has been three decades since the United Nations' (UN) Declaration of 8 March as International Women's Day and the subsequent period as the International Women's Decade. This day is celebrated in India and the world over with talks and seminars, and is an occasion to both assess the year's progress and make projections for the coming year. The class-oriented grassroots movements of the 1960s and 1970s and the UN Declaration's directive to assess the status of women in different countries spurred the Indian state to appoint a Committee on the Status of Women in India. The publication of the Committee's report (1974), 'Towards Equality: The Status of Women in India', was a catalytic force, setting in motion the women's movement which reverberates even today. The disenchantment with the findings in the report despite constitutional guarantees was a wake-up call for many urban, educated, middle-class women to take stock of the conditions of women's lives since the closure of women's activism soon after independence. The outcome was the mushrooming of autonomous women's groups across the country. By 1985, it was estimated that there were as many as 55 autonomous women's groups all over the country.

The immediate issue to seize the imagination of these politically non-aligned groups was violence against women. Dowry deaths, custodial rape, female foeticide, eve teasing, and the *devdasi* system were signalled out for attention. The other issues that were addressed included demographics and population figures: lop-sided sex ratios, women's reproductive health, high infant and maternal mortality rates, sterilisation abuse, and the imposition of untested contraceptives such as Depo Provera on unsuspecting women. In 1988, women's groups spoke out against the inadequate health services for women, and the ensuing problems such as death and complications during pregnancy, abortion, childbirth and family planning operations.

Another issue of interest was that of giving women a fair deal at work, which emphasised improving working conditions, providing crèches, giving equal pay for equal work, and strengthening the bargaining power of women in the informal sector. Feminist economists pointed to the need for making women's work visible and including women's unpaid work at home in the nation's Gross Domestic Product (GDP) considerations. Further, an assortment of social problems addressed included media portrayals of women, socialisation and gender stereotyping, women's rights in the family, women's political participation, and scrutinising personal (family), criminal and labour laws for gender bias.

To achieve their ends, women activists adopted a variety of strategies and methods. These included holding rallies, protest marches, *dharnas*, street plays, *yatras*, seminars, conferences, exhibitions, training workshops, media coverage, public campaigns, agitations, demonstrations, etc. The main purpose behind their efforts was to increase awareness and raise consciousness, organise women and help the victims of patriarchy. Their aim also included bringing about concrete changes in the condition of women in the family and society. At a theoretical level, women were interested in examining the roots of their oppression; they not only questioned cultural norms and traditions, but also went beyond them to trace their subordination in structural patterns of patriarchy.

A demand for the passage of new laws and amendments to the old ones was perceived as a centrepiece to ameliorate the subordinate condition of women. Laws pertaining to violence against women rightly received the first share of attention. In 1983 Section 498-A was introduced in the Indian Penal Code (IPC), which stated that cruelty to one's wife is a cognisable, non-bailable offence punishable by up to three years of imprisonment and a fine. Cruelty was redefined as both mental and physical. In addition, post-mortem examination was made compulsory on the body of a woman who died within seven years of marriage. The Central government also ordered compulsory investigation and post-mortem in cases of married women who died under unnatural circumstances during the first five years of marriage. It became mandatory for the police to register unnatural deaths of married women as murder. Though Section 498-A was brought in to curb dowry and related deaths, women use it to deal with domestic violence in general. The New Rape Bill, 1983, made amendments to the rape law as incorporated in the Indian Penal Code (IPC) of 1860. The definition of rape was expanded and custodial rape was given the attention it deserved. Under Section 376 of the Indian Penal Code, two types of punishment were chalked out for rapists. The minimum punishment for a rapist is seven years rigorous imprisonment, which may go up to 10 years or life in case of custodial rape, gang rape and rape of a minor. Forced sexual intercourse with a separated wife was punishable by up to two years. This period also saw the drafting of new bills, particularly the Women's Reservation Bill. In the short run, laws did seem to create some heightening of consciousness among the police force, the courts, the lawmakers and the general public. However, in the long run, these laws have fallen short of meeting the expectations of women's groups.

Besides amendments to existing laws, women were able to see the fruits of their labour in concrete terms. In the 1980s, family courts were set up for speedy justice in matters of divorce, maintenance, child custody, etc. In the early 1980s women's cells were opened at police stations in Mumbai, followed by the rest of Maharashtra and Rajasthan. Here the police and social workers collaborated to help women in distress through counselling, legal aid, action, etc. Apart from women's cells, women's groups set up similar centres for victims of domestic violence. Women brought pressure on the state to create a department for women's affairs, change the definition of work to include many aspects of women's work hitherto considered invisible, and sought participation to influence development policies and Five-Year Plans.

An important gain of the period was the clearing of the 33 per cent reservation for women in *Panchayati Raj* and local bodies. Sustained media coverage of women's problems and issues generated the much-needed public awareness. Many NGOs working for the poor and other marginalised groups were sensitised to women's issues, which helped bring girls and women to the centre of their efforts.

This period also marked the beginning of the feminist journal *Manushi,* and saw the beginnings of networking among autonomous women's groups and activists to build solidarity, share information, seek insights and strengthen their resolve to better women's lives. They forged alliances with other social justice movements without submerging women's concerns. The women's movement also went beyond the issue of gender-class dichotomy to more philosophical ones like identity, the construction of knowledge, and sexuality.

Although the autonomous women's groups focused exclusively on women's concerns, there were other players interested in women's issues. These included international agencies (UN, UNDP, UNIFEM, etc.), the State and its representatives like the police, the judiciary and women's wings of political parties, and, particularly, the grassroots non-governmental organisations (NGOs). In the 1980s indigenous NGOs, with their thrust on development from below and eradication of poverty, had on their rolls some women who had been active in the women's movements and/or left movements. They played a role in bringing the girl child and women to the centre of these groups' focus. Kamat (2003) writes that the agenda of the NGOs was development with social justice, and that they aimed at promoting livelihood and health along with consciousness raising campaigns, the structural analysis of power and inequality, and the demand for political rights. The role of the NGOs was also to bring the variety of development programmes and schemes floated by the government to the notice of the poor and the disenfranchised.

In the late 1970s, activism found its cognitive component in the establishment of Women's Studies Centres in the university system, under the aegis of the University Grants Commission. The establishment of the Research Centre for Women's Studies at the SNDT Women's University in Mumbai marked a beginning, with teaching, research, documentation, extension work, training programmes and seminars being their forte. Unlike women activists who dealt with women as victims, the academic had the opportunity to educate the young and thereby prevent victimisation. The institutionalisation of feminism was pursued with the hope of reaching out to the youth of the nation. The beginning of the first Women's Studies Centre led to the establishment of the Indian Association of Women's Studies (IAWS), and its first conference was held in Mumbai in 1981 at the SNDT Women's University. There have been many conferences since then, with the last and 11th one being in Goa in 2005. The newsletter published by IAWS goes a long way in keeping the momentum, sustaining solidarity, informing and updating on recent research, events and happenings. The decade of the 1980s also marked the launching of the first academic periodical devoted exclusively to gender issues, the *Indian Journal of Gender Studies*.

The activities of all these groups and institutions made a permanent mark on the conscience of the country. They made visible the oppression women faced at all levels of their lives—those of the family, community and society. The reaction to women's presence in the public sphere moved from tolerance to acceptance, provided it did not seriously interfere with women's domestic and childcare roles. Women activists succeeded in breaking the silence surrounding private issues such as wife battering and birth control. Women's education and occupation, rather than their bodies, were emerging as markers of their social identity. There was also the confidence accompanying the belief that there is nothing inevitable about women being in second place. They could become leaders in their households, communities, and even in public places.

The long struggle for social transformation was not without its difficulties and setbacks. The main obstacles were lack of financial resources, lack of experience in dealing with enormous issues, the negative labelling of feminists, patriarchal resistance (hostility, apathy) at every level, as manifested in the mindsets of the police force, the judges, the politicians, the men in the families, as well as resistance from women victims themselves. There was also the gradual realisation that laws may be less than effective in mitigating women's distress. The social base of the women's movement remained narrow partly due to the failure to recognise the tremendous diversity among Indian women.

In short, the contemporary women's movement grew out of a diverse conditions, a diverse set of actors, and addressed a broad range of issues using a variety of methods and strategies to achieve awareness building, improvement of women's condition and gender equality. In this struggle they have chalked up several achievements and had to contend with many setbacks. Little did many of them realise that they would be confronted with forces way beyond their control, which would dramatically change the conditions of their struggle.

The late 1980s and 1990s have been a time of reflection on the work of the previous decades—the changes introduced, their impact on women's lives, the resources (time, money, effort, skills) invested, and the hard won gains. More significantly, it has been a time of facing new challenges, seizing new opportunities and dealing with persisting problems. The new challenges—adoption of the structural adjustment package (SAP), neo-liberal globalisation, introduction of information and communication technologies (ICTs), and majoritarian fundamentalism—colluding headlong with patriarchy, have compounded women's problems manifold. While these have radically altered the conditions under which women live, there is little systematic research available on the impact of these on women's lives. I now turn to a discussion of the role of these factors in affecting women, and touch on some of the issues that persist from the earlier two decades. This is followed by an overview of some gains that have been registered, and those lost by the women's movement. Some unfinished business and neglected issues are touched upon, followed by a look at the fresh challenges ahead of us, and concluding remarks.

Four Transforming Events

On 6 December 1991, the Finance Minister announced the terms aimed at the structural adjustment of the Indian economy, stipulated by the International Monetary Fund stand-by credit of $2.2 billion. Among other measures, the package included export promotion, government spending cuts, privatisation, un-restricted imports and currency devaluation. The impact of SAP on both urban and rural women has been sparsely documented. In urban areas the most visible result has been the establishment of export processing zones (EPZs), and women's involvement in labour-intensive manufacturing of electronics, textiles, footwear, etc., in these zones. A United Nations Conference of Trade and Development (UNCTAD) study, using International Labour Organisation (ILO) data, estimates that by 2003, there were more than 37 million workers employed in these zones, with the share of women workers ranging from 50 to 90 per cent. Since the export activity is not restricted to EPZs, the actual number may be even higher. The market-oriented demand for labour (especially unskilled and semi-skilled) in which women are engaged makes the nature of work temporary, forcing many into the informal sector. As demonstrated in East Asia in the 1990s, women are able to secure employment only during rapid expansions, employment that is usually transitory, insecure and performed under harsh conditions. In rural areas the shift from subsistence to cash crops for export has displaced rural women from their traditional farming lands, and many work as wage labourers on these estates, often for wages half those of men. Another hallmark of the SAP has been government cutbacks in health, education and food subsidies, which have affected the urban and rural poor (PIRG 1994). Cuts in health care means that women are expected to carry the additional burden of providing these services. According to the 2001 Census, male literacy (75.85 per cent) is higher than female (54.16 per cent), and hence education cutbacks means girls are more affected. The cut in food subsidies means that the prices of basic food commodities soar, and women are left with balancing the family budget.

SAP brought in concerns about the feminisation of poverty, and globalisation threatens to make the gap between the haves and the have-nots even wider. The ongoing phase of globalisation was speeded up in 1991 as the Indian economy opened up to the world market. Like SAP, the impact of economic and cultural globalisation on women has not been subjected to systematic study. However, certain trends are quite clear. The rounds of the National Sample Survey (NSS) done in the mid-1990s point to growing disparities despite the high economic growth. Since the majority of women are in the informal sector, they are excluded from the new economic drive. The tragic face of this inequality and the growing feminisation of poverty manifests itself in sex tourism, the transnational migration of women who are concentrated in service sectors such as domestic work, entertainment and the sex industries, trafficking, and as mail-order brides. The globalisation of women's labour, as manifested in the flesh trade and trafficking in women, is now a worldwide problem. For women working in their home country, foreign direct investment jeopardises their future as women in the service sector are faced with the prospect of unemployment once foreign investors leave the country. Globalisation has generated opportunities for local producers and entrepreneurs to reach international markets, but by and large the gains of globalisation are concentrated in the hands of those women who are urban, educated, fluent in English and have access to capital. Poor women are usually unable to seize the long-term opportunities offered by this turn of events.

With the acceleration of economic globalisation, cultural globalisation, especially that marked by the new media, also entered India. Between 1990 and 1999 access to television grew from 10 to 75 per cent for the urban population. The number of television channels grew from one state-run channel reaching 300,000 homes in 1991 to more than 70 cable channels reaching 24 million homes in 1999. With the easing of foreign exchange restrictions, Hollywood captured 10 per cent of the feature film market (Derné 2005). Indian commentators were apprehensive that the new media would transform the cultural scenario, especially family and gender arrangements. Although the impact of the new media is yet to be addressed systematically, a study done on young non-elite Indian men provides some insights. Derné (ibid.) found that middle-class male youth with little or no English language skills and no global connections interpret new media messages in the contexts of the institutional realities they live in. Given their limited financial autonomy and family institutions in which most marriages are arranged, young men, while thrilled at the prospect of romance, distance themselves from new media celebrations of love matches. In contrast, these men are attracted to new media celebrations of male dominance as manifested in the intensification of the cultural objectification of women and the culture of male violence. He concludes that changes resulting from globalisation are more likely to follow from changed structural realities than from the introduction of new cultural meanings. On the other hand, Ganguly-Scrase (2003) studied the impact of liberalisation and globalisation on lower middle-class families in Bengal, and found that while this class is cognisant of the fact that they are unable to accrue the benefits of the consumer lifestyles of the middle class, some young women feel empowered in terms of greater opportunities and freedoms as reflected in the emerging diversity of role models shown on television. These images do not radically subvert gender relations, but provide a degree of assertiveness and agency that young women find attractive.

The verdict, as to whether women are the losers or net gainers of economic and cultural globalisation, is far from clear. It has brought benefits for a section of women, but by and large has intensified existing inequalities and insecurities for many poor women who represent two thirds of the world's poorest people. Frances Raddy of Israel, moderator of the plenary session on 'Globalization: Economic Values and Poverty' at the Women's Worlds Conference 2005 in Seoul, South Korea, stated that ideally globalisation should signal the world coming together with the ultimate purpose of creating a win-win situation for all. However, the world is still far from its ideal and globalisation processes continue to marginalise certain groups, women being one such group. It has created economic and social divisions among women, making it difficult to sustain women's solidarity (Lim 2005).

As mentioned earlier, SAP and neo-liberal globalisation signalled a decreased state expenditure in the social service sector. This has led to an increase in the number of NGOs, which have taken over the role of the State in providing adequate assistance for social welfare. My own reading has come up with as many as 34 priorities of international donor organisations, ranging from drug abuse to road traffic management. Kamat (2003) states that the neo-liberal policies have resulted in the blunting of the radical content of the NGOs and caused the trend towards their professionalisation and de-politicisation. In other words, instead of consciousness raising of structural obstacles to their condition and organising the marginal groups for what is rightfully theirs, the shift has been to focus on individual capacity building to empower them politically and economically and incorporate women's interests within current developmental practices. The popularity of the micro-credit programme must be seen in the context of this new ideology. What are by-passed are issues of access and control over productive resources such as time, money, networks and technologies, which are much stronger bases of women's empowerment. Some experts argue that this kind of push increases women's income but does not lead to human rights.

The tools held most responsible for speeding up globalisation are the new ICTs. While some experts have argued that ICTs are crucial for speeding up development, for most others the buzzword of the information society is the digital divide. Among the various divides, the one most relevant for feminists is the gender divide, which also includes many other divides (rural/urban; class, religious, ethnic). However, while everyone speaks of the gender divide, hard gender-based data is practically non-existent.

In a comprehensive report titled 'Gender, Information Technology and Developing Countries: An Analytic Study', Nancy Hafkin and Nancy Taggart (2001) discuss a variety of problems and prospects. The issues of concern where the divide is manifested covers questions of access, training, use, production and design of technologies. The second concern is the impact of new technologies on women's work, and third, the possibilities these offer for new economic opportunities. The most common barriers to access, training and use are literacy and education, English language facility, cost, time, geographical location, socio-cultural norms and technical skills. The impact of ICTs on women's work focuses on the gendered division of labour, the feminisation of IT occupations, and enhancing women's ongoing economic activities. ICTs' potential for affecting women's ongoing economic activities and political empowerment has been recognised, but it is still more in the realm of rhetoric than reality. The Hafkin and Taggart report mentions the uses of ICTs in women's farming, trade and entrepreneurship activities. Women farmers could increase productivity by using information on improved technologies, agricultural inputs, weather and markets. Traders and other entrepreneurs can find marketing information and disseminate information about their business, for example, women's handicrafts can find niche markets. IT-enabled communication businesses offer promise for women entrepreneurs following the model of *Grameen* mobile phones in Bangladesh. The new technologies have the potential for networking, social and political advocacy, and strengthening women's participation in the political process. It is particularly relevant in increasing the transparency and accountability of the government. These new technologies have the potential for making a difference in women's lives, provided ICT policies are gender-sensitive. Making access to technology and its products affordable is an important starting point. Improving infrastructure and subsidised training can go a long way in taking advantage of the opportunities opened by these technologies. However, while ICTs hold promise for women, they have brought in their wake the possibility of misuse as exemplified by cyber porn, cell baseness and, more recently, the Short Message Service (SMS) divorce.

Women's organisations working to promote ICTs in the women's movement as tactical tools for social transformation focus on two ideas, namely bridging the digital divide and use of these technologies by feminists. The use of ICTs to address feminist issues was first recognised when women from the preparatory phase of the World Women's Conference in Beijing used the tools for networking and political advocacy across national boundaries. More recently, in India, the interventionist role of ICTs to generate and record complaints against members of the medical community indulging in selective sex determination tests and selective abortion of female foetuses is underway under the 'Save the Girl Child Campaign' (Jain 2005).

There is a divergence of opinion on whether the women's movement is doing its two-bit to lessen the divide and use ICTs to address feminist issues. Heike Jensen has this to say:

> Paradoxically and dangerously at the same time that many feminists and women's movements throughout the world have de-prioritized media and ICT issues, the global influence of the new digital and networked

media on all aspects of life, from the economy to politics to culture to the creation of knowledge, has reached unprecedented proportions.

Lin McDevitt-Pugh has a different view

Increasingly more organizations and individuals are addressing the interconnection between ICTs and feminist issues. The size of the group must expand if we are to effect the necessary changes. Importantly, the level of participation by women must come from the North must increase, for the simple reason that the North dominates the development of policy. It is a matter of solidarity and a matter of capacity. (IIAV International News 2005: 5)

In response to the growing globalisation and presumed or real historical wrongs, Hindu or majoritarian fundamentalism took firm root with the demolition of the Babri Masjid in 1992 and the setting up of the right-wing Hindu nationalist *Bharatiya Janata Party* (BJP)-led coalition in Delhi in 1999. The construction of the 'new' Indian woman by the right-wing groups, women's participation in these groups, and backing by the BJP has been a source of concern to Indian feminists. The agenda of right-wing groups to create a Hindu nation has diverted attention once again to women as repositories of culture and tradition. Tradition is a mixed bag of messages, and in the construction of the Hindu woman's identity and role these groups draw on aggressive female figures from Hindu myths and religion, while simultaneously co-opting the modern language of the women's movement. The construction of the new Hindu woman as strong and assertive, educated and employed, has created an aura of empowerment, which matches in many ways the vision of the Indian feminists. Where they part, however, is the end purpose of this agency. Unlike Indian feminists, for right-wing groups women's empowerment is not for their own betterment, but in the service of a communal project to defend Hindu faith and the Hindu nation. Their participation in violence against Muslims and their support of their men in the gang rapes of Muslim women has shaken the very foundation of women's solidarity and the principles of democracy, secularism and equality from which the women's movement draws its strength.

This communal project has served a variety of functions. Its focus is on divisions rather than on respect and tolerance for diversity, the hallmarks of the women's movement. Second, it prioritised Hindu identity over Indian identity, which deepened the anxieties of minorities, a fear that makes it difficult for Muslim women to challenge the gender inequality enshrined in the Muslim Personal Law. Given the communally charged climate, they are compelled to sideline their own issues in the interests of their community. Third, the call for a Uniform Civil Code (UCC) (an opportunity to impose Hindu identity, according to some) by Hindu right-wing groups has also forced Indian feminists to put this issue on the back burner. Lastly, the use of religion to pursue political ends has taken away from women their spirituality, a resource many women depend on in their hour of difficulty.

Old Issues and Gains: A New Garb

As though facing the new challenges posed by India's integration into the world market is not enough, women are also still grappling with old issues and are faced with the spectre of losing some gains made in the previous decades. I turn to some of these now.

Violence against women—dowry harassment, domestic violence, rape, eve-teasing, declining sex ratios, female foeticide—continues to haunt feminists and make demands on their energies. It is particularly disconcerting to many feminists to discover that dowry harassment and female foeticide occur in the elite strata of society and in economically advanced states like Punjab and Haryana, when many had nourished the hope that economic progress would mitigate some of the social ills. In dealing with violence in the earlier decades of the women's movement, three issues had come forth. One was the burnout of activists as a result of the insurmountable problems involved in helping victims of violence. Another was the low rate of convictions across the board (rape, dowry, sex selection) under the revised laws. Third, though minor, the misuse of some of the laws by women is another cause of concern among activists; women have misused Section 498-A of the IPC to get back at their husbands and in-laws, and despite stringent provisions enlisted in the Pre-conception and Pre-natal Diagnostic Techniques (PPNDT) Prohibition of Sex Selection Act, 1994, implicit methods to convey the sex of the child has made a mockery of the Act.

The new forms of violence that need attention are acid throwing, honour killings, sexual harassment at the workplace, stalking, national and transnational trafficking in women, adult films on television, indecent portrayal of women in the new media, and sex tourism from the West, to mention just a few. Cyber porn and cell-phone misuse are other emerging problems. Despite the knowledge that legal empowerment is of limited value, the need for amendments and new laws to tackle violence against women persists among women's groups. In January 1992, the National Commission for Women (NCW) was set up as a statutory body to review the constitutional and legal safeguards for women, recommend remedial legislative measures, facilitate the redressal of grievances and advise the government on all policy matters affecting women. This Commission has been pivotal in drafting Bills on behalf of women.

The draft of the Domestic Violence Against Women (Prevention) Bill 1999 prepared by the Women's Rights Initiative expands the definition of domestic violence. It attempts to institutionalise the mechanisms of help for the victims, and vests power in the very institutions that have been gender insensitive in the past. Women's groups have critiqued the Bill on several counts. The Bill provides for in-camera proceedings, but women's groups with experience in cases of rape argue that these block the entry of people supporting the concerned woman when she is testifying. The Bill makes provision for a third party to impose cases on a woman's husband or partner. It has been the experience of women's groups that legislation of this kind is often misused to target men from Dalit and minority groups (Pappu 2000). The Protection of Women from Domestic Violence Bill, 2005, was introduced in the Lok Sabha in August 2005, and seeks to go beyond Section 498-A of IPC. It extends legal protection to not just the wives of abusers, but also to sisters, widows, mothers, etc. Most importantly, it safeguards the rights of women to secure housing in their matrimonial homes, regardless of whether they have any title to such houses. The measure also empowers a magistrate to pass protection orders in favour of the aggrieved person.

In 1997 the Supreme Court laid down guidelines to deal with sexual harassment at the workplace. The response from institutions and organisations to this directive was, at best, lukewarm. In April 2003 the government directed the NCW to prepare a draft Bill. The Protection Against Sexual Harassment of Women Bill was submitted to the Ministry of Human Resources Development in September 2004. The draft Bill aims to protect women in all sectors. The NCW recommended that a local complaints committee at the district level should be expected to take care of rural workers and workers in the informal sector of the economy. However, women's groups have felt that women in the informal sector of work may not be adequately protected. Besides, they state that the Bill is incomplete as third parties or service users in the case of hospitals, restaurants, banks, etc., are neglected in the draft Bill. Also overlooked is sexual harassment in custodial situations such as police stations and mental hospitals. To some extent the draft Bill does streamline the process of inquiry and suggests guidelines to make these as fair and painless as possible. Another plus point of the Bill is that it directs the employer to ensure that the complainant, supporter or witness to sexual harassment is not victimised in and at the end of the proceedings. However, clear-cut guidelines on the conduct of the inquiry are needed (Tejani 2004).

The need to safeguard women against violence will continue to dog women. The question is, what else is needed besides laws? The State of the World Population 2005 Report of the United Nations Population Fund (UNFPA) has indicated the need for investing in women's education, health care, equal rights in marriage and family, and labour laws to empower women and reduce the incidence of gender violence. Given the economic growth of 8 per cent in 2004, this should not pose a problem for the government.

As globalisation has drastically altered the conditions in developing countries under which the struggle for gender equality must be carried out, four concepts besides legislation and the use of ICTs have become popular in the post-liberal period—gender mainstreaming, gender budgeting, empowerment and human rights. In 1984, the UN General Assembly instructed the newly-established fund within the United Nations Development Program (UNDP), the United Nations Development Fund for Women (UNIFEM), to ensure women's involvement in mainstream activities. The Platform of Action resulting from the 1995 Beijing World Conference on Women expanded this concept and called it gender mainstreaming, that is, the mandatory application of gender perspectives to all legal and social norms and standards, policies of development, research, planning, advocacy, implementation and monitoring. In this way, the gender factor is no longer to be only a supplement to development, but will be central to it (Sadler 2004). In 2000, the follow-up Beijing +5 Conference further expanded the application of the mainstreaming concept in providing gender equality worldwide.

Another important mechanism by which to arrive at gender equality has been the concept of gender budgeting, that is, focusing attention in the process of budget formulation on whether a particular fiscal measure will increase or decrease gender equality or leave it unchanged (Elson 2003). Gender Budget Initiatives (GBIs) not only identify target expenditures or allocate more money to women, but also aim to break down and identify the differentiated impact and incidence of general public revenue and expenditure on women and men ... (and) significantly contribute to overall objectives like equity, equality, efficiency, transparency, the realisation of social, economic and cultural rights, and good governance (Bridge 2004), and hold policy-makers more accountable for their action (Zahidi 2005).

Kamat (2003) has argued that the post-liberal period has been characterised by a marriage of convenience between professional NGOs and international capital interests. These NGOs have popularised the neo-liberal notion of empowerment, which implies a focus on individual capacities and needs, rather than raising consciousness around structural-based injustices and organising marginalised groups for their betterment. The individual is projected as both the problem and the solution to poverty rather than as an issue of the state's policies and international trade. According to Kamat, individualising the process of empowerment to entrepreneurial capacity building to access the market reduces the concept of public welfare to an aggregate of individual gains.

The fourth perspective through which to attain gender equality is that of Human Rights. Its advocates are engaged with the protection of women's human rights and function to change conditions at both the individual and systemic (structures, policies and practices) levels under which women live.

In India, government-led initiatives include legal ones, as described above, and gender budgeting. As far as gender budgeting is concerned, in October 1996 the Planning Commission directed Central ministries/departments and the states to identify a 'woman component' in the various schemes and programmes with which they were concerned to achieve the objective of empowering women during the Ninth Plan. Apart from the Women's Component Plan, which covers only the planned expenditure of the government, the concept of gender budgeting has gathered momentum for analysing the entire budgetary process through a gender lens. In October 2000 a number of studies on gender budgeting were commissioned along the model set by the National Institute of Public Finance and Policy (NIPFP). The initiative for a gender sensitive budget analysis began in 2000 with a workshop on 'Engendering National Budgets in the South Asian Region' in Delhi, in collaboration with UNIFEM and other national and international agencies. This culminated in the presentation by the Union Minister for Finance, Dr Chidambaram, in Parliament of the budget 2005–2006, which for the first time in the history of the country included a separate chapter on gender budgeting (Nakray 2005).

Other gains include the 73rd and 74th Constitutional Amendments (1993), which guaranteed one-third reservation for women in local bodies. There are today over a million women in the panchayat bodies. Another is the passing in the Lok Sabha of the Hindu Succession (Amendment) Bill, 2005, which gives Hindu women equal rights of inheritance in ancestral property. The Bill was passed in August 2005 with a directive from the Centre to the states to follow suit. The impact of this Bill remains to be seen.

A gain of the earlier decades, fast becoming illusory, was the opening of Women's Studies Centres at various universities across the country. By the turn of the century, the UGC supported 34 centres and four cells in various universities across India. It directed that these centres be renamed as 'Women and Family Studies Centres', a move that has taken activists and women academic by surprise and put a marginal discipline in a quandary as it struggles in the face of a variety of contradictory pulls and pushes. Poonacha (2003), in a critique of the UGC directive, states that the attachment of the word family has questioned the main project of the Women's Studies programme, namely a critical inquiry into the societal structures that uphold male privileges, and has diluted its cognitive role into welfare-based activities. The personnel who (wo)man these centres also suspect that the UGC expect them to nurture values that preserve the family, by now identified by feminists as the most oppressive site for women, rather than contribute to its break-up by empowering women. Poonacha further argues that their gradual demise may be due not only to their embeddedness in patriarchal institutions, but also to the drying up of funds and lack of gender sensitive and politically-oriented womanpower. At the Women's Worlds 2005 Conference in Seoul, Korean feminists claimed that the successful institutionalisation of the Women's Studies discipline has led to the rapid spread of feminism in Korean society as a whole. With the UGC directive renaming these centres, we may be in danger of relapsing.

Unfinished Business and Neglected Issues

As women count their gains or losses, they are faced with a number of unfinished businesses. Data from the Inter-Parliamentary Union ranks India rather dismally at 134 among 183 countries in terms of percentage of women legislators (8.3 per cent) in the Parliament. The Congress-led United Progressive Alliance (UPA) government in its Common Minimum Programme had made a commitment towards women's reservation in the country's political bodies, and the Bill to make this a reality was first introduced in Parliament in 1996. Since then the debate around the purpose of one-third reservation for women in State Assemblies and Parliament continues without any concrete outcome in sight. Discussion and resistance to the Bill centres around various suggestions: quotas for Muslim and SC/ST women, rotating the reserved one-third seats by lottery before every election so that a different one-third is picked at each election; having one-third women contest in political parties rather than reservation; and lastly, the suggestion to increase the number of seats in Parliament so as to accommodate women without undermining the existing male strength. The issue of quotas to resolve issues of representation is a stormy one, and according to some opens up a Pandora's box because while quotas challenge the privileged, the few who benefit from the opening of new opportunity structures are themselves advantaged. Each suggestion has its merit and demerit and the debate and discussion goes on. Until a consensus emerges in political circles and women's groups, delay will be the order of the day. Many activists suspect that the most likely reason for its stalling is the threat it poses to male power and privileges.

Since the 1970s the feminist movement in India has been sporadically engaged in debates around personal laws to bring about a secular solution to women's problems. In 1974, in its report, the Committee on the Status of Women in India recommended the enactment of the UCC as a solution to discriminatory laws against women in the personal laws of respective communities, and ever since this has been a subject of discussion in the women's movement. Between 1975 and 1995, the heightened communal context in which personal laws, especially the Muslim Personal Law, have been discussed has made the women's groups distance themselves from the UCC. Instead, the feminists have taken diverse positions on the matter, recommending reform within the different personal laws, or reform of all laws affecting women (family, criminal and employment laws), or subjecting all personal laws to systematic scrutiny instead of just targeting the Muslim Personal Law. Gangoli (2003) writes that this impasse is partly due to the fact that since the 1950s the debate around the UCC has become frozen around individual rights, citizenship and national integration on the one hand, and minority rights and cultural diversity on the other.

As we face the manner of unfinished businesses, globalisation has forced us to look at several hitherto unaddressed and neglected issues. Here I touch on one issue, which I see as critical for the future of all women. It is estimated that almost three billion people, that is, close to half the world's population, are below the age of 25; 85 per cent of them live in developing countries. Despite the size of this group, little research and activism has been specifically directed to these emerging adults, especially the teenage girl. The issues facing the urban and rural poor girl child, such as education, nutrition, early marriage, early motherhood and health are well-known, and are being addressed by various fora. As the urban middle-class youth collides with cultural diversity in the age of globalisation, urgent attention needs to be centred around their issues: identity questions, consumption of new technologies, creation of new gender arrangements centring on issues of romance and sexuality, opening of new career opportunities with easy cash in hand, to mention a few. The attention on the adolescent and the emerging adult assumes greater significance, as there are no specific policies to empower teenage girls. Besides, even before the task of defining the new emancipated woman is completed, it has been confounded by the sweep of the global media, which, with its images and values of the West, have a strong influence on the young, and often misrepresent what the ultimate liberation for women necessitates. In an interview at the Women's Worlds Conference 2005 in Seoul, Vicky Randall, the author of *Women and Politics*, stated that old feminists have to let young feminists do things their own way. She encouraged young women to explore the realms of problem solving in gender issues. According to her, there are many ways of approaching and addressing gender issues—young women will have to create their own solutions (Park 2005).

Facing Fresh Challenges

The challenge during the earlier decades of the women's movement was to make women part of the national mainstream. While this still remains a distant goal, the new challenge is to make them global citizens, a seemingly insurmountable and unenviable task, but which nonetheless must be undertaken. In this attempt the need for investment in female education and capacity building, especially training in ICT-related skills and English language skills, will be critical. The need to explore potentials for networking across national boundaries, made possible by the new technologies, will go a long way in facilitating the globalisation of feminist activists and academic. In this respect, despite all odds, women of South Asian countries are coming together, as exemplified by the conference on Violence Against Women held in Delhi in 2004. Networking among activists and feminist academics in certain regions of Asia, such as Southeast Asia, Japan and Korea, is considerably stronger than in South Asia. Cooperation, networking, meeting and discussing shared problems such as trafficking in women across borders is an absolute must to better the condition of women and bring peace, progress and prosperity to the region.

As mentioned earlier, work in the IT software and IT-enabled services sectors is stratified with women at the low skills and men at the high skills end. Women need to brainstorm as to how to go about increasing their enrolment in science and engineering, especially the fields of information and communication technologies, to improve their standing in the value chain.

With the coming of the global media, the continued monitoring and effort to minimise its negative impact remains a formidable new challenge before Indian feminists. The new cultural input wrought by the new media equates empowerment with possession of consumer goods, having a certain (read Western) body and image, and fulfilling individual as opposed to group-based needs. While feminists are furious about such preoccupations, many middle-class women find this empowering. More research needs to be done not only on how women are portrayed, but also on how the audience receives these messages. Another challenge is to expand women's leadership. Few women are visible in leadership positions despite the lowering of barriers to such leadership positions. The question of women's leadership development, their emergence and contribution in the corporate world, business and professional fields, non-profit organisations and higher education need to be considered and discussed.

Lastly, while the existence of diversity among women is now etched on our minds, what needs to be pursued are policies, programmes and actions to empower women from marginalised ethnic and religious minorities. The Indian women's movement has experienced a slump, and workshops and seminars are needed to gather creative and optimal ideas for resurging and revitalising the activism.

Concluding Remarks

In advancing gender justice, the work of the United Nations and related agencies has converged on three closely interconnected areas: strengthening women's economic capacity, with a focus on new technologies and the new trade agenda; promoting women's leadership and political participation; and eliminating violence against women. These concerns have been very much reflected in the thinking and efforts of women activists in the Indian subcontinent in the past three decades. The overall outcome of this effort, however, is less than encouraging. What is India's ranking on women's empowerment on a measure of a global gender gap index? Among 58 nations, it gets a lowly rank of 53. Among the various indices of empowerment, it performs worst on economic participation and educational attainment, better on political participation, and moderately on economic opportunity and health and well-being (World Economic Forum 2005). According to the Human Development Report 2005, in terms of the Human Development Index (HDI), which includes measures like life expectancy, education and per capita GDP, India ranks 127 out of 177 countries with an HDI value of 0.602. In short, it figures near the bottom of the group of medium human development countries. This poor showing seems all the more disconcerting as India ranks as one of the fastest growing economies in the world. It is quite clear from this that the challenges and problems facing women activists and organisations in the globalising era are enormous. However, there are now new tools and methods available to address some of these. There is also recognition that women alone are not primarily responsible as the agents of social change; the role in making a difference rests heavily with transnational corporations, international financial institutions, and the United States.

A counterpoint to the activism has been the research output in women's studies and gender studies, which highlight the emergence of three different theoretical underpinnings of and debates on the gender question in India. One is the pull between scholars who choose to focus exclusively on the category of gender and those who emphasise the interaction of gender with class, caste, religion, etc. Second, the epistemological roots of work on gender are not based entirely on feminism, but draw on strands of broader issues of social justice. Lastly, there is considerable emphasis on the role of the state and international agencies in fostering gender equality. Research attention has focused on topics fuelled by priorities set by women's activism and has been a forte of sociologists, economists and historians. This has resulted in a variety of research approaches ranging from participant observation, interviews, questionnaires, and use of secondary reports and data. The methods can be classified under three overlapping trajectories—historical analysis, analysis of specific cases and quantitative analysis. Large-scale surveys covering several states have only recently been undertaken (Purkayastha et al. 2003). The emphasis has been quite rightly on applied research, however, this needs to be supplemented by basic research to complete the picture of women's lives.

What lies before Indian women's groups is the task of nurturing young women and men, who too often assume that all that needed to be done has been done. Second, working in a global context demands more regional and global networking and sharing to come up with a common set of ideas and strategies. Lastly, a globalised context also means that we have to think in different and innovative ways to address many of the issues. The road ahead is a long one. I end with a mild note of despair and lots of hope, best exemplified in the words of feminists from other parts of the world. Filomena Steady from Sierre Leone said in her speech at the Women's Worlds Conference 2005: 'Women's work is never done. Feminists' work will never ever be done.' (Lee 2005: 1). Sharon Z. Rader of the United States added, 'There's a lot of work to be done. And I think women have many gifts to transform the world. We should be strong and offer more to the world' (Kim 2005: 7).

References

Bridge, 2004. 'Gender and Development: Gender and Budgets', In-Brief Issue, No. 12, available at http://www.bride.ids.ac.uk/dgb 12.html.

Derne, Steve. 2005. 'The (Limited) Effect of Cultural Globalization in India: Implications for Culture Theory', *Poetics*, 33: 33–47.

Elson, D. 2003. 'Gender Mainstreaming and Gender Budgeting', Paper presented at Conference of the European Commission, 'Gender Equality and Europe's Future'. Brussels.

Gangoli, Geetanjali. 2003. 'Muslim Divorce and the Discourse Around Muslim Personal Law', in Imtiaz Ahmad (ed.), *The Sociology of Divorce*. New Delhi: Sage Publications.

Ganguly-Scrase, Ruchira. 2003. 'Paradoxes of Globalization, Liberalization and Gender Equality: The Worldviews of the Lower Middle Class in West Bengal, India', *Gender and Society*, 17(4): 544–66.

Hafkin, Nancy and Nancy Taggart. 2001. *Gender, Information Technology and Developing Countries: An Analytic Study*'. Washington, D.C.: United States Agency for International Development.

International Information Centre and Archives for the Women's Movement (IIAV). 2005. 'A German Feminist ICT Inquiry', *International News*, 6 (2), October: 5.

Jain, Divya. 2005. 'Fighting Female Foeticide through ICT', *i4d*, 3 (3), March: 17–20.

Kamat, Sangeeta. 2003. 'The NGO Phenomenon and Political Culture in the Third World', *Development*, 46 (1): 89–93.

Kim, Soo-hyun. 2005. 'Embracing Who We Are and All Being Created', *The Daily Newspaper*, IX International Interdisciplinary Congress on Women, 4. Ewha Womans University, Seoul, Korea.

Lee, Eun-joo. 2005. 'Speakers Change the World with Passion', *The Daily Newspaper*, IX International Interdisciplinary Congress on Women, 6. Ewha Womans University, Seoul, Korea.

Lim, Rhie-young. 2005. 'Globalizing to Embrace the World', *The Daily Newspaper*, IX International Interdisciplinary Congress on Women, 5. Ewha Womans University, Seoul, Korea.

Nakray, Keerty Yogendra. 2005. 'Gender Budgeting and Women's Empowerment: A Study of *Sarva Shiksha Abhyan* in Mumbai', Master in Philosophy (Planning and Development) thesis. Mumbai: Dept. of Humanities and Social Sciences, Indian Institute of Technology.

Pappu, Rekha. 2000. 'Feminist Initiatives in Legislation: A Perspective from India', *Asian Women*, 11: 49–60.

Park, Sook–young. 2005. 'Everything from Family to Third World Politics' (interview with Vicky Randall), *The Daily Newspaper*, IX International Interdisciplinary Congress on Women, 4. Ewha Womans University, Seoul, Korea.

Poonacha, Veena. 2003. 'Women's Studies in Indian Universities: Current Concerns', *Economic and Political Weekly*, 38 (June): 2653–58.

Public Interest Research Group. 1994. 'Structural Adjustment Policies: Who Really Pays', Delhi: PIRG.

Purkayastha Bandana, Mangala Subramaniam, Manisha Desai and Sunita Bose. 2003. 'The Study of Gender in India: A Partial Review', *Gender and Society*, 17 (4): 503–24.

Sadler, J. 2004. 'UNIFEM's Experiences in Mainstreaming for Gender Equality', available at ⟨http://www.unifem.org/index.php?f page pid=188⟩.

Tejani, Sheba. 2004. 'Sexual Harassment at the Workplace: Emerging Problems and Debates', *Economic and Political Weekly*, October: 4491–94.

Zahidi, Saadia (Interview). 2005. 'Women's Empowerment: Measuring the Global Gender Gap World Economic Forum', Source http://www.weforum.org/pdf/global-Competitveness-Reports/Reports/gender-gap.pdf.

Section I

Re-constructing Gender

Economic reforms have integrated India into the world economy and neo-liberal globalisation has resulted in flooding the Indian market with consumer goods and other relics of materialism. This has brought about an unprecedented transformation in the social and cultural fabric of society, and speeded up by intense connectivity resulting from the new information and communication technologies. What is the impact of these new sweeping changes as the middle class aspires to be global citizens? The transformation brought on by colonialism resulted in education becoming the hallmark of individual modernity. Discourses of tradition and modernity have existed simultaneously and often in contradiction with one another; neo-liberal globalisation has added an altogether new dimension to this ongoing dialogue. The production of global goods and culture has ramifications for contemporary urban life, particularly in relation to young men and women.

This changing scenario is problematic for the youth of the society in terms of their identity and role, gender relations and equations. This opening of doors to different worlds has brought in its wake new opportunities and options; but this very euphoria of expansion contains challenges for conflict, confusion and despair. The choices the young have to make are not easy ones, as they are propelled in different directions by global, national and local forces. J.J. Arnett (2002), in his reflections on the psychology of globalisation, highlights three issues. First, as a consequence of globalisation many young adults develop a bicultural identity, one rooted in their local culture and the other stemming from their relation to global culture. Second, globalisation has resulted in an increased identity confusion among the young in non-western nations. Lastly, in every society there are people who choose to maintain their own cultural identity, unsullied by global values, by associating with like-minded persons. The middle class has the best opportunities for education, but being educated may not make the task of resolving questions of identity and role any easier as family, peer and media pressures, together with new organisational structures and technologies at the workplace, work at cross purposes on the young.

As the young aspire to be global citizens their identity is shaped both by what often seems a contradictory integration of competence and performance on the one hand, and being well-groomed on the other. While the need for competence sends them scrambling to the best schools and colleges, the need to be well-groomed sees them at the doors of beauty clinics and, in extreme cases, under the scalpel of a plastic surgeon. Job performance and the image makeover are pitted against a global benchmark. To what extent does this global cultural system translate into the young losing touch with their feminist roots, which the older generation had worked hard to accomplish? We may have to go full circle once again to discover our true worth. New gender roles for women may mean becoming more efficient at multi-tasking. More relaxed gender relations may mean teenage pregnancies, fear of rejection, coping with rejection, and developing appropriate interpersonal skills for the young adolescent and emerging adult. In the early days of feminism women were urged to become more like men; globalisation equates possessions with self-worth, which translates into keeping up with everyone.

The first section is labelled Re-constructing Gender. The focus of three of the four articles is on the young, and all four articles use different methodologies to address their objectives. Meenakshi Thapan, in 'Adolescence, Embodiment and Gender Identity: Elite Women in a Changing Society', focuses on the adolescent girl, a much neglected population in scholarly literature. In the shaping of gender identity in the post-globalisation period, schoolgoing girls are the major receivers of the impact of re-colonisation, media and new peer pressures on the one hand, and the patriarchal pull of the family on the other. She argues that the young are not merely receptacles of the contradictory information, but rather active agents in making choices that shape their self-image. The author uses the concept of 'habitus'—a set of internalised dispositions, structured yet open to change, to make her point. In the chapter on 'Male Hindi Filmgoers' Gaze: An Ethnographic Interpretation of Gender Construction', Steve Derné and Lisa Jadwin explore two ideas. One, that since cinema halls in India are male-dominated spaces, they provide opportunities for asserting male privileges expressed in men being agents and women objects of their gaze. However, the objectification is qualified by a distinction male filmgoers make between women whom they define as legitimate objects of their gaze, and those not legitimate. Second, the issue is further complicated when men themselves become objects of scrutiny as they identify with heroes and are expected to show the same. U. Vindhya, in her chapter 'Women as Emblems of Culture and Nation: Conceptions of the Hindu Right and the Democratic Women's Movement', traces the conception of women as politically active and militant in the service of the Hindu nation by right-wing organisations on the one hand, and the construction of women as independent and autonomous by the Indian women's movement on the other. The two sets of constructions clash in important ways, and the author argues for a need to place the women's movement's visions of secularism and equality at the centre of the nation's consciousness, both for the sake of women and for a united nation. Any migrant community, especially its young, is faced with the task of dealing simultaneously with two cultures. The empirical work by Shamita Das Dasgupta, titled 'Gender Roles and Cultural Continuity in the Asian Indian Immigrant Community in the US', describes the project of preserving their ethnic identity undertaken by Indian migrants to the United States by focusing on the construction of gender relations. The author takes both a gender and a generational approach in coming to terms with the issues involved. She argues that while attitudes towards women's role in society show some generational and gender difference, the issue of dating is a bone of contention between the generations and genders. She highlights the nature of negotiations undertaken to strike a balance between preservation and change.

Reference

Arnett, J.J. 2002. 'The Psychology of Globalisation', *American Psychologist*, 41: 295–315.

ONE

Adolescence, Embodiment and Gender Identity: Elite Women in a Changing Society*

Meenakshi Thapan

Introduction

This chapter seeks to understand the complexities in the articulation and constitution of gender identity among elite and educationally advantaged adolescent women in urban India.[1] The social context in which this takes place is fraught with dilemmas and contradictions, reflecting the cultural and social turmoil in contemporary Indian society. As economic reforms have opened up the Indian economy, an influx of consumer goods and artefacts of material culture, and their accompanying social and psychological characteristics, have wrought a transformation in the social and cultural fabric of contemporary urban India.

Discourses of tradition and modernity have existed simultaneously, and often contradictorily, since the country attained political independence from the British in 1947. However, liberalisation of the Indian economy has added a new impetus to this discourse, particularly in relation to women. It is precisely in this period of transition that the possibilities for both 'recolonisation' and resistance open up. Recolonisation is characterised by a mix of global elements translated into socially and culturally acceptable, and thereby legitimate, ideas, values and practices in everyday life. The phenomenon of globalisation, and its implications for urban India over the last decade, offers one example of the recolonisation of women (Bhattacharya 1994; Chaudhuri 1998; John 1998).

The production of a global culture has consequences for everyday life in contemporary urban India. Education processes and media culture play a significant role in this production. A new global media provides the symbols, myths, resources, ideas and images for the construction of both a common culture and individual identities. Thus, the upper-class, English-speaking, educationally advantaged urban elite in India emphasises the 'secular' (modern), non-traditional (contemporary), liberated (Westernised) and 'trendy' aspects of everyday life. The cosmopolitan, urbane, 'civilised' Indian social agent, who is part of a globalised network of relations, constitutes the elite section of the new middle class, which has now become the crucial component of a secular, modern India.[2] This new middle-class Indian emphasises all that is modern in the world today, and this includes a view of the Indian woman, which transcends the earlier perceived place of women in the domestic world.

This new view of Indian womanhood defines women, amongst other things, as being 'of substance', and includes a more visible and public view of women in the workplace, both within new spheres of work such as design and fashion, journalism and social activism, and through entry into the traditionally male preserves of the military, police, banking, and other allied occupations.[3]

*Originally published in the *Women's Studies International Forum*, Vol. 24, Nos 3/4, May–August 2001, pp. 359–71. Reprinted with permission from Elsevier.

This emphasis on women's public roles is largely at variance with the middle and upper-class nationalist construction of the cultural domain in terms of an inner and an outer sphere. In everyday life these refer both to the home and the world, with the home representing our spiritual self and our true identity. Women are constructed at the centre of the inner world, whereas the exterior domain of 'material interests,' treachery and intrigue is the domain of men (Chatterjee 1993: 238ff).[4] Global culture enters the home and erodes that which is sacred, the inner sanctum, the woman, through a re-articulation of her identity as more directed to the outer world, as defined in the Western world—and this can be seen as a process of recolonisation.

In contemporary India so-called 'old' modes of contact (including religious practices, cultural tradition and social custom) and apparently 'new' ones (most significantly, educational processes and the visual and print media) shape, influence, structure and construct gender identity in particular and varied ways. Both modes of contact, I suggest, are forms of recolonisation of social agents in postcolonial societies. The re-iteration of the 'old' characteristics of colonialism include, for example, an emphasis on the education of women, not necessarily for their individual empowerment, but for the purposes of having educated and aware mothers and wives who can be harbingers of social and cultural development that will contribute to national progress. The process of recolonisation is significant because it reproduces the characteristics of colonialism in a redefined mode in postcolonial societies, thereby ensuring continuous hegemony over cultural, social and economic domains.

The characteristics of modern Indian family life have also changed, from the traditional extended family living together to the more commonly visible nuclear family.[5] This has resulted in perhaps greater bonding between members of the nuclear family due to the absence of a large and overbearing network of kin relations, but in no way does this suggest a marked transformation in the articulation of the roles and functions of various members of the nuclear family. The work of Indian feminists and scholars such as Leela Dube (1988), Zarina Bhatty (1988), Sudhir Kakar (1988), Kamala Ganesh (1989), Shahida Lateef (1990) and Jasodhara Bagchi (1995) has shown the contribution of cultural and social values, in differing religious and social contexts, to the development of gender identities. These values include an emphasis on female submissiveness and passivity, and particular role-specific identities, and tend to reproduce gender asymmetry and a classical femininity that is continuously looking to the external, social world for its own nurturance and sustenance. In a sense, these processes of socialisation also ensure that the gendered self does not seek to consciously develop an interior world of political awareness that may challenge social constructions of identity. Thus contemporary middle-class, urban India finds itself in a safe, patriarchal haven as far as the politics of the family is concerned. The family remains the cradle of nurturance, comfort and security that it has always constituted[6].

A discussion of gender identity in contemporary India can be articulated, at one level, in the register of the everyday in urban society. In the recasting or refashioning of the educationally advantaged Indian adolescent young woman, there are certain continuities and discontinuities between the contemporary and inherited social and cultural practices pertaining to the social construction of gender identity. In much the same way as Indian womanhood has been characterised as an ambivalent state, wherein women are both revered and oppressed, worshipped and molested, free to express themselves in different domains and yet voiceless, the educationally advantaged young woman also finds herself in an ambivalent state. She is simultaneously a part of tradition, ritual and customary practices while experiencing the more contemporary world through both the education she receives, and the diverse images and texts presented by the visual and print media and the peer group culture she is part of. By accepting and idealising certain values based on what appear to be 'novel' images and representations, she not only displays her exposure to modernity, but also her departure from classical forms of idealisation. This dilemma gives rise to conflicting sets of expectations about her identity as a young woman in relation to familial and socio-cultural factors, and in relation to her peers at school.[7]

In the first section of this chapter, I will consider the methodology used for data collection and then examine the conceptual resources that provide the theoretical underpinnings for my research. Thereafter, I turn to my material and to the question of gender identity in relation to familial and socio-cultural factors. In the following section I examine my material in the context of gender identity and peer group cultures at school, and then I analyse the material with reference to Westernisation and recolonisation. I conclude with a discussion of the main points raised throughout the chapter.

Methodology and Conceptual Framework

It was only in the early 1980s that psychologists such as Carol Gilligan highlighted the psychological development of young women as part of a theory of adolescence. Psychologists like Erik Erikson had earlier focused on male adolescents in formulating their theories of adolescence, and did not seek to differentiate between women and men. The term 'adolescence' itself was a masculine construct based on masculine images. Crucial defining concepts such as 'self, identity, relationship, sexuality, morality, creativity, achievement and even development itself were drawn for the most part from a man's perspective or reflected the viewpoint of a male child' (Gilligan 1995: 196). While the sociologist James Coleman (1961) did include young women as a distinct category in his work, his primary focus was on the 'value climate' of each of the 10 US schools he studied rather than women per se. Thus, Carol Gilligan's work (Gilligan 1982, 1988) was a major landmark in adolescent studies, highlighting the neglect of young women and focusing on the different dimensions of female adolescence. She has, in fact, suggested that by not studying women, what has been missed is an understanding about 'relationships' and their significance in young women's lives.[8]

This chapter seeks to begin to explore and understand the world of the educationally advantaged urban Indian adolescent young woman, a somewhat neglected category in studies of Indian society. The term 'educationally advantaged' refers to that category of individuals who not only have access to the education of their choice (e.g., private as opposed to state-funded schooling), but also have the privilege of pursuing their educational goals to fruition. This is not common across India, but is a distinct part of the lives of girls who belong to the middle and upper middle class in urban Indian society.[9]

The chapter is based on young women's perceptions and lived experience in relation to their families, peer group, schooling and aspirations. Data was collected through a written questionnaire distributed randomly to women students from different coeducational public (i.e., fee-paying) schools in New Delhi, and also to students in a boarding school in southern India. The students are all aged around 16–17 years. They were asked questions about their family structure, their relationships with their fathers and mothers and what these mean to them, their aspirations and how they relate these aspirations to their potential family role in the future, the kinds of books and music they like, their popular heroes and heroines, and their leisure-time activities. They were also asked specific questions about their self-image, the qualities they perceive that make them desirable to young men, how they assess the young men in their peer group, and their expectations from young men in terms of the kinds of relationships they might like to have with them. It should be noted that the questions relating to young men were asked of both young women and their teachers at school, but not of young men themselves.

Although I am aware that a questionnaire may not be the best mode of collecting information on the above topics, and group discussions or interviews may have drawn out the intricacies and complexities of the women's lives in greater detail, practical considerations dictated its use. In presenting the perspectives of the young women I have used excerpts from their questionnaires without making any changes to their writing and in an anonymous fashion, because that undertaking was given to them.

Habitus, Embodiment and Gender Identity

A key question at the heart of much feminist theorising today is the extent to which gender identity is rooted in a body that is female as opposed to male, thereby biologically determined, or in a continuously evolving and changing self that undoubtedly has a material existence but is also emotionally and socially constituted. Although psychologists such as Erik Erikson have traditionally argued that there is a crystallisation of identity during the later stages of adolescence, feminist scholarship argues that identity is not a fixed, immutable state of being.

The concept of 'habitus' developed by Pierre Bourdieu helps us to understand how certain general dispositions are internalised and reproduced by the embodied subject. The habitus is defined by Bourdieu (1977) as 'systems of durable, transposable dispositions, structured structures predisposed to function as structuring structures, that is, as principles of the generation and structuring of practices and representations which can be objectively 'regulated' and 'regular' without in any way being the product of obedience to rules ...' (p. 72). The habitus is developed first in the family, which plays a significant role in the constitution of gender identities. Relations of power are not imposed in an institutionalised manner but effected through forms of 'symbolic violence' (a form of domination), wherein there is an element of complicity on the part of the embodied subject. However, as Bourdieu points out, habitus is an 'open system of dispositions that is constantly subject to experiences, and therefore, constantly affected by them in a way that either reinforces or modifies its structures' (1977: 133). The habitus is, therefore, very much a 'generative structure' (McNay 1999: 100) that allows for the 'elements of variability and potential creativity immanent to even the most routine reproduction of gender identity' (ibid.: 101).

Embodiment, 'a lived matter of gender' (Hughes and Witz 1997), is crucial to the experience and perception of gender identity. As Lois McNay puts it:

> At the point of overlap between the physical, the symbolic and the sociological, the body is a dynamic, mutable frontier. The body is the threshold through which the subject's lived experience of the world is incorporated and realized and as such, is neither pure object nor pure subject. (1999: 98)

As object, the body and its image are part of 'formally identical objects interacting in the infinity of space and time', but as subject, the same body and body-image are 'immeasurably enriched with the inner content of lived experience' (Ferguson 1997: 6).

Veena Das has argued that 'the sense of being a woman is internalised' through the double perspective of 'the body as object and the body as subject' (1988: 193). The socialisation process in Indian society reflects the manner in which the bodies of men and women are socially viewed, thereby assigning different values to the masculine and the feminine body (ibid.: 193ff). A young woman's experience of her gendered identity therefore rests very much on her body, both in terms of body image and the experience of her embodiment in her relations with others in everyday life. Gender is, therefore, not only perceived and experienced, but also 'deeply inscribed on our bodies' (McNay 1999: 98), our thoughts, our experiences, our very existence. This perhaps suggests an element of determinism in the extent to which dominant norms prevail upon and shape the trajectories of our identities. However, although the embodied social agent is constituted by dominant norms and values, these do not in any way point to their complete and total hold over the social agent. In other words, while the significance of the role of dominant norms and values cannot be denied, at the same time it is possible that there is a space for an 'active and creative relation between the subject and the world' (McNay 1999: 100). This is possible through the habitus, which, as a generative structure, perceives and often creates the possibilities for change. In this manner, the habitus provides the space for relative autonomy, although this chapter will also show us the dark areas and shadowed edges between domination and creativity in relations with significant others in everyday life. The possibilities for creation and transformation are indeed not only present, but part of our modes of functioning in everyday life. Our circumstances and relations in different contexts, however, impose limitations on our abilities to make use of these possibilities in a truly creative manner.

Familial Gender Identities

Fathers, Mothers, and Daughters: The Reproduction of Patriarchy

The responses of the young women in my sample point to the cohesive and all-encompassing nature of the Indian family as experienced by the elite, and to the reproduction of existing patriarchal norms and values. There are certain complexities in their articulation of their familial relationships, and, among other things, these highlight a lack of close or intimate communication with their father, his inability to understand their long-term goals and aspirations, and a general feeling of aloofness and distance from him. It is a somewhat problematic relationship with the father wherein he is respected and admired, but is not always around for a close relationship:

- My father—somebody who I always look up to for care, love, helping me make my decisions. His perfection in whatever he may do, compels me to make him my role model. [...] Since I have always seen my Dad work very hard in his jobs; and he mostly came back home late, I certainly did spend more time with my mother. She is from where I belong, my shelter, my friend. She is a very patient and understanding listener; I can talk my heart out when with her. Of course we share an undestructable bond.

- My father is one person I have always looked up to. My mother is my ideal. Her values, outlook of life, character is out of the world. She is most understanding and we have a perfect daughter–mother relationship.

- My father is like a pillar behind me. He is the sole motive behind the deed/work I do. He is an encouragement for me and a friend with whom I can discuss my problems [...] [My mother is my] best friend. She is always with me; whenever I need her. I can discuss my problems with her and share my feelings with her. She is the one to whom I depend entirely upon. She encourages me, helps me to fight back after defeat and controls me from doing what is no good for me.

While the father is an ideal support, it is in fact with their mother that these young women find friendship and from whom they draw strength and courage. This aspect of the relationship is repeated in almost all the responses, that is, a friendship based on the ability to talk to the mother and confide in her.

- I love her very much. She supports and guides me in the steps I take for my future. Clear, however, that she's a separate person whose opinions and advice I'm free to take or leave. My mother talks to me about her day and various issues on her mind. I love listening. I talk about almost anything under the sun, I love her listening. My mum leans on me for emotional support. I love to be strong. I love the relationship my mama and I have. My relationship with my father is less intense. I love him very much but I don't know him as a person. Discipline was mostly handled by my mother. Papa spent weekends with us, we watch him paint, he teaches us electronics of carpentry or driving. We bug him or do him favours with great glee. In a way he balanced the relationship I have with my mother. Showing me a different kind of passion for work than my mother's. And music. My papa's music is my music. I grew up to it and I love it. He always makes me feel proud. 'You're my girl,' he'd say. 'You'll be a good lawyer,' or 'a good mechanic', or a good whatever I did well at that point of time. He makes me feel strong, secure and loved. He has hopes for me I suppose, but he doesn't say anything about it. He just says, 'find what you love, go after it like mad.'

- I think of my father as a man who does not influence me much as I have never had a very close or personal relationship with him. I, however, admire him a great deal, because he's dedicated to his work and in some ways his family, is absolutely fit even at this age (46) and is incredibly fun to be with. I would love to be like him.

- My communication with my mom is fine. Affection—fine. I don't share many of my ideas with anyone. Same goes for my thoughts. Plans for the future are shared, however. My communication with dad—rare. Affection—fine. No sharing of ideas or thoughts or plans for future.

Other young women say,

- [About her father] 5'11" with the most striking eyes ever. Straightforward and frank. Humorous. Very caring about his parents and his in-laws. Very punctual, hardworking and a bit short-tempered. Handles the accounts, etc. [...] I am not as close to my father as I am to my mother, however, it's a very friendly relationship. I would regard him as my advisor. We have discussions often and I enjoy them. [...] There are several qualities I admire about him and it is enjoyable to be in his company. [...] [Mother] We agree on several aspects so it's a very loving relationship that exists. I love and respect her very much.

- My mum and I are very close. She even tells me things my dad doesn't know. I can tell her anything. She is very ambitious for me. She wants me to solidly stand on my own two feet. She doesn't like women who depend on their husbands! Feminist! She allows me to go out with guys and all. She's not conservative but her clothes always seem very Indian—loves her culture.

- My dad has a big ambition for me. He is the only one who can see right through me. He wants me to always be independent and responsible. He never gives up on me. He is very encouraging [...]. He is very affectionate but never often kisses me.

In this last response, there is an indication of regret; perhaps earlier in the relationship her father had been more demonstrative in his affections. Apart from the obvious emphasis on the patriarchal norm of a masculine role model, the young women's desire for deeper emotive relationships with their fathers is also an indication of the significance of relationships in their lives. The fathers' opinions, appreciation of their efforts and encouragement does count for a great deal in their lives, shaping their life experiences and relations with others. Bonding with their mother does not rule out their desire for a similar relationship with their father, which they consider necessary, but cannot have due to both his preoccupation with work and a social and cultural socialisation that does not encourage close or intimate relationships between fathers and daughters.

The complexity characteristic of recolonisation as a hegemonic tool is apparent in the dual-edged manner in which it manifests itself within the urban Indian family. On the one hand the young women's responses indicate a yearning for a closer relationship with their father, and on the other hand they view their father as an ideal role model worthy of emulation. This longing for proximity with their father is based on the images derived from global culture and contemporary perspectives on intrafamilial relations; it is generally not valued or encouraged by indigenous cultural norms and values which, in fact, exhort young women not to speak before their fathers. Simultaneously, there is an idealisation of the masculine figure—'physically fit', 'striking' (in appearance), who 'does the accounts', a workaholic, a personification of great strength and determination, a provider for the family one who holds authority in the family—all of which indicate a clear reproduction of the patriarchal norm and ideal. A young woman's relationship with her father, it has been suggested, is 'only one strand in the great complexity of interfamilial relations that contribute to the construction of social and sexual identity in contemporary times' (Mann 1996: 80). It is from these relationships and from young women's relationships with other men in the family that the basis for relationships with men in different contexts is formed.

Careers and the Family

Clearly, the language of the young women's constructions of masculinity and femininity reflects the power relations embedded in identities. The generative habitus develops sex role stereotypes and limits the subject's own aspirations, although there is indeed a struggle between a desire to be independent and a desire to be like their mothers. Although a young woman may not subscribe to the view that some professions are more appropriate for women than for men, she may be well aware of the division that is created by the internalisation of a heterosexual norm focusing on marriage and children:

- ... coz I think a mother should spend time with her children coz that is an important time and that is when a child learns the most.

- I guess the husband should be a little dominating as well as caring, for women often like being dependent on their husbands. The wife on the other hand should take care of the family for a mother's love has no substitute.

- Girls sometimes just have a knack for doing some stuff like making jewellery or designing clothes although boys too do these things. Girls are mostly more gentle in nature too, so maybe they excel in social work or baby sitting, etc.

It appears, then, that gender identity is firmly entrenched as a social and cultural construction through the process of socialisation in the family and community. In other words, the habitus reproduces the structures and values of the patriarchal society in which it is embedded. Insofar as the habitus is a lived category, we can argue, however, that there is an element of creativity, struggle, and perhaps surprise even in the most routine reproduction of gender identity. Young women no doubt struggle with social and familial definitions and expectations, and experience conflict and dilemmas as they struggle to redefine and shape their identities in different contexts and situations.

In accordance with her aspirations and desires, one young woman ranks her three career preferences as: (1) Neuroscientist; (2) Neurosurgeon; (3) Neurologist. She explains, 'I love Maths and Sciences. I wasn't influenced by anyone, instead it was the topic that got me going.' The training for any of these choices would obviously require a great deal of time and hard work, of which she is no doubt aware. At the same time, she cannot see herself abandoning the family and her obligations to the family. The family is as important to her as her career, in fact more so:

- Well, I suppose it is important to handle a career as well as take care of the family. In my opinion the family should come before one's career. Therefore, before dedicating one's self to the career it would be wiser to think about the family first.

Similarly, another young woman lists her career choices as: (1) Engineer; (2) C.A. [Chartered Accountant]; (3) Hotel Management; and explains, 'My sister is doing engineering. I love science and would like to pursue it. I would love to do BIO-MEDICAL ENGINEERING.' However, she also expresses a struggle between her career aspirations and her commitment to her family:

- A career is very important for me, I don't want to depend on anyone else. [...] I think it is very important to have a career that is compatible with family life. If your work makes you very busy, you tend to neglect your family which leads to separation and lack of closeness.

These young women have selected a career in no uncertain terms, but at the same time are at pains to emphasise their commitment to their families and the need for their career to be compatible with their family responsibilities. This refrain can be heard in the responses of others as well, who indicate a wide variety in their choice of professions from journalism, teaching, writing, the legal profession, to business, chartered accountancy, fashion designing and architecture, but who do not want to be seen to be giving up their families:

- It is very important to have a career that is very compatible with family life as families are very important in everyone's lives.
- It's damn important [to have a career compatible with family life]. I'd love to take care of my parents later. I want to make them proud of me. But I would love to have time to spend with them too.
- If I ever have kids they will come first—other than that I don't really wish to be tied down with a family or such. I wish to travel, etc.

These responses may indicate the all-encompassing nature of the Indian family that somehow keeps young girls trapped within its complacent world of warmth and contentment. Yet these responses also include the voice of the creative social agent who wants and seeks a close relationship with her father and is extremely happy when she has it. There is also the voice of the educationally advantaged and socially aware social agent, who clearly understands and knows her choice of career, but keeps a check on her aspirations so as to enable a 'balanced' life. The transitory space created by modernity opens up her career options and perhaps provides her with a host of opportunities to which she did not earlier have access, but her rootedness in a tradition that glorifies the family and relationships within the family inhibits her complete immersion in the external world.

Gender and Peer Group Cultures at School

Schooling is a site where gender ideologies are transmitted through peer group cultures and through teachers, via the hidden curriculum of school practice. The heterosexual norm promoted by the young women's ideal family types, with father as provider and advisor, a pillar of strength, and mother as nurturer, carer and communicator, is reinforced by peer group approval/disapproval of particular ways of behaving, acting and being in school.[10]

Images of One Another

Young women and men have preconstructed images of one another that are based to a large extent on family stereotypes, social expectations, and the visual and print media. By and large, young women acknowledge that having a 'good figure' is a passport to popularity at school among both young men and other women. One young woman adds, 'Most boys are like that,' suggesting that little else could be expected from young men than a focus on women's bodily qualities. However, those women whose self-image extends beyond their physical embodiment resent this:

- There are boys countable on your fingers who appreciate loyalty, good nature and sensibility. Majority go for a good figure, short skirts and physical appearance.
- Boys base their opinions on good looking girls/feminine girls/'cool' girls (stylish)/good figure. Very few go for sense of humour.
- In all the schools I've been to, boys seem to give the most importance to the way a girl looks, not just a pretty face but also what she wears. They also give importance to the feminty (*sic*) of a girl. Studies or a sense of humour doesn't seem too important. It's more the physical outlook.

At the same time, young women showed an equal interest in young men's physical characteristics, appreciating men who are 'good-looking', have 'good height and stuff', a 'good physique', a 'macho personality', are 'chivalrous', have 'charming ways of talking, movement'. However, they also mentioned appreciating men's social skills, such as their ability to be friendly, have an 'easy and open manner of speaking', a 'sense of humour', and not being 'antigirls'. Seeking to break free from socio-cultural stereotypes, some women found different ways of expressing their expectations:

1. In school guys have to be humorous.
2. Boys have to be 'nice' and not rude.

Nonetheless, the young women often found it difficult to reject conventional imagery completely. Indeed, there was a tension between the idealisation of men's physical attributes (conventional masculinity) and the idealisation of their social skills (contemporary masculinity), as the following quotes reveal:

- They gotta be good at football. Good-looking guys are appreciated. They have to talk nicely and not be shy. Friendly, outgoing, not mean guys are always welcome, too.

1. Should be a good friend
2. Never to bitch behind back. No male chauvanism
3. Gives you another chance
4. Good height and stuff

Young Women's Self-image

The young women's self-images are essentially grounded in their embodiment, wherein the body as object and the body as subject are simultaneously present. The young women's assessment of their image contains many aspects of their identity:

- I'm a confident girl. Not worried about looks at all. I love being tom-boyish—I am (though my mum doesn't like it too much). I have a medium ego. Except with boys I don't allow male chauvanism to take over me. I'm fat—YUCK. Need to reduce ... I'm fat. But that's it. I like my height. I'd be very happy if I could reduce. I don't exactly crave for a 'figure', but I'd like to look healthy and strong (more guyish I suppose).

- I am not happy with the way I look. My hair is too frizzy and I'm way too short. People mistake me as a junior and that's really insulting.

- Chubby, breasts on the small size, sexy legs, smooth delicate collarbones, very woman. Over all if I was slimmer I'd be pretty nice figured. Hips good for childbearing and shoulders strong for working and fighting.

- I haven't given much thought to my appearance although people find me good-looking. However my image in the mirror is of a young, mature, no-nonsense human being who knows her goals and are all set to achieve it. I look at me and know myself well. The image has a touch of arrogance and poor communication skills.

These young women are certainly aware of their 'womanly' characteristics grounded in their embodiment, and yet at the same time assert their independence from this embodiment. They also know how to express these multiple characteristics, whether it is in terms of different body parts or in terms of confidence, strength, or even looking more 'guyish'. These characteristics are asserted un-selfconsciously and often together, so that a heightened femininity does not necessarily imply a lack of confidence or strength. However, there is a troubling concern with weight, the adolescent preoccupation across cultures, and for some women this overrides everything else:

- [I am] fat, ugly and stupid. (I'm a neurotic—just kidding!!). No sometimes I develop a FAT-O-PHOBIA (a word I have made up myself) although I'm underweight at the minute. I like my hair ('coz I bleached it) ... Thats about it!!! ... Sometimes I exercise a lot also I'm no way overweight but I would like to be thinner ...

- I am obsessed about my weight ... because the first thing a person is judged by is his/her physical appearance. (Matter of First Impression).

The obsession with weight here is overwhelming, both in terms of the emphasis on being thin as well as in terms of the desire for the perfect body image. There is a frightening contradiction in the first response, where a woman asserts simultaneously that she is already underweight and yet would like to be thinner. The second response makes clear the context within which bodily perfection is desired, namely the assessment of one's embodied self by the other. Physical body weight is, in the young women's minds, related to creating the right 'impression', and thereby ensuring a place in the social networks of friendship and inclusion. Clearly, a sense of failure is experienced if the body does not match up to the perceived expectations of others. The 'wrong' impression may perhaps result in exclusion and is not desirable at all—a clear link is manifest between embodiment, self-image and relationships. There is also an anxiety about being really all wrong:

- I'm short, not too dark, high cheek bones, pinochio nose, weird walk, knock kneed, bowlegged, busty ... I'm not like I'm really happy. But I'm not bitter about it. I'm bitter about my walk, bust. The rest is fine and I can get along with it.

Thus, 'looks' are central to peer group cultures, whether in terms of young women's self-image, their perceptions of young men, or how they consider young men to perceive them. Teachers' definitions of peer group cultures confirm this overriding concern with modes of self-presentation and appearance, citing peer group pressure and family cultures as the two most important factors. As one teacher put it, 'Peer group pressure is very strong. [It] Influences the way you dress, your ideas on issues, sexual preference.' According to this teacher, the criteria dictating the popularity of young women were: having the right male idol (in 1999, Leonardo di Caprio); being allowed out late; going to parties; wearing the right length of skirt (short); waxing (legs); and plucking eyebrows. Another teacher in the same school confirmed that peer pressure centres on women 'looking good', which requires waxing their legs, plucking their eyebrows, wearing their shirts outside their skirts or jeans, and anything else which is 'antiestablishment', such as chewing gum and adopting an attitude of 'defiance towards the school'. The peer group, therefore, provides the strength for collective resistance and rebellion that is exhibited in very specific ways through gestures, bodily display, or plain disobedience. However, this resistance is not directed at breaking stereotypes or reproductions of gender identities, but only in joining the gang, as it were, in a collective voice against the authority associated with the school establishment.

The approval of 'friendship groups' and other peers 'counts a lot' for this age-group of young women and men, primarily because they want to blend in with their peers rather than stand out. As one teacher explained, 'In the same way as the like-minded stick together, the like-bodied stick together.' The image young women and men strive for is to 'look cool, act cool' but, as one teacher explained, what this means is differentiated by gender. For young men it implies 'not listening to teachers, not giving in home-work, not wearing regulation uniform', whereas for young women it includes wearing short skirts, listening to Western music, waxing the hair off their legs, making friends with the opposite sex. Both young men and women are clearly adhering to the dominant characteristics associated with a stereotypical masculine and feminine image: the young men being riotous, rebellious and defiant, while the young women are more concerned with self-presentation.

Westernisation and Recolonisation

Contemporary media culture shapes identity in many conflicting, competing, and formative ways. Ella Shohat has argued that, 'In a transnational world typified by the global circulation of images and sounds, goods and peoples, media spectatorship impacts complexly on national identity, communal belonging and political affiliations' (1997: 209). Clearly, it also impacts on gender identity. The ideal male body espoused by the young women in this study is not a classically Indian body, clothed in Indian clothes, but very much a body grounded in Western culture. This body is appropriated from popular cinema, television serials, and novels: Leonardo di Caprio from the film *Titanic*; Howard Roark from Ayn Rand's novel *The Fountainhead*. Young women make a romantic association with Western images of hegemonic masculinity through popular culture, and the perfectly formed, physically fit, healthy, preferably white, glamourous, and wealthy male becomes the ideal through which the gendered body is recolonised.

The young women's understanding of their own embodied selves is also shaped by contemporary global media culture. The plump and even voluptuous female body associated with physical well-being and a deeply sensual sexuality and fertility in classical Indian thought, and reflected in popular art and cinema until the 1960s and 1970s, does not find any place in the idealisation of embodiment by young women in contemporary India. This earlier imagery has been replaced by a recolonised version that, although grounded in Western cultures, is adapted to acceptable norms and representations in Indian culture.

The fiction young women read at private schools begins with the Sweet Valley series of high-school novels based in the United States, takes in Western historical romantic fiction authors such as Georgette Heyer, Louisa May Alcott, Daphne du Maurier, and moves on to Ayn Rand, Danielle Steele and Sidney Sheldon. All provide them with countless images of the ideal Western women, the ideal Western man and the ideal relations between them, and these images are reinforced through television, popular cinema and magazines. Adverts on Indian television and in women's magazines are a central trope in the recolonisation of the Indian woman and her reconstruction along lines deemed appropriate for an increasingly globalised but nonetheless specifically postcolonial culture.[11] As Chaudhuri (1998) explains, [The advertisement] 'has passed the frontier of selling goods and services and has become involved with the teaching of social and personal values.' Alongside the new or 'recast' image of a consuming nation is a similarly refashioned woman.

Adverts are produced through market forces that seek to instil, or even enforce, a particular lifestyle through explicit statements, as well as suggestive nuances, of visual and textual excesses. In women's magazines, body imagery is strikingly conveyed primarily through adverts and fashion photography. The impact of much of this imagery is to make us conscious of our bodies in terms of shape, size, weight, skin colour or texture, and associated characteristics. The female gaze is preoccupied with the visual imagery of one's self and of others, and there is a continuous assessment of whether these images match up to others' expectations or to the socially prescribed ideal. Of course, the 'new' Indian woman is simultaneously engaged in making her identity in her own way by struggling with conflicting and ambivalent images, Western constructs, and her own desires and aspirations.[12]

The English language plays a crucial part in the dissemination of global cultural forms. Western culture is made accessible to the elite young women in this study through their excellent grasp of the English language. During the colonial period, hegemonic processes established the superiority of the English language in India. Its status has been reinforced, and further legitimised, primarily because of the cultural capital that is seen as being attached to an English education. Such an education allows access not only to higher education and a choice of professional occupations, but also to an entire cultural discourse that comes along with an English education. Those who have access to this education are wittingly and unwittingly trapped, and those who are excluded spend all their working time trying to secure access. This is another crucial aspect of recolonisation insofar as colonialism continues its hegemony over subjects by creating a recolonised postcolonial mind through the social and cultural reproduction of the dominant language and culture.

Conclusion

This chapter has sought to understand the processes in families and schools that contribute to the reproduction and creation of a class and gender-specific habitus, as well as the factors that lead to the formation of gender identities located in the transitory moment of both reproduction and change in contemporary Indian society. It has been argued that the family is the ground on which the heterosexual patriarchal ideal is nurtured and sustained, but that peer group cultures informed by global media are also important to young women's perceptions of their embodied selves and gender identity. Grounded in global media images, family preferences and social expectations, young women (and young men) consciously create, devise and formulate their own rules for conduct, appearance and self-presentation, and seek to comprehend and develop their gender identities.

In the reproduction of prevailing structures and processes, the habitus also allows space for struggle, contradictions and conflicts. Thus, although it may appear that the young woman's identity in India is firmly entrenched in the family and in tradition, she is simultaneously engaged in the task of redefining her identity as she sees it. Young women now seek to understand and reformulate their relations with their fathers and with young men at school. There has been an opening up of career choice for elite women, and, as a result, of their roles at home and at work, at least to some extent. The young women respondents' identification of their bodies as not only womanly but also strong and powerful, meant for working and fighting, is part of their attempt to reformulate their own identities contrary to familial and social expectations.

This lived experience of educationally advantaged urban young women remains embedded in a particular social class that shapes their consciousness in many different ways—perhaps critical and liberated in some situations, but limited and oppressive in other social contexts. Woman's identity is, therefore, very much a social construction as well as an emotional and personal perception. The postcolonial other that recolonises our bodies and identities is not a distant other who seeks to oppress us, but thoughts, perceptions and ideas that have become our own over a period of time, primarily through the processes of education and the influence of the media.

The colonial construction of the Indian woman, well documented by scholars, ensured control, regulation and Westernisation in certain obvious ways. The resultant identity was circumscribed, limited and had to find different ways of freeing itself from self-enclosing and all-encompassing social strictures. The postcolonial construction of womanhood is a very similar phenomenon, although its surface reality is presented in the garb of a modern and liberated female identity. This new construction is projected through the media primarily in terms of an enhanced physical appearance and a sexual identity as now constituting the core of the modern Indian woman's identity. The resulting ambivalent construction of the Indian woman as one who is liberated and yet somehow adheres to traditional norms and values is thus a faithful reproduction of what has gone before. What is new, however, is not so much the experience of struggle as the articulation and awareness of this struggle by young women in postcolonial cultures, who seek to produce new cultural forms and practices in the process of constructing themselves as women.

Notes

1. This chapter is based on data from a questionnaire survey of 25 female adolescents in public schools in urban India, as well as on interviews with teachers in two such schools.
2. In a recent article, Satish Deshpande (1998) has examined the main functions of the middle class in post-independence and postcolonial India.
3. Advertisements on Indian television and in women's magazines, such as *Femina* and *Cosmopolitan*, increasingly emphasise the role of women in the public sphere, although they also place a great deal of emphasis on the body beautiful, beauty culture and beauty contests. Thus, although elite women have a new occupational space, their objectification has not ceased.
4. Partha Chatterjee has emphasised that the European powers failed to colonise the 'inner, essential, identity of the East which lay in its distinctive, and superior, spiritual culture' (Chatterjee 1993: 239). He has also argued that while 'imitation and adaptation to Western norms' was often a necessity, this was not allowed to happen at home as it would be 'tantamount to annihilation of one's very identity' (ibid.: 239). See also Saigol (1994) for an understanding of the construction of women's identity in Muslim nationalism.
5. In a recent article, A.M. Shah has used census data to show that the preponderance of joint households has increased, and that a larger number of people live in joint households than nuclear ones (Shah 1999: 1180). However, among the educationally advantaged, urban elite in India, there appears to be a greater preponderance of nuclear households, although more research is needed in this area. Not a single respondent in my sample indicated joint household residence.
6. This is somewhat at variance with the status of the family in contemporary Western society, where it is acquiring a new historical form, the postfamilial family (Beck-Gernsheim 1998: 54). However, this may not be embraced by North American and British Indians. Patricia Uberoi's article (Uberoi 1998) on contemporary commercial Hindi cinema points to the felt need among such diasporic communities for the rearticulation and regeneration of patriarchal and patrilineal family values among its possibly wayward, Westernised youth. Clearly, the significance of place as location is important in understanding the Indian family.
7. See Hudson (1984) for a discussion of the dilemmas created by the different connotations attached to the terms femininity and adolescence as discourses.
8. Gilligan's work has also addressed the importance of 'moral questions' in adolescence, which she suggests is a crucial time for a 'moral education' (Gilligan 1988). See also Gilligan et al. (1990) and Gilligan (1995).
9. For an assessment of the contemporary educational status of young women in India, see the collection of essays in Wazir (2000).
10. Although the relationship between body imagery and sexuality is imbricated in gender identity, this aspect of young women's lives is not the focus of my chapter. I have discussed it elsewhere in the context of women's experience of violence in intimate relationships (Thapan 1997).
11. Srilata has argued that in 'post-liberalization India, we mark the emergence of a differently normative female subject' who exists in the space of a 'cosmopolitan modernity'. Although this 'new woman' is 'apparently unmarked in terms of caste, religion and language, a complex and elaborate semiotic system operates to produce her as essentially "Indian" and ... as the normative new Indian' (1999: 61).
12. I have examined elsewhere how gender identity is both constructed and experienced by women through the medium of textual imagery and visual representation in women's magazines in contemporary India (Thapan 2000).

References

Bagchi, Jasodhara (ed.). 1995. *Indian Women. Myth and Reality*. Hyderabad: Sangam Books Ltd.

Beck-Gernsheim, Elisabeth. 1998. 'On the Way to a Post-familial Family', *Theory, Culture and Society*, 15 (3–4): 53–70.

Bhattacharya, Malini. 1994. 'Women in Dark Times: Gender, Culture and Politics', *Social Scientist*, 22 (3–4).

Bhatty, Zarina. 1988. 'Socialisation of the Female Muslim Child in Uttar Pradesh', in K. Chanana (ed.), *Socialisation, Education and Women. Explorations in Gender Identity*, pp. 231–39. New Delhi: Orient Longman Ltd.

Bourdieu, Pierre. 1977. *Outline of a Theory of Practice* (Translator, R. Nice). Cambridge: Cambridge University Press.

Chatterjee, Partha. 1993. 'The Nationalist Resolution of the Women's Question', in K. Sangari and S. Vaid, (eds), *Recasting Women. Essays in Colonial History*, pp. 233–53. New Delhi: Kali for Women.

Chaudhuri, Maitrayee. 1998. 'Advertisements, Print Media and the New Indian Woman', *Social Action*, July: 239–52.

———. 1999. 'The World of Advertisements and Globalisation: A Look at the Print Media, in R.M. Sethi (ed.), *Globalisation, Culture and Women's Development*, pp. 239–56. Jaipur: Rawat Publications.

Coleman, James S. 1961. *The Adolescent Society*. New York: The Free Press.

Das, Veena. 1988. 'Femininity and Orientation to the Body'. in K. Chanana (ed.), *Socialisation, Education and Women. Explorations in Gender Identity*, pp. 193–207. New Delhi: Orient Longman Ltd.

Deshpande, Satish. 1998. 'After Culture. Renewed Agendas for the Political Economy of India', *Cultural Dynamics*, 10 (2): 147–69.

Dube, Leela. 1988. 'Socialisation of Hindu Girls in Patrilineal India', in K. Chanana (ed.), *Socialisation, Education and Women. Explorations in Gender Identity*, pp. 166–92. New Delhi: Orient Longman Ltd.

Erikson, Erik H. 1968. *Identity: Youth and Crisis*. New York: Norton.

———. 1979. *Identity: A Reissue*. New York: Norton.

Ferguson, Harvie. 1997. 'Me and My Shadows: On the Accumulation of Body-images in Western Society Part Two – The Corporeal Forms of Modernity, *Body and Society*, 3 (4): 1–31.

Ganesh, Kamala. 1989. 'Seclusion of Women and the Structure of Caste', in Maitrayi Krishnaraj and Karuna Chanana (eds), *Gender and the Household Domain*. New Delhi: Sage Publications.

Gilligan, Carol. 1982. *In a Different Voice*. Cambridge: Harvard University Press.

———. 1988. 'Prologue. Adolescent Development Reconsidered', in Carol Gilligan, Jane Victoria Ward and Jill McLean Taylor (eds), *Mapping the Moral Domain. A Contribution of Women's Thinking to Psychological Theory and Education*, pp. vii–xxxix. Harvard: Center for the Study of Gender, Education and Human Development.

———. 1995. 'The Centrality of Relationship in Psychological Development: A Puzzle, Some Evidence and a Theory', in Maud Blair, Janet Holland and Sue Sheldon (eds), *Identity and Diversity: Gender and the Experience of Education*, pp. 194–208. Clevedon: Multilingual Matters Ltd. in Association with the Open University.

Gilligan, Carol, Nona P. Lyons and Trudy J. Hanmer, (eds). 1990. *Making Connections. The Relational Worlds of Adolescent Girls at Emma Willard School*. Cambridge: Harvard University Press.

Hudson, Barbara. 1984. 'Femininity and Adolescence', in Angela McRobbie and Mica Nava (eds), *Gender and Generation*, pp. 31–53. London: Macmillan.

Hughes, Alex and Anne Witz. 1997. 'Feminism and the Matter of Bodies: From de Beauvoir to Butler', *Body and Society*, 3 (1): 47–60.

John, Mary E. 1998. 'Globalisation, Sexuality and the Visual Field', in Mary E. John and Janaki Nair (eds), *A Question of Silence? The Sexual Economies of Modern India*, pp. 368–96. New Delhi: Kali for Women.

Kakar, Sudhir. 1988. 'Feminine Identity in India', in Rehana Ghadially (ed.), *Women in Indian Society*, pp. 44–68. New Delhi: Sage Publications.

Lateef, Shahida. 1990. *Muslim Women in India. Political and Private Realities*. New Delhi: Kali for Women.

Mann, Chris. 1996. 'Girls' Own Story: The Search for a Sexual Identity in Times of Family Change', in Janet Holland and Lisa Adkins (eds), *Sex, Sensibility and the Gendered Body*, pp. 78–95. New York: St. Martin's Press.

McNay, Lois. 1999. 'Gender, Habitus and the Field', *Theory, Culture and Society*, 16 (1): 95–117.

Saigol, Rubina. 1994. 'Boundaries of Consciousness: Interface between the Curriculum, Gender and Nationalism', in N.S. Khan, R. Saigol and A.S. Zia (eds), *Locating the Self: Reflections of Women and Multiple Identities*. Lahore: ASR.

Shah, Arvind M. 1999. 'Changes in the Family and the Elderly', *Economic and Political Weekly*, 15 May: 1179–82.

Shohat, Ella. 1997. 'Post-third-worldist Culture: Gender, Nation and the Cinema', in M. Jaqui Alexander and Chandra Talpade Mohanty (eds), *Feminist Genealogies, Colonial Legacies, Democratic Futures*, pp. 183–209. New York: Routledge.

Srilata, K. 1999. 'The Story of the "up-market" Reader: Femina's "New woman" and the Normative Feminist Subject', *Journal of Arts and Ideas*, 32: 61–72.

Thapan, Meenakshi. 1997. 'Femininity and its Discontents. The Woman's Body in Intimate Relationships', in Meenakshi Thapan (ed.), *Embodiment. Essays on Gender and Identity*, pp. 172–93. New Delhi: Oxford University Press (under the auspices of the Nehru Memorial Museum and Library, New Delhi).

———. 2000. 'The body in the Mirror: Women and Representation in Contemporary India', in Neera Chandhoke (ed.), *Mapping Histories. Essays in Honour of Professor Ravinder Kumar*, pp. 337–64. New Delhi: Tulika.

Uberoi, Patricia. 1998. 'The Diaspora Comes Home: Disciplining Desire in DDLJ', *Contributions to Indian Sociology*, 32 (2): 305–35.

Wazir, Rekha (ed.). 2000. *The Gender Gap in Basic Education*. New Delhi: Sage Publications.

TWO

Male Hindi Filmgoers' Gaze: An Ethnographic Interpretation of Gender Construction*

Steve Derné and Lisa Jadwin

Laura Mulvey's contention that film-viewing technologies contribute to the power of the male gaze was a central focus of film theory throughout the 1970s and 1980s (VanZoonen 1994: 88). Mulvey argued that the gaze of the camera, the gaze of men within a narrative on the screen, and the gaze of male spectators in cinema halls all create the woman as a spectacle for male desire. Drawing on psychoanalytic theory, Mulvey (1975 [1988]: 61) identified scopophilia—'using another person as an object of sexual stimulation through sight'—as one of the primary pleasures of cinema. She argued that the 'determining male gaze projects its phantasy on the female figure', subjecting it to a 'controlling and curious gaze' (ibid.: 62, 59). Assuming that films' 'preoccupations reflect the psychical obsessions of the society' that produces them, Mulvey (ibid.: 59, 60) analysed screening conventions and camera angles to argue that films position men to look and women to-be-looked-at. She argued that the technology of film advances mechanisms for looking, multiplying the pleasures produced by looking, hence empowering men, since they are the ones who are already positioned to look.

Without necessarily embracing Mulvey's psychoanalytic assumptions, feminist theorists and activists often identify men's objectification of women as an important component of male power. Catharine MacKinnon (1989: 124) argues, for instance, that 'sexual objectification' is 'the primary process of the subjection of women'. A range of feminist researchers have shown how the 'to-be-looked-at-ness' (Mulvey 1975 [1988]: 59, 62), which the male gaze creates, harms women's self-image and sense of well-being. Often these researchers link this process to media portrayals of women (e.g., VanZoonen 1994: 87; Walters 1995: 56; Wolf 1991). MacKinnon and others show that the objectification of women in pornography and other media plays an important part in prompting male violence. Recognising the role of objectification in women's subordination, feminist activists in the USA, India and elsewhere have criticised films, advertising and beauty contests that project women as sex objects (e.g., Gandhi and Shah 1992: 68–75).

At the same time that feminist research and activism have been highlighting how the objectification of women supports male power, film theory's turn towards an empirical study of the audience's actual pleasure has surprisingly neglected to address Mulvey's influential argument. Mulvey conceived of 'the pleasures of the male/masculine spectators ... as the *direct* result of the way they are positioned by the cinematographic mode of address' (VanZoonen 1994: 92), but 15 years of empirical audience-reception studies show that audiences are not always successfully positioned by cultural products themselves. Rather, cultural products are interpreted in diverse ways (for reviews of this literature see Press 1994, Moores 1993, VanZoonen 1994). Despite the influence of Mulvey's argument, we have few audience-reception studies of cinemagoers or of

*Originally published in *Contributions to Indian Sociology*, Vol. 34, No. 2, 2000, pp. 243–69.

the male audience. While many useful studies examine how readers interpret books (e.g., Christian-Smith 1990; Radway 1984) and magazines (McRobbie 1982) and how viewers watch television (Mankekar 1993; e.g., Press 1991), Shaun Moores's (1993: 33) review of the literature on the 'anthropology of [popular culture] consumption' reveals a striking absence of 'qualitative empirical work on the public settings of cinema spectatorship'. Just as surprisingly, reception researchers have devoted little attention to how the mainstream male audience interprets popular culture. Birmingham school researchers' interest in understanding the struggles of oppressed groups prompted them to focus on studying women and working-class men. Other researchers conducted reception studies of women to understand what women gained from popular culture texts which appeared to bolster stereotypes that oppress them (VanZoonen 1994: 97). Perhaps because male pleasures seemed easily understood by examining texts themselves, there have been few studies of men's reception, as men (Moores 1993: 49).

Certainly, film theorists have tempered and debated Mulvey's early formulation. Mulvey herself (1988b [1981]) has subsequently recognized, for instance, that films also position women filmgoers to gaze at on-screen images. It is nonetheless striking that her influential argument about cinema shapes men's gaze has not as yet been empirically addressed through a study of male filmgoers in cinema halls.

This chapter considers whether films prompt a controlling male gaze that objectifies women through an ethnographic study of filmgoing men in India—the country with the world's largest film audience and the largest production of feature films. Consistent with Mulvey's argument, the first author's interviews with Indian male filmgoers and participant observation in Indian movie houses, as well as our consideration of Hindi-film fan magazines show that Indian films do indeed facilitate men's controlling gaze, which is an important part of male power. While MacKinnon (1989: 139) highlights pornography as a privileged sphere that encourages the objectification of women, our study suggests that mainstream cinema may play at least as important a role in encouraging objectification.

While emphasising that men's filmgoing pleasures are complicit in male dominance, this ethnographic study reveals that other processes are also at work. Driven by an anxious uncertainty about their Indianness, men do not make *all* women the object of the gaze, but instead distinguish between those whom they see as legitimate objects of the gaze, and those whom they feel should be protected from it. This suggests that issues of national identity (in addition to gender) shape the nature of the gaze. This study also shows that while men enjoy gazing at women, they also gaze at on-screen men and even come to see themselves as controlled by others' looks. Ethnographic evidence suggests, then, that the dynamics of the gaze are more complex than Mulvey's original formulation would suggest.

Studying Men in Indian Cinema Halls

Following the lead of reception researchers, we combine a textual analysis of commercial Hindi films with interviews and fieldwork conducted with male filmgoers in India in 1991. We supplement this with a consideration of fan magazines, popular journalism and mainstream film reviews, allowing us to balance our interpretations with indigenous ones.

Textual Analysis

Janice Radway's combination of ethnographic and textual analysis drove the success of her study of romance reading that prompted the recent wave of audience-reception studies. Radway (1986: 99) insists that one must 'begin with a real audience's conscious, surface interpretations', but she also identifies the importance of the analyst's textual interpretation. Our study is supported by a textual analysis of popular films that played in India between 1986 and 1991.

Much of this analysis focuses on Hindi-film love stories, which were the biggest hits of this period (Derné 1995b). The unprecedented success of *Ram Teri Ganga Maili* (which was released in December 1985) ushered in a wave of love stories that dominated the Hindi film world for the next six or seven years, culminating with the 1990s blockbuster, *Maine Pyar Kiya (I Fell in Love)*. Like most love stories, these films celebrate the love of a hero and heroine that overcomes the objections of parents. As in most love stories, the heroine is a traditionally modest Indian woman who respects family hierarchies, while the hero transgresses family authority and flaunts a lifestyle that many Indians would see as unacceptably 'Westernised' (see also Thomas 1995: 161–72). We focus especially on hit social films like *Maine Pyar Kiya* that have attracted a broad audience.

However, we also analyse action films and less prestigious social films that continued to play to large, if less diverse, audiences during the height of the success of love stories. Unmarried men are intensive users of film culture, sometimes seeing films 20, or even 30 times a month, and seeing their favourite film dozens of times (Derné 1995b, 1995c). Action films and B movies are unlikely to be seen by women and less likely to be seen by married men, but they still have an important influence on unmarried men, who often see every release at least once. Indeed, because the cinema hall is more male-dominated during screenings of such films, they may play a particularly important role in prompting men's objectification of women.

Fieldwork and Interviews with Filmgoers

Recent reception studies show that to understand reception from the viewpoint of actual audiences, one must examine the situational contexts in which popular culture is used and interpreted (Moores 1993: 32; Radway 1984). Following this insight, Steve Derné conducted participant observation with filmgoers in the north Indian city of Dehra Dun. For three months in the summer of 1991, he hung around the six movie houses in Dehra Dun. The movie houses included two plush, air-conditioned, relatively expensive cinema halls that catered to men and women of all classes by showing prestigious social films; one dilapidated movie hall which lacked even functioning fans, but still attracted fair audiences of poor urban men with its low prices and fare of B movies and action film revivals; and a relatively comfortable theatre that showed first-run action films to almost exclusively male audiences of various classes. Derné participated in filmgoing rituals, buying tickets, watching people watch films, and participating in tea-shop discussions in and around all of these theatres. He played the role of participant observer with people of a range of classes from the relatively expensive balcony sections that cater to families and middle-class people, and the less expensive floor seats that are mostly patronised by young men and the urban poor (Derné 2000).

Derné conducted taped interviews with 22 male filmgoers, whom he interviewed in and around movie houses.[1] Since the bulk of the Hindi film audience consists of young men, it is not surprising that most of the men whom he met (and subsequently interviewed) were young and unmarried.[2] Eighteen of the men were Hindus, two were Muslims and two were Sikhs. About 41 per cent (9/22) of the men were still in school, recently graduated, or unemployed. The employed men represented a wide range of jobs (transport, masonry, carpentry, tailoring, selling fruit), and four of the 13 employed men were solidly middle class. Derné asked men why they enjoyed the filmgoing experience and who they saw films with. He asked men to tell him about their favourite films, and their favourite heroes and heroines. He asked why they disliked particular films, heroes and heroines, and about the themes they found salient in *Maine Pyar Kiya*.

Consideration of Indigenous Commentaries

Indian film has sparked a large amount of commentary in fan magazines and popular journalism. Reception researchers Harrington and Bielby (1995) have shown the usefulness of considering fan magazines as a complement to interviews and textual analyses. When Derné was in India between 1986–87 and 1991, he collected many of the two dozen popular magazines that focus on the film industry, allowing us to consider questions like the following: What trends do film magazines emphasise? What sorts of criticisms are apparent in magazine questioning of film heroes and heroines? How do film directors and film stars choose to present their films and image to fans? What parts of films do letter-writers emphasise as appealing or appalling?

Fan magazines, of course, do not reflect the desires and concerns of fans in any direct way. Indeed, they probably play a role in inciting these desires. Still, we use popular fan magazines to suggest that the trends we identify through textual analyses are salient. We use them to provide further support for the conclusions we draw from interviews.

Given the reception work which suggests that broad cultural judgments about cultural products influence reception (e.g., Mankekar 1993: 488; Moores 1993: 38; Press 1994; Radway 1984), we also consider reviews of films and commentaries on films that appear in mainstream Indian newspapers and magazines like *India Today* and the *Times of India*. These sources give us access to the broader discourses about film that occur in the wider community.

A note about recent developments. We focus on the films which were most popular during the first author's period of field research and do not offer an in-depth consideration of more recent developments. Prompted by the tremendous success of *Aankhen* (1993), subsequent to this research, there was a period in which many films included raunchy comedy and smutty lyrics (Chandra 1993; Katiyar 1994; Saari 1994). Filmmakers have increasingly shown heroines in clothing styles (like miniskirts) that in previous eras would have been rejected as too Westernised or too revealing (Chakravarti 1998; Chopra 1997). In recent years, Hollywood films have, for the first time, been hits in some of the urban centers (Chandra 1995; Ray 1998). Certainly, scholars should consider how these changes might transform the Hindi film world.

But important continuities remain. Action films continue to attract male viewers with their themes of violence and revenge, but love stories continue to be the biggest hits (Uberoi 1998: 314). As in the earlier period, viewers see these love stories as more serious films, and they appear to attract a broader audience (Uberoi, forthcoming). As in the 1980s and early 1990s, love stories continue to focus on balancing love with respect for family authority. As in earlier love stories, heroes continue to seek consent to marry from the guardians of their beloveds (e.g., *Pardes* 1997; *Dilwale Dulhania Le Jayenge* 1995; see Uberoi 1998, forthcoming). While mid- and late 1990s heroines often appear in jeans and mini-skirts that the men whom the first author interviewed in the early 1990s rejected as excessively revealing, their relative modesty and commitment to family duty continue to be contrasted with anti-heroines' excessive sexuality and disregard for the concerns of family authorities (e.g., *Dil to Pagal Hai* 1999; *Hum Aapke Hain Kaun* 1994; ibid; also Chopra 1997). While heroes increasingly embrace fashions that are associated with Western lifestyles (e.g., Chakravarti 1998), filmmakers continue to contrast heroes' controlled sexuality and willingness to check their own feelings to meet family obligations with the womanizing and selfishness of Westernised villains (e.g., *Pardes*; *Dilwale Dulhania Le Jayenge*; *Hum Aapke Hain Kaun*). Even though some mid- and late-1990s heroes and heroines are depicted as living abroad, they continue to mediate between India and the West by embracing traditional family arrangements (e.g., *Dilwale Dulhania Le Jayenge*; *Pardes*; *see* Uberoi 1998).

Male Indian Filmgoers' Gaze at Women

Consistent with Mulvey's expectations, Hindi films position male viewers to gaze at on-screen women by making women the object of both the camera's gaze and the gaze of men within the narrative. Like on-screen male characters, men in cinema halls gawk at women who display themselves in sexy dances. As Mulvey (1975 [1988]: 62) argues, the on-screen woman functions 'on two levels: an erotic object for the character within the screen story, and as erotic object for the spectator within the auditorium, with a shifting tension between the looks on either side of the screen'. For instance, *Shahenshah* [*King of Kings*, 1988] shows an on-screen male audience staring at the heroine dancing in a wet sari in a swimming pool in the villain's plush residence. At screenings of *Shahenshah*, which played in revival at a Dehra Dun theatre catering to poor urban men, men gawked at the heroine as they rustled in their seats. A mainstream journalist's description of Shilpa Shirodkar's dancing captures a similar scene in *Trinetra* (1991): 'Nothing seems to come between a tipsy Shilpa and the camera as she writhes on the floor—surrounded by a crowd of men with lust filled eyes and tongues hanging out' (Jain 1991: 33). The screenings of *Trinetra* that Derné observed at a plush Dehra Dun cinema hall catering to a middle-class audience prompted male spectators to squirm in their seats, staring spellbound at Shilpa's dancing. He observed similar behaviour among men at the full range of cinema halls in Dehra Dun, suggesting that it is shared by men of a range of classes.

The complaints of Indian film critics and journalists reveal a concern that such scenes prompt men's controlling look. One columnist complained about the way men stared at Shilpa Shirodkar as she entered a studio—even though she was dressed in a 'sober' *salwar kamiz*. The columnist reported that the men 'ogled' her with 'hungry looks': 'I could see lust in their eyes and that is a very dangerous sight to see in the morning.' The columnist recognised such looks as part of men's control:

> That morning I realized we were still far, far away from the civilized society we are living in or are claim-ing to live in, and *parampara* [tradition] and *sanskriti* [culture] and all those high sounding words can go into the dustbins of the politicians and the social workers ... who are out to serve society. (Ali 1991: 10)

Male filmgoers confirm the pleasure of scopophilia when they talk about their favourite heroines. About half of the men whom the first author interviewed mentioned dancing ability or a beautiful body as the reason for a particular heroine being their favourite.[3] For instance, one unmarried 22-year-old called Dimple Kapadia his favourite heroine because 'her body is sexy', while another unmarried 20-year-old said that he was seeing *Prem Qaidi* [*Love Prisoner*, 1991] daily because he was intoxicated with the excellence of the girl (*larki*) in the film. A shoe repairman in his 20s who sees films daily said that he loves Karisma Kapoor in *Prem Qaidi* because 'she's beautiful'. 'She's not at all modest [*sharmati*],' he said, perhaps referring to how she dances in a swimsuit in the film. 'She's like an American girl.' By contrast, one 17-year-old complained of a film he disliked by saying that the heroine was unattractive (*akarshan*). (While younger, less affluent men were more likely to comment on the sexiness of their favourite heroines' bodies, the gawking of men of diverse classes in a range of theatres suggests that scopophilic pleasure is actually not class-specific). The discredit attached to the sexiness of Hindi films (Derné 1995c) suggests, moreover, that men may over-emphasise socially acceptable reasons, like acting skills, when talking about their favourite heroines. Shilpa Shirodkar said in a fan-magazine interview that while the audience 'love[s] to ogle at a sensuous woman on screen, when the lights come on, you'll only hear them praising an actress' acting ability' (Iyer 1991: 79). What is surprising, then, is that so many male filmgoers admit to liking their favourite heroines because of their bodies! Certainly, the woofs and catcalls that men let out during dance scenes indicate how much they enjoy staring at women.

Men's descriptions of how women must restrict their movements in order to appear correct 'in the eyes of society' (Derné 1995a: 30–35, 50–51) suggests that a controlling gaze is an important component of male power in India. A 28-year-old husband whom Derné interviewed in Banaras, India, in 1987[4] described looks from every direction as urgently compelling women to follow 'social restrictions':

> If [a woman] goes out on her own wish, people will point fingers at her over this. If she moves around with a strange man, people will point fingers at her. If she doesn't obey her elders, people will point fingers at her .... If the woman wants to do any work outside, then fingers begin to be raised at her from every side because the main responsibility of building or ruining a child is on the woman.

For this man, like others, controlling looks create an imperative that restricts women, limiting their opportunities. Decades of research in India show that restrictions on women's movement outside the home makes it difficult for them to participate fully in political, educational and economic life (e.g., Derné 1994: 223, n1 for a review), and the demands of a controlling look are an important force behind these restrictions.

Certainly, men are not a homogeneous group, all of whom objectify women. But by prompting the objectifying gaze of some men, films play a role in limiting women's movements.

Protecting Women from the Gaze

But do Indian men make all women the object of their gaze? Do they see some women as legitimate objects of the gaze, and others as so valuable that they should be protected from it? Does a concern with maintaining a sense of Indianness (in addition to a sense of masculinity) shape men's gaze?

Anxieties about Indianness

Identification with Indian tradition is an essential part of many Indians' self-conceptions (Derné 1992: 44–47; Kakar 1982: 214). But for men today, the secure feeling of belonging that a sense of Indianness provides is sometimes threatened by often imagined movements towards impersonal and bureaucratic economic forms (Nandy 1989: 4; Roland 1988: 17–18) and gender equality (Calman 1992: 12; Mankekar 1993: 484), both of which Indians associate with Western cultures. Several psychoanalysts show that Indian men often experience anxiety over conflicting lifestyles and normative frames (Alter 1992: 238; Kakar 1982: 214; Nandy 1989: 2; Roland 1988: 25).

Indeed, in talking about their family lives, many of the Hindu men whom Derné interviewed in Banaras in 1987 expressed uneasiness about changes which they feel are being brought about by a 'Westernised' elite that has embraced 'modern' principles. They complained that the growth of immorality and selfishness threatened joint-family harmony, and blamed modern education for encouraging women to challenge their husbands' authority and insist on moving freely outside the home (Derné forthcoming). They claimed that the alien forces of materialism and greed have led parents of sons to focus more on getting a good dowry than arranging appropriate marriages. One 26-year-old husband complained, for instance, that traditional Hindu arranged marriages are being challenged by *filmwalle* [filmmakers and filmgoers] and 'government' officials, like then prime minister Rajiv Gandhi, whom he described as 'trying to mix Indian culture with dirt'. Although the tensions that men describe are probably an inherent part of joint-family living, arranged marriages and restrictions on women's movements outside the home,[5] 'many men nonetheless imagine a happier era in which brothers lived harmoniously together, parents found suitable spouses for their children, and women happily accepted the restrictions placed on them. For many men, such gender and family relations are defining features of Indianness.

Even though these interviews focused on family life, men still voiced frustration with the corruption they associate with bureaucracy—a frustration that is widespread in India today (Alter 1992; Wadley 1994: Chapter 5). In talking about laws that seek to combat dowry, a married 30-year-old emphasised the confusing and money-based maze of India's legal system:

> The Government of India has [outlawed dowry,] but [the legal system's] process is so back and forth that nobody wants to go anywhere near it. The process of law is so injurious and costly that not a single good person wants to go there.

Often, men linked corruption to an abandonment of traditional religious values in favour of the city-based materialism and lack of respect that they believe to be imported from the West. In describing the evil of dowry demands, a 76-year-old complained of the influence of materialism and the decline of old ways:

> India is becoming more and more like Western places. There is an increasing attraction to the artificial and materialistic [*bhautikavadi*]. No one moves according to the heart [*hrdaya, dil*] and soul [*atma*] anymore. Instead, people move according to what they see in the outer world, whether it is eating, clothing, or life-style. Now there is no following of the old things. Now they are taking the new things.

This broad concern with the alien and corrupting influence of materialism, city life and bureaucracy produces anxiety among men who must after all participate in these very spheres.

Engagement with films often reveals ambivalence about modern lifestyles. Filmgoers often exhibit a fascination with the West, sporting Westernised clothes like Nike t-shirts, Rayban sunglasses, and shirts with American flags or messages in English (like 'Because I'm the Best that's Why'). One 23-year-old college student even said that he sees films partly to educate himself 'about what it means to be modern'. Yet filmgoers also complain that films are too violent, too sexy, or simply 'not good for Indian culture'. Young men's almost obsessive filmgoing may reflect their attraction to modern ways, while the obsessive complaints about films (e.g., Derné 1995b: 182–84) reflect an unease with departures from Indian traditions. The married 26-year-old who complained that filmmakers are trying to mix Indian culture with dirt nonetheless said that he enjoyed the sexy *Ram Teri Ganga Maili*, a film regularly criticised by both media and common people for having exposed the breasts of the heroine. A married 29-year-old whom the first author interviewed in 1987 similarly said that he enjoyed *Ram Teri* 'very much', yet complained that cinema was too 'intoxicating'.

Emphasising Modest Women

While films construct women characters who are made to 'expose' themselves to men's looks, the most popular films also highlight the modesty of other (more Indian) women characters. The most popular films of the last 25 years contrast traditionally modest Indian heroines with 'Westernised' Indian women who are too immodest and forward. The 1990s *Maine Pyar Kiya* [*I Fell in Love*], one of the three biggest hits of the last 25 years, contrasts a modest heroine who can claim protection from the gaze with an immodest 'anti-heroine',[6] who exposes her body in an effort to manipulate men.

Maine Pyar Kiya shows the heroine, Suman (played by Bhagyashree), as a traditionally modest village woman. Suman wears traditional saris or (more often) *salwar kamizes* that protect her body from men's gaze. When her father takes a job as a diesel mechanic in Dubai, Suman goes to Bombay to stay with an old friend of her father's. Soon after her father leaves, Prem (played by Salman Khan), a son of the family she is staying with, returns from America. Unaware that he has returned, Suman stumbles into a bathroom that the hero is using. Embarrassed at catching him exposed, she lectures him that he should lock the door to protect himself from being seen by others.

The filmmakers emphasise Suman's modesty as distinctively Indian by contrasting her with Sima, the modern daughter of one of Prem's father's business associates. The filmmakers portray Sima (whose name means 'limit' in Hindi) as a modern woman, who boldly tries to win Prem's affections by wearing Western clothes that expose her legs. The audience first sees a cigarette-smoking Sima drag racing with her father against cars piloted by Prem and his father. As they drive, her father tells Sima of his plans to get control over Prem's father's company by marrying Sima to Prem. Sima tells her father to 'act out friendship' for Prem's father while she 'acts out love [*mohabbat*]' for Prem. When Sima comes upon Prem changing clothes in his bedroom, she (unlike Suman) is not embarrassed: rather, she spreads out on Prem's bed, and tries to use her red lipstick, short hair and short red dress to seduce him.

Film journalists describe the appeal of *Maine Pyar Kiya* and other recent hits by emphasising the modesty of female characters like Suman. One writer for a mainstream magazine reported that 'what seems to have really got to people is [*Maine Pyar Kiya*'s] advocacy of a *particularly Indian* virtue moth-balled for a long time: sharam (coyness)' (Jain 1990: 65).[7] This writer describes the 'key scene' as the one in which Prem gives Suman a skimpy dress to wear. 'At this point, the camera goes behind the girl as she draws open the cloth. The camera sees nothing except her covered back and [Prem] in a state of rapture. But he quickly gathers himself and drapes the cloth around her. Modesty restored' (ibid.).

The salience of the celebration of modest Indian women is apparent in Indian actresses' preoccupation with defining themselves in opposition to modern women who expose their bodies. In Hindi-film magazines, actresses like Bhagyashree (who played *Maine Pyar Kiya*'s Suman) repeatedly emphasise their modest image:

Today, I am in a different position because I have a different image. When producers sign me, they want something different. Bhagyashree is completely different from those who wear miniskirts. (Tandan 1991: 19)

In nearly all of her film-magazine interviews, Bhagyashree reiterates the same point:

My image is very honorable [*sammanapurn*] and dignified [*garimaya*]. I would never think of becoming a sex symbol. Therefore, any producer who wants me to wear a miniskirt is wasting his time [*bekar*]. (*Chitralekha* 1991: 36)

Other actresses are similarly careful to emphasise their modesty. Manisha Koirala quit a film to protect her 'royal image [English phrase]' because she was 'not prepared to expose herself to the public's view' (*Filmi Kaliyan* 1991a: 32). Chandni similarly emphasised that she is 'not prepared to expose for any price' (*Filmi Kaliyan* 1991b: 14). The salient distinction is between the *salwar kamiz* and sari, which protect the body from men's gaze, and miniskirts, bikinis and form-revealing jeans. As Shilpa Shirodkar, a heroine who is often criticised for exposing, puts it, 'the fight is invariably between a mini and a sari' (Iyer 1991: 79).

Fan-magazine writers praise heroines who act appropriately Indian by protecting their modesty. They question actresses about any racy scenes they have appeared in, and about whether they will kiss or expose. The following criticism of one actress who exposes 'too much' is typical:

> What Shilpa Shirodkar did in ... *Trinetra* was shocking to say the least. One enlightened collegian was on the brink of losing her cool and said: 'What does she think she is Madonna or Samantha Fox ...? Is she come here to show her talent or to shamelessly display her body?' (Ali 1991)

In making the comparison with Madonna and Samantha Fox, the columnist identifies the heroine who 'crosses all limits of decency' (ibid.) with the shameless West.

Handling Ambivalence about Western Ways

Films of the 1980s and early 1990s, then, encourage men to distinguish between shameless women who willingly expose themselves to men's look and modest women who should be protected from the gaze of men. Even when men are attracted by modern lifestyles and participate in modern bureaucracies and educational systems that sometimes seem alien and corrupt, they still identify themselves as Indian because of their marriage to a modest, sari-wearing wife who toils for them at home (Derné 1999a).

While men are titillated by sexy dancing and posters of heroines showing leg, *all* of the men whom Derné interviewed in 1991 praised modest heroines like *Maine Pyar Kiya*'s Suman because of their *distinctively Indian* modesty. One unmarried 22-year-old college student, despite wearing jeans and a t-shirt with an English slogan, nevertheless complained of Western influences on Indian women:

> According to the Indian culture, [women] should wear *salwar kamizes*. Wearing jeans and smoking cigarettes are things of a different country and are separate.

An unmarried 20-year-old similarly focused on the importance of Indian women wearing clothing that covers the body. Sima, he says, 'is not up to the standards of our Indian culture. Our tradition demands saris and *salwar kamizes*.' According to another 20-year-old, 'jeans and skirts should be banned and Indian culture should be restored'.[8]

Men's taste in heroines is similarly consistent with their preference for modest traditional women who protect themselves from being looked at. Each man who identified a heroine he disliked named those, like Kimi Katkar, who are famous for 'exposing'. Men complained that some heroines 'wear bikinis one film after another' (unmarried 19-year-old), or that some actresses are 'openly used to attract the audience for a reason other than their acting' (unmarried-24-year-old). Of the heroines men mentioned as their favourites—Madhuri, Sridevi, Rekha, Smita Patil, Dimple, Bhagyashree and Juhi Chawla—none has a reputation for exposing.[9]

As VanZoonen (1994: 92) notes, Mulvey sees the gaze as shaped exclusively by gender. Our analysis suggests that national identity may also play a role in shaping the gaze's direction and dynamics. Rather than assuming that gender alone shapes the gaze, researchers should address other salient identities as well.

While many men appear attracted to heroines' modesty, modesty also acts as a signifier for women's commitment to fulfilling family duties. An 18 year old high school student said that he liked 'the role taken by Suman because she serves her family in a good way. She is one who understands (*samajhdar*).' A 20 year old who likes 'women who wear salwar kamizes' said that 'a modern woman would not be able to do the good work of serving the family (*ghar*).'

Of course anyone familiar with Hindi films in more recent years will recognize the steady loosening of the standard of modesty for heroines. Yet Indian films continue to show Indian women as more committed to modesty and family duty than their Westernised counterparts. Only in the early 1980s did film makers begin to show heroines on motor bikes (Thomas 1995: 181n8). Only in the mid-1980s did heroines' screen kisses become more common. By the late 1990s film-makers routinely showed heroines wearing the mini-skirts and jeans that the men whom the first author interviewed rejected as excessively revealing in the early 1990s. But one mainstream critic described this change as mere 'Hollywood-inspired gloss' which did not change the 'desi (Indian)' 'core.... The presentation may be MTV but the values are still 100% traditional' (Chopra 1997). In the recent hit *Dil To Pagal Hai* the heroine Madhuri Dixit is a 'trendy leotard-clad dancer who refuses to settle for an arranged marriage' but she is still committed to family duties and is willing 'to sacrifice her love to please her foster parents'. In another recent hit, *Raja Hindustani*, the heroine engages in the 'longest kiss in Hindi movie history', but although she is 'an educated city girl' she still refuses to divorce her 'uneducated small-town' husband 'despite his boorish behaviour'. Uberoi's (forthcoming) recent work on 1994' superhit *Hum Aapke Hain Koun* ...! Similarly shows individual desires to meet family duties. The signifiers associated with heroines' commitment to family duty may change, but the imperative remains that heroines maintain that commitment, suggesting its importance to Hindi film audiences.

As VanZoonen (1994: 92) criticizes Mulvey's original formulation for seeing the gaze as shaped exclusively by gender. Our analysis confirms that national identity may also play a role in shaping the gaze's direction and dynamics: anxious about their Indianness, many men distinguish between Westernized women whom they see as legitimate objects of the gaze and distinctively Indian women whom they believe deserve to be protected from it. For many men, attachment to such women is a sign of their Indianness, the study confirms, then, recent film studies work which argues that gender is not the only salient identity that shapes the gaze.

Maintaining Male Dominance

While films define modest Indian women as deserving protection from the gaze, this doesn't diminish the male gaze's role in bolstering male dominance. First, films encourage men to root their sense of Indianness in having a subservient wife who cooks and cleans for them at home, thus supporting patriarchal family structures. Films encourage men to find their Indianness in women's traditionalism, and suggest that they can compensate for a lack of power within alienating bureaucracies by emphasising their power over their dependent wives (see also Derné 1999a).

Second, for most husbands the distinction between women who should be protected from the gaze and those who can be unabashedly stared at is fluid, allowing husbands to objectify their wives. Even the sensitive Prem asks Suman to wear a revealing dress for him. Before he comes to his senses and covers her exposed body, his insistent stare invokes an expression of pain on Suman's face. A 27-year-old husband whom the first author interviewed in 1987 praised Indian women's subservience as a key part of India's tradition. India's 'most wonderful tradition', he said, is that 'even when there are difficulties' a woman's shyness [*sharm*] will prevent her from complaining about anything in her *sasural* (father-in-law's house). A woman, this man opined, understands whatever happens in her husband's home as gold, 'even if it is dirt'. While praising the distinctively Hindustani 'shyness [*sharm*] and deference [*lihaj*]' that give women 'status [*man*] and prestige [*maryada*]', the man nonetheless expected his wife to expose herself for him whenever he wants: 'A wife should do whatever her husband wants. If her husband wants her to wear jeans and a t-shirt, then she should dress that way.' This man, like some of the filmgoers whom Derné interviewed in 1991,[10] insisted that the woman who is appropriately modest in public be willing, like Suman, to expose herself to her husband's gaze in private. Men externalise the alienness of Westernisation by projecting it onto too-modern characters like Sima, allowing them to gaze at their modest wives as well.

Third, men who protect modest women by shielding them from controlling looks effectively limit women's freedom of movement. For Indian women, it is imperative to keep out of men's gaze to avoid being 'branded' (Iyer 1991) as someone as loose as Shilpa Shirodkar. To avoid being ogled by men, women have had to limit their participation in political and economic life, a limitation which has hampered their ability to gain independent power. As Parameswaran's (1997) recent ethnography shows, college-age women often feel unable to move freely about Indian towns because of 'cheap guys peering ... [and] whistling' (in the words of one college student). Even when women gain jobs in the modern economy, male bosses may limit their opportunities for advancement as they try to protect women by refusing to send them to district jobs or preventing them from doing research work on site (e.g., Liddle and Joshi 1986: 134–37). While men may want to protect modest 'Indian' women from a controlling look, such 'protection' limits their public opportunities.

The Male Body as the Object of the Gaze

Mulvey's emphasis on female bodies as the object of the gaze obscures how male bodies are also made the object of the male audience's inquiring look. In her original formulation, Mulvey (1975 [1988]: 63) argued that 'the principles of the ruling ideology' mean that 'the male figure cannot bear the burden of sexual objectification'. In a later essay, Mulvey (1981 [1988]) considers how films may position women viewers to gaze at screen images, but she still fails to consider how male images may be sexually objectified for the male audience. But cinema, as Steven Cohan (1993) argues, has always been invested in the spectacle of the male body.

Indeed, displays of the male body are important in Hindi films. Film stars, fan magazines and the popular Indian press all comment on male actors' strong bodies. In *Maine Pyar Kiya*, the hero's body is on display (as he works out or punches punching bags) more than the body of either the heroine or the anti-heroine. Fan magazines repeatedly reprinted stills of a shirtless Prem pictured with the heroine kneeling at his waist. An interest in the male body is apparent in fan-magazine discourse. One fan-magazine writer commented that the hero Sunny Deol is 'beautiful [*khubsurat*] and strong [*mazbut*] just like his father, [the actor] Dharmendra' (*Sine Ganga* 1991). In a fan-magazine interview, hero Sunjay Dutt proclaimed that 'If you have a great body which can be displayed, then I don't think there's anything wrong in flaunting it' (Jain 1991: 29). Popular fan magazine *Stardust* featured a spread on a naked Jackie Shroff (ibid.: 32), while another film magazine assessed a hero's chances of success by questioning whether an actor has a hero's 'physique' (Gokuldas 1991).

Some evidence suggests that these bodily displays are enjoyed by female viewers. Like most fan magazines, *Filmi Kaliyan* (a fan magazine that seems from its advertisements to be directed at a female audience) emphasises recent displays of the male body. For instance, the magazine's editors posed the following rhetorical question:

What is happening, Sunny Deol? In every film you're in, the heroine doesn't expose [*ang pradarshan*], but you do! That's okay, you can give the heroine the argument, 'If I have muscles [English, transliterated into Hindi], then why not show them?' (*Filmi Kaliyan* 1991c)

The editor of *Movie* magazine said that he featured a spread 'showing the macho men and their magnificent muscles' because 'women readers had written in asking for' it. 'Women,' he said 'are finally asserting their voyeuristic rights. The feedback to the article was fabulous' (Jain 1991: 32). Consistent with Mulvey's more recent work and feminist discussions of the gaze in the West (VanZoonen 1994: 87–88), women filmgoers may also make male stars the object of their gaze.

For most unmarried men, filmgoing is a practice that celebrates their bonds with each other. Young male filmgoers joke, dance and roughhouse together. They hold hands and put their arms around each other in and around cinema halls. Unmarried men fighting to buy tickets or push their way into movie houses often press tightly against each other. Film themes and film-world discussions may contribute to an emphasis on homosocial attachment. Fan magazines question stars about whether they are homosexual (e.g., Kumar 1991: 47; *Cineadvance* 1991: 11), and film themes celebrate closeness between male friends—a closeness that some viewers recognise as including a homoerotic component (Dissanayake and Sahai 1992: 95). Hindi films show a great deal of physical horseplay between men, and the ubiquitous all-male dance scenes often have an erotic element. In a context that encourages homosocial attachments, young men seem to enjoy objectifying the beautiful male bodies they see on the screen.

Film journalist Madhu Jain (1991: 32) opens her article on sex in Indian cinema by describing how the camera focuses on Jackie Shroff's groin as he dances suggestively, 'thrusting his pelvis back and forth'. Perhaps prompted by such camera angles, the male audience seems to enjoy gazing at male bodies. In *Pyar Ka Devta* [*God of Love*, 1991], which screened at a Dehra Dun theatre catering to the working class, the hero Mithun Chakraborty leads an all-male dance of automechanics. Mithun, as one journalist puts it, is famous for his 'pelvic movements' (ibid.). During screenings of the film in Dehra Dun, the audience whistled and clapped throughout the dance—a reaction that closely paralleled the responses of male audiences to on-screen women's sexy dancing.

In interviews, men say they like heroes who look good. Nearly half of young male filmgoers said that the ability to fight and dance is what makes a hero their favourite. Several commented on how heroes who fight and dance well display excellent bodies. One 22-year-old said, for instance, that Sunny Deol is his favourite actor 'because his acting is the best, and his body is also the best. When he dances, his body comes out. His body is the best.' A 17-year-old said that Anil Kapoor is his favourite 'because he is manly [English]'.[11]

The fact that many male filmgoers get very attached to their favourite heroes implies that many make on-screen images the object of their affection. Men gush that these heroes have particularly special qualities. An unmarried 24-year-old described the action hero Amitabh Bachchan as having 'his own talent and his own way of acting. He doesn't copy anyone.' A married 32-year-old similarly described the romantic hero Jeetender as his favourite because he 'moves deep into the story'. They wear the names of their favorites on their shirts, and paint them on their autorickshaws. Popular hero Mithun Chakraborty (1992), who specialises in homoerotic dances, told how one of his fans has even tattooed his name on his hand. So while male filmgoers like to gaze at women, they seem to enjoy gazing at men as well.

Male Filmgoers as Objects of the Gaze

However, while on-screen male figures may be the object of filmgoing men's gaze, they may also prompt an identification that leads male filmgoers to see themselves as framed by the look of others. Filmgoing is a time for many men to promenade about, displaying themselves. Around cinema halls, men often groom their hair in the rear-view mirrors of motor scooters, or in the glitzy mirrors that are prominent in cinema-hall lobbies or flashy hair salons that surround cinema halls. Men like to wear cologne as they walk about cinema halls with their combs sticking out of their pockets. Filmgoing men, then, seem particularly concerned with how they are seen by others.

This emphasis on styling hair and wearing cologne is also encouraged by films, film heroes and film-world media. The press sometimes comments on the colognes that heroes wear (*Illustrated Weekly of India* 1988). Films often show heroes putting on cologne and grooming themselves in mirrors. In a fan-magazine interview, Sunjay Dutt (1991: 96) described his changing hairstyle: 'Earlier, I had this very soft floppy hair falling on my eyes, and everyone thought it looked very cute. Then people told me, you've got nice expressive eyes. Why don't you push your hair back? But I was bored by then. So, on my next trip abroad I had it cut in spikes in the front. Oh Man! You should have seen the look on people's faces.' While Dutt doesn't always conform to social pressures, he nonetheless sees himself largely as the object of people's gaze. In another fan magazine, a less well-known hero commented on the martial arts and swimming he does to develop his biceps. Like Dutt, this hero was aware of how he is seen. 'Yes, I do notice women reacting to my physique all the time' (Kalarikal 1992: 39).

Like film stars, common men seem very concerned with maintaining appearances. In wide-ranging interviews about family life that the first author conducted in 1987, men often talked about their concern with how they are seen by society. When discussing whether they will marry for love, talk to unrelated women, or separate from their parents, men repeatedly talked about what is and isn't right in society's eyes, what activities are seen with 'good eyes' and what seen with 'bad eyes'. They hoped to avoid activities that are seen with a hateful look and wanted to do things that are seen approvingly (Derné 1995a: 38–40). It is not only Western women and Indian women who are shaped by being made the objects of a gaze, then. To some extent, Indian men are, too.

Male Bodies and Male Power

By focusing on how men gaze at male characters and see themselves as framed by a controlling look, we do not mean to imply that films are any less implicated in male dominance. Mulvey (1975 [1988]: 62) argues that 'in a world ordered by sexual imbalance, pleasure in looking has been split between active/male and passive/female'. While on-screen men are made the object of a gaze, they are nonetheless portrayed as active: male actors like Salman Khan in *Maine Pyar Kiya* display muscles that allow them to act in the world, whether by manipulating heavy machinery or participating in boxing matches. When the editors of a fan magazine aimed largely at women question Sunny Deol about 'exposing' more than the heroines in his films, they reveal an assumption that it is usually the heroine who is made the object of the gaze. The editors go on to say that it is 'okay' for this hero to expose because what he is exposing is his muscles.

The discrepancy between men who display biceps and women who display breasts and legs highlights men's control of violent force. When critics indict women for exposing in Hindi films, they refer to wet saris or swimsuits that expose the outlines of their breasts, or to miniskirts that display their legs. Mandakini, the heroine of 1986's major hit, *Ram Teri Ganga Maili*, was repeatedly asked about the scenes in which her character exposed her breasts as she bathed in a thin sari under a waterfall and later nursed her child (*Cineblitz* 1987; *Madhuri* 1986). These scenes were often discussed by people whom the first author spoke with in Banaras and Delhi in 1986 and 1987. In 1991, Karisma Kapoor was regularly criticised in fan magazines for doing a dance sequence in a swimsuit. By contrast, when critics describe men who expose, they talk about 'biceps' and 'muscles'. What men are exposing, then, is male power. In *Maine Pyar Kiya* Prem ends a physical workout by punching a punching bag. To emphasise how the violence could be directed at the modest heroine, the film shows the heroine's head snapping back each time Prem punches the bag.[12]

Men's bodily displays, then, are in the context of active violence that may bolster male power. As Messner (1992: 15) and others argue, men often maintain power over women by elevating the 'male-body-as-superior through the use (or threat) of violence'. Not only do films display the male body as men work out by punching punching bags, but they also display controlling male bodies and controlled female bodies in the rape scenes that are a standard part of most films (Kakar 1989: 33; Khanzada 1991). Feminist groups' protests of violence in Hindi films is testament to the role such scenes may play in perpetuating violence against women (e.g., Gandhi and Shah 1992: 77).

While films may make both male and female bodies the object of the gaze, then, the different ways that bodies are objectified plays a role in how the gaze works.[13]

Being objectified as a passive object encourages a *controlling* look. Being portrayed as an active body may provoke an interested gaze, but one without the same impulse to control. When the hero of *Maine Pyar Kiya* gazes at the heroine standing passively in a skimpy dress, she responds with a look of pain. When the heroine gazes at the hero's active body working out with a punching bag and begins to say she loves him, he pushes her against the wall and demands that she finish professing her love. Whether an objectified body is presented as active or passive, then, shapes the gaze that it prompts.

Conclusion

Because it is a male-dominated space, the cinema hall may be particularly important for constructing the objectification of women. At cinema halls, men usually outnumber women by four to one, and often by as much as 10 or 15 to one. While closeness between men in cinema halls allows young men to play with homosocial bonds, this predominantly male context also allow men to emphasise male privilege (Bird 1996). Similar to American men's relationships in all-male settings, the erotic bond between men may be neutralised through erotic talk that objectifies women (Messner 1992: 96). In India, young unmarried men who are so involved in filmgoing that they often see several films a week, sometimes use this space to leer at women, making them the objects of their gaze. In a Banaras cinema hall, the first author once saw a group of three college women leave the balcony abruptly because of men's harassing stares. In Dehra Dun, too, the first author once saw a fight break out in a packed elite cinema balcony because several college-age men were verbally taunting several women (see also Manuel 1993: 43). Cinema halls, then, are a privileged site for men's objectification of women—a process which MacKinnon rightly sees as a fundamental basis of male power.

MacKinnon (1989: 118) argues that the social construction of sexuality identifies a woman 'as one whose sexuality exists for someone else, who is socially male'. By contrast, this construction of sexuality defines men by their use of others as objects: 'Woman through male eyes is sex object, that by which man knows himself at once as man and as subject' (ibid.: 123). In India, cinema provides a model of 'doing gender' (West and Zimmerman 1987), in which men are active, looking subjects and women are passive, looked-at objects. Cinema halls provide a space in which interactions accomplish this construction of gender. This study, then, confirms Mulvey's argument that the male audience derives scopophilic pleasure from looking at on-screen women, and that this dynamic encourages the objectification of women that bolsters male power. However, this study also shows that while films create woman as the spectacle of male desire, male filmgoers often make distinctions between the women whom they define as legitimate objects of the gaze, and those whom they believe should be protected from it. This suggests that the gaze's direction is shaped not just by gender identity, but by national identity as well.

This study also shows that many male filmgoers do more than identify with the hero who makes the heroine the object of his gaze. Identifying with the hero's interest in appearing beautiful, male spectators also come to see themselves as framed by others' controlling looks. In addition, many male (and female) filmgoers gain scopophilic pleasure from gazing at men on the screen. Still, this objectification of men's active biceps and muscles may not prompt the same sort of controlling look as the cinematic objectification of women's legs and breasts. Hence, researchers should consider not just the direction of the look of audiences and on-screen characters, but the different ways that men and women are made the objects of spectacle as well.

Notes

1. The interviews were conducted in Hindi and lasted about 30 minutes. Assisted by two Dehra Dun correspondents for a regional Hindi newspaper, the first author approached men who were waiting in line to buy tickets at cinema halls.
2. All but two were in their teens or 20s, and all but three were unmarried.
3. Of the 22 men, six either didn't name a favourite heroine (e.g., 'I like them all', 'Heroes are important—not heroines'), or couldn't say why they like their favourite (e.g., 'Even I can't say why I like her'.) Of the remaining 16, eight mentioned their favourites' dancing ability (five) or body and beauty (three). Other reasons given include the types of films their favourites' act in (four respondents), their favourites' acting ability (seven respondents), and their favourites' charm (three respondents). (Several men gave more than one reason for a heroine being their favourite.) Fan magazines also comment on heroines' bodies (e.g., *Cineblitz* 1992). On the importance of heroines' bodies, see also Ahmed (1992: 308).
4. The first author's 1987 interviews were with 49 upper-middle-class, upper-caste Hindu men (Derné 1995a: 3–5).
5. Older ethnographies (Luschinsky 1962) and recent analyses of nineteenth-century folk theatre (Hansen 1992) and women's long-standing oral traditions (Raheja and Gold 1994) indicate that such tensions are an inherent part of Indian family practices.
6. This term was suggested by a film distributor in Dehra Dun.
7. Coyness is the writer's translation. *Sharm* also connotes shyness and modesty.
8. Of course, all heroines may be seen as non-traditional in that they work in the paid labour force. They all act in front of the camera. But in the context of the Hindi film world, actresses like Bhagyashree limit their exposure: they do not wear bikinis or miniskirts, nor do they do waterfall scenes. Indeed, heroines like Bhagyashree may mediate between the excessive traditionalism of women who don't work in the paid labour force and the excessive modernity of heroines like Shilpa Shirodkar who expose their bodies on film.
9. Research by Kimmel (1987) and others shows that men often handle a feeling of powerlessness in the economy by controlling women.
10. One unmarried 22-year-old filmgoer said, for instance, that 'the heroine who adapts [English: adopt] by wearing jeans is like many girls today. It is only wearing jeans every day that is bad.'
11. Other analysts make the same mistake. VanZoonen's (1994) discussion of Mulvey's argument includes sections on men gazing at women figures, women gazing at men figures, and women gazing at women figures, but does not consider men gazing at men figures.
12. In this scene, the film equates love with male violence. When Suman says the 'I' and the 'love' of 'I love you', Prem punches the bag and her head snaps back in pain.
13. There are other reasons, of course, for why men's gaze is more controlling than the gaze of women. First, public looks demand more of women than it does of men. When men talk about how they themselves might induce a look of hatred from society, they cite extreme public crimes, like murder or theft. But for women, it is simply going outside the home that prompts a critical look (Derné 1995a: 30–31). Second, because men have social power, their demands are more threatening. As Kaplan (1983: 31) argues, 'men do not simply look; their gaze carries with it the power of action and of possession which is lacking in the female gaze.' This highlights the fact that cinema images alone do not constitute male power. Rather, men's powerful social position allows them to act on the fantasies they see on the screen, making women the object of a controlling gaze.

References

Ahmed, Akbar S. 1992. 'Bombay Films: The Cinema as Metaphor for Indian Society and Politics', *Modern Asian Studies*, 26: 289–320.

Ali. 1991. 'Ali's Notes', *Screen*, Bombay, 28 June: 10.

Alter, Joseph S. 1992. *The Wrestler's Body: Identity and Ideology in North India*. Berkeley: University of California Press.

Bird, Sharon R. 1996. 'Welcome to the Men's Club: Homosociality and the Maintenance of Hegemonic Masculinity', *Gender & Society*, 10: 120–32.

Calman, Leslie. 1992. *Toward Empowerment: Women and Movement Politics in India*. Boulder: Westview.

Chakraborty, Mithun. 1992. 'Mithun Chakraborty: Chhoti Chhoti Baatein' [Small talk, Hindi Transliterated into English], *Movie* 10 (8): 75.

Chakravarti, Sudeep. 1998. 'Americana: Like, this is it!' *India today*, 9 February: 42–45.

Chandra, Anupama. 1993. 'Aankhen: Surprise Winner.' *India today*, 15 July: 57.

———. 1995. 'Dubbing: Audible Success', *India today*, 15 November: 114–17.

Chitralekha. 1991. 'Bhagyashri ab age kahin nahin?' August: 35–36.

Chopra, Anupama. 1997. 'Bollywood: Bye, bye Bharat', *India today*, 1 December: 53–54.

Christian-Smith, Linda K. 1990. *Becoming a Woman through Romance*. New York: Routledge.

Cineadvance. 1991. 'At the Midway Mark in 1991: A Continuing Crisis', 28 June: 10–11.

Cineblitz. 1987. 'Mandakini Grilled', September: 80–85.

———. 1992. 'Ritu Shivpuri Hits Out', August: 16–18.

Cohan, Steven. 1993. 'Masquerading as the American Male in the Fifties: *Picnic*, William Holden, and the Spectacle of Masculinity in Hollywood Film', in Constance Penley and Sharon Willis (eds), *Male Trouble*, pp. 203–32. Minneapolis: University of Minnesota Press.

Derné, Steve. 1992. 'Beyond Institutional and Impulsive Conceptions of Self: Family Structure and the Socially Anchored Real Self', *Ethos* 20 (3): 259–88.

———. 1994. 'Arranging marriages: How Fathers' Concerns Limit Women's Educational Achievements', in Carol Chapnick Mukhopadhyay and Susan Seymour (eds), *Women, Education, and Family Structure in India*, pp. 83–101. Boulder: Westview.

———. 1995a. *Culture in Action: Family Life, Emotion, and Male Dominance in Banaras, India*. Albany: SUNY Press.

———. 1995b. 'Popular Culture and Emotional Experiences: Rituals of Filmgoing and the Reception of Emotion Culture', in Carolyn Ellis and Michael G. Flaherty (eds), *Social Perspectives on Emotion* (Vol. 3), pp. 171–97. Greenwich, CT: Jai Press.

———. 1995c. 'Market Forces at Work: Religious Themes in Commercial Hindi Films', in Lawrence A. Babb and Susan S. Wadley (eds), *Media and the Transformation of Religions in South Asia*, pp. 191–216. Philadelphia: University of Pennsylvania Press.

———. 1999a. 'Handling Ambivalence toward 'western' Ways: Transnational Cultural Flows and Men's Identity in India', *Studies in Symbolic Interaction*, 22: 17–45.

———. 1999b. 'Making Sex Violent: Love as Force in Recent Hindi Films', *Violence Against Women*, 5: 548–74.

———. 2000. *Movies, Masculinity and Modernity: An Ethnography of Men's Filmgoing in India*. Westport, CT: Greenwood Press.

Dissanayake, Wimal and Malti Sahai. 1992. *Sholay: A Cultural Reading*. New Delhi: Wiley Eastern.

Dutt, Sunjay. 1991. 'My Page', *Stardust*, 20, 10 (July): 96–99.

Filmi Kaliyan. 1991a. '*Filmi Samachar*', August: 12–14.

———. 1991b. 'Manisha Koirala', August: 31–34.

———. 1991c. '*Yah kya ho raha hai?*' September: 90.

Gandhi, Nandita and Nandita Shah. 1992. *The Issues at Stake: Theory and Practice in the Contemporary Women's Movement in India*. New Delhi: Kali for Women.

Gokuldas, Meena. 1991. 'Deepak Tijori: "I am not a Manipulator"', *Tinseltown* II, 7 (August): 17–18.

Hansen, Kathryn. 1992. *Grounds for Play: The Nautanki Theatre of North India*. Berkeley: University of California Press.

Harrington, C. Lee and Denise D. Bielby. 1995. *Soap Fans: Pursuing Pleasure and Making Meaning in Everyday Life*. Philadelphia: Temple University Press.

Illustrated Weekly of India. 1988. 'The bubble gum brat', 27 November: 8–17.

Iyer, Meena. 1991. 'Shilpa: Branded for Life!' *Cineblitz*, August: 76–79.

Jain, Madhu. 1990. 'Cinema: Return to Romance', *India today*, 15 May: 62–69.

———. 1991. 'Cinema Turns Sexy: Films become Increasingly Raunchy, Ribald and Explicit', *India today*, 15 November: 28–34.

Kakar, Sudhir. 1989. *Intimate Relations: Exploring Indian Sexuality*. New Delhi: Penguin.

———. 1990 [1982]. *Shamans, Mystics, and Doctors*. Delhi: Oxford University Press, Second Edition.

Kalarikal, Aruna. 1992. 'Let's Talk about Sex, Akshay [Kumar]', *Movie*, 10, 8 (August): 38–40.

Kaplan, E. Ann. 1983. *Women and Film: Both Sides of the Camera*. New York: Methuen.

Katiyar, Arun. 1994. 'Film Lyrics: Obscene Overtures', *India today*, 15 January: 67–68.

Khanzada, Farida. 1991. 'Roopesh Kumar: A Long Night's Journey', *Screen* (Bombay); 5 July.

Kimmel, Michael S. 1987. *Changing Men: New Directions in Research on Men and Masculinity*. Thousand Oaks, California: Sage Publications.

Kumar, Harish. 1991. 'Court Martial [An Interview with Javed Jaffrey.]', *Stardust*, 20, 20 (July): 45–47.

Liddle, Joanna and Rama Joshi. 1986. *Daughters of Independence: Gender, Caste and Class in India*. New Brunswick: Rutgers University Press.

Luschinsky, Mildred Stroop. 1962. 'The Life of Women in a Village of North India: A Study of Role and Status', Ph.D. dissertation, Cornell University. Ann Arbor: University Microfilms.

MacKinnon, Catharine A. 1989. *Toward a Feminist Theory of the State*. Cambridge, MA: Harvard University Press.

Madhuri. 1986. '*Chumban charcitaen kya kahati hain'*, *Madhuri*, 27 April: 10–19.

Mankekar, Purnima. 1993. 'Television Tales and a Woman's Rage: A Nationalist Recasting of Draupadi's, 'disrobing', *Public Culture*, 5: 469–92.

Manuel, Peter. 1993. *Cassette Culture: Popular Music and Technology in North India*. Chicago: University of Chicago Press.

McRobbie, Angela. 1982. '*Jackie*: An Ideology of Adolescent Femininity', in Bernard Waites, Tony Bennett and Graham Martin (eds), *Popular Culture: Past and Present*, pp. 263–83. London: Croom Helm.

Messner, Michael A. 1992. *Power at Play: Sports and the Problem of Masculinity*. Boston: Beacon Press.

Moores, Shaun, 1993. *Interpreting Audiences: The Ethnography of Mass Consumption*. London: Sage Publications.

Mulvey, Laura. 1988 [1975]. 'Visual Pleasure and Narrative Cinema', in Constance Penley (ed.), *Feminism and Film-theory*, pp. 57–68. New York: Routledge.

———. 1988b [1981]. 'Afterthoughts on "Visual Pleasure and Narrative Cinema" inspired by *Duel in the Sun*', in Constance Penley (ed.), *Feminism and Film-theory*, pp. 69–79. New York: Routledge.

Nandy, Ashis. 1989. *The Tao of Cricket: On Games of Destiny and the Destiny of Games*. New Delhi: Penguin.

Parameswaran, Radhika. 1997. 'Public Images, Private Pleasures: Romance Reading at the Intersection of Gender, Class, and National Identities in Urban India', Ph.D. dissertation, School of Journalism and Mass Communication, University of Iowa.

Patwardhan, A. 1995. *Father, Son, and Holy War* (First Run/Icarus Films).

Penley, Constance and Sharon Willis. 1993. 'Introduction' in Constance Penley and Sharon Willis (eds), *Male Trouble*, pp. vii–xix. Minneapolis: University of Minnesota Press.

Press, Andrea. 1991. *Women Watching Television: Gender, Class and Generation in the American Television Experience*. Philadelphia: University of Pennsylvania Press.

———. 1994. 'The Sociology of Cultural Reception: Notes toward an Emerging Paradigm', in Diana Crane (ed.), *The Sociology of Culture: Emerging Theoretical Perspectives*, pp. 221–46. Oxford: Blackwell.

Radway, Janice A. 1984. *Reading the Romance: Women, Patriarchy, and Popular Literature*. Chapel Hill: University of North Carolina Press.

———. 1986. 'Identifying Ideological Seams: Mass Culture, Analytic Method, and Political Practice', *Communication*, 9 (1): 99–123.

Raheja, Gloria Goodwin and Ann Grodzins Gold. 1994. *Listen to the Heron's Words: Reimagining Gender and Kinship in North India*. Berkeley University of California Press.

Ray, Durga. 1998. '"Titanic" Mania has Reached India', *India Abroad*, 15 May: 48.

Roland, Alan. 1988. *In Search of Self in India and Japan: Toward a Cross-cultural Psychology*. Princeton: Princeton University Press.

Saari, Anil. 1994. 'Movies are Back in a Big Way', *India Abroad*, 22 April: 40.

Sine Ganga. 1991. '"*Age Savdhan Rahunga!"—Sani Deol*', August: 15.

Tandan, Chanda. 1991. '*Bhagyashri. Mayapuri*', 11 August: 19.

Thomas, Rosie. 1995. 'Melodrama and the Negotiation of Morality in Mainstream Hindi Film', in Carol A. Breckenridge (ed.), *Consuming Modernity: Public Culture in a South Asian World*, pp. 157–82. Minneapolis: University of Minnesota Press.

———. Forthcoming. 'Imagining the Family: An Ethnography of Viewing *Hum aapke hain koun …!*' in Rachel Dwyer and Chris Pinney (eds), *Pleasure and the Nation: The History and Politics of Popular Culture in India*. Delhi: Oxford University Press.

Uberoi, Patricia. 1998. 'The Diaspora Comes Home: Disciplining Desire in *DDLJ*', *Contributions to Indian sociology* (n.s.) 32: 305–36.

VanZoonen, Liesbet. 1994. *Feminist Media Studies*. London: Sage Publications.

Wadley, Susan S. 1994. *Struggling with Destiny in Karimpur, 1925–1984*. Berkeley: University of California Press.

Walters, Suzanna Danuta. 1995. *Material Girls: Making Sense of Feminist Cultural Theory*. Berkeley: University of California Press.

West, Candace and Don H. Zimmerman. 1987. 'Doing Gender', *Gender & Society*, 1: 125–51.

Wolf, Naomi. 1991. *The Beauty Myth: How Images of Beauty are used Against Women*. New York: William Morrow.

THREE

Women as Emblems of Culture and Nation: Conceptions of the Hindu Right and the Democratic Women's Movement*

U. Vindhya

Introduction

A matter of considerable concern to the women's movement in recent years has been the rise of militant women within right-wing Hindu political formations. A serious examination of the political writings of the right-wing Sangh Parivar, a group of political parties and social organisations favouring the ideology of the Hindu right, points to designs for a majoritarian, authoritarian and markedly militaristic state order that is basically incompatible with notions of democracy and social justice (Sarkar and Butalia 1995). Although the Bharatiya Janata Party (BJP), one of the affiliates of this combine, has been voted out of power after ruling for five years, a more long-term concern than that of gaining political power is the fundamental political and cultural transformation of its upper-caste/middle-class constituency on the basis of a communalistic interpretation of Hinduism. Communalism, as employed by the right-wing, is essentially a political project, which uses religion as a denominator of the political community. It is this larger and more critical project that opens up a space for the political importance of the women of the Sangh combine.

The emergence of women's activism within the Hindu right has in fact led the contemporary democratic women's movement to reassess certain assumptions about women's relationship with violence, religion and politics. It has led to no less than a questioning of the long-held notions of sisterhood of all women, and their identification with ideals of equality and social justice. It is now clear that the right-wing combine's vision of the desirable role and identity of women is opposed to the conception of the contemporary women's movement, which is broadly based on pro-left and secular principles. In a sense, the opposition between the ideology of the Hindu right and that of the contemporary women's movement revolves around a contest over the constitution of gender identities—over the claim to define who and what Indian women should be.

An attempt is made in this chapter to highlight the implications of women's involvement with strident right-wing ideologies like that of the Sangh Parivar, and to emphasise the importance of placing the women's movement's visions of secularism and equality at the centrestage of popular consciousness.

From the time of the social reform movement of the nineteenth century till the present day, the behaviour of women in India continues to be an important focus of public attention. Anxiety has been further generated in current times by globalised lifestyles and the seeming erosion of 'traditional' values (Uberoi 1996). However, the primary site for the iconisation of women as symbols of culture and tradition in contemporary India is in the context of communal identity politics. Much has been written about the ways in which

*This is a revised version of the paper published in *Asian Women*, Vol. 12, Summer 2001, pp. 165–76.

fundamentalist discourse is rearticulating a traditional identity for women in our society (Bacchetta 1996; Kapur and Cossman 1993; Sangari 1993; Sarkar 1991; Sarkar and Butalia 1995; Sethi 2002). More disturbing is the fact that politically and methodologically, the assertive and often violent participation of women in right-wing campaigns has thrown many of our assumptions about the category of 'women' and their agency into disarray. This is particularly so since women had always been perceived as victims of violence and their public, political activity and participation as a positive, liberating force (Sarkar and Butalia 1995). Contrary to these assumptions, however, the past decade has witnessed a large-scale movement among women of the right who bring with them not only an informed consent and agency, but a militant activism favouring communal forces. The gender ideology and women's activism within the Hindu right have therefore raised disturbing questions for the contemporary women's movement, which, despite its fragmented and splintered nature, continues to base its character on the hard-won gains of secular and democratic struggles.

Hindutva's Conception of Women

According to the Sangh Parivar thesis, all those whose *punyabhoomi* (holyland) lies outside the territories of Bharat (India) can never be trusted enough to be loyal to their *pitrabhoomi* (fatherland). Therefore, following the principle of exclusion, such people cannot be Indians. It is the native Hindus, whose identity is seen to flow from centuries of traditional wisdom of the Hindu scriptures of Bharat, who are considered the legitimate residents of this land, according to the philosophy of Hindutva (Golwalkar 1966).

The years of Muslim and colonial rule are attributed to the absence of Hindu nationhood. Golwalkar, the most well-known ideologue of the Rashtriya Swayamsevak Sangh (RSS), an organisation established in 1925 which continues to be the most effective organiser of the politics of the Hindu right, writes, for instance, that the weakness of Hindu society lies not in the Brahminical order, casteism, illiteracy or women's subordination and such other social practices, but in its 'absence of national feeling' (Golwalkar 1939: 47). The current social, economic and political malaise is also seen as a result of the policy of surrender to and appeasement of the minorities. The answer to this crisis, according to Hindu fundamentalism, is to build a strong Hindu *rashtra* or state wherein Hindu culture and pride can be restored to its earlier glory.

As long ago as 1939, Golwalkar had advocated the following as a solution to what is perceived as 'the Muslim problem':

> From this standpoint, sanctioned by the experience of shrewd old nations, [he had earlier approvingly referred to the example of Hitler's methods in Nazi Germany] the foreign races in Hindusthan must either adopt the Hindu culture and language, must learn to respect and hold in reverence Hindu religion, must entertain no idea but those of the glorification of the Hindu race and culture, i.e., of the Hindu nation, and must lose their separate existence to merge in the Hindu race; or may stay in the country, wholly subordinated to the Hindu Nation, claiming nothing, deserving no privileges, far less any pre-ferential treatment—not even citizens' rights. (ibid.: 47–48)

In present times, even prior to the Gujarat pogrom, Pokhran (the site of India's launch of its nuclear programme, ostensibly to arm itself in an attempt to intimidate its Muslim enemy, Pakistan) and Kargil (the site of India's war with Pakistan in 2001 and subsequently promoted by the then ruling BJP as a symbol of Hindu nationalism), have been evoked as symbols of conquest and potency. Appeals and veiled threats have also been made to the minorities in order to get them join the 'mainstream' by taking pride in a common Hindu ancestry and being under a common umbrella of a *swadeshi* church.

Militant Hindutva is thus perceived as a solution to the nation's ills. Such an ideology, bolstered by slogans like *Garv se kaho hum hindu hain* (Declare with pride that we are Hindus), conveniently glosses over issues of profound social inequality within Hindu culture such as the hierarchy of the caste system and the subordination of women, to cite two major examples. The crisis of identity, long since fuelled by the tradition/modernity, Western/Indian dischotomy, is now seen to be resolved and forged in the foundry of a Hindu identity. Those who do not fit into this mould are obviously to be excluded.

For fundamentalism, the constitution of a gender identity is significantly connected to the project of constituting communal identity. The formation of women's identity within the discourse of communalism is, however, not monolithic. Kapur and Cossman (1993) have observed that even within the Sangh Parivar, there are at least two distinctive discourses constituting the Hindu woman—one, a moderate one and the other a fundamentalist one. In both these discourses, the underlying common thread is the perception of women as *matri shakti* or mother power. Women are exhorted to be strong and powerful, not only in the family, but also in the community. Women are accorded a particular role: as dutiful wives and self-sacrificing mothers in the family, and as *stri-shakti* (woman power) to restore the glories of an ancient past and the pride of the community. As Kapur and Cossman have observed,

> The constitution of the new Hindu woman—a woman who may be educated, and who may work outside of the home, a woman who is strong and powerful, inside her family, and her community—is still a woman constituted through traditional discourses of *matri shakti*, as mother and wife, and of Sita, as chaste, pure and loyal. (ibid.: WS–41)

Such a conceptualisation fits in well with the ways in which the specific histories of colonialism, the nationalist movement and conflicted community relationships have reconstituted patriarchies (Rege 2003). Feminist scholarship has underscored the agenda of cultural nationalism from pre-independence times to the reverberations still echoing to the present, wherein women are considered the symbols of cultural purity. This construction of women as either mothers to be venerated or as objects whose sexuality was to be regulated and protected from 'outsiders' is a legacy inherited from the nationalist era and one that continues to be resurrected for various uses even today (Chaudhuri 2003). At the heart of this conceptualisation is the belief that women are the primeval sources of creation as '*nirmatri*' and power as '*prakriti*' and '*adishakti*' (Sethi 2002). For a '*nirmatri*' to demand rights equal to her own creation (men) is to despoil the divinity associated with her status. The conception of 'feminist' agency is thus guided by the ideal of '*nari shakti*', or woman power, rather than '*nari mukti*' or emancipation of women. For this power is to be used in defence of the motherland (the epitome of all virtues) and against the moral turpitude represented by the Muslim invasion and western colonialism in various stages of our history. The 'enemy' is as relevant today in the form of both the perceived Muslim proliferation in our country and onslaught from our Muslim neighbour, and 'cultural corruption from the west' (Sethi 2002).

A crucial dimension in the construction of womanhood in Hindu culture is its strong links to the pantheon of goddesses. In contrast to the androcentric monotheistic representation of the Judeo-Christian tradition, Hindu culture adheres to a polytheistic pantheon and gives goddesses an important role in it. Reference is made not only to the existence and worship of the goddesses, but also to their representation in 'feminist' ways—as complementary 'female principle', as autonomous female agent, or as powerful cosmic force (Kapur and Cossman 1993). Clarion calls to emulate the goddesses invested with powerful and often destructive energy, such as Kali, do not appear to be discordant with the equally widely prevalent models of female meekness, subordination and obedience in the form of the *pativrata* ideal derived from the mythological Sita-Savitri-Anasuya paradigm.

As Sethi (2002) points out succinctly, emphasis on the fiery goddesses and on women as sisters-in-arms in the crusade of Hindu nationalism does not mean that the conventional roles of mother and wife are given any less priority. She says that on the contrary,

> it was their foregrounding as Hindu mothers and wives that made possible this shift to militancy ... as wives, their bravery was to shame and shake their men out of their slothful cowardliness by putting into question their masculinity and ability to protect their women and religion ... as mothers, they were per-fectly suited to nurture in the young, the qualities of fearlessness, patriotism, love for the nation and of course hate for the Muslim. (p. 1548)

Women's organisations within the Hindu right such as the Durga Vahini and the Sevika Samithi lay claim to this ancient lineage of mother goddesses in order to empower themselves. The reference to the concept of *strishakti* or the tradition of *virangana* is thus often made to buttress the argument that a certain kind of feminism was already available in our tradition. India's presumed pristine past—an 'ancient' and 'glorious' Hindu culture and religion—is evoked to underscore the futility of the language of rights in (western) feminist principles.

As feminist scholars have noted, fundamentalist organisations today, taking advantage of women's close association with religion, are floating outfits like the Hindu Mahila Sammelan and the Durga Vahini. These groups highlight women's role as mothers, progenitors and, more importantly, as defenders of the faith. An entire range of images and symbols is deployed to indicate the desirable qualities and practices in a woman—from the powerfully evocative homage to Bharat Mata or Mother India who combines the goddesses Durga and Parvati and the physical mother, to references to historical figures such as the warrior queen Lakshmibai of Jhansi, and her valour on the battlefield against the colonisers (Sethi 2002).

The mission of these women has been to support their men in the fight for a Hindu *rashtra* or state, and for 'teaching a lesson to the enemy'. Scholars have noted that the self-perception of these women regarding their political roles in the making of the Hindu nation are largely couched in terms of their association with procreation and productive wombs—mothers of heroes and male martyrs (Sarkar 1995b). The activism of women is thus sought to be contained within the rhetoric of 'the glorified mother', who presumably has the onerous and divine duty of socialising children in the right direction—of imparting 'samskaras' so that they can be shaped into 'patriots' and 'men of character' (Sethi 2002).

Tracing the structure, activities and dynamics of these women's organisations, scholars have drawn attention to the manner in which they foreground the role of the mother as divinely ordained—for safeguarding revered Hindu values of duty towards and protection of the motherland. Women's role is thereby seemingly expansive, going beyond the family to embrace the nation, and ultimately moving towards god. Nationalism and religiosity thus coalesce, without, however, eroding or diluting the duty and reach of the 'mother' (Sethi 2002). The mother is 'powerful', in so much as she combines in her the sacred task of upholding 'Hindu culture' through nurturing the 'right kind of Hindu values' in her children. Such power does not, of course, cause any disturbance in the overall arrangement and distribution of social and economic power. Empowerment of women is thereby seen to flow from their commitment to their divinely ordained duties as mothers. Viewed from this context, women's participation in political life is looked upon favourably as long as it serves the interests of Hindutva. In one stroke, then, not only does it make women's status appear enhanced and 'glorified', but it also aims to undermine the women's movement that is premised on goals of equality, the language of equal rights, and the need for collective action to achieve these goals.

In an ironic inversion of women's former invisibility in the domain of public violence, large numbers of women have been active and visible not only in the rallies and campaigns, but also in actual episodes of violent attacks against Muslims. The complicity has also involved an informed assent to such brutalities against Muslim women as, for example, the gang rapes in Bhopal and Surat in 1992 and 1993, and more recently in the Gujarat pogrom of 2002. The new communal phase in the years following the demolition of the Babri Masjid in 1992 has thereby witnessed women's self-constitution as active political subjects in dangerously unprecedented ways (Chakravarti 1992).

Feminist scholars have engaged with the vexing question of whether this movement, despite the growing commitment of certain sections of women to it, genuinely expresses the empowerment of women or reflects a manipulated, constructed 'false' consent and intentionality (Chhachhi 1994; Kapur and Cossman 1993; Sangari 1993). Underlying this unease is the feminist conceptualisation of patriarchal religions as the vehicles of women's oppression. Added to the unease are recent developments in this new context that seemingly appear to empower women politically. Thus, phenomena like the membership and participation of women in large numbers in the organisations allied to the Sangh Parivar, the promotion of 'feminist' qualities (of strength and assertion in women), the xenophobic rhetoric of Hindutva propagated by leaders, including women leaders such as Uma Bharati and Sadhvi Rithambara, bring to the fore the question: on whose behalf are women's strength and action being channelled and used? It has also been observed that sanction for women's active participation in political life is presently most readily forthcoming from right-wing groups. These developments have thus raised several questions regarding women's empowerment, and the desirability of autonomous action in the service of the right-wing organisations (Sangari 1993).

Among women of a specific milieu (upper-caste, middle-class and urban, particularly in north India), the movement has provided a degree of empowerment, a sense of confidence, and opportunities for larger solidarities. It has brought them into activist, public roles and has allowed them to go beyond a purely domestic or feminine identity (Sarkar 1995b). At the same time, this limited yet real empowerment leads them to a complicity with fascist intolerance and violence, and towards the creation of an anti-democratic social and political order. The feminist critique has pointed out that if assertion and strength of women are to be located only within the framework of *stri-shakti*, thereby continuing a tradition of violence, power and militant heroics, they can be easily utilised for promoting communal ends, committed to 'freeing' the 'Hindu nation' of 'Muslim and other enemies' (Sangari 1993). As Sarkar (1995b) observes, 'Eventually, it is going to lead these women, in the name of the feigned authenticity of indigenism, to resisting notions of justice, even for their own sex' (p. 210). In fact, the present context is one which sees women of the Hindutva organisations steering clear of contemporary women's agitation for enlargement of gender rights and justice. The secular underpinnings of the women's movement associated with the feminist language of democratic rights and justice are viewed as 'western', and thereby opposed to the 'Indian/Hindu' construction of womanhood.

Although religion has become a means for women to negotiate entry into hitherto restricted political domains beyond the confines of the household, this empowerment of women nevertheless continues, to be constrained by patriarchal interests. The unequal power relations within the institution of marriage and practices such as dowry and female foeticide continue to be unquestioned. There are contradictory pulls within the Hindutva movement that make it imperative to foreground women while at the same time limiting and containing the consequences of their politicisation in the form of increased prominence and bargaining power within the family. As Sarkar (1995a) points out succinctly,

The language in which the Hindu right restates its patriarchal purposes points to a larger imperative. The assertion of the greater dignity ... of the chaste and good Hindu woman covertly substitutes for and ultimately displaces, a demand for equal rights. The Hindu right depends on a seemingly radical contestation of 'modern secularism', a critique of modernity that opposes the liberal theories of rights that it considers an alien and alienating colonizing influence. In their place it tries to claim the existence of 'traditional' notions of community obligations and mutuality. The claim can establish itself thorugh a suppression of the historical realities of caste and gender asymmetries. (p. 213)

The Hindu right, however, does not directly oppose the demands for equal rights as that would shatter the notion of a nurturant Hindu community. Basing its opposition on different grounds, it denounces notions of social equality and gender justice because of their 'alien' origins, as they have come to this country through the colonial connection and western education. In the context of Hindu patriarchy, uncontaminated by western influence, concepts like that of gender rights take a backseat in order to ensure community supremacy.

Such an orientation not only goes against the secular and democratic objectives of our constitution, but is also opposed to the history and practice of the contemporary women's movement whose roots lie in principles of egalitarianism and democratic secularism. The goals of a secular and democratic feminism are thus opposed to Hindu communalism, or communalism of any religion for that matter. It does not subscribe to the use of religious revivalism for electoral politics, which is what the Sangh Parivar is doing in a violent and divisive manner.

It is becoming increasingly clear that the contemporary politics of Hindutva is expansionist and adaptable, and has selectively incorporated various progressive elements in order to enlarge its appeal to hitherto ignored sections like women, lower castes and minority communities for its own political interests. The women's movement has been particularly alert to these moves. It is aware that fundamentalist organisations, taking advantage of the ferment in women's consciousness, are today making a bid to channelise the nascent awareness about women's rights for their own purpose and agenda. In a modernizing postcolonial nation, the influence of majoritarian religious discourse and practice can be countered only by a cogent and visible secular alternative. To highlight religion as the sole available identity would be to give up the hard-won gains of democratic and secular struggles in post-independence India.

The Contemporary Women's Movement in India

The post-independence women's movement can be traced to the political and economic crisis of the mid and late 1960s. After the initial euphoria of independence had worn off, evidence of the crisis of governance in the form of increasing poverty, unemployment and price rise led to a radicalisation process wherein a variety of struggles in the 1970s against price rise and unemployment, and for land reforms and civil and political rights following the Emergency period (1975–77) were launched. This period also witnessed the marshalling of evidence around the devaluation of women in the form of growing gender disparities in literacy rates, employment opportunities and life expectancies (Committee for the Status of Women in India 1974). The documentation of this evidence coincided with the global attention that was being paid to the question of women in the development paradigm (Mazumdar 1985).

While the thrust of the nineteenth-century social reform movement was on an understanding of women as representatives of culture and tradition, and as the pillars of family and society—the movement concerned the issues of sati, widow marriage, child marriage, etc.—the contemporary women's movement had from the 1970s shifted to a recognition of women's role in the productive sphere. It emphasised issues of wages, working hours, factory legislation, etc. In fact, it was issues of survival— for land, work and wages, for protection of the environment, and against sexual and family violence—that had dominated the concerns of the women's movement in the post-independence years. Violence against women—ranging from dowry murders, rape and sexual harassment, to custodial rape by the police—provided the rallying point for mobilising women in the early phase of the movement (Agnihotri and Mazumdar 1995).

Although initially confined to urban, middle-class, educated women, these efforts provided a visibility to 'women's issues' that had not been seen since the early years of independence. Protests against instances of violence not only emphasised a feeling of 'sisterhood' against what was the most visible form of oppression of women, it also showed up the universality of such oppression. The emergence of a separate 'women's movement' served to highlight women's specific oppression in relation to men, preventing it from being submerged amid all the other unequal relations existing in society. Furthermore, in instances of rape in particular, cases like those of Mathura, Maya Tyagi and Rameeza Bee revealed the class, caste and religious biases of agencies of the state such as the police and the judiciary. It was in keeping with the pro-left and democratic leanings of the women's movement to emphasise the excesses and violations committed by both the Indian state and the ruling classes, because both could considered as key players in the exploitation of the weaker sections of society—thereby creating a consciousness of women's oppression amongst men, and a consciousness of class oppression amongst women. A crime like rape could be interpreted as a weapon to terrorise and brutalise disadvantaged sections of society as part of the structural violence directed specifically by men from privileged sections against women of weaker sections.

It was in fact because of the left and democratic underpinnings of the women's movement that violence against women was not simply interpreted as a generic *male* violence vis-à-vis women as in the west, but viewed as *patriarchal* violence located within the intersecting levels of caste, class, religion and gender. The same secular basis of the contemporary women's movement has prompted women's groups in recent years to express their support and engage in concrete intervention for assistance and justice in the recent pogroms in Gujarat, for instance (Phadke 2003).

Since the 1980s, with the ascendancy of Hindutva politics on the one hand and the assertion of Dalit and minority identities on the other, the questions of caste, religion and culture has begun to engage the Indian women's movement. These questions began to pose a big challenge to both the theory and praxis of the movement. It was increasingly being realised that there is no single monolithic ideology of gender. Since gender is constructed at the intersections of class, caste, ethnicity and religious group, feminist scholars began to argue that gender exhibits itself in the context of lives that are shaped by a multiplicity of influences which cannot be neatly sorted out and which are rarely experienced as discrete and isolated. In practice, women's actions have often been against interconnecting relations of inequality, and have involved many aspects of resistance around daily life and culture that are not simply about gender. The category of 'Woman' thus appeared almost empty. The recent debate over 'which women' should be included in the 'Women's Reservation Bill' is illustrative of the evolving dilemmas of contemporary feminist political practice. Furthermore, the celebration of the 'feminine principle' and supposedly 'womanly' qualities, ethics and cognition began to appear rather too simple. The problem is not that these tend to reinforce an essentialism of gender attributes that is questionable, but that by viewing different forms of experience and understanding through the grid of gender opposition, the sexes are polarised in a manner which is artificial and divisive.

Political practice in India in recent years has shown often enough that caste, religious or class identity has tended to prevail over gender identity. Therefore, seldom have women rallied as 'women'. Rather, whether it was in debates like that on the Uniform Civil Code, or in issues such as the anti-Mandal upper-caste agitation or in Hindu right-wing mobilisation, women have tended to mobilise either as upper/lower caste or

Muslim/Hindu. The women's movement thus had to engage with the question of identifying its constituency. While in its early years the women's movement had set about charting its course with a (seemingly) single constituency and a relatively uncomplicated agenda of achieving equality of opportunity for (all) women, the agenda is now embedded within a complex matrix of other identities.

A crucial question thus raised is—if women do not form a homogenous group, how is it possible to unite them towards a common goal? How can the differences between women based on their caste, religion and class identities be reconciled without losing sight of their solidarity on the grounds of a common gender-specific oppression? There are no easy answers to these questions. A national body like the Indian Association for Women's Studies (IAWS), established in the early 1980s with both academics and activists in the context of an emerging women's movement, not only took up issues of violence, legal reform as a strategy for change, work participation and the impact of public policies on different sections of women, but also examined questions concerning caste, religion and gender. After more than two decades the IAWS now consists principally of women academics and researchers, and a few representatives of autonomous groups. The reason for this change in composition lies not so much in women's studies being taken over as yet another academic discipline without much connection to social reality or relevance, signifying a snapping of the organic link between theory and practice, research and activism but perhaps has more to do with the intractable question of the representative character of the women's movement. Over the years, the women's movement has been challenged by women of Dalit and minority communities as being predominantly representative of upper-caste and Hindu women. The IAWS, being primarily an academic body, has therefore been viewed with greater suspicion about its ability to represent the interests of all sections of women.

Be that as it may, it is only fair to state that the campaigns undertaken by the women's movement in recent years have attempted to mitigate the everyday struggles of women. Issues of women's work, health, education, rights, violence against them, etc., were taken up. These are issues of everyday concern affecting women across different stratifications like caste, class and religious group, although in varied ways. Issues of gender equality and human rights of women have therefore emerged as universal concerns despite the multiple positioning of women. More importantly, these issues address the fundamental problem of asymmetrical power relations between men and women, regardless of their social location. Despite the challenge to its representative character, the task before the Indian women's movement is to develop modes of analysis and strategies that will engage with both the generality of women's situations and the specific aspects of the struggles of women from different strata.

The concepts of equal rights and gender justice, which have gained a certain visibility and recognition due to the struggles for democratic rights, have to be safeguarded and pushed forward in light of the attempts of the Hindu right to redefine the meanings of equality and secularism. Nor can the splintering of the Indian women's movement be allowed to blur its visions of secularism and equality.

References

Agnihotri, I. and V. Mazumdar. 1995. 'Changing Terms of Political Discourse: Women's Movement in India, 1970–1990s', *Economic and Political Weekly*, 30 (29): 1869–78.

Bacchetta, P. 1996. 'Hindu Nationalist Women as Ideologues: The "Sangh" and the "Samiti" and their Differential Concepts of the Hindu Nation', in K. Jayawardene and M. de Alwis (eds), *Embodied Violence: Communalizing Women's Sexuality in South Asia*, pp. 126–67. New Delhi: Kali for Women.

Chakravarti, U. 1992. 'Khurja Riots 1990–91: Understanding the Conjuncture', *Economic and Political Weekly*, 27(18): 445–57.

Chaudhuri, M. 2003. 'Gender in the Making of the Indian Nation-state', in S. Rege (ed.), *Sociology of Gender: The Challenge of Feminist Sociological Knowledge*, pp. 341–66. New Delhi: Sage Publications.

Chhachhi, A. 1994. 'Identity Politics, Secularism and Women: A South Asian Perspective, in Z. Hasan (ed.), *Forging Identities: Gender, Communities and the State*, pp. 144–75. New Delhi: Kali for Women.

Committee on the Status of Women in India (CSWI). 1974. *Towards Equality*. New Delhi: Government of India.

Golwalkar, M.S. 1939. *We and our Nationhood Defined*. Nagpur: Bharat Publications.

———. 1966. *Bunch of Thoughts*. Bangalore: Vikrama Prakashan.

Kapur, R. and B. Cossman. 1993. 'Communalising Gender/engendering Community: Women, Legal Discourse and Saffron Agenda', *Economic and Political Weekly*, April 24: WS 35–44.

Mazumdar, V. 1985. *Emergence of the Women's Question*. Occasional Paper No. 2. New Delhi: Centre for Women's Development Studies.

Phadke, Shilpa. 2003. 'Thirty Years on Women's Studies Reflects on the Women's Movement', *Economic and Political Weekly*, 25 October: 4567–76.

Rege, S. 2003. 'Introduction: Feminist Challenge to Sociology: Disenchanting Sociology or "for sociology"?' in S. Rege (ed.), *Sociology of Gender: The Challenge of Feminist Sociological Knowledge*, pp. 1–50. New Delhi: Sage Publications.

Sangari, K. 1993. 'Consent, Agency and the Rhetoric of Incitement', *Economic and Political Weekly*, 1 May: 867–82.

Sarkar, T. 1991. 'The Woman as Commercial Subject: Rashtra Sevika Samiti and Ramjanmabhoomi Movement', *Economic and Political Weekly*, 31 August: 2057–62.

———. 1995a. 'Heroic Women, Mother Goddesses: Family and Organization in Hindutva Politics', in T. Sarkar and U. Butalia (eds), *Women and the Hindu Right*, pp. 11–34. New Delhi: Kali for Women.

———. 1995b. 'The Rashtra Sevika Samiti and Ramjanmabhoomi', in G. Pandey (ed.), *Hindus and Others*, pp. 24–45. Delhi: Viking Penguin India.

Sarkar, T. and U. Butalia (eds) 1995. *Women and the Hindu Right*. New Delhi: Kali for Women.

Sethi, M. 2002. 'Avenging Angels and Nurturing Mothers: Women in Hindu Nationalism', *Economic and Political Weekly*, April 20: 1545–52.

Uberoi, P. 1996. 'Introduction: Problematising Social Reform, Engaging Sexuality, Interrogating the State', in P. Uberoi (ed.), *Social Reform, Sexuality and the State*, pp. ix–xxvi. New Delhi: Sage Publications.

FOUR

Gender Roles and Cultural Continuity in the Asian Indian Immigrant Community in the US*

Shamita Das Dasgupta

*With a makara-crested crown on my brow, Holding in my right hand bow
and arrow I stood majestically and said, 'I have come from a far country.'*
Rabindranath Tagore, *Sea-Maiden*

Over three decades have passed since the Immigration and Nationality Act of 1965 liberalised the legal channels of Asian Indian migration to the US. Since that time, this immigrant minority group has been able to carve a niche for itself as a technical and financial force. Current US demographic accounts unequivocally declare that Asian Indian immigrants who came to the US after 1965 have successfully acculturated to the North American environment (Agarwal 1991; Helweg and Helweg 1990; Jensen 1988). But, however well-adjusted in the United States, Asian Indian immigrants seem to insist on keeping vital their ties with their heritage. These links are maintained physically through frequent trips to the homeland, while psychological closeness is maintained by reinventing 'Indian culture' on foreign soil (Bhattacharjee 1992). In addition, by developing a network of religious institutions cultural associations and social gatherings, Asian Indians have adopted a pattern of renewing their commitment to their native culture (Mehra 1992).

As years pass and the post-1965 immigrants age in the US, a new generation of Asian Indians, the 'second generation', has started to make its presence felt. This 'second generation' consists of individuals who are born and/or brought up in the US. With the children of immigrants coming of age, the task of retaining a distinct ethnic identity has become decidedly more complex. New issues such as dating, marriage, individualism, obedience to parents' wishes, responsibility towards extended families, etc., are emerging as critical concerns within Asian Indian communities as the second generation approaches adulthood (Kar et al. 1995/1996).

For the past 30 years that the Asian Indians have been in the US, they have tried fiercely to maintain a sense of ethnic self-identity in the face of the assimilatory forces of the US. Yet, they now face their greatest threat of cultural erasure at the hands of their relatively more 'Americanised' children. Consequently, their foremost challenge has become the successful transfer of culturally significant behaviours as well as identity to a generation of young adults reared in the US. Therefore, groups and subgroups based on language, caste cultures and religion have been formed in the community to encourage and sponsor esoteric practices among the members and instil these values in the second generation. Cultural celebrations and communal festivals that used to serve as avenues to assuage immigrant nostalgia have now taken on the added purpose of familiarising the next generation with their Indian heritage and traditions. Besides relying on such incidental learning, many communities have begun to initiate organised 'youth forums' to explicitly acquaint the second generation with their parents' cultural beliefs.

*Originally published in *Sex Roles: A Journal of Research*, Vol. 38, Nos 11–12, June 1998, pp. 953–74. Reprinted with permission from Springer Science and Business Media.

Ethnic Identity and Immigrants

Ethnic identity can be understood as a part of the self that consciously anchors an individual to a particular ethnic group (Rotheram and Phinney 1987; Tajfel 1981). Central to this identity is a sense of belonging, as well as a commitment, to the group's values, beliefs, conventions and customs (Eisenbruch 1984; Phinney 1990). Uba (1994) contends that the maintenance of traditional culture by a minority group and the adoption of a stable ethnic identity is integrally linked. In fact, minority groups actively establish a positive ethnic identity by distinct in-group behaviours, regardless of its social and financial cost (Hutnik 1986). However, the strength of commitment to this identity may differ from person to person according to two factors: the degree to which one is devoted to various aspects of the natal culture, and the degree to which one is identified with the dominant group (Berry 1997; Hutnik 1986; Sue and Sue 1990; Uba 1994). Thus, the apparent faithfulness to traditions that Asian Indian immigrants exhibit is hardly a peculiar whimsy. Rather, it is an affirmation of their ethnic identity, a critical psychological aspect of the minority individual in society (De Santis and Ugarriza 1995; Kibria 1987, 1993; Sue and Sue 1990; Tajfel 1981; Uba 1994). The above theories of ethnic identity not only shed light on attitudes and behaviours of the post-1965 Asian Indian immigrant community in the US, but also explain within-group variations. They explain why an Asian Indian immigrant may abide by unwavering filial duties and family coherence, yet be quite aggressive and individualistic at work. Or why some Asian Indians seem to be more at home with the American culture than others.

A frenetic adherence to significant traditional values to the exclusion of the dominant groups' characteristics is a feature of most new immigrants (Nicassio 1985; Phinney 1990; Sue and Sue 1971). Sue and Sue (1971) label groups expressing such behaviour as 'tranditionalists', and assert that this is a common form of ethnic identity among many Asian Americans. In addition, they identify three other categories of immigrant identity based on the degree of internalisation of the dominant cultural norms: (*a*) assimilationists, who adopt critical behavioural norms of the dominant group to the exclusion of ethnic characteristics; (*b*) bicultural, who amalgamate both the ethnic and dominant groups' features; and (*c*) marginal, who feel alienated from both cultures. Hutnik's (1986) categorisation of strategies for ethic identification, even if labelled differently, are virtually indistinguishable from the former typology: (*a*) dissociative (traditionalist); (*b*) assimilative (assimilationist); (*c*) acculturative (bicultural); and (*d*) marginal.

The process of ethnic identity development also follows a distinct course. Phinney (1990) offers a three-step model of ethnic identity development that delineates the initial stage as uninspected ethnic identity, the second as exploration, and the last as consolidation. In the first phase, the minority group unquestioningly conforms to its own values and norms. As acculturation progresses, the second phase of identity development emerges when the group begins exploring its relationship with the dominant culture. The third phase entails incorporation of identity that may merge both cultures, and yet exhibit uniquely individualistic characteristics. Although developmental, the stages are not necessarily hierarchical—that is, an individual may revert to a previous phase from a higher level. Moreover, this development may extend beyond the life of the immigrant and take a couple of generations to complete.

Background

I have to give greatly in utter daring—This girl is not to satisfy the demands of the Present, Therefore if it is not to your liking. Its appraisal can be left to the Future. And yet with what I have, I must not only pay off my debts to the Present, But hope that this Present may be in my debt.
Rabindranath Tagore, *Newcomer*

A number of studies conducted in the US and Canada indicate that although immigrants from India have adapted significantly to their environment, they have retained their taste for traditional food, along with their values concerning home, family, children, religion and marriage (Kar et al. 1995/1996; Kaul 1983; Kurian 1989; Moghaddam and Taylor 1987; Naidoo 1985, 1986; Saran 1985; Segal 1991; Sodowsky and Carey 1987, 1988; Wakil et al. 1981). In addition, many scholars claim that Asian Indian immigrants have transplanted old-world gender ideologies and clearly dichotomised gender roles in their adopted country of residence (Agarwal 1991; Buchignani 1983; Kar et al. 1995/1996; Kurian 1989; LaBrack 1988; Naidoo 1980, 1985, 1986; Ralston 1988; Sodowsky and Carey 1987, 1988). Other studies with Asian Indian immigrants to North America have found that first-generation women support gender equality, as well as general principles of feminism (Dasgupta 1986; Naidoo 1986; Siddiqui and Reeves 1986). Despite such findings regarding the egalitarian gender beliefs among adult immigrant women, many second-generation women tend to complain about the restrictive gender role prescriptions imposed on them. In her study of immigrants and their children, Agarwal (1991) states that although 'several women [first generation] said their immigration to the United States brought them independence and liberation from the institutional repression of women in India . . . the second generation Indian woman feels that old-world gender roles are still rigidly being upheld for her' (p. 52). This phenomenon can perhaps be explained by examining the gender-specific role that daughters of immigrants are given in the preservation of Indian ethnic/cultural identity. Mani (1992) claims that the maintenance of traditions and identity have historically been placed on South Asian women's shoulders. As the keepers of South Asian culture and heritage in the US, the roles of second-generation daughters are therefore monitored more strictly than those of sons. Fears of cultural obliteration by 'Americanisation' and exogamy have played a large role in imposing such constructions on the female gender role. This gender imbalanced expectation is coming to a head as the second-generation Asian Indian women approach adulthood.

A manifestation of this intergenerational crisis is the Asian Indian community's exaggerated concern with the practice of dating. Some studies report that Asian Indian parents resist marital integration by refusing to allow their children to date and mix freely with their non-Indian peers (Kar et al. 1995/1996; Kurian 1986, 1989; Sharma 1984; Siddique 1977; Stopes-Roe and Cochrane 1987). This restriction is more pronounced for females than males (Menon 1989) since ' . . . the popular definition of a "good Indian girl" is one who does not date, is shy and delicate, and marries an Indian man of her parents' choosing' (Agarwal 1991: 52). From debates in community newspapers to the 'youth sessions' of cultural conferences, dating appears to be at the root of a raging intergenerational controversy. This tug-of-war is often coded as a maintenance of 'traditional' Indian values vs. assimilation into 'Western' ones. In a series of letters to the editor printed in *India Abroad* on the subject, one reader opines, 'Indian tradition is not consistent with dating. Should we not be proud of that tradition?' (May 1992: 3). Another steers a middle course, 'I feel it is not advisable to completely wipe out the old traditional Indian values by becoming a part of mainstream America; but nor is it advisable to be absolutely rigid and just refuse to change, irrespective of the consequences' (June 1992: 3). The speaker at a Parents-Youth Forum in New Jersey invoked the story of Kunti[1] from the Hindu epic *Mahabharata* in response to a youngster's question as to why Indian parents disapprove of dating:

Dating, as [just] defined by youth, does not include all these commitments: physical, mental, and spiritual, and therefore is impermissible [sic]. Another way to look at it is [that] any act, when it is doubtful or ambiguous, should be avoided due to fear, guilt, or responsibility of a bad result. (December 1992: 7)

Purpose of Study

The Asian Indian community has lived but a little over two decades in the US. Although the bias of the immigration policies led to the congregation of a middle class, educated, and homogeneous group of individuals here, the Indian community is still a minority with values and norms that are distinguishable from the Euro-American majority. As a new minority immigrant group, the Asian Indians have become deeply engrossed in articulating their cultural/ethnic identity.

A significant aspect of the process of ethnic identity consolidation is the desire to perpetuate it by socialising the next generation into accepting some key practices and rituals of the native culture (De Santis and Ugarizza 1995; Kar et al. 1995/1996; Phinney and Rotheram 1987; Spencer 1987). Currently, the Asian Indian community is deeply involved in this process with its youth, and consequently, significant importance is given in various Asian Indian conferences to discussions on how to foster allegiance to Indian culture in the second generation. For instance, in a Conference on Family sponsored by the National Federation of Asian Indian Organisations, Domadia (1988) recommends exposing children to Indian cultural, social and religious programmes, practising religion on a daily basis at home, and teaching them consistently about approved living behaviour (e.g., food, language, religion, dress, etc.) as integral to teaching them about the beliefs and culture of their parents.

This study was undertaken to evaluate the success that immigrants have achieved in instilling Indian cultural views in their children. Beliefs regarding gender equality and dating practices were identified as points of significant contrast between the ethnic and dominant cultures' norms, and, therefore, key aspects of Asian Indians' ethnic identity. It was also presumed that this difference and the ensuing psychological acculturative stress would provoke major intergenerational conflicts between the immigrant and the second generation (Berry and Annis 1974; Rosenthal 1987). Thus, this study was conducted to assess the synchrony of these two attitudes in the immigrants and the second-generation Asian Indians, and the potential for intergenerational discord around these issues.

The role of the author in this study is literally that of participant observer. I am one of the early Asian Indian immigrants to this country, having arrived here in 1968. I have watched the community develop and change over the years. The struggles of other Asian Indians, settling down, resolving identities, raising children to fit both the worlds of East and West, have also been mine. In addition, I am one of the co-founders of the first agency in the US that focuses on violence against South Asian immigrant women.[2] Most of the questions addressed in this chapter emerged through my work with this organisation. I have adopted a method of study that utilises the experiences of the community as expressed in its various conferences, the media and anecdotes, in addition to formal assessment tools. I have tried to locate myself 'in particular, actual places, knowing the society only from within' (Smith 1990: 33).

Objective

Since the continuation of ethnic/cultural identity depends upon invoking loyalties to the traditions of the parents, the imparting of certain core values/attitudes to the second generation has become critical for Asian Indian immigrants. The most fundamental of such values are those regarding gender roles and miscegenation. This study was conducted to explore the similarities in the attitudes towards women and dating among Asian Indian immigrants and their children. In both immigrants and their offspring, a positive correlation between these attitudes was anticipated. That is, if an individual held a liberal attitude towards women's role in society, it was anticipated that s/he would also have higher acceptance for dating as a practice. It was, again hypothesised that the parents and their children would closely resemble each other's views on both these values.

A number of South Asia scholars have pointed to the anxiety the practice of dating provoked in Asian Indian immigrants (Buchignani 1983; Kar et al. 1995/1996; Kurian 1989; Kurian and Ghosh 1983; Saran 1985; Segal 1991; Sikri 1989; Sodowsky and Carey 1987, 1988; Vaidyanathan and Naidoo 1990), while others have pointed to the unequal gender ideologies they seem to support (Agarwal 1991; Buchignani 1983; LaBrack 1988; Kurian 1989; Naidoo 1980, 1985, 1986; Ralston 1988; Sodowsky et al. 1987, 1988;). A corollary hy-pothesis, stating that higher levels of anxiety would accompany the rejection of dating and egalitarianism, sprang from these findings. The rationale for this expectation was that attitudes contradicting the dominant culture's customs and practices would generate internal conflicts or acculturative stress in immigrants and their children, resulting in heightened levels of anxiety (Krishnan and Berry 1992). Thus, a secondary objective of this study was to correlate the levels of anxiety felt by both generations with their attitudes towards dating and women.

Sample

The North Eastern corridor of the US, especially the tri-state areas of New York, New Jersey and Connecticut, has a high concentration of Asian Indians. Forty-six families[3] from this area participated in the study by responding to three questionnaires: Attitudes Toward Women Scale (Spence et al. 1973), a dating sale (Bardis 1962), and IPAT Anxiety Scale (Cattell and Scheier 1961). Forty-three men (fathers) and 41 women (mothers) who were foreign-born immigrants from India, and 29 men (sons) and 34 women (daughters) of the second generation participated by filling out these questionnaires. The Asian Indians who participated in this study were primarily well-educated professionals belonging to the upper and middle classes. Forty-three families (approx. 93.5 per cent) in this sample were Hindus, while the rest (approx. 6.5 per cent) of the group was comprised of Jains, Christians and Muslims. The sample was a mixture of Bengali, Gujarati, Punjabi, Tamil, Kannada, and a few other regional or linguistic groups. All fathers held white-collar jobs, as did the majority of mothers who were engaged in occupations outside the home. Only 10 mothers were full-time homemakers. Among the second-generation participants, 55 per cent were foreign born and all except one were students.

Although the primary data for this study was collected through questionnaires, there are some additional sources. Discussions from a few parent-youth forums organised in New Jersey in 1992 have been collected as support for the quantitative analyses. Voices of individuals from some of these sessions have been excerpted here.

Questionnaires

One of the questionnaires utilised in this study, the short version of Attitude Toward Women Scale (AWS), has 25 questions. It is designed to elicit agreement of the respondent on a 4-point scale. Although the questionnaire was standardised on American populations, it has been used in studies with Asian Indians (Das et al. 1997; Dasgupta 1986; Dasgupta and Jain 1997). Items on this scale have been judged by independent researchers to possess adequate face validity for Asian Indian populations. Some items are, for example,

'Swearing and obscenity are more repulsive in the speech of a woman than of a man', 'Intoxication among women is worse than intoxication among men', 'A woman should be as free as a man to propose marriage', 'In general, the father should have greater authority than the mother in the bringing up of children', 'The modern girl is entitled to the same freedom from regulation and control that is given to the modern boy', etc. (see Table 4.1).

TABLE 4.1
Summary of Demographic Characteristics and Measures by Groups

	Groups			
Variables	*Mothers*	*Fathers*	*Sons*	*Daughters*
Number of participants	41	43	29	34
Age				
Mean	42.3	46.8	16.3	17.0
SD	4.0	3.7	2.0	2.6
Marital status married	40.0	42.0	0	0
SES (a)				
Mean	80.2	79.4	77.9	78.5
SD	12.2	12.5	14.6	14.1
Education (b)				
Mean	16.6	18.1	10.6	11.4
SD	2.6	2.3	2.0	2.4
AWS				
Mean	56.3	51.9	53.2	60.9
SD	9.1	15.9	16.1	8.6
DAT				
Mean	27.6	34.3	59.8	50.2
SD	14.1	18.7	20.2	16.9
AQS				
Mean	33.0	25.8	28.4	38.6
SD	9.9	9.4	10.7	12.0

Notes: (*a*) Duncan's (1961) index was used to measure the socio-economic status of all participants. This scale assesses SES through occupations, with 1 being lowest and 100 highest.

(*b*) Years of education translates as follows: up to 12 = school grades; 13 = HS graduated; 16 = four-year college degree; 18 = master's degree; 21 and over = doctorate degree.

The second measure, a Dating Scale (DAT), was similarly constructed for American populations. Since the purpose of using the questionnaire was to assess a participant's acceptance of the practice of dating, which is generally perceived as a western custom, validation with Asian Indians was not essential. However, a sample of the items in this questionnaire do indicate their applicability for an immigrant population: 'Every person should be allowed to choose his or her dating partner freely and independently', 'Girls should be allowed to ask boys for dates', 'It is all right for a girl to wait for her date in a public place', 'Dating couples between 18 and 20 should be allowed to stay out as late as they wish', 'It is all right for dating partners to talk about sex', etc.

The third measure, the IPAT Anxiety Scale (AQS), has been used with Indians with norms available (Hundal et al. 1970; Hundal et al. 1972). However, it has not previously been used with Asian Indian immigrant populations.

Results

All four groups, fathers, mothers, sons and daughters, were included in a stepwise discriminant analysis with the three measures mentioned above. The most statistically significant function consisted of DAT, which had a standardised Discriminant Function Coefficient (DFC) of 1.0. The second function, which was also statistically significant, identified AQS (Anxiety Scale) as the major contributor to this function (DFC = .93). Results of multiple regression with DAT and all other variables yielded sex (beta = .28, T = 2.23, p = .03) and age (beta = –.27, T = –2.19, p = .03) as the two most statistically significant variables (adjusted [R.sup.2] = .131). Results of multiple regression with AQS identified sex (beta = –.45, T = –3.8, p = .001) as the only statistically significant variable (adjusted [R.sup.2] = .191). Further narrative analyses of the three areas of scrutiny are presented below:

Attitudes towards Women

Where attitude towards women was concerned, there seemed to be great intergenerational similarities between parents and children. The belief in the gender equality of both mothers and fathers was positively correlated with that of their children, regardless of age. However, mothers' egalitarianism seemed to be mitigated by their children's age. That is, the older their children, the more conservative mothers became regarding women's roles. Since mothers' own age was not linked to this relationship, it can only be speculated that as adolescents grew older, their mothers started to experience the pressures of socialising them in traditional gender roles. In the process, they themselves turned towards conservatism.

In the second generation, location of early development seemed to have an effect on their attitude towards women. Children born in the US held more liberal views about women's roles in society than their foreign-born counterparts. It is possible that the early years spent in India had ingrained in the youngsters a slightly more dichotomous gender-role ideology than that which their US-born counterparts had a chance to internalise.

The adolescent daughters in this study seemed to hold significantly more egalitarian values than sons. Agarwal's (1991) study of second-generation Asian Indians supports this finding. The young women she interviewed were not only cognisant of the unequal treatment of the sexes, but were also quite vocal in their objections to sexism.

Attitudes towards Dating

On their attitude towards dating, the participants of the study sequestered along generational lines with the sons showing the greatest acceptance of dating and mothers the least. Daughters and fathers stayed between these two extremes. The rejection of dating by both parents' groups indicates the resistance immigrants feel towards this mode of heterosexual interaction. The remarks of Laxmi,[4] an Asian-Indian professional woman, is revealing of the general sentiments of parents. While addressing a roomful of youngsters on the practice of dating, this paediatrician and mother of three adolescents said,

As a representative of parents here, I want to say we love our children. We care for our children. I am not telling our neighbour Tony or Harry not to go for dating, because they are not my children. [To] all the children I want to say: trust us, because we want the best for our kids.

Venkataraman, an Asian Indian immigrant and father, said,

> Children talk about going out on date(s) and tell us that we don't know anything about the US culture. What do they know about their cultural background? I think they are lost . . . . If dating is an exploration, they are going the wrong way.

Contrary to original expectations, attitudes towards women and acceptance of dating were not statistically linked in the fathers' group, or in the second-generation adolescents. However, the relationship found support among mothers. Thus, mothers who possessed higher tolerance for gender equality also showed higher acceptance for dating behaviour in their children. Furthermore, even though mothers seemed to be most reluctant to accept dating, adolescents of both sexes were more influenced by mothers' attitudes than fathers'. This particular finding is evidence of the important role mothers play as primary socialising agents in the Asian Indian community. Regardless of their occupational responsibilities outside the home, the critical duty of childrearing has obviously remained ensconced within the domain of Asian Indian women's work.

In the second generation, sons showed the most favourable attitude towards dating. That young women showed more reservation towards dating than their male counterparts indicates quite directly a gender bias in socialisation. '[T]hose parents who did let their children date admitted to maintaining separate standards for their sons and daughters' (Agarwal 1991: 49). Mani (1992) echoes these sentiments,

> . . . the fear of dating that consumes many South Asian families is primarily a fear of women dating. Although many parents may worry about interracial marriage for what it might imply for them in old age, there is little attempt to control men's sexuality. Women, meanwhile, are quite frequently policed with the stick of tradition: it is women who are called on to preserve the ways of the old country. (p. 13)

A study on dating and arranged marriages conducted by Dr J. Motwani points clearly to the differential treatment of sons and daughters in the Asian Indian community. Sixty per cent of the total youngsters surveyed favoured both dating and choosing their own partners. Twenty-five per cent of girls wanted to date but restrained themselves, reporting that they did so due to parental disapproval and prohibitions. Furthermore, 50 per cent of girls were dating without their parents' knowledge, as opposed to 80 per cent of boys who were doing the same (as reported in Domadia 1988).

Undoubtedly, a reason for instilling inhibitions about dating in girls more than in boys is due to Asian Indian parents' obsessions with maintaining sexual chastity. Dr Prasad, a professor of engineering conducting a youth forum in New Jersey, stated, 'From an Indian culture point of view, dating involving physical relationships before marriage is not permissible.' Segal (1991) notes this fear in Asian Indian parents and believes most Indian immigrants who are not quite familiar with the practice tend to conflate dating with sexual activity. During a parent-youth forum, a physician and father commented on what he believes to be the actual motivation for dating: 'Why do men want to see women, for sex; why do they want to go out with them, for sex; why do they want to marry them, for sex again'. Although the remark may have been made mockingly, it does represent the dread some parents feel about exposing their children, especially daughters, to the evils of premarital intimacy through dating. Domadia (1988) asserts that added to this fear of sexual intimacy is that of sexual assault:

> [S]ince girls tend to be more vulnerable physically parents tend to be more protective. Teenage rape and pregnancy are a big scare and pitiful condition for those involved. These two factors alone scare parents into forbidding dating, no matter the situation. (p. 67)

Interestingly, young adults seem to be aware of their parents' confusion with this unfamiliar practice. Sunita, a 21-year-old college student, asserted,

> I don't believe that meeting people is only for sex . . . . Dating is a preliminary for marriage, but what you do is to meet many different kinds of people and see what you want in a spouse. I don't think dating only one person will automatically lead to marriage . . . . I think you want to know what you want in your mate.

Although many men and women of the second generation recognise their parents' apprehension with dating, it is not easily tolerated. A college student writes,

> [D]ating and the desire to be with the opposite sex is a natural urge and it would be a gross injustice not to allow adolescents to fulfill this urge. The adolescent child may feel lonely and may need the companionship of the opposite sex in order for his/her life to feel complete . . . . It is like a parent, whose mouth is full of candy, telling his child not to eat any candy because it is bad . . . . [T]he hypocrisy of the disapproval of adolescent dating becomes quite evident. (Tamaskar 1988: 69)

This study indicates that it is not just the daughters of the community who are internalising strictures regarding dating. The older adolescents of both sexes in this sample showed more conservatism regarding dating than younger ones. This trend towards conservatism with age may suggest that parents have been somewhat successful in inculcating their children with Indian cultural values, and that this process becomes more rigorous as their adolescents approach marriageable age.

Anxiety

Refuting the hypothesis of this study, conservatism in attitudes towards women and dating did not have any relationship with anxiety. On the contrary, liberal attitudes towards dating and women showed a significant relationship with anxiety in first-generation immigrants. In the mothers' and fathers' groups, egalitarian values were accompanied by high degrees of anxiety. This finding indicates that Asian Indians who embrace egalitarian/non-traditional/non-conformist values experience significant stress.

The results are consonant with Krishnan and Berry's (1992) study of acculturative stress in Indian immigrants in the US Midwest. In their sample, assimilationist individuals who preferred espousing values of the host culture to the exclusion of their native ones experienced higher acculturative stress compared to the integrationists who maintained the values of both cultures. Examining the nature of the Asian Indian immigrant community from another angle may also clarify this finding. Bhattacharjee (1992) claims that the construction of the immigrant nation in the US by the post-1965 Asian Indian bourgeoisie has meant reinventing ideological familiar 'essentials'. Within this recreation, the image of the Indian woman as the essence of chastity, purity, family values, etc., has been crucial. Cultural and political organisations within the community have expended great resources to maintain and promote this idealistic image of women, and therefore they resist any challenges to it (ibid.). Regardless of whether they are explicitly excommunicated, individuals who threaten this immigrant ideology stand the risk of psychological marginalisation. Considering the important social, cultural and ideological role that the community plays in the lives of immigrants, the anxiety felt by first-generation Asian Indians who strongly believe in gender equality is easily understood.

The above explanation is further supported by the finding that, although the fathers in this study were less conservative than mothers on the issue of dating, their level of anxiety increased in proportion to their spouses' liberalism. That is, the more accepting mothers were towards this practice, the more anxious fathers became. However, the converse relationship did not hold true. Fathers' attitude towards dating did not seem to influence mothers' levels of anxiety. From these findings one can speculate that fathers' increasing anxiety in relationship to mothers' acceptance towards dating might in turn put pressure on the latter to constrain their liberalism. This supposition is supported by the fact that mothers in this study did not seem to escape anxiety by assuming a liberal stance towards dating. Higher levels of anxiety accompanied mothers' non-traditional attitude towards dating.

In their assessment of quality of life, Kar et al. (1995/1996) report that the second-generation Asian Indians experience a high level of stress arising from intergenerational and interracial conflicts. However, among the second-generation young adults in the current sample, daughters were much higher in anxiety than sons. In fact, on the variable of anxiety, the participants were clearly separated along gender lines, with mothers and daughters exhibiting higher anxieties than fathers and sons. Krishnan and Berry (1992) also reported higher acculturative stress in women than men. In light of the fact that '. . . the burden of negotiating the new world is borne disproportionately by women, whose behavior and desires, real or imagined, become the litmus test for the South Asian community's anxieties or sense of well-being' (Mani 1992: 13), this finding is no surprise (see Table 4.2).

TABLE 4.2
Summary of Significant Results of Three Measures by Groups

	r	p
Mothers' AWS with children's age	−.35	.002
Mothers' AWS with own DAT	.54	[less than] .001
Mothers' AWS with own AQS	.64	[less than] .001
Mothers' DAT with children's DAT	.36	.002
Mothers' DAT with children's AWS	.22	[less than] .05
Mothers' DAT with own AQS	.41	[less than] .001
Mothers' DAT with fathers' AQS	.27	[less than] .02
Fathers' AWS with children's AWS	.30	.01
Fathers' AWS with own AQS	.38	.001

Conclusion

This study was inspired by a concern that the post-1965 Asian Indian community has been voicing consistently: cultural continuity by perpetuating traditions. Research on US minority groups suggests that adherence to familiar customs and conventions are part of a process of ethnic identity development that all immigrant groups experience. In fact, 'traditionalism', or ardent clinging to old behaviours, beliefs and attitudes, is considered to be the earliest stage of a multi-tiered trajectory of acculturation in a new country. However, this development process is neither static nor linear. In fact, external as well as internal pressures to change and adjust mark the immigrant experience.

Among the Asian Indians, a new immigrant community, the maturation of the US-born and raised second generation has posed a dilemma. For the first time, the immigrant parents have had to deal with an internal threat to the continuation of their identity and beloved culture. Thus, the immigrant parents have been attempting to ensure the transmission of cultural/ethnic values to the next generation. Since the survival of the community as a distinct ethnic group is dependent on the children's faithfulness to traditions, tremendous efforts are being expended to inculcate them with certain beliefs and customs.

With the help of 46 educated, middle-class families, this study explored the extent of synchrony between Asian Indian parents and children on two critical values: attitudes towards women and dating. A secondary goal of the study was to assess the levels of anxiety both parents and children experienced in conjunction with these attitudes. The following is a summary of the findings:

1. On their attitudes towards women's roles in society, parents and children were highly similar to each other. Furthermore, the second-generation women's belief in gender equality was significantly stronger than their male counterparts'. Although mothers in the sample also scored higher than fathers and sons on this scale, their liberalism seemed to dwindle as their children became older. Both mothers' and fathers' attitudes toward women had close correlation with their children's.

2. The practice of dating seemed to divide parents and children along generational lines. Sons were the most accepting of dating and mothers the least. Although imbued with strong reservations, mothers' attitudes seemed to influence children's attitudes towards dating quite significantly, whereas fathers' views had no such effect. Older children generally showed more conservatism towards dating than younger ones.

3. Women of both generations revealed more elevated levels of anxiety than their male counterparts. Interestingly, egalitarianism and liberal acceptance of dating were both related to higher levels of anxiety in the immigrant parents. Although less anxious and more liberal regarding dating than the mothers, the fathers' anxieties increased with the non-traditionality of their wives' attitudes towards dating. The same relationship was not repeated with regard to gender roles.

Despite intergenerational differences in attitudes towards dating, Asian Indian families in this study project a general picture of harmony and shared values. Although disagreement around the issue of dating would indicate some discord between parents and children, the community still reflects intergenerational amity. The close resemblance between parents and children's views on women's roles and the increasing conservatism of older adolescents regarding dating seem to issue from parents' unfamiliarity with the practice and their fear of sexual intimacy. Thus, a solution to this discord may lie in both parties meeting each other halfway: the parents taking time to learn about dating, and the children taking time to teach them in realistic terms. As Gautam, a 19-year-old college student said in a youth forum, 'It is a two-way relationship. It takes two to tango . . . . I talk to them [parents] which means that I trust them, which means they have to trust me . . . . [T]he way to teach your parents is to be their role model. Raise your parents well!'

However, the profile of the Asian Indian community is hardly one of fixed and mindless acceptance of traditions. Rather, lively negotiations and reconciliations mark the community's process of acculturation. For example, in the 1997 Bengali Conference of North America convened in Philadelphia, PA, the immigrant organisers arranged an 'ice-breaking mixer' for young adults, obviously in response to the changing realities of the new country. A compromise between the two generations is also evident in the formation of organisations by young Asian Indians that allow inter-sex mixing within the parameters delineated by the older members. The informational brochure of one such organisation in the East Coast, Sangam, declares,

Unlike generations past [however,] our roles as men and women in the workplace and at home are not clearly defined. No longer is the man solely the 'breadwinner,' and the women solely the 'homemaker'. Women face the pressure of increasing responsibilities in the workplace while continuing to cultivate most aspects of family life . . . . At times when we most need to communicate with our partners, friends or colleagues, we find ourselves at a loss for words, action and understanding. On a large scale, the inability of men and women to effectively communicate and resolve the tensions created by increased responsibilities and our dual cultures can result in discord within marriages and a breakdown of the family.

These ventures are, obviously, attempts on the part of both the second generation and the immigrants to successfully combine the contradictory processes of transformation and preservation.

When it comes to gender, however, the potential for conflict within the community is significantly alarming, and may warrant further examination. In the present study, although parents and children were highly analogous in their views of gender equality, the differential treatment of women within the community did pose a serious concern. The results indicate that both generations of Asian Indian women are being penned in by some traditional gender role expectations that are pervasive in the community. In her explorations within another recent immigrant community, the Vietnamese, Kibria (1987, 1993) reports similar findings. Her studies indicate that among Vietnamese refugees, women experience singular conflicts that generate from the contradictions between patriarchal family ideologies and personal bids for autonomy. Fan (1996) also reports that Asian women in Hawai'i manage their lives with 'a nexus of complex social, economic, and cultural conditions characterized by class division, racial discrimination, and patriarchal tradition' (p. 70).

Within the Asian Indian community, too, women seem to negotiate their lives by balancing similar discrepancies in group and personal expectations. For instance, regardless of their workload (31 mothers in this study held full-time positions outside the home), mothers shoulder the primary responsibilities of socialising their children, bearing the heavy burden of inculcating them with the community's dictates regarding appropriate 'Indian' behaviour. Yet, they seem to hold more liberal gender values than the fathers and sons. Similarly, daughters, although stronger in their egalitarian convictions, are placed in a position where they cannot express themselves fully.

These differences in the attitude towards gender equality between the young men and women of the second generation indicate future difficulties. Presuming that a significant number of marriages between second-generation Asian Indians will take place in years to come, such conflicting attitudes towards women may translate into mismatched expectations between marriage partners (Dasgupta and DasGupta 1996). Agarwal's (1991) study of the second generation seems to foretell these findings. The elevated level of anxiety that Asian Indian women of all ages expressed in this study testifies to the disproportionate psychological stress they are enduring.

It is important to recognise that the power of the immigrants' dream of cultural continuity is not lost on the second generation. As the children of the immigrants grow up, they are bound to create a balance between their heritage and surroundings in their own way. However, the belief that changes will occur only with subsequent generations while the original immigrants remain steeped in traditions overlooks the dynamic process of acculturation currently continuing within the community. The assumption that Asian Indian immigrants are consummate traditionalists seems to survive contradictory indicators such as their unequivocal financial and social achievements in this country. To a large extent, the source of this persistent belief is the immigrants' vehement rejection of dating and non-traditional gender roles. Following Sue and Sue's (1971) explication of biculturalism as a process of adaptation, this attempt by the immigrants to preserve certain critical attitudes, values and behaviours may be best understood as 'judicious biculturalism', a course of action utilised to control the rate and level of assimilation into the new culture. The method is characterised by vigorous involvement on the immigrants' part to control their environment and direct the progress of their own acculturation. Thus, rather than being a passive participant in his/her own 'Americanization', the immigrant should be considered an active and empowered force controlling, negotiating and organising his/her own experiences to optimise adaptation.

Furthermore, this process is being transferred successfully to the next generation, and is apparent as students on college campuses organise around their amalgamated identity as 'Indian–American'. Agarwal (1991) states, 'In college, a majority of second generation Indians come to terms with their Indian background and start to view it more positively' (p. 82). The parents themselves are, of course, actively participating in this process of their children's adaptation by creating a space for them in the community's functions and celebrations. The proliferation of youth curricula and forums within Asian Indian conferences and festivals is an example of this involvement. The fact remains that no matter how wide the differences in values, the immigrants can hardly reject their children's realities. Neither can the second generation afford to renounce their parents' values completely. The healthy survival of the Asian Indian community and ethnic identity depend on sympathetic mutual understandings between both generations.

> *In the night you followed the path Never trodden before; You saw the sign in the sky And alone you went; . . . In the narrow path of New Life, You are the forerunner, ignoring all limits, Conquering the impassable. In every step resounds the great yea; 'I am! I am~'*
> Rabindranath Tagore, *The Forerunner*

Notes

1. Kunti, before her marriage to Pandu, had given birth to Karna. Soon after his birth, fearing social sanctions, she abandoned him. Later, as a queen, she went on to become the mother of the Pandavas, her legitimate children. The Kauravas, the sworn enemies of the Pandavas, subsequently befriended Karna. Before the great Kurukshetra battle, Kunti regretted that her offsprings, unknown to each other, were on warring sides.
2. Manavi is the first organisation in the US to address the issues of family violence in South Asian communities in the US. It is located in New Jersey.
3. In 38 participating families both parents responded to the questionnaires, whereas in eight, only one parent did. Among these eight families, two had lost one parent to death and the rest had only one parent who agreed to cooperate with the study.
4. All names have been changed to protect the participants' identities.

References

Agarwal, P. 1991. *Passage from India: Post 1965 Indian Immigrants and their Children; Conflicts, Concerns, and Solutions*. Palos Verdes, CA: Yuvati Publications.

Bardis, P.D. 1962. 'A Dating Scale', *Social Science*, 37: 44–47.

Berry, J.W. 1997. 'Immigration, Acculturation, and Adaptation', *Applied Psychology: An International Review*, 46: 5–68.

Berry, J.W. and R.C. Annis 1974. 'Acculturative Stress', *Journal of Cross-Cultural Psychology*, 5: 382–406.

Bhattacharjee, A. 1992. 'The Habit of Ex-nomination: Nation, Woman, and the Indian Immigrant Bourgeoisie', *Public Culture*, 5: 19–44.

Buchignani, N. 1983. 'Determinants of Fijian Indian Social Organization in Canada', in G. Kurian and R. Srivastava (eds), *Overseas Indians—A Study in Adaptation*, pp. 68–89. New Delhi: Vikas.

Cattell, R.B. and I.H. Scheier. 1961. *The Meaning and Measurement of Neuroticism and Anxiety*. New York: Ronald Press.

Das, A., S.D. Dasgupta and H.I. Siegel. 1997. 'Motherhood Across Oceans: Attitude Toward Gender and Motherhood among Asian Indians'. Presented at the Conference of Eastern Psychological Association, Washington, D.C.

Dasgupta, S.D. 1986. 'Marching to a Different Drummer? Sex Roles of Asian Indian Women in the United States', *Women and Therapy* (Special Issue: The Dynamic of Feminist Therapy), 5 (2/3): 297–311.

Dasgupta, S.D. and S. DasGupta. 1996. 'Women in Exile: Gender Relations in the Asian Indian Community in the U.S.', in S. Maira and R. Srikanth (eds), *Contours of the Heart: South Asians Map North America*, pp. 381–400. New York: Asian American Writers' Workshop.

Dasgupta, S.D. and S. Jain 1997. '"Ahimsa" and the Contextual Realities of Woman Abuse in the Jain Community', Presented at the 26th South Asia Conference, Madison, WI.

De Santis, L. and D.N. Ugarriza. 1995. 'Potential for Intergenerational Conflict in Cuban and Haitian Immigrant Families', *Archives of Psychiatric Nursing*, 9: 354–64.

Domadia, P.M. 1988. 'Attitude towards Dating'. Proceedings: Conference on Family and Youth, 2–3 July, Cleveland, Ohio, Silver Spring, MD: National Federation of Asian Indian Organizations in America, pp. 67–68.

Duncan, O.D. 1961. 'A Socioeconomic Index for all Occupations', in A.J. Reiss, Jr. (ed.), *Occupations and Social Status*, pp. 109–38. New York: Free Press.

Eisenbruch, M. 1984. 'Cross-cultural Aspects of Bereavement. II: Ethnic and Cultural Variations in the Development of Bereavement Practices', *Culture, Medicine, and Psychiatry*, 8: 315–47.

Fan, C.C. 1996. 'Asian Women in Hawai'i: Migration, Family, Work, and Identity', *NWSA Journal*, 8: 70–84.

Helweg, A.W. and U.M. Helweg. 1990. *An Immigrant Success Story: East Indians in America*. Philadelphia: University of Pennsylvania Press.

Hundal, P.S., A. Singh and M. Singh. 1970. 'Factor Analytical Study of Tests and Anxiety', *Psychological Reports*, 26: 875–78.

Hundal, P.S., Y. Sudhakar and K. Sidhu. 1972. 'Factor Analytical Study of Measures of Anxiety, Intelligence and Academic Achievement', *Journal of Psychological Researches*, 16: 28–34.

Hutnik, N. 1986. 'Patterns of Ethnic Minority Identification and Modes of Social Adaptation', *Ethnic and Racial Studies*, 9: 150–67.

India Abroad. 22 May 1992. 'We don't have to date', *Letters to the Editor*, p. 3.

———. 5 June 1992. 'Steering a Middle Course', *Letters to the Editor*, p. 3.

Jensen, J.M. 1988. *Passage from India: Asian Indian Immigrants in North America*. New Haven, CT: Yale University Press.

Kar, S.B., K. Cambell, A. Jimenez and S.R. Gupta. 1995/1996. 'Invisible Americans: IndoAmerican Quality of Life', *Amerasia Journal*, 21: 25–52.

Kaul, M.L. 1983. 'Adaptation of Recently Arrived Professional Immigrants from India in Four Selected Communities in Ohio', *The Journal of Applied Social Sciences*, 7: 131–45.

Kibria, N. 1987. 'New Images of Immigrant Women: A Study of Women's Social Groups among Vietnamese Refugees', *Working Paper* No. 173. Wellesley, MA: Wellesley College, Center for Research on Women.

———. 1993. *Family Tightrope: The Changing Lives of Vietnamese Americans*. Princeton, N.J.: Princeton University Press.

Krishnan, A. and J.W. Berry. 1992. 'Acculturative Stress and Acculturation Attitudes among Indian Immigrants to the United States', *Psychology and Developing Societies*, 4: 187–212.

Kurian, G. 1986. 'Intergenerational Integration with Special Reference to Indian Families', *Indian Journal of Social Work*, 47: 39–49.

———. 1989. 'Changing Attitude towards Asian Immigration with Special Reference to Canada', Paper presented at the First Global Convention of People of Indian Origin, New York.

Kurian, G. and R. Ghosh. 1983. 'Child-rearing in Transition in Indian Immigrant Families in Canada', in G. Kurian and R.P. Srivastava (eds), *Overseas Indians —A Study in Adaptation*, pp. 128–38. New Delhi: Vikas.

LaBrack, B. 1988. 'Evolution of Sikh family form and Values in Rural California: Continuity and Change 1904–1980', *Journal of Comparative Family Studies*, 19: 287–309.

Mani, L. 1992. 'Gender, Class, and Cultural Conflict: Indu Krishnan's Knowing Her Place, *SAMAR*, Winter: 11–14.

Mehra, A. 1992. 'Hindu Revival in an Alien Land', *Little India*, 2: 10–12, 14, 16–20, 22–23.

Menon, R. 1989. 'Arranged Marriages among South Asian Immigrants', *Sociology and Social Research*, 73: 180–81.

Moghaddam, F.M. and D.M. Taylor. 1987. 'The Meaning of Multiculturalism for Visible Minority Immigrant Women', *Canadian Journal of Behavioural Science*, 19: 121–36.

Naidoo, J.C. 1980. 'East Indian Women in the Canadian Context: A Study in Social Psychology', in K.V. Ujimoto and G. Hirabayashi (eds), *Visible Minorities and Multiculturalism: Asians in Canada*, pp. 193–218. Toronto, Canada: Butterworth.

———. 1985. 'Contemporary South Asian Women in the Canadian Mosaic', *International Journal of Women's Studies*, 8: 338–50.

———. 1986. 'Value Conflicts for South Asian Women in Multicultural Canada', in L. Ekstrand (ed.), *Ethnic Minority and Immigrant Research*, pp. 132–46. Lisse, The Netherlands: Swets & Zeitlinger.

Nicassio, P. 1985. 'The Psychosocial Adjustment of the Southeast Asian Refugee: An Overview of Empirical Findings and Theoretical Models', *Journal of Cross-Cultural Psychology*, 16: 153–73.

Phinney, J.S. 1990. 'Ethnic Identity in Adolescents and Adults: Review of Research', *Psychological Bulletin*, 108: 499–514.

Phinney, J.S. and M.J. Rotheram. 1987. 'Children's Ethnic Socialization: Themes and Implications', in J.S. Phinney and M.J. Rotheram (eds), *Children's Ethnic Socialization: Pluralism and Development*, pp. 274–92. Newbury Park, CA: Sage Publications.

Ralston, H. 1988. 'Ethnicity, Class and Gender among South Asian Women in Metro Halifax: An exploratory Study', *Canadian Ethnic Studies*, 20: 63–83.

Rosenthal, D.A. 1987. 'Ethnic Identity Development in Adolescents', in J.S. Phinney and M.J. Rotheram (eds), *Children's Ethnic Socialization: Pluralism and Development*, pp. 156–79. Newbury Park, CA: Sage Publications.

Rotheram, M.J. and J.S. Phinney 1987. 'Introduction: Definitions and Perspectives in the Study of Children's Ethnic Socialization', in J.S. Phinney and M.J. Rotheram (eds), *Children's Ethnic Socialization: Pluralism and Development*. Newbury Park, CA: Sage Publications.

Saran, P. 1985. *The Asian Indian Experience in the United States*. Cambridge, MA: Schenkman Publ. Co., Inc.

Segal, U.A. 1991. 'Cultural Variables in Asian Indian Families. Families in Society', *The Journal of Contemporary Human Services*, 72: 233–41.

Sharma, S.M. 1984. 'Assimilation of Indian Immigrant Adolescents in British Society', *The Journal of Psychology*, 118: 79–84.

Siddiqi, M.U. and E.Y. Reeves. 1986. 'A Comparative Study of Mate Selection Criteria among Indians in India and the United States', *International Journal of Comparative Sociology*, 27: 226–33.

Siddique, C.M. 1977. 'Structural Separation and Family Change: An Exploratory Study of the Immigrant Indian and Pakistani Community in Saskatoon', *Canada. International Review of Sociology*, 7: 13–34.

Sikri, A. 1989. 'Dating: A Scary Cultural Gap', *India Abroad*, 13 October: 19.

Smith, D.E. 1990. *The Conceptual Practices of Power: A Feminist Sociology of Knowledge*. Boston, MA: Northeastern University Press.

Sodowsky, G.R. and J.C. Carey. 1987. 'Asian Indian Immigrants in America: Factors Related to Adjustment', *Journal of Multicultural Counseling and Development* (Special Issue: Cross Cultural Counseling: The International Context, Part 2), 15 (3): 129–41.

———. 1988. 'Relationships between Acculturation-related Demographics and Cultural Attitudes of an Asian-indian Immigrant Group', *Journal of Multicultural Counseling and Development*, 16: 117–36.

Spence, T., R. Helmreich and J. Stapp. 1973. 'A Short Version of the Attitudes toward Women Scale (AWS)', *Bulletin of Psychonometric Society*, 2: 219–20.

Spencer, M.B. 1987. 'Black Children's Ethnic Identity Formation: Risk and Resilience of Castelike Minorities', in J.S. Phinney and M.J. Rotheram (eds), *Children's Ethnic Socialization: Pluralism and Development*, pp. 103–16. Newbury Park, CA: Sage Publications.

Stopes-Roe, M. and R. Cochrane. 1987. 'The Process of Assimilation in Asians in Britain: A Study of Hindu, Muslim and Sikh immigrants and their Young Adult Children', *International Journal of Comparative Sociology*, 28: 43–56.

Sue, D.W. and D. Sue. 1990. *Counseling the Culturally Different: Theory & Practice* (2nd edn.). New York: John Wiley & Sons.

Sue, S. and D.W. Sue. 1971. 'Chinese American Personality and Mental Health', *Amerasia Journal*, 1: 36–49.

Tagore, R. 1987. 'Sea-maiden', in W. Radice (trans.), *Rabindranath Tagore, Selected Poems*, pp. 94–95. Middlesex, England: Penguin Books.

———. 1974a. 'The Forerunner', in A. Bose (trans.), *Later Poems of Rabindranath Tagore*, pp. 111–20. New York: Minerva Press.

———. 1974b. 'Newcomer' in A. Bose (trans.), *Later Poems of Rabindranath Tagore*, p. 40. New York: Minerva Press.

Tajfel, H. 1981. *Human Groups and Social Categories*. Cambridge, England: Cambridge University Press.

Tamaskar, V. 1988. 'Attitudes towards Dating in the 80's', in Proceedings: *Conference on Family and Youth*, 2–3 July. Cleveland, Ohio. Silver Spring, MD: National Federation of Asian Indian Organizations in America.

Uba, L. 1994. *Asian Americans: Personality Patterns, Identity, and Mental Health*. New York: The Guilford Press.

Vaidyanathan, E. and J. Naidoo. 1990. 'Asian Indians in Western Countries: Cultural Identity and the Arranged Marriage', in N. Bleichrodt and P.J.D. Drenth (eds), *Contemporary Issues in Cross-cultural Psychology*, pp. 37–49. Amsterdam, The Netherlands: Swets & Zeitlinger.

Wakil, S.P., C. M. Siddique and F.A. Wakil. 1981. 'Between Two Cultures: A Study in Socialization of Children of Immigrants', *Journal of Marriage and the Family*, 43: 929–40.

Section II

Violence

Violence against women has taken many forms and expressions. The earlier decades were given over to confronting, describing and enumerating it. There was also analysis of the roots of violence against women, her secondary status in society being the primary reason. The consequences of all this were amendments in archaic laws, and the evolving of support systems for the victims of violence. The focus in the later decades was on innovative strategies to deal with this persistent menace, as exemplified by women's slum *panchayat*s in Delhi, police slum *panchayat*s in Mumbai, the recruitment of women in the police force, getting women victims to assume greater responsibility in the solution to their problems, especially that of domestic violence, and training in self-defence techniques. The effectiveness of these new strategies awaits evaluation. At the root of violence against women were patriarchy and unequal power between the genders. Together with patriarchy, violence is now seen more as a consequence of neo-liberal globalisation—the rapid socio-economic changes resulting in alienation, fear and insecurity that finds expression in aggressive ways. Violence or the threat of violence was considered a male strategy to keep women in their place and to check their movements, but now it seems more a price that has to be paid for the freedom women seem to enjoy. Just as the dynamics behind male violence have changed, so have women's views about it. Today, women are less inclined to accept male views on violent behaviour ('she must have asked for it'), and less ashamed to speak up about it.

The safety of women in urban India can be gauged by events in Mumbai, which until recently was considered a women-friendly metropolis. Going by police statistics (which rarely give a correct estimate because of under-reporting), Mumbai has registered an increase in crimes against women by 22 per cent in the first quarter of 2005, with sexual abuse being at the top on the list, particularly in relation to minors. At the close of the last millennium, new forms of violence were brought to the fore, like date rape, rape of minority women during communal riots, honour killings (in the case of inter-caste and inter-religious marriages), trafficking in women, sexual harassment at the workplace, the greater social stigma attached to women with HIV/AIDS, and cyber violence, to mention a few. Some experts stretch the definition and take the stand that the market-driven economy itself is a form of violence, especially against poor women. Again, cosmetic surgery can be construed as a form of self-inflicted violence.

As date rape and rape among acquaintances increases, the line between force and consent blurs, making it harder for women to punish their perpetrators. In a repeat of the 1970s and 1980s, the year 2005 saw rapes of college girls and minors by the police. Increasing the representation of women in the police force and addressing the issue of alcohol abuse among men in uniform are the new methods expected to bring down these crimes. Trafficking in women, a major fallout of the neo-liberal paradigm, requires transnational effort and cooperation, difficult to come by as South Asian solidarity eludes the power brokers. Women, being vulnerable, are unable to protect themselves from unsafe sex and fall easy prey to HIV/AIDS. Some experts and women activists perceive legalising prostitution as a way of controlling this dreaded disease. If the research published in *Lancet*, a reputed British medical journal, is to be believed, 10 million female foetuses were aborted in India in a period of 20 years, between 1984 to 2004. This deplorable practice is more common among educated, middle-class urban families with a girl child. Socio-economic development is no match for the cultural pressure to have a son, and greater access to and affordability of pre-natal reproductive techniques have made things that much easier.

In developed countries, anonymous cyber violence, which includes online insults, sexual harassment, slander, etc., is growing, and there is a felt need on the part of governments to put safeguards in place. Closer to home, in the guise of managing cybercafes, young men subscribe to adult websites, download and transfer pornographic images and video clips to mobile phones, and profit by selling these as porn MMSes.

So pressing is the problem of violence against women that in late 2005, the National Commission for Women began advertising its services to victims of violence in local and national newspapers, providing its full address and telephone number. Besides helplines, the need of the hour is systematic research to throw light on these emergent forms of violence.

The second section in this book is titled 'Violence'. Jane Rudd, in her chapter 'Dowry-murder: An Example of Violence against Women', examines the phenomenon of dowry-murders as an example of the ways in which violence against women is perpetuated on a global scale. The author examines the traditional and the current dowry systems, and highlights the role of economic factors in its escalation. As the patriarchal structure is fortified by capitalist inputs, she argues that women need to understand and address its effects across nation-states. The author recommends that the example of the Indian women's movement in combating violence against women be universalised as a model for the prevention of violence against women. The interview article 'When Homes are Torture Chambers: Vimochana's Work with Domestic Violence' by the group *Vimochana* provides insights into the work of one women's organisation to assist victims of domestic violence. It mentions the setbacks encountered by the activists, their burnout, and the uncooperative role played by the police and courts. Some of the hurdles are in the form of the victims themselves, which makes the task much more difficult for those involved in their assistance. 'Sexual Harassment at the Workplace' by Vibhuti Patel highlights women's efforts to bring sexual harassment at the centre of the consciousness of policymakers. She traces the legislative changes and details the Supreme Court guidelines arising from the *Vishaka* judgment. Results of surveys undertaken on the nature and prevalence of sexual harassment at the workplace are briefly highlighted. The chapter zeroes in on the recommendations of the National Commis-sion of Women for the safety of women students on campuses, and describes the concrete initiatives taken at various universities to safeguard women students' interests.

'Empowerment Approaches to Gender-based Violence: Women's Courts in Delhi Slums' by Veronica Magar is a descriptive study of an Indian non-governmental organisation (NGO) working in tandem with *mahila panchayat*s or women's courts—a traditional, indigenous form of conflict resolution that has adapted feminist principles, and deal with domestic violence. Using interviews with NGO staff and victims of violence together with observations of the NGO activities, the author provides insights into slum women's understanding of the causes of violence, and the manner in which victims address this violence. Reconciliation with the husband is the preferred alternative, but when provided with the empowerment framework with its focus on capacity building and access to resources, women openly challenge their subordination in the family and become their own teachers in developing a better understanding of gender-based violence. This new understanding helps women say a categorical no to any kind of violence no matter what the reason, and in the process helps them redefine their traditional roles.

FIVE

Dowry-murder: An Example of Violence against Women*

Jane Rudd

Introduction

This chapter examines the phenomenon of dowry-murders in India as an example of the ways in which violence against women is perpetuated on a global scale. Violence against women is seen in many forms across nation-states. Dowry-murder is but one example that can be utilised to increase international awareness of the severe effects of violence against women. Dowry-murder is the killing of a woman, ostensibly for not bringing sufficient dowry to the marriage. It is the culmination of a series of prior domestic abuses by the husband's family (Narayan 1997).

An examination of the patriarchal system and the role of women within that system, particularly at the point of marriage and the bestowment of dowry, illuminates the problems of dowry-murder and patriarchy that are a common part of daily life in India. The social mechanisms of male domination and female subordination perpetuate the imbalance of power between men and women in day-to-day events (Ong 1990). As Tsing and Yanagisako (1983) point out, marriage, a common life event, is particularly important in the analysis of inequality because it is the point at which gender inequalities are negotiated and the division of labour is defined.

Numerous cultural explanations of dowry-murder have been given in recent years. Narayan (1997) cautions against seeking cultural explanations for violence against women in Third World countries when similar research conclusions are not made for violence against women in Western countries. The 'deadening essentialism of much historical and contemporary Western representation of the Third World has confirmed ... an abiding suspicion of primarily cultural explanations of social phenomena' (Mani 1990: 32). This is especially true when fatal forms of violence are discussed, which are sometimes dismissed as 'death by culture' (Narayan 1997: 84). In fact, women in multiple classes and across nations are often caught in a patriarchal/capitalist system that leads to them being controlled by multiple forms of violence (Mies 1986).

Western researchers who compare domestic abuse in both the United States and in India are a good example of this bias. Narayan (1997) states that in the United States, domestic abuse, rather than homicide by a partner, is emphasised. The emphasis in the United States is on providing shelters and educating about the breadth of domestic abuse to include '... verbal, emotional, and psychological abuse' (ibid.: 91), as well as physical abuse and murder. As a result of the social services available to women in the United States, the shelter movement has received a great deal of attention, and domestic partner murders have been less widely publicised. In India, the balance is seen as being entirely different. The women's movement in India

*Originally published in *Women's Studies International Forum,* Vol. 24, No. 5, September–October 2001, pp. 513–22. Reprinted with permission from Elsevier.

began to widely address the issue of violence against women in the 1970s, and dowry-murder had more of an impact than other forms (ibid.). Hence, their focus is on domestic murder rather than domestic abuse in general. However, there are many similarities between the two countries regarding violence against women.

An example of the similarities is that in the United States, violence against poor women of colour is often disregarded, but when it occurs against white women of the middle classes, it is given a great deal of attention. For instance, in my own state, Connecticut, Tracy Thurman, a middle-class, suburban battered wife who was maimed and almost killed by her husband, gained notoriety, and was effective in changing laws regarding police action against batterers ('Man kills wife', 1993). Her cause was taken up by a battered women's shelter located in a suburb. On the other hand, the urban battered women's shelters, housing mainly women of colour, had had similar incidences that received little or no press. It is certainly true that 'the experience of violence by minority women is ignored, except to the extent it gains white support for domestic violence programs in the white community' (Crenshaw 1997: 187). This class-based imbalance in the reporting of crimes also exists in India. Narayan (1997) sees dowry-murders as a mainly middle-class phenomenon, and as such, they receive more media attention than such crimes as police rape, which happens more often to women who are poor. Narayan believes 'that public unfamiliarity with this issue combined with its heinousness and its predominantly middle-class occurrence make dowry-murder one of the most publicly visible issues of those addressed by women's groups in India' (ibid.: 93). It is also understood that dowry-murders occur with poor women in India, yet they receive far less attention than that with middle-class women.

The question then arises as to how to assess the extent of and/or increase of violence against women in any given country. This sort of debate is most likely to come from Western women seeing abuse as worse in developing countries, which arises from their need to see themselves as safer than the 'other'. As a result: 'Domestic violence against Indian women thus becomes most widely known in Western contexts in its most extreme incarnation, underlining its "Otherness"' (ibid.: 101). However, as Narayan (ibid.) points out, the level of reported homicide by a partner is in fact similar (in proportion to each country's population) in both the United States (mainly due to gun-related domestic violence) and India—approximately 5,000 a year in India and 1,400 in the United States. Therefore, 'These figures at least made plausible the claim that "death by domestic violence" in the U.S. seems to be numerically as significant a social problem as "dowry-murders" are in India' (ibid.: 99).

All we do know about dowry-murders, and still with not a great deal of certainty, is that '... dowry-murders seem to be a fairly recent phenomenon that seem to have come into "systematic" existence in the last three decades, and that seem to be on the increase' (ibid.: 103). It is the understanding of this author that until women realise that the patriarchal structure permeates violence against all women, we will continue with this marginal debate.

Causes of violence against women have generally been attributed to inequality between men and women, hierarchical family relationships, early marriage, and women's isolation (Vasquez y Tamayo, cited in Carrillo 1993). Connors (1987, cited in ibid.: 106) also addresses causes such as 'the context of social structure, institutions and codes of conduct', which leave women 'in a position of inferiority to men, responsible to and in need of protection by them'. I would suggest that these are not the causes, but the institutional results of violence against women.

Endless biological, psychological and cultural arguments have been raised to explain women's lack of status. It is true that 'there is no field of activity and no country in which women have obtained equality with men' (Sivard 1985: 5, quoted in Carrillo 1993: 99). The most plausible explanation for this is structural control. In a global survey of women's groups in developing countries, it was seen that violence against women 'was the most frequent concern raised by women' (Carrillo 1993: 100). To explain dowry-murders as a cultural phenomenon is to ignore the larger picture of worldwide violence against women. In addition, such a label merely increases the '... perceived sense of entrapment and dependence that sets women's experiences with violence, and battering in particular, apart from men's experiences' (Fernandez 1997: 436). In fact, Fernandez (ibid.) gives a more global perspective: 'Gender-based economic inequality, husbands' control of the family wealth and decision making, and restricted access to divorce for women are found to be strong predictors of wife beating in the 90 societies studied by Levinson' (1989, cited in ibid.: 436).

To address violence against women within nation-states, there are global themes addressing oppression and violence that need to be understood. Mies (1986) describes the need of the capitalist patriarchal system to maintain control over women's lives in order to increase 'growth' or continued wealth accumulation, thus ensuring an endless supply of free or low-wage labour. Mies' (1986) analysis speaks to the actual causes of violence against women. She explains that the 'global division of labor under the dictates of capital accumulation' (ibid.: 2) is a condition that perpetuates violence against women. Women's labour has been rendered 'invisible', despite their role in supporting the patriarchal/capitalist system. Men maintain this position and 'try to accumulate wealth and productive capital, based not on economic but on direct coercion, and on the extension of patriarchal control over women' (ibid.: 4). This control is ensured through the threat or actuality of violence.

Violence as a form of control directly affects women's participation in the development process. In reality, 'Gender violence, whether in its most brutal or more subtle forms, is a constant in women's lives' (Carrillo 1993: 100). This chapter will show how violence against women in India is perpetuated by the patriarchal-capitalist conundrum. It will also discuss the Indian women's movement's efforts to counteract this phenomenon. This analysis can be applied to the effort to dispel violence against women across nation-states.

The Traditional Dowry System in India

To begin the discussion of violence against women in India with dowry-murders is to ignore the abuses present in a young girl's life, as well as in her married life up until dowry-murder occurs. In India, due to the crushing financial burden of the dowry expectation, a daughter is often neither welcomed nor valued by her natal family. This manifests itself when health and educational decisions are made within the family. There continues to be a discrepancy in the sex ratio of the Indian population due to poor healthcare and nutrition for girls and women. Currently, there are 94 females for every 100 males in India (United Nations 1998: 88). Miller (1981: 134) states, 'Where dowry is the custom and the practice, the high masculinity of sex ratios will express the devaluation of daughters.' In fact, the rejection of girls begins before birth. Palriwala (1985) indicates that medical clinics throughout the country provide amniocentesis tests that are used to detect the gender of a foetus. Those that are female are often subsequently aborted because the eventual financial burden of a woman makes a female infant highly undesirable. Related to this is female infanticide (Miller 1981). Palriwala (1985: 11) states, 'Rather than female infanticide alone, dowry now leads to adult female homicide'. UNICEF has recently documented the worldwide abuse of women in these multiple forms and in many countries; however, their report is quick to acknowledge that little is being done to prevent such abuse (UNICEF 2000).

In the recent past, young girls were accorded substantial religious power, and could gain respect through their moral behaviour, which gave them a measure of value in their affinal home. The young girl was able to perform the Bhai Tika ceremony in which she prayed for the gift of long life for her brother (Bennett 1983).

A girl's 'sacred' status was used to justify restricting her movements in the form of purdah. Women who have high moral standards, demonstrated in their strict purdah, become a source of status for their husbands. Purdah maintains male dominance in a patriarchal system despite its original intent, which was to protect women from outside forces (Hale 1989; Jacobson 1982; Omvedt 1990). Even when actual veiling is no longer practised, sexual seclusion is still the norm, thus effectively curtailing women's public access. Women cannot own land, and they have more limited access to education and to work outside the home. In short, they are dependent and tied to their husbands and families. As Jacobson (1982: 85) aptly describes it, 'feminine seclusion and veiling are integral aspects of patterns of economic activity, kinship structures, inheritance roles, social hierarchy and religious ideology'. The debate over the merits/demerits of purdah for women continues. Hale (1989: 367) feels that if women 'manage to adjust to their situation and to make something of their lives [this] is a credit to their resilience, but to claim from this that women enjoy and accept the restrictions placed upon them is not justified'.

In the traditional dowry system in India, dowry was said to 'connote female property or female right to property which is transferred at a women's marriage as a sort of pre-mortem inheritance' (Tambiah 1973: 64). Each stage of the marriage process was infused with religious meaning, sacralising and integrating the kinship system within the socio-economic sphere. In India, when a gift or *dakshina* is given to a Brahmin priest, it is given without reciprocation, which blesses the giver and renders the gift sacred. The same principle applied to dowry. A father received no material gain when he properly dowered his daughter, but he did achieve status and family honour, along with blessings. Religious values, then, were extremely important in perpetuating the Indian marriage and dowry system.

Dowry in India has always been a way of demonstrating, and sometimes obtaining, status. As Goody notes, 'dowry, especially direct dowry, is always an instrument and product of stratification' (Goody 1983: 258). However, because the giving of one's daughter and her dowry constituted a holy act, dowry was limited to the most holy of castes, the Brahmins. Tambiah (1973) suggests that restricting dowry to the Brahmin caste was ordained by the ancient scripts of the *Manu* Smriti (a holy text). Other castes utilised the 'inferior' tradition of bride-price, in which the family of the bride received gifts from the family of the groom as compensation for losing their daughter (ibid.). Thus, dowry was a status symbol of the highest caste and was deeply connected to the caste system.

Dowry's traditional role as a symbol of status and caste, however, was closely circumscribed. Dowry was formerly confined to specific gifts for specific purposes. The dowry itself consisted of: (*a*) a portion destined for the bride called *stridanam*, or women's wealth, which contributed to her status, and (*b*) a portion destined for the groom and his family, referred to as *dakshina*, which included gifts, given only on special occasions after the marriage.

With the escalation of monetisation, women in India lost ritual power (and with it kinship power) and gained nothing in terms of economic control, thus losing what little power was theirs. As a result, women have become vulnerable to being treated as replaceable objects. They are seen as commodities, providers of cash (Veena Oldenburg, personal communication, 1987). When the supply of cash diminishes, they are in a tenuous position that can lead to criticism, abuse, and finally, dowry-murder. Dowry-murder is the culmination of domestic abuse and follows a series of prior serious abuses (Narayan 1997).

The Current Dowry System in India

Dowry in India today remains a compelling force in the life of Hindu families (Stein 1988). In fact, marriages with dowry are continuing despite the Dowry Prohibition Act of 1961 that made dowry illegal. However, with the changing socio-economic structure, dowry has changed shape and meaning to the point where Srinivas sees it as a 'modern monstrosity', which people attempt to legitimate 'by linking it up with an ancient and respected custom' (Srinivas 1983: 13).

Dowry-giving in India has increasingly deteriorated into a bargaining system in which bridegrooms go to the highest bidder. The bride's position in the family is even more tenuous than it was in the past, and a woman is increasingly viewed as merely a way to bring in cash. Once this cash is depleted, brides become an expendable commodity. The driving force behind this process is the growth of the cash-based economy, which has commercialised dowry and further lowered the status of women, despite new laws and educational opportunities designed to assist them.

One of the effects of the cash economy is a redefinition of the social hierarchy. Whereas caste formerly determined social status, class now takes precedence (Srinivas 1983). Education and an expanding economy, as well as government employment, have created an urban middle class. The centuries-old tradition of dowry becomes one way for an upwardly mobile family to demonstrate its wealth and make ties among higher social groups (Paul 1985).

Because dowry is no longer limited to certain social groups, the acceptable amount of dowry to be given with a bride is no longer fixed; it now varies and often escalates. Furthermore, the bulk of the dowry is now delivered in cash—fuelling the greed of the groom's family. Rather than taking out a bank loan (to be paid back with interest), the groom's family may turn to dowry as a loan they do not need to repay (Veena Oldenburg, personal communication, 1987).

A family can use the cash to repay a debt incurred from the education of their son (Meinzen 1980), to establish the groom in his own business, or to pay their own daughter's dowry (Stein 1988). In fact, 'Dowries are now quite openly justified as being necessary for the payment in turn of the grooms' sisters' dowries' (ibid.: 480). None of the dowry goes directly to the woman, who becomes increasingly defined as a means by which to obtain cash.

Historically, gifts were continually passed from the bride's family to the groom's, usually on holidays. This aspect of dowry is now the most threatening to women. Gifts are continuous, and since they are not specified, there can often be disagreements as to what is given versus what is expected, now that the emphasis is on consumption rather than spirituality. Palriwala indicates that 'dowry has come to encompass the entire marital relationship and customary gift exchange between affines' (Palriwala 1985: 71). These gifts, given on special occasions, are now often demanded on the basis of an 'inadequate' dowry given at the time of the marriage. Brides can be criticised and mistreated by their affines for not continuously providing what were by past standards enormous amounts of dowry.

These disputes can then escalate into wife murder—freeing the husband to remarry for a more lucrative dowry. In more urban settings, marriages are now arranged with strangers (Stein 1988). The family is no longer assessed through 'local reputation' (ibid.: 477), and marriages 'are contracted without even the feeble social constraints that at one time might have inhibited the mistreatment of a young woman in an alien family' (ibid.).

Another distinction of marriage arrangements is between women's treatment in the north and south of India. In the north Indian cultural system 'dowry was regarded as the collective property of a woman's in-laws' (Banerjee 1999: 662). The difference in dowry between the north and south exists in part 'because couples were often related [in the south, so] a woman's property was never completely alienated from her family' (ibid.). This still does not mean that women themselves gained from it economically, and in general, 'Every possible arrangement is made to ensure the overwhelming dominance of the groom and his family over the wife in an Indian marriage' (Stein 1988: 476). Mies (1986: 160) agrees, 'The relationship between the bride-giving and the bride-receiving families is never an egalitarian one.' In sum, dowry is part of the class system and the 'maintenance of the superiority of higher groups over lower' (Stone and James 1995: 126).

Hale (1989: 373) puts it even more forcefully: 'The implicit message is that female power is benevolent only when subject to male control, but destructive and violent when uncontrolled.' According to Hale, with the invasion of India by the Muslims in the tenth century, the Brahmins tried to exert even more control. She (ibid.: 374) believes, 'Male power over women depends upon two controls, property and sexuality, and both forms of control were intensified.' While Hindus and Muslims believed in the containment of women's sexuality, the 'British introduced the alien western notion of women as inferior, and so added a derogatory component to their subjugation' (ibid.).

Traditionally, a woman attained higher status when she produced a son, but according to a study by Ghadially and Kumar, 36 per cent of women had children and 11 per cent were pregnant when they were killed by their marriage partners (1988, cited in Stone and James 1995: 131). In the urban setting, having children is costly and so no longer seems to be of economic benefit, especially when the consumer mentality takes precedence (Stone and James 1995). 'So long as [women's] valuation rests primarily in their being vehicles of property transmission, they will remain vulnerable to dowry harassment and murder' (ibid.: 133). Stone and James' main point here is that women's ability to produce children, which was necessary in a rural agrarian economy, is no longer advantageous in the urban settings of modern India.

Fertility used to be regarded as a source of women's power, but this is no longer the case. Rather than supporting women, the Dowry Prohibition Act (1961) 'was passed as a measure to facilitate the implementation of the traditional ideal of marriage for all women' (Stein 1988: 480). The Succession Act of 1965 entitled women to inherit equally with their brothers, and it legalised divorce. These laws have, however, changed little of the practical reality for women (Mies 1986). Rather, the current legal protection for women is overridden by socio-cultural and economic pressures. Women are considered selfish if they do not turn over their share of inheritance to their brothers, and divorce remains a social taboo. Dowry, a primary means of economic advancement for both families, ensures that the patriarchal marriage system has remained intact. The problem is, as Hale (1989: 371) points out, that 'the laws are virtually unenforceable in the patriarchal and hierarchical society of India'. Moreover, 'Attempts to introduce legal parity in inheritance without significant change in women's economic and political power sets the stage for manipulation of legal provisions at the expense of women' (Banerjee 1999: 674). While some considered dowry an economic safety net for women (Narayan 1997), due to the control exercised by her husband and in-laws, a woman could rarely turn her own dowry property (such as jewels) into wealth.

The issue of whether the modern variant of dowry should be regarded as a woman's inheritance or a net transfer of assets to a man's family is an important one for the analysis of gender stratification; if a dowry constitutes a woman's inheritance it represents empowerment of women, but if it constitutes a transfer of financial assets it implies a continuation of the asymmetrical power relationship between men and women (Banerjee 1999: 663). Since land is mainly inherited by males, it provided no direct economic benefit for women. In addition, women had little opportunity to deal in economic matters due to their confinement to their homes. Therefore, neither male inheritance nor female dowry holds direct economic benefit for women in India.

According to Hale (1989: 378): 'The principle of dowry affirms explicitly that the woman's inheritance does not go to her, but to her husband's family. It represents a total reversal of the matrilineal principle of inheritance through the female line.' Instead, women and their dowry are a means to continue the capitalist-patriarchal system. Not only do they not benefit from the dowry, but they are now also in danger of being harassed or even killed for more dowry (Stone and James 1995). Mani (1990: 35) makes a similar point about sati (wives burning themselves on their husbands' funeral pyres): 'for both officials and missionaries, women were not really at issue. Women rather provided ground for development of the other agendas.' In other words, women were used to inject religious or political 'meaning' into society. Billing (1992, cited in Banerjee 1999) favours the adoption of the term groom-price to distinguish the present practice from classical dowry. Groom-price specifically refers to a de facto transfer of ownership of property from the bride's family to the groom (and/or his family) as a condition for marriage. Banerjee (1999: 664) makes her point of view clear on this issue:

> If dowry property is absorbed by a woman's in-laws (as it frequently is) and recycled to pay for other marriages, then we must regard it as a permanent transfer of assets from a woman's family to a man's family. Regardless of the provisions of the inheritance law, the idea of dowry as female inheritance is contradicted by everyday practice, and one must concur with Billing's view that modern dowry is a form of groom-price.

As Mies (1986: 169) explains, women 'themselves, their whole person, their labour, their emotionality, their children, their body, their sexuality were not their own but belonged to their husband ... they ... were property; therefore, ... they could not be owners of property. Combined with sanctions against divorce, and the cultural prohibition against women living on their own, these economic factors mean that women have few resources if conjugal life becomes unbearable or life threatening.

The Economic Factors in Dowry-murder

While India was seen as backward by the British, in fact, any 'underdevelopment ... was the direct result of an exploitative unequal ... relationship' (Mies 1986: 39). Oldenberg gives an example of this exploitation. She demonstrates that dowry began escalating during the colonial period (1870–1947) when the British instituted taxation, forcing many families to mortgage their land in order to make payments (Oldenburg 1993). To relieve the increasing financial pressure of this period, dowry demands increased. The initiation of tax laws forced landowners to deal in cash crops, rather than in the exchange of goods. Moreover, as property was privatised for the benefit of the colonialists, and export-driven agricultural production replaced subsistence production, the indigenous economy further declined (Sen and Grown 1987: 31). Although dowry continued to escalate (between 1950 and 1970), it was not at a rapid rate. This was because India had a measure of overall economic stability, based on the Indian government's effective policy of economic diversification, orientation to internal growth, and the availability of capital (Bagchi 1987, cited in Banerjee 1991).

However, since the economic crisis of the 1970s, dowry escalation—and with it dowry-murder—has increased exponentially. This crisis can be attributed to several economic pressures. First, US economic aid to India was suspended as a result of the Pakistan/East Pakistan conflict (in which the United States allied with Pakistan). Second, as a result of the same conflict, India became home to 10 million refugees and 100,000 POWs. Resources intended for social programmes were diverted to the military, while food imports from the United States were renounced in response to its hostility towards India during the crisis (Nayar 1989: 328–29). Third, agricultural production decreased, and industrial production increased at the slow rate of 3.5 per annum (ibid.: 328). Finally, in 1973, OPEC significantly increased oil prices, which further aggravated the stifling economic conditions. Consequently, from 1970 to 1975, economic stagnation prevailed—inflation increased, per capita income decreased, and public discontent, riots and alienation from the government became the norm. Consequentially, a state of emergency was called and the Congress National Party was ousted (ibid.).

Banerjee (1999: 668) further explains shifts in the economy and their relationship to dowry-murder: 'The wage labor market transferred economic power from the family to the market and enhanced the power of other economic institutions at the expense of the family', and thus 'a family's economic viability came to depend on its ability to generate cash income either through commercial production of commodities or through participation in the wage labor market, or both' (p. 667). Hale (1989: 667) adds to this discussion— 'Key institutions of the peasant economic and social system began to unravel under the combined effects of demographic growth, commercialization, urbanization, employment change, migration, and schooling'. As the need for cash increases ' ... agriculture has shifted to intensive capitalist production of cash crops using advanced technology' (Hale 1989: 364), rather than crops for local consumption.

The structural adjustment policies recommended by the International Monetary Fund and the World Bank beginning in the 1970s and continuing into the present day have severely increased poverty (Daines and Seddon 1991). In fact, 'those who were most disadvantaged and vulnerable were suffering dispro-portionately from what the Bank tended to refer to easily as "the social costs of transition"' (ibid.: 1). Along with the effects of structural adjustment, western countries have also imposed a Malthusian population control policy on developing countries in what Kuumba and Bahati (1999: 449–50) calls 'reproductive imperialism', or 'foreign domination ... that manipulates population processes coercively in the interests of maintaining racial domination, capitalist labor interests, and male dominance'.

On a familial level, this crisis translated into an increased need for cash to keep up with inflation, fewer jobs for sons whose parents had paid high prices for education, and a general feeling of desperation to main-tain present living standards. These pressures, combined with the already low status of Indian women, con-tributed to the escalation of dowry-deaths. Such economic crises are common in other countries, and have led to other forms of violence and oppression against women. Dowry-murders are a cogent example of the political-economic-patriarchal mix that continues to ensure a lower status for women.

The Role of the Women's Movement

Women's movements have been far more successful than history has recorded (Carroll 1989). The least recorded are 'those aspects that would provide ... knowledge of women's resistance to patriarchy' (ibid.: 3). Throughout the eighteenth, nineteenth and twentieth centuries, women have been involved in protest movements, but were 'invisible' and only credited with their participation and even leadership after the fact (Daines and Seddon 1991). It is well known that 'with notable exceptions, women have remained virtually invisible in most contemporary accounts of popular protest' (ibid.: 29).

Women in India have certainly been involved in protest movements in historical times, and are increasingly so in the present day (ibid.). A turning point was when the report by the commission on the Status of Women in India came out in 1974, and women directly began to address issues of violence against women (ibid.). 'Women's groups in India have succeeded in publicizing the phenomenon of dowry deaths in the media and in criminalizing some kinds of violence against women' (Banerjee 1999: 664). As a result of this, two laws were favourably amended in 1986: the Indian Penal Code states that a woman's death any time within the first seven years of marriage will be investigated, and the Dowry Prohibition Act now requires the government to maintain statistics on dowry-deaths (ibid.).

The Women's Movement in India is concerned with a myriad issues affecting women. They have addressed poverty, employment, health, and legal and political issues, to name just a few (Katzenstein 1989). However, '... it was the focus on violence against women, beginning in the late 1970s, that propelled the movement forward and endowed it with much of its present strength' (ibid.: 54).

Initially, the philosophy of the women's movement in India disagreed with the push for equality between men and women (Stein 1988), but in the mid to late 1970s, Indian women began to take '... positions far more politically sophisticated than those of their western counterparts' (ibid.: 482). They began to realise the extent of dowry-murder, rape, '... child marriage, ... extreme overwork, exploitation and undernourishment to which poorer women in the Indian subcontinent were ... subjected' (ibid.). Spouse abuse was addressed as an issue in the context of dowry-murder as well as separately from dowry-murder 'in the context of male drinking and alcoholism' (Narayan 1997: 92).

The Indian women's movement has been successful largely because they have been able to name the issues women confront, which has led to other parts of the society having to address them, in particular the press, producing 'new meanings in interaction with the political system of which it is a part' (Katzenstein 1989: 70). The movement now includes women representing many organisations, both rural and urban, as well as academics, activists, and women from all classes. It has been successful in bringing together such disparate groups of women such as grassroots activists and researchers, a feat with which western feminists continue to struggle (ibid.). Actually, 'Many, indeed most, of the research and activist projects address issues facing rural and poor women' (ibid.: 58). In fact, women's voices and agendas are now a central focus in larger social movements in India such as 'the new farmers' movement, the anti-caste movement and the environmental movement' (Omvedt 1990: 34).

The Indian women's movement has adopted 'an ideology of radical pragmatism' (Katzenstein 1989: 70) in their attempts to help women. Many societies where 'battering is barely even identifiable as a social phenomenon [and] is considered a normal part of marriage' are now developing awareness and successful prevention strategies as a result of women's movements (Hirschman 1997: 198). Simply put, 'when there are people in the community to whom a woman can complain and ask for help in cases where violence is threatened, the incidence of violence is reduced' (Rao 1997: 1176).

The dilemma in addressing violence against women in India and, indeed worldwide, is the dichotomous nature of the solution that is needed. As Bush (1992: 587–88) states, 'reform aimed at protecting individual women is one goal while the other is lasting structural change in gender relations within nation states'. When feminist agendas to assist women are joined with the power of the state, the feminist agenda is frequently diluted (Bush 1992). This means that structural questions that address the capitalist-patriarchal stronghold are not pursued, and there is less empowerment of the women needing assistance from the women's movement.

If this is indeed the case, it would seem that it is imperative that all activity designed to assist women be maintained outside the structure of the patriarchal system Katzenstein (1989: 63) puts it forcefully: 'Whether in India or elsewhere, when the state or political parties "sponsor" feminist concerns, concerns about violence against women are rarely a priority.' In addition, legal interventions do not empower, but often, in fact, further endanger women. 'The notion that women need to be protected by men in the form of [the] criminal justice system strengthens traditional gendered relations of power' (Bush 1992: 606).

Conclusions

I have used the phenomenon of dowry-murder as an example of women's experience of violence. It is not just a problem of dowry giving, 'but a pathology or a syndrome rooted in history and gender inequality in a patriarchal society' (Oldenburg 1993: 151). Violence against women is broader even than one country, or one event such as marriage.

Certainly, a theme for women in all nation-states is the control exercised over them by the capitalist patriarchal system. In everyday life, 'the more complete and effective a system of oppression is, the less aware of it as oppression its victims are' (Hirschman 1997: 203). The point at which women make changes 'makes them vulnerable to violence' (Carrillo 1993: 111). This can be seen cross-culturally in the examples Carrillo (1993) gives of women who begin to gain economically through development projects. In the United States, it is commonly known among shelter workers that when women get ready to leave the abuser, they are at a heightened risk of violence. Yet breaking free of their family constraints leads them to be defined 'as public sexual property', whereas before that women were seen as private property within the marriage (Hale 1989: 375). The 'patriarchal bargaining' (Kandiyoti 1988: 274) refers to the fact that when women vie against each other within the family for the minimal power that is theirs in a system of oppression, there is no solution. That is why the women's movement in India is a prime example to other countries to continue to develop awareness as well as attempt to change the patriarchal system.

Even as we address specific remedies for dowry-murder, we need to look at violence against women in all countries and keep in mind that 'institutionalization of women's movement demands and organization may diminish the capacity of such movements to control the social construction of domestic violence against women by providing protection without empowerment' (Bush 1992: 587). This is but one dilemma women face as they work to change the capitalist-patriarchal structure.

The UN document 'Forward Looking Strategies' (1985, cited in Carillo 1993: 103) favours a preventive approach that includes economic assistance to women and structures on national levels to deal with the question of domestic violence. While such assistance may be of value, 'constructing alternative relations of support and solidarity and development of forms of countervailing power' (Daines and Seddon 1991: 9) may bring more lasting change. Since large-scale structural change will be slow, women's groups that develop into movements can ensure gendered participation that will lead to lasting change. It's true that few 'solutions' to the problem of violence against women are at hand, but as aptly stated by Omvedt:

> All the basic conditions of women's oppression and exploitation—control of property and the means of production, control over political power and the means of violence, control over their own bodies and the means of reproduction—are at least coming on to the historical agenda. (1990: 39)

Rather than looking at provincial causes of violence against women, women need to maintain this agenda across nation-states, and look for common global solutions to this critical issue.

References

Banerjee, Kakoli. 1991. 'Introduction', in Nirmala Banerjee (ed.), *Indian Women in a Changing Industrial Scenario*, pp. 11–26. London: Sage Publications.

———. 1999. 'Gender Stratification and the Contemporary Marriage Market in India', *Journal of Family Issues*, 20 (5): 648–76.

Bennett, Lynn. 1983. *Dangerous Wives and Sacred Sisters*, New York: Columbia University Press.

Bush, Diane. 1992. 'Women's Movements and State Policy Reform Aimed at Domestic Violence against Women: A Comparison of the Consequences of Movement Mobilization in the U.S. and India', *Gender and Society*, 64: 587–602.

Carrillo, Roxanna. 1993. 'Violence against Women: An Obstacle to Development', in Meredith Turshen and Briavel Holcomb (eds), *Women's Lives and Public Policy: The International Experience*, pp. 99–113. Westport, CT: Greenwood Press.

Carroll, Berenice. 1989. '"Women take Action!" Women's Direct Action and Social Change', *Women's Studies International Forum*, 12 (1): 3–24.

Crenshaw, Kimberle. 1997. 'Intersectionality and Identity Politics: Learning from Violence against Women of Color', in Mary Shanley and Uma Narayan (eds), *Reconstructing Political Theory: Feminist Perspectives*, pp. 178–193. University Park, PA: The Pennsylvania State University Press.

Daines, Victoria and David Seddon. 1991. 'Survival Struggles, Protest and Resistance: Women's Responses to "austerity" and "structural adjustment"', *Gender Analysis in Development Sub-series*, 4: 1–42.

Fernandez, Marilyn. 1997. 'Domestic Violence by Extended Family Members in India', *Journal of Interpersonal Violence*, 12 (3): 433–55.

Goody, Jack. 1983. *The Development of Family and Marriage in Europe*. Cambridge, UK: Cambridge University Press.

Hale, Sylvia. 1989. 'The Status of Women in India', *Pacific Affairs*, 62 (3): 364–81.

Hirschman, Nancy. 1997. 'The Theory and Practice of Freedom: The Case of Battered Women', in Mary Shanley and Uma Narayan (eds), *Reconstructing Political Theory: Feminist Perspectives*, pp. 194–210. University Park, PA: The Pennsylvania State University Press.

Jacobson, Doranne. 1982. 'Purdah and the Hindu Family in Central India', in Hanna Papanek and Gail Minault (eds), *Separate Worlds*, pp. 82–109. Delhi: Chanakya Publications.

Kandiyoti, Deniz. 1988. 'Bargaining with Patriarchy', *Gender and Society*, 2: 274–90.

Katzenstein, Mary Fainsod. 1989. 'Organizing against Violence: Strategies of the Indian Women's Movement', *Pacific Affairs*, 62 (1): 53–71.

Kuumba, M. and Bahati. 1999. 'A Cross-cultural Race/Class/Gender Critique of Contemporary Population Policy: The Impact of Globalization', *Sociological Forum*, 14 (3): 447–63.

Mani, Lata. 1990. 'Multiple Mediations: Feminist Scholarship in the Age of Multinational Reception', *Feminist Review*, 35: 24–41.

Meinzen, Ruth. 1980. 'Norms and Realities of Marriage Arrangements in a South Indian Town', *Economic and Political Weekly*, 7: 1137–44.

Mies, Maria. 1986. *Patriarchy and Accumulation on a World Scale: Women in the International Division of Labor*. Atlantic Highlands, NJ.: Zed Books, Ltd.

Miller, Barbara. 1981. *The Endangered Sex*. Ithaca, NY: Cornell University Press.

Narayan, Uma. 1997. 'Cross-cultural Connections, Border-crossings, and "death by culture"', in Uma Narayan (ed.), *Dislocating Cultures/Identities, Traditions, and Third-world Feminism*, pp. 83–117. New York: Routledge Press.

Nayar, Baldev. 1989. *India's Mixed Economy: The Role of Ideology and Interest in its Development*. Bombay: Popular Prakashan.

Omvedt, Gail. 1990. 'Violence against Women: New Movements and New Theories in India', *Interpress Magazines*, 1–42.

Oldenburg, Veena. 1993. 'Dowry Murders in India: A Preliminary Examination of the Historical Evidence', in Meredith Turshen and Briavel Holcomb (eds), *Women's Lives and Public Policy: The International Experience*, pp. 145–57. Westport, CT: Greenwood Press.

Ong, Aihwa. 1990. 'Japanese Factories, Malay Workers: Class and Sexual Metaphors in West Malaysia', in Jane Monnig Atkinson and Shelly Errington (eds), *Power and Difference: Gender in Island Southeast Asia*, pp. 385–422. Stanford, CA: Stanford University Press.

Palriwala, Rajni. 1985. 'Women are not for Burning: The Anti-dowry Movement in Delhi', in 'Anthropological Perspectives on Women's Collective Actions: An Assessment of the Decade, 1975–1985', pp. 9–17. Wenner-Gren International Symposium No. 99, November, Mijas, Spain.

Paul, Madan. 1985. 'Dowry and Position of Women in India with Special References to Delhi', in Indian Association for Women's Studies (eds), *Women and the Household*, pp. 13–14. Mysore: Indian Association for Women's Studies.

Rao, Vijayendra. 1997. 'Wife-beating in Rural South India: A Qualitative and Econometric Analysis', *Social Science Methods*, 44 (8): 1169–80.

Sen, Gita and Caren Grown. 1987. *Development, Crises, and Alternative Visions*. New York: Monthly Review Press.

Srinivas, Mysore. 1983. *Some Reflections on Dowry*. Delhi: Oxford University Press.

Stein, Dorothy. 1988. 'Burning Widows, Burning Brides: The Perils of Daughterhood in India', *Pacific Affairs*, 61: 465–85.

Stone, Linda and Caroline James. 1995. 'Dowry, Bride-burning, and Female Power in India', *Women's Studies International Forum*, 18 (2): 125–34.

Tambiah, Stanley J. 1973. 'Dowry, Bridewealth and Women's Property Rights', in Jack Goody and S.J. Tambiah (eds), *Bridewealth and Dowry*, pp. 61–98. Cambridge, UK: Cambridge University Press.

Tsing, Anna and Sylvia Yanagisako. 1983. 'Feminism and Kinship Theory', *Current Anthropology*, 24 (4): 509–29.

UNICEF Issues Report on Worldwide Violence Facing Women. 2000. *The New York Times*, p. 15.

United Nations. 1998. 'World Statistics Pocketbook', Department of Economic and Social Affairs (Vol. 18, p. 88), Statistics Division.

SIX

When Homes are Torture Chambers:
Vimochana's Work with Victims of Domestic Violence*

Vimochana

Many of those who have worked over a period of time providing legal, emotional, or other help to women in distress, especially to women who are victims of domestic violence, quickly burn out because attempting to rebuild broken or severely damaged lives is very difficult and often heartbreaking. This is especially so in a country like ours where the police and courts provide very little relief. Often, these government agencies even add to the injustice by protecting those committing atrocities. However, there are some organisations like Vimochana of Bangalore who are able to sustain their commitment to bringing justice for women despite all the setbacks they face, not just from external forces, but even from the women victims themselves, who they try to help.

I conducted this interview with Celine Suguna of Vimochana a few months ago to provide our readers a glimpse into the very difficult and complex task of helping women in distress.

Vimochana's experience in Bangalore also confirms *Manushi*'s experience in Delhi—that, as part of complex domestic disputes, a few women are beginning to misuse many of the laws enacted (especially the provisions of Section 498) to protect women victims of domestic violence in an attempt to hurt innocent men.

This is an early warning for the women's movement, which, if ignored, is likely to produce a severe backlash.

Several of our readers are involved in work similar to Vimochana's. We invite them to share their experiences and provide us with additional insights into the challenges we face, and the ways in which we can revise our strategies in order to be more effective in combating domestic violence.

—Madhu Kishwar

- Tell us about the work done by Vimochana in helping women in distress. Has your emphasis changed over the years? Do you think the assumptions you started with are valid today?

Vimochana has been working for 20 years on women's issues. Our focus has been on domestic violence and sexual harassment at the workplace. Initially, we operated as an office-based counselling organisation. But soon enough, we got fed up with armchair theorising and decided to personally investigate the cases that came to us. The transition brought many shocks. The first was the sight of burnt bodies of young girls and women. Our initial attempts at investigation were not easy.

Since we were strangers, the relatives of victims were often apprehensive and reluctant to talk to us. Their immediate question would be, 'What are you here for? Are you going to bring our daughter back?' Our effort was to get them to pursue the matter through the police and the courts, but they were uncooperative because pursuing the case meant spending money. The girl's family would rather do a *puja*, garland

*Originally published in *Manushi*, No. 110, January–February 1999, pp. 17–24.

the girl's photograph, cry, and then forget about it. The number of families that dismissed such episodes as their fate and did not want to find out what happened to their children really hit us hard.

We also learnt that the police never provided any help in such incidents. In fact, they would make matters worse by declaring the case a suicide or giving out stories of stove bursts, even when there was no kerosene stove in the house! We would try to hold a protest demonstration in front of the guilty person's house or his workplace to demoralise him. But the police would tell us that they had to stop us, since we were taking the law into our own hands. We were also confused and shocked by the working of the judiciary.

- What was the response of the neighbours when you held such demonstrations? In Delhi, we have almost always got a very positive response from neighbours to such protest actions and calls for social boycott of such families.

The neighbours just remained curious onlookers. In the beginning, some people came out openly to support us, but they didn't act in an organised manner.

The victim's family would prefer to compromise and settle for some money. This demonstrated to us how women and their role in the society are viewed. It also explained a bitter reality. Right from her birth, a girl grows up in a highly restricted environment, especially in the rural areas. She is not allowed to attend high school in an attempt to prevent her from mixing from boys for fear that she might lose her virginity.

It seems the only responsibility parents feel towards their daughter is to ensure that she stays a virgin so that her family can find a suitable match and marry her off as soon as possible. They cry at her wedding at the thought that their duty to their daughter is over. They are of little help if there is trouble in her marriage. Such an approach can easily lead to suicidal tendencies in the daughter if she faces ill-treatment at her in-laws', since she know that she is not welcome at her parents' home. When a daughter has to be taken back in her natal home, she is viewed as a liability. The parents' approach is guided by their conditioning, which makes them believe that since she has left her husband, other men will now make advances towards her.

- Don't brothers and their wives become resentful if the girl comes back? In north India, we have found that the role of the *bhabhi* (brother's wife or sister-in-law) is very vicious, and plays an important role in keeping women from seeking support and shelter in their parental home.

The resentment comes from both the *bhabhi*s and her brothers. They already have old parents to look after. Then there are their own children. They don't want any more responsibility, especially one they consider a burden. Their familiar argument is: in our social set-up, the woman's only place is in her husband's house.

We learnt that a woman is gagged by the dictates of her family, her community and her society. And if she tries to seek help from the so-called law-enforcing agencies, the police or the judiciary, she does not get anywhere. The police might register a cursory First Information Report (FIR) and pass on the work to the forensic department, which will hand its report to the judiciary. Such matters are rarely taken seriously if a proper case is not made in the original FIR, which requires effort and investigation by the police. But usually everybody just keeps passing the buck and nothing ever results from seeking help from the law.

The police blame the forensic department, who in turn say they acted on the FIR provided to them. And the judiciary will not be satisfied with evidence that does not meet every legal nicety. Moreover, evidence is presented during the last stages of a court proceeding. We have not had a case that was completed within six months or a year—we have cases pending in the courts for more than 14 years. I recall a murder case where eight or 10 years after the incident they produced in court a little piece of burnt wood and said this was used as a weapon. Obviously, the case fell flat, as they didn't present the sort of evidence that convinces the court. A judge can make a decision only on the basis of evidence provided by whoever is assigned the task.

Another reason for lack of evidence is that in many such cases, the women's parents are not informed immediately even if they live nearby and the victim is battling for life in a hospital. They learn of her fate only after she is dead. In the hospital, the in-laws pretend that it was a natural death, and deny that it had anything to do with dowry.

When the police constable comes over to take a dying declaration, the husband (the usual suspect) has fled or is in hiding. His brothers, sisters and parents plead that 'it all happened in a moment of anger but there are children to be taken care of, so please don't take the man away'. They also seek to give assurances to guarantee his good behaviour in the future. For the victim, this is the first time she hears her in-laws talk nicely to her.

When a woman decides to kill herself, she is pushed into the decision through bigamy, sexual harassment or an uncaring husband. Nevertheless, she has this *Savitri* attitude—she would prefer to just end her life and let her husband get away with his criminal behaviour. This stops her from giving a dying declaration indicting the husband for her misery, and this is just the sort of thing the police don't want to acknowledge or understand. These women don't tell the truth.

There was this victim who was brought to the hospital with her hands and legs badly burnt. She kept repeating, 'No, my husband came to save me.' The way she said it, one knew that she was trying to hide something and protect him.

The police and the courts ask for eyewitnesses. But we've had a case where they even rejected an eyewitness account and said it was not admissible. This happened in a village on the outskirts of Bangalore. A relative of the girl was walking past the house when he saw her crying. Seeing bruises on her body he asked her what had happened. She said, 'My husband beat me in the morning.' This was the day she died. But the judge ruled against admitting the witness in the court because, he held, 'He is an interested party.'

Most often you cannot have totally foolproof evidence of a crime that is so highly personalised and private.

- When did Vimochana start providing legal aid?

A long time back. In the initial few years after we started, we would approach the police and the courts. Either they didn't have the time, or they were not in a position to provide us a fair hearing. Their training doesn't equip them to investigate adequately, and they only ask the husband's family to give their version of what happened. As a result, biases are allowed to operate all the time, particularly male biases.

We initiate direct legal action only when the victim is dead, or when we know for certain that she won't survive. We gather evidence and get the indictable man, the in-laws, or all the defendants arrested. We also initiate legal action in cases of beatings, burns and injuries.

You'd be horrified to know the extent to which some of these people will go. We know of cases where they put a *surtula* (brand) on the woman, others where they heated a steel ladle (used for making *dosa* or *chapatti*) and burned her in her private parts with it.

After such torture they taunt the woman to visit a doctor because they know she is too fearful or embarrassed to try. Then there are cases where the man will beat up the woman, breaking her teeth, chopping off an ear, a finger, or some other part of her body. These men don't plan such attacks; they do it at random. In all such cases, we provide medical care and emotional help. We even try talking to the man. We learnt to do this gradually. Initially, our approach was guided by anger and disbelief and our common refrain was, 'What kind of a person is this? We shouldn't let him go scot-free.' We learnt our lesson the hard way.

- What is the lesson you learnt?

I will tell you the story of Shashikala [name changed], who was a nurse married to a doctor. They had three children. Though they lived together, she was the one who looked after the children and even built a house with the money she earned. However, the house was registered jointly in both their names. Then this man went away and married a young girl in Kerala. The girl's brothers wrote threatening letters to the nurse demanding that she leave the house, as her husband had married their sister. But the nurse didn't pay any heed and carried on with her life. She was a strong-willed woman, she attended and spoke at Vimochana meetings. She even started a Vimochana centre in her village.

In fact, she maintained that she would not rest till the husband was put behind bars. She came to us and we filed a case on her behalf. The Karnataka and Kerala police worked on it. Evidence was collected from Kerala, where she went accompanied by another member of Vimochana. Around Christmas, when the date of the hearing neared, her husband returned and publicly asked for her forgiveness by falling at her feet and crying. Under the influence of the Christmas spirit, she forgave him.

She let him back into her house and they started living together. We didn't know this had happened. Soon after this reunion, when we met her, she appeared quite composed and happy—not the angry person we knew. We also met her husband and he melodramatically told us how he had done his wife a great injustice and was now really repentant. He said he wanted to find a way to be nicer to her after all that had happened. We just advised her to be careful, unaware that they were living together.

In the last week of April, the police telephoned us to say that this woman had died.

- Dead? Did he kill her?

He made her drink brandy laced with some harmful substance. When she vomited it out, he gave her an injection, apparently to show the children that he cared for her. And he would give his shady injection to her every day. In a few days she grew very weak and could not even speak. Finally, the neighbours intervened and said she should be taken to a hospital. Even there, he made sure that he gave her that injection regularly. The children saw him with a syringe and injection in his coat pocket. He would insist on helping the paralysed woman to the bathroom. He had her shifted to a nursing home against the doctor's wishes.

- Any case against that husband?

Yes. The Superintendent of Police, a woman named Prabha Rao, assured us that the police is going to get this man punished.

- How do you sustain your faith that women can be helped when you see such things happening so often?

Shashikala's case was a nightmare. It hurt us because she was also a friend. But we learnt our lesson. And after all this, we had to sit with this man and divide the house, so that at least the children could get their share.

Of course, we followed the case and he was arrested, but he managed to secure bail. It was a case of slow poisoning. To detect it, the forensic department needed 10 ml of blood. In this case they took just 1 ml. We were asked to produce the syringe used for the injections.

The children were not in favour of their mother visiting Vimochana and seeking our advice. The eldest daughter, who was 16 then, was angry that her mother was letting strangers know about their personal life. The children eventually forgave their father. They let their mother's death pass with a feeble excuse, 'What to do? After all, he is our father and we have to forgive him.' Now the man is living with his second wife, and also continues his medical practice. He also got a share in the house.

- So what did you learn from this whole incident?

We found that very few women are allowed to stay single even if they want, so there is really no option other than marriage. And when a woman relates to a man sexually, it becomes the most intimate and important relationship in her life. In Shashikala's case, what we find difficult to accept is the fact that she didn't tell us the truth when her husband started to live with her, despite our telling her that if she wanted to revive this relationship, she should go ahead but be cautious. After all, even if her husband comes across as a wretched fellow, we cannot force our decisions on his wife. Shashikala was possibly afraid that we would be disappointed and become less friendly and supportive of her if she did not live up to the image she had created of herself. People will always have their own perceptions of how others will respond to their decisions. We cannot pretend to decide for them. But now we understand these difficulties, and therein lies the big chance in the way we function today.

We find that a woman who has survived a violent assault is usually very angry and often appears ready to seek justice at that point in time. But the moment we try to file a case to take legal action against her guilty husband, she retracts her statements and withdraws. There was the pathetic case of Laxmi, whose husband made a habit of simultaneously beating Laxmi while blasting the radio at full volume to deflect the neighbours' attention. She seemed to derive a sadomasochistic pleasure out of this sordid treatment. Fortunately, she finally decided to escape the abusive relationship by running away. When she came to us, her body bore telltale bruises. We took her to the police commissioner and filed a case against her husband, with her consent. When the police arrested the man, Laxmi started crying and pleading with the police, who admonished her for pleading for her husband.

There are numerous instances of women who go back to live with their husbands after they have been released from jail. If they see us in public, these women smile weakly and turn away. Later, they might telephone to apologise for not acknowledging us on the street because their husbands have promised to treat them well only if they promised in turn to cut themselves off from Vimochana. We tell them they don't have to be afraid, since they don't need to buy a membership in Vimochana to get our assistance. We are pleased to know our effort has helped in some way and made the abusive husbands realise they ought to mend their ways. But we also tell them that if their husband misbehaves again, they needn't hesitate to call on us.

This approach has given some sort of leverage to women, a handle over their lives. With the cost of living soaring, it is not possible for a single woman, unless she is rich, to sustain herself and run a household. Our emphasis in the last six to seven years has been to first listen to the woman's story, then approach the husband and get his version.

- Do you go to the husband's house?

We first send a message. Very few of these men are decent enough to reply. When we visit them at home, they shout at us and claim that we are interfering in a personal matter. We let them exhaust themselves ranting and raving. Soon, they calm down and narrate their woes. Usually, it turns out that both husband and wife have lied to us.

In fact, it is virtually impossible to get at the truth during the first meeting. It takes several sittings before we get to see the real picture. In cases of sexual abuse, women are hesitant to speak openly about what they have undergone. We have to talk to them in private and give them the confidence to come out of their shells. We tell them about male and female sexual problems, including problems concerning impotency and lack of satisfactory sexual experience. We have had to deal with real horror stories.

- Such as?

A man insisting on putting an egg in the woman's genitals during intercourse.

We talked to a doctor, but he could not provide a satisfactory explanation for this behaviour. It's just a plain perversion. In our society, sex is still a taboo subject. Our society, it seems, is prepared to tolerate sexual perversion rather than disseminate correct information on the subject. We are so inhibited that both men and women will put up with their sexual problems endlessly rather than discuss them, even with those they trust most, such as their parents, sisters, or brothers.

- What do they do then?

In cases of sexual abuse, the silence of the victims keeps them locked in a situation they desperately want to escape from.

In this particular case, we wrote down the husband's and the wife's respective stories on paper to know if either of them back-tracked or said something new. It was not until we had reached a kind of settlement in the presence of their parents that the truth emerged. When she was about to leave with her husband, she shouted out that if we were to let her go, she would commit suicide rather than put up with this form of perverted sex. This was the first time she mentioned her real problem. All we had heard till then were lies and concoctions.

- How do you cope with such sordid domestic melodramas?

We provide help out of our conviction that there is a genuine need for such help. Otherwise the police, the lawyers and the courts will harass and extract money under the pretext of securing them justice. The failure of the existing machinery for redressal is too apparent for us to ignore the plight of the victims of domestic violence.

There are also cases where women are the offenders, such as in a situation where a woman tries to steal or lure another woman's husband. Our aim is to be free of any kind of gender bias. Otherwise, some women will have the impression that just because they are women they can use our organisation to further harass their victims. We have to work objectively to get the facts of the case.

- For instance?

Say a man is having an extramarital affair and his wife tells us to file a false case of dowry harassment against the husband to get even with him. Such cases are common among middle and upper-middle class people. They make pathetic spectacles of themselves. Of course there is a large number of cases of spouses cheating on each other even among the poorer sections of society, but somehow they don't turn as vindictive towards each other and display better sense by being more willing to reconcile with and to tolerate each other's indiscretions if they don't get completely out of hand.

As they live on the margins of survival, their bonds are strengthened by their daily struggle. Even if they cannot provide adequate care for each other, they remain concerned. It's quite the opposite for the moneyed class. In the upper-middle class, money becomes the bone of contention in a troubled marriage. Most shocking is the behaviour of couples concerning their children, who they think will be content to ignore a lack of parental love and concern provided they are given all the comforts money can buy. We have seen mothers refuse their responsibility to look after their children unless they are adequately compensated. We tell such people to go and hire legal aid to settle each other, instead of wasting our time.

- You mean mothers too neglect children and use them as a tool for bargaining?

Yes. There are couples with plum jobs in multinational companies earning hefty salaries who, on separation, will treat their responsibility for their children as a liability. These are very fickle human relationships, which have been sustained until then under the veneer of superficiality and with an eye on each other's bank balances.

- Have you encountered marriages with just a single problem—maladjustment, where there is no abuse of the sort you described earlier? Especially maladjustment on the woman's part, where she can't stand her in-laws, or desires a different lifestyle, for example. Do they resort to the misuse of anti-cruelty or anti-dowry laws as we have experienced in Delhi?

Yes, there have been cases of that sort as well. For example, we had a case where this woman knew her husband was seeing other women, but she kept quiet to protect the family's reputation. When she could not bear it any longer, she went to the police, who told her to press dowry harassment charges against him. Her lawyer also advised her to do this, and put it in her petition.

When we get such cases, our investigations often reveal that there is no evidence for such charges. Many a time the situation is actually the reverse, for example, cases where the woman has all the control over the family finances, and the man has been forced to obey her dictates. Such cases don't stand up during the evidence stage.

- But the police sometimes arrest the husband even in a false case, and make threats of arresting other members of the family in the hope of getting bribes.

We know the police encourage such cases as they are looking for ways to extract bribes. So we try to avoid the police and the courts as far as possible. Only when we need an injunction order or maintenance, a visit to the police station or the courts is a must. Otherwise, we tell the couples coming to us to sort out their problems between themselves, and that we will assist and advise only if their aim is to act honestly. We tell them to resolve the issues and avoid needless mudslinging.

- Whereas lawyers will insist on telling lies …

They will even traumatise the children by making them witnesses. So we have to assure the couples of our commitment to help them out of their trouble and emphasise our availability whenever they need to discuss their problems. It's in the lawyer's interest to let the case drag on in court as it increases his opportunities to charge higher fees. So people cooperate with us, except when they are blinded by their egos and cannot look beyond their craving for revenge, the attitude that 'I want to teach her a lesson'.

- Isn't it the other way round too, with 'I want to teach *him* a lesson'?

Oh, women can be equally vicious. When the estranged couple has the money and the resources, they don't mind using it to play a power game, or, more egotistically, to prove who can last longer in a dispute.

However, when the woman is clear in her mind that she does not want to live with the man and files for divorce, she tries to take away all her belongings. Otherwise, the man may report the matter to the police, who in turn will immediately confiscate the woman's belongings for as long as the case lasts in the court. A woman on a salaried job does not have the financial resources to start an independent life from scratch.

- What are the other types of cases where women were the offending party and tried to misuse Vimochana?

There was a case where a young Brahmin girl complained to us about a young Muslim man, who she said was troubling her. According to her, every time a marriage proposal came her way, this Muslim boy would arrive at her place to harass the family. She said that after cheating her into pregnancy, the least this fellow could do was leave her alone. Her family had this man arrested, and also tried to give the case a communal overtone by publicly projecting the situation as one in which a Muslim boy was trying to harass a Hindu girl.

Eventually we got to the bottom of the case, and it turned out to be very different. The Muslim boy was already engaged when he met the Hindu girl. Their mutual attraction led to a love affair, and the girl became pregnant. The boy cancelled his engagement, earned the wrath of his family, and had to start living separately from them. The most amazing aspect was how the girl was able to hide her pregnancy and deliver her baby without the knowledge of her parents. When she had labour pains, she simply went with her boyfriend to the hospital, telephoned her parents to say that she was staying at a friend's place, and returned home after the delivery. The parents never got wind of it.

In the meantime, the boy's sister helped with the care of the child. In spite of her promise to return to him, the girl did a complete turnaround and refused to have anything to do with the Muslim boy or their child. While she fancied him, it was all hunky-dory. The moment it became inconvenient, she backed out of the relationship and dumped the man. To top it all, she had the audacity to portray herself as the victim and seek our help.

What we regret most is the misuse of the strict anti-dowry laws. Ironically, as a women's organisation, we were at the forefront in demanding such legislation. One visit to the Bangalore Central Jail and its gross misuse becomes evident. We found that out of 30 cases, eight pertained to dowry deaths, and in each such dowry case, at least six or more members of a family have been jailed. There are too many trumped-up charges. There are cases where the girl has died at her parents' house, and it was made out to be a dowry suicide case.

- What precautions do you take to prevent such misuse?

We never initiate legal action on the basis of one person's story. We make sure that we get the other person or party to share their version with us. Even in cases of death where we get the alleged offender arrested, we make it a point to meet the person in jail and know all the details.

- How have you sustained yourself? What's your motivation?

All of us in the group know each other well, and there is a very strong bond between us. Even if I am not well, I cannot stay at home, I get a craving to reach here. However, all the women working with us must be sincere about the work and actually believe in it. We took on some people who had been through traumatic experiences in their lives, thinking they would make good counsellors, but it is not that simple. These people had preconceived notions, which they would apply in all cases, when in reality each case is different and has its own complexities. Therefore, now we assign individuals to counsellors based on the latters' specific abilities and knowledge, be it in child custody, alcoholism, drug abuse, marriage counselling, or other areas.

SEVEN

Sexual Harassment at the Workplace

Vibhuti Patel

Introduction

Sexual harassment at the workplace (SHW) is a major occupational hazard affecting women all over the globe. In spite of its prevalence, it remains the most unattended, trivialised crime, where the offender goes scot-free as victim blaming is the name of the game. In the Indian context, the situation is even more serious as 92 per cent of working women are in the informal, unorganised sector where they don't get any statutory protection, and where the law of the jungle prevails. To provide a safe and sexual harassment-free work environment is a duty of the employer not only from the human rights perspective, but also from the point of view of efficiency and productivity. In this context, it is extremely important to make a serious examination of the socio-cultural, economic, psychological and legal implications of SHW.

SHW has remained one of the central concerns of the women's movement in India since the early 1980s (Patel 2002). During this period, militant action by the Forum Against Oppression of Women (Mumbai) against the sexual harassment of nurses in public and private hospitals by patients and their male relatives, ward-boys and other hospital staff; of airhostesses by their colleagues and passengers; of teachers by their colleagues, principals and management representatives; of doctoral students by their guides, and so on received a lukewarm response from the trade unions and adverse publicity in the media (FAOW 1991). However, this trivialisation did not deter the women's rights activists. An increasing member of working women started taking systematic action against SHW. *Baailancho Saad* ('Women's Voice') in Goa mobilised public opinion against the chief minister, who allegedly harassed his secretary, through demonstrations, rallies and sit-ins till the minister was forced to resign. In 1990, the same organisation filed a public interest litigation to bring amendments in the antiquated rape law that defined rape in the narrowest sense of 'penile penetration into the vagina'. Several women's groups came forward in support of a new concern about a variety of sexually violent acts against women, including SHW (Chorine et al. 1999).

During the 1990s, the most controversial and brutal gang rape at the workplace involved a Rajasthan state government employee who tried to prevent child marriage as part of her duties as a worker of the Women Development Programme. The feudal patriarchs who were enraged by her (in their words: 'a lowly woman from a poor and potter community') 'guts' decided to teach her a lesson and raped her repeatedly (Samhita 2001). After an extremely humiliating legal battle in the Rajasthan High Court, the rape survivor did not get justice and the rapists—'educated and upper caste affluent men'—were allowed to go free. This enraged a women's rights group called Vishakha, which filed public interest litigation in the Supreme Court of India (*Combat Law* 2003).

Some noteworthy complaints of SHW that came into the national limelight were filed by Rupan Deo Bajaj, a high profile IAS officer in Chandigarh, against 'super cop' K.P.S. Gill; an activist from the All India Democratic Women's Association (AIDWA) against the environment minister in Dehra Dun; an airhostess against her colleague Mahesh Kumar Lala in Mumbai and an IAS officer in Thiruvananthapuram, against the state minister. In all of these cases, men, who were more powerful in the economic and/or political hierarchy, harassed the women victims.

Before 1997, women experiencing SHW had to lodge a complaint under Section 354 of the Indian Penal Code that deals with the 'criminal assault of women to outrage women's modesty', and Section 509 that punishes an individual/individuals for using a 'word, gesture or act intended to insult the modesty of a woman'. These sections left the interpretation of 'outraging women's modesty' to the discretion of the police officer. In 1997, the Supreme Court passed a landmark judgment in the Vishakha case, laying down guidelines to be followed by establishments in dealing with complaints about sexual harassment. The court stated that these guidelines were to be implemented until legislation is passed to deal with the issue (Mathew 2002). Later on the same judgment came in handy when Apparel Export Promotion Council vs. A.K. Chopra, 1999, came for hearing in the Supreme Court of India. In this case of SHW, a woman employee had complained of sexual harassment by her boss.

Pursuant to this, the Government of India requested the National Commission for Women (NCW) to draft the legislation. A number of issues were raised regarding the NCW draft; ultimately a drafting committee was set up to prepare a fresh draft. Several women's organisations are part of this committee, including Majlis from Mumbai, which was asked to make the draft. Women's organisations and women lawyers associated with trade unions in Mumbai have collectively worked on the draft with Majlis. Of particular concern whilst working out the draft has been to include the unorganised sector and incorporate provisions of the labour law. The bill to be introduced in Parliament is known as the Protection against Sexual Harassment of Women at the Workplace Bill, 2006. It provides for the prevention and redressal of sexual harassment of women at the workplace, or arising during and in the course of their employment and matters connected thereto, in keeping with the principles of equality, freedom, life and liberty as enshrined in the Constitution of India, and as upheld by the Supreme Court in *Vishakha* vs. State of Rajasthan [1997(7) SCC.323] and as reflected in the Convention on the Elimination of all Forms of Discrimination against Women (CEDAW), which has been ratified by the Government of India.

Scenario in the Post-Vishakha Guidelines Period

As a result of the *Vishakha* guidelines, a lot of research work and journalistic articles have started appearing in the last decade. Voluntary organisations such as the India Centre for Human Rights and Law (Mumbai), Sakshi (Delhi) and Samhita (Kolkata) have been in the forefront so far as the primary database on the subject is concerned. They also regularly conduct training programmes on SHW for the government bodies, police, civil society groups and the corporate world. The Research Centre for Women's Studies and Maharashtra State Commission for Women have prepared research reports on SHW in the government and municipal hospitals in Mumbai.

A survey on SHW by a Delhi-based counselling centre, Sakshi, which provides legal and psychological support to the victims of sexual offences has been widely disseminated. Sakshi's report is based on calls received on their telephonic hotline services, and women who have sought its help over a period of five years come from a cross-section of the population—students, organised and unorganised-sector workers, office employees and professionals. The Sakshi report throws up some worrying data: 80 per cent of respondents revealed that SHW exists, 49 per cent had encountered (when faced with SHW, they managed to narrowly escape the situation) SHW, 41 per cent had experienced (they had to put up with) SHW, 53 per cent women and men did not have equal opportunities at the workplace, 53 per cent were treated unfairly by supervisors, employers and co-workers, 58 per cent had not heard of the Supreme Court's directive of 1997, and only 20 per cent of organisations had implemented the *Vishakha* guidelines (Dalal 2003).

Controversy over SHW by the senior manager of Infosys (Nair 2003); by the chairman and managing director of NALCO (Ramanujan 2004); the Medha Kotwal petition on SHW of a Ph.D. student by her guide at M.S. University, Vadodara; complaints against a senior professor at Lucknow University (*The Times of India* 2003); and complaints about SHW by the film star Sushmita Sen against the CEO of Coca-Cola have all alerted employers to the economic burden of and efficiency loss from SHW. Still, most private companies refrain from investing funds and making space for counselling for such committees. Though the cases are handled by the Human Resource Departments of the companies/institutions, the employers find the arguments around loss of economic efficiency, productivity, and monetary loss due to the compensation to be paid to the victim of SHW most worrying. Women's groups, human rights organisations and trade unions are concerned about the devastating impact of SHW on the victim.

After considerable media publicity, the consistent work of a women's organisation—Swadhar—in providing support to the victims, and the personal involvement of Professor Pushpa Bhave, a renowned activist scholar of Mumbai, the manager of Infosys and managing director of NALCO were suspended. In the case of the Ph.D. student of M.S. University, no one from Vadodara was ready to stick out his/her neck and Dr. Medha Kotval, Director of Alochana—a women's resource centre based in Pune—filed a public interest litigation with the help of the India Centre for Human Rights and Law. The case is still pending. The same has been the fate of a case of SHW in Lucknow University. The film star Sushmita Sen managed to get a large sum as compensation from Coca-Cola after enormous media coverage on the issue. Consistent follow-up by the victim and her supporters, judicious functioning of the grievance committee, and/or publicity in the print and electronic media have played a crucial role in delivering speedy justice to the victims of SHW.

A Sophia Centre for Women's Studies and Development study shows that awareness and implementation of the Supreme Court's guidelines is very low among students, housewives and employers, and that there is a need to spread awareness about the same. A report by Samhita, a women's organisation based in Kolkata, which throws light on the Bhanwari Devi case, has highlighted to the state and civil society the gravity of the menace of SHW (SCWSD and ICHRL 2003).

Recently, the Times Foundation in Mumbai organised a workshop for the corporate world on SHW. The testimonies of several participants at the workshop revealed that SHW is prevalent even in companies where the victims are highly educated and have considerable economic leverage. Similar views have been expressed in a business journal (*Business Today* 2002).

On 20 October 2004, students beat up an anatomy professor from Versova, Andheri, for alleged sexual misconduct. They had invited the attention of the management to it, but no action was taken against the harasser. The students were so enraged that they collectively decided to punish the offender (*The Indian Express*, Mumbai *Newsline* 2004). Such incidents have now become routine matters in educational institutions. Either students beat up the harassers or parents file criminal complaints at the police station to get the accused arrested.

Realising that the state initiative to make employers accountable for sexual offence is an urgent need to promote the safety of women at the workplace, the NCW and state Commissions of Women have taken a lead in organising capacity-building workshops for potential member secretaries, chairpersons and members of the sexual harassment grievance redressal cell. Allocation of rooms and budgets are provided by the government departments to create structures and mechanisms for preventive measures in cases of SHW, and promotive measures ensure a sexual harassment-free work environment.

There is a need to gender-sensitise our society so that the victim does not feel guilty and is encouraged to report any form of harassment. The victim's privacy must be protected. The police and the judiciary, in particular, need to be gender-sensitised. There should be speedy redressal and an increase in the conviction rate. Women themselves should be made aware of their right to a safe and harassment-free work environment. The concept and definition of sexual harassment should be clearly laid down, and the redressal mechanism made known to women in each and every sector of the economy. Structures and mechanisms should also be created for women in the unorganised/informal sector to combat SHW. Despite bold judgments by the Supreme Court, there is no sexual harassment complaints committee at most workplaces, even in the government sector. The apex court must direct the various workplaces to form sexual harassment committees within a stipulated time-frame.

Definition of Sexual Harassment at Work

The Supreme Court directive of 1997 clearly and unambiguously provides an answer to the question 'What is sexual harassment'?

As defined in the Supreme Court guidelines (*Vishakha* vs. State of Rajasthan, August 1997), sexual harassment includes such unwelcome sexually determined behaviour as: physical contact, a demand or request for sexual favours, sexually coloured remarks, showing pornography and any other unwelcome physical, verbal or non-verbal conduct of a sexual nature, for example leering, telling dirty jokes, making sexual remarks about a person's body, etc.

The Supreme Court directive provided a legitimate space for the hidden truth about SHW to surface; earlier one had only heard about victim blaming, witch-hunting and blackmailing. Now women are fighting back tooth and nail. The electronic and print media have become extremely responsive to the issue of SHW. I worked as member secretary of the Women's Development Cell (WDC) of the University of Mumbai from 2002–2004, and managed 14 orientation programmes for teachers, students and staff of colleges and the university departments. The WDC has twin objectives of prevention of sexual harassment and promotion of empowerment of women among 377 colleges and university departments of the University of Mumbai. My first-hand experiences with providing support to women survivors of SHW has convinced me that we need to counter the myths about SHW with concrete facts, case studies and a database. The list of myths and facts are provided below.

Myths and Facts about Sexual Harassment

Myth1: Women enjoy eve-teasing/sexual harassment.
Fact: Eve-teasing/sexual harassment is humiliating, intimidating, painful and frightening.

Myth 2: Eve-teasing is harmless flirtation. Women who object have no sense of humour.
Fact: Behaviour that is unwelcome cannot be considered harmless or funny. Sexual harassment is defined by its impact on the woman rather than the intent of the perpetrator.

Myth 3: Women ask for SHW. Only women who are provocatively dressed are sexually harassed.
Fact: This is the classic way of shifting blame from the harasser to the victim. Women have the right to act, dress and move around freely without the threat of attack or harassment.

The most popular slogan of the women's rights movement of the past three decades has been: However we dress, wherever we go, 'Yes' means 'Yes' and 'No' means 'No'.

Myth 4: Women who say 'no' actually mean 'yes'.
Fact: This is a common myth used by men to justify sexual aggression and one-sided sexual advances.

Myth 5: Sexual harassment is not really an issue. It doesn't hurt anyone.
Fact: Persons subjected to sexual harassment experience a wide range of physical and psychological ailments. There are economic consequences for the victim's physical and mental well-being, and the organisation's productivity, efficiency and work ethic.

Myth 6: Sexual harassment is 'natural' male behaviour. Man is the hunter and woman the prey.
Fact: Men are not born knowing how to sexually harass others. It's learned within the context of a sexist and patriarchal environment that perpetuates control over women's sexuality, fertility and labour.

Myth 7: Women keep quiet. That means they like it.
Fact: Women keep quiet to avoid both the stigma attached to having been sexually harassed, and retaliation from the harasser. Women are afraid that they will be accused of provoking it, of being victimised, of being called liars and made the subject of gossip.

Myth 8: If women go to places where they are not welcome, they should expect sexual harassment.
Fact: Discriminatory behaviour and abuse is unlawful. Women have equal access to all work facilities. A safe workplace is a woman's legal right.

The *Vishakha* guidelines categorically state that:

It is the duty of the employer or other responsible persons in the workplace or institution to prevent sexual harassment and provide mechanisms for the resolution of complaints. All women who draw a regular salary, receive an honorarium, or work in a voluntary capacity in the government, private sector or unorganised sector come under the purview of these guidelines.

Complaints Mechanism

As per the directive, all workplaces are required to have an appropriate complaints mechanism with a complaints committee, special counsellor, or other support services. A woman must head the complaints committee and no less than half its members should be women. The committee has to include an NGO/individual familiar with the issue of sexual harassment. The complaints procedure must be time-bound, and confidentiality must be maintained. Complainants/witnesses should not experience victimisation/discrimination during the process.

Preventive Steps

The *Vishakha* directive also categorically recommends discussion on sexual harassment at workers' meetings, employer-employee meetings, etc., and prominent display of the guidelines to create awareness about the rights of female employees. The employer is required to assist persons affected in cases of sexual harassment by outsiders. It demands that Central and state governments adopt measures, including legislation, to ensure that private employers also observe the guidelines and prominently display names and contact numbers of members of the complaints committee.

Employers' Responsibilities

The state demands that the employer recognise sexual harassment as a serious offence, the responsibility of the company/factory/workplace to prevent and deal with sexual harassment at the workplace, and the liability of the company, etc., for sexual harassment by the employees or management. Employers are not necessarily insulated from that liability because they were not aware of sexual harassment by staff. The employers are required to formulate an anti-sexual harassment policy, which must include the statements: 'Freedom from sexual harassment is a condition of work that an employee is entitled to expect. Women's rights at the workplace are human rights.'

There are four perspectives on SHW, as explained below:

TABLE 7.1
Four Perspectives on SHW

		Organisational	
Feminist	*Legal*	*View A*	*View B*
1 Power relation, male over woman	1 Exploitative	1 Inter-personal	1 Inter-personal
2 Constitutes economic coercion	2 Involves both implicit and explicit terms of employment	2 Consists of misinterpretation or misunderstanding of person's intentions	2 Improper use of power to extort gratification
3 Threatens women's livelihood	3 Used as a basis for employment decisions	3 'Love affair gone sour'	3 Treats women as sex objects
4 Reflects women's subordinate status in society	4 Produces consequences from submission to/or refusal of advances	4 Personal matters. Why should organisation get involved?	4 Coercive, exploitative, improper
5 Asserts women's sex role over her work role	5 Promotes intimidating, hostile or offensive work environment	5 Can hurt reputation of accused	5 Asserts women's sex role over work role
6 Parallels rape			6 Aberrant behaviour

As the above classification reveals, the feminist perspective on SHW focuses on unequal power relations between men and women that signify subordination of women and male dominance for patriarchal control over women's sexuality and labour. The feminist analysis of SHW sees it as a weapon in the hands of men to keep women in a perpetual state of humiliation, terror and subjugation. The legal perspective highlights the exploitation of women, which involves both implicit and explicit terms of employment, while the organisational perspective consists of either 'misinterpretation or misunderstanding of person's intentions', or 'improper use of power to extort gratification'. The feminist perspective promotes women's agency while the other two see women as 'victims' who need to be protected.

NCW Recommendations on Safety of Women in and around University Campuses

During the last decade, animated debates and discussions have taken place on socio-cultural, social, economic and legal aspects of sexual harassment at the workplace. The National Commission and State Commissions for Women have taken major initiatives in this regard. They have asked all educational institutions to provide a safe and sexual harassment-free environment for women employees and students.

In response to sexual violence against three women students in three different places within one week on Delhi University campuses in 2002, the NCW called an emergency meeting to discuss the safety of women at educational institutions. In the first case, an M.B.B.S. student was forcibly kidnapped in a car and raped in an isolated brick and mortar structure near the campus. In the second case, a stalker kidnapped a student of law. She lodged a police complaint against him and his friends. In the third case, a college girl was gang-raped by the workers on the campus and thrown in the bushes. In all three cases, the authorities responded quickly and there were massive protests by the students. In all these cases, the accused have been arrested and the cases are waiting for the final judgments.

The recommendations that emerged out of the meeting convened by the NCW with the Principal Secretary (Home), Delhi Police Commission and heads of educational institutions regarding strategies to prevent the occurrence of rape and sexual harassment in and around campuses are as follows:

- The NCW demanded from the police that more PCR (Police Constabulary Reporting) vans be deployed to patrol educational institutions, and along the lines of women's helplines, college help-lines also be provided and its number be prominently displayed.

- It recommended that educational institutions must ensure proper lighting in and around their premises, as darkness is conducive to crime. The height of hedges must be reduced in campuses for proper visibility. The NCW also demanded from school and college authorities that an internal security committee be constituted, headed by the head of the institution, a police officer and student represen-tatives who must be invited for meetings to review the security arrangements. If the need arises, other government departments like the Public Works Department (PWD), Metropolitan Council for Devel-opment (MCD), etc., may be invited to review the security arrangements.

- Sensitisation of media is given top priority by the NCW as a repeated relay of incidents relating to violence against women has negative repercussions on society, especially on children. NCW directed the media to not intrude on the privacy of the victim.

Delhi University has passed an ordinance based on its policy against SHW, with clearly defined rules and procedures. It has mentioned a range of disciplinary actions to punish the culprit (employee), including warnings, written apologies, bond of good behaviour, adverse remarks in the confidential report, debarring from supervisory duty, denial of membership to statutory bodies, denial of re-employment, stopping of increments/promotion, reverting, demotion, suspension and dismissal. For student culprits, the punishment could be in the form of warnings, written apologies, bond of good behaviour, debarring entry into hostels/ campuses, suspension for a specific period of time, withholding results, debarring from exams, debarring from contesting elections, debarring from holding posts such as member of a committee, of courses, membership of a college union, expulsion, denial of admission, declaring the harasser to be 'persona non grata' for a stipulated period of time, and other such relevant mechanisms (Court Meeting 2003).

Conclusion

Sexual harassment at the workplace is prevalent in both developing countries and the industrialised world. Even though the offence of SHW has existed in India for a long time, this is the first time that it has been recognised as an infringement of the fundamental rights of a woman under Article 19(1) (g) of the Constitution of India 'to practice any profession or to carry out any occupation, trade or business'. Due to the efforts of the women's movement and human rights concerns, an increasing number of women are reporting such cases and fighting legal battles in the lower courts, high courts and the Supreme Court of India. Articles 14, 15 and 21 of the Indian Constitution safeguard against all forms of discrimination. In recent times, the Supreme Court has given two landmark judgments—*Vishakha* vs. State of Rajasthan, 1997, and Apparel Export Promotion Council vs. A.K. Chopra, 1999, in which it laid down certain guidelines and measures to ensure the prevention of such incidents. Despite these developments, the problem of sexual harassment is assuming alarming proportions and there is a pressing need for domestic laws on the issue.

India is rapidly advancing in its developmental goals, and more and more women are joining the workforce. It is the duty of the state to provide for the well-being and dignity of its citizens to prevent frustration, low self-esteem, insecurity and emotional disturbance, which in turn could affect business efficacy, leading to loss of production and loss of reputation for the organisation or the employer. In fact, the recognition of the right to protection against sexual harassment is an intrinsic component of the protection of women's human rights. It is also a step towards providing women independence, equality of opportunity, and the right to work with dignity.

In the last 50 years, various international human rights organisations have focused on promoting and protecting women's rights. The United Nations has acknowledged that women's rights are synonymous with human rights. The same was reiterated in the Beijing Declaration. Most international women's human rights movements have raised their voice against the abuse and violence perpetrated against women in general. In 1979, the UN General Assembly adopted the Convention on the Elimination of all forms of Discrimination Against Women (CEDAW). Areas where discrimination was found to be rampant include political rights, marriage, family and employment. The convention emphasised that discrimination and attacks on a woman's dignity violated the principle of equality of rights.

Keeping pace with international developments, The Protection Against Sexual Harassment at the Workplace Bill, 2006, has already been introduced in the Indian Parliament. Women's groups have begun lobbying with parliamentarians to get it passed as an Act in the winter session of Parliament. For any sexual harassment law to be successful in India, it is important to be aware of the difficulties confronting our society and ways to overcome them. India is a patriarchal society and lacks sensitivity to women's needs, and hence most cases of sexual harassment remain unreported. The provision of a legitimate democratic space for women at the workplace to speak out against this nerve-wracking occupational hazard is very important.

In any society, it is the fundamental right of people to be able to lead their lives with dignity, free from mental and physical torture. To ensure this, transgressors must pay for their unsolicited sexual advances. A two-pronged strategy of gender-sensitisation of the decision-makers on SHW and prompt punishment of the offender is the most effective way to create safe work environments. At the same time, organisations such as Men Against Violence and Abuse, which conduct gender-sensitisation programmes and self-defence classes to combat sexual harassment at the workplace, must be encouraged (Sadani 2003). To effectively prevent SHW we need both a top-down initiative by the state and employers, and the bottom-up, civil society initiatives from citizens' groups, women's organisations and trade unions.

References

Chorine, Christine, Mihir Desai and Colin Gonsalves. 1999. *Women and Law*, Vols. I & II. Bombay: Socio-legal Information Centre.

Combat Law. 2003. *The Human Rights Magazine*, Special Number on Violence Against Women, September–October.

Court Meeting. 2003. 'Amendments to Ordinances and Appendices to Ordinances', No. 19. XV D Sexual Harassment, University of Delhi.

Dalal, Suchata. 2003. 'Bias in the Boardroom', *The Sunday Express*, 18 May.

FAOW. 1991. *Moving ....But Not Quite There—Evaluation Report of One Decade 1980–1990*. Mumbai: Forum Against Oppression of Women.

Gupte, Manisha and Renu Khanna. 2002. *Process Documentation of Gender Training of Dilaasa*. Mumbai: Centre for Enquiry into Health and Allied Themes (CEHAT).

Mathew, Mini. 2002. *Sexual Harassment at Workplace*. Mumbai: India Centre for Human Rights and Law.

Nair, Meera. 2003. 'The Seamier Side of Office Life—This Woman's Day Let's Do Away With the Groping, Lecherous Advances Made by Male Colleagues at the Workplace', *The Indian Express*, 6–12 March.

Patel, Vibhuti. 2002. *Women's Challenges of the New Millennium*. Delhi: Gyan Publications.

———. 2004. 'Crusade of University of Mumbai Against Sexual Harassment at Place of Work'. Paper presented at seminar on 'An Interdisciplinary Approach to the Unexplored Areas Related to Women', sponsored by University Grants Commission and organised by Maniben Nanavati College for Women, Mumbai, 31–31 July.

Ramanujan, Sweta. 2004. 'NALCO: Sexual Harassment Victim Takes Heart from Family and Friends—Working Woman Shows Grace Under Pressure', *The Indian Express*, 23 February.

Report. 1999. *Workshop on Prevention of Sexual Harassment of Women at Workplaces*. University of Mumbai: Department of Adult and Continuing Education and Extension.

Sadani, Harish. 2003. 'Man Against Violence and Abuse-MAVA', *Urdhva Mula*, Vol. 2 (2), December.

Sadashivan. 1999. 'Policy for Prevention of Sexual Harassment in Educational Institutions and for Dealing with Cases of Sexual Harassment', Mumbai: Bombay University College Teachers' Union.

Samhita. 2001. *The Politics of Silence*, Training Manual by SAMHITA—A Women's Group, Kolkata.

Sophia Centre for Women's Studies and Development and India Centre for Human Rights and Law. 2003. 'Sexual Harassment of Women at the Workplace'. Mumbai: Department of Sociology, Sophia College.

The Times News Network. 2003. 'Disclosures—What is Sexual Harassment', *The Times of India*, 15 June.

Women Development Cell. 2002a. 'Orientation Program on Women's Rights: Laws that Protect', 6–7 August 2001, organised by Department of Adult and Continuing Education and Extension in collaboration with Ghanshyamdas Saraf Girls' College, University of Mumbai.

———. 2002b. *Report for 1991–2001*. Department of Adult and Continuing Education and Extension, University of Mumbai.

EIGHT

Empowerment Approaches to Gender-based Violence: Women's Courts in Delhi Slums[*]

Veronica Magar

The man has been given a higher position in our society. He always keeps that in mind.
He beats even those who have not harmed him .... Nothing like it anymore! There has
been a lot of weeping—now there is a lot of courage.
Women's court organizer

To maintain the control of men over women, gender-based violence has been sanctioned and perceived as normal conduct in most cultures worldwide (Heise et al. 1999). The combination of high incidence and low visibility in the public eye makes it one of the most pressing social problems of this era. Through grassroots mobilisation, women's non-governmental organisations (NGOs) have emerged as dynamic institutions working against deeply ingrained gender inequities to address violence over the last two decades. Representing a counterforce against the social norm of violence against women, NGOs represent the key agents of citizen initiative and social reform.

This descriptive study of an NGO in India interprets how women from Delhi's poorest regions are redefining traditional understandings of female roles in ways that are resulting in dramatic shifts at the local level. In particular, the chapter contributes to the study of empowerment frameworks through insight into a unique model of self-governance designed for women, by women. It focuses largely on a resistance initiative of an NGO consisting of slum-dwellers themselves who work within the social fabric of their communities. They not only counsel abused women, but also hold perpetrators accountable through a feminist variant of an indigenous form of resolving conflict, known as *mahila panchayats*, or women's courts.

An exploration of contemporary intervention strategies illustrates that among the most effective forces acting against gender-based violence are pro-feminist NGOs, who are working to slowly change the power imbalance between men and women at the grassroots level. The literature on local initiatives against gender-based violence in India shows that four main types of prevention strategies have been employed. The first is the anti-dowry campaign, which, when it began in the early 1980s, galvanised women to take action around individual cases brought to public attention through the media (Agnes 1992; Datar 1993; Kelkar 1992).

A second strategy relates to providing aid and support to individual women in crisis (Kumar 1995). Although many of these organisations engage in street theatre, songs and demonstrations to influence attitudes among their constituency, much of their energy is consumed with individual women's needs (Heise 1996). Not unlike many women's groups worldwide, including, for example, shelters in the United States, less time is available for community-based social change activities when concerns over the woman's protection takes precedent.

[*]Originally published in *Women's Studies International Forum*, Vol. 26, No. 6, November–December 2003, pp. 509–23. Reprinted with permission from Elsevier.

The third strategy discussed by Omvedt (1990) consists of rural social movements, in which women assert their rights within larger movements. For example, some Dalit (formerly, untouchable caste) movements assume a feminist perspective as an important organising principle among their constituency. Their central objectives are generally related to issues addressing the needs of all those perceived as marginalised, and not solely women.

The fourth relates to legal and criminal justice system reform, initiated by NGOs with a broad policy orientation. These efforts have brought about advanced dowry-related laws. The Dowry Prohibition Act, passed in 1961, criminalises the giving and taking of dowry. Amendments in the early 1980s recognised abetting suicide as a special crime, made cruelty to a wife a cognisable, non-bailable offence, and made police investigation mandatory on cases in which a woman died within seven years of marriage. However, the effectiveness of these amendments have been limited when it comes to securing convictions (Agnes 1992; Devi Prasad and Vijayalakshmi 1988; Heise 1996; Van Willigen and Channa 1991). Social and legal norms still support the use of violence as a means of control in marriage. It is generally agreed that law-enforcement officers are bribed into colluding with perpetrators, thereby preventing most women from obtaining proper redress (Ahuja 1998; Thapalyal et al. 1987). Critics believe that the legal reform focuses on dowry and, more recently, on pro-women property and inheritance laws (Van Willigen and Channa 1991), and ignores the need to change socio-cultural beliefs held by the mass of society, which supports gender-based violence despite certain illegalities. Studies investigating the characteristics and extent of gender-based violence among the urban poor in northern India are lacking. Moreover, the relative scarcity of research on gender-based violence interventions within the subcontinent has made it difficult to effectively explore strategies towards individual- and community-level social change. This study will help fill this gap by using an empowerment model to examine a unique community-based intervention strategy, known as women's courts, based in an NGO operating out of four Delhi slum localities.

Study Methods

The principal question motivating this study was to see how gender-based violence is being addressed by an exemplary NGO in Delhi slums. Data was combined from in-depth interviews with both NGO staff and women seeking help at the NGO, and observations of NGO activities, including *mahila panchayat* hearings and counselling sessions. Over a five-month period, in-depth interviews were conducted with 31 key informants (18 staff and 13 women), while observations were made of 16 *mahila panchayat* hearings, 22 home visits, a three-day emergency visit outside of Delhi, a two-day *mahila panchayat* workshop, and approximately 18 counselling encounters between staff or *mahila panchayat* members and women seeking help at the NGO. Observations were documented by two investigators, expanded, and transcribed within 24 hours. Interviews were taped and transcribed verbatim. Descriptive codes corresponding to items in the empowerment framework and 'kinds of cases' identified by informants were created and assigned to text.

A matrix-based approach to analysis was used, in which variables and coded text from the documents were extracted, and then interpreted by comparison among cases (Miles and Huberman 1994). Matrices display data in a condensed format to assist in drawing conclusions such as noting patterns and themes. Through systematic recording of data for each case, matrices reduce the possibility of selective reading. Analysis of the textual data in the documents as in well as in the interviews and observations was facilitated by the use of dtSearch, a computer software programme that organises texts systematically for search and retrieval purposes.

A Feminist Empowerment Framework

Whether intentional or not, women's NGOs that provide services and are engaged in policy change generally use a feminist framework as an explanatory model for understanding gender-based violence. According to Yllo (1993), 'feminist academic work, theoretical analyses, and methodological debates flow out of feminist practice.' Indeed, social action, usually in local communities, has been the fundamental source of feminist insight into gender-based violence. Since the late 1970s, feminist theorists have perceived gender-based violence by a male as one of the many means to attain power through social control (Dobash and Dobash 1979). Women's empowerment is recognised as a key element that challenges this norm (Batliwala 1994). Accordingly, the empowerment framework used in this study serves as a guide for the data collection and analysis of the *mahila panchayat*'s violence intervention strategies.

Empowerment is a social process involving change in an individual, organisation, community and society as a whole. Studies have shown that a transformation process happens through participation and collective expertise, and therefore cannot happen in isolation (Batliwala 1994; Purdey et al. 1994; Schuler and Syed 1993, 1994). NGOs play a role as catalysts in this process, which depends on community leaders near the process, rather than highly trained experts who are not engaged in the context (Elliott 1987). The theoretical model developed for this study builds on the work of Schwerin (1995), Kabeer (1999) and Stein (1997). Edward Schwerin derived his understanding of empowerment from the 'transformational politics' and 'mediation' discourses of leading researchers in the empowerment field. His framework highlights individuals' attitudes and capabilities, which enable participation in various types of collaborative behaviour, which in turn empowers the participants. The empowerment process consists of two levels: (*i*) the level of individual capacities observed in individual attitudes and capabilities; and (*ii*) the level of group capacities. Individual attitudes, including self-esteem and self-efficacy/agency along with specific types of skills, knowledge and political awareness, are key ingredients to achieving empowerment at these two levels (Kieffer 1984; Rappaport 1985, 1995; Stein 1997; Zimmerman 1996).

According to feminist theorists, women's empowerment entails a process of change in which patriarchal relations are challenged, in an effort to end men's traditional role over women, particularly at the household level (Batliwala 1994). Kabeer (1999) describes women's empowerment as a process through which women acquire the ability to make strategic life choices. The empowerment model described in this study integrates Kabeer's reflection on strategic life choices, which implies the possibility of alternatives for any given decision. Choice is presented in terms of three interrelated dimensions that include resources (pre-conditions), agency (process) and achievements (outcomes).

NGOs do not rely on a single input; usually a complimentary package of resources and services are provided to ensure that goals are met (Kabeer 1994). As individual and group capacities are enhanced, women's empowerment becomes capable of emerging as a political force that challenges and transforms existing power structures. NGOs are therefore integral to achieving-both individual and group/community-level achievements to attain empowerment (Fetterman 1996; Kieffer 1984; Rappaport 1995; Schuler and Syed 1993; Stein 1997). The desired results are to see favourable changes among both individuals and communities so that the eventual transformation of society can take place. Figure 8.1 illustrates the relationship between individual and group capacities, and how they produce achievements in the empowerment model referred to in this study. The following is a discussion of the elements contained in the empowerment model.

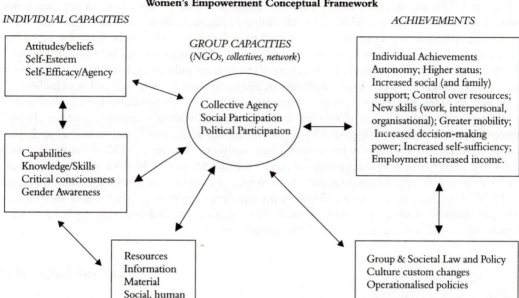

FIGURE 8.1
Women's Empowerment Conceptual Framework

INDIVIDUAL CAPACITIES

Attitudes/beliefs
Self-Esteem
Self-Efficacy/Agency

Capabilities
Knowledge/Skills
Critical consciousness
Gender Awareness

GROUP CAPACITIES
(*NGOs, collectives, network*)

Collective Agency
Social Participation
Political Participation

Resources
Information
Material
Social, human

ACHIEVEMENTS

Individual Achievements
Autonomy; Higher status;
Increased social (and family)
 support; Control over resources;
New skills (work, interpersonal,
organisational); Greater mobility;
Increased decision-making
power; Increased self-sufficiency;
Employment increased income.

Group & Societal Law and Policy
Culture custom changes
Operationalised policies

Note: Women's empowerment is an outcome of a process whereby individual attitudes (self-esteem and self-efficacy) and capabilities (knowledge skills and political awareness), combined together with collaborative actions (social and political participation) and reciprocally influenced by resources (information, material, and social/psychological) result in a transformation into desired achievements (individual, group and societal).

Individual Capabilities

As Figure 8.1 indicates, attitudes and capabilities are key attributes of individual empowerment. 'Individual capability' may be limited if a woman lacks support from either her marital or natal family. Abused women are often disadvantaged due to diminished self-esteem, which gradually erodes as abusive relationships progress. The impairment of a woman's self-esteem places her at risk for several mental health problems. Self-efficacy (or agency) is the experience of oneself as a cause agent, not in terms of skills but rather in terms of one's judgments of what one can do with whatever skills she has (Bandura 1995). It refers to one's capacity and motivation to define her own life choices and pursue her goals, despite the opposition that she faces (Kabeer 1999). It is basic to an individual's mental health and has also been linked to democratic political participation (Schwerin 1995). Within Delhi slums, self-esteem and self-efficacy are demonstrated by a woman's ability to assert her individual concerns and interests during counselling sessions, interviews and *mahila panchayat* hearings. At more advanced stages, women demonstrate self-esteem and self-efficacy through participating in NGO activities and supporting other survivors of violence through counselling, legal advice, representation at police stations, and public shamings.

Knowledge and skills are personal competencies required for social empowerment, and enable women to survive and accomplish goals. In the NGO context, this would include knowledge of the rights of women and Indian laws related to dowry, property, financial maintenance, marriage and divorce. These kinds of knowledge and skills are necessary for a woman to understand how to take action on her own behalf. A woman's level of knowledge is evidenced by her ability to articulate those laws and rights that are most relevant to her immediate set of circumstances. According to the model, skills can be defined as a coordinated series of actions that help to attain goals or accomplish tasks. A woman seeking help from the police or a social service agency requires skills to negotiate herself through the judicio-legal system, access government and non-governmental services, obtain entitlements, and secure safety for herself and her children.

In the past, most researchers have left gender awareness out of models pertaining to empowerment. This model brings in the work of Kabeer (1994), and her discussion of 'women's empowerment from below'. In the place of political awareness suggested by Schwerin, gender awareness is emphasised as an important kind of political awareness necessary for women's empowerment. Kabeer (pp. 232–66) posits that women must develop 'power within' by recognising the gender inequalities within the domestic domain. An aspect of gender awareness is critical consciousness, a special type of empowering knowledge first introduced by Freire (1970). It enables women in the slums—who experience oppression as a result of their low caste, poverty and status as women—to transform their consciousness and mobilise collectively by developing their own concepts of social justice (Freire 1970; Kabeer 1994).

Group Capabilities

Social and political participation through collective behaviour has the potential to transform individuals as well as societies (Rappaport 1995). Social participation provides a context in which women can attain the support necessary for them to change their situation. Moreover, in the context of violence, it also provides a safe space for them to develop new capabilities, which help them enhance their self-esteem and self-efficacy. If empowerment is to take place, developing individual capacities cannot occur in isolation from enhancing group capacity. As illustrated in Figure 8.1, social and political participation have a reciprocal relationship with individual attitudes and capabilities. As individual capabilities are enhanced, so are group capabilities. Due to the nature of service-oriented organisations, it is important to observe whether dependency, rather than self-sufficiency, is reinforced within the groups (Kabeer 1994). Group agency occurs when they seek to access resources and services independently, demanding accountability from those who govern and make policies, and lobbying for changes in policies that subordinate women. Good governance practices exist, observed through women's redefinition of power. That is, power is shared through collective responsibility and accountability which have emerged through new decision-making processes (Batliwala 1994). Societal transformation is achieved through group agency when women's empowerment becomes a political force.

Resources

Having access to resources represents important attributes for empowerment. Correspondingly, increasing empowerment means increasing access to essential resources. These are tangible assets such as economic resources (income, dowry, maintenance allowance and inheritance), basic household necessities (food and medication), social services and information. Kabeer emphasises the need to go beyond simple 'access' indicators in order to understand how resources are translated into the actual realisation of choice. Having control, otherwise described as 'having say' in relation to the resource in question, must be understood when defining the relationship between resources and empowerment.

Achievements

Also missing from Schwerin's model but included in the study model are 'individual' and 'group achievements.' Achievements are derived when an empowerment framework is effectively implemented. Stein's (1997) empowerment framework includes variables representing potential individual- and group-level changes. Adapted to this study's model, the changes she describes are represented as achievements for a more comprehensive interpretation of what needs to take place for empowerment to occur. An effective empowerment process is meant to transform the individual by developing the necessary attitudes, knowledge and skills for personal competence. Kabeer (1999) states that a woman's achievements relate largely to her ability to make meaningful choices that she can achieve not only in concrete and material terms, but also in a context in which she would consider achievements in the realm of possibilities available to her. These might include, but are not limited to, the following: higher status and autonomy within the marital family; increased social support from a woman's natal family and other women; control over family resources, including a part of her husband's wage; legal literacy and ability to navigate through the judicio-legal system; greater mobility outside the home; increased decision-making power within the family; increased self-sufficiency or employment.

Because it is also a group process, empowerment must lead to transformation of the community as well. Community transformation includes achievements like stronger group identities, leadership, and the ability to influence policy that affects society at large. Within the NGO, this would include increased membership, improved leadership, heightened community support, and more *mahila panchayats*. Moreover, behaviour and attitudinal changes related to gender-based violence would be observed among law-enforcement officers, community leaders, as well as individual families.

To gain an understanding of effective gender-based violence intervention from an empowerment perspective, this study uses qualitative methods to explore empowerment processes at the individual and group levels. An empowerment framework is used because it assumes that individual and group capacities interact to influence individual and community behaviour towards social change. Accordingly, the items in the model are mutual and interdependent, whereby an individual's changing attitudes and capabilities will influence collective behaviour. Reciprocally, as social change takes place in groups such as the NGO, family and community, individual behaviour is influenced.

The Study Site: A Women's Advocacy Organisation

This chapter helps document the passage of a Delhi-based NGO from a small, informal group consisting of part-time volunteers to a large, feminist establishment which has now become a significant figure on Delhi's landscape—especially in the eyes of the thousands of the city's women living in the slums. This is accomplished by looking closely at how they have addressed violence, methods that have helped the organisation grow into a vibrant, feminist force. In 1979, this NGO began with a handful of volunteers who provided counselling and help to survivors of gender-based violence. Since their work was born out of a politicised reaction against the Indian government's forced sterilisation programme, a feminist and social justice perspective remains the cornerstone of their activities. Similar to their roles with victims of the sterilisation campaign, the health workers provided advocacy, consciousness-raising activities and social support to survivors of gender-based abuse until 1993, when case workers were hired to staff the resisting-violence project. Except for a few part-time lawyers who run law classes and provide counsel to exceptional cases, the project is staffed and coordinated by women from the slums themselves, who have little or no formal education. Extremely well-seasoned and articulate—many of whom are survivors of violence themselves—they wield influence in support of women's rights within the communities they live in.

Domestic violence disputes have been traditionally regulated through the *baradari panchayats* (traditional caste-based village-governing councils) and by joint families themselves (Van Willigen and Channa 1991). The *mahila panchayats*, a modified departure from the male-dominated *baradari panchayats*, were developed in 1993 by this NGO in four slum localities where it has had a 20-year presence. NGO staff were trained to manage cases, educate and raise the consciousness of its members, and develop and support *mahila panchayats* in each of the four slum localities in which it operates. Three NGO staff handle approximately 5–10 new cases each week. They provide emotional support, legal advice and conflict resolution through the *mahila panchayat*. Husbands are generally obliged to 'sit' with their wives before the *mahila panchayat*, where a hearing is held and rulings are made. Up to 25 members volunteer to convene weekly and hold hearings to solicit information, including desired outcomes, from both parties in order to provide a formal order that the couple is expected to abide by.

Results

Based on 16 *mahila panchayat* hearings, the matrix analysis (Table 8.1) illustrates the variation of cases observed, in terms of primary complaints and case resolution. Insufficient resources—whether from lack of financial

TABLE 8.1
Mahila Panchayat **Hearings, by Complaints, Reconciliation with Husband,**
Mahila Panchayat **Ruling, and Quotes, in Delhi Slum**

	Primary Complaints Brought to the NGO	Age	Years Married	Reconcile?	Mahila Panchayat Ruling	Quotes from Mahila Panchayat
1	Dowry demands; beatings; restriction against toilet use; husband (and in-laws) denies paternity, provides no maintenance	24	2	yes	Husband pays maintenance; no beating; build another latrine	'Everyone uses the same latrine! Why can't she? Why did you try to burn her? Why did you leave your first wife? And, why are you now talking of getting a third one?'
2	Dowry demands; in-laws abuse and throw out; daughter not wanted; drenched self with kerosene	21	4	yes	Husband, wife move out of in-laws' house	'Don't blame Kamla for pouring the kerosene. She couldn't handle the harassment... it just got out of hand.'
3	Husband drinks, brother-in-law wants property, thrown out, beatings	28	10	yes	Woman should lodge a formal complaint at the police station	To neighbour: 'See if you really want to help her, you will have to do this little work, anyway the signatures will be hers, so you don't have to worry... we will help you'.

(Table 8.1 continued)

(*Table 8.1 continued*)

	Primary complaints brought to the NGO	Age	Years married	Reconcile?	Mahila panchayat ruling	Quotes from mahila panchayat
4	In debt (Rs 50,000). Sons fight over inheritance. Eldest son favoured because he has sons; younger son has only daughters	34	5	NA	Collect rent to pay debt; live with different son every 6 months; divide inheritance equally	'You should treat both sons equally .... For your daughter you have given so much that now you are in debt. For your daughter-in-law, you have given her nothing and even want to kick her out.'
5	Husband's brother took sisters' inheritance and spent it on lotteries. Kamla's nephew moved in her house, but is not paying rent	50	30	NA	If property is in woman's name, couple should vacate. NGO lawyers assist	'The mahila panchayat is very efficient...why did you wait so long. We would have given you more time and helped you if you cooperated.'
6	Husband has second woman and not paying financial maintenance	37	15	yes	Monthly financial maintenance required	To husband: 'Speak, you will soon see that we are impartial.... We can't make you stop your affair, but we do require you support your family.'
7	Husband drinks and is jealous. He will not allow her to leave the house without his permission	28	9	NA	Woman's side must be heard before decision is made	To husband: 'I see your point. But, if your wife is suffering, only she knows about it and can tell us. We have to hear side as well.'
8	Husband beats, drinks. She threatened suicide, wants separation. Husband is financially dependent on her and wants her to stay	52	35	no	A formal divorce is required	To husband: 'If you would have kept her properly, why would she come here?' To woman: 'You have taken a good decision. You have thought, what you want, on your own.' To woman: 'Why are you doing all this at such and old age.... It is a sin to leave your husband.'
9	Woman and 3 children (hungry, gaunt, and tattered) live with widowed sister-in-law. Husband and father-in-law beat, drink. Husband has heroine addiction. Third hearing	22	7	yes	Husband must provide maintenance and discontinue beating. If he does not obey, in-laws will keep children	'She is giving you one more chance. If you beat her and the children and drink alcohol, then it will be too late'.

(*Table 8.1 continued*)

(Table 8.1 continued)

	Primary complaints brought to the NGO	Age	Years married	Reconcile?	Mahila panchayat ruling	Quotes from mahila panchayat
10	Husband has a second woman who is pregnant	22	8	yes	Husband is responsible for maintenance of both women	'The society and law doesn't consider your relationship with Anita a marriage at all. You can have only one wife. But for us, both are equal. Because both are women.'
11	Husband drinks, plays lottery, and does not provide maintenance. She and children are destitute. He returns home every few months and forces her to have sex	31	18	yes	Husband should provide maintenance and stop forcing intercourse	To Husband: 'Look at your children. They are living from other people's handouts. They go to bed hungry. Times are hard. What will it take for you to care for them.'
12	Husband burned woman. He kidnapped children and remarried.	32	15	yes	Husband should provide main-tenance and return children	To Shehnaz: 'It is not enough to get maintenance ... you should get your children back. What will you do when you are old?'
13	Dowry demands; husband denies paternity; sexual harassment from husband's brother who threatened to kill her	25	1	yes	Husband must get paternity test, stop abuse and provide maintenance	To Husband: 'You think you can deny who the father is? What will you say when the blood test says it is you?'
14	Widow and mother of four adults sons, in need of maintenance from them	65	–	NA	All four sons must provide maintenance	To woman: 'By raising your children you carried out your responsibility. Now they will do their duty. All four sons must contribute so that one of them does not pay all the money.'
15	Husband beats and tried to burn woman. He kidnapped child and abandoned her since attachment to a second woman	22	4	yes	Husband should provide maintenance and stop abuse	To husband: 'You are very slick. You think we don't see truth? We know that you are wrong. You think we are stupid here?
16	Husband beats and drinks heavily	35	16	yes	Husband should stop abuse and provide maintenance	To husband: 'Don't think we are scared. We will stay here as long as it takes to get the truth.'

maintenance, dowry demands, or property disputes—were common to all the cases. A lack of financial maintenance from the husband accompanied by abuse was the most commonly reported problem (11). Of these, six women reported that their husbands spent household resources on alcohol and/or gambling, and four channelled resources to women with whom they were romantically involved. While the five dowry-related cases were reported by younger women (between 21 and 25 years of age) who had been married on an average for three years, the six women whose husbands were reported to drink heavily tended to be older (28–52 years of age), and had been married on an average for 15 years. In five of the 16 cases, the husband and/or in-laws either denied paternity or expressed reluctance to keep the woman's daughter(s), because they represented a drain on family resources. Three elderly women reported property-related problems from younger family members, who were ostensibly attempting to usurp her property or were living on her property but not contributing to the household resources. Alleging that his wife was romantically involved with another man, one man wished to obtain the *panchayat* support in preventing his wife from leaving the household premises without his permission.

In all the cases, the *mahila panchayat* required that women receive financial maintenance. In addition to obtaining maintenance, providing debt-repayment strategies and legal counsel related to acquiring property are two examples of methods the *mahila panchayat* used to empower women to obtain resources. Most of the women (10) who brought disputes against their husbands wanted to reconcile. The two not disposed to reconciliation were those who obtained financial maintenance through other means: one was the primary wage earner, and the other received money from her brother.

Creating Social Change through a Woman's NGO

The NGO's intervention occurs at two levels: individual capacity building through case management, and group capacity building, namely through NGO activities in the slum-based offices and ad-hoc trials convened by the *mahila panchayats*. The NGO staff and *mahila panchayats* engage the husbands as part of the woman's empowerment process. Husbands comply with the *mahila panchayats* as an outcome of the collective process.

If the accused husband does not appear at his hearing when he is asked to, he receives a registered letter notifying him of the new date. A typical letter usually reads:

Dear [Husband's Name],

Your wife came to us and told us her problems. She said you beat her all the time. Why do you do this? What is your problem? Come to our office and tell us so we can help solve your problem.

Thank you, [Signature]

P.S. If you do not come, we will take further action. Come to our office at: [Date/Time].

Furthermore, traditional *panchayats* have a long history and a prominent place in the lives of slum dwellers, providing a context to realise collective behaviour. Resembling the structure of a traditional village council, the *mahila panchayat* similarly commands authority and respect in the locality. When a woman and her husband appear at the hearing, they assume the traditional roles of accused and accuser. The *mahila panchayat* provides the setting and framework where group-level empowerment is possible. In addition to hearings, activities such as consciousness-raising and groups' case-sharing meetings occur daily. Women who have higher levels of individual capacities became socially and politically engaged in the NGO's activities. For example, six months prior to introducing herself to the NGO, Vimlesh began her long weekly journeys to the closest *mahila panchayat* site where she studied the hearings held for women with stories similar to her own. After several months of vicarious encounters, she presented her case and successfully obtained maintenance from her husband's family through the *mahila panchayat*. Having been engaged in the process which led to a favourable outcome, she began organising a *mahila panchayat* in her own community several miles away. Despite her limited experience and education, she was hired by the NGO as permanent staff.

The NGO staff's knowledge of Indian personal law and skill in handling the judicio-legal and police systems enhances their authority in the community and strengthens their ability to assert themselves against traditional norms. For example, asking a father who denies his infant daughter's paternity to recognise his daughter as his own, demanding that he stop beating his wife and challenging him when he lies about the beatings could not be done without knowledge coupled with self-efficacy. By modelling behaviour and providing support, NGO staff and *mahila panchayat* members transfer their knowledge and skills to women who seek help.

Women's Empowerment through the *Mahila Panchayat*

Women are required to understand their legal rights in order to make an informed decision—often for the first time—on their own behalf. Women who once had a vague awareness of their rights related to dowry, property, financial maintenance, marriage and divorce often become well-versed in the law and their rights. Deepa was physically abused and denied food by her husband and in-laws during the initial months of her marriage. Unlike most cases, she was not able to obtain maintenance from her husband and father-in-law as they were both addicted to heroin and unemployed. After helping her obtain health services and medication to cure her from tuberculosis, the NGO provided her with a loan to open a small cigarette and candy stall across from her natal home. Deepa describes the impact of her new-found knowledge:

> The *mahila panchayat* is very new. Previously it was only the men's *panchayat*. Nobody cared about the woman. She would be beaten by her own family. Now a woman has risen even higher than a man in all fields. Now she understands everything. She knows the law and she knows what belongs to her .... The man used to say, 'I'm the earner, I'm feeding five children.' Today the woman is doing the same .... The man isn't the boss anymore. Now she is his equal, speaks up, and tells him to be quiet. It is the woman who suffers. Why should she shut up?

By gaining knowledge and skill capabilities in relation to her rights as well as running her own cottage industry, Deepa has increased her level of autonomy and self-sufficiency. Deepa's narrative suggests a shift in women's roles since the arrival of the *mahila panchayat* in her community.

Providing women with intangible resources such as social and emotional support represents a large portion of the NGO's work. Given its reputation in the slums, gaining a woman's trust is generally not difficult to achieve. The NGO staff and *mahila panchayat* often replace a woman's own family if parental support is not forthcoming. For example, young women who reject their parents' wishes for an 'arranged marriage' may rely on the NGO staff and *mahila panchayat* to replace their families during the wedding ceremony with the groom of their choice. In these cases, an NGO staff may offer her services as the official witness to the 'love marriage'.

Similarly, the *mahila panchayat* often represents the woman's most supportive advocate, throughout her long hearing process. Geetanjali had been married six months when problems with her husband and in-laws began. Although she had requested the NGO's help towards reconciliation with her husband, as her hearing concluded she began expressing apprehension at returning to her marital home.

> Geetanjali (to *mahila panchayat* member): Sister, in front of you, he's acting so good. I don't want to go to that home. I want to live somewhere else. I will not go there. They'll burn me, I tell you. All of them have a meeting upstairs. He looks for excuses to fight with me and beats me up.

> MPms: You must trust us. We won't let that happen. Why do you think we're here? We will continue to check on you so that nothing will happen. Like many cases before, we will make sure of it.

> Geetanjali's mother: She must move back with her husband. She can't continue staying with us .... She is a married woman.

> MPm (to Geetanjali): Tell us if you are unhappy. If you're not satisfied, we won't mind ripping up this ruling. It's your decision.

This segment of the *mahila panchayat* hearing illustrates how social participation provides opportunities to fulfill individual needs in order to enhance feelings of personal control. The *mahila panchayat* members solicited Geetanjali's trust by displaying their commitment to her well-being and safety. Moreover, they demonstrated their allegiance to her decisions, even if it meant opposing her parents.

At least a minimal degree of self-esteem and self-efficacy was revealed by the study participants, evidenced in their initiative to seek help from the NGO in the first place. As their relationships with staff and *mahila panchayat* members progressed, women's abilities to assert individual concerns, interests and personal goals became evident. Over a two-year period, Vimla, who is 28 years old, made several reconciliation attempts with her husband. She endured several years of abuse from her husband and brothers-in-law, all of whom drank heavily and dwindled family resources by playing the lottery. She currently works and lives with her two children in her mother's house, where her brothers reside.

Vimla reports:

> My in-laws wouldn't let me work. They tortured me a lot. I went [on my own] to the police. But they didn't write up a report, saying it was a family matter. Instead of helping me, they accepted [bribes] from my husband's family. Even when I returned with my brother, the police directed me to the dowry cell where they instructed me to reconcile with my husband. Each time I went to the police my brothers-in-law bribed them and each time they developed more courage to hurt me. At times I felt they were trying to kill me. Finally I came [to the NGO], and a medical examination was done. My in-laws were arrested and my father-in-law lost his job .... I kept thinking that he would improve so I tolerated a lot .... Now, I dislike [my husband] so much that I would rather die than live with him again. If he wants to give something to the children, that's fine. I want [financial] maintenance only for the children. But I won't take anything from him, as a wife. I manage to take care of myself now.

Vimla's narrative highlights how individual transformation occurs through collective participation within the NGO context. When she began soliciting help from the police, her goal was to obtain maintenance and reconciliation with her husband. Through group participation, she developed the capabilities for personal competence and attitudes for dealing with problems. With NGO support, she moved out of her marital home and earned her own income, becoming self-sufficient in a relatively short period of time. By combining knowledge of the law, skills in managing law enforcement, and information regarding her rights, the NGO played a critical role in Vimla's advance towards individual achievement.

The *mahila panchayat* decision, or compromise contract, in the form of a signed resolution statement is generated from the couples themselves. According to an NGO staff member, 'They formulate the decision. ... If [the *mahila panchayat*] drafts the rulings, tells them what we think, what to do, they will blame us if it doesn't work out. It's more likely to succeed if they write the decisions themselves.' The final edict is written on a *mahila panchayat* letterhead which the plaintiff, opponent and family representatives sign. Each side keeps a carbon copy. The following is an example of a declaration obtained from a husband, which formed the basis of the final edict:

> I respectfully state that my domestic problems will not continue. I will not make any more mistakes like this. I promise to give my wife Rs 500/month. I will not physically or verbally abuse my wife anymore. I will not suspect her of cheating on me and I will let her visit her relatives. If there are any more such incidents, I'll be answerable to you.
>
> Rakesh [Date]

In addition to thwarting a husband's perceived right to physically abuse his wife, as evidenced in Rakesh's agreement, the *mahila panchayat* compels the husband to relinquish part of his wage under her control. This is accomplished by enforcing entitlement laws through a collective process recognised by the community, namely the *mahila panchayat*. The official judicial-legal system is usually bypassed.

Unless a woman's life is threatened, which is usually the case in dowry cases, law-enforcement officers are generally considered ineffective and are therefore avoided in most instances. The NGO usually maintains control over resources. Ten of the 11 *mahila panchayat* cases in this study did not involve law enforcement. Lila is one such example. After her first husband died, she encountered extreme abuse from her brothers-in-law. Having no financial means to care for them, she left her two daughters at her in-laws' and escaped to her father's house. She describes how her police encounter unfolded:

> The officers at the police station started taunting me. They said, 'aren't you ashamed of yourself, to leave your daughters behind like that? Do you call yourself a mother?' With the [*mahila panchayat*] sisters by my side, I responded, 'Aren't you ashamed of yourself to speak like that when you haven't written a report since I first arrived?' The NGO handled my case without the police and things went much better.

Lila's narrative demonstrates two important points. First, her bold reply to the police suggests that she had acquired sufficient self-efficacy to experience herself as a cause agent. She accomplished this within the context of the collective support of the *mahila panchayat* members accompanying her. Second, the judicial-legal system was bypassed in favour of a socially-just participatory process as reflected in the *mahila panchayat*, in which she was able to achieve a higher level of well-being. Indeed, Lila received financial maintenance from her in-laws for her daughters through *mahila panchayat* manoeuverings and not through law enforcement as she had originally attempted.

Gender Awareness

Awareness of gender inequity is best observed by the NGO staff and *mahila panchayat* members through their understandings of the perceived causes of violence, which in turn reveals how gender-based violence is addressed by them. Since they are not seen as the cause, factors outside the actual violent behaviour, such as dowry-giving, heavy drinking and a second wife, are generally given minimal attention. With reference to an abusive husband who harassed his wife for more cash from her father, one NGO staff member claimed, 'with or without dowry she would still be taunted, beaten, or killed. She is targeted simply because she's a woman.' Similarly, a husband's heavy drinking pattern and spending of family resources on lottery and gambling are not the focus of the NGO's interventions. When counselling a client with these complaints, an NGO staff member warns, 'don't be deceived .... Alcohol is only his excuse. The day that [your husband] wants to fight to make you do something and create drama, he drinks alcohol.' Another staff member purports, 'a husband may be drunk as ever when he rapes his wife, but it's not the bottle that does the deed, he is the one responsible.' As described above, *mahila panchayat* hearings are largely focused on exposing gender inequities in the familial relationships and holding husbands accountable for their crimes. Lila, whose distressing police experience enhanced her trust in the NGO, describes how her consciousness about women's roles evolved through participation and connection with the NGO.

I realised when I joined the *sanstha*, the truth about life. I have seen and experienced all the restrictions placed on women by the family .... Before I joined the *sanstha*, I knew nothing, it was like living in a dark cell. Even in my [natal] family, I thought things were supposed to be like this. After joining, I started thinking. It was like I came towards a light from darkness.

An Unseasoned *Mahila Panchayat*: Lessons Learned

A seasoned *mahila panchayat* under the leadership of a local NGO generally supports women's efforts towards self-determination. However, an unskilled *mahila panchayat* is not immune to social pressures upholding men's violent behaviour against women. In such instances, the husband may persuade one or two *mahila panchayat* members, who in turn influence the larger group. For example, Reshem's case (no. 8) was heard in front of a newly-formed *mahila panchayat*, which lacked skills in critical consciousness. Throughout the hearing, Reshem was condemned by members for wanting to leave her husband. The *mahila panchayat* members succumbed to Reshem's husband's emotional appeals, and persuaded Reshem to remain home with him.

Husbands and *Mahila Panchayats*

In general, *mahila panchayats* and NGO staff create change by confronting husbands who perpetrate violence against their wives. In doing so, they model skills that are necessary when standing up to family members and police, while also instilling consciousness related to gender equity. In addition to the newly-understood information about the law and their rights, women acquire material resources as these rights are practised.

One of the *mahila panchayat*'s most effective contributions is holding perpetrators accountable for criminal offences against women. Husbands accused of battering their wives to extort money from her family generally deny their abusive behaviour or rationalise it in order to legitimise their conduct. They are challenged, particularly as they fabricate the truth, elude accountability for transgressions against their wives, or wrongly transfer the blame on their wives or someone else. Excerpts from *mahila panchayat* hearings illustrate:

Husband: She doesn't get up from the bed until I leave for work. So, I never get any breakfast. She doesn't bring me tea .... She won't make me *rotis* (flat bread) unless I press her feet.

NGO staff: See, I know you are not the innocent one that you pretend to be. You mean to say, she'll eat all alone and not even ask you for food? You tell me! Why did you leave your first wife.

Husband: She left me on her own will.

NGO staff: No woman marries to leave her husband! She doesn't move out unless the situation gets out of hand!

MPm: How can you accuse [your wife] of sleeping with her own brother?

Husband: I never said this .... My mother goes out to work. I go out to work. She's there alone. What do I know what she does with him when I'm not around.

NGO staff: (angry) She manages the household! Understand?

NGO staff: We notice that you don't hold your own child ... didn't even look at her.

MPm: You say she's not yours, but we see that she looks just like you (husband reaches for child).

Husband: [My wife] relieves herself on the floor at home and doesn't clean it up ....

MPm: Why are you lying? No one speaks to us like that! Lies! Don't you know! The *mahila panchayat* is like a god!

In these short segments, the *mahila panchayat* exposes the deeply ingrained gender-biased beliefs held by men in this study. By contesting the view that violence against women is a legitimate part of male prerogatives in maintaining control over women, the *mahila panchayat* profoundly challenges the belief that such violence falls in the realm of normal and acceptable behaviour. Within this pro-feminist model, *mahila panchayat* members impart knowledge and critical consciousness to men, affecting their gendered expectations and attitudes. Because they are savvy about the law and articulate in challenging husbands' dominant roles in marital relationships, men generally agree to comply with *mahila panchayat* rulings.

Segments from four of the 16 hearings illustrate:

Husband: [My wife] goes to her mother's house without asking me. All I want her to do is to ask me before she goes anywhere.

NGO staff: How much will you obey her? Will you give her your salary every month?

MPm: See it has to be both sided. If she obeys you, you should also obey her.

Husband: Okay, but she should also listen to me if I obey her.

Husband: She comes and goes from the house on her own will. If I have ever beaten her up, it's because she did something wrong.

MPm: You are shrewd .... (angry) And when you do something wrong?

MPm: Is there someone there to beat you?

Husband: I don't know what else to do ....

Woman: He shouldn't beat me because he loves another woman.

Husband: I am her husband. You're saying I shouldn't beat her at all, no matter what she does?

NGO staff: She's your wife, not a cow to be beaten.

Husband: So what do I do if I can't beat her?

MPm: You don't beat her, you come to us if you have problems.

These verbal exchanges reveal the *mahila panchayat*'s role in bringing to light the gendered beliefs husbands hold. In each exchange, husbands justified their male prerogative to use violence as a matter of right. By profoundly challenging the notion that such violence is inevitable and in the natural order of things, the *mahila panchayat* prompted the bewildered husbands to begin thinking about alternative beliefs. For example, in the last scenario, in which the *mahila panchayat* restricted him from beating his wife, the perplexed husband requested instruction on what to do short of using violence. In essence, while gaining knowledge of their wives' rights, the husbands were also engaging in a process of raising consciousness.

Husbands are not only admonished, but also have their own difficulties acknowledged. The *mahila panchayat* gains its power in part by providing resources such as social support to husbands. Providing reinforcement to behaviour that complies with *panchayat* directives helps husbands develop new skills in their family relationships.

MPm: Tell me why you beat her?

Husband: See, I'm an ordinary man. I only earn Rs 1,500 washing dishes in a canteen.

MPm: That's OK—it's honourable work and is nothing to be ashamed of.

Husband: I drive the rickshaw all day and come home completely mentally fatigued. When there is fighting, between my mother and wife, I can't handle it. I'm trying to do the right thing.

MPm: You are a good man.... You should not feel this heaviness.

Conclusion

This chapter uses an empowerment model to demonstrate the effectiveness of a community-based strategy that seeks not only to empower women, but also to hold perpetrators accountable and change social norms. It is the women activists performing these roles who have helped institutionalise a middle-class welfare initiative into a new framework, which systematically impacts how poor women in contemporary Delhi slums deal with male oppression inside their homes.

Gender-based violence in the home is widely perceived as a matter of a husband's and his family's right. The narratives demonstrate that survivors who seek help at the NGO accept this tenet as an unfortunate phenomenon, but nevertheless one that families with girls must accede to. The fact that there is virtually no institutionalised alternative with effective methods of recourse for women illustrates the extent to which such violence is accepted as standard comportment. The *mahila panchayat* continually challenges deeply in-grained attitudes reflecting gender inequality, thereby re-conceptualising violence by lowering the threshold of what is considered normal behaviour.

Through consensus, *mahila panchayat* members develop a critical consciousness among its members by discussing cases as well as practising a just system of jurisprudence modelled on a traditional system, which they have appropriated as their own. New *mahila panchayat* members model their behaviour after NGO staff and seasoned *panchayat* members. They gain a sense of accomplishment and pride in applying their new-found knowledge and skills in doing what is right. The ideology and feminist precepts, which are discussed in meetings throughout the week, are practised everyday through encounters with women seeking help.

It is not unlikely, however, for a hearing to suddenly shift unfavourably, especially in cases where the husband is perceived sympathetically by the *mahila panchayat*. Therefore, the participation of leaders from the community who are well-grounded in critical understandings of women's oppression in poor contexts is essential if *mahila panchayat*s are to achieve their goal of empowering women. If such leaders are otherwise unavailable, a response not unlike the one held by the community at large—excusing abusive behaviour and undermining women's rights to safety—can be expected to ensue. The *mahila panchayat* opinion in Reshem's case, for example, was swayed as a result of her persuasive husband's justifications, despite his wrongdoings. A woman who transgresses social norms, as Reshem did when she asserted her intention to leave her husband in the face of his emotional outpourings, must be assured that her rights will be upheld and the members will not submit to traditional beliefs about women living independently. Continuous monitoring by experienced leaders, especially during the initial years of the development of *mahila panchayat*s, are critical to ensure that the latter does not create another obstacle for women to obtain justice. NGOs are best positioned to play this leadership role.

NGO staff and *mahila panchayat* members do not put their efforts into ending dowry-giving or alcohol abuse because they see it as a pretext, and not the cause for violence. Instead, gender-based violence is addressed by focusing on changing gender inequalities. Husbands are held accountable by challenging patriarchal behaviour in public fora, and by making the husbands equally responsible for determining what they want as well as how to resolve their conflicts.

Women's perceptions that something is wrong are validated by the *mahila panchayat*, an outside authority, which challenges the conventional notion of what it means to be a woman. This includes younger women who are expected to 'adjust' to their homes where they must remain, despite the risk of abandonment and severe abuse. It is not assumed, for example, that a young wife is at fault in her dispute against her in-laws. The *mahila panchayat* provides a space where she claims agency by establishing an equal relationship with her husband—both verbalise their complaints, both apply conditions to their resolutions, and both sign a compromise contract in the form of a *mahila panchayat* ruling.

As it is a local governing council, the very nature of a *mahila panchayat* takes up public space. Hearings are held in the community and are accessible to everyone. The women claim group agency not only by exerting their influence openly, but also by doing so in sensitive areas formerly considered private, and therefore outside the realm of external intervention. The benefits that the *mahila panchayat* members provide the community by claiming public space are immeasurable. Generally, older women wield a lot of influence as mothers and mothers-in-law in the context of family affairs, however, they rarely exert that influence openly, publicly, or directly (Mandelbaum 1988). Outside the realm of private discourse, *mahila panchayat* members unwittingly act as role models for other women, particularly mothers-in-law involved in case disputes. In so doing, the *mahila panchayat* provides a forum for women to view other ways of being a mother and mother-in-law.

Having made this private act public, husbands and in-laws are held accountable, in most cases for the first time ever. Mothers-in-law and other family members are expected to comply with *mahila panchayat* directives in keeping with what their sons have committed to, both in the hearing and on paper. Once a woman has made her case public through the NGO, in-laws would not risk harming their daughter-in-law for fear of getting caught. From a slum dweller's perspective, the presence of the *mahila panchayat* ensures that gender-based violence cannot continue to take place with impunity.

Unlike other prevention strategies, the *mahila panchayat* empowerment strategy—through the aegis of the NGO—addresses the individual needs of women while also implementing strategies for social change. National-level laws have inadequate exposure and have been unable to regulate policies enhancing women's rights. By publicly challenging women's subordination by the husband and in-laws, women become agents in developing a new understanding of gender-based violence—that physical and emotional abuse against women, for any reason, is unacceptable.

References

Agnes, Flavia. 1992. 'Protecting Women against Violence? Review of a Decade of Legislation, 1980–89', *Economic and Political Weekly*, 27 (17): WS 19–WS 33.

Ahuja, Ram. 1998. *Violence against Women*. New Delhi: Rawat Publications.

Bandura, Albert. 1995. *Self-efficacy in Changing Societies*. Cambridge, NY: Cambridge University Press.

Batliwala, Srilatha. 1994. 'The Meaning of Women's Empowerment: New Concepts from Action', in G. Sen, A. Germain and L.C. Chen (eds), *Population Policies Reconsidered: Health, Empowerment, and Rights*. Boston: Harvard University Press.

Datar, Chaya. 1993. 'The Women's Movement in Maharashtra: An Overview', in C. Datar (ed.), *Struggle for Violence*, pp. 1–50. Calcutta: Stree.

Devi Prasad, B. and B. Vijayalakshmi. 1988. 'Dowry-related Violence Towards Women—Some Issues', *Indian Journal of Social Work*, 49 (3): 271–80.

Devraj, Ranjit. 2000. 'No Way but Down for India's Slumdwellers', *Asia Times Internet Services*. Available at www.atimes.com/ind-pak/BG20Df01.html.

Dobash, Russell P. and Rebecca Emerson Dobash. 1979. *Violence against Wives: A Case against the Patriarchy*. New York: New York Free Press.

Elliott, Charles. 1987. 'Some Aspects of Relations between the North and South in the NGO Sector', in *World Development* 15(1): S57–S68.

Fetterman, David M. 1996. 'Empowerment Evaluation: An Introduction to Theory and Practice', in D.M. Fetterman, S.J. Kaftarian and A. Wandersman (eds), *Empowerment Evaluation: Knowledge and Tools for Self-assessment and Accountability*, pp. 3–46. Thousand Oaks: Sage Publications.

Freire, Paulo. 1970. *Pedagogy of the Oppressed*, New York: Seabury Press.

Finney Ruth. 2000. *Breaking the Earthenware Jar: Lessons from South Asia to End Violence against Women and Girls*. New York: UNICEF Regional Office for South Asia.

Heise, Lori L. 1996. 'Violence against Women: Global Organizing for Change.' in J. Edleson and Z. Eisikovits (eds), *The Future Intervention with Battered Women and their Families*, pp. 7–33. London: Sage Publications.

Heise, Lori L., Mary Ellsberg and Megan, Gottemoeller. 1999. 'Ending Violence against Women', (Population Reports Series L, No. 11, Johns Hopkins University School of Public Health, Population Information Program, Baltimore.

The Hindu. 2001. 'Slum Relocation Plans Go Awry' 22 October.

Kabeer, Naila. 1994. *Reversed Realities: Gender Hierarchies in Development Thought*. London: Verso.

———. 1999. 'Resources, Agency, Achievements: Reflections on the Measurement of Women's Empowerment', *Development and Change* 30: 435–64.

Kelkar, Govind. 1992. *Violence against Women: Perspectives and Strategies in India*. New Delhi: Manohar Publications, Indian Institute of Advanced Study.

Kieffer, Charles. 1984. 'Citizen Empowerment: A Developmental Perspective', in Julian Rappaport and Robert Hess (eds), *Studies in Empowerment*, pp. 9–36. New York: Haworth Press.

Kumar, Radha. 1995. 'From Chipko to Sati: The Contemporary Indian Women's Movement', in A. Basu (ed.), *The Challenge of Local Feminism: Women's Movements in Global Perspective*, pp. 58–86. Boulder: Westview Press.

Mandelbaum, David G. 1988. *Women's Seclusion and Men's Honor: Sex Roles in North India, Bangladesh, and Pakistan*. Tucson: The University of Arizona Press,

Miles, Matthew B. and Michael A. Huberman. 1994. *Qualitative Data Analysis* (2nd edn.). Thousand Oaks: Sage Publications.

Omvedt, Gail. 1990. *Violence against Women: New Movements and New Theories in India*. New Delhi: Kali for Women.

Purdey, Alice F., Gyan Bahadur Adhikari, Sheila A. Robinson and Phillip W. Cox. 1994. 'Participatory Health Development in Rural Nepal: Clarifying the Process of Community Empowerment', *Health Education Quarterly*, 21 (3): 329–43.

Rappaport, Julian. 1985. 'The Power of Empowerment Language', *Social Policy*, 16: 15–21.

———. 1995. 'Empowerment Meets Narrative: Listening to Stories and Creating Settings', *American Journal of Community Psychology*, 23 (5): 795–807.

Schuler, Sidney Ruth and Hasemi Mesbahuddin Syed. 1993. *Defining and Studying Empowerment of Women: A Research Note from Bangladesh* (Working Paper 3). Washington, DC: John Snow International.

———. 1994. 'Credit Programs, Women's Empowerment, and Contraceptive use in Rural Bangladesh', *Studies in Family Planning*, 25 (2): 65–76.

Schwerin Edward. 1995. *Mediation, Citizen Empowerment, and Transformational Politics*. Westport: Praeger.

Schwerin, Edward. 1995. *Mediation, Citizen Empowerment, and Transformational Politics*. Westport: Praeger.

Stein, Jane. 1997. *Empowerment and Women's Health: Theory, Methods and Practice*. London: Zed Books.

Thapalyal, Abha, Prabha Rani and Ruth Vanita. 1987. 'A Study of Twenty Cases', *Manushi*, 40: 18–24.

Van Willigen, John and V.C. Channa. 1991. 'Law, Custom, and Crimes against Women: The Problem of Dowry Death in India', *Human Organization*, 50 (4): 369–77.

Yllo, Kersti A. 1993. 'Through a Feminist Lens: Social Structure and Family Violence', in R.J. Gelles and D.R. Loseke (eds), *Current Controversies on Family Violence*, pp. 47–63. Newbury Park: Sage Publications.

Zimmerman, M.A. 1996. 'Empowerment Theory: Psychological, Organizational and Community Levels of Analysis', in Julian Rappaport (ed.), *Handbook of Community Psychology*. New York: Plenum.

Section III

Media

On 8 March 2006, as part of the celebration of International Women's Day, I attended a conference on women's empowerment organised by the Confederation of Indian Industry (CII) in Mumbai city. The themes of the conference centred on corporate leadership, poor women, work-life balance issues, and the media. Media representatives (film, newspaper, radio) made it quite clear to the audience that the balance of power in the world of media has been changing. Although no concrete figures were forthcoming, the message was that since the integration of the Indian economy into the world market, the Banking and Finance sector had taken the lead in economically empowering women. The media has now followed this trend. As Shekhar Gupta, editor in chief of the *Indian Express*, stated, if numbers determine empowerment, then women are more powerful as they exceed the men in this sector of the economy. The media, according to him, has provided women with a level playing field.

Besides equal representation and creating new job opportunities, the media is faced with a number of issues and challenges. First, what role has the media played in representing women's issues, and has it continued with its earlier task of raising the nation's awareness about women's problems? Second, how does the media project women, especially in advertisements and non-news sections? Last, the question of censorship, which is close to the hearts of many, especially parents who watch their young spend hours before the television. In all these issues media personalities and the audience felt the need to grapple with the balance between the media's dangers and responsibilities. Farzana Contractor of *The Afternoon Despatch & Courier* stated that each medium is different in its level of evolution when it comes to representing women, and the print media seems to have done much better in doing justice to women's issues partly because of its longer history and therefore maturity, and partly because its readership requires a certain level of education. On the other hand, television has emerged as the medium capable of making the most impact. It does not require much education, she stated, to watch a serial on television. This is a medium at a low level of evolution in the context of representing women's concerns adequately. While there was agreement on the fact that the media has done justice to many of the issues confronting women and given adequate coverage to women's campaigns, there was also disenchantment with the idea that reportage too often focuses on the success of corporate women or those from the world of entertainment. A strong need was felt to represent ordinary women and their struggles, as it is they who are creating a quiet revolution. Given the current drive towards glamour, entertainment and corporate profit, my impression is that both the representation of women and the coverage of women's concerns is bound to get worse before it gets better.

In most cases, censorship by media representatives was considered ineffective, and the need for self-censorship was felt to be crucial as readers and viewers guide themselves through a plethora of what is presented to them, be it cinema or television. The other question is, is the purpose and role of the media to reflect the mood of the times, or to tread a new and different path? The answer is somewhere in the middle and the debate goes on.

The third section is designated **Media**, and the first chapter by Mallika Das is titled 'Men and Women in Indian Magazine Advertisements: A Preliminary Report'. Few researchers have examined gender role portrayals in advertisements from developing countries, and Das's article attempts to fill the vacuum. Over 1,000 magazine advertisements from the late 1980s to the mid-1990s were examined to provide a time frame for the analysis. The author concludes that gender portrayals have changed over the years, but are still quite stereotypical. The portrayal is informed by the nature of the product in question. The chapter ends with some interesting parallels between Indian magazine advertisements and those from other nations. In her article, 'The Women's Movement and the Press in India: The Construction of Female Foeticide as a Social Issue', Rashmi Luthra analyses both the press coverage and the activist's interpretations of this issue, and finds a considerable overlap between the two sources, resulting in the press serving the women's campaign quite well. This overlap flows from the elite nature of both the English press and the urban activists. At the same time, however, both these agents of change overlook ordinary women's response to such oppressive practices. According to Luthra, this invisibility springs from the separation of elite, urban, educated activists and the constituency they claim to serve. In the next paper, 'Portrayals of Sexual Violence in Popular Hindi Films 1997–99', Srividya Ramasubramanian and Mary Beth Oliver use characters and sexual scenes as units of analysis to establish links between celluloid impressions of sexual violence, and the way these may be linked to gender and romantic love. The authors conclude that viewers leave the cinema halls convinced that it is normal for men to be aggressive with the women with whom they are romantically involved. 'Packaging the Contemporary Woman in Television Fiction: Deconstructing the Role of "Commerce" and "Tradition"' is the title of the next paper prepared by the Centre for Advocacy and Research in Delhi. It traces the phenomenal growth of satellite television since the early 1990s, the growing popularity among women of women-oriented soap operas, and their impact at the conscious and material levels. It provides new theoretical paradigms for researchers interested in examining the link between television serials, and the women consumers of these serials. The results of the Centre's monitoring of these shows highlight that despite their modern veneer, it is the supremacy of the joint Hindu family that is upheld.

NINE

Men and Women in Indian Magazine Advertisements: A Preliminary Report*

Mallika Das

Studies from developed nations indicate that women are generally portrayed in advertisements as homemakers, dependent on men and sex objects, while men are portrayed as dominant, authoritative figures. However, very few researchers have examined role portrayals in ads from developing countries. This study examined the portrayal of women and men in Indian magazine ads. Over 1,100 magazine ads from a wide range of magazines in 1987, 1990 and 1994 were examined. Results indicate that although the portrayals of women and men in Indian magazine ads have changed over the period, they are still portrayed in stereotypical ways. Role portrayals in Indian magazine ads seem to be influenced by the nature of the product being advertised. Similarities and differences between role portrayals in Indian magazine ads and those from other nations are also discussed.

Introduction

Past research indicates that both women and men are portrayed in stereotypical ways in magazine advertisements in most parts of the world (e.g., Bretl and Cantor 1988; Courtney and Lockeretz 1971; Cutler et al. 1995; Goffman 1976). Men and women appear in different roles, in different settings, and for different types of products (Bretl and Cantor 1988; Courtney and Lockeretz 1971). Although strong similarities in gender-role portrayals in ads have been noted across cultures, several differences have also been identified (Milner and Collins 1998; Wiles et al. 1995). For example, Swedish magazine advertisers seem more comfortable showing men and women in a greater variety of non-working roles than Dutch and US advertisers do (Wiles et al. 1995).

There is some empirical evidence to show that role portrayals in advertisements in the Asian media may not mirror these findings (Cutler et al. 1995; Ford et al. 1998; Sengupta 1992). For example, Cutler et al. (1995) found that although females were portrayed in stereotypical ways in Korean magazine ads (when compared to ads from the US), they were also less likely to be shown as sex objects and as likely to appear in ads for durable goods as men. Further, as Hofstede (1980) indicates, the cultural values of Asian nations such as India are significantly different from those of countries like the United States, Canada and Britain. Thus, it is likely that portrayals of men and women in Indian ads may differ from that found in western countries.

*Originally published in *Sex Roles: A Journal of Research*, Vol. 43, Nos. 9/10, November 2000, pp. 699–718. Reprinted with permission from Springer Science and Business Media.

An exhaustive survey of the literature in marketing and related fields found a general paucity of research on marketing in the country (as noted by Brokaw and Lakshman 1995), and yielded only two studies on gender-role portrayals in the Indian media. Both were somewhat limited in scope. For example, Matthew (1990) focused only on how the Indian male market could be segmented, and the kind of male role portrayals preferred by each segment. This study found that Indian men could be classified into three groups—'the career-driven', the 'self-seekers', and the 'home-lover'—and each group preferred ads that portrayed men as being similar to themselves and disliked ads that portrayed men as being very different from themselves. The only other study on role portrayals in Indian ads focused solely on the portrayals of Indian housewives, and hence was also limited in its scope. Munshi (1998) examined the way Indian housewives were portrayed in television ads in India in the 1990s, and found that the portrayals had changed slightly over the period. She found that 'the representation of (the Indian) woman has been played around with, but not changed in a structural or substantial way. She is still pictured in the roles she has fulfilled from way back when' (Munshi 1998: 587). The major difference, according to Munshi, is the addition of a 'tongue-in-cheek humour, (and) a hint of parody' (ibid.). Neither of these two studies examined gender-role portrayals of men and women in ads. This study hopes to fill this gap in the literature.

Since magazines are the primary vehicles for advertising in India (Sanghavi 1990), gender-role portrayals in magazine ads—as opposed to television, radio or newspaper—were the focus of this study. As role portrayals in advertising have been found to differ by product (Cutler et al. 1995), this study also focused on examining role portrayals in Indian magazine ads across different product types. Thus, the present study aimed to (*i*) examine male and female role portrayals in Indian magazine ads; (*ii*) examine how these portrayals have changed over the years by comparing ads in three different time periods—1987, 1990 and 1994; (*iii*) examine whether these gender-role portrayals varied across product categories; and (*iv*) compare the role portrayals in Indian magazine ads to those found in other countries.

The Present Study

Past research indicates that men and women are portrayed very differently in advertisements. For example, studies conducted in the United States and Britain indicate that women in magazine ads are portrayed as (*i*) being dependent on and needing the protection of men; (*ii*) not making important decisions; (*iii*) homemakers and in home-settings rather than outside the home; and (*iv*) sex objects (Belkaoui and Belkaoui 1976; Courtney and Lockeretz 1971; Sullivan and O'Connor 1988). Similar results have been found in studies of ads from countries such as Italy (Furnham and Voli 1989), Australia (Mazella et al. 1992), Japan (Ford et al. 1998), Korea (Cutler et al. 1995), Hong Kong, (Sengupta 1992) and Portugal (Neto and Pinto 1998).

Until recently, only a few researchers (e.g., Kolbe and Albanese 1997; Skelly and Lundstrom 1981; Vigorito and Curry 1998; Wolheter and Lammers 1980) had focused on men's images in advertisements. Gender identity for men is often associated with the competitive realm of work rather than the emotional realm of family (Bernard 1981), and to how well a man provides for his family (Vigorito and Curry 1998). Perhaps due to this, men in the media are depicted in occupational rather than nurturing roles (ibid.). They are also shown as autonomous, and are pictured outdoors or in business settings more often than at home (Fejes 1992; Fowles 1996; Kolbe and Albanese 1997).

Given the prevalence of gender-role stereotypes in other nations, and the fact that advertisers in Asia have not been as sensitised to gender-role stereotyping as those in western nations (Cutler et al. 1995; Mitchell and Taylor 1990), it is hypothesised that

H1: In all three time periods, women and men will be portrayed more often in traditional, stereotypical ways in Indian magazine ads (i.e., in traditional feminine and masculine roles respectively), rather than in neutral or non-traditional ways.

Past research also indicates that the portrayals of women and men are influenced by the nature of the product being advertised. Product type seems to affect gender-role portrayals in two ways. First, the frequency with which men and women appear in ads seems to vary depending on the nature of the product being advertised. In general, women are found more often in ads for home products, baby items, cosmetics and food items, whereas men are seen more often in ads for 'masculine' products such as automobiles, alcohol, insurance, financial services and business products (Craig 1992; Dominick and Rauch 1972; Fowles 1996; Furnham and Bitar 1993; Mwangi 1995; Schneider and Schneider 1979). Women have also been found to appear more frequently in ads for non-durable products than for durable products (Cutler et al. 1995). Second, there is some evidence that the nature of gender-role portrayals is also affected by the type of product being advertised. For example, women are more likely to be portrayed stereotypically in ads for publishing, recreation, clothes and cosmetics, but less likely to be portrayed stereotypically in ads for tobacco, travel, food and financial services (Mitchell and Taylor 1989).

Several ways of categorising products can be found in the literature. Generally, products are classified into goods versus services, consumer versus industrial, durable versus non-durable, or some combination of these (Cutler et al. 1995; Srivastava and Schoenbachler 1999). Although these classifications have their advantages, a classification that is based on male and female purchase roles would be of more relevance for a study on gender-role portrayals. Based on the participation of husbands and wives, family decisions have been categorised into husband-dominant, wife-dominant, joint (or syncretic) and autonomic, where either partner is equally likely to make the decision alone (Qualls 1987). Research indicates that generally products such as automobiles, liquor, financial investments, and insurance are husband-dominant decisions, whereas food, appliances, cosmetics and jewellry are wife-dominant ones. Joint decisions are most likely to occur in the case of houses, vacations and major furniture, whereas autonomous decisions are more common in the case of clothing (Foster and Olshavsky 1989; Qualls 1987). Since the role played by women when they purchase traditional 'female-oriented' products may be in line with gender-role stereotypes, it is reasonable to expect ads for such products to portray women in traditional ways. A similar pattern can be expected in the case of men in ads for 'masculine' products. Thus it was hypothesised that

H2: In all three time periods, the frequency with which women and men appear in Indian magazine ads will vary depending on the nature of the product being advertised. Specifically, women will appear more often in ads for products traditionally considered to be 'feminine' (or female-oriented), and men will appear more often in ads for products traditionally considered to be 'masculine' (or male-oriented).

H3: In all three periods, the nature of gender-role portrayals of women and men in magazine ads will vary depending on the type of product being advertised. Specifically, women will be shown in traditional ways more often in ads for 'feminine' products and men will be portrayed in traditional ways more often in ads for 'masculine' products.

Recently, some researchers have argued that changes have occurred in the way males and females are portrayed in advertisements. There is evidence showing that in some western nations, women are being portrayed in less stereotypical ways in ads (Mitchell and Taylor 1989), and appear more often in non-traditional roles (Allan and Coltrane 1996; Bretl and Cantor 1988). A similar softening of stereotypical portrayals has been reported in ads from Japan (Ford et al. 1998). Further, women's increased participation in the workforce has led to their becoming major purchasers of several products like automobiles, insurance and financial services. Guns, cars, motorcycles, computer games and equipment, golf equipment, financial services, and many other once-masculine products are now designed and advertised with women in mind (Bellizzi and Milner 1991; Myers 1996).

Similar trends can be expected in India for two reasons: (*i*) several of the trends found in western nations (e.g., increases in the number of working women and their educational levels) are also found in India; and (*ii*) the opening up of the Indian economy has led to an increased exposure to the western world (Jacob 1992). In fact, Munshi (1998) found that portrayals of women in Indian television ads were changing, albeit slowly. Based on these reasons, it is hypothesised that

H4: Male and female role portrayals will 'soften' or become less stereotypical over the years. This will be reflected in the types of roles males and females are portrayed in and the type of products they appear for. Specifically, (*a*) women and men in Indian magazine ads will be portrayed less often in traditional, stereotypical roles in 1990 and 1994 than in 1987, and (*b*) women and men will appear more often in ads for non-traditional and neutral products in 1990 and 1994 than 1987.

Research Methodology

The advertisements were content analysed to examine how women and men were portrayed in Indian magazine ads. Content analysis has been used extensively to evaluate stereotypes and other issues related to advertising (e.g., Allan and Coltrane 1996; Mitchell and Taylor 1989).

Sample

As mentioned earlier, this is part of an ongoing study on several aspects of advertising in India, which began in 1987 with ads being collected at approximately three-year intervals. Ads from popular Indian magazines published in 1987, 1990 and 1994 were included in the study. Each year's sample consisted of ads from over 20 different English language magazines over a four-month period. These included the top circulation magazines (Media Reports 1995) in each category (e.g., film magazines, men's magazines, news magazines and women's magazines). All ads (half page or more in size) with at least one male or female figure in them were included in the study. Since this study aimed to examine how gender roles varied across different products, the emphasis was on having as wide a range of products as possible. Hence, as in several other studies (e.g., Cutler et al. 1995; Furnham and Bitar 1993; Kolbe and Albanese 1996, 1997; Neto and Pinto 1998), repetitive ads were excluded. This yielded a total sample of 635 ads with at least one woman in them (191 in 1987, 249 in 1990, and 195 in 1994), and 541 ads with at least one male in them (57 from 1987, 232 from 1990, and 252 from 1994). Gender-role portrayals of only the key male or female figure or both in an ad were analysed.

Categories of Role Portrayals

To enable cross-cultural comparisons, this study utilised the same categories used by previous researchers (e.g., Lysonski 1985; Mitchell and Taylor 1989). For female-role portrayals, there were nine mutually exclusive categories—women as sex objects, engaged in non-traditional activities in non-work settings (e.g., buying a car), career-oriented, authority figures (or 'experts'), dependent on males, housewives, concerned with physical attractiveness, neutral (or shown as equal to men), and other. Male gender-roles were classified into 10 mutually exclusive categories—dominant over women (as 'protectors', decision-makers, etc.), authority figure (or 'experts'), family man (e.g., in household setting, but doing traditional 'male' chores), frustrated male, sex-appeal, career-oriented, having outside work-life interests, in non-traditional roles within the home, neutral, and other. This classification system, originally proposed by Lysonski (1985), provided the opportunity for cross-cultural comparisons focused on male and female role portrayals, and was suitable to the Indian context. Descriptions of the categories are provided in the Appendix.

Product Categories

Product categories used in the study were again based on past research studies (Lysonski 1985; Mitchell and Taylor 1989). The products advertised were classified into clothing and fabrics, female hygiene, beauty aids and cosmetics, men's toiletteries, household items and appliances, food and beverages, tobacco and alcohol, insurance/financial/medical services and industrial goods, jewellry, footwear, automobiles and related items, travel, and other.

Coding

Two white undergraduate students, one male and one female, coded each ad. The coders were given detailed descriptions of the role portrayal categories and three sets of 25 trial ads for training purposes. The inter-rater reliability had reached over 80 per cent by the end of the training period. This was followed by an analysis of the actual ads. Disagreements between them were resolved through discussion by the coders themselves, without the researcher's intervention.

Results

The number of ads in Indian magazines appear to have increased dramatically during the period under study. There were only 248 ads in 1987 (with males or females or both), whereas there were 481 in 1990 and 447 in 1994. The proportion of ads with a male appearing in them increased significantly (from 23 per cent in 1987 to 48 per cent in 1990 and 56 per cent in 1994), whereas the proportion of ads with women decreased significantly (from 77 per cent of the ads in 1987 to 51.8 per cent in 1990 and 43.7 per cent in 1994).

Gender Role Portrayals

To test Hypothesis 1, the female role categories were collapsed into three groups: 'traditional' (which included 'dependency', 'housewife', 'concerned with looks', and 'sex-object' categories), 'neutral' (i.e., 'neutral' and 'other' categories), and 'nontraditional' (i.e., 'nontraditional', 'career-oriented', and 'authority figure' categories, in which women were portrayed in positive, non-traditional ways). These categories form a continuum of gender-role portrayals, with traditional on one end and non-traditional on the other.

As there were very few ads portraying men in non-traditional roles, male role categories were grouped into three slightly different ones: 'traditional-macho—dominant' (which included the 'sex-appeal' and 'dominant over female(s)' categories), 'traditional-other' (i.e., 'authority figure', 'family man', 'career-oriented', and 'involved in sports/recreational activities' categories), and 'neutral' ('neutral', 'frustrated male', and 'other' categories), where men were not shown in stereotypical ways. These categories (combined with non-traditional portrayals) also form a continuum, with the most negative portrayal being macho-dominant, followed by the traditional-other, neutral and non-traditional categories. As there were only six non-traditional portrayals over the three time periods, these were not included in the analysis.

As shown in Table 9.1, females were portrayed most often in traditional roles in all three time periods (p [less than] .001). This was followed by neutral and, finally, non-traditional portrayals. The lowest percentage (52.8 per cent) of traditional portrayals were in 1994. As indicated in Table 9.1, males were also portrayed most often in traditional ways in all three time periods (p [less than] .001). Thus, the results support the first hypothesis that men and women will be portrayed in traditional ways in all three time periods.

TABLE 9.1
Modified Female and Male Role Portrayal Categories by Year

Role Portrayal Category	Year of Publication			Total
	1987	1990	1994	
Female portrayals				
Traditional	158 (82.7)	133 (53.4)	103 (52.8)	394 (62.0)
Neutral	23 (12.0)	82 (32.9)	84 (43.1)	189 (29.8)
Nontraditional	10 (5.2)	34 (13.7)	8 (4.1)	52 (8.2)
Total	191 (100)	249 (100)	195 (100)	635 (100)
Chi-square	210.98	59.06	77.75	
df	2	2	2	
p	[less than].001	[less than].001	[less than].001	
Male portrayals				
Macho-dominant	22 (38.6)	83 (35.9)	68 (27.5)	173 (32.3)
Traditional-other	6 (10.5)	92 (39.8)	115 (46.6)	213 (39.8)
Neutral	29 (50.9)	56 (24.3)	64 (25.0)	149 (27.9)
Total	57 (100)	231 (100)	247 (100)	535 (100)
Chi-square	14.63	9.12	19.54	
df	2	2	2	
p	[less than].001	[less than].001	[less than].001	

Gender and Frequency of Appearance

To test the second hypothesis, the product categories were collapsed into three groups: primarily female-oriented (jewellery, feminine hygiene, food/beverages, household appliances and cosmetics), neutral—that is, joint/autonomous decisions (e.g., clothing/fabrics, travel, other), and primarily male-oriented products (e.g., tobacco, insurance/financial/industrial, and automotive). Chi-square analysis indicated that the frequency with which women and men appeared in ads varied significantly (p [less than] .01) by product type in all three years (Table 9.2). In all three time periods, women appeared more often in ads for female-oriented products and men appeared more often in ads for male-oriented products. Interestingly, in the case of neutral products, no consistent pattern was found; females outnumbered males in neutral product ads in 1987 but in 1990 and 1994, males outnumbered females in this category.

TABLE 9.2
Frequency of Appearance of Males and Females by Product Type

Modified Product Type	Year of Publication							
	1987		1990		1994		Total	
	Female	*Male*	*Female*	*Male*	*Female*	*Male*	*Female*	*Male*
Female interest								
n	117	24	92	32	73	32	282	92
%	83.0	17.0	71.9	28.1	69.5	30.5	75.4	24.6
Neutral								
n	70	28	126	159	97	137	292	324
%	71.4	28.6	44.2	55.8	41.5	58.5	47.5	52.5
Male interest								
n	4	5	31	37	25	83	60	125
%	44.4	55.6	45.6	54.4	23.1	76.9	32.4	67.6
Total								
n	191	57	232	249	252	195	635	541
%	77	23	51.8	48.2	43.6	56.4	54	46
Chi-square	9.95		28.29		47.50			
df	2		2		2			
p	[less than] .01		[less than] .01		[less than] .01			

Role Portrayals by Product Type

To test the third hypothesis, the male and female role portrayals were collapsed into two categories (traditional and non-traditional/neutral). This reduced the chances of low cell counts. In the case of women, significant differences in role portrayals based on product type were found in 1990 and 1994 (Table 9.3). Women were more likely to be portrayed in very traditional ways in ads for female-oriented products in these years. (In 1987, the results were not significantly different.) For example, in 1990 65.9 per cent of the ads for female-oriented products showed women in traditional roles, but only 35.5 per cent of the ads for male-oriented products portrayed them in such a manner.

Interestingly, in all three years, the way men were portrayed did not vary significantly depending on the type of product being advertised; hence the results are not provided. Thus, the results only partially support the third hypothesis that role portrayals will vary depending on the type of product being advertised.

Role Portrayals—Trends Over the Years

Chi-square analysis indicated that there were significant differences in the way women and men were portrayed in 1987, 1990 and 1994. As shown in Table 9.4, women were portrayed more often in traditional ways in 1987 than in 1990 or 1994 (p [less than] .001). The proportion of traditional role portrayals (of women)

TABLE 9.3
Female Role Portrayals by Product Type Modified Role Categories

Modified Product Type	Year of Publication					
	1987		1990		1994	
	Traditional	NT	Traditional	NT	Traditional	NT
Female interest						
n	94	21	60	31	47	25
%	81.7	18.3	65.9	34.1	65.3	34.7
Neutral						
n	59	11	62	64	52	45
%	84.3	15.7	49.2	50.8	53.6	46.4
Male interest						
n	4	0	11	20	3	22
%	100	0.0	35.5	64.5	12.0	88.0
Total						
n	157	32	133	115	102	92
%	83.1	16.9	53.6	46.4	52.6	47.4
Chi-square	1.03		10.64		21.2	
df	2		2		2	
p		ns		.005		[less than] .001

Note: NT = Nontraditional.

TABLE 9.4
Trends in Role Portrayals Across Years

Year	Male Portrayals		Female Portrayals	
	Traditional	Neutral/NT	Traditional	Neutral/NT
1987				
n	28	29	158	33
%	49.1	50.9	83.1	16.9
1990				
n	175	57	133	116
%	75.4	24.6	53.6	46.4
1994				
n	183	69	103	92
%	72.6	27.4	52.6	47.4
n	541		635	
Chi-square	15.864		50.356	
df	2		2	
p		[less than].001		[less than].001

Note: NT = Nontraditional.

had decreased from 83.1 per cent in 1987 to 52.6 per cent in 1994. In the case of men, although there were significant differences in portrayals over time (p [less than] .001), the results were not in the hypothesised direction. Men were portrayed least often in traditional ways in 1987, with under 50 per cent of the ads portraying them in traditional roles in 1987. By 1994, this proportion had increased to 72.6 per cent. Thus, overall, the results only partially support hypothesis 4a.

Did women and men appear more often for neutral and non-traditional (for them) products in later years? As Table 9.5 shows, females did appear more often in ads for non-traditional products (i.e., both male-oriented and neutral products) in 1990 and 1994 than in 1987. The percentage of neutral/non-traditional product ads with a female in them increased from 38.7 per cent in 1987 to 62.6 per cent in 1994 (p [less than] .001). However, the opposite was true in the case of men. Men were less likely to appear in ads for non-traditional products (i.e., female-oriented and neutral products) in 1994 than in 1990 or in 1987 (p [less than] .001). Thus, the results only partially support hypothesis 4b.

TABLE 9.5
Trends in Frequency of Appearance Across Years

	Product Type			
	Males		Females	
Year	Traditional Products	Neutral/NT Products	Traditional Products	Neutral/NT Products
1987				
n	5	52	117	74
%	8.8	91.2	61.3	38.7
1990				
n	37	195	92	157
%	15.9	84.1	36.9	63.1
1994				
n	83	169	73	122
%	32.9	67.1	37.4	62.6
n	541		635	
Chi-square	26.989		31.415	
df	2		2	
P		[less than].001		[less than].001

Note: NT = Nontraditional.

Discussion

Female and Male Role Portrayals—Trends Over the Years

As the results indicate, the portrayals of women and men in Indian magazine ads have changed over a period of time. Although some stereotypical portrayals (e.g., 'housewives', 'concerned with looks') decreased in the 1990s, women were more likely to be portrayed as sex objects in this decade. It is also interesting that non-traditional portrayals did increase in 1990, but dropped to below-1987 levels in 1994. The softening of female role portrayals thus seems to be primarily due to increases in neutral portrayals (rather than increases in portrayals of women as being career-oriented, authority figures, or engaged in non-traditional activities). Women were less likely than men to be present in ads for neutral or male-oriented products in the 1990s than in 1987. However, the dramatic increase in the number of ads for such products (even with the lower female representation in them) has led to the appearance of a softening in female portrayals. The fact that the least traditional portrayal of women was found in 1990 (rather than in 1994) makes one wonder whether we will see a return to the more traditional portrayals in the late 1990s. Further longitudinal research is required to understand the trends in Indian ads. Overall, the results of this study are in line with those found by Munshi (1998), that is, that the portrayal of women has changed, but only slightly.

Male role portrayals in Indian magazine ads seem to have undergone more significant changes than have female role portrayals. Five major changes in male role portrayals were identified. First, contrary to expectations, males were portrayed more often in traditional ways in 1990 and 1994 than in 1987. Second, although 'sex-appeal' was the most common role category for men in all three years, there seems to be a trend toward a less negatively stereotypical portrayal of men in Indian magazine ads. For example, the frequency with which men were portrayed as being dominant over females came down significantly (from 8.8 per cent in 1987 to 1.2 per cent in 1994), and there were at least a few ads (2 per cent) showing them in non-traditional roles in 1994. Third, men were portrayed in a greater variety of roles (though not too often in non-traditional ones) in 1994 than in previous years. For example, in 1987 there were few or no ads portraying men as career-oriented, or being involved in sports/outside activities. By 1994, the picture had changed and men were more often likely to be portrayed in these roles. Fourth, men were less likely to be portrayed in neutral ways in 1994 than in 1987. The reduction in the number of ads in which men were portrayed in neutral ways (from 50.9 per cent in 1987 to 25 per cent in 1994) indicates a trend towards more clear-cut male portrayals in ads. The fact that there were significantly more ads for neutral products (for which neutral portrayals of both men and women are more suitable) in the 1990s than in 1987 makes this even more interesting. Finally, the variety of products that they appear for has also increased over the years. For example, men appeared more often for products such as jewellery and footwear in 1994 than in 1987. All these trends seem to indicate that men are being targeted more often, in more clear-cut and less- stereotypical ways by Indian marketers than ever before.

Product Type and Gender-Role Portrayals

The nature of the product being advertised seems to influence female role portrayals, but not male ones. Women were portrayed in more traditional, stereotypical ways in ads for products aimed primarily at females. This might be appropriate for these products as 'these roles provide an appropriate usage environment' for them (Wortzel and Frisbie 1974: 45). Traditional portrayals of women for such products are more likely to be viewed favourably by all women (ibid.). However, women were also portrayed in traditional ways in ads for neutral products. This might reflect the fact that several of the products considered 'neutral' were probably targeted more towards women than towards men. For example, products like footwear are often targeted more at women than at both sexes.

Comparison with International Trends

The results of this study indicate that there are similarities and differences in the way women and men are portrayed in Indian magazine ads and the way they are portrayed in other countries. The similarities seem to be that (*i*) overall, men and women in Indian ads are also portrayed in stereotypical ways; (*ii*) the stereotypes in India also seem to be changing and softening, albeit slowly; (*iii*) as in the case of western ads, women and men appear for different types of products in Indian ads; and (*iv*) role portrayals seem to be affected by the nature of the product in the case of women. However, differences could also be found between role portrayals in Indian and western magazine ads. In the case of male role portrayals, the following major differences were found:

(*i*) Although men in Indian ads are portrayed in a traditional manner, they are probably portrayed less often in a macho-dominant manner in Indian magazine ads than in ads from countries such as

Britain, the United States, and other western nations. Contrary to expectations, Indian print ads also seem to portray men more often in neutral (or men and women as equals) roles than those in other countries (Mitchell and Taylor 1989).

(*ii*) Men were not shown very frequently as involved in sports and other recreational activities in Indian ads. For example, a recent study of male role portrayals in the United States found that men were most often portrayed in athletic roles (Kolbe and Albanese 1997). Only 11.4 per cent of the Indian ads showed men in such a role. However, it should be pointed out that this type of portrayal was more common in 1994 (15.5 per cent) than in previous years ([less than] 9.5 per cent). This may indicate that role portrayals in India are starting to follow the trends found in western nations.

(*iii*) Unlike in other nations, male portrayals in India seem to have undergone more significant changes than female role portrayals have. In the 1990s, men seem to appear for more products and in a greater variety of roles in Indian ads. Although they appeared more often in traditional ways, they were not portrayed very negatively. This seems contradictory to findings from other nations, which indicate that male portrayals have changed to a lesser extent than female role portrayals over the past few decades (Lammers and Wilkinson 1980; Wiles et al. 1995).

What would account for these differences? The increased appearance of men in Indian ads may be due to two reasons. First, India is one of the fastest growing markets for consumer durables and several 'male-oriented' products such as insurance, medical, industrial, and technology-related products (Bullis 1997; Ramesh 2000), and because men are more often considered the primary decision-makers for such products, it is understandable that there would be an increase in the number of ads with men in them. There is some evidence to show that when advertisers target men for such products, they include greater information cues in the ads than when they target women (Srivastava and Schoenbachler 1999). This, again, indicates that men are considered to be the primary decision-makers for such products. Second, the number of ads in business and general interest magazines in India has increased tremendously while the number in women's magazines has remained more or less constant. Both these factors could have led to an increase in the number of men appearing in Indian ads.

The lower incidence of highly negative portrayals of men (and women) may be attributed to the religious and cultural differences between India and most western nations. As Kurien (1999) notes, 'Hinduism and Indian culture are pluralistic, and therefore, the patriarchal model of gender is not the only model in India' (p. 45). Further, although India is a patriarchal society, women are respected and negative portrayals of women (e.g., as sex objects or being dominated by men) are not necessarily appreciated. Similar findings (i.e., of less negative portrayals of men and women) have also been found in other Asian countries. Thus, such portrayals might not be seen as appropriate in the Asian context.

The portrayal of women in Indian magazine ads also differed somewhat from those found in other nations. Two major differences in female role portrayals were noted:

(*i*) Some of the common stereotypical portrayals seem less prevalent in Indian ads. For example, unlike in British magazine ads (Lysonski 1985; Mitchell and Taylor 1989), women were more likely to be portrayed in 'neutral/other' ways and less likely to be portrayed as sex objects in Indian magazine ads. Women were also less likely to be portrayed in 'dependency' roles in Indian ads than in British ads. It is noteworthy that these results are similar to those found in two other Asian countries—Korea and Japan—where, again, females were less likely to be portrayed in very negative stereotypical ways than they are in western nations. As mentioned earlier, the religious and cultural differences between India and western nations may account for this finding.

(*ii*) The polarising trend (i.e., a tendency to portray women in dependency and housewife roles and in non-traditional activities, career-oriented, and authority figure roles) found in British magazine ads (Mitchell and Taylor 1989) was not found in this study. In India, the trend seems to be to portray women less often as housewives or as concerned with looks, but not more often in non-traditional, career-oriented, or authority figure roles either. Instead, there seems to be an increase in neutral portrayals of women, due in part to the dramatic increase in the number of ads for such products. This might be attributed to the fact that although Indian society is changing, it is still patriarchical, and dramatic changes (such as portraying women in non-traditional ways) may not be accepted as easily in Indian society as in western ones. As Munshi (1998) notes, any change in role portrayals of women have to be done 'while being posited clearly within dominant ideology, not from without' (p. 587). Furthermore, as Ramu (1988) and Bharat (1995) found, Indian men and women, regardless of their educational level or career status, hold conservative perceptions of women's roles within the family. Thus, although portraying women in neutral ways may be acceptable to Indians, portraying them in non-traditional ways may not.

Implications and Suggestions for Future Research

From a practitioner's point of view, the results raise some critical questions. Are the ads reflecting the needs and values of their target market? Are they effective? For example, Indian males see themselves as 'career-driven', 'self-seekers', and 'home lovers' (Matthew 1990). Yet, the role portrayals in Indian magazines are not consistent with these male self-images. If, as Matthew (1990) found, Indian men relate better to ads that are closer to their own self-images, the lower incidence of 'family men' and 'career-oriented' portrayals may lead to problems.

Similarly, questions can be raised about the effectiveness of female role portrayals in Indian magazine ads. There are several factors that should have led to even more liberal portrayals of women in these ads. The increasing number of middle-class consumers and their higher levels of education should, as in other countries, result in a more egalitarian marital ethic in India (Sullivan and O'Connor 1988) and more liberal portrayals of women. Further, women are major decisions-makers in India and make decisions based on several criteria (Dholakia 1986). As Brokaw and Lakshman (1995) note, due to various societal factors, more joint decisions are to be expected in India than in other patriarchal societies. Research in other countries indicates that women—both those with traditional and non-traditional views—tend to prefer a modern, less traditional portrayal for products that do not require a traditional portrayal. All of these should have led to more liberal, non-traditional portrayals of women in Indian magazines. Yet, the results of this study indicate that women are still portrayed in very traditional ways. Even more importantly, their overall influence—if frequency of appearance in ads is an indicator of this—seems to be declining. This is even more interesting as most of these magazines target middle to upper-class Indians. Indian advertisers should perhaps re-examine their current ways of portraying men and women in ads for as Pollay and Lysonski (1993) note, 'a lack of identification with the roles portrayed may reduce the attention, credibility, retention and subsequent recall of any advertisement' (p. 39).

The findings may be of use to multinational companies attempting to enter the Indian market. This study indicates that there are clear differences between the current gender-role portrayals in Indian and western magazine ads and hence, different message and image strategies may be required in the Indian context.

Unlike most studies in the area, the present study was not totally cross-sectional in nature. In fact, as mentioned earlier, it is an ongoing study with ads being collected at approximately three-year intervals. The preliminary results reported here indicate that there might be an advantage in examining such phenomena over frequent intervals, rather than at one or two points in time. For example, 1990 seems to be an unusually 'modern' year in Indian ads. The trends found in 1990 seem to have reversed themselves to some degree by 1994. Thus, researchers should be cautious when reporting the results from one or two points in time. Finally, the impact of magazine-type on gender-role portrayals was not dealt with in this chapter. Current research indicates that the nature of the magazine may have an impact on role portrayals and how consumers react to them (Vigorito and Curry 1998). This needs to be examined in greater detail in the Indian context.

References

Allan, K. and S. Coltrane. 1996. 'Gender Displaying Television Commercials: A Comparative Study of Television Commercials in the 1950s and 1980s', *Sex Roles*, 35 (3/4): 185–203.

Belkaoui, A. and M. Belkaoui. 1976. 'A Comparative Analysis of the Roles Portrayed by Women in Print Advertisements: 1958, 1970, 1972', *Journal of Marketing Research*, XII: 168–72.

Bellizzi, J.A. and L. Milner. 1991. 'Gender Positioning of a Traditionally Male-dominant Product', *Journal of Advertising Research*, 31 (3): 74–72.

Bernard, J. 1981. 'The Good-provider Role: Its Rise and Fall', *American Psychologist*, 36: 1–12.

Bharat, S. 1995. 'Attitudes and Sex-role Perceptions among Working Couples in India', *Journal of Comparative Family Studies*, XXVI (3): 371–88.

Bretl, D.J. and J. Cantor. 1988. 'The Portrayal of Men and Women in U.S. Television Commercials: A Recent Content Analysis and Trends Over 15 Years', *Sex Roles*, 18: 595–609.

Brokaw, S.C. and C. Lakshman. 1995. 'Cross-cultural Consumer Research in India: A Review and Analysis', *Journal of International Consumer Marketing*, 7 (3): 53–81.

Bullis, D. 1997. *Selling to India's Consumer Market*. Westport, CT: Quorum Books.

Courtney, A.E. and S.W. Lockeretz. 1971. 'A Woman's Place: An Analysis of the Roles Portrayed by Women in Magazine Advertisements', *Journal of Marketing Research*, VIII: 92–59.

Craig, R.S. 1992. 'The Effect of Television Day Part on Gender Portrayals in Television Commercials: A Content Analysis', *Sex Roles*, 26: 197–211.

Cutler, B.D., R.G. Javalgi and D. Lee. 1995. 'The Portrayal of People in Magazine Advertisements: The United States and Korea', *Journal of International Consumer Marketing*, 8 (2): 45–55.

Dholakia, R. 1986. 'Brand Names or Cognition? A Look at Information Processing Behaviour of Indian Mothers and Sons', *Management and Labor Studies*, 11 (1): 115–21.

Dominick, I.R. and G.E. Rauch. 1972. *The Image of Women in Network TV Commercials*. Cambridge, MA: Blackwell.

Fejes, F.J. 1992. 'Masculinity as Fact: A Review of Empirical Mass Communication Research on Masculinity', in S. Craig (ed.), *Men, Masculinity and the Media*. Newbury Park, CA: Sage Publications.

Ford, J.B., P.K. Voli, E.D. Honeycutt, Jr. and S.L. Casey. 1998. 'Gender Role Portrayals in Japanese Advertising: A Magazine Content Analysis', *Journal of Advertising*, 27 (1): 113–25.

Foster, I.R. and R.W. Olshavsky. 1989. 'An Exploratory Study of Family Decision Making Using a New Taxonomy of Family Role Structure', in T.K. Srull (ed.), *Advances in Consumer Research XVI*, pp. 665–70. Proro, UT: Association for Consumer Research.

Fowles, J. 1996. *Advertising and Popular Culture*. Thousand Oaks, CA: Sage Publications.

Furnham, A. and N. Bitar. 1993. 'The Stereotyped Portrayal of Men and Women in British Television Advertisements', *Sex Roles*, 29 (3/4): 297–310.

Furnham, A. and V. Voli. 1989. 'Gender Stereotyping in Italian Television Advertisements', *Journal of Broadcasting and Electric Media*, 33: 175–85.

Goffman, E. 1976. *Gender Advertisements*. NY: Harper.

Hofstede, G. 1980. *Cultures and Organizations*. London: McGraw-Hill.

Jacob, R. 1992. 'India is Opening for Business', *Fortune*, 16 November.

Kolbe, R.H. and P.J. Albanese. 1996. 'Man to Man: A Content Analysis of Sole-male Images in Male-audience Magazines', *Journal of Advertising*, XXV (4): 1–20.

———. 1997. 'The Functional Integration of Sole-male Images into Magazine Advertisements', *Sex Roles*, 36 (11/12): 812–36.

Kurien, P. 1999. 'Gendered Ethnicity: Creating a Hindu Indian Identity in the United States', *American Behavioral Scientist*, 42: 4.

Lammers, H.B. and M.L. Wilkinson. 1980. 'Attitudes toward Women and Satisfaction with Sex Roles in Advertisements', *Psychological Reports*, 46 (3, pt 1), June, p. 690.

Lysonski, S. 1985. 'Role Portrayals in British Magazine Advertisements', *European Journal of Marketing*, 19 (7): 37–55.

Matthew, V. 1990. 'Faces of the Indian Male: A Study of Stereotypes', *Journal of the Market Research Society*, 32 (2): 217–25.

Mazella, C., K. Durkin, E. Cerini and P. Buralli. 1992. 'Gender-role Stereotyping in Australian Television Advertisements', *Sex Roles*, 26: 243–59.

Media Reports (1995. Table 3A, p. MR/95/3A/3–4). MRUC.

Milner, L.M. and J.M. Collins. 1998. 'Sex Role Portrayals in Turkish Television Advertisements: An Examination in an International Context', *Journal of Euro-Marketing*, 7 (1): 1–28.

Mitchell, P.C.N. and W. Taylor. 1990. 'Polarising Trends in Female Role Portrayals in UK Advertising', *European Journal of Marketing*, 24 (5): 41–50.

Munshi, S. 1998. 'Wife/mother/daughter-in/law: Multiple Avatars of Homemaker in 1990s Indian Advertising', *Media, Culture and Society*, 20 (4): 573–91.

Mwangi, M.W. 1995. 'Gender Roles Portrayed in Kenyan Television Commercials', *Sex Roles*, 34 (3/4): 205–14.

Myers, G. 1996. 'Selling a Man's Wold to Women', *American Demographics*, April: 36–42.

Neto, E. and I. Pinto. 1998. 'Gender Stereotypes in Portuguese Television Advertisements', *Sex Roles*, 39 (1/2): 153–64.

Pollay, R.W. and S. Lysonski. 1993. 'In the Eye of the Beholder: International Differences in Ad Sexism Perceptions and Reactions', *Journal of International Consumer Marketing*, 6 (2): 25–43.

Qualls, J.W. 1987. 'Household Decision Behavior', *Journal of Consumer Research*, September: 264–79.

Ramesh, J. 2000. 'India Ahead of Germany', *India Today*, 29 May: 35.

Ramu, G. 1988. 'Marital Roles and Power: Perceptions and Reality in an Urban Setting', *Journal of Comparative Family Studies*, 19: 207–28.

Sanghavi, V. 1990. 'The Coming Crunch', *Advertising and Marketing*, 1 (10): 18–21.

Schneider, K. and S. Schneider. 1979. 'Trends in Sex Roles in Advertising', *Journal of Marketing*, 4: 79–84.

Sengupta, S. 1992. 'Role Portrayals of Women in Magazine Advertisements', *Media Asia*, 19 (3): 145–55.

Skelly, G.U. and W.J. Lundstrom. 1981. 'Mate Sex Roles in Magazine Advertising: 1959–1979', *Journal of Communication*, 31: 52–57.

Srivastava, T. and D.D. Schoenbachler. 1999. 'An Examination of the Information and Thematic Content of Consumer Print Advertising in India', *Journal of International Consumer Marketing*, 12 (2): 63–86.

Sullivan, G.L. and P.J. O'Connor. 1988. 'Women's Role Portrayals in Magazine Advertising: 1958–1983', *Sex Roles*, 18: 181–88.

Vigorito, A.J. and T.J. Curry. 1998. 'Marketing Masculinity: Gender Identity and Popular Magazines', *Sex Roles*, 39 (1/2): 135–52.

Wiles, J.A., C.R. Wiles and A. Tjernlund. 1995. 'A Comparison of Gender Role Portrayals in Magazine Advertising: The Netherlands, Sweden and the USA', *European Journal of Marketing*, 29 (11): 35–49.

Wolheter, M. and H.B. Lammers. 1980. 'An Analysis of Male Roles in Print Advertisements Over a 20-year Span: 1959–1978', in J.C. Olson (ed.), *Advances in Consumer Research*, Ann Arbor, MI: Association for Consumer Research.

Wortzel, L.H. and J.M. Frisbie. 1974. 'Women's Role Portrayal Preferences in Advertisements: An Empirical Study', *Journal of Marketing*, 38: 41–46.

Appendix

Role Portrayal Categories [*]

Female Role Portrayal Categories

Dependency: Women as dependent on protection by/reassurance from a male; or as making unimportant decisions.

Housewife: Women as housewives/concerned with housekeeping tasks.

Concerned with physical appearance: Women as attempting to appear youthful; as concerned with cosmetics/jewellery/fashion.

Sex objects: Women as sex objects whether or not sex is related to product; high emphasis on sex appeal.

Non-traditional (non-work settings only): Women engaged in non-traditional activities (e.g., buying a car, fixing appliances, engaged in sports).

Career-oriented: Women engaged in professional/non-professional occupations (but not shown as experts/spokespersons); as committed to their jobs and concerned with their performance.

Authority figure: Women as experts in a field (and not just employed or career-oriented); as 'voice of authority'/product representatives. Includes celebrity sponsors.

Neutral: Ads showing men and women as being equal with neither shown as dominant (e.g., men and women enjoying a soft drink in a restaurant).

Other: Ads that do not fit into any of the above categories.

Male Role Portrayal Categories

Sex Appeal: These ads use a theme of sex appeal, that is, men showing physical strength being 'cool', or men as womanisers, or both.

Dominant over women: Men as having power over women—includes those that depict men as being in control of decisions (for his family/spouse), men as protectors (of spouse/partner), or men offering reassurance to women, or a combination of these.

Authority figure: Same as for females.

Family man: Men in household settings (but not performing non-traditional household chores); men performing traditional activities around the house or day-to-day activities like eating.

Frustrated male: Ads portraying men as dissatisfied with life in general or his job.

Sports/non-work activities: Men as being involved in sports/recreational activities.

Career-oriented: same as for females

Non-traditional (non-work): Same as for women, but activities that are non-traditional for men (e.g., cooking, feeding a baby, taking a child for swimming).

Neutral/equal: same as for females.

Other: Ads that do not fit into any of these categories.

(*) **Source:** Lysonski, S. (1985). Role portrayals on British magazine advertisements *European Journal of Marketing*, 19 (7): 37–55.

TEN

The Women's Movement and the Press in India: The Construction of Female Foeticide as a Social Issue*1

Rashmi Luthra

The urban women's movement in India has been successful in publicising various women's issues through the press, including dowry-related murders, rape and the selective abortion of female foetuses (Balasubrahmanyan 1988; Joseph and Sharma 1994). Due to the efforts of women's groups in alliance with other progressive groups, the coverage of women's issues in the Indian press steadily increased during the 1980s (UNESCO 1989; Joseph and Sharma 1994). Although there have been studies documenting the quantity and quality of this coverage (Joseph and Sharma 1994; Balasubrahmanyan 1988), this study goes into greater depth by analysing both the press coverage and the activists' own framing of the female foeticide issue, interrogating the ways in which these relate to each other, and the limitations each present in terms of the radical potential of the women's movement in India. Activist interpretation of female foeticide is placed within the larger context of the contradictory relationship between the Indian women's movement and the mass of ordinary Indian women, and the ways in which this contradictory relationship informs the news coverage of the issues are explored. Feminists have begun to look seriously at issues of the representation of women within the Indian women's movement, including the difficulties and contradictions involved in the process of representation (Narayan 1997; Sunder Rajan 1993). This study focuses on the coverage of the female foeticide issue to gain further insight into this process of representation.

Although the Indian press has been amenable to publishing stories on women's issues, it has often chosen to concentrate on the sensational and political aspects of the issues rather than on the larger implications in terms of gender (Joseph and Sharma 1994). In this way, the Indian press has participated in the 'symbolic annihilation' (Tuchman 1978) of women and of a gender perspective (Women's Feature Service 1993), as have the mainstream media from the US (Rakow and Kranich 1991), Tanzania (Gallagher 1981), Kenya (Steeves 1997; Worthington 1995), Sri Lanka and the Philippines (UNESCO 1989), among many other countries. Even so, the Indian English press has been an important instrument in bringing the issues of the urban Indian women's movement into the public discourse, and in influencing legislation on women's issues. It is therefore important to look at the relationship between the press and the women's movement in India.

This chapter focuses in particular on the English Indian press coverage of the campaign in the state of Maharashtra to ban the use of sex determination tests for the purpose of detecting the sex of the foetus (which is coupled with the selective absorption of female foetuses termed 'female foeticide' by women's movement activists). The various issues surrounding the campaign have been analysed in depth by Patel

*Originally published in *Women's Studies in Communication*, Vol. 22, No. 1, Spring, 1999, pp. 1–24.

(1989b), Shukla et al. (1987), Parikh (1990) and Luthra (1993, 1994). Community-based studies of sex determination and sex selective abortion in the context of an urbanising village have provided insights into the economic, social and cultural dynamics underpinning the practice (Khanna 1995, 1997). This chapter focuses on a different facet by looking specifically at the press coverage of the campaign, and relating this to the activists' own interpretations of the issue.

Women's groups, in alliance with people's science groups and progressive doctors, lawyers and journalists waged the campaign against sex determination and sex pre-selection. The campaign has been recognised for its success in cultivating the support of sympathetic journalists, and in using the press to create pressure on the state to pass a law banning the tests (Parikh 1990). This case study of the coverage of female foeticide shows that even though the Indian press modified the language of the activists to make it palatable to readers and gave emphasis to certain aspects of the campaign over others to suit news conventions, it on the whole echoed the main contours of the activists' own interpretations of the issues. And yet, as will be seen, despite the fact that the coverage was quite amenable to the activists' framing of the issues, it presented no threat to the larger hegemonic system. This was accomplished partly by the selective use of certain elements of the campaign, and partly by virtue of the fact that even the activists' own framing of the issue muted certain questions such as the contradictory relations between the state and the women's movement, and the elite character of the Indian women's movement, which renders problematic 'ordinary' women's agency. To understand this, it will be useful to understand the history of the Indian women's movement, and its relationship to the mass of 'ordinary'[2] Indian women.

The Indian Women's Movement

Movements for women's rights in India date back to the early nineteenth century. These movements have generally been classified into three periods or eras—the social reform era of the nineteenth century, the nationalist period of the early twentieth century leading up to Indian independence in 1947, and the new women's movement that started in the 1970s and is ongoing (Kumar 1993). Social reformers in the nineteenth century agitated for widow remarriage, women's education, increased age at marriage, and abolition of sati (widow immolation), among other issues directly relating to women's quality of life within upper-caste families. These reforms were mainly directed at the elite sector of Hindu society, and were rarely initiated by groups of women themselves (ibid.).

During the nationalist movement, women's issues were welded with the nationalist agenda at various junctures. The nationalist period also gave the impetus for women politicians and organisers to test and develop their leadership and organising skills. Women came out in large numbers to support the civil disobedience actions initiated, among others, by Mahatma Gandhi (Kumar 1993; Jayawardena 1986).[3] Large numbers of women, many of them belonging to the Communist Party, emerged as militant revolutionaries. Early in this period, in 1926, the All India Women's Conference was established to tackle the issue of women's education, but it quickly broadened its scope to include various women's issues such as the restraint of early marriage, women's inheritance rights, conditions of working-class Indian women (such as mine workers), and women's franchise. The AIWC was an explicitly non-political organisation, and by the late 1930s had settled into a reformist pattern with a mainly social welfare orientation (Kumar 1993).

Immediately following the nationalist period, there was a lull in the movement for women's 'social upliftment'. Though thousands of women participated actively in militant sharecroppers' movements such as the Telangana movement in Andhra Pradesh in 1948–50, and though women engaged in anti-alcohol agitations in the early 1960s in the Uttarkhand area (a mountainous region in Northern India), this was in general a period of scant activity in the area of women's rights.

In the 1970s the women's movement burgeoned once again, and this time both its contours and potential consequences were drastically different. Beginning with the anti-price rise demonstrations in the late 1970s, women's groups began forming and protesting on various visible issues through the 1970s and 1980s. Especially in the major cities such as Delhi, Bombay and Calcutta, the focus of the urban movement was often 'atrocities' committed against women. Several groups protested the rape of women, particularly custodial rape and class rape (rape by policemen of women citizens and rape by landowners of lower-caste landless women, for example). When it become clear that the scourge of dowry murders was spreading, more groups formed and protested against this latest form of women's direct oppression. There has also been activity in the area of reproductive rights, including resistance to hormonal contraceptives like Depo Provera.

Also in the 1970s, landless labourer movements and Dalit (anti-caste) movements, as well as the environmental, people's science, and health movements gained impetus at the grassroots level. Within some of these grassroots movements, women took the forefront in the battles against landlords, hired hoodlums, government contractors, and other vested interests. This was amply clear in the Chipko environmental movement and the Bodhgaya movement to redistribute land to the landless, among others. Beyond this, women began to articulate their separate demands within these movements. In order to participate effectively in the political sphere and ensure that gains are fairly distributed between men and women as a result of the struggles, women realised that they had to forge a separate voice while at the same time supporting the larger struggles of which they are an indispensable part. For example, in the Bodhgaya struggle, after it became clear that when landless men received a small share of land they only beat their women more, the women insisted that land titles be registered in their names (Kishwar and Vanita 1984).

In both the grassroots movements and the more urban, relatively elite-focused women's movement, the necessity of forging alliances between different people's movements while simultaneously maintaining some autonomy for the women's struggle has been recognised, although the exact relationship with political parties and other activist organisations has been debated for some time within the women's movement (Kumar 1993). The nature of the relationship between the women's groups and the mass of Indian women is highly contradictory, and it varies between different facets of the movement, with the rural and working-class based movements organised by left political parties (and generally dominated by men) with a stronger mass base than the more urban, more elite autonomous women's groups. The women's groups are themselves keenly aware of their separation from the mass of Indian women (Kumar 1993; Omvedt 1993). Kumar says that 'one of the deepest sorrows' of women's movement activists has been the recognition that they are fighting for legal reforms that 'may never be embedded in social practice' (Kumar 1993: 5). Omvedt (1993) writes that there is a gap between the urban, middle-class feminists and the working-class urban and rural women whose exploitation feminists attempt to articulate. This gap is reflected even in the liberation songs written by the feminists, which lack a 'bottom' perspective.

The urban women's movement therefore finds itself in a generally contradictory position in the Indian postcolonial context. Its focus on legislative reform has for the most part implied working with the state rather than confronting it, and it has also implied the use of the elite English language press as an instrument to create pressure on legislators. Its main focus on issues of atrocities against women has tended to constrain its critique of society to this sphere, leaving out of its purview questions regarding the role of the state, the caste and class system, etc.[4] Its struggle against patriarchy has been framed in the context of particular issues like dowry murder, rape, female foeticide and reproductive rights. Although the interrogation of these issues threatens the Indian patriarchal system up to a point and can provide openings for a more wide-ranging discussion, the press can also easily report on these issues in ways that sit comfortably within its vaguely liberal ideology, in ways that do not pose an overarching threat to its elite audience. Analysis of the Bombay press shows that the press can cover a women's issue in ways sympathetic to the women's movement without challenging basic divisions and contradictions within Indian society, such as the role of the state in women's lives, or the class character of the women's movement and its contradictory relationship with the women it seeks to represent.

The separation of the urban women's movement from the mass of Indian women encourages a construal of the ordinary Indian woman as a muted, passive symbol, a construction that is easily picked up and used within the elite discourse of the English language press. In some instances the urban Indian women's movement has taken great pains to retain the agency of the woman victimised by societal practices, for instance in the depiction of the suffering woman in the campaign against sati, a woman depicted in movement agitational propaganda as 'a burning woman seeking to escape, not a spectacle but the subject of action and agency' (Sunder Rajan 1993: 31). At other times, however, there has been a tendency to depict the woman as devoid of agency, as primarily a victim (ibid.). At any rate, agitational propaganda has to contend with the tension between subject-constitution and object-formation with regard to the ordinary Indian woman (ibid., borrowing from Spivak), and press accounts tend to select descriptions that fit into the object-constitution mould, accentuating the passive aspects of the representation of the ordinary Indian woman while further muting representations suggesting their agency and their capacity for resistance, as the following textual analysis will make clear.

Method

My analysis is based on a close scrutiny of 53 articles in the Indian English press and 15 circulars and papers brought out by members of the Forum Against Sex Determination and Sex Pre-selection Methods, which waged the campaign to ban the tests in the state of Maharashtra. I also analysed three documentaries brought out by activists, 'A Cry Strangled', 'Ayata', and 'Samadhan', and the content of three posters created by the activists. The press articles come from English language dailies based in Bombay, the capital of Maharashtra. Since the Maharashtra campaign was the first such campaign in the country and is therefore the focus of this chapter, it was considered appropriate to limit the analysis to dailies from the state.[5] The publications include *The Times of India, The Indian Express, The Daily* and *The Indian Post*. The articles range from August 1986 to June 1989, covering the entire period during the media campaign to have the sex determination tests banned in Maharashtra (the first such campaign in the country). All articles pertaining to the campaign in the four dailies within the specified time period were included in the analysis.

Textual analysis was used to elicit patterns, with particular attention paid to the way in which the issue of female foeticide was framed, whose terms were predominant in this framing, which ideologies constituted these frames, how the framing was accomplished, what came within the purview of the frames, and what was left out. Ultimately, this was related to the larger questions about media, social movements and the hegemonic process. The use of qualitative textual analysis made it possible to look at the use of emphasis, inflection, narrative techniques and other ways in which the framing of the issue was done.

Press coverage was analysed in conjunction with the conference papers, press releases and documentaries put out by activists working for the ban to see to what extent the press coverage matched or contradicted the activists' rhetoric. This was crucial in deriving the central insights regarding the ways in which the press coverage modified activists' language while echoing the main themes of the campaign, and also the ways in which the activists' own interpretations muted certain contradictions.

Newspaper staff wrote the majority of the newspaper articles included for analyses. In addition, there were seven letters to the editor, six articles authored directly by campaign activists, and two articles authored directly by an academic opposed to the ban. There were also two articles by a columnist, who was clearly self-identified as opposing the ban. When identifying news frames, the main focus was on articles (including editorials) by newspaper staff, since these point most directly to the framing decisions made by the news-paper personnel, although letters and articles authored directly by activists and opponents were also included in the analysis. Of the 53 articles, 22 were from the *The Times of India*, 10 from *The Indian Express*, 13 from *The Indian Post*, and eight from *The Daily*.

Press Coverage of the Movement: The Predominant Frames

In this section I locate the frames that recur throughout the coverage, frames that make available particular interpretations of the issues of sex determination and sex-selective abortion, the campaign, and the women's movement more generally, and at the same time make other interpretations less likely. I also examine the degree to which activists' interpretations (as culled from activist literature) mesh with the news frames. In the next section I discuss further both the newspapers' and activists' framing of the issue, what was left out of the purview of both sets of interpretations, and the implications of the boundaries of the discourse on female foeticide.

Establishing the Dimensions of the Problem

A recurrent strain in the coverage is a description of the dimensions of the problem, the extent to which the tests and selective abortions have spread within the social system. The dimensions of the problem are de-scribed with phrases such as 'an alarmingly high rate of female foeticide' (Setalvad 1988b) and a 'flood of female foeticides' (Vanaik 1986). The tests themselves are referred to as having 'escalated dramatically' in frequency ('Not Enough', 1986), and the clinics as having 'mushroomed' ('Sex Tests Banned', 1988; Desai 1988; 'Amniocentesis Muddle ...' 1986). There are frequent references to the easy availability of the tests, and their spread across classes and regions. These claims are often supported with statistics documenting the growth of clinics and the rise in the numbers of selective abortions of female foetuses.

As the activist literature points out, the problem of sex determination through selective abortion is a difficult one to establish as an 'issue' because of its invisible aspect (Shukla and Kulkarni 1986). In contrast, ill-treatment of girl children and adult women, or atrocities like dowry murder or rape, can be seen by all concerned and are therefore more open to criticism. Realising the invisibility of the phenomenon, the activists took pains to make the problem visible by conducting several studies documenting its growth. By using statistics from these and other studies, using phrases and metaphors to convey the enormity of the problem, and by con-stantly linking the tests with selective abortion, the news stories helped accomplish the intent of the activists to articulate the sex determination-selective abortion nexus as a public issue. The alignment of activist strategy and newspaper coverage suggests activists' influence on coverage. In addition, all the main elements of the coverage—the depiction of the tests as proliferating, (Patel 1986a, 1986b; Shukla et al. 1987; Bhate 1987), the citing of statistics and studies (Patel 1986b; Shukla et al. 1987; Bhate 1987), and the analogy between female foeticide and infanticide (Patel 1986b; Bhate 1987)—are present in the activist literature as well, which also suggests activists' influence on news frames.

Establishing the Gravity of the Problem

In addition to showing how widespread the practice of sex determination through selective abortion is, the coverage repeatedly establishes the gravity of the problem by attaching criminality to it and showing it as morally objectionable, and by pointing out its adverse consequences. Sex determination and selective abortion are collectively referred to in the coverage as the 'evil' (Setalvad 1988a), the 'abhorrent practice' (Setalvad 1988c), as an 'obnoxious practice' (Mehta 1989), as a 'terrible practice' (Sadasivam 1988), as 'an evil and anti-social and also criminal practice' ('Amniocentesis Muddle ...' 1986), and as 'murder' (ibid.). Headlines such as 'Amniocentesis: Invitation to Murder' (Puri 1988), and 'Born to Die' (Desai 1988) add to the aura of criminality attached to the practice. The term 'female foeticide' is used routinely without quotation marks, legitimating the activists' construction of sex-selective abortion as a crime. In addition, selective abortion is depicted as a modern, more efficient and more acceptable version of eliminating females than female infanticide ('Female Foeticide Returns with Respectability', 1987; D' Monte 1988; 'Amniocentesis Muddle ...,' 1986). Drawing parallels with more visible and recognisable 'atrocities' helps to remove the cloak of normalcy attached to the practice.

The attachment of criminality to selective abortion echoes the activist stance directly. Activist literature uses the terms 'female foeticide' and 'femicide' routinely when referring to selective abortion. A paper by an activist describes selective abortion as a 'modern method of massacring female fetuses on a massive scale' (Patel 1986b). Posters brought out by activists show huge injections pointed, gun-like, at the female foetus (shown in the documentary 'Ajata.') One poster depicts a decapitated doll with the caption above saying, 'Sentenced to death', and the caption below saying 'Found guilty of being a girl'. The text of the poster refers to the parents as 'executioners'. Another poster spells out the equation as 'female foeticide or murder of the unborn female child'. Although the language is less harsh in the news stories, there is a definite attachment of criminality to selective abortion.

The news coverage points out the adverse consequences of the tests and of selective abortion. The possible health hazards for the woman and foetus are mentioned repeatedly ('Amniocentesis Muddle', 1986; 'Female Foeticide Returns with Respectability', 1987; Chougule 1989; Sen 1988; Setalvad 1988b; 'Sex Tests Banned', 1988; Sharma 1988; Shivdasani 1989). The worsening of the women-men sex ratio is also mentioned repeatedly as a possible adverse consequence of the spread of the phenomenon ('Amniocentesis muddle ...,' 1986; 'Bill of pre-natal tests passed', 1988; Chougule 1989; D'Monte 1988; Desai 1988; 'Female foeticide returns with respectability', 1987; Setalvad 1988b; Sharma 1988; Shivdasani 1989; 'State promises to ban sex tests', 1986; Vanaik 1986). One article in *The Times of India* leads with the following:

> In a recent television interview on sex-determination (SD) tests, one social activist and member of the Women's Centre in Bombay, Ms. Vibhuti Patel, effectively dramatised the problem when she declared that such tests followed by abortion of female fetuses would soon render women in India an 'endangered species.' (Vanaik 1986)

The depiction of the practice as a crime, and the repeated references to the adverse consequences for women and for the society, apart from echoing the activist literature (Patel 1986a, 1986b, Ravindra 1986; Bhate 1987), establishes the sex determination-selective abortion nexus as a problem worthy of public attention, and worthy of action, especially in the legislative arena.

Establishing the Protagonists and Antagonists

From the beginning, the news coverage uses the frame of conflict. The very use of the term 'female foeticide,' taken directly from the women's groups, sets up a conflict between the innocent female foetus victim and those who would inflict harm upon her. Aside from attaching criminality to the practice and thereby providing justification for a ban, the term also sets up a confrontation between the female foetus and the criminals, between good and evil. If there is a crime involved, someone must be responsible.[6]

Although the omniscient point of view is used in writing the stories, the stories generally portray the Forum activists as protagonists and the doctors performing the tests as the villains. The exceptional few doctors supporting the Forum's stance are clearly differentiated from the majority of unscrupulous doctors. Doctors are referred to as 'quacks' (Puri 1988), and stories refer to their 'misuse of power' (Vanaik 1986) and 'private medical abuse' ('Must Be Banned', 1987). The greed and unscrupulousness of the doctors are cited as reasons for the spread and persistence of the practice ('Amniocentesis Muddle', 1986; Chougule 1989; D'Monte 1988; Desai 1988; Puri 1988; Setalvad 1988b, 1988c; Sharma 1988; Vanaik 1986). The practice is referred to as 'big business' (Vanaik 1986), as a 'money-making racket' ('Amniocentesis Muddle ...', 1986), as a 'commercial venture' (Chougule 1989), and the doctors are referred to as a 'cartel' (Desai 1988).

In the interest of 'balance', the opposition does get the opportunity to have its case heard in the news stories. However, the opposition is contained in ways usually subtle but sometimes more obvious, which tilt the balance in favour of the activists. In stories that use a 'debate' format, presenting arguments from both the activists and their opponents, techniques are used to lend legitimacy to the activists' stance and detract legitimacy from the opposition's stance, thereby endorsing the former. For example, a *Times of India* article ('Female Foeticide Returns with Respectability', 1987) devotes seven paragraphs to arguments given by medical practitioners against the ban and seven paragraphs to arguments in support of a ban (the entire article consists of 20 paragraphs). There is an apparent symmetry, a semblance of balance in the way the article is structured. However, certain framing devices tilt the balance in favour of the activists' stance. The lead paragraph makes a clear parallel between female infanticide and female foeticide, followed by five paragraphs explaining the rapid spread of the tests, the misuse of the tests for the wrong purpose, and some societal problems that may result from the spread of the tests. The stage is already set for a sympathetic hearing of the activists' arguments at this point. The seventh paragraph begins with a strong series of arguments by doctors defending the tests, introduced with the statement. 'The medical profession insists on maintaining ethical neutrality on the issue', and continuing for the next seven paragraphs. The activists' stance is then introduced in the 14th paragraph with the statement. 'These medical arguments betray an incredible unfamiliarity with the Indian social reality.' Arguments supporting the ban then run for seven paragraphs, until the end of the story. Both the lead and the statement immediately preceding the activists' arguments serve the purpose of dismissing the arguments made by the medical practitioners, and indirectly endorsing the activists' arguments. Other devices contributing to the legitimation of the activists are the use of frequent attribution when the opponents' arguments are presented, such as 'they say' and 'they argue', serving to distance the opponents' arguments from the writer's own voice, and the relative absence of such attribution when the activists' arguments are presented, serving to subtly align the activists' stance with the writer's own stance. The fact that the activists have the last word in the article, in addition to the lead being sympathetic, lends further weight to their stance.

The opposition is heard more directly in four articles in the *The Times of India*. Dharma Kumar, an academic who was a known opponent of the campaign to ban the tests, sent two articles (Kumar 1989a, 1989b). A columnist who clearly identifies himself as opposing the ban wrote the other two (D'Souza 1988, 1989).

In these four articles, we hear a direct indictment of the activists' approach, and a direct refutation of their arguments. They are referred to as 'a certain type of feminist', as 'fundamentalists' (Kumar 1989b), as 'starry-eyed' feminists (D'Souza 1988), as a 'vocal, if misguided, feminist lobby' (D'Souza 1989), and as 'aggressive feminists'. The campaigns are characterised as fanatical and self-indulgent (Kumar 1989b), as 'materialism' (ibid.) and as 'less rational than emotional' (D'Souza 1988). Their success in pressuring the state government to pass legislation is described as having 'succeeded in writing their prejudice into law' (D'Souza 1988). Even though these four articles question the motives and good sense of the activists and carry the potential to sully their image, the fact that they are part of a very small minority of articles, coupled with the fact that the authors are clearly self-identified as opponents of the ban, keeps the critique of activists and the campaign at the margins of the coverage. Dharma Kumar's first article, published on 9 December 1988, is followed by two articles directly refuting it, one by an author clearly self-identified as a supporter of the campaign, published on 26 December 1988 (Taneja 1988), and another by a Forum activist, published on 14 January 1989 (Patel 1989a). A lengthy letter follows Dharma Kumar's second article, published on 11 February 1989, to the editor sent by activists in the Forum Against Sex Determination in Gujarat (the state neighbouring Maharashtra), published on 17 February 1989 (Tanushree et al. 1989). The two articles and the letter provide a scathing critique of Dharma Kumar's motives and arguments, identifying her as part of a larger 'tribe' (ibid.) that is 'essentially right wing' (Taneja 1988), whose leanings are 'facist' (Tanushree et al. 1989), whose perspective is 'reactionary' (Taneja 1988) and whose arguments smack of 'social Darwinism in its crudest form' (ibid.). D'Souza's first article, published on 10 January 1988, is followed by an article by Forum activist R.P. Ravindra, published on 14 February 1988. Ravindra's article directly refutes D'Souza's. The opportunity given to supporters of the ban to directly refute the opponents of the ban serves to contain the opposition, even as the very presence of opponents' articles serves to create a semblance of balance.

Establishing the Complicity of Indian Society

The blame for the spread of the tests is laid on unscrupulous doctors willing to ignore the ethical implications and long-term consequences of their actions for the sake of profit. There is another, more abstract, antagonist held responsible for the spread and persistence of sex determination and selective abortion in Maharashtra and the rest of India—the traditional values of Indian society. It is repeatedly pointed out in the coverage that a test that is intended primarily for the detection of genetic abnormalities has been misused for sex determination in the Indian context, a context that is variously described as 'a patriarchal society where male attitudes and values dominate' (Setalvad 1988c), a place where 'extremely backward social values ... predominate' (Vanaik 1986), a place where 'the marriage of advanced medical technology and backward social values creates many a horrifying offspring' ('Not Enough', 1986), where 'traditional socio-cultural prejudices' ('Female Foeticide Returns with Respectability', 1987), 'archaic value systems' (Desai 1988), and 'medieval values' (Ravindra 1988) predominate. The repeated parallels made between female infanticide and female foeticide ('Amniocentesis Muddle ...', 1986; D'Monte 1988; 'Female Foeticide Returns with Respectability', 1987) also serve to reinforce the notion that it is the traditional, feudal aspects of Indian society that are responsible for the perverse use of modern technology, that the modern technology of amniocentesis, when introduced into a tradition-bound society, becomes simply a modern-day version of an ancient practice. Press coverage stresses backwardness as the main contextual factor responsible for the spread of the tests, with a few oblique references to patriarchy ('The Male Factor', 1988; Setalvad 1988c; Vanaik 1986), and passing references to modernity in the form of a 'penchant for adopting the latest technology' (Desai 1988) and 'rampant medical consumerism' (Sharma 1988). Despite frequent references to the perverse use of modern technology, the technology itself, and modern science more generally, appear as blameless and neutral. It is the archaic values that are blamed for putting the technology to use for a vicious purpose.

In contrast, the activist literature subsumes the critique of tradition under the critique of patriarchy. In the activist literature, particularly the articles by women's movement activists, both modernity and tradition are held responsible for fuelling the demand for the tests, and both are seen as being harnessed in the service of patriarchy. For example, Vibhuti Patel explains that, 'the uncontrollable lust of consumerism and the commercialization of human relations have combined with patriarchal power over women to reduce Indian women to easily dispensable commodities' (Patel 1989b: 6). Commercialisation and consumerism have worsened the dowry problem, which feeds into son preference, which in turn fuels female foeticide. The combination of 'patriarchal values and capitalist profit hunger' are seen as having 'created a scenario which has potentialities of destruction' (Patel 1986a; 'Women's Movement', n.d.). Both the 'strongly patriarchal structure' in collusion with 'India's pursuit of the capitalist path of development' which leads to a 'money-crazy environment', are seen as fuelling the demand for the tests. Rather than representing technology and science as neutral, the activist literature, particularly pieces written by women's movement activists, speak of how advances in technology have been used to discriminate against women in various countries at various times historically (Shukla and Kulkarni 1986), saying that the 'misuse of many inventions and discoveries of science against the people is an integral part of the present social structure of society' (Lata and Harpal n.d.), and that 'the very paradigm of Science has imbibed the values and prejudices of the ruling elites' (Ravindra 1986). Patriarchy is seen as existing in many different societies, and as taking the form of male preference in South Asia (Shukla and Kulkarni 1986). This construction avoids the depiction of India as atavistic and as isolated in its discrimination of women.

The women's movement in India has taken pains to develop a critique of modernity along with a critique of traditional values, and the activist literature includes this critique, so that both modernity (read alternately as capitalism) and the feudal aspects of Indian society are held responsible for subjugating women.[7] While both the activist literature and the press coverage include derogatory references to traditional values, patriarchy and consumerism, the critique of traditional values is amplified in the press coverage and the critiques of modernity and patriarchy are attenuated.

Establishing the Innocence of the Indian Woman

Placing the blame on doctors on the one hand, and on the Indian social structure and its values on the other allows the coverage to depict the ordinary Indian woman in consonance with the activists' principal representation of her: as a blameless, innocent victim. Women are depicted as facing health hazards when undergoing procedures for sex determination ('Amniocentesis Muddle', 1986; Chougule 1989; 'Female Foeticide Returns with Respectability', 1987; Sen 1988; Setalvad 1988b; 'Sex Tests Banned', 1988; Sharma 1988; Shivdasani 1989), as being 'victims of rampant medical consumerism' (Sharma 1988), as being oppressed (Shelley 1987; Vanaik 1986), as 'expendable' within Indian society ('Amniocentesis Muddle', 1986), in fact as being an 'endangered species' (Vanaik 1986). The construction of woman as victim is particularly evident in the articles and letters in the press authored directly by Forum activists (Duggal and Gupte 1987; Gupte 1987; Patel 1989a; Ravindra 1988; Taneja 1988; Tanushree et al. 1989). In these articles, the activists take great pains to show that women are the victims of patriarchy rather than the perpetrators of a crime against the female foetus. The activists explain that women's participation in the practice of selective abortion results from direct coercion by family members, and from indirect coercion created by oppression and the internalisation of oppression. Their 'choice' to abort the female foetus cannot be seen as an authentic choice; it is forced upon the women by society, say the activists, and therefore female foeticide always represents coercion of the women. Manisha Gupte (1987) puts it this way:[8]

> Often a choice can be another name for implicit coercion. When a woman undergoes amniocentesis by her own choice, she is herself a victim of patriarchal values. It can be argued that she can find her place in the sun only through mothering sons, and that she has a lot to lose when she bears a daughter.

Even in an article that includes interviews with women who have opted for sex pre-selection and/or selective abortion, the women's choices are construed as internalised oppression so as to absolve them of blame (Duggal and Gupte 1987). Their choices are explained in this way: 'Their pro-male stance is not because of a strong, personal belief. It just demonstrates the way the social system has reared them into accepting a male-dominated society as the means of order and the core of control.'

In activist literature and documentaries, a similar construction of the ordinary Indian woman is apparent. The literature stresses that there is no point in blaming the masses, particularly the women; rather, the finger should be pointed at the scientists, technocrats, doctors and the government, who help in propagating the situation by advocating population control (Patel 1986b; Ravindra 1986). The literature includes a discussion of the societal context of women's choices (Patel 1986b; Ravindra 'S.D. Test: Myths v. Reality' (n.d.); Bhate 1987), suggesting that such choices are forced upon the women by society. This is in consonance with the interpretation prevalent in news stories. Although the documentaries and posters created by activists also tend to depict the ordinary Indian woman as a blameless victim, the depiction is not as seamless; there are occasional glimpses of the possible collusion of the woman in the decision to abort the female foetus, and occasional glimpses of the possibility of resistance on the part of the ordinary, non-feminist, non-activist, woman. These instances are rare, exceptions rather than the rule, and yet they are present. The posters, for example, address parents directly, and this address includes the woman as mother. When posters proclaim, 'This is the lovely girl you did not want', followed by the statement '50 per cent of the *women* abort because they do not want girls' [emphasis mine], or when they speak of the parents turning into executioners and plead, 'Your daughter is your child too. Let her be born,' they are including adult women in the address. This opens up the possibility of both culpability and resistance on the part of the women. There is also at least one instance of a more direct depiction of a woman trying to resist pressure to abort the female foetus in the mini-feature film 'Samadhan' (Shankar). She finally prevails with the help of a female gynaecologist, who lectures the husband about the issue. Even these few instances of resistance in the agitational propaganda are eclipsed in the news coverage, which presents a consistent picture of the woman as a blameless victim lacking in agency.

The activist literature suggests that the press representation of the ordinary Indian woman as a blameless victim is in keeping with the activists' strategic requirements. One of the primary functions of press coverage was to pressure legislators to pass a law banning the tests. The activists wanted to be sure that the law did not end up penalising the woman, since they in fact saw her as coerced in various ways, and penalising would thereby amount to victimising the victim. It therefore made sense for them to stress the lack of culpability of the adult woman in selective abortion.[9] Activists also found it necessary to show the woman's decision as coerced so that they could effectively counter the doctors' justification that in offering the tests they were respecting women's choice. The rhetoric they employed, which formed the basis for press coverage, made sense given their strategic requirements and the discursive environment within which they were working. An unintended consequence of this strategy was to amplify the depiction of the ordinary Indian woman as a passive, blameless victim, and to mute the representation of the woman as being capable of conscious choice, and even resistance. The activists assumed the role of resistance, with the ordinary Indian woman being able to speak only through them, in ways that suited the strategic requirements of the movement. The press, in turn, in giving sympathetic coverage to the movement, further legitimated the movement activists, and further muted the agency of the ordinary Indian woman.

Discussion

The coverage of the female foeticide issue by the English elite press in Maharashtra, India, appears to be an instance of a well-orchestrated use of the media by a social movement. News frames used in representing the issue were in close consonance with the approach of the Forum on the issue. The main contours of the coverage were in keeping with the premises of the activists' own interpretations of the issue as presented in activist literature and agitational propaganda.

Several plausible explanations for the meshing of frames of interpretation between movement discourse and press discourse on female foeticide can be offered. At the immediate, concrete level, the concerted effort made by Forum activists to make alliances with sympathetic journalists, to issue press releases, and send articles and letters to the press paid off in terms of sympathetic coverage. Both the supporters of the movement ('Ban on Sex Tests Major Legislation', 1988; Parikh 1990) and detractors (D'Souza 1988) acknowledged their success. The ability of the campaign to utilise the press to have their own articles and letters published could also have been facilitated by the relative 'looseness' in the framing process in the Indian press. Joseph and Sharma (1994) allude to this explanation when they say that in certain instances, editorials contributed by activists in the women's movement have been published intact because they can easily slip through in the absence of clearly defined editorial policies. Yet another facilitating factor may have been the characteristics of the issue itself; its more invisible and more subtle aspects, compared to other atrocities against women such as rape and bride burning, may have made it less amenable to sensationalisation, leading the press to rely more directly on activists' own interpretations of the issue. Invisibility may also have made it possible for activists to construct the 'facts' of the issue.

At a more structural level, the comfortable meshing of movement frames with press frames may be explained by the nature of the relationship between the Indian women's movement and the elite press in India, and further, the elite character of the urban Indian women's movement itself. The coverage of the female foeticide issue brings up questions of the oppression, the vulnerability and relative powerlessness of women within Indian society. It attempts to direct the readers' moral outrage at the discrimination heaped upon women and the injustice certain sectors of society perpetuate against women. It offers a sporadic and mild critique of patriarchy (milder than the activists' version), and a very mild critique of the government's actions (milder even than the activists' own mild critique). Neither the activist literature nor the press coverage offer a sustained, far-reaching critique of patriarchy, the state, or the class and caste system. Therefore, neither the activist discourse nor press discourse transgresses the boundaries of middle-class liberal morality. Both discourses stay within the 'vaguely liberal' but markedly elite domain, with elite activists claiming to represent the interests of the ordinary Indian woman. The press can incorporate the activists' articulation with relative ease because this articulation itself remains well within the boundary of liberal middle and upper-class welfarist definitions of women's upliftment, without challenging class or caste divisions directly, and without challenging the role of the state in women's lives. The activists' construction of the issue fits well within the general ideological mould of the elite press in India. From the post-Emergency period in the late 1970s to the late 1980s, there has been a liberal consensus in the Indian press that has led to a steady stream of investigative stories on the deprived sections of the Indian population, such as landless labourers and tribals (Joseph and Sharma 1994). In women's issues presented as such, the press gains the opportunity to appear progressive, without the political fallout that would result from taking a truly progressive stance like questioning the caste or class hierarchy, or questioning the very basis of the patriarchal system, or questioning the role of the state in social change, etc.[10] Following Steeves' (1997) insight, expansive hegemony allows for the expression of feminist resistance without presenting an overarching threat to the system itself, including its patriarchal aspects.

While bringing women's issues to the public forum, the accommodation between activist discourse and press discourse creates certain important absences. For example, neither the activist literature nor press coverage addresses the contradictions involved in using the legislative and coercive power of the government to enact women's agendas, and neither addresses the contradictions involved in this route to change the condition of Indian women. The discussion of such contradictions is left to the alternative press such as the women's journal *Manushi* (Kishwar 1994, 1995).[11] Another absence in the coverage, as has already been noted, is that of the voice of the ordinary woman, the woman opting for sex determination and selective abortion, or the woman resisting it. The positioning of the women's groups as the ordinary woman's legitimate representatives dictates a construction of the issues that plays down the contradictions in women's own lives, and that emphasises the inability of the ordinary women to perceive and articulate their own oppressive situation and their inability to resist oppressive practices. This construction encourages identification with the causes taken up by the women's movement, but also discourages the coverage of ordinary women's own understandings of their situation, and instances of resistance by these women. Khanna (1995), while doing a community-based anthropological study of the use of sex determination techniques and sex-selective abortion in Shahargaon, discovered a few isolated instances of Jat women who had resisted the practice of selective abortion in their own small but courageous way, in a situation fraught with pressures to have sons. One Jat woman left her affinal (husband and in-laws') home and went to her natal (her own mother and father's) village to avoid an ultrasound exam. Another woman refused to cohabit with her husband after he forced her to abort a female foetus. Yet another woman asked her unborn daughter's forgiveness the night before the abortion. Though limited, such acts of resistance indicate openings, possibilities for social change at the personal and community levels, just as the politically sophisticated and well-orchestrated campaign of the activists provide openings for social change in the more public arenas of the press and the legislature. And yet representations of this kind of resistance are missing from the coverage.[12] The absence of such representations is damaging, because it serves to reinforce the separation of the urban women's movement from its constituency of ordinary Indian women, and therefore leaves the urban women's movement open to critiques by conservative forces. The right can then represent the women's movement as being alienated, Westernised, maternalistic (D'Souza 1989; Kumar 1989b), and so on, and represent themselves as the defenders of women's choice. Such representations gain credence to the extent that the women's movement is perceived as removed from the mass of Indian women.[13]

Certain absences originate in the activist discourse itself, as is apparent from the discussion above. Other absences are created by the way in which the press selects and modifies elements of the activist discourse. For example, as shown in the textual analysis, the press coverage tends to attenuate the already moderate critique of patriarchy offered in the activist literature, while amplifying the critique of traditional Indian values. The resultant framing of the issue encourages the location of the root causes of female foeticide in the feudal remnants of the Indian social structure, rather than in patriarchy itself. Further, the press coverage attenuates the critique of modernity offered in activist discourse. Narayan points out that Indian feminists were very careful in their depiction of sati to locate the 'thoroughly modern economic, political, and patriarchal agendas' involved (1997: 73). The women's movement activists in Maharashtra were similarly careful to discuss the modern aspects of female foeticide, and the ways in which capitalism and modernity have fuelled the phenomenon. By nearly eclipsing the discussion of modernity and at the same time amplifying the critique of traditional Indian values, the press coverage encourages the location of the root causes of patriarchy in feudal aspects of India rather than encouraging an examination of the ways in which both tradition and modernity strengthen patriarchy. Finally, although the activist discourse itself creates a separation between the activist woman and the ordinary woman, showing only rare glimpses of her capacity for agency, press coverage eclipses the ordinary woman's agency altogether.

In sum, then, the analysis suggests that the urban women's movement in India has been able to successfully use the press to bring certain issues to the public forum. This has enabled them to make alternative meanings available to some degree, thereby influencing the 'evolution of hegemony' (Steeves 1997: 100). On the other hand, the easy adaptability of their discourse by the press, and its further softening within the coverage, creates certain absences that may limit the radical potential of the critiques offered by the women's movement. Further, this analysis suggests that the discourse on women's issues is constrained not only by press ideology, norms and conventions, but also by limitations in the women's movement's own discourse, and that both should be examined for ways to better exploit the radical potential of the women's movement.

Notes

1. For inspiration and materials I am greatly indebted to Manju Parikh, Sonal Shukla and Vibhuti Patel, and to all the Forum activists who worked hard in waging the campaign against female foeticide.
2. The term 'ordinary' is being used here to differentiate activist women who are involved in women's groups from women in Indian society generally. Although a class difference is also connoted, whereby activist women are generally elite and 'ordinary' women are often not, within the context of the female foeticide issue the distinction is not based as much on class as on involvement with the women's movement. Since women of all classes have been undergoing the tests and selective abortions, activists in the women's movement see themselves as representing this broad constituency of women.
3. This short account of the Indian women's movement glosses over various contradictions within the different phases of the movement. Sangari and Vaid (1989) and Jayawardena (1986) have pointed out various contradictions within both the nineteenth-century social reform movement and the participation of women in the nationalist movement. Within both, there was a mix of reformist and conservative ideologies. Both led to contradictory results in terms of the legitimation of the class and caste structure, as well as in the lives of the women whose lot they were meant to improve.
4. This is admittedly a simplified sketch of the urban women's movement, and is meant only to convey the main emphases of the movement. There are groups, for example, that devote themselves to working with working-class women, women in the slums, etc. And some of these groups, foremost among them the Self Employed Women's Association, do confront government authorities such as the police directly. Also, the urban movement has taken up the issue of rape in police custody, which implies a direct clash with the policing arm of the state. In most such cases, the groups attempt to influence certain state institutions such as the judiciary and the legislative arm to create changes that will reform the other errant state institutions (such as the police).
5. The only exception to this is an article by Anjali Puri from the *Indian Express*, Delhi. This article was included in the analysis because it referred directly to the campaign in Maharashtra, and served to illustrate a pertinent point.
6. The term 'female foeticide' brings up important contradictions. Although it highlights the injustice of the act of selective abortion, it cannot also avoid echoing the language of the 'pro-life' lobby in India and elsewhere, which has also used the imagery of abortion as a crime against the foetus, as murder of the foetus. The activists lobbying against selective abortion in India are vehemently against curtailing the general right of women to have easy access to safe abortions, and the right of women to decide when to get an abortion. They are against selective abortion as a discriminatory act, and not as a crime against the foetus per se. Although Joseph and Sharma (1994) indicate that the activists were well aware of this contradiction, and their reluctance to frame the issue as violence against the foetus had led to restricted coverage, my analysis of the press coverage shows a straightforward use of the term 'female foeticide' throughout the coverage, without any indication of the contradictions involved.

7. For a very interesting discussion of the ways in which urbanisation (as an aspect of modernisation) has intensified son preference rather than reducing it, providing new reasons to value sons and devalue daughters, see Khanna (1997).

8. For an extended discussion of the discourse of 'choice' surrounding the female foeticide issue, see Luthra (1993).

9. The Maharashtra Regulation of Pre-natal Diagnostic Techniques Act that resulted from the campaign did end up allowing for the woman herself to be fined Rs 50, but the activists attended throughout to make sure the woman was not penalised. This created pressure for them to represent the woman as a blameless victim of familial and societal pressure.

10. Joseph and Sharma (1994) point out that even the superficial liberal consensus of the post-Emergency period was in the process of being eroded by the early 1990s, with the press more concerned with formal politics, scandals and the lifestyles of the rich and famous today than with the plight of deprived sections of the population. This may make it much more difficult for women's groups to get a hearing, particularly on their own terms.

11. Ammu Joseph and Kalpana Sharma (1994) have made a similar observation while studying the coverage of the dowry issue in the Indian English language press. They found that
    The unquestioning acceptance of law as a tool of social reform was also evident in much of the editorial comment .... The unwritten, but generally accepted, social compact that governs many of the positions taken by the mainstream media of such issues is an acceptance of the State as the arbiter in dealing with crimes against the so-called weaker sections. Dissenting voices, which actually question the motives of the State and its agencies and highlight structures which perpetuate patriarchy and oppression, appear only in the alternative media—in magazines like *Manushi*. (p. 42)

12. The regional presses may offer more potential in the long run to engage in a dialogue with the Indian community, and particularly with unconverted, non-feminist, Indian women. These newspapers and magazines are published in the vernacular in different regions, and as Joseph and Sharma (1994) note, they use the idiom of the people, and can therefore speak more directly to them at an emotional, and not just an intellectual level. But the little research that has been done on the treatment of women's issues by the regional presses indicates the generally conservative bent of these presses, including their conservative approach to women's issues (Balasubrahmanyan 1988; Joseph and Sharma 1994).

13. In studying a special issue of a Kenyan newspaper, Worthington (1995) found a definite difference between the way elite women and poor women are depicted. The elite women are presented as expert sources, whereas the poor women are depicted as specimens of the female gender (Worthington 1995; Rakow and Kranich 1991). This is similar to the division between elite activist women and ordinary women found here.

References

'Amniocentesis muddle: Growing Protest against Test Abuse'. 1986. *The Daily* (Bombay), 11 August.

Balasubrahmanyan, V. 1988. *Mirror Image: The Media and the Women's Question*. Bombay: Centre for Education and Documentation.

'Ban on sex tests major legislation'. 1988. *The Times of India* (Bombay), 25 January.

Bhate, K. 1987. 'Sex Determination Tests: A New Challenge before Indian Women's Movement'. Paper presented at the 5th International Conference on Women and Health, San Jose, Costa Rica.

'Bill on pre-natal tests passed'. 1988. *The Indian Express* (Bombay), 14 April.

Centre for Development of Instructional Technology (CENDIT). *Ajata* [Film]. New Delhi, India: CENDIT.

Chougule, A.L. 1989, 'Return of the Sex Test', *The Daily* (Sunday Daily magazine section), 11 June.

D'Monte, D. 1988. 'World without Women', *The Indian Post* (Bombay), 18 June.

D'Souza, J.B. 1988. 'Should there be a Choice?' *The Times of India* (Bombay), 10 January.

———. 1989. 'Why must Wanting a Son be Rendered Criminal?' *The Times of India* (Bombay), 7 June.

Desai, N. 1988. 'Born to Die', *The Indian Post* (Bombay), 7 October.

Duggal, R. and M. Gupte. 1987. 'The XYZ of Sex', *The Indian Post* (Bombay), 31 May.

'Female foeticide returns with respectability'. 1987. *The Times of India* (Bombay), 4 August.

Gallagher, M. 1981. *Unequal Opportunities: The Case of Women and the Media*. Paris: UNESCO.

Gupte, M. 1987. 'Neither Dead, nor Buried', *The Indian Post* (Bombay), 28 May.

Jayawardena, K. 1986. *Feminism and Nationalism in the Third World*. New Jersey: Zed.

Joseph, A. and K. Sharma. 1994. *Whose News? The Media and Women's Issues*. New Delhi, India: Sage Publications.

Khanna, S.K. 1995. 'Prenatal Sex Determination: A New Family-building Strategy', *Manushi: A Journal about Women and Society*, no. 85 (January–February): 23–29.

———. 1997. 'Traditions and Reproductive Technology in an Urbanizing North Indian Village', *Social Science Medicine*, 44: 171–80.

Kishwar, M. 1995. 'When Daughters are Unwanted: Sex Determination Tests in India', *Manushi: A Journal about Women and Society*, no. 86 (January–February): 15–22.

Kishwar, M. and R. Vanita. 1984. *In Search of Answers: Indian Women's Voices from Manushi*. New Jersey: Zed.

Kumar, D. 1989a. 'Ban on Sex Test Clinics Unwise'. *The Times of India* (Bombay), 9 December.

———. 1989b. 'Logic of Sex Tests—Feminist Distortions'. *The Times of India* (Bombay), 11 February.

Kumar, R. 1993. *The History of Doing: An Illustrated Account of Movements for Women's Rights and Feminism in India 1800–1990*. New Delhi: Kali for Women.

Lata and Harpal. n.d. 'Campaign against Sex Determination and Pre-selection Techniques—Forum Against Sex Determination and Sex Pre-selection Techniques'. Mimeo (available from Women's Centre, B–104, Sunrise Apartments, Vakola, Santa Cruz [East], Bombay 400 055, India).

Luthra, R. 1993. 'Toward a Reconceptualization of "choice": Challenges by Women at the Margins', *Feminist Issues*, 13: 41–54.

———. 1994. 'A Case of Problematic Diffusion: The Use of Sex Determination Techniques in India', *Knowledge: Creation, Diffusion, Utilization*, 15: 259–72.

'The male factor', 1988. *The Times of India* (Bombay), 11 February.

Mehta, G. 1989. 'Gujarat Tops in Female Foeticide', *The Times of India* (Bombay), 4 February.

'Must be banned'. 1987. *The Times of India* (Bombay), 16 December.

Narayan, U. 1997. *Dislocating Cultures: Identities, Traditions, and Third World Feminism*. New York: Routledge.

'Not enough'. 1986. *The Times of India* (Bombay), August.

Omvedt, G. 1993. *Reinventing Revolution: New Social Movements and the Socialist Tradition in India*. New York: M.E. Sharpe.

Parikh, M. 1990. 'Sex Selective Abortions in India: Parental Choice or Sexist Discrimination?' *Feminist Issues*, 10: 19–32.

Patel, V. 1986a. 'Amniocentesis and Women's Movement'. Paper presented at the meeting of the National Council on Women's Studies, Punjab University, Chandigarh, India.

———. 1986b. 'New Reproductive Technology and its Impact on Women'. Paper presented at the Workshop on Feminist Perspectives on Women, Health and Reproduction, Bombay, India.

———. 1989a. 'Sex Tests Endanger Women's Rights'. *The Times of India*, 14 January.

———. 1989b. 'Sex-determination and Sex-preselection Tests in India: Modern Techniques for Femicide', *Bulletin of Concerned Asian Scholars*, 21: 2–10.

Puri, A. 1988. 'Amniocentesis: Invitation to Murder', *The Indian Express* (Delhi), 7 January.

Rakow, L.F. and K. Kranich, 1991. 'Woman as Sign in Television News', *Journal of Communication*, 41(1): 8–23.

Ravindra, R.P. 1986. 'Refined Techniques of Femicide'. Mimeo (available from Women's Centre, Bombay, India).

———. n.d. 'S.D. Tests: Myths v. reality. Mimeo'. (available from Women's Centre, Bombay, India).

———. 1988. 'How can a Society Advocating Female Infanticide Move towards Equality of the Sexes?' *The Times of India* (Bombay), 14 February.

Sadasivam, B. 1988. 'Doublespeak on Sex Tests', *The Indian Post* (Bombay), 29 April.

Sangari, K. and S. Vaid. 1989. 'Recasting Women: An Introduction', in K. Sangari and S. Vaid (eds), *Recasting Women: Essays in Indian Colonial History*, pp. 1–26. New Delhi: Kali for Women.

Sen, M. 1988. 'Sex Test Debate Gains Force', *The Times of India* (Bombay), 12 February.

Setalvad, T. 1988a. 'Bill Soon to Ban Amniocentesis', *The Indian Express* (Bombay), 14 March.

———. 1988b. 'Sex Test Ban a Welcome Move', *The Indian Express* (Bombay), 13 January.

———. 1988c. 'Campaign against Sex Test Pays', *The Indian Express* (Bombay), 15 April.

'Sex tests banned'. 1988. *The Times of India* (Bombay), 1 January.

Shankar, M.K. *Samadhan* [Film]. Bombay, India: Aditya Creative Film Makers.

Sharma, K. 1988. 'The Problem with Girls', *The Indian Express* (Bombay), 18 December.

Shelley, M. 1987. 'What Price, Sex Tests', *The Daily* (Bombay), 5 April.

Shivdasani, S. 1989. 'Politics of Sex Tests', *The Daily* (Bombay), 14 March.

Shukla, S. and S. Kulkarni. 1986. 'Social Implications of Sex-determination Tests: Advances in Medical Field Supporting Backward Social Values'. Mimeo (available from Women's Center, Bombay, India).

Shukla, S., S. Kulkarni and V. Patel. 1987. 'Abuse of New Technology', *Seminar*, 331: 14–17.

Spivak, G.C. 1988. 'Can the Subaltern Speak?' in C. Nelson and L. Grossberg (eds), *Marxism and the Interpretation of Culture*. London: Macmillan.

'State promises to ban sex tests'. 29 November 1986.

Steeves, H.L. 1997. *Gender Violence and the Press: The St. Kizito Story*. Athens, Ohio: Ohio University Center for International Studies (Monographs in International Studies, Africa Series No. 67).

Sunder Rajan, R. 1993. *Real and Imagined Women: Gender, Culture and Postcolonialism*. London and New York: Routledge.

Taneja, N. 1988. 'Female Foeticide No Democratic Right', *The Times of India* (Bombay), 26 December.

Tanushree, L. Shah, B. Ahmedi and D. Marlankar. 1989. 'Against Female Foeticide'. [Letter to the editor], *The Times of India* (Bombay), 17 February.

Tuchman, G. 1978. *Making News: A Study in the Construction of Reality*. New York: The Free Press.

UNESCO. 1989. *World Communication Report*. Paris: UNESCO.

Vanaik, A. 1986. 'Female Foeticide in India: Sex Determination Leads the Way'. *The Times of India* (Bombay), 20 June.

Women's Feature Service. 1993. *The Power to Change: Women in the Third World Redefine their Environment*. New Jersey: Zed.

Worthington, N. 1995. 'Classifying Kenyan Women: Press Representations of Gender in Nairobi's *Daily Nation*', *Women's Studies in Communication*, 18: 65–84.

ELEVEN

Portrayals of Sexual Violence in Popular Hindi Films, 1997–99*

Srividya Ramasubramanian and Mary Beth Oliver

The incidence of sexual violence against women is greater in societies with male-dominated ideologies and a history of violence, as is the case in India (Burt 1980; Check and Malamuth 1985; Linz and Malamuth 1993). The number of registered cases of sexual crimes against women in India increased from 67,072 in 1989 to 84,000 in 1993 ('Crimes Against', 1996). In 1995 alone, more than 25,000 cases of molestation and 12,000 cases of rape were reported in the capital city of New Delhi (West 1996). It is estimated that well over 80 per cent of sexual crimes go unreported ('Atrocities Against', 2002). For example, only 7,643 of the estimated 50,000 instances of violence against women were reported to the police even in Kerala, a south Indian state with the highest women's literacy rate (ibid.).

One specific form of sexual harassment called 'eve-teasing' is prevalent, especially in urban India.[1] The term eve-teasing is used to refer to the sexual harassment of women in public places such as the streets, public transportation, parks, beaches and cinema halls. This type of public harassment by a lone man or gangs of men includes verbal assaults such as making passes or unwelcome sexual jokes; non-verbal assaults such as showing obscene gestures, winking, whistling and staring; and physical assaults such as pinching, fondling and rubbing against women in public places ('Eve-teasing,' 1999; Stevens 1984). In addition, in several instances eve-teasing has been followed by more violent assaults such as rape and murder. In trying to construct the profile of an eve-teaser, it is interesting to note that about 32 per cent of eve-teasers are college students ('Films', 1998).

The severity of these incidents, coupled with their high prevalence, resulted in the legal declaration of eve-teasing as a punishable offence by the state government of Tamil Nadu in 1999, where it was announced that offenders would be penalised with up to one year of imprisonment or a fine of Rs 10,000 or both ('Ordinance', 1999). Despite the seriousness of these incidents, research suggests that they are frighteningly commonplace. For example, a recent survey revealed that approximately 90 per cent of college women in New Delhi have experienced sexual harassment in some shape or form ('Films', 1998). Yet, it is estimated that only about one in 10,000 eve-teasing occurrences are reported to the police ('Atrocities Against', 2002).

The primary reasons why women abstain from reporting incidents of sexual violence are the unwieldy medico-legal process, concerns about continued violence, and fear of stigmatisation (Prasad 1999).

Mass Media and Sexuality in India

The variables that give rise to sexual violence in India are undoubtedly numerous and complex. However, for feminist media scholars, the idea that popular cinema plays a significant role in shaping notions about gender roles and gender identities within the Indian context is of special interest and concern (Bagchi 1996;

*Originally published in *Sex Roles: A Journal of Research*, Vol. 48, Nos 7/8, April 2003, pp. 327–37. Reprinted with permission from Springer Science and Business Media.

Ram 2002). Cinema has been a dominant medium in India because of the sheer size and reach of its indigenous film industry. The Indian film industry produces about 800 feature films annually—the highest in the world (National Film Development Corporation n.d.). Not only does India produce the largest numbers of films in the world, but a sizeable amount of film consumption is also common among almost all age groups, socio-economic backgrounds, and geographical locations within India (Derné 1995). It is estimated that every week approximately 90–100 million Indian viewers go to the cinema halls to watch films (Nair et al. 1999). Many cinemagoers ritualistically make as many as 20–30 visits to the cinema hall in a month, and repeatedly view a favourite film several dozens of times (Derné 1999; Khare 1985). Moreover, Indians films are popular not just in India, but also amongst the Indian diaspora in countries such as the United States, United Kingdom, Canada, Fiji, Dubai and Singapore (Bist 2002). Indian-made films constitute the majority of the films watched by Indians; only about 5 per cent of Indians watch non-Indian (mostly Hollywood) films (Anjum 2002).

Apart from cinema halls, films also reach the Indian household through countdown shows on television that feature film-based song-and-dance hit numbers (Nair et al. 1999). In addition, access to cable television has also grown very rapidly in the last decade, with a penetration of over 50 per cent of the urban Indian market as of 1997 (ibid.). Furthermore, over 85 per cent of the cable television operators routinely screen two films a day through their own private local channels to attract their customers (ibid.).

The importance of sexual portrayals in motion pictures is particularly relevant to Indian audiences, not only because these portrayals are viewed in abundance, but also because issues of sexuality are rarely discussed in other contexts (Derné 1999). According to Derné (ibid.), Indian film portrayals form a 'privileged arena for construction of sexuality' for the common person, and serve as primary sources of information about how men and women are to behave in sexual relationships (p. 548). A recent study sponsored by UNICEF and Save the Children Fund in the Indian subcontinent showed that the film medium is influential, especially among teenaged boys, in teaching notions about masculinity, power and violence in relationships with women (Poudyal 2002). Similarly, researchers in the North American context have found that children and adolescents use media narratives (especially teen magazines and prime-time television programmes) as sexual scripts for learning about dominant norms concerning gender, love and sexuality (Carpenter 1998; Pardun 2002; Ward 1995; Wood 2001; Wood et al. 2002).

Feminist scholars are particularly concerned that popular films in India too often portray women in stereotypical roles of subordination, accepting sexual violence as a normal part of relationships with men (Dasgupta and Hegde 1988; Gandhi and Shah 1992). Further, they have pointed out that men's abuse of women is often glorified within Indian cinema (Derné 1999). More specifically, critics have pointed out that the repeated glamorisation of eve-teasing in films as a macho manifestation of a tough-acting, college student hero, who initially upsets the heroine but finally wins her attention, has fostered a climate supportive of such acts in real life (Birla 2001; 'Films', 1998; Ravindran 2001). Although many critics have voiced concerns, very few researchers have dealt with sexually violent portrayals in Indian films. In a rare study of its kind, Derné (1999) conducted a qualitative content analysis study of a select few Hindi films in which violence and sexuality were often intertwined. He suggested that these films conveyed the notion that force and physical aggression were legitimate means of expressing romantic love. Therefore, sexual violence was not only 'normal', but also 'expected' in romantic relationships between heroes and heroines.

Links between Media and Sexual Violence

Although little systematic research has explored the causal influences of Hindi films on sexual violence in India specifically, there is research in other cultures, particularly North America, which has explored the role of consumption of media portrayals of sexuality on viewers' behaviours. In this regard, some researchers have suggested that there is no causal relationship between access to sexually explicit material and the incidence of sexual crimes (Kutchinsky 1991), that effects are observed only for individuals who are pre-disposed to be aggressive (Zillmann and Sapolsky 1977), or that harmful effects are observed only for ex-plicitly violent portrayals (Donnerstein et al. 1987). However, results of meta-analytic research suggest that there is a relationship between media consumption of sexually explicit materials (and particularly violent materials) and a number of variables related to sexual violence. These analyses reported that exposure to sexually explicit media (both violent and non-violent) was associated with increased rape-myth acceptance and increased subsequent aggression, especially among angered participants (Allen et al. 1995a; Allen et al. 1995b). In addition, researchers have also reported that consumption of sexually explicit media (both violent and non-violent) may lead to increased sexual callousness, the disregard or contempt for a woman's right to deny sexual access (Zillmann and Weaver 1989). Similarly, other researchers have argued that the consumption of media portrayals of sexual violence may lead to target desensitisation, the belief that certain individuals are appropriate, natural and safe targets of violence, and are deserving of aggression (Check and Malamuth 1985; Donnerstein and Berkowitz 1981). Behavioural effects of exposure to sexually explicit material can take the form of imitation of new behaviours as well as lowered inhibitions to try out already learned behav-iours (Russell 1988). Finally, other researchers have examined the idea of sexual objectification, and have reported that the viewing of pornography can lead some male viewers to interpret subsequent interactions with women in inappropriate sexual or erotic terms (McKenzie-Mohr and Zanna 1990).

In summary, although most of the research on the effects of sexual portrayals suggests that some types of explicit images, particularly those that contain aggression, can lead to harmful effects on viewers, there are some inconsistencies in the literature that have made it difficult to determine causal effects. These differences have been attributed to the types of stimulus materials employed, the types of populations studied (e.g., rapists/non-criminals, hyper-masculine men, whether or not the participants are under the influence of alcohol, propensity to use force), the environment, and additional cultural factors (Harris and Scott 2002). Despite these factors, however, meta-analytic research that synthesised the body of literature in this area suggested that exposure to media portrayals of sexually explicit material can have a variety of effects on viewers' attitudes and behaviours, many of which are causes for concern (Allen et al. 1995a; Allen et al. 1995b; Harris and Scott 2002).

The Present Research

Given the dearth of research on the effects of sexual violence with respect to popular Indian films and the need to investigate the effects of sexually explicit media amongst diverse populations, there is a need for re-search in the area of mediated sexual violence in India. The literature on the effects of filmed sexual violence generally supports claims that Hindi films may be a contributory factor in sexual harassment. However, this would be true only if Hindi films actually depicted the types of images that are thought to play a role in in-fluencing notions about sexuality in the Indian context. Hence, the first step in exploring this issue is to examine the types of portrayals that are commonly depicted in the films. At this point it is unclear if popular films meant for mass consumption would have any sexually violent material in the first place, in particular since people of all age groups (rather than just adults) view popular Hindi films, one might expect that Hindi films would be unlikely to show sexual images. On the other hand, if Hindi films do provide an outlet for 'discussions' of sexual behaviours that serve to reinforce traditional views of women, then one might expect that Hindi films would be likely to show violence against women as normal, and perhaps even enjoyable.

Consequently, the purpose of this exploratory study was to examine the manner in which popular Hindi films portray sexual violence, and the way in which violence might be associated with gender and romantic love. Specifically, we examined the following research questions:

RQ1: What proportion of sexual scenes contains violence?

RQ2: Is there a relationship between gender and the likelihood of being the primary victim of sexual violence?

RQ3: Is there a relationship between character role and the likelihood of being the primary perpetrator of sexual violence?

RQ4: Is there a relationship between severity of sexual violence and character role of the primary perpetrator of sexual violence?

RQ5: Against what type of character roles are heroes most likely to perpetrate sexual violence?

RQ6: Is there a relationship between scene type and severity of sexual violence?

Method

Sample

A sample of nine full-length feature films was randomly selected from a population of top-10 box office hits in the Hindi film industry released in the years 1997, 1998 and 1999.[2] Within each of these three years, three films were randomly selected. Because we were interested in mass entertainment, especially films viewed by adolescents, films rated 'U' (universal audience) and 'UA' (public viewing with parental guidance for children under age 12) were included in the study, but those rated 'A' (films restricted to adult audiences) were excluded (National Film Development Corporation n.d.; see Table 11.1 for a list of the films analysed).

TABLE 11.1
List of Films Analysed in this Study

Year	Film Title
1997	*Pardes*
	Border
	Hero No. 1
1998	*Bandhan*
	Pyaar To Hona Hi Tha
	Kuch Kuch Hota Hai
1999	*Biwi No. 1*
	Hum Aapke Dil Mein Rehte Hain
	Sarfarosh

Units of Analysis

Two units of analysis were examined in this study: characters and sexual scenes. A scene was defined as a division of the film that presents continuous action in one place, such as a single situation or unit of dialogue in the film (e.g., love scene or fight scene). As we were interested in examining the nature of violence within the context of sexual interactions, only sexual scenes (both violent and non-violent) were coded. The entire film was watched to locate the presence of sexual scenes. One hundred and eight such scenes were included in this study. A sexual scene was defined as one in which two or more characters were involved in activities such as having sex, kissing, petting, initiating or suggesting sexual contact, displaying nudity, engaging in sexual talk, bathing in an erotic way, wearing provocative or revealing clothes, or shown as a sexual object of gaze. This included actual depictions, suggestions of, and preparation for sexual activities. No instances of homosexual relationships were portrayed in any of the films selected. Therefore, only heterosexual relationships were considered within the scope of this study. Also, because we were interested in examining sexual interactions between individuals, two or more characters had to be present in a scene for it to be considered a sexual scene. For example, a woman undressing for a bath was not considered for the study, but if a man undressed a woman, it was included within the study.

The second unit of analysis was the character. Seventy-seven characters were coded in this study. Only those characters who were shown speaking and were present in a sexual scene were included in the study. Characteristics of characters, such as gender and type of character role, were coded. Characters were observed for the entire film before coding their characteristics.

Coding Scheme

A coding scheme was created for the variables of interest: presence of sexual violence, primary perpetrators/victims, gender, character role, severity of sexual violence, and fun/seriousness of scene.

Presence of Sexual Violence

Sexual scenes were of two types: mutually consenting scenes and sexually violent scenes. Mutually consenting scenes were those in which the characters involved showed interest in or expressed no objection to engaging in the sexual behaviour, and there was no harm to any of the people involved. In contrast, a sexually violent scene was any sexual scene where there was actual depiction of, suggestion of, or preparation for sexual violence. Sexual violence was defined from the victim's perspective as any forced sexual act that was inappropriate, offensive, and/or harmful. Offensiveness to the victim was assessed using verbal and non-verbal expressions of disapproval, anger, or disgust (e.g., saying no, crying, pushing away, clenching fists). This included (but was not limited to) acts such as rape, verbal comments, kissing, disrobing, touching, staring, rubbing against, and obscene gestures. Rape was defined as the actual depiction of, suggestion of, or preparation for forced sexual intercourse.

Sexual violence was not just limited to rape, but also included sexual harassment, eve-teasing and domestic violence. Sexual harassment was defined as inappropriate, offensive, and/or harmful sexual behaviour within the context of a workplace or academic environment wherein a power differential existed between the parties involved. For example, the sexual harassment of a student by a professor or of a subordinate by a boss was coded as sexual harassment. Eve-teasing was defined as sexual behaviour displayed in public places (especially between strangers or acquaintances who are not committed to a relationship) that was inappropriate, harmful, and/or offensive to the victim. Domestic violence was defined as sexual aggression (e.g., forced kissing, disrobing, pinching) between couples who were in an intimate, committed sexual relationship (e.g., boyfriend/girlfriend, fiancé/fiancee, husband/wife), and where the victim was hurt and/or offended by the sexual act.

Severity of Sexual Violence

Sexually violent scenes were further categorised as severe or moderate. Severe violence included actual depictions of, suggested, attempted, or preparation for rape or eroticised murder. Moderate sexual violence included all other forms of sexual violence, sexual harassment, eve-teasing and domestic violence—that did not involve rape or murder.[3]

Primary Perpetrators/Victims in a Sexually Violent Scene

All sexually violent scenes had at least one perpetrator and one victim. The perpetrator was the one who initiated sexual aggression. A perpetrator was defined as someone who actually used, suggested the use of, attempted to use, or made preparations for using aggression in a sexual context. The victim was defined as the character who expressed lack of consent to the sexual act, and/or was harmed by the act. It is important to note that sexual violence was defined more in terms of the harm caused to the victim rather than the intention of the perpetrator. This meant that even if the perpetrator did not intend to cause harm to the victim, it was considered as sexual violence if the victim was harmed.

Character Role

Every character was coded as playing one of five character roles: hero, heroine, villain, comedian, or supporting character. A hero was defined as a character who played the role of the main, leading, male protagonist of the film. The heroine was defined as the main, leading, female protagonist in the film. The villain was anyone who was an antagonist (man or woman). A comedian is a character who is similar to a 'sidekick' in Hollywood films, and was one whose role in the narrative was to provide comic relief (man or woman). Supporting characters included anybody who did not fall into the classification of hero, heroine, villain, or comedian. In a given film, more than one person could play these roles. For example, there were some films with two heroes.

Fun/Seriousness of the Scene

To understand fully the context within which sexuality was introduced into the plot of the films, it was crucial to code for the type of scenes that depicted sexuality. The sexual scenes were classified as either fun scenes or serious scenes. Serious scenes included drama, action and mystery. Fun scenes included comedy, romance and song-dance. Romance was defined as scenes that showed sexually attracted, dating, engaged, or married couples interacting with each other in a romantic fashion. Action was defined as scenes that showed fights, physical aggression, or violence. Comedy was defined as scenes that depicted jokes and humour. Song-dance scenes were defined as musical episodes accompanied by dances by characters in the film. All other scenes were coded as drama scenes. Typically, drama scenes showed conflict, were dialogue-oriented, and involved emotions such as anger or sadness.

Coding Reliability

All coding and data reported here was conducted by the first author, who was trained in coding procedures and was familiar with the descriptive booklet.[4] To examine reliability, a secondary coder fluent in the language of the films but unaware of the specific research hypotheses independently coded six of the nine films. Inter-coder reliability was calculated by computing the percent agreement for the five variables examined in this study: presence of sexual violence (83 per cent), character role (78 per cent), severity (95 per cent), gender of character (93 per cent), and fun/serious (78 per cent).[5]

Results

Presence of Sexual Violence

The first research question concerned the prevalence of sexual violence. An examination of the sexual scenes analysed showed that slightly less than half of the sexual scenes (40.7 per cent, N = 44) contained violence (see Table 11.2). The most common form of sexual violence depicted was eve-teasing (57 per cent of sexually violent scenes, N = 25). Approximately 11 per cent of the sexually violent scenes contained severe sexual violence such as rape or eroticised murder (N = 5). It should be noted here that one film (*Border*) showed only mutually consenting sexual scenes whereas *Hero No. 1* depicted 72.2 per cent of the sexual scenes as violent. However, most films depicted approximately 40 per cent of the sexual scenes as sexually violent, suggesting that although there is clearly variation in the percentage of sexually violent scenes portrayed, the majority of these films contained a substantial proportion of sexual scenes containing violence.

TABLE 11.2
Summary of Results

Sexual scenes	
With violence	40.7 per cent
Without violence	59.3 per cent
Gender of primary victims of sexual violence	
Women	77.0 per cent
Men	23.0 per cent
Character role of primary victims of sexual violence	
Heroines	95.0 per cent
Other roles	5.0 per cent
Primary perpetrators of sexual violence	
Heroes	67.8 per cent
Villains	32.2 per cent
Primary perpetrators of moderate sexual violence	
Heroes	78.2 per cent
Villains	21.7 per cent
Portrayal of moderate sexual violence	
Fun	69.2 per cent
Serious	30.7 per cent

Gender and Primary Victim of a Sexually Violent Scene

The second research question asked if there was any relationship between gender and the primary victim in sexually violent scenes. A chi-square test of the primary victims in sexual scenes revealed that women were more likely than men to be victims. Namely, of all victims coded in sexually violent scenes, 77 per cent were women and 23 per cent were men—[chi square] $(1, N = 43) = 12.30$, $p < .001$, [V.sup.*] $= 0.29$ (see Table 11.2). For example, in *Kuch Kuch Hota Hai*, a typical college-based eve-teasing is used as a means to enhance the sexual appeal of the heroine Tina (played by Rani Mukherjee). When Tina enters the college campus wearing a very short mini-skirt and tight top, she is accosted by a gang of men in her college who stare at her legs, whistle, hoot, and make lewd remarks at her even though she expresses her disgust at their behaviour. However, it appears that the intention of the scene is more to invite the audience to view the heroine as a sex object rather than to empathise with her experience.

Character Role and Primary Perpetrator

The third research question focused on the relationship between the character role (hero vs. villain) and the primary perpetrator in sexually violent scenes. A chi-square analysis of heroes and villains showed that heroes (67.8 per cent) were more likely than villains (32.2 per cent) to be the primary perpetrator in sexually violent scenes. However, these differences only approached statistical significance—[chi square] $(1, N = 28) = 3.57$, $p = .06$, [V.sup.*] $= 0.13$ (see Table 11.2). For example, films such as *Biwi No. 1* and *Hum Aapke Dil Mein Rehte Hain* show the hero eve-teasing women by singing lewd songs, making sexual remarks, and touching the heroine in sexual ways despite knowing that the heroine does not like these acts. On the other hand, in *Pardes*, the evil, villainous boyfriend tries to force his fiancee to have sex with him and rips off parts of her clothes after taking her to a hotel room. However, such depictions are much fewer than those instances where the hero is the perpetrator.

Character Roles and Severity of Sexual Violence

The fourth research question examined the relationship between character of the primary perpetrator and the severity of sexual violence portrayed. A chi-square analysis of character role and severity of sexual violence revealed that villains were more likely to be featured as perpetrators of severe sexual violence, whereas heroes were more likely to be featured as perpetrators of moderate sexual violence. Specifically, primary perpetrators in severe scenes were more often villains (80.0 per cent) than heroes (20.0 per cent), whereas primary perpetrators in moderate scenes were more often heroes (78.2 per cent) than villains (21.7 per cent)—[chi square]$(1, N = 28) = 6.39$, $p < .05$, [V.sup.*] $= 0.48$ (see Table 11.2). In films such as *Kuch Kuch Hota Hai* and *Hero No. 1*, there are several instances in which the hero eve-teases attractive young women to win their attention. These acts are treated in a very casual and trivial manner. However, later in the same film (*Hero No. 1*), the hero is shown to be enraged when the villains try to rape another young girl in the streets. The sexual violence in the latter scene is dramatised as something evil and wrong.

Character Role and Primary Victim

The fifth research question focused on the types of character roles against whom heroes were most likely to perpetrate sexual violence. All sexually violent scenes where the hero was the primary perpetrator were selected for this analysis. A chi-square analysis of the primary victims in these scenes revealed that heroines (95 per cent) were much more likely to be the victim than other characters (5 per cent)—[chi square] $(1, N = 19) = 15.21$, $p < 0.001$, [V.sup.*] $= 0.85$ (see Table 11.2). For example, a typical scene showing a boy-girl romantic confrontation using eve-teasing can be seen in *Hero No. 1*. The hero waylays the unsuspecting heroine (both are strangers to each other until this point in the story) at the airport, follows her around to the train station, makes obscene passes at her, rubs against her body, and even sits on her lap in the train, even though all through the sequence, the heroine constantly expresses her disapproval of these actions by the stranger (hero). As the entire encounter is against the background of a catchy song-and-dance sequence, the sexual harassment is presented to the audience as light-hearted fun.

Severity of Sexual Violence and Fun/Seriousness of Scene

The sixth research question asked if there was a relationship between severity of sexual violence and the type of scene. The findings suggest that severe sexual violence is more likely to be portrayed as serious, whereas moderate sexual violence is more likely to be portrayed as fun. Specifically, a chi-square analysis revealed that severe crimes were more often portrayed as serious (80.0 per cent) than as fun (20.0 per cent), whereas moderate crimes were more often portrayed as fun (69.2 per cent) than as serious (30.7 per cent)—[chi square]$(1, N = 44) = 4.64, p < .05$, [V.sup.*] = .33 (see Table 11.2). For instance, in *Bandhan*, the hero (played by Salman Khan) constantly eve-teases the heroine (played by Rambha), but the entire situation is couched in slapstick comedy, which distracts the viewer from the sexual harassment per se. On the other hand, later in the same film when the villains stop the heroine in an isolated field and eve-tease her, the scene takes on more serious proportions with dialogue and drama rather than song and dance.

Discussion

The results of this study lend support to the idea that a substantial proportion of sexual scenes in popular Hindi films depict sexual violence, even in those films meant for viewing by audiences of all age groups or with parental guidance if under 12 years. However, it is not just the amount of sexual violence in the films that is the cause of concern, but the nature of these portrayals.

First, these films indicate a gender divide when it comes to perpetrators and victims of sexual violence. Almost all films show female characters as victims of sexual violence, whereas male characters are shown as perpetrators of these incidents. This seems to be consistent with traditional gendered beliefs in India that women should be submissive and men should be aggressive in social relationships. This repeated pairing of women with violence is problematic because it might reinforce existing beliefs that it is acceptable to aggress against women, and that women should tolerate violence from men.

Another aspect of these portrayals that is a cause for concern is that the perpetrators of sexual violence were not just villains, but also heroes. Heroes were somewhat more likely than villains to be the primary perpetrators in sexually violent scenes. It is a cause for concern that heroes, who often represented the essence of 'ideal manhood' and male sexuality, were perpetrators of sexual violence. This lends some support to the idea that being aggressive is depicted as 'being manly'.

The idea that heroes would be shown engaging in sexual violence is cause for concern as social learning perspectives suggest that when likable, attractive characters such as heroes perpetrate sexual violence on screen, they are more likely to be imitated by viewers. That is, research on social learning from media portrayals suggests that viewers are more likely to emulate behaviours that they see in the media when the modelled behaviour is portrayed as rewarded (see Bandura 1994). This line of reasoning suggests that film portrayals of women as victims of sexual aggression are particularly problematic, because such behaviour might be learned and imitated by the viewers. In addition, the viewer's modelling of a media character's behaviours is particularly likely to occur when the character is portrayed as attractive, likable and heroic. In terms of the present research, this suggests that Indian male viewers may be especially likely to emulate the sexually violent behaviour perpetrated by heroes.

Heroes and villains differed in the types of sexual violence that they perpetrated. Heroes were more likely to perpetrate moderate crimes such as eve-teasing, sexual harassment and domestic violence, whereas villains were more likely to perpetrate severe crimes including rape and eroticised murder. Thus, moderate sexual violence seems not to be condemned, and might even be rewarded. As we saw above, heroes, by definition, seem to protect moral good and fight evil. Therefore, the association of heroes with moderate sexual violence may run the risk of sending a message to viewers that only severe crimes are bad, and that moderate sexual violence is not bad (and may be even perceived as good). Therefore, these findings suggest that audiences consider only rape and eroticised murder to be crimes, but that eve-teasing, sexual harassment and domestic violence may be socially acceptable sexual behaviours. Furthermore, moderate sexual violence is often depicted in the context of fun and happiness, whereas severe sexual crimes are depicted as serious and dramatic. This pairing of fun with moderate sexual violence implies that such crimes are not bad, but enjoyable for all involved.

Moreover, the finding that heroes more often aggressed against heroines than against any other characters is consistent with the argument that aggression is portrayed as a desirable attribute in Hindi films. It should be noted that in all the films in this study, the hero and heroine were romantically involved. This suggests that it was appropriate, normal, and perhaps even romantic for men to aggress against the women with whom they were romantically involved. From the perspective of sexual script theory, these portrayals may suggest to viewers (especially young adults, adolescents and children) that these recurring themes of violence among romantically involved couples in the media represent acceptable ways of behaving in sexual relationships. The films analysed in the current study were not adult films, but those rated U and UA. Thus, it is highly likely that these films' audiences include younger age groups, who are also likely to be learning social norms related to gender and sexuality. Moreover, as mentioned previously, eve-teasing statistics report that about one-third of the perpetrators in real life are college-age youth ('Films', 1998). This situation suggests that social learning and sexual script theories might be at work, although clearly experimental research needs to be conducted to determine the specific nature of the effects that these films may be having on their viewing audiences.

Although the results of this study indicate that moderate sexual violence such as eve-teasing, domestic violence and sexual harassment by men against women is very often portrayed as appropriate, enjoyable and romantic, there are several limitations that deserve attention and suggest directions for future research. First, only top-10 box office hits were chosen for the analysis. It can be argued that more (or fewer) types of films could have been included in defining what is popular. However, the use of top-10 box office films allowed for the examination of films that are clearly popular among a wide viewing audience, both within India and amongst the Indian diaspora in countries such as the United States, United Kingdom, Canada, Singapore and Dubai.

Second, we examined popular films in the Hindi language only and did not include regional Indian language films. Even though there are very large numbers of films produced each year in regional languages (especially Telugu and Tamil), their popularity and audience reach is smaller than that of Hindi films. Nevertheless, future researchers could benefit by including these two-regional-language films to get a regional sample of sexually violent portrayals.

Another limitation of this research is the small sample of films analysed. This limitation reflects the fact that Hindi films often average three to four hours in length, which makes them time-consuming to analyse. However, the longer film length meant that the numbers of scenes and characters analysed in a given film were also proportionately higher. Nevertheless, future studies would undoubtedly benefit from the inclusion of a larger sample of films.

An additional limitation of this study is that we coded only sexual scenes within the films. Although the use of sexual scenes as a unit of analysis was appropriate for the questions examined in this study, it restricted the generalisability of our findings because it was not possible to say whether sexual scenes contained more or less violence than the non-sexual scenes. On the one hand the potential effect of sexual violence may largely depend on the amount of violence in the film overall, with violence in the sexual scenes having only arguably different effects than the violence running throughout all types of scenes. On the other hand, one might argue that any portrayals of sexual violence have the potential to affect viewers. Nevertheless, an examination of violence across all scenes, sexual and non-sexual, should be taken into consideration by future researchers.

Finally, a content analysis such as this one can only describe the portrayals that exist on screen. The method is limited in its ability to predict attitudinal and behavioural changes that could result from exposure. At best, the results can only be seen as indicative of the likely effects on the audience. We cannot in any way claim that the increase in sex crimes is due to the sexual violence portrayed in films. Such conclusions are best made using experimental methodologies.

Despite these limitations, the results of this exploratory study seem to suggest that Indian films tend to present moderate forms of sexual violence to its audience as normal, fun and heroic. The effect that such sexually violent portrayals have on viewers is an area of study that is deserving of research attention. Overall, our data supports the criticism that eve-teasing in Indian films is not generally portrayed as a crime that ought to be punished, but rather as an act of romantic love aesthetically woven into the narrative as fun and enjoyable.

Notes

1. Although it is entirely possible that the word eve-teasing might refer to the Biblical story of Adam and Eve, we prefer to spell eve-teasing with a small 'e' rather than a capital 'E' because this is the spelling used by Indian journalists.
2. While we were making a random selection of three of the top-10 box office hits of 1997, the film *Virasat* was selected at first, but it was not accessible. Therefore, it was replaced with another randomly selected film, *Border*.
3. It is important to point out that our use of the terms severe and moderate is not meant to imply that 'moderate' acts are trivial. Rather, both severe and moderate acts are understood to represent sexual violence. However, our use of the term severe in this context refers to acts such as rape and murder, which are extreme forms of sexual violence that result in lasting physical harm to the victim.
4. In this study, the primary coder was responsible for coding all of the data that was presented in this chapter. The additional coder was employed as a way of assessing the primary coder's reliability. Although researchers often have coders resolve disputes and arrive at a mutual decision, there are numerous instances where an additional coder is employed as a means of reliability computation or where multiple coders were employed, with their independently coded data collected after reliability checks had been conducted (e.g., Fouts and Burggraf 1999; Larson 2001; Scharrer 2002; Schlenker et al. 1998).
5. There was disagreement among the coders concerning the unit of analysis for two of the sexual scenes. This disagreement is reflected in the reliability indicators. Gender was coded as male/female. There was some disagreement between coders regarding the gender of transvestites, bisexual persons and transgendered individuals, which reduced the reliability of this measure.

References

Allen, M., D. D'Alessio and K. Brezgel. 1995a. 'A Meta-analysis Summarizing the Effects of Pornography: II. Aggression after Exposure', *Human Communication Research*, 22: 258–83.

Allen, M., T. Emmers, L. Gebhardt and M.A. Giery. 1995b. 'Exposure to Pornography and Acceptance of Rape Myths', *Journal of Communication*, 45 (1): 5–26.

Anjum, Z. 2002. 'Hollywood Calling, Bollywood Falling', *Aaj Magazine*. Retrieved 13 August 2002, from http://www.aajmag.com/hollybollywood.html.

'...ocities against women on the rise in state'. 2002. *The Hindu*, 11 April. Retrieved 12 August 2002, from the Lexis-Nexis Academic Universe database, http://web.lexis-nexis.com/universe.

Bagchi, A. 1996. 'Women in Indian Cinema'. Retrieved 12 August 2002, from http://www.cs.jhu.edu/~bagchi/ women.html.

Bandura, A. 1994. 'Social Cognitive Theory of Mass Communication', in J. Bryant and D. Zillmann (eds), *Media Effects: Advances in Theory and Research*, pp. 61–90. Hillsdale, NJ: Erlbaum.

Birla, P. 2001. 'Helping Kids Get Street-smart on Sex Education'. Retrieved 18 August 2002, from the Health Education Library for People website: http://www.healthlibrary.com/news/25_31_march/31_sex.ht.

Bist, R. 2002. 'Bollywood Takes on the World'. Retrieved 6 December 2002, from Asia Times (Online) website: http://www.atimes.com/atimes/South_Asia/DJ12Df01.html.

Burt, M.R. 1980. 'Cultural Myths and Supports for Rape', *Journal of Personality and Social Psychology*, 38: 217–30.

Carpenter, L. 1998. 'From Girls into Women: Scripts for Sexuality and Romance in Seventeen Magazine, 1974–1994', *Journal of Sex Research*, 35: 158–68.

Check, J.V.P. and N.M. Malamuth. 1985. 'An Empirical Assessment of Some Feminist Hypotheses about Rape', *International Journal of Women's Studies*, 8: 414–23.

Crimes against women rise in India. 1996. Xinhua News Agency, 27 August. Retrieved 11 February 2002, from the Lexis-Nexis Academic Universe database, http://web.lexis-nexis.com/universe.

Dasgupta, S.D. and R.S. Hegde. 1988. 'The Eternal Receptacle: A Study of Mistreatment of Women in Hindi Films', in R. Ghadially (ed.), *Women in Indian Society: A Reader*, pp. 209–16). New Delhi: Sage Publications.

Derné, S. 1995. *Culture in Action: Family Life, Emotion and Male Dominance in Banaras, India*. Albany: State University of New York Press.

———. 1999. 'Making Sex Violent: Love as Force in Recent Hindi Films', *Violence Against Women*, 5: 548–75.

Donnerstein, E. and L. Berkowitz. 1981. 'Victims' Reactions in Aggressive Erotic Films as a Factor in Violence against Women', *Journal of Personality and Social Psychology*, 41: 710–24.

Donnerstein, E., D. Linz and S. Penrod. 1987. *The Question of Pornography: Research Findings and Policy Implications*. New York: Free Press.

'Eve-teasing—The menace refuses to die'. 1999. *The Hindu*, 12 June. Retrieved 12 August 2002, from the Lexis-Nexis Academic Universe database, http://web.lexis-nexis.com/universe.

'Films, TV serials have contributed to increasing acts of eve-teasing'. 1998. *The Hindu*, 22 September. Retrieved 11 February 2002, from the Lexis-Nexis Academic Universe database, http://web.lexis-nexis.com/universe.

Fouts, G. and K. Burggraf. 1999. 'Television Situation Comedies: Female Body Images and Verbal Reinforcements', *Sex Roles*, 40: 473–81.

Gandhi, N. and N. Shah. 1992. *The Issues at Stake: Theory and Practice in the Contemporary Women's Movement in India*. New Delhi: Kali for Women.

Harris, R.J. and C.L. Scott. 2002. 'Effects of Sex in the Media', in J. Bryant and D. Zillmann (eds.), *Media Effects: Advances in Theory and Research*, (2nd edn), pp. 307–31. Mahwah, NJ: Erlbaum.

Khare, V. 1985. 'The Dinman Hindi Film Inquiry: A summary', in B. Pfleiderer and L. Lutze (eds), *The Hindi Film: Agent and Re-agent of Cultural Change*, pp. 139–48. New Delhi: Manohar.

Kutchinsky, B. 1991. 'Pornography and Rape: Theory and Practice? Evidence from Crime Data in Four Countries where Pornography is Easily Available', *International Journal of Law and Psychiatry*, 14: 47–64.

Larson, M.S. 2001. 'Interactions, Activities and Gender in Children's Television Commercials: A Content Analysis'. *Journal of Broadcasting and Electronic Media*, 45: 41–56.

Linz, D. and N.M. Malamuth. 1993. *Pornography*. Newbury Park, CA: Sage Publications.

McKenzie-Mohr, D. and M.P. Zanna. 1990. 'Treating Women as Sexual Objects: Look to the (gender-schematic) Male Who has Viewed Pornography', *Personality and Social Psychology Bulletin*, 16: 296–08.

Nair, N.K., A.K. Barman and U. Chattopadhyay. 1999. 'Study on Copyright Piracy in India'. Retrieved 11 August 2002, from the Government of India, Department of Education. Website: http://www.education.nic.in/htmlweb/cr_piracy_study.

National Film Development Corporation. n.d. 'Cinema History'. Retrieved 11 February 2002, from http://www.nfdcindia.com/history.htm.

'Ordinance against eve-teasing issued'. 1999. *The Hindu*, 30 July. Retrieved 11 February 2002, from the Lexis-Nexis Academic Universe database, http://web.lexis-nexis.com/universe.

Pardun, C.J. 2002. 'Romancing the Script: Identifying the Romantic Agenda in Top-grossing Movies', in J.D. Brown, J.R. Steele and K. Walsh-Childers (eds), *Sexual Teens, Sexual Media: Investigating Media's Influence on Adolescent Sexuality*, pp. 211–25. Mahwah, NJ: Erlbaum.

Poudyal, R. 2002. 'Boys on Film: Challenging Masculinities in South Asia'. Retrieved 11 August 2002, from http://www.id21.org/society/6arp1.html.

Prasad, S. 1999. 'Medicolegal Response to Violence against Women in India', *Violence Against Women*, 5: 478–506.

Ram, A. 2002. 'Framing the Feminine: Diasporic Readings of Gender in Popular Indian Cinema', *Women's Studies in Communication*, 25 (1): 25–52.

Ravindran, V. 2001. 'Victims of Whims', *The Hindu*, 10 September. Retrieved 12 August 2002, from the Lexis-Nexis Academic Universe database, http://web.lexis-nexis.com/universe.

Russell, D.E. 1988. 'Pornography and Rape: A Causal Model', *Political Psychology*, 19: 41–73.

Scharrer, E. 2001. 'Tough Guys: The Portrayal of Hypermasculinity and Aggression in Televised Police Dramas', *Journal of Broadcasting and Electronic Media*, 45: 615–34.

———. 2002. 'Men, Muscles and Machismo: The Relationship between Television Violence Exposure and Aggression and Hostility in the Presence of Hypermasculinity', Media Psychology, 3: 159–88.

Schlenker, J.A., S.L. Caron and W.A. Halteman. 1998. 'A Feminist Analysis of Seventeen Magazine: Content Analysis from 1945 to 1995', *Sex Roles*, 38: 135–49.

Stevens, W.K. 1984. 'For Women of India, a Rite of Spring is Sour', *The New York Times*, 17 March, p. 24. Retrieved 11 February 2002, from the Lexis-Nexis Academic Universe Database, http://web.lexis-nexis.com/universe.

Ward, M. 1995. 'Talking about Sex: Common Themes about Sexuality in the Prime-time Television Programs Children and Adolescents View Most'. *Journal of Youth and Adolescence*, 24: 595–615.

West, J. 1996. 'Police "tease" is Slapped in Jail: India Applies the Law to Curb Gropers', *Sunday Telegraph*, 11 August. p. 25. Retrieved 11 February 2002, from the Lexis-Nexis Academic Universe database, http://web.lexis-nexis.com/universe.

Wood, J. 2001. 'The Normalization of Violence in Heterosexual Romantic Relationships: Women's Narratives of Love and Violence', *Journal of Social and Personal Relationships,* 18: 239–61.

Wood, E., C.Y. Senn, S. Desmarias, L. Park and N. Verberg. 2002. 'Sources of Information about Dating and Their Perceived Influence on Adolescents', *Journal of Adolescent Research*, 17: 401–17.

Zillmann, D. and B.S. Sapolsky. 1977. 'What Mediates the Effects of Mild Erotica on Annoyance and Hostile Behavior in Males?' *Journal of Personality and Social Psychology*, 35: 587–96.

Zillmann, D., and J. Weaver. 1989. 'Pornography and Men's Sexual Callousness Toward Women', in D. Zillmann and J. Bryant (eds), *Pornography: Research Advances and Policy Considerations*, pp. 95–126. Hillsdale, NJ: Erlbaum.

TWELVE

Packaging the Contemporary Woman in Television Fiction: Deconstructing the Role of 'Commerce' and 'Tradition'*

Centre for Advocacy and Research

Introduction

> *To the Indian mass media a woman's body is not only a locale for violence, exclusion and abuse but also the site for the construction of modernity and an upper-caste (Brahminical) Hindu nation. The 'new' woman is intrinsically related to the 'true' identity of the nation and hence it becomes necessary for the oppressive patriarchal tradition to patrol and monitor the woman's body and sexuality.*
> (Radhakrishnan 2001)

In her analysis of the media's coverage of women's news/issues and the women's movement within the broader socio-cultural and political scenario in Indian society, Bathla states,

> ... most of the issues facing women are missing on the media agenda and those which are covered are mainly event-oriented .... In event-oriented coverage, the structures that produce oppressive conditions for women are left unquestioned and 'issues' appear simply as 'accidents' or 'incidents' .... Media is not facilitating the endeavours of the (women's) movement to bring women's issues to the attention of policy-makers and the public. In other words, it does not act as 'agenda-setter' for women's issues and the movement thus also denying them participation in the democratic processes.' (Bathla 1998)

> While serials seem to have mechanistically absorbed the more topical or sensational aspects of issues which the women's movement has taken up .... There is no understanding in the serials of the systematic nature of women's oppression. The fundamental premise of the women's movement that the personal is political finds no echo. Issues, attitudes and radical re-articulations thrown up by the movement have been incorporated into the traditional ways of looking at the women's question. This process of assimilation not only tames oppositional ideas but creates the illusion that change has been affected. (Dhanraj 1994)

For a long time, both feminist scholars/activists as well as social scientists studying gender perspectives related to the media have been preoccupied with issues related to women and media representation. Their central concern has been the extreme marginalisation or deliberate trivialisation of women in the media.

*Originally published in *Economic and Political Weekly*, Vol. XXXVIII, No. 17, 26 April 2003: 1684–711.

Since the late 1990s, women are being drawn into the media in large numbers. They also constitute the central subject/object when it comes to media content and commercial media planning. Simultaneously, we find a continuing stereotypical portrayal of women on TV. Gender roles propagated by mass media still adhere to the patriarchal ideology of women as wives, mothers and daughters. Though contemporary and more modern situations/contexts are used in the narratives of the serials and advertisements, what remains unchanged is the representation of women within the traditional spaces of the household and patriarchy. All of this makes it imperative for us to re-read the messages that the media conveys to the viewer.

The Impact of Satellite Television

India first experienced the potential of satellite television during the 1982 Asian Games. It was to be almost a decade before Indian television underwent another revolutionary change: this was in 1992 when we watched CNN's coverage of the Gulf War via satellite dishes and cable TV connections. Since then, there has been no looking back. By 2002 there were an estimated 40+ million homes which had access to 50–70 cable and satellite channels. According to the National Readership Survey (NRS), cable and satellite sub-scription has now penetrated 50 per cent of all TV homes (www.indiantelevision.com, 2002).

Even as satellite TV has offered the Indian viewer access to a vast number of different channels and genres of programming 24 hours a day, it has also played a role in alerting transnational business to the size and potential of the Indian market. Privately-owned satellite TV channels have thus become the bulwark of a new consumerism. Unlike Doordarshan, which, as a government-funded public service broadcaster, has traditionally propagated the political and development ideology of the Indian state, private satellite TV channels appeal to the viewer as a consumer in a liberalised India where personal choice has become a new ideology. Satellite TV has opened the doors to new values, new attitudes and aspirations.

Satellite TV has also created an environment in which the audience is made to feel that it matters, and that it is a part of the content decision-making process. Viewers actively participate in TV debates, discussions with politicians, talk shows, musical events, talent shows, contests, etc. Page and Crawley (2001) have cited examples from their field surveys in which young girls and boys have expressed their desire to participate in shows, even if it is just as members of the audience. VJs from the music channels were definite reference points for style and fashion in music and dress, hairstyle, language, etc.

For their part, Hindi satellite entertainment channels have played an active role in the commodification of everyday life by stimulating interest in their characters' lifestyles, relationships, wealth, clothing, and the personal likes and dislikes of the stars. It has also played a significant role in bringing out into the open issues like human rights, women's rights, questions of choice and career, sexuality, and relations with others (ibid.).

Women and the Media

We can say without fear of contradiction that television is essentially a female bastion. One of the main offshoots of the phenomenal growth of satellite TV has been the media focus on women—both as a key target audience that needs to be delivered to the advertiser and as the main protagonists. Together, television and advertisers target women viewers, aggressively and with reason. The ratings of some of the more recent prime-time soaps[1] indicate a very high percentage of women viewers.[2] It has also been found that women are more 'regular' in TV viewing,[3] and that they are heavier consumers of cable television than men, which means that the 'modern' storylines of the soap operas are playing to very full female houses! Thus, 70 per cent of TV ad revenue target women directly, and prime-time television is dominated by women-oriented family soaps (*The Telegraph* 2003). Programming chiefs of popular TV channels concede that they keep women in mind when they fill in prime-time slots.

In a recent study by CFAR on responses of women to beauty ads on television,[4] women respondents from three cities stated that they get most of their information about products from TV ads. Television has created a range of spectator positions for women. A key finding was that the strongest personality perception and aspiration to emerge from women consumers in relation to ads featuring women are those depicting women as 'bold' and 'independent'. However, others categorised the same ads as depicting images that are 'sexy' 'glamorous' and denoting a desire for 'protection'.

Similarly, with TV serials/soaps, earlier Hindi soaps such as *Tara, Hasratein, Saans, Shanti*, and *Aurat* projected women in the different roles of wife, mother and homemaker. They also dealt with issues of working women, divorce, extra-marital relationships, sexual harassment, rape, abortion—and women fighting for their rights. More recent soaps like the highest-rated *Kahani Ghar Ghar Ki, Kyunki Saas Bhi Kabhi Bahu Thi, Kusum, Kasauti Zindagi Kay*, etc., have explored the notions of sexuality, violence and conflicts within the context of the family. The serials deal with issues women come across in their everyday life. While these serials do raise controversies (due to the stereotypes they reinforce), they also allow women from different strata and walks of life to identify with the same issues. The identification is not just at the level of consciousness, but also at the material level. Page and Crawley (2001) state that clients in beauty parlours specifically demand hairstyles from serials like *Surabhi, Shanti* and *Tara*. Ritu Dewra, the costume designer from serials like *Desh Mein Nikla Hoga Chand* and *Shagun*, says that viewers come to her asking for costumes worn by the female protagonists of these serials (*Dainik Bhaskar* 2003). Similarly, women are wearing accessories and jewellery similar to those worn by female protagonists of serials. For example, the distinctive *bindi*s worn by the character 'Ramola', played by Sudha Chandran, in *Kahin Kissi Roz* have become trendsetters among many women (*The Indian Express* 2003).

Theoretical Paradigm

The new consumer culture and spectator positions initiated by satellite television have thrown up for researchers and activists alike numerous possibilities on how we need to explore the emerging relationship between women as a key audience segment and the media. In earlier studies of mass media and communication, the audience-viewer relationship was defined as a passive-active one. However, this premise has been challenged and replaced by the active participation of audiences in selecting and often rejecting media messages.

The popularity and appeal of TV serials/soaps for a large section of people are derived from the fact that various genres and components/programmes are intrinsic to the socio-cultural experience of the audience (Kumar 1981). The interaction of audiences with the media is not in their capacity as isolated individuals, but as individuals who belong to different (interlocking) groups—family, language, religion, caste, class, political parties, professional associations, and the like. These groups exercise a strong influence on our thinking and behaviour. Audiences/viewers thus come with a 'social baggage'. They 'read' the messages of the media in terms of their own experiences; they 'negotiate' its various meanings, accepting or rejecting or 're-reading' the open and latent layers of meaning.

Faroukh Sheikh (noted actor), in an interview to *Lucknow Times* (*The Times of India* 2003), states that while he is sceptical about the impact of cinema on the public, TV allows for a strong identification. He finds that when he travels, people force him to go over even the smallest situation in *Ji Mantri Ji* (the serial he starred in), and though much of it is comic, they apparently insist on investing it with deeper meanings. Media must, therefore, be seen as a personalised product, to which each consumer gives the attribute they think it deserves. Realising this the producer factors in many fundamental susceptibilities—be it melodrama, conflict, stress, extreme exuberance, gaiety, nostalgia, search for identity, etc.—to create an internal, emotional, highly personalised and selective association to hook the viewer.

Over the years, feminists and others involved in the women's movement have brought the discourse surrounding politics within the family out into the public domain. Of late this discourse has also included the discrimination men face within the patriarchal structure.[5] Thus, the family is considered a site of domination, subordination and discrimination. The growing concern in the women's movement over the discriminatory nature of the family, especially towards women, has been accentuated by popular culture—films and entertainment TV. Feminists and others working for gender equality have accused both of playing a reactionary role as far as the portrayal and depiction of women and men are concerned.

However, media research must go beyond auditing media content from the perspective of quantifying acts of omission, bias, stereotyping, violations and distortions. We must consider how the media is able to create a day-to-day communication with a cross-section of the audience, and, in particular, with women living under very challenging and stressful circumstances, using tried and tested symbols, identifiable associations, safe narrative structures, and a mundane and everyday situational framework. How can these everyday engagements with the mass media shape and distort societal consciousness towards women and their position in the family? What do women perceive as their role? How much does that role perception influence their day-to-day discourse on rights, responsibilities and obligations within the family and outside?

'Responsibility' versus 'Rights'

The Centre for Advocacy and Research (CFAR) has been consistently monitoring and analysing television content since 1995. In our latest monitoring study on prime time Hindi soaps,[6] we found that the core structure of the daily soap is built around a repackaged and larger-than-life *Indian* (read Hindu) family. Feminists have regarded these soaps as an ideological tool, used by the media to reinforce the public's deep-seated traditional bearings and, in some instances, legitimise behavioural standards that are prejudicial to women. In many instances, television fiction employs the idiom of empowerment to draw attention to the day-to-day disagreements and conflicts that exist and develop between women and men, both within the family and outside it. This process, full of conflict, not only brings women to the forefront of the narrative, but also by default involves etching out the male characters and their reactions to the constant shifts in the pattern of responsibilities.

Upon closer examination we will find that the disagreements concern expanding and reclaiming the 'responsibilities' of the female character rather than her 'rights', so that the core values of patriarchy and male domination remain intact.

For example, in our ongoing study of the depiction and treatment of the aftermath of the rape of a blind girl by two of the family members in *Kahani Ghar Ghar Ki*, the daughters-in-law of the household have been depicted as very bold, independent, and fighting for justice for the rape victim, even if this means opposing their husbands and taking the issue of domestic violence to court. Their mother-in-law applauds them for preserving the family honour. However, underlying the applause and bravado is the reiteration of a woman and wife's traditional responsibility as the gatekeeper of honour, family values and norms. Thus, Maaji (mother) proclaims that the daughters-in-law are there to bring their husbands back on the right path if the latter go astray.

It is assumed that this process of re-affirming 'responsibilities' rather than 'rights' for women will find a greater groundswell of approval with women viewers. The popularity of these soaps amongst a cross-section of viewers—urban, small town, big town—led us to analyse why these soaps, which have been termed as highly regressive by those working for women's empowerment, enjoy deep engagements with viewers, and in many ways have even responded to viewers' emotional and psychological needs. Our research findings indicate that much of the popularity of these soaps comes from the manner in which the family is constructed. The family in TV fiction is shown at a crossroads: it is striving to maintain its traditional strengths within the strife of the post-modern era, where the only certainty is that everything is in a state of flux. In television drama serials, faith in the traditional values of the Indian family system has been renewed in a number of ways—from the dress codes to the central issues addressed by the serials. However, the process of reasserting the values of the traditional family through a series of conflicts and disagreements exposes its inherent hypocrisies and gender biases against women. Are we then stating that such representations are pro-women? Are we implying that serial producers endorse modernity and change? No. A closer scrutiny of the texts will reveal that tradition is depicted as being more in harmony with an Indian woman's persona and needs. What is being stressed is the need to rediscover and reinvent tradition in order to bring about the 'right' kind of 'change'.

The problem with this approach is the way 'change' is packaged. In the packaging process the family is constantly under threat. The conflicts within the family and their resolution lie at the core of the narratives. These narratives follow a dialectic process by which tradition undergoes a sort of modern *agnipariksha* (In the mythology, *Ramayana*, after being rescued from the clutches of King Ravana, Sita, the wife of king Rama, was asked to step into fire and prove her chastity. She came out unburned and was declared pure. Though originally a test that women were put through, it has become a symbolic ritual that is used to test the 'purity' of anything of concern.) and comes out with its fingers burnt but more resilient, albeit changed. TV fiction uses 'traditional spokespersons' (normally an older family member or a chosen younger one), traditional methods of family bonding, and rituals and customs like fasting in a contemporary situation to resolve issues. Thus, it is important for us to engage with this packaging process which represents the family in a mode of transition, a transition that works towards re-establishing the traditional family with all its gender and power constructs.

Depiction of Women

The pivotal characters in most serials are females. They are repositories of how 'Things Are Done' in the husband's family. Parvati's role in *Kahani Ghar Ghar Ki* illustrates the point. She is the perfect wife, daughter-in-law, mother, sister-in-law, etc. She must look after the entire extended family and does so with astonishing élan. Again and again the women work to restore the core values of the family, which are threatened by one or other member of the family.

At a superficial level, the family in TV serials is pro-active in its attitude towards women. Many female characters are shown to be authoritative, some deliberately scheming and manipulative, but seldom openly submissive. However, for all their assertiveness, female characters display all the traditional trappings: from their saris and *bindi*s to their fasting rituals and *pooja*s, observation of daily courtesies and protocols, and family celebrations. This is precisely where the packaging occurs.[7]

In most serials we can broadly observe a return to a fairly rigid gender characterisation along the expected stereotypes of women and men. Thus, in terms of distribution along geographical space, the serials reassert that a woman's place is in the home. It is both her life and her domain. Approximately 80 per cent of the female characters are confined to the kitchen, living room, dining room and bedrooms (see Table 12.1). They enter the professional space only when they have to save their spouses or family from the clutches of others (e.g., Parvati in *Kahani Ghar Ghar Ki* moved out of her marital family and joined Pallavi—the 'bad' woman and her sister-in-law— in order to destroy the latter so that her husband Om and his family could regain what was rightfully theirs).

TABLE 12.1
Gender Representation Across Location

Location		Presentation		
	Male		Female	
Sitting room	38	38%	33	32.67%
Dining space	9	9%	10	9.90%
Bed room	19	19%	22	21.78%
Kitchen	1	1%	7	6.93%
House compound	6	6%	7	6.93%
House corridor	1	1%	2	1.98%
Public space	18	18%	17	16.83%
Office	8	8%	3	2.97%
Total	**100**	**100%**	**101**	**100%**

Notes: Male representation within the premise of the home is 74 per cent.
  Female representation within the premise of the home is 80.19 per cent.

Moreover, this affirmation of the traditional is portrayed as an expression of consumer choice rather than compulsion. In the serial *Kusum* (Sony), the eponymous female protagonist refuses to attend to any of her professional chores on the day she fasts. Even when her husband insists she break the fast by midnight, she refuses: 'Your well being is the only reason I go to the temple and fast. I will only eat at daybreak'. As long as the women represent tradition they can be strong, assertive and the point of power in the serial. In portraying them as strong, 'active' personalities, the producers lend them a veneer of modernity—another aspect of the packaging process.

Conflict as a Contemporary Hook

Any meaningful qualitative analysis of the depiction and treatment of gender in television fiction needs to be conducted in the context of the core structure of the narrative. The drama serial, especially daily soaps, thrive on the generation of conflict and its eventual resolution. This is the source of suspense, the 'hook', which holds the viewers' attention captive. In this area of conflict resides the family, which is constantly under threat from the deceit and ambitions of its individual members. Over 80 per cent of the scenes from the monitored samples dealt with conflicts concerning the family, and over 50 per cent were specifically related to marriage (see Table 12.2).

TABLE 12.2
Break-up of Issue

Issues	Frequency		Frequency of Conflict	
In and around marriage (affecting family)	92	73.6%	57	61.4%*
Issues concerning family (other than marriage)	24	19.2%	7	21.9%**
Others (career, business deals, drug racket, potential love affair)	9***	7.2%	–	–

Notes: Frequency scene-wise (125 scenes)
    *Out of 92 scenes
    **Out of 24 scenes
    ***Out of the 9 scenes 4 dealt with purely professional relationships

Within this narrative the structure of the family is pivotal. The family on TV is almost invariably a joint family, primarily Hindu. This joint family is predominantly a male construct. The women's families are largely absent from the screen—in *Kyunki Saas Bhi Kabhi Bahu Thi* and *Kahani Ghar Ghar Ki* the daughters-in-law have absentee families. Serials such as *Koshish Ek Aasha, Kutumb, Heena,* and *Saanjjhi* see women with parents, but no other family. The female protagonist in *Kohi Apna Sa, Kyunki Saas Bhi Kabhi Bahu Thi, Koshish,* and *Kahani Ghar Ghar Ki,* have either single parents—a widower or widow—or have been brought up by a grandmother or aunt. In *Kahin Kissi Roz,* the lead female character, Shaina, is an orphan. Thus, the joint or extended family which dominates Hindi serials is essentially the family of the lead male characters, and the women are defined only in terms of their husbands' families. Once they have entered their marital home, they leave their past behind. Women have no discrete universe of their own.

This centrality of the traditional, joint/extended family is also played out through the depiction of geographical space. Over 30.8 per cent of all scenes in the monitoring sample (15 episodes) occur in the central sitting room (often in the presence of the entire family), 26.47 per cent of scenes take place in the bedroom (see Table 12.3). This occupation of the central space in the house and TV frame is symbolic of the family's premier position in serials, especially those by Balaji Telefilms: *Kyunki...., Kahani...., Kkusum, Kutumb, Kasauti Zindagi Kay,* and *Kohi Apna Sa.*

TABLE 12.3
Space Distribution (Scene-wise)

Location	Frequency	
Sitting room	42	30.88%
Dining space	15	11.02%
Bed room	36	26.47%
Kitchen	4	2.94%
House compound	8	5.88%
House corridor	2	1.47%
Public space	19	13.97%
Office	10	7.35%
Total	**136**	**100%**

Note: 78.66 per cent of the locations are within the premise of the house.

The joint family consists of couples who inhabit their own separate units, but come together to resolve all issues. There is a great blurring of the public and the private. In *Kohi Apna Sa,* the entire family is summoned by the grandfather to discuss his grandson's marriage to a woman of his choice, as opposed to the family's candidate. The entire family—his sons and their wives, his grandsons and their wives, etc.—gather in the central hall, or drawing room. Interestingly, each couple is thereafter shown to discuss the issue within the confines of their individual rooms. This movement from the collective space of the central living room to the individual domain of the bedroom is part of the packaging process. The individual space represents modernity, while the collective space represents tradition. However, the dominant space is the collective. It is this collective force that is reinforced again and again as the family asserts itself over and above the individual. Family is, therefore, the key site of the narrative. It is critical to assess how within the family structure the conflicts, the marital discords, and flare-ups between members of the family are treated, and the manner in which the family intervenes to resolve them.

In the above-mentioned example of *Kohi Apna Sa*, a daily soap on Zee TV, the personal decision by a male protagonist (Rahul) to marry a woman he loves rather than settle for a nominee of the family leads to a major conflagration in the family. The dramatisation of this conflict intersperses both tradition as well as contemporary issues. The conflict over the marriage is dramatised in such a manner that it is represented not as an inter-generational war, but a violent conflict among peers and cousins, all of whom are young men. The conflict spreads to the mothers of the men, and the extended family is involved in internal strife. Tradition is used to resolve it. For instance, as we saw earlier, the main scene takes place in the presence of the larger extended family, with the head of the family presiding over it. The hierarchical roles are maintained: the older siblings are the most authoritative, the sons take on the defence of their mothers, and their wives are either silenced or told not to meddle in matters.

Given the strict division of the family along hierarchical lines, the elders are the founts of wisdom and authority in the family. The grandfather, the grandmother, and then the mother and father use their position as elders to assert their will within a contemporary paradigm. However, it is packaged in a manner that enables the defenders of tradition to co-opt modern values. Thus, in *Kohi Apna Sa* it is the grandfather who decides that the new wife (Priyanka) should live in her marital home on the grounds that she is not being accorded the respect a daughter-in-law deserves. The decision of the grandfather is final, and there is no question of anyone challenging it.

In a fundamental issue such as marriage, it is the men who retain their 'rights'. In our example, the young man's decision to marry is challenged, but he is not deprived of his personal rights. It is the new wife who is stripped of hers. Her mother is unwilling to let her stay in her home, her husband is not in a position to bring her into his home, and at no point does she assert her right to her husband's home as his lawfully-wedded wife. There is no attempt to empower the woman or the young couple. The aim is to reaffirm the family, and not disturb the status quo or the entrenched norms and values. However, this is done in a manner that (at least superficially) fuses modernity with tradition in order to be acceptable to the urban middle-class viewer, who forms the bulk of the audience for these serials.

The women in the narrative structure of the soaps are either the victims of the conflicts within the family, or the agents of its troubles. The family conflict plays either upon their vulnerability, or on their hegemonic role as perpetrators. In two episodes of *Kyunki Saas Bhi Kabhi Bahu Thi* we are constantly reminded of the 'stability' and 'precariousness' of marital relationships. On one hand, the episodes dramatise the sense of marital fulfilment experienced by the elderly couple (Baa and Babuji). On the other hand, Gayatri (one of the daughters-in-law of the Virani family) is determined to break up the marriage of her son (Hemant) on the grounds that the daughter-in-law (Pooja) is a *manglik*—an astrologically incompatible sign for the marital partner.

The characters are shown discussing the matter openly among themselves and as separate units—Gayatri and her husband (JD), Gayatri and Hemant, JD and Hemant, Hemant and his wife (Pooja). The men—be it the father or the son—remain unconvinced of Gayatri's position. However, they decide that it would be difficult to bring the women around (woman viewers are deliberately co-opted in this decision). They neither vehemently oppose the women, nor actively support them. Pooja, the woman at the centre of this persecution, prefers to depend on the quiet resistance of her husband rather than demand her rights or assert her beliefs. The men's evasive attitude and the woman's passivity are constructed in such a way that passivity appears to be the 'intelligent' way of dealing with the problem. It legitimises the harassment and violations that are inflicted on the daughter-in-law and, to a lesser extent, on the son. The underlying notion is that the family has the prescriptive right to test and try the 'compatibility' of the couple to protect itself from any 'adverse' or 'malefic' influences.

Conclusion

- The family is being packaged and marketed as a 'dynamic entity' that allows for continuity and change. There is no contradiction here. The fusion is achieved through a constant dialectic between the two. The family is first presented as the 'ideal'. Then, through a series of conflicts, the family is undermined and threatened. In the process many aspects of the family and its relationships are minutely explored and exposed.

- Within this narrative structure (with conflict as the hook), both traditional as well as modern symbols are used. There is a deliberate selection of values, some affirmed, and some dismissed, and change is 'packaged' to ensure a convenient degree of modification whereby the family as an institution remains unchallenged, even though individuals may be affected in different ways.

- The packaging process involves incorporating the past and present, the old and new, tradition and modernity, in a lived fashion. Viewers are locked into family relationships of their own, which are often mirrored in these serials. The family drama deconstructs the family and reveals the enormous pressures it faces in a modern context. This type of familiar representation of the family and the characters is one of the main levels of engagement viewers have with these serials.

Owing to the identification with the situational engagements, viewers' identification with the images/representations is both at the material level and at the level of consciousness. In this day-to-day representation, viewers find new values, aspirations and spectator positions. Given this type of identification with the serials—where gender constructs are reinforced along stereotypical lines despite their being cloaked in the garb of modernity; where, in the process of initiating consumer culture, programme-makers and channel executives ignore the impact this type of identification can have on viewers when it comes to family, marriage and individual rights—it becomes important for us to actively engage in their deconstruction.

The serial producers' insistence on the depiction of everything, be it marriage, sexuality or even the generation gap, mainly in terms of the family, prevents TV narratives from exploring gender issues in the modern context. Unless we understand the process of how content is packaged, it is difficult to assess viewers' response or engagement with it. Also, any critique of content will not prove useful unless we are also able to understand what viewers encourage producers to create. The deconstruction needs to be done through an analysis of the situational context rather than through the storyboard. Decoding the contextual structure of these family dramas needs to be done if we want to use the television as a powerful instrument for raising consciousness about 'gender rights'.

Notes

1. *Kahani Ghar Ghar Ki* (Star Plus), *Kyunki Saans Bhi Kabhi Bahu Thi* (Star Plus), *Kasauti Zindagi Kay* (Star Plus), *Desh Mein Nikla Hoga Chand* (Star Plus), *Kehta Hain Dil* (Star Plus).
2. According to TAM ratings, for the week ending 1 February 2003, in the Hindi belt the percentage of female viewers (of their selected sample) above the age of 15 is as follows: *Kahani Ghar Ghar Ki*—22.89, *Kyunki Saas Bhi Kabhi Bahu Thi*—20.61, *Kasauti Zindagi Kay*—21.44, *Desh Mein Nikla Hoga Chand*—24.16 and *Kehta Hain Dil*—16.18. In comparison, the male and female viewership taken together bring down the percentage of viewership. This indicates the low viewership among males. According to TAM ratings, for the same time period, in the Hindi belt the percentage of male and female viewers above the age of 15 (of their selected sample) taken together is as follows: *Kahani Ghar Ghar Ki*—19.84, *Kyunki Saas Bhi Kabhi Bahu Thi*—18.09, *Kasauti Zindagi Kay*—16.49, *Desh Mein Nikla Hoga Chand*—18.99 and *Kehta Hain Dil*—14.82.
3. In a study of viewing habits by Media Advocacy Group (renamed as Centre for Advocacy and Research), published in May 1994.
4. A survey on responses to beauty ads on TV was conducted by CFAR in September 2001 in Delhi, Ahmedabad and Lucknow amongst students (25 per cent), homemakers (25 per cent) and working women (50 per cent). The sample consisted of an equal representation of married and unmarried women across socio-economic categories. The survey was conducted amongst 300 respondents between the age group 16–30 years.
5. In the gender discourse, studies on men have stated that within the paradigm of masculinity, certain forms of masculinity are constructed as the hegemonic type, and the others are subordinate or variant types. Within the family it is the role of men as breadwinner and father that is considered the hegemonic types. Adolescent boys and young men are subordinated to this hegemonic type (Almeida 1996; Dasgupta 2002; Kandiyoti 1994; Mitchell 1994; Osella and Osella 1998).
6. CFAR, along with ASMITA (Nepal) and PROSHIKA (Bangladesh), conducted a monitoring research study of 50 hours and 30 minutes (101) episodes of prime-time fiction during the early months of 2002. In all, 52 episodes from satellite TV channels and 49 episodes from terrestrial channels were monitored. Along with this, 15 episodes across nine prime-time serials were qualitatively monitored. The data in this chapter pertains to the 15 episodes. The figures are approximate values. It should be noted that though the total number of scenes across the 15 episodes is 125, while calculating the data scenes have been recounted to show the diversity of issues, relationships, conflicts, locations, etc. The characters that have been taken for providing data are the characters that are relevant to particular episodes.
7. The 'packaging process' does not exclude men. In most cases of conflict the men perform their role to maintain the balance in the family, while it is the women who are the main sources of imbalance. In playing out this role in the world of TV fiction, a man's position is also in the confines of the house. Over 70 per cent are shown within the household premises (see Table 12.1). Importantly, being portrayed as victims or oppressed is not a woman's prerogative. Often, a male character who is forced into a contract or compromise marriage is depicted as being as much a victim as the woman. Anurag Basu in *Kasauti Zindagi Kay*, Abhay and Yash in *Kkusum*, and Sameer in *Heena* have to act against their own wishes and marry girls of their parents'/grandparents' choice due to the ill-health of or pressure from the latter.

References

Almeida, Miguel Vale de. 1996. *The Hegemonic Male: Masculinity in a Portuguese Town.* Oxford: Bergham Books. Providence.

Bathla, Sonia. 1998. *Women, Democracy and the Media: Cultural and Political Representations in the Indian Press.* New Delhi: Sage Publications.

Dasgupta, Chaitali. 2002. 'The Neighbourhood Boys Club', in Radhika Chopra (ed.), *From Violence to Supportive Practice: Family, Gender and Masculinities in India.* United Nations Development Fund for Women (UNIFEM), New Delhi: South Asia Regional Office.

Dhanraj, Deepa. 1994. 'A Critical Focus', in Ammu Joseph and Kalpana Sharma (eds), *Whose News? The Media and Women's Issues.* New Delhi: Sage Publications.

Indiantelevision.com, 2002. 'Urbanites spend less time in front of telly—NRS 2002', in indiantelevision.com's Breaking News. Posted on 17 June 2002. http://www.indiantelevision.com/headlines/y2k2/june/june65.htm.

Kandiyoti, Deniz. 1994. 'The Paradoxes of Masculinity: Some Thoughts on Segregated Societies', in A. Cornwall and N. Lindisfarne (eds), *Dislocating Masculinity: Comparative Ethnography*. London and New York: Routledge.

Kumar, J. Keval. 1981. *Mass Communication in India*. Bombay, Delhi, Bangalore, Calcutta, Hyderabad, Madras: Jaico Publishing House.

Krishnamurthy, Ajanta. 2003. 'Remote Control', *The Telegraph*, 18 January.

Mitchell, Jon P. 1998. 'Performance of Masculinity in a Maltese Festa', in F. Hughes-Freeland and Mary M. Crain, *Recasting Ritual: Performance, Media, Identity*. London and New York: Routledge.

Nandini. 2003. 'Sajte hain serial Ritu Dewra kay kapro mein', *Dainik Bhaskar*, 30 January.

Osella, Caroline and Filippo, Osella. 'Friendship and Flirting: Micro-politics in Kerala, South India' in *The Journal of the Royal Anthropological Institute*: 4(2).

Page, David and William Crawley. 2001. *Satellites Over South Asia: Broadcasting Culture And The Public Interest*. New Delhi: Sage Publications.

Radhakrishnan, Chitra. 2001. 'The Image of Women in Indian Television'. *Women in Action*, No. 1. http://www.isiswomen.org/pub/wia/wia101/media.html.

S.S. Singh. 2003. 'Ramola Is A Trendsetter', *The Indian Express*, 6 January.

Devanshi Seth. 2003. 'Films Can Never Reform Society', *The Times of India*, 21 February.

Annexure–I

The following article is part of a Seminar Report titled 'Towards Empowerment? A Regional Initiative on Women and Media', 2002, conducted by the Centre for Advocacy and Research (New Delhi), PROSHIKA (Bangladesh), ASMITA (Nepal), and supported by the Japan Foundation.

Project Team

Centre for Advocacy and Research, India
Akhila Sivadas
Meeta Parti
Shyamala Shiveshwarkar
Rizwan Parwez
Chaitali Dasgupta
Maithreyee Saha
Sandhya M.

PROSHIKA, Bangladesh:
Nargis Jahan Banu

Bangladesh Centre for Development Journalism and Communication:
Md. Nayeemul Islam

ASMITA, Nepal:
Manju Thapa

Research Advisors:
Shailaja Bajpai, Media Critic and Columnist
Shubhra Gupta, Media Critic
Udita Das, Data Analyst

Published by:

Centre for Advocacy and Research, F-19, 3rd Floor, Kalkaji, New Delhi-110019.
telefax: 011-26292787, 26430133, 26229631.
E-mail: cfarasam@ndf.vsnl.net.in

Annexure-II

Brief storylines of the serials mentioned in the article.

(The storylines pertain to the period of the research. Some of the serials have been taken off air or their storylines have changed subsequently.)

Serial: Kohi Apna Sa
Channel: Zee TV
Production House: Balaji Telefilms

By a quirk of fate, three childhood friends, Khushi, Shruti and Sanjana, marry three brothers in the same extended family. The economic status of the three units, which reside under one roof, differs dramatically. The three girls also come from varying backgrounds. Khushi belongs to an upper-class family and is married to the richest of the brothers. Shruti, an orphan who lives with a widowed aunt, marries the least affluent brother. Sanjana, the only friend who is shown to be working, marries the young brother, whose family belongs to the professional middle class.

Kohi Apna Sa is the story of these three friends and how their relationship withstands the stresses of their situation in their married home.

Serial: Kutumb
Channel: Sony
Production House: Balaji Telefilms

Kutumb starts off as a campus romance with Pratham and Gauri indulging in the typical '*nok-jhonk*' so familiar to us from Hindi movies. The name of the game is humiliation, and Pratham does his best to put out Gauri. After one trick too many, Gauri and Pratham have to marry in order to 'save' Gauri's 'honour'.

On their wedding night, Gauri announces that the game has just begun, that their marriage is not the end, but the beginning of Pratham's miseries. Gauri does not allow him to touch her, and gives him an earful whenever he tries to get near her, but maintains a very cordial relationship with his family. Her mother-in-law becomes her best ally. Much to Pratham's displeasure, she encourages Gauri to continue with college.

Serial: Kkusum
Channel: Sony
Production House: Balaji Telefilms

Kkusum, a young middle-class girl who earns her living as a lowly employee in a big construction firm, is 'selected' by the firm owner's wife to be her daughter-in-law because of her strong 'kundali'. Mrs. Kapoor believes that Kkusum's luck will save her son Abhay from all potential dangers. Much against Abhay's wishes, the marriage is contracted for one year. However, Kkusum, with her pliant nature and devotion, wins his friendship. They become friends and colleagues at work, and things are going smoothly till Esha walks into their life. She starts off with being Kkusum's friend, but soon betrays Kkusum's trust and becomes sexually involved with Abhay.

Serial: Kahani Ghar Ghar Ki
Channel: Star Plus
Production House: Balaji Telefilms

A family drama drawn on the lines of the great epic Ramayana. Om and Parvati, the eldest son and daughter-in-law of the family, are the thread which keeps the family together.

Serial: Kyunki Saas Bhi Kabhi Bahu Thi
Channel: Star Plus
Production House: Balaji Telefilms

A family drama set in a Gujarati business family. It tells the tale of the Viranis—Babuji and Baa with their children, grandchildren, and now great-grandchildren.

Serial: Kasauti Zindagi Kay
Channel: Star Plus
Production House: Balaji Telefilms

A family drama set in a Bengali media family. It is a tale of two lovers—Anurag and Prema. Anurag succumbs to his mother's pressure and marries Komolika. Torn between love and 'duty', the story of the two lovers goes on.

Serial: Kahin Kissi Roz
Channel: Star Plus
Production House: Balaji Telefilms

The story begins with Shaina, an orphan, marrying Kunal from the Sikand family. Strange things happen after she comes into the house. The story is full of suspense. Upon making inquiries Shaina comes to know that her husband had been married earlier to another woman, who had apparently died in a fire. As the story unfolds, the truth comes out in the open—it was Ramola Sikand, Kunal's stepmother, who had set fire to his earlier wife for money. However, the girl had not died, and instead the maid in the kitchen had. It turns out that Shaina is actually Kunal's first wife who goes through cosmetic surgery and returns to avenge her attempted murder. Initially Shaina suspects her husband for having tried to murder her as she had seen his former girlfriend's car outside their house when the kitchen had caught fire. She confides in Ramola, but later comes to know that it was Ramola who had tried to kill her. From this point begins the *saas-bahu* war. The story moves on with Kunal and Shaina going against Ramola Sikand. Ramola Sikand decides to kill Kunal and brings in his lookalike, a village lad.

Serial: Heena
Channel: Sony
Production House: RT Entertainment

Sweet, docile Heena is rejected by her husband on their wedding night because he is in love with another woman. However, with great endurance, she tries to win over Sameer with her determination to be a good wife. She remains in character even when Sameer divorces her, and she is offered a proposal of marriage by Akram, her husband's friend. She accepts the proposal and marries Akram, but is shown to have residual feelings for Sameer. Akram is shown as suspecting Heena of softening towards Sameer. Heena, the 'perfect wife', neither raises her voice nor tries to clarify anything. She just suffers in silence.

Serial: Saanjjhi
Channel: Zee TV
Producer: Neena Gupta

Middle-aged, childless 'thakur' Amar Singh is persuaded into taking a 'second wife' in the hope of an heir. Kanak, his 'barren' wife, resolves to make the much younger Hansa (who marries because in exchange Amar promises to free her father from debt) miserable. She treats the younger woman with acute hostility, and employs all sorts of ruses to make Hansa give up and run away. But she fails, and Hansa sticks on. The 'thakur' tries to strike a balance between the two women. He doesn't want to deprive his first wife of her 'wifely rights', and gives her physical and emotional attention. At the same time he tries to protect Hansa from Kanak's wrath.

Serial: Koshish Ek Aasha
Channel: Zee TV
Production House: Balaji Telefilms

A young girl, Kajal, is tricked into marrying a 'mentally retarded' man. She rebels, but is forced to remain with him because of her concern for her mother's illness. Soon she discovers that her husband's illness was 'curable', but that his stepmother had been trying to prevent his recovery in order to safeguard the interests of 'her own' children. Kajal vows to fight for her husband's rights.

Section IV

Neo-liberal Globalisation

At the heart of neo-liberal globalisation are two important issues—economics and culture. The earliest icons of this unfolding transformation were McDonalds and Coca-Cola, symbolising what India's new landscape would look like. Penetrating deeper into the Indian psyche and social fabric were corporate-led international beauty pageants and, more recently, the celebration of Valentine's Day. Outwardly celebrating beauty, talent and romance, these Western-inspired commercial ventures are a backlash against feminism, and a gift-wrapped neo-traditional push towards unequal gender relations. This heady mix of commerce, culture and new gender agreements await research from scholars. In the meantime, some research effort has been directed towards more piecemeal and uni-dimensional aspects of this change.

The impact of neo-liberal policies on urban and rural women has been sparsely documented. Evidence from a number of countries has shown that export-led growth has created wage employment for women in substantial numbers. Their income, quality of life, and status have improved. However, gender parity in terms of wages and other benefits has not got better (Swamy 2004). Besides poor working conditions put women's health and safety at risk, and directives against unionisation weaken employees' bargaining power. Economic globalisation exacerbates the situation created by economic reforms, and produces stark inequalities within and between nation-states. It also aggravates pre-existing occupational segregation by gender, and in this shifting occupational structure, while educated English-speaking women have benefited with the opening of new jobs in the IT software sector and IT-enabled services sector, they are ghettoised at the low end of the value chain. The banking and financial sectors followed by the media and service sectors such as tourism have also opened new job opportunities for women, but this again is confined to a sub-set of urban women.

Coming on the heels of economic globalisation has been cultural globalisation, especially the entry of new media. The media not only reflects realities, but also constructs new ones. *Baywatch* beauties and desperate housewives may now co-exist with *saas* and *bahu*. The globalisation of the Indian media has meant that the portrayal of women has changed. Advertisements, for example, register a shift from representing women as homemakers and mothers to portraying women as sex objects (objects of consumption) on the one hand, and as avid consumers of global goods and services on the other. The sprinkling of professionals point to the emergence of a new westernised, tech-savvy, globally aspiring middle-class woman. Media, with its need for corporate advertising support and pressure to increase readership/viewership, maintain a competitive edge and, to appear to be seemingly moving with the times, has spawned a western-inspired culture of health, beauty, fitness and fashion that many young women aspire for, but have difficulty keeping up with. The pursuit of unrealistic ideals has transformed women's self-image and body consciousness, a body which until recently they were taught to ignore or be ashamed of, but which is now placed at the centre of their psyches.

As the world becomes a global village, common issues confront all nation-states. Issues such as peace, poverty, environmental degradation, climate change and HIV/AIDS, highlighted at the World Social Forum (WSF) and the World Economic Forum (WEF) held at the beginning of 2006, are closely tied to gender and women's issues. To take one example, HIV/AIDS started as a disease affecting gay men, but sex workers were soon implicated, and now it is the unwary housewife who is most likely to fall victim to it. Globalisation and its negative side-effects have been ushered in at the behest of multinational corporations, and some members at the two world forums have clearly made them accountable for cleaning up the mess.

Section four is named Neo-liberal Globalisation, and the first chapter, 'Showcasing India: Gender, Geography and Globalisation', is by Rupal Oza. It examines the 1996 Miss World beauty contest, with a focus on the protests that characterised this event. The author argues that in response to India's globalisation effort, these protests appealed to a commitment to the nation-state, and revealed the manner in which women and sexuality became inseparable from imagining India in the discourses of both the supporters and the opponents of the contest. Sharmila Rege in her chapter 'More than Just Tacking Women on the "Macro-Picture": Feminist Contributions to Globalisation Discourses' expounds the theoretical underpinnings and origins of three debates on globalisation, and looks at the distinctive feminist contributions to these debates. The author recommends integrating gender into the discourse of globalisation, and not just stapling women on its macro-structural models. Rina Bhattacharya in her study 'Gender and Employment in the Context of Globalisation: Some Facts and Figures' describes the scenario of women's employment and unemployment status flowing from the structural adjustment policies and India's subsequent globalisation. She argues that indicators such as workforce participation rate, employment status, the growing number of women in the unorganised sector, all point to the marginalisation of women. She concludes that while the work participation rate among women is on the rise, the opportunities fall short of expectations. The chapter 'Globalisation and Women in India in the Nineties' by Gabriele Dietrich is from the perspective of activists in the women's movement working with marginalised groups, especially women. The author presents the overall economic, political and cultural climate in the 1990s, and provides findings of alternative surveys, which debunk some of the government's claims about economic growth. The focus on profit-driven growth coupled with militarisation and communalisation has jeopardised people's right to a livelihood. The chapter ends with a feminist critique of capitalist development, and suggestions for alternative development models.

Reference

Swamy, Gurushri. 2004. 'International Trade and Women', *Economic and Political Weekly*, 6 November: 4885–89.

THIRTEEN

Showcasing India: Gender, Geography and Globalisation*

Rupal Oza

On a cool late November evening in Bangalore, India, a city held under siege by a 12,500-strong security contingent, Irene Skliva from Greece was crowned Miss World 1996. Since August of 1996, when it was announced that India was to host the Miss World pageant, controversy and debate had surrounded the issue. Members of political parties and particular national and local women's organisations, farmers, students, and trade unions from various parts of the country demonstrated, wrote petitions, filed public interest litigations in court, and threatened to damage the venue of the pageant. Opposition to the pageant spanned a broad enough spectrum to accommodate an entire range of concerns. For instance, opposition to imperialism, resentment against the retreating role of the state, high inflation, threatened Indian culture, and an anxiety with the 'foreign', all crystallised in response to the pageant. Conversely, for the state and domestic capital the pageant provided an international opportunity to 'showcase' the new, liberalised India to the world. The pageant, therefore, was a site at which political protest and anxiety with 'globalisation' as well as the opportunity to showcase India to the world were articulated. It is in this tension between sentiments of proving national worth on the one hand, and the protests against the pageant on the other that I examine the staging of discourses of gender, nation, sexuality and place in this chapter.

A month prior to the event, in the *The Times of India*, a major English-language newspaper, an advertisement for the pageant read, 'the time has come for the world to see ... what real India is all about, Indian hospitality, Indian culture, Indian beauty, Indian capability'.[1] What is striking about the advertisement is the statement that 'real' India—its capability and culture—will be showcased through an international beauty pageant. Recent work on beauty pageants, rather than dismissing these events as misogynist cultural kitsch, reveals that 'these contests showcase values, concepts, and behavior that exist at the center of a group's sense of itself and exhibit values of morality, gender, and place' (Cohen et al. 1996: 2). Pageants are spectacles whose performances showcase the important ways in which gender and sexuality are linked with geography. Whether pageants are performed at the national scale, such as the Miss America Pageant (Banet-Weisner 1999), or as local community events (Wu 1997), they are remarkably similar in the ways in which they link gender and sexual identity with particular places.

In this chapter, I examine the 1996 Miss World beauty pageant and, in particular, the protests that marked the event. While the pageant itself showcased gender and the nation, I am more concerned with the way in which the protests invoked a fidelity to nation and place in response to globalisation. There are three analytical tasks with which I engage: first, I explore the way in which the pageant signified globalisation in India

*Originally published in *SIGNS*, Vol. 26, No. 4, Summer, 2001, pp. 1067–96. Reprinted with permission from the University of Chicago Press.

and became the target of local opposition; second, I trace the politics of opposition and its attempts to redefine the nation in globalisation; and third, I reveal the manner in which gender and sexuality became inextricable from imagining contemporary India in the rhetoric of the supporters of as well as the opposition to the pageant.

The pageant provides an excellent empirical opportunity to examine the contours of globalisation and local opposition in India. Rather than implicitly endorsing local opposition to globalisation, I argue for a critical understanding of the formation of 'the local' in the politics of opposition. Within anthropology, Akhil Gupta and James Ferguson (1997) have argued the need to destabilise and denaturalise the fixity of place, identity and culture. Drawing on this assessment in combination with geographical literature on space, I critically examine how opposing groups' ideological and political positions manifest themselves by considering 'place' as fixed and bounded.[2] Towards this effort, then, I examine the ways in which opposition to the pageant employed a politics of place, whereby local opposition was spatially manifested as preserving the nation against the larger forces of globalisation. In so doing, the nation in opposition to globalisation rested on deeply problematic constructions of gender and sexuality. Three problems arose from these constructions. First, women's bodies and sexuality became the material and discursive sites where the nation was performed, values were contested, and borders and boundaries were policed and controlled.[3] Second, the nation's resistance to globalisation was structured on and through maintaining oppressive gender and sexual codes. Such oppositional praxis alerts us to the ways in which some structures may 'borrow' from each other, at times across different scales, to perpetuate structures that are oppressive to women.[4] Finally, the formulation of such oppositional praxis reinforced the idea that spaces such as the nation or the global are discrete and fixed 'places', rather than persistently dynamic and mutable.

I begin with a brief outline of the analytical category of globalisation and suggest the way that the pageant was considered iconic of globalisation in India. Next, I outline the rhetoric that the organisers and the state used to support the pageant, primarily as a vehicle to showcase the 'new' India to the world. It is here that the nation is reconstructed primarily as Hindu, and gendered in terms of masculine capability and feminine compassion. If the support of the pageant sought to create a fixed identity of the nation in globalisation, in the opposition to the pageant this was further evident. In this section, I examine the opposition stemming from those allied with feminist and other progressive groups, and those allied with the Hindu right-wing political party, the Bharatiya Janata Party (BJP). Finally, I dismantle the fixed notion of place and nation that emerged in the rhetoric of the supporters and the opposition in the face of globalisation. I argue that this fixed notion had to do with a concern for belonging and an attempt to fortify against border crossings, which is indicative of an anxiety with sexual transgression in globalisation. I suggest that a more nuanced understanding of geography and globalisation will open opportunities for oppositional politics that preclude considering place and position as fixed and immutable, and local resistance as always subversive. The political concern with such a project is that of formulating a nuanced politics of opposition, one that is responsive to both the possibilities and predicaments that globalisation generates.[5]

The research for this chapter was conducted in 1996 over a period of four months preceding and during the Miss World pageant in Bangalore. I interviewed officials, participants, organisers, set designers, and several opposing groups. In addition, I drew on the extensive media coverage in newspapers and magazines, and on ethnographic observations of the pageant. As a researcher and participant, I worked with some of the progressive and left-allied women's organisations to mobilise opposition to the pageant. I am, therefore, implicated in the complex politics generated from the protests against the pageant.

Globalisation and the Pageant

We live in a world where everyone seems to be watching satellite television and drinking Coke; it is also a world where making, claiming, and maintaining local identity and culture is increasingly important.

(Cohen et al. 1996: 2)

There is now a significant literature on globalisation supporting the claim that greater mobility and faster circulation of capital mark the contemporary era.[6] According to David Harvey (2000), globalisation per se is not new, and can be dated back at least to 1492 with the internationalisation of trade and commerce. This current phase, however, is significant for the profound reorganisation of geography, where prior configurations of borders and boundaries are being rapidly reshaped, effecting change in the politics of gender, class and place. These changes have caused some to speculate on the demise of prior configurations of boundaries such as the nation-state (Appadurai 1996), while others see this more as a 'nexus' between global and local scales (Wilson and Dissanayake 1996).

In this chapter, I consider globalisation in terms of the ways in which place is reconfigured. This is not to suggest that globalisation is a one-way process whereby the global 'creates' the local, precluding its converse (the local creates the global), but rather that globalisation is considered here as the dynamic reorganisation of borders and boundaries from the most local and intimate scale of the body to that of the global.[7] In the reorganisation of these borders, prior established boundaries are challenged, and the politics around public spectacles such as the pageant afford the possibility of opening new and perhaps more emancipatory spaces of political expression. My focus here is on the assertion of place in response to globalisation. In my analysis, I examine place in terms of the scales of the body and the nation, and I look at how these borders overlap and signify each other. My attention, then, is on boundaries that were being formed and contested in response to the pageant as iconic of globalisation and on how particular boundaries, such as the nation-state, were forcefully established against others.

The factors that contributed to the pageant as an icon of globalisation in contemporary India arose from the intersection of complex political, economic and cultural changes. These changes began roughly in the mid-1970s with a series of economic liberalisation policies, and led up to globalisation in the early 1990s.[8] The distinction between a period of 'economic liberalisation' and one of 'globalisation' is somewhat arbitrary, since globalisation per se in India can be traced back to the beginning of its history of trade with various parts of the world. The difference between the two, however, is based on the emphasis on marketing India in the early 1990s as an important global destination for foreign investment, as against the domestic liberalisation policies of the 1970s and 1980s that set the precedent for the changes initiated in 1991.

The early 1990s were preceded by a decade and a half of significant political and economic changes, made manifest particularly in the policy shift from investment in infrastructure development to an emphasis on consumer durables. Beginning with Indira Gandhi's regime and continuing later with her son Rajiv Gandhi's government, this change in policy combined materially and discursively a discourse of modernity with the middle class in India. According to Purnima Mankekar, the emphasis on consumer durables during the mid-1970s was based on 'the premise that India could become a modern nation when its citizens acquired middle-class lifestyles through the acquisition of consumer goods' (1999: 75). By the mid-1980s, the policy changes and attention to the middle class were evident. For instance, one magazine reported that, for the first time in India, the prime minister understood the importance of owning a colour television in the aspirations of the middle class (Ninan 1985). Along with the political visibility of the middle class, the late 1980s also witnessed the dramatic rise of the religious right. Through a series of often violent campaigns, the Hindu right repeatedly sought to define the nation in terms of a unified virile masculine Hindu identity.

Subsequent to the economic liberalisation of the 1970s and 1980s, the economic reforms initiated in the early 1990s were anticipated by a series of factors manifested most particularly in the depletion of foreign exchange reserves (Jalan 1991). Advised by the International Monetary Fund and the World Bank, India initiated aggressive measures to attract foreign direct investment. Following the economic logic established in the 1980s, that of the middle class and consumer durables, the economic policies of the 1990s renewed their emphasis on India's consumer base, projecting it as a 'land of opportunity'.[9] For instance, one investment brochure declared the emergence of a 'new' India, claiming: 'India today is a whole "new" country. Vibrant. Active. Alive .... You can feel a sense of urgency permeating just about every sector. A determination to catch up.'[10]

In addition to these dramatic changes in the political economy, city landscapes and cultural politics also witnessed a shift. Retail outlets replaced local brand names with multinational merchandise; across cities, billboards advertised Citibank and Levi's jeans, while walls and store shutters were painted over with Coca-Cola and Pepsi logos, marking the urban landscape with perceptible signs of an opening economy. One of the most dramatic changes witnessed in cultural politics was the privatisation of television. From the three state-run channels available in metropolitan areas in 1987, by 1996 approximately 40 international and domestic satellite and cable channels, such as CNN, BBC, Zee and STAR TV, made their presence felt.[11] The increase in channels led to a burgeoning of the television software industry to fill the available airtime, and presented an alternative to the imported English-language fare of soap operas and game shows.

This dramatic change in the visual spectrum fostered a discourse of public anxiety at multiple locations, from the parliament and print media to public interest groups and some women's organisations.[12] This discourse was primarily focused on measures to control 'obscenity and violence' on satellite and cable television. Women and children recurred persistently in the rhetoric as those most in need of protection against the corrupting influence of the new media. Of even greater concern was that several satellite channels were beamed from outside of Indian borders and thus were structurally outside the jurisdiction of the state, which limited its ability to control the medium.[13] By 1996 this concern with television resulted in four writ petitions filed by a few women's organisations in the Delhi High Court against several satellite and cable companies (see Oza 1999). These petitions claimed that the satellite and cable channels violated the 1986 Indecent Representation of Women (Prohibition) Act and the Customs Act, and thus threatened the integrity of Indian borders. These court cases were significant because they were able to intertwine, ideologically and symbolically, the representation of women with the integrity of the nation's borders, and solidified the link between women and the nation's borders within the state apparatus. These cases were part of a larger and increasingly conservative campaign begun in the early 1990s, which echoed the concern with Indian borders. From banned advertisements and film songs to the burning of Maqbool Fida Husain's tapestries—in protest of his rendering of a Hindu goddess in the nude—these instances of censorship in popular culture signalled systematic measures to curtail women's sexuality and sexual expression.[14]

Each of these instances, and particularly the rhetoric of opposition to the Miss World pageant, was remarkable for the manner in which representations of women's bodies and sexuality were considered a threat to borders. In some of the Hindu right's opposition to the pageant, the perceived threat to borders resulted in efforts to protect Indian culture and tradition. For the progressive women's groups, the pageant signified the threat of the re-entrenchment of imperialism in the country. Significantly, for both groups, this concern with borders were gendered and sexualised. For the Hindu right the threat was expressed in terms of rampant transgressive women's sexuality and body exposure, while for the progressive organisations the concern was with the commodification of women's bodies and the spread of the sex trade. In both cases, the borders of the nation were symbolised through women's bodies. Such concern with borders and scales demonstrates, according to Sankaran Krishna (1996), a 'cartographic anxiety'. Instances such as the pageant, therefore, allow a way to understand how globalisation was negotiated and contested, and the manner in which borders were constantly recreated and policed at the scale of the gendered and sexualised body.

The opposition to the pageant, therefore, arose from a broad context of concerns that coalesced in the protests surrounding the pageant. High inflation, increasing rural poverty, and the rise of the Hindu right combined with images of '*Baywatch*', cellular phones and Citibank billboards to create a fractured and dislocated image of a globalising nation.[15] Consumers and activist groups were faced with the question: 'To whom should [we] address [our] protests?' (Butalia and Chakravarti 1996: 5). Oppositional praxis was frustrated on the one hand by the state's retreating role and, on the other, by often inaccessible corporate owners. It is within this context, then, that the pageant became a viable target for opposition to globalisation, because the event made visible the alliance between the state and domestic and global capital. Measures such as providing financial assistance for tourist spots, rather than infrastructure and extensive police protection for the pageant, visibly reinforced state alliances with corporate capital. Due to the visibility of such alliances and the identification of the specific companies that sponsored the event, it was possible to name and identify the companies and people responsible for the pageant. The ability to name and identify was significant, because it was then possible to implicate particular people and power relationships in the social and discursive critique of the pageant.

Showcasing India: The State, ABCL, and the Miss World Organisation

For the state, the managers and the sponsors, the opportunity to showcase India to the world through the pageant crystallised multiple agendas. For each, the opportunity was saturated with the promise of a worldwide audience. The collaboration between the managers of the event, the state and domestic capital was thus forged to safeguard this opportunity. For instance, Amitabh Bachchan Corporation Limited (ABCL), the Indian event managers of the pageant, claimed, 'the pageant will showcase India and will provide a tremendous opportunity for Indian tourism, as a global audience of nearly 3 billion will watch this show'.[16] For Godrej, the official domestic sponsor of the event, the pageant was an opportunity to expand its large domestic market beyond India's borders. Meanwhile, where the state was concerned, the pageant would help put Karnataka on the global tourist map. The chief minister of Karnataka justified the pageant by claiming it would 'elevate the spirit of Indian women', adding that the pageant would be like a traditional Indian *mela* (a carnival or fair), and that it should be viewed as an international *mela* where 'there will be buyers and sellers' (quoted in Menon 1996: 13).

The pageant served as a tele-visual exhibit for a worldwide audience of 2.3 billion. It was carefully marketed as an opportunity for India to be 'exhibited' on the world stage—to be viewed and experienced from afar (Mitchel 1989: 220). In a telling instance, Julia Morley, the managing director of the Miss World organisation, stated that the pageant allowed the opportunity for 'many people to know about Indian women. And I think that it's good that people have been able to get to know the Indian woman *without visiting*.'[17] As with exhibitions, the pageant allowed spectators the distance of viewing India 'without visiting', a window through which

India came packaged and ready to be consumed. Gender and sexuality occupied a carefully balanced position in the language of the pageant; on the one hand there was the veiled eroticism of viewing India without visiting, while on the other the participants' sexual codes were held in check through traditional displays of femininity and compassion. The discourse of the political and economic opportunities that the pageant would generate was able to balance a particular tension between the erotic possibilities of exoticised land and geography, and strictly controlled displays of the respectable sexuality of the participants within its borders.[18] The pageant presented, therefore, the opportunity for erotic, voyeuristic pleasure 'without visiting'.

The idea of 'showcasing India' generated strong sentiments of proving masculine capability. For instance, Amitabh Bachchan, the chief executive officer of ABCL, claimed, 'I wanted to prove that an Indian show can be a world class event …. I've heard so many people treating India as a backward country that I wanted to prove them wrong …. They will realise that we can do it better than a western country' (quoted in Sanghvi 1996: 17).[19] The pageant, as an international exhibit of India that also provided the opportunity to prove Indian capability, tapped into a particularly middle and upper-class engagement with a discourse on India's worth in the global arena. By articulating the reasons for hosting the pageant in terms of Indian capability, Bachchan was seeking the endorsement of the middle and upper classes for the event.

The pageant sought to construct India as a modern and economically liberalised nation. These representational efforts were attentive to the shift in the balance of power in the post-Cold War era, and therefore were at great pains to demonstrate a nation that determined its own modernity.[20] The selection of the venue of the pageant—Bangalore—was crucial towards these efforts. As a modern metropolis that did not show the scars of the communal riots from a few years earlier, Bangalore, which exports thousands of software engineers all over the world, claimed to be India's Silicon Valley. Therefore, strategically removed from associations such as the communal riots that would mark the nation as 'primitive' and 'third world', Bangalore's burgeoning computer industry was the icon of modern India. Modernity in India, however, was not to be confused with Westernisation and a loss of tradition. An extravagantly designed stage on which the main pageant would be held and telecast worldwide achieved this balance. The stage, designed to reflect India's ancient culture, drew on the architectural motifs of traditional temples and caves. In addition, the theme of the pageant, 'Kanyakumari to Kashmir', was crafted to show India's cultural diversity, and, according to an official press release, sought to 'project unity amidst diversity to remind the people of mother Earth that all human beings belong to one big global family'.[21]

According to Liisa Malkki, international spectacles such as the Miss World pageant and the Olympic games serve as ceremonial arenas for nations—in this case for India—to take their place among the 'family of nations' (1994: 50). Therefore internationalisms, in essence, are not about a dissolving of national borders towards the larger goal of a unified humanity, but about the recognition of the nation in the international, thus reinforcing particularly nationalist paradigms in the global era.[22] Within the international arena of the pageant, therefore, India was not only to prove masculine capability, but also to display feminine compassion. To this end, the pageant was advertised as 'beauty with a purpose'. In India, the pageant would raise money to be shared by the Spastics Society of Karnataka and the Variety Club International. Both agencies raise funds to help children. The ABCL organised a children's party for the 88 international contestants in 'a touching function … commemorating the concern for the child who is not normal'.[23] Raising money for children through an international beauty pageant inevitably highlights the assumption of an implicit connection between women and children. The contestants are shown as women with a natural compassion for children, an image that also serves to contain their sexuality within respectable boundaries. Children with disabilities are meant to evoke immediate support and empathy, and are politically safe avenues of support.

In her discussion on international beauty pageants, Sarah Banet-Weiser comments on the way in which contestants are linked with geography. Each contestant embodies an exotic locale worth visiting, particularly with reference to Third World countries (Banet-Weiser 1999). As the host country, India displayed its cultural diversity in the encompassing theme—Kanyakumari to Kashmir—which spans the length of the nation, peppered with exotic tourist destinations. The portrayal of a unified geography, however, erased the landscape of conflict, so that borderlands such as Kashmir were co-opted within the universal theme of the pageant—'peace on Earth, and belonging to one big global family'. Furthermore, the unified rhetoric erased India of minority groups, and thus crafted the country as primarily Hindu. In one particularly telling instance, during an interview with the stage designer Sabu Cyril, I asked whether the ancient Indian motifs used for the set design also included those from Mughal architecture.[24] In reply, he claimed that 'Mughal was not art of Indian culture'. Cyril's judgements of what constitutes Indian culture brought into focus the recent history of Hindu and Muslim conflicts in India. Thus, the Indian dance forms and the stage design were to show a markedly Hindu India that did not acknowledge Muslim influence and presence as constitutive of Indian culture.

The reconstruction of the nation as Hindu was an attempt to link space with ideology. Satish Deshpande suggests that 'successful spatial strategies are able to link, in a durable and ideologically credible way, abstract (imagined) spaces to concrete (physical) spaces' (1998: 250). Conflict and protest around spectacles such as the pageant thus expose how meanings are created that link places, and borders around places, to particular ideologies and identities. In one significant response to the protests surrounding the swimwear part of the pageant, spaces and the nation's borders were fortified against obscenity and transgression. The objections to obscenity and vulgarity in the swimwear event, raised primarily by the political right, resulted in the event being moved outside of India's borders to Seychelles, a small island country in the Indian Ocean. The integrity of Indian borders was therefore maintained, and shielded against any obscenity. The protests as well as the decision to hold the swimwear event outside India's borders reinforced a linear logic whereby body exposure is akin to obscenity and, by extension, a threat to the nation. The shift in the event reinforced a linking of conservative gender and body codes with the nation and its borders.

The pageant, therefore, was framed within complex structures of power that made safeguarding the event, as well as its success, paramount. In efforts to make the event successful, the alliances of the state with domestic and international capital were most visible. Efforts by the state, for instance, included the allotment of one hundred million rupees by the central government 'to beautify its tourist spots' for the pageant.[25] Financial assistance specifically meant for the pageant stood in stark relief against prior requests to the central government for infrastructure support in Bangalore. In addition, faced with increasing protests by both the right and left coalitions against the pageant, the state mobilised a 12,500-member police force in Bangalore consisting of central paramilitary contingents, including National Security Guard personnel, to safeguard its opportunity to advertise the new India. It was the first time in India that the police force was mobilised with such extensive detail to protect what was, in essence, a private multinational venture.

The pageant, for its supporters, was a vehicle to showcase liberalised India to the world. For the state, the pageant advertised India as a tourist destination; for ABCL, it served as an opportunity to display Indian capability; and for the corporate sponsors, the pageant would help create worldwide markets. To create these opportunities, structural alliances between the state and capital were forged, while choreography and set design helped to reinvent India as primarily Hindu, erased of other communities. For those opposed to the pageant, in these multiple registers some of the anxieties with globalisation were reflected.

The Opposition: Cultural Protectionism and Imperial Domination

Feminist theory has destabilised the notion of gender as a stable category. In its place, critical work on gender now reflects on gender performativity (Butler 1990). The controversy over the pageant created a space where the meaning of gender and sexuality in contemporary India was expressed and debated. Consequently, as a public arena, the pageant was significant for the important political positions about gender and sexuality that emerged from the pageant itself, as well as in the protests. While for the organisers and the state the event would showcase India, for the opposition, the pageant signified a threat to the nation. The opposition to the pageant emerged from many different political positions, producing a complex discourse on gender and sexuality in contemporary India.

Groups opposing the pageant included students, farmers, unions, the political religious right, and a series of women's organisations that formed a loosely defined progressive coalition. The sharpest distinctions emerged between the political religious right and the progressive coalition, which strategically distanced itself from the right. While these groups diverged ideologically and politically on several issues, in several instances the progressive group's rhetoric came surprisingly close to the views expressed by the political right. The resultant blurring of boundaries between the progressive coalition and the political right indicates the ways in which the right effectively used some feminist politics to construct its opposition. It also indicates the challenge of formulating a coherent and nuanced radical critique of the pageant.

In a period of tremendous flux, the contours that defined the nation (in terms not only of political economy but also cultural politics, gender and sexuality) were in transition. The pageant provided a stage on which to define these contours and secure meaning and identity for the space within its boundaries. Within this context, the opposition to the pageant mapped onto women's representation and body politic the debate of globalisation in India. Concerns with perforated borders and the loss of autonomy with political, cultural and economic changes were displaced onto women's sexuality and bodies. Therefore, containment entailed securing the female body and sexuality against transgression.

Among the various groups that voiced their protest of the pageant, none received as much media attention as the political religious right—the BJP and Mahila Jagran, a women's organisation allied with the BJP. The BJP's form and articulation of protest, which included threats to destroy the venue of the pageant, self-immolation, strikes and mass violent demonstrations, resulted in extensive media coverage. According to the BJP and Mahila Jagran, the Miss World pageant was a 'show of obscenity' and 'against Indian culture'. In a large BJP demonstration in Bangalore, placards read 'Stop Miss World Pageant—Save National Honour' and 'Big B (Amitabh Bachchan] means bring bad culture to Bharat' (Srikanth 1996: 1).

The progressive women's coalitions, allied with the political left, categorically distanced themselves from the right-wing arguments, and focused their critique of the pageant on imperialism, arguing that the pageant encouraged the entry of multinational corporations into the country. The Centre for Indian Trade Union voiced a typical position adopted by the political left: 'Selection of India/Bangalore for the Beauty Pageant to select Miss World is nothing but an attempt to smoothen [sic] the entry of Multi Nationals into our country in a big way. It is also an attempt to divert the attention of the toiling people from their real problems adversely affecting their livelihood.'[26]

A significant aspect of the differences between the various groups that were critical of the pageant was the ways in which their political campaigns were organised. Political campaigning and demonstrations by the religious right gained immediate attention in the media, and often the positions adopted by progressive organisations were deliberately left out. Opposition to the pageant was consequently most visibly marked by a rightist political position with relatively few alternate arguments. In the face of the primarily right-wing position visible in the media, progressive and left-allied political organisations sought to present a different opinion and critique of the pageant. For instance, the All India Democratic Women's Association (AIDWA), a women's organisation allied with the political left, made a point of presenting an alternative to the right-wing political position. In a press release, AIDWA claimed: 'We do not agree with those who are opposing the contest in the name of "Indian culture" and "Indian womanhood". We reject the notion of any one definition of culture, womanhood, and tradition being imposed on women'.[27] Instead, AIDWA focused its critique on state expenditure on the pageant, and sought to expose to public scrutiny the state's priorities and its alliance with global and domestic capital.

However, in the strategic rejection of the political right-wing's version of culture, progressive groups relinquished the issue of culture, so that the only visible opinion about culture was the conservative view of threatened Indian tradition. In the context of rapid political, economic and cultural changes, about which there already existed concern with the corrupting impact of the media, the political right effectively mobilised sympathy for its concern for threatened Indian culture. Moreover, indigenous notions of sexuality that draw on a rich tradition of myth and legend remained silent in discourses of the opposition, so that it became easier for the right-wing to claim that any discourse on sexuality was other, foreign, and not within the parameters of what is considered Indian culture.

A significant distinction between political parties affiliated with the religious right, such as the BJP, and those that distanced themselves from the right was the particular ways in which their arguments against the pageant framed gender and body politics.[28] For the right-wing, such concern was primarily a link between body exposure and the perceived threat to the sanctity of the nation. An extremely vocal right-wing opponent of the pageant, Pramila Nesargi, a BJP member of the legislative assembly in Bangalore, articulated the political right's position as:

The portions of the body which has to be covered, which women knows which has to be covered, which in the society it should not be shown it should not be meant for public places, and in other words, such portion of the body which will arouse the sensual or the sexual parts of man that must not be shown'. (quoted in Menon 1996: 13)

Nesargi's statement affords a particular kind of slippage between women's sexuality, body exposure and femininity, such that 'women must know' which parts of their body should be covered so as not to 'arouse' men. They prescribe a certain kind of femininity that controls women's bodies and sexuality, since men's sexuality is naturalised as uncontrollable. Women's bodies, sexuality and femininity, then, are intricately woven together so that the perceived transgression of any one threatens others, and subsequently threatens Indian culture. This is the other slippage evidenced in the BJP's arguments: exposure of certain parts of the female body was perceived as a threat to Indian culture and, by extension, to national sovereignty.

Conversely, for women's organisations, gender and body politics were expressed primarily in terms of the commodification of women and exploitation by structures of patriarchy and capital. However, in some instances, the rhetoric of a few organisations mirrored the slippage between women's bodies and sexuality articulated by the political right. For instance, the Active Opposition Association, a consortium of six women's organisations in Bangalore, alleged that 'the concept of prosperity of tourism through the exhibition of beautiful bodies is questionable. This is not the prosperity of sex trade in the country'.[29] Other organisations voiced a similar rhetoric, asking: 'Do we need to be watched and admired on such issues or as a nation hosting an almost pornographic show for the benefit of a few organisations who want to exploit us for profit?'[30] Such positions assume that the exhibition of women's bodies will inevitably lead to 'sex trade' in the country; they articulate the slippage between exposure of women's bodies and the encouragement of deviant sexualities, which are a threat to the nation.

Significant similarities in rhetoric between the political right and the progressive coalitions also occurred because of the ways in which the right borrowed and adapted particular feminist agendas to suit their terms. For instance, most progressive groups that criticised the pageant and its impact were concerned with the commodification of women and the exploitation of women through patriarchy and capital. The political right used the argument against the commodification of women to suggest that the selling of women's bodies offended Indian culture. For example, AIDWA based their critique on the claim that 'the media attention that they (the pageant's contestants] receive contributes greatly to the commercialisation of social relations and the commodification of women and their bodies that in turn reinforce their subordinate status'.[31] In another instance, Mahila Sangharsha Okkuta (MSO), a consortium of 15 women's organisations in Bangalore, linked the pageant with multinational business and the denigration of women, stating that,

> at the altar of capital, a women's body is turned into a saleable commodity .... It is this market created fraudulent image of beauty that we resist. An image that is falsely liberating and modern but which in reality pushes women into stereotypical, subordinate roles.[32]

Adapting these arguments about the commodification and exploitation of women's bodies to fit the agenda of the right-wing, Nesargi claimed: 'In India women are not meant to be sold. Women are not treated as a commodity available for sale in the bazaar. If she sells herself, either her flesh, or body or beauty, she is offending every law in India .... Beauty cannot be sold' (quoted in Menon 1996: 13). The distinction between the two positions was that for the right, the commodification of women was an offence against Indian culture, while for the women's groups the commodification of women was a consequence of capitalist relations of power.

However, political arguments concerning the commodification of women's bodies need to be rethought. The problem with this conceptualisation, besides its conservative reenactment, is that it rests on the assumption that there are 'pure' spaces outside a commodified realm. This inevitably raises questions: what would be outside of commodification? Why and how must women occupy this realm? Furthermore, this outside of commodification then allows quite easily for the right to claim that women must occupy some sanctified, pure realm; this argument is politically dangerous precisely because it easily slips to fit the religious right-wing agenda.

While the political positions adopted by the religious right and the progressive organisations often came close and were at times remarkably similar, a significant arena of difference between them has been their positions on women and work. Historically, women's paid and unpaid labour has been an important site of political struggle for progressive groups.[33] Conversely, the right has continued to recreate the public-private division, with women's primary responsibility structured from within the domestic sphere. This reiteration of the inside-outside division has been perpetuated in spite of the presence of more women in public spaces, some occupying prominent political positions in the right-wing political apparatus. Tanika Sarkar (1993) points out that, with several women in such prominent positions, more women within the right-wing political movement have mobility in the public spaces earlier deemed closed to them. While the inclusion of women in the public and their agency in the right-wing political movement may be seen as signs of progressive factions within a conservative movement, Sarkar cautions against such claims, stating that 'limited public identity and mobility that has become available to these women is made conditional on their submission to a new form of patriarchy' (ibid.: 42). Therefore, political organising has to be attentive not only to what kinds of gender and sexual politics are enabled, but also through which structures they are enabled.

In the context of the pageant, I am concerned with the particular gender and sexual politics that were sanctioned conditional to new grids of oppression. A particularly interesting instance of such grids was evidenced when a prominent BJP member of parliament, Uma Bharti, voiced her protest of the pageant, stating that she was against 'Westernisation', not 'modernity', in India. She distinguished modernisation from Westernisation, saying: 'We want women to become doctors, engineers, IAS [Indian Administrative Service] and IPS [Indian Police Service] officers and ministers. But we don't want them to smoke, drink and adopt Western styles of living'.[34] While Bharti's carefully crafted distinction is emblematic of the crisis perceived in the contemporary moment, attempts to articulate the distinction between modernity and Westernisation have historically recurred since the middle of the nineteenth century. Partha Chatterjee (1989: 237), for instance, claims that within the nationalist struggle the woman question, in the middle of the nineteenth century, was resolved with the separation of the outside material sphere from the internal spiritual sphere. Women occupied the inner spiritual sphere and were shielded from the influences of Western civilisation. Post-independence, the issue of India's modernity was evidenced in Nehru's rhetoric by the importance given to institutions and heavy industry, and towards the latter part of the century this recurs in the vision of his grandson, Rajiv Gandhi, for India's modernity realised through computerisation.

The reason for the recurrence of this debate on Indian modernity as distinguished from Westernisation, Chatterjee argues, is because 'of the way in which the history of our modernity has been intertwined with the history of colonialism[;] we have never quite been able to believe that there exists a universal domain of free discourse, unfettered by differences of race or nationality' (1997: 275). The recurrence of this debate in contemporary India and through various points in history is indicative of the persistent desire to craft an Indian modernity.

The anxiety with crafting a specifically Indian modernity is particularly evident in both Nesargi's and Bharti's statements, where modernity is distinguished from Westernisation, and this distinction is effected through the intersections of gender, class and caste. Women are encouraged to join respectable middle-class public service professions such as medicine and engineering, but not to smoke or drink. Women's participation in waged labour is encouraged, but only as prescribed from within particular parameters through which India's modernity is defined. Thus, while Indian borders must be open to economic investment, Western value systems, seen as corrupting influences, must be policed and even censored. This dichotomy is enacted on women's bodies and representational praxis; women must balance the desired modern against the undesirable Western values. For the political right, then, women are used to define modernity, but are not active participants in crafting India's modernity.

The concern that women will adopt Western styles of living is a ruse for the anxiety related to women's sexuality in liberalised India. The balancing of Westernisation versus modernity is particularly indicative of Bharti's statement that modernity in terms of women as doctors and lawyers is acceptable, but women smoking or drinking and adopting Western values is not. Defining 'smoking or drinking' as Westernisation echoes vamp images in Hindi films from the 1960s and 1970s (Mazumdar 1996). The image of the vamp, according to Ranjani Mazumdar, 'was the visible intrusion of the West into the cinematic space of Indian films, signifying an unrestrained sexuality and license, given to vices "unknown" to "Indian" women' (ibid.: 29). The recurrence of women's bodies as a site of control and containment is registered in other geographic locations.[35] For instance, Aihwa Ong remarks that in Malaysia, 'women's bodily containment was key to the envisaged order that would contain those social forces unleashed by state policies and the capitalist economy' (1990: 270).

The opposition between Westernisation and modernisation, therefore, placed in public discourse regulatory norms about body and sexuality. Smoking and drinking were associated with transgressive sexuality, and the contamination by Western cultural influences made possible through globalisation. It is through public spectacles such as the pageant that norms and ideas about sexuality and gender are fixed or, in the words of Butler (1993), 'materialised'.[36] In place of gender construction, Butler contends that gender is materialised through 'a process ... that stabilises over time to produce the effect of boundary, fixity, and surface we call matter' (ibid.: 9). My concern with the fixity of 'matter' on the body stems from the ways in which bodies and sexualities then become regulated and prescribed within structures of state, patriarchy and capital.

In the context of the pageant, such fixity was evident when the Bangalore High Court ruled in a landmark judgment that the pageant could not be stopped but would, however, be monitored by the director general of Police for Indecent Exposure of Women. Although the court ruled against the political right's petition to have the pageant banned, the judgment nevertheless served to endorse the concern that exposure of women's bodies constitutes obscenity and indecent exposure, and therefore must be policed. Such judgments by structures of the state are crucial because particular ideas of gender and sexuality become, in the words of Davina Cooper, 'embedded within the state's technologies of power' (1995: 2).

Sexuality, Nation, Globalisation

Thus far I have argued that the pageant was iconic of globalisation in India for those who supported as well as those who opposed the event. For the supporters, the pageant provided an international forum to advertise India's capability to stage a world event successfully, and its compassion in raising money for disabled children. The contours of the nation defined here, it was hoped, would draw the world's attention to the new 'modern' India, and secure its future as a world tourist destination. Meanwhile, for the opposition, the pageant as an icon of globalisation in India signified a threat. The discourses of the opponents and the supporters of the pageant defined the contours of the nation through women's bodies and sexuality. From both, there emerged a particular politics of place that accorded primacy to the nation in globalisation, and, in so doing, asserted boundaries that were deeply problematic, for gender and sexual politics warrants a more nuanced understanding of the politics of place that precludes an automatic endorsement of local opposition to globalisation.

Politics of place is critical to formulating oppositional praxis. That is, oppositional praxis locates itself in some place—defined through an ideological, political and geographical grid. According to Stuart Hall, 'the rediscovery of place, a past, of one's roots, of one's context, [is] a necessary moment of enunciation' (1991: 36). He adds, 'I do not think the margins could speak up without first grounding themselves somewhere'(ibid.). The opponents of the pageant grounded themselves and located their critique in the nation. The politics of opposition that ensued from this locational grid thus reestablished the contours of the nation in a period when the sanctity of boundaries were perceived to be under threat. The political right and the progressive coalition therefore constructed their opposition to the pageant by arguing for the autonomy of the nation. Within the framework of globalisation, then, local opposition was formulated as the nation against globalisation. However, for the two groups, the nation as local opposition signified different things.

For the political right, the pageant afforded the public possibility to articulate a national Hindu identity in a period of change. Women's bodies became the trope of 'mother India', who had to be protected against the contaminating influences of globalisation. For members of the progressive coalition, this was more complicated. Their articulation of the nation-state as their place of opposition was based on an argument that the pageant symbolised the imperialist power of globalisation. Their concern with globalisation was the dissolving power of the nation-state; consequently, their opposition attempted to reassert the responsibility of the nation-state. The progressive coalition's political opposition recognised the impossibility of doing away with the nation in globalisation; they, thus, acknowledged that the jurisdiction of the state is still the only structural unit of power with whom they can negotiate issues of rights and responsibility. Consequently, much of the opposition to the pageant focused on the funds allocated to the pageant by the federal and the state governments, and the deployment of 12,500 security personnel. The structure of their position, however, was predicated on the following linear argument: the pageant symbolised globalisation, which encouraged imperialism, resulting in the commodification of women and the encouragement of sex trade. Within this structure, opposition to commodification and sex trade entailed implementing structural measures prohibiting events, images and representational praxis deemed to commodify women. Since only the state has the jurisdiction to implement these measures, the progressive coalitions sought to draw the state's attention to its responsibility towards women. Thus, unlike the political right-wing—for whom women were symbolic signifiers of the nation and, therefore, must be protected and policed—for the progressive coalition opposition to the pageant was based on opposition to structures of patriarchy and imperialism. The different ways the political right and the progressive coalition linked gender with the nation-state emerged from different critiques. For both the coalitions, clearly, there are both structural and discursive ways in which gender and the nation-state were linked. However, the difference I want to highlight is the way in which the opposing groups constructed their critique of globalisation by connecting gender with the nation-state.

For political organising, the position of gender implicated, symbolically and structurally, in the nation-state raises the question: can radical feminist politics emerge from within nationalist discourses? Why, for instance, do both right and progressive political parties critique the pageant at the site of women's bodies and sexuality because of a perceived threat to a nation? My attempt here is not to suggest that radical feminist politics is realisable only by 'wishing away' the nation.[37] Rather, my aim is to point out that our efforts to rethink contemporary feminist politics and praxis attempt a reworking of their imbrication within the nation-state. Such rethinking is possible through a critical look at the politics of place as played out in the opposition to the pageant. Two threads of argument follow: first, opposition to the pageant and, by extension, against globalisation rested on the identity of the nation as conceived in terms of desexualised womanhood. Second, this construction set up the nation in opposition to globalisation as a fixed and bounded sphere of power.

While beauty pageants clearly reinforce traditional and limited notions of sexuality and gender that, in turn, reinforce the cosmetics industry with its narrow heterosexual notions of beauty, these qualities do not account for their continued popularity or, as Mary John points out, for 'the aspirations and anxieties symptomatic of the desire for beauty' (1998: 375). In India, beauty pageants have gained immense popularity in the past few years, with pageants occurring in schools, at community events, and as part of inter-collegiate competitions. These pageants, quite successfully, link beauty and femininity with group identity. This is even more evident in international beauty pageants, where each woman is representative of a nation. For instance, Rhenuma Dilruba, the Miss World contestant from Bangladesh, stated, 'I was chosen from among 1,000-odd women in Bangladesh. This is to prove how liberal we are'.[38] Through her participation as a representative of Bangladesh, she embodied, quite literally, national qualities of liberalism. In another interesting instance, Joan Rani Jeyraj, who is of Indian parentage but was born and brought up in Zambia and had recently decide to live in India, claimed, 'I think I'm representative of India because I made a choice to make it my home'.[39] For Jeyraj, representing the nation is based on deciding which place is 'home'. Being considered to represent the nation on an international stage is a powerfully strong sentiment that anchors a complex frame of justifications and desires.

Responding to the opposition's criticism that the women who participated in the pageant were exploited, Jeyraj defended the pageant and justified the participation of the contestants by saying, 'I do not think that the women here feel exploited. I do not think that 88 countries could have forced the women to come here. It was each one's individual choice to come here'.[40] The discourse of individual choice and freedom to participate forcefully asserts the agency of the 88 contestants. Agency and individual choice attempt to counter the argument that the contestants' willingness to participate simply indicates the extent to which they have absorbed the ideas of the beauty industry, suspending their own agency and judgment. However, it simultaneously suggests that freedom and choice are unmediated by social structures and constraints. There is also the assumption, as with other international events, that all 88 contestants participate in a fair contest, where each is given equal consideration. In the 1996 Miss World pageant, however, some of the African contestants challenged this assumption, alleging that the Indian media paid them little attention in contrast with the media frenzy that surrounded other participants. For instance, Miss Tanzania claimed: 'The Indian Press has totally ignored us (black Africans) from the day we have landed in your country. Just about everyone in the press is paying attention only to the whites'.[41] Structures of racism are thus ignored in the discourse of 'free and fair' participation. This complicates the assumption that for each of the contestants, 'willingness to participate' means the same thing, and that each occupies the position of a participant within the structure of the pageant in the same way.

These dual conceptions force us to understand the contestants' willingness to participate 'as neither complete victims nor entirely free agents' (Banet-Weiser 1999: 23). The opposition, however, predicated its arguments on considering the 88 contestants of the pageant as victims erased of autonomy over their bodies and sexuality. This was a critical facet of the opponents' positions because it allowed the argument that women's bodies and sexuality must be controlled in public. For instance, in her response to the rights of women over their bodies and sexuality, Nesargi of the political right-wing BJP claimed that a woman is free to use her body, 'at her home. Free to do within the four walls … free to do in her bedroom. Not before the public where youngsters are there, young children are there, where they will have an impact on the minds, weaker section of the society'.[42] The progressive coalition asserted that the representation of women's bodies and sexuality in public encouraged prostitution and commodified women. For both, there is a direct link between the representation of women's bodies and sexuality and its 'effect', and, consequently, the assumption that the reception of images and representations is unmediated by discursive practices and structures, and open to multiple interpretive frames.

Therefore, women's engagement with desire and pleasure through events such as the pageant remained silent in the discourse of the opposition. Instead, a desexualised Indian womanhood as emblematic of the nation became an effective icon to protect the nation against globalisation (John 1996: 373). A desexualised iconic figure does not threaten the nation with sexual transgression. This desexualised narrative was most particularly evidenced in the rhetoric of the political right, which held that women's modernity is acceptable but not Westernisation—which was symbolic of uncontrolled sexuality. Conversely, while the progressive coalitions were critical of the conceptions of womanhood adopted by the right, they too did not consider women's agency and sexuality, so that the primary arguments about women's sexuality concerned commodification and the threat of sex trade. In effect, then, for the progressive coalition, women remained desexualised. By fashioning resistance to globalisation in terms of desexualised icons and symbols, the right affected a slide whereby this resistance was predicated on erasing women's autonomy over their bodies and sexualities.

The construction of resistance at any level that is predicated on structures of oppression or suppression at other levels or is contained through them is problematic from the start. Equally problematic are the assumptions of political hierarchy whereby gender and sexual politics are put on hold against the priority of local resistance to the overarching force of globalisation. The underlying assumption here is that gender and sexuality can be put on hold, or that gender and sexuality are not already constitutive of globalisation and local resistance. The political hierarchy in this context, then, is a ruse for denying agency to gender and sexuality. These issues have been raised in the context of the struggles for women's rights and the structural place of the women's movement within nationalism.[43] Therefore, conceptually progressive politics, when framed in terms of local resistance to globalisation and yet dependent on adherence to hegemonic structural positions within a 'new' patriarchy, is politically dangerous and theoretically precarious.

My second thread of argument entails examining geography and the politics of location that was played out in the opposition to the pageant. Events like the pageant have significance because they allow the public possibility to deepen the contours of national imaginings and to colour in homogenous identity. The possibility of imagining the nation, according to Gupta, 'involves the creation of a new order of difference, a new alignment of "self" in relation to "other"' (1997: 196). This self-other distinction was fundamental for constructing a politics of opposition. It entailed a dynamic drawing of boundaries, enclosing the nation from the outside influence of globalisation. These boundaries of the nation, as I have argued, were predicated on the construction of the nation in terms of desexualised womanhood. In the construction of the self-other distinction, the other is rendered outside the boundaries and is therefore always suspect. For instance, in her study of refugees, Malkki (1997) points out that attachment to place is naturalised, while displacement is pathologised. Drawing on this construct, attachment and belonging to a nation is naturalised, whereas the borderlands of the nation occupied by those who transgress or are refugees are suspect. It is this construction of the self versus the other that is reminiscent of India's persistence in crafting its own modernity. Particularly in the perceived threat from globalisation, the construction of the nation entails fixing or solidifying the identity of the self, and of constantly defining boundaries and borders that mark the self-nation from the other global.

The pageant symbolised a threat to the self so that the defence was based on fortifying the self as the nation against the outside. In so doing, the nation became defined and prescribed through fixed contours. This self-nation-other-global distinction raises the question: who in the nation feels invaded, and who is protected by fortifying the nation's boundaries?[44] Particular structures of class, caste, gender and sexuality are implicitly assumed to stand for the nation. These structures fix the location of the opposition where other configurations of these structures become erased. Furthermore, the concern with the threat from the other becomes a trope that is then available to level against a multitude of others. In addition, the concern with perforated boundaries assumes that the boundaries around the nation have not historically been made and remade in a process that peoples the articulation of multiple modernities. Finally, the nation-global distinctions are gendered so that the nation is coded as enclosed and feminine, while the global is coded as free-floating and masculine, mirroring the public-private divide. In the vision of more emancipatory politics, rather than envisioning the politics of place as the production of fixed locations, we may instead consider using Caren Kaplan's terms—location as an 'axis' (1996: 183). In such a formulation, the nation can be envisioned not as fixed and enclosed, but as dynamic and open.

Conclusion

In this chapter I have argued that the pageant was considered iconic of globalisation by the state and the organisers as well as by the opposition to the pageant. The pageant and the opposition effectively opened to scrutiny the debate about women's sexuality and autonomy in a period of tremendous political and economic change. A focus on women's bodies and representation contained and controlled the concern with rapid change in the country. For the opposition, the symbol of desexualised womanhood fortified the nation in globalisation, and effectively secured the borders and boundaries of the nation against sexual transgression. In so doing, the opposition to the pageant refashioned gender and sexuality to fit new forms of patriarchy, which were structured to accommodate the concern with the 'contaminating' influence of globalisation in India.

A politics of opposition fashioned through new forms of oppression, such as in the case of the pageant, where the arguments against globalisation were predicated on erasing women's agency and sexuality, is deeply problematic. This framework, I argue, was based on a particular politics of place, where the nation was ideologically and symbolically fixed and immutable. The structure of such oppositional praxis forecloses the possibility of considering globalisation and the nation as mutually constitutive spaces where location is not considered fixed, but as 'axis'. The insistence on generating a nuanced politics of place stems from an argument against the assumption of 'pure' spaces of agency or oppression on either side of globalisation or local opposition. Therefore, public spectacles such as the pageant are important sites of political intervention because they create the possibility of articulating new spatial geographies.

Acknowledgements

I would like to thank Rehana Ghadially for including this essay as part of this collection. I am also grateful to *SIGNS* for permission to reprint this article. To Paula Chakravartty, I am grateful for her contribution to this chapter. In addition, I would like to thank Lawrence Grossberg, Hillary Hinds, Ranjani Mazumdar, Arvind Rajgopal and Jackie Stacy for their comments. I am indebted to Karen Barad, Leela Fernandes and Laura Liu for sustained engagement with this piece and for their support.

Notes

1. *The Times of India*, 24 October 1996.
2. Emerging geographic literature examines space and structure intersectionally. See, for instance, Liu 2000. For a critique of resistance, I particularly draw on Abu-Lughod 1990.
3. For the way in which women and nation are collapsed in pageants, see Banet-Weiser 1999. With regard to gender, nation and sexuality, see Parker et al. 1992.
4. Inderpal Gresal and Caren Kaplan (1994) draw our attention to the way various patriarchies may collaborate to reinforce oppressive practices.
5. I draw on Arif Dirlik's (1996) use of the terms *promise* and *predicament* in relation to globalisation.
6. See, among others, Appadurai 1996; Featherstone 1990; Harvey 2000; Wallerstein 1991; Wilson and Dissanayake 1996.
7. For an interesting account of the production of the global through nationalist imagination, see Fernandes 2000.

8. For further details, see Kohli 1989.
9. For an account of the politics of gender, commodity, class and caste politics in advertising, see Rajagopal 1999.
10. Director General of Tourism, quoted in 'Tourism in India' (New Delhi: Government of India, 1996), p. 1.
11. For an extensive review of these changes, see Oza 1999.
12. I do not refer to anxiety in this sense as personal or intimate; rather, it is 'public', where concern is expressed *in the name of* public morality, Indian tradition, and the nation.
13. Measures by which satellite and cable television can and should be regulated were a significant part of the debate in formulating the Broadcast Bill. The bill emerged in response to a landmark Supreme Court directive where the court claimed that the airwaves were public property, and should thus be governed by an autonomous body. For further details, see Oza 1999.
14. Some of these instances include controversy around the popular Hindi song '*Choli ke peeche*', banned advertisements and confiscated magazines, and later the controversy around the film *Fire*.
15. A national sample survey suggests that rural poverty increased steadily, from 35.04 per cent in 1990–91 to approximately 44 per cent by 1993–94, and that those constituting the rural poor increased from 230 million in 1987–88 to 245 million by 1993–94. For further details, see Ghosh 1996. The average rate of inflation between 1991 and 1995 was 10.6 per cent. For further details, see Upadhyay 1996.
16. Amitabh Bachchan Corporation Limited press release, 4 November 1996.
17. Press conference, 4 November 1996, New Delhi, India. Emphasis added.
18. For similar arguments about eroticised land, see Alexander 1994.
19. Bachchan was one of the biggest superstars of Indian cinema during the 1970s and 1980s.
20. For a detailed account of Indian modernity created through television discourses in the 1980s and early 1990s, see Mankekar 1999.
21. Amitabh Bachchan Corporation Limited press release, 'Miss World Spectacle', November 1996, Bangalore, India.
22. *Ibid.*
23. Amitabh Bachchan Corporation Limited press release, 'Children's Party Adds a Human Touch to Miss World', 14 November 1996, Bangalore, India.
24. Sabu Cyril, interview by author, 16 November 1996, Bangalore, India.
25. *The Times of India*, 7 October 1996. One hundred million rupees is approximately three million US dollars.
26. Centre for Indian Trade Union pamphlet distributed at a mass demonstration against pageant, 'Mass Protest by CITU Beauty Contest Heralding the Entry of Multi-nationals in a Big Way', 17 November 1996, Bangalore, India.
27. All India Democratic Women's Association (AIDWA) press release, 16 November 1996, Bangalore, India.
28. I would like to acknowledge Laura Liu for drawing my attention to this point.
29. Pamphlet distributed by the Active Opposition Association, 'Who is the World Beauty Contest For?' Bangalore, India.
30. Pamphlet distributed during a Communist Party of India (Marxist) and AIDWA demonstration, 17 November 1996, Bangalore, India.
31. *Ibid.*
32. Pamphlet distributed by Mahila Sangharsha Okkuta, 'Women Protest Beauty Contest', 30 September 1996, Bangalore, India.
33. Since structural adjustment in 1991, more attention has been given to the impact of the reforms on women's labour. See Shah et al. 1994 and John 1996.
34. *The Times of India*, 25 October 1996, p. 1.
35. See, for example, Ong 1990 and Layoun 1994.
36. Gender is constantly being fixed and unfixed; by highlighting the pageant I do not mean that there are not other spaces but, rather, that the pageant was a critical space in the contemporary moment.
37. My use of 'wishing away' is drawn from Leela Fernandes's comments at a panel discussion on 'Developing Women's Studies: Confronting the Legacies of Colonialism, Imperialism and Racism' at the University of Pennsylvania conference, 'Unleashing Our Legacies: Exploring Third World Feminisms', Philadelphia, March 1998.
38. *The Hindu*, Bangalore, 24 November 1996, p. 4.
39. *Express Magazine*, Delhi, 17 November 1996, p. 1.
40. *The Hindu*, Bangalore, 24 November 1996, p. 4.
41. *The Asian Age*, Mumbai, 18 November 1996, p. 3.
42. Pramila Nesargi, interview by author, 29 November 1996, Bangalore, India.
43. In particular, see McClintock 1997.
44. Doreen Massey directs this question to those who perceive a threat to home and homeland in globalisation. See Massey 1994.

References

Abu-Lughod, Lila. 1990. 'The Romance of Resistance: Tracing Transformations of Power through Bedouin Women', *American Ethmologist*, 17 (1): 41–55.

Alexander, M. Jacqui. 1994. 'Not Just (Any) Body Can Be a Citizen: The Politics of Law, Sexuality and Postcoloniality in Trinidad and Tobago and the Bahamas', *Feminist Review*, 48 (Autumn): 5–23.

Appadurai, Arjun. 1996. *Modernity at Large: Cultural Dimensions of Globalisation*. Minneapolis: University of Minnesota Press.

Banet-Weiser, Sarah. 1999. *The Most Beautiful Girl in the World: Beauty Pageants and National Identity*. Berkeley: University of California Press.

Butalia, Urvashi and Uma Chakravarti. 1996. 'Censorship and Free Expression: Balancing the Extremes', *Voices*, 4 (2): 4–6.

Butler, Judith. 1990. *Gender Trouble: Feminism and the Subversion of Identity*. New York: Routledge.

———. 1993. *Bodies That Matter: On the Discursive Limits of 'Sex'*. New York: Routledge.

Chatterjee, Partha. 1989. 'The Nationlist Resolution of the Women's Question', in Kumkum Sangari and Sudesh Vaid (eds), *Recasting Women: Essays in Colonial History*, pp. 233–53. New Delhi: Kali for Women.

———. 1997. 'Talking about Our Modernity in Two Languages', in Partha Chatterjee, *A Possible India: Essays in Political Criticism*, pp. 261–85. Delhi: Oxford University Press.

Cohen, Colleen Ballerino, Richard Wilk and Beverly Stoeltje (eds). 1996. *Beauty Queens on the Global Stage*. New York: Routledge.

Cooper, Davina. 1995. *Power in Struggle: Feminism, Sexuality and the State*. New York: New York University Press.

Deshpande, Satish. 1998. 'Hegemonic Spatial Strategies: The Nation-Space and Hindu Communalism in Twentieth-Century India', *Public Culture* 10 (2): 249–84.

Dirlik, Arif. 1996. 'The Global and the Local', in Wilson and Dissanayake (eds), *Global/Local: Cultural Production and the Transnational Imaginary*, pp. 21–45, Durham, N.C. and London: Duke University Press.

Featherstone, Mike (ed.). 1990. *Global Culture: Nationalism, Globalization and Modernity*. London: Sage Publications.

Fernandes, Leela. 2000. 'Nationalizing "The Global": Media Images, Cultural Politics and the Middle Class in India', *Media, Culture, and Society*, 22 (5): 611–28.

Ghosh, Arun. 1996. 'The Macro Economic Situation in India', in Alternate Survey Group (ed.), *Alternative Economic Survey 1995–1996*, pp. 1–7, Delhi: Delhi Science Forum.

Grewal, Inderpal and Caren Kaplan (eds). 1994. *Scattered Hegemonies: Postmodernity and Transnational Feminist Practices*. Minneapolis and London: University of Minnesota Press.

Gupta, Akhil. 1997. 'Song of the Non Aligned World: Transnational Identities and the Reinscription of Space in Late Capitalism', in Gupta and Ferguson (eds), *Culture, Power, Place: Explorations in Critical Anthropology*, pp. 179–99. Durham, N.C. and London: Duke University Press.

Gupta, Akhil and James Ferguson (eds). 1997. *Culture, Power, Place: Explorations in Critical Anthropology*. Durham, N.C., and London: Duke University Press.

Hall, Stuart. 1991. 'The Local and the Global: Globalization and Ethnicity', in Anthony D. King (ed.), *Culture, Globalization, and the World System: Contemporary Conditions for the Representation of Identity*, pp. 19–39, Binghamton: State University of New York at Binghamton, Department of Art and Art History.

Harvey, David. 2000. *Spaces of Hope*. Berkeley: University of California Press.

Jalan, Bimal. 1991. *India's Economic Crisis: The Way Ahead*. Delhi: Oxford University Press.

John, Mary E. 1996. 'Gender and Development in India, 1970s–1990s: Some Reflections on the Constitutive Role of Contexts', *Economic and Political Weekly*, 31 (47): 3071–77.

———. 1998. 'Globalization, Sexuality, and the Visual Field', in Mary E. John and Janaki Nair (eds), *A Question of Silence: The Sexual Economics of Modern India*, pp. 368–96. New Delhi: Kali for Women.

Kaplan, Caren. 1996. 'Postmodern Geographies: Feminist Politics of Location', in Caren Kaplan, *Questions of Travel: Postmodern Discourses of Displacement*, pp. 143–87. Durham, N.C., and London: Duke University Press.

Kohli, Atul. 1989. 'Politics of Economic Liberalisation in India', *World Development*, 17 (3): 305–28.

Krishna, Sankaran. 1996. 'Cartographic Anxiety: Mapping the Body Politic in India', in Michael J. Shapiro and Hayward R. Alker (eds), *Challenging Boundaries: Global Flows, Territorial Identities*, pp. 193–214. Minneapolis: University of Minnesota Press.

Layoun, Mary. 1994. 'The Female Body and "Transnational" Reproduction; or, Rape by Any Other Name?' in Grewal and Kaplan, *Scattered Hegemonies: Postmodernity and Transnational Feminist Practices*. Minneapolis and London: University of Minneapolis Press, pp. 63–75.

Liu, Laura Y. 2000. 'Organizing around Multiple Forms of Identity: Community Groups Serving New York City's Chinatowns', Paper presented at the annual conference of the Association of American Geographers, Pittsburgh.

Malkki, Liisa. 1994. 'Citizens of Humanity' Inernationalism and the Imagined Community of Nations', *Diaspora*, 3 (1): 41–68.
———. 1997. 'National Geographic: The Rooting of Peoples and the Territorialization of National Identity among Scholars and Refugees', in Akhil Gupta and James Ferguson (eds), *Culture, Power, Place: Explorations in Critical Anthropology*. Durham, N.C., and London: Duke University Press, pp. 52–74.
Mankekar, Purnima. 1999. *Screening Culture, Viewing Politics: An Ethnography of Television, Womanhood, and Nation in Postcolonial India*. Durham, N.C. and London: Duke University Press.
Massey, Doreen. 1994. *Space, Place, and Gender*. Minneapolis: University of Minnesota Press.
Mazumdar, Ranjani. 1996. 'Is There a Type beyond the Stereotype? Women in Hindi Cinema', *Voices*, 4 (2): 29–32.
McClintock, Anne. 1997. 'No Longer in a Future Heaven', in Anne McClintock, Aamir Mufti and Ella Shohat (eds), *Dangerous Liaisons: Gender, Nation, and Postcolonial Perspectives*, pp. 352–96. Minneapolis: University of Minnesota Press.
Menon, Parvathi. 1996. 'Pageant and Protests', *Frontline*, 13 December, pp. 4–16.
Mitchell, Timothy. 1989. 'The World as Exhibition', *Comparative Studies in Society and History*, 31 (2): 217–36.
Ninan, T.N. 1985. 'Rise of the Middle Class', *India Today*, 15 December.
Ong, Aihwa. 1990. 'State versus Islam: Malay Families, Women's Bodies, and the Body Politic in Malaysia', *American Ethnologist*, 17 (2): 258–76.
Oza, Rupal. 1999. 'Contentious Bodies: Globalization, Sexuality and the Politics of Culture in India'. Ph.D. dissertation, Rutgers University.
Parker, Andrew, Mary Russo, Doris Sommer and Patricia Yaeger (eds). 1992. *Nationalisms and Sexualities*. New York: Routledge.
Rajagopal, Arvind. 1999. 'Thinking about the New Indian Middle Class: Gender, Advertising and Politics in an Age of Economic Reform', in Rajeshwari Sunder Rajan (ed.), *Signposts: Gender Issues in Post-Independence India*, pp. 57–100. New Delhi: Kali for Women.
Sanghvi, Vir. 1996. 'Why I brought Miss World to India', *Sunday*, 17 November, 12–21.
Sarkar, Tanika. 1993. 'Women's Agency within Authoritarian Communalism: The Rashtrasevika Samiti and Ramjanmabhoomi', in Gyanendra Pandey (ed.), *Hindus and Others: The Question of Identity in India Today*, pp. 24–44. New Delhi: Viking.
Shah, Nandita, Sujata Gothoskar, Nandita Gandhi and Amrita Chhachhi. 1994. 'Structural Adjustment, Feminisation of Labour Force and Organisational Strategies', *Economic and Political Weekly*, 29 (18): 39–48.
Srikanth, B.R. 1996. 'Uma Vows to Kill to Stop Miss World', *The Asian Age*, 25 October, p. 1.
Upadhyay, V. 1996. 'Rise in Prices', in Alternate Survey Group (ed.), *Alternative Economic Survey, 1995–96*, pp. 31–34. New Delhi: Delhi Science Forum.
Wallerstein, Immanuel. 1991. *Geopolitics and Geoculture: Essays on the Changing World-System*. New York: Cambridge University Press.
Wilson, Rob and Wimal Dissanayake (eds). 1996. *Global/Local: Cultural Production and the Transnational Imaginary*. Durham, N.C., and London: Duke University Press.
Wu, Judy Tzu-Chun. 1997. 'Loveliest Daughter of Our Ancient Cathay!: Representations of Ethnic and Gender Identity in the Miss Chinatown U.S.A. Beauty Pageant', *Journal of Social History*, 31 (1): 5–31.

FOURTEEN

More than Just Tacking Women on to the 'Macro-Picture': Feminist Contributions to Globalisation Discourses*

Sharmila Rege[1]

In the 1970s and 1980s, the most urgent task for feminists reviewing the social science discourse was that of addressing the questions of the 'invisibility' of women. More than two decades after the emergence of second wave feminist political activism and scholarship, one would imagine that feminists would no longer have to contend with questions of invisibility and legitimacy of gender as a category of analysis. In the 1990s, gender index had become a crucial factor of assessment, be it for the World Bank or the Human Development Report. The much-celebrated 'success' of women's micro-credit programmes has meant that gender needs and planning have become imperative for all projects in the NGO sector. The decade has also been marked by visibility of upper-class/caste women in 'public'—be it in the anti-Mandal protests or the violence and looting during the Gujarat carnage. As Tharu and Niranjana (1994) have commented, 'women are suddenly everywhere' (p. 93), and yet this visibility is not something at which feminists can take heart. It seems to raise more problems than ways out for a theory of gender. A theory of gender in times of globalisation has to contend with old questions of the 'invisibility' of gender, new questions of contesting the 'hypervisibility' of the market and inverted feminisms, as also the questions of conceptualising 'differences among women'. Consider, for instance, the conversation between Will Hutton and Anthony Giddens on the character of globalisation. Hutton says, 'The growth in personal household services is the result of the emergence of the two-earner household who have to buy in services because the woman is no longer at home' (quoted in Lutz 2002: 90). The automatism in the phrase 'household services have to be bought' suggests the persistence of the older questions —of invisibility and the absence of gender as a category of analyses. The only visible woman in Hutton's statement, 'the woman who is no longer at home'—the professional middle-class woman—stands as if for all women, making invisible the gender-race character of the domestic services that have to be bought in. The rise of right-wing and market feminisms on the one hand and the significant political assertions and theoretical interventions of Third World and Dalit feminists on the other have challenged this assumed universality of gender oppression.

Feminist analyses of globalisation that seek to contest the assumed universality of gender oppression must account for relations of power not only between men and women, north and south, but also between women. In the last two decades or more, feminist analyses has mapped the dynamics of gender, race and global capital; the dynamics of caste, gender and global capital is emerging as an urgent area of inquiry. The analyses of the impact of the New Economic Policy on Dalits (Guru 2000; Jogdand 2001; Teltumbde 2001; Narsalay 2002) have focused on caste and livelihoods, and the reconstitution of land relations and urban spaces. The National Federation of Dalit Women (NFDW) [NGO Declaration on Gender and Racism 2001]

*Originally published in the *Economic and Political Weekly*, Vol. XXXVIII, No. 43, 25 October 2003, pp. 4555–563.

underlines the intersections between community, race and poverty as vital to understanding the implications of globalisation for women in generally and especially Dalit women. The NFDW has thus suggested a materially and methodologically more meaningful juncture of feminist, labour and Dalit studies. This chapter does not even attempt a summary of the current state of all these discussions on globalisation; the very scope of the discussions would make such a task impossible. Given that the immediate task is to review the perspectives that theorise the connections between globalisation and gender, the challenge is to underline the ways in which a feminist focus suggests new insights and perspectives on established ways of seeing. We begin by mapping some of the major features of contemporary globalisation on which there is basic agreement among social scientists, and outline the different foci of the new analytical paradigms suggested by them. This makes possible a comparison with feminist perspectives on globalisation—so that in the final analyses the distinctively feminist contributions to current globalisation debates and politics, which have not always been clear, may be drawn out.

Debates on Globalisation: Through a Feminist Lens

Debates on globalisation can no longer be confined to the academic, as the term has circulated in diverse ways into business, political and journalistic discourses. Within academic debates, too, as there are no clear-cut lines of contestation, categorisation of trends and positions remains broad. A broad classification between globalists who see contemporary globalisation as a real and historical development and the sceptics who see it as an ideological construction has been suggested (Held et al. 1999). Two broad trends, albeit internally differentiated, one more biased towards international political economy and the other towards the sociological and cultural aspects of globalisation, have been traced (Marchand and Runyan 2000). Across the different classifications and trends, despite major differences with respect to matters of historical interpretation and normative argument, there seems to be a basic agreement on some key issues, processes and actors involved in globalisation. The important issues over which there is substantial agreement have been summarised as follows:

- The global economy with the capacity to work as a unit in real time on a planetary scale as historically distinct from the world economy.
- The importance of neo-liberal ideology in influencing the direction of globalisation.
- Cultural ramifications of global capital as recognised by both homogenisers and heterogenisers.
- TNCs, states and financial institutions as the main driving force in globalisation.
- The role of ICTs, of knowledge, information, affect and communication as contributing to global-isation, and increasing and transforming the velocity and reach of social and cultural networks.
- Global migrations as a major process through which the new transnational political economy is being reconstituted.
- The witnessing of an environmental crisis and a risk society and consciousness of a global condition.
- Distinct patterns of stratification; the global military hierarchy dominated by the US, the political and economic hierarchy between the OECD and non-OECD states, and within the OECD the G-8 having the greatest control over networks.
- Transformation in the management of production, distribution and the production process, which transforms the nature of labour.
- The proliferation of nation-states and the loss of the nation-state as the sole site of sovereignty despite it remaining a critical player. (Brah 2002; Marchand and Runyan 2000)

To a feminist reviewer there are at least two interesting observations, perhaps one seemingly more obvious, to be made from this summary of the main features of the globalisation discourse. The first observation, that feminist scholars hardly figure in these accounts though feminists have extended the debates from different perspectives (Adam 2002; Brah 2002; Dietrich 1996; Ghosh 1994; Krishnaraj 1988; Rai 2002; Sen and Grown 1985; Shiva and Mies 1993), is perhaps more predictable than the second. Feminist analyses have directly and indirectly drawn upon these debates and have expressed its debt to the 'second and critical' wave of literature on globalisation, especially in contesting the prevalent and tenacious myths about the predetermined logic of globalisation. However, as Adam (2002) has argued, the fact that recent prominent discourses of globalisation do not speak to the feminist debates is apparent, as the econo-techno and institutional processes outlined as having a pervasive, if uneven, impact are treated as being gender neutral. Further, though the authors of institutional globalisation, especially those who have concentrated on the globalisation of poverty (Choussudovsky 1997), have given some attention to the gendered impact of globalisation, their analysis leaves the depth of gendered experiences largely untouched. This is particularly surprising since feminist scholarship, at least since the 1980s, had focused on the internationalisation of manufacture, production and feminisation of the off-shoring of labour. In a sense the gendered lens of these scholars had laid bare the nexus between the dismantling of the proletariat in the First World, and the formation of an off-shore feminised proletariat as both an operational reality and an analytical strategy (Sassen 2000). The first observation thus suggests that we explore the lack of dialogue with the feminist discourse on globalisation. Does this lack of dialogue with the feminist discourse stem from a disparate set of concerns? What are the blind spots created by this apparent lack of dialogue?

The second and less predictable observation about the dominant discourse of globalisation concerns its dispersed character. There are wide gaps between the language of the academic communities and the everyday understanding of the experiences of global forces by the poor (Appadurai 2000). The same may be said of the analyses of global conditions in the discourses located in the north and those in the south, including the south in the north (Pieterse 2000). There seems to be a growing divorce between academic debates and the vernacular discourses, with the common metaphor for globalisation in the booklets published in regional languages being imperialism or neo-colonialism (Rege and Chavan 2001). In contrast, much of the feminist discussions on globalisation seem to step back from the abstractions that constitute academic practice to consider the problems of the global everyday. The discussions seek to democratise the knowledge about globalisation, thus bridging academic research, policy discourse concerning trade, labour and environment, movement literature, and advocacy efforts. There have been several efforts by feminists to democratise knowledge about globalisation. Reports like 'Womenspeak: United Voices Against Globalisation, Poverty and Violence in India', annotated bibliographies on the impact of the structural adjustment programme (Lingam et al. 2001), several documents brought out in regional languages on the occasion of the Global March 2000, are all cases in point. In Maharashtra, for instance, at mass gatherings of women such as those organised on the International Women's Day and the 'Bhartiya Stree Mukti Divas' (Indian Women's Liberation Day), the impact of globalisation on women and marginalised communities in India has been highlighted, and detailed resolutions against structural adjustment policies passed. Feminist discussions on globalisation across the different sites of advocacy, resistance marches, academic writings, conference proceedings and resolutions passed in mass meetings intersect and flow into each other. The intersection and dialogue between issues and perspectives across the varied sites of the academic, organisational, political and advocacy efforts are apparent. This observation leads us to rephrase the question raised earlier as—is it a different set of concerns and/or a different mode of analyses that constitutes the distinctive character of the feminist contributions to the debates on globalisation? We shall argue that it is a mode of relational analysis that makes feminist contributions distinctive, and make a case for combined conceptual forces that would help make connections and trace the naturalised assumptions in the debate on globalisation.

Globalisation: Mapping Feminist Perspectives and Concerns

In tracing the feminist studies on globalisation while refraining from a 'stages or phases' approach, at least three discrete and overlapping perspectives may be mapped. There is, no doubt, internal differentiation in positions within perspectives, and considerable overlap between the three perspectives. However, their theoretical genealogies and legacies are distinctly located—more specifically in development studies, the postcolonial/Third World/transnational studies, and practices and post-communism transitology studies. The first, which may be outlined as a gender and political economy of the development perspective, has documented and theorised the underside of globalisation through women's experiences of the Structural Adjustment Programme (SAP) in Asia, Africa and Latin America. The second, which may be called a transnational feminist perspective, draws upon postcolonial analyses of uneven and dissimilar circuits of culture and capital. It seeks to provide a position from which to argue for a comparative, relational feminist praxis that is transnational in its response to and engagement with global processes of colonisation. The third perspective, which may be outlined as gender perspectives between states and markets, draws upon the experiences of women living through the post-communist transitions. It seeks to underline the specificity of their situation, and suggests the need to develop paradigms that go beyond women as losers or winners of the transition. We shall briefly outline the areas and issues explored by each perspective, and then pull together the important issues in the feminist discourse of globalisation.

Gender and the Political Economy of Development Perspective

In the mid-1980s 'The Women and the Household in Asia' series established the centrality of the household as the concrete site of the production and reproduction of social life. In noting the variations within and across households, this collection documented and analysed home-based production across traditional activities and new technologies (Singh and Kelles-Vitanen 1987). Women's labour in the free trading zones, food processing, coir and garment export industry in the Asian region came to be documented. This series remains one of the early documentations of the global political economy as the interaction of reproductive and productive economies. This also marked the beginning of a South Asia framework in feminist studies; a kind of regional feminist internationalism that has gained momentum in the last decade. It also set the household as the locus of feminist interrogations of the global economic regimes. In the 1990s, while there were some feminist reflections on macro-economic policy (Dewan 1999; Ghosh 1994; Krishnaraj 1996), the feminist focus was largely on the effects of the Structural Adjustment Policy. The effects of SAP, especially as they directly and indirectly shape gender relations inside and outside the household, came to be underlined. This engagement with globalisation as lived experience is closely related to the special relationship between gender and development studies.

Studies in the field of development, in contrast to globalisation studies, are tuned in to gender, and their own development has been closely linked to the second wave of feminist theorisation (Adam 2002). This is reflected in the feminist challenges to the growth model posed by the basic needs approach (Nussbaum 1999), feminist environmentalism (Agarwal 1992), and eco-feminist and post-development critiques of development. The eco-feminist (Shiva 1989) and Marxist feminist critiques of the gendered nature of capitalist accumulation and the international division of labour (Mies et al. 1988) have become central to the development discourse. Feminist perspectives on globalisation vary in the emphasis they place on anti-capitalism as anti-industrialism, the importance of a politics of place, and the possibility of strategic engagement with the community, state and international economic institutions (Rai 2002).

Gender and development perspectives that draw from a socialist feminist tradition have made a significant contribution towards outlining the gendered character of the processes of global restructuring. Research in this tradition has been guided by questions about the material structures and practices—the sites, so to say, of global restructuring in specific places, as also the sites and strategies of resistance. Feminist analysis has mapped labour, livelihood and security, household, sexuality, and the state as some of the major sites of global restructuring. The structural deformation of subsistence production, and the transfer of access of natural resources from poor women to multinationals has been documented as having deleterious effects on the food security system (Bhattacharya 1994). The impact of market-driven agricultural prices, reduction of food subsidies and targeting strategies in the public distribution system for women in poorer households has been noted. The institutionalisation of SAP through the international legal regimes saw feminist analyses developing a political and normative case against the gendered phenomenon of environmental damage and commodification of social knowledge (Mies and Shiva 1993). Global market systems, it has been argued, are hyper-masculinised sites that recognise only certain forms of knowledge that lead to economic emasculation in the marketplace. Male populations of the Third World are feminised; the suicides of cotton farmers and their invisible widows are cases in point (Rai 2002). The impact of the displacement of female agricultural labour in terms of increased violence both at home and work has been another area of concern (*Womenspeak* 2000).

Considering that violence and discrimination against girls by their own families is not a new phenomenon, research has sought to trace the increased intensity and wider spread of such practices (Banerjee 2002; Kapadia 2002). It has been noted, for instance, that even among castes and in regions where dowry was so far unknown, dowry has become the central achievement of a consumerist subject, an important diacritic of translocal modernity (Kapadia 2002). Most of the studies contest the neo-liberal mantra of market-led growth by foregrounding indicators like women's access to land, property, credit, employment, environment, education, health and housing. It is argued that women pay a disproportionate share of the costs of economic globalisation while being excluded from its benefits. Macro issues of health policy have been traced to the micro mechanisms of consumption, production and distribution of healthcare within households (Karlekar 2000). Cuts in public spending have been traced to the expansion of women's work outside the home, longer hours of work, daughters foregoing school for care work, and increased malnourishment and violence (Afshar and Dennis 1991; Beneria 1999; Deshmukh-Ranadive 2000; Elson 1989; Grown et al. 2000; Moser 1989). This concern with the impact of SAP on social security has shaped into specialised studies of budgets, and state and central government expenditure patterns from gender perspectives (Patel 2002; Prabhu 1994).

There is a wealth of studies on gendered global labour markets, especially on the feminisation of labour, the conditions of labour, and ideologies of femininity operating in the export promotion zones. The feminisation of labour and the concentration of women in assembly lines in FTZs, sweatshops, homework, domestic service and the sex industry, resulting in female migration and gendered vulnerability, has been documented. The feminisation of labour, its flexibilisation and casualisation are underscored as being structural to the new international division of labour (Gothoskar 2000; Mitter and Rowbotham 1995; Shah et al. 1994; Streefkerk 2001). It is the control over and flexibility of women's labour, and the ability to lay off and recruit as and when needed that guides the preference for female labour. It has been argued that the process of feminisation of export employment in East Asia peaked in the early 1990s. However, even before the financial crisis began to have an impact on economic activity, women workers were disproportionately prone to job loss. The crisis adjustment period has seen a large number of women workers in this region working on their own account or on a subcontracting basis (Ghosh 2002). The feminisation of export-oriented employment has taken a particularly regressive form in India, pointing to the limits of aggregative models of social policy in contexts of differentiated populations. Gender differentiation acts in a more complex manner because of the interrelationships within households. In India, where the marginal utilisation of women workers is in the lowest-paid parts of the production chain, the feminisation of work has been marked by an organisational structure of outsourcing and home-based work. Thus, women are deprived of all benefits of outside employment, be it healthcare or collective bargaining (Ghosh 2002).

The gendered impact in specific spheres like electronics, ICTs, teletrade and teleworking are being explored (Banerjee 1996; Mitter 2000) with a specific focus on understanding gender, flexi-time and the use of new tools. The role of the family, state and trade union structures in distributing IT-related employment has been explored (Mitter 1995). The new opportunities and kinds of double burden that rapid changes taking place in the concept of the workplace, especially related to teleworking, bring for women have been documented (Gothoskar 2000). The assumption that the mobility and flexibility of the ICT sector are, 'virtues' where women workers are concerned is being interrogated (Kelkar et al. 2002). Feminist analyses have sought to unmask the gendered character of the neo-liberal discourse, underlining the gendered metaphors and symbolism that naturalise the relations of dominance. Neo-liberal discourse draws upon gendered binaries in privileging finance over manufacture, market over state, the global over the local, and the consumer over the producer. For instance, the market is represented as robust as against the feminised state, which is represented as a drag on the economy that must be subordinated. The state thus seeks to re-masculinise itself through a role akin to that of the private sector, minimising welfare and increasing its role of surveillance and coercion (Marchand and Runyan 2000). The changing form and nature of the nation-state and the rise of right-wing parties and state-sponsored fundamentalisms have thus been areas of focus in feminist debates on globalisation (Moghdam 1996a). The emphasis on family values placed by neo-nationalisms not only regulates and mobilises women, but also consolidates the private sphere that services late capitalism (Chakravarti and Sangari 1999). Domestic labour is a part of the dependable social relations in which the market is embedded, as women's labour provides the buffer against the depredations of the market. It is apparent that the gendered critique of SAP goes beyond considerations of the impact of SAP on women to cover discussions on the interrogations of neo-liberal economics. Feminist analyses have charted out concrete ways in which the gender biases of micro, meso and macro-level institutions such as the household, governments, firms and markets operate.

A focus on the effects on women's lives underlines the paradoxes of global restructuring. Deregulation has been accompanied by an increased regulation of reproduction, austerity by consumerism, and a feminised workforce with increased levels of malnutrition and violence against women. The feminist focus on the household underscores the paradox of the home, which is at once the 'haven' and worksite for flexibilised labour. The gender and political economy of the development perspective on globalisation builds upon two older phases of gendering the recent history of economic internationalisation. As Sassen (2000) argues, development literature after Boserup had underlined that far from being unconnected, the subsistence sector and modern capitalist enterprise were articulated through a gender dynamic.

The second phase in the 1980s emerged with the scholarship that underlined connections between the internationalisation of production and feminisation of the proletariat, especially in the garments and electronics industry. The focus had been on how offshoring and feminising restricts any collective gains for the female proletariat. In the last decade the focus has been on the impact of debt and debt servicing as systematic features on the lives of women. Sex work, entertainment and export of domestic workers are significant sources for the alternate circuits of profit-making and revenue generation for the states in indebted economies. These alternate circuits of survival sex and entertainment work, and immigrant domestic work suggest the feminisation of survival (Sassen 2000). Thus, the history of economic internationalisation through a gendered lens lays bare the nexus between patriarchies and the capitalist enterprise, both as an operational reality and analytic strategy. Such an analytic strategy has guided feminist analyses to draw out generalisations about the impact of SAP. These generalisations have no doubt a crucial significance, especially for policy implications; but essentialist generalisations may turn out to be counterproductive. The effects of globalisation on the lives of women have been multiple, contradictory, inclusionary and exclusionary (Afshar and Barrientos 1999), and cannot be overlooked. Essentialist generalisations about the feminisation of poverty can lead to the reduction of gender to the problem of poverty (Jackson 1996). Women then come to be used both nationally and internationally, as instruments to manage poverty. This discovery of poor women's economic efficiency then ends up effectively collaborating with views of marginalised men as 'irresponsible'. Those working at the interface of gender and development have to refigure priorities, not by insisting on some putative 'pure' economy, but by broadening feminist conceptions of the economy itself (John 1996). In order to grasp the present situation of flux, intellectual practices that fix differences, whether between spaces, sexes or countries, have to be interrogated. Moving beyond dichotomies requires that the symbolic, institutional and subjective dimensions of gender be considered (Davids and Van Driel 2001). We need to recall that if the trap of gender collapsing into women is to be avoided, feminist analyses of the processes of globalisation will have to involve more than the complex relations of power between men and women. The complex relations of power that exclude some men from the dominant order of patriarchy and those between women in different class, caste and ethnic locations need to be considered.

Post-Colonial/Transnational Feminist Perspectives

Transnational feminist perspectives use the term 'transnational' over international in order to reflect on and destabilise the boundaries of nation, race and gender. This perspective has sought to analyse how inequalities of class, gender, nationality, sexuality and ethnicity are created through movements over time and space in particular ways. This is contrasted with socialist and liberal conservative models of internationalism. Transnational feminist perspectives are, it is argued, clearly different from international feminism, which has often evoked a 'difference as pluralism model'. In such a model, Third World women have always borne a disproportionate burden of difference. Global feminism, which assumes global sisterhood, is also different from transnational feminism, which emphasises the uneven, unequal and complex relations between women in diverse parts of the world. It builds upon the feminist analysis of the new international division of labour (Leacock and Safa 1986), underlining how capitalism depended on sexism in order to be global. The focus now is on migration and diasporas—unsettling the assumed categories of consumption and production as well as tradition and modernity. In different ways, transnational feminist practices seek to unravel the global-ised histories of gender and power. Race and gender, then, are not only matters of identity politics, but also discourses with concrete effects within the history of imperialism (Grewal and Kaplan 2000).

The perspectives of post-colonial/transnationalist feminisms provide a relational and comparative con-ception of identity, culture and history to understand specific processes of domination and subordination. The unit of analysis is shifted from local, regional and national cultures to relations and processes across cultures (Mohanty 1991).

Analyses of incorporation of Third World women into the global division of labour at different geo-graphical ends—Silicon Valley and the lace makers in Narsapur—outlines the relationship between job typing and social identity of the workers concentrated in low-paying, unsafe and invisible sectors of labour. Inherent to globalisation is the 're-domestication' of women, made apparent in home-based work and ideologies of Third World mothers in Silicon Valley (Alexander and Mohanty 1997). Thus, much of what is narrated in the language of immigration and ethnicity is a series of processes that have as much to do with the globalisation of economic, cultural activity and identity formation, as with the increasingly marked racialisation of market segmentation. Often, transnational feminists underline the ways in which components of the production process in the advanced global economy, which take place in immigrant work environments, are not recognised as part of the global information economy (Sassen 2000).

The analyses of domestic workers in the North (Anderson 2000; Lutz 2002; Phizacklea 1998) have pointed to global care chains as a crucial aspect of the international division of labour. This domestic service sector in Europe is different from earlier appearances in that the domestic workers are mainly migrant women—suggesting, as transnational feminists argue, the intersectionality of class, gender and ethnic differences in globalised labour markets. Feminist scholars have traced the denial of green cards to domestic workers, and the long-term chain of care and dependencies that follow.

The feminisation of migration has also translated into a sexualisation of women's labour. There have been efforts to map the sexual economy routes from places of dislocation to places of greater accumulation. The travel money, the debt bondage that it ensures—a geography of their recruitment across borders is traced, and this is also traced as the routes of circuits of survival at the margins of pan-capitalist reality (Biemann 2002). The 1980s and 1990s has witnessed a boom in prison construction and a sharp rise in women prisoners in Europe and North America. Transnational feminist analyses have drawn attention to the new regimes of accumulation and discipline of the prison-industrial complex, which draws upon the systems of racial and patriarchal exploitation. The connections between the fundamental shift in the role of the state, the intricate web of relations of the prison-industrial complex, and the US-led global war on drugs are underlined. These processes are seen as constitutive of a corporate maximisation of profits (Sudbury 2002), and of the global feminisation and racialisation of poverty. The focus on the labour of Third World women in the north, it is argued, underlines the limits of any simple class analysis. The effort thus is to underline the centrality of gender within the historical processes of globalisation, and women's agency in social move-ments in opposition to globalisation. One of the significant contributions of this perspective is the focus that it brings to the mapping of gender and race parameters of global capitalism. Studies have sought to map how women's work is constitutively defined in terms of gender, race and caste parameters, and the ways in which capitalist ideology, processes and values come to be naturalised through this. Thus, transnational feminists have conceptualised the 'scattered yet connected hegemonies' (Grewal and Kaplan 2000) of global economic institutions, nation-states, patriarchal households and other structures, traditional or juridical legal, which support exploitation.

Transnational feminist practices have no doubt made a major contribution in underlining white femin-ism as situated, local and partial. However, several questions emerge—are transnational feminist practices limited by their contestation of generalisations? Do they privilege the discursive over the material? One of the seminal texts of transnational feminism is Mohanty's (1984) essay 'Under Western Eyes'; an essay that dismantled hegemonic western feminism's construction of Third World feminisms. Revisiting this essay 16 years later in the context of privatisation and corporatisation of public life, Mohanty (2002) sought to trace the challenges facing a transnational perspective in the 21st century. She argues for a feminist solidarity model that remains as committed as before to struggles that critique the effects of discursive colonisation on the lives of marginalised women. However, the challenge now is to see how specifying differences can make way for the theorisation of universal concerns. Transnational perspectives undoubtedly, have to guard against the earlier 'sisterhood is global' format that now appears in the mantra of human rights. The crucial task for such perspectives is to specify the differences in the articulations of gender, women's bodies and labour. Having made the differences visible, efforts must be directed towards theorising this visibility as a process of articulating a more inclusive anti-capitalist politics.

A more recent trend in feminist transitology studies has argued that feminist scholars, like the mainstream ones, have rarely analysed the so-called transitions to post-communism in a comprehensive manner. Feminist scholarship on post-socialist societies has argued that the ways in which the transitions shift the very boundaries of state and civil society, public and private, national and international, need deliberation (True 2000). In the last decade several studies have emphasised the loss of former socialist rights to employment, living wages, child-care, and other public services as disproportionately affecting women in central and eastern Europe (Aslanbeigui et al. 1994). The absence of women in political institutions and that of women's organisations and movements has been noted. In such a context, the diffusion of western democracy in central and eastern Europe has been seen as producing a masculine public sphere (Einhorn 1992; Funk and Mueller 1993; Mies and Shiva 1993; Moghdam 1996b).

A more recent trend in feminist transitology studies has argued that mainstream feminist scholars have approached the study of post-socialism from a teleological rather than a gender perspective. The whole focus, they argue, has been on women as victims and as losers, creating thereby a category of victimised women not unlike the earlier construction of Third World women 'under western eyes'. The importance of analyses of global economic integration as it takes place on gendered terrain is not undermined. However, the importance of directing efforts towards locating women's emerging sense of agency and feminism at the intersection of state repression and the liberal democratic market economy is highlighted. Incorporation into a gendered global division of labour as well as patterns of gender segregation under socialism, it is argued, have shaped the emergence of new forms of feminism or 'gender humanism' (Beck 2000). The various configurations of struggles against neo-liberalism, which emerge from a context that is devoid of critiques of patriarchy but rooted in experiences of gender equality under socialism, are outlined as areas requiring further deliberation.

Having outlined the three feminist perspectives, we shall return to the questions raised earlier in the chapter regarding the distinctive character of feminist contributions to the debates on globalisation.

Gendering Globalisation: More than Just Tacking Women onto the 'Macro-picture'

As noted earlier, the grand theories of globalisation have erased gender as integral to social and economic dimensions, thus leading to an implicit masculinisation of macro-structural models. What, then, are the implications of ignoring gender as an analytical lens? The feminist documentation of the impact of SAPs has made visible the increasing burden of women's unpaid work and the crisis of social reproduction. This challenges the notion that paid production economy can function in isolation from the world of home-bound labour. Analyses of women's labour brings into focus the four areas of labour that are generally overlooked: subsistence, unpaid work, domestic production and voluntary work (Beneria and Feldman 1992), and helps to foreground the 'productive' economy and the gendered nature of production. The liberal discourse, which, while constructing the market as private sphere and the state as public, makes invisible the private household or lumps it with civil society, is contested. Situated feminist studies that critique the effects of globalisation on local grounds reconfigure the private and public divide, and stretch the boundaries of what is considered the appropriate domain of the global.

The transnational feminist perspectives provide a global social analytic and helps to guard off reductionist analysis. Such an analytic is global in two senses; first, it engages with 'national' and local histories as they imbricate in a world system fashioned by imperialism and colonialism. Second, it understands the social as the intersection of the political, economic and cultural/ideological, none of which can be reduced to the other. It provides a heuristic model of imperialism that draws attention to the concreteness of particular historical conjunctures, whose dynamics are shaped not by some predetermined foundations whether structural or discursive, but by the outcome of specific struggles in history (Sinha 2000: 1078). The writing of particular groups of women workers in the global division of labour outlines the interests of contemporary transnational capitalism and its strategies of recolonisation. These strategies, which draw upon indigenous social hierarchies to construct, reproduce and maintain ideologies of skilled/unskilled, feminine/masculine, are constitutive of the processes of globalisation. For all their transformative power, the material and cultural forms of globalisation do not have a homogenised effect. The processes are dialectical, occurring on concrete culturally occupied locals, and with socially embedded human beings. This is evident in the uneasy fusion of enfranchisement and exclusion, of xenophobia and the prospect of world citizenship without the protectionism of nationhood. How do we make sense of the unanticipated ways of inclusion and marginalisation, of the magnification of class differences and undercutting of class consciousness (Comaroff and Comaroff 2002: 298). Feminist perspectives from post-socialist societies guard against an overdetermined reading of homogenised effects, and have suggestions for the study of the interplay between regional and global markets, fundamentalist forces and local identities (Molyneux 1994; True 2000). Across the different feminist perspectives, a relational mode of analysis is what sets them apart from the mainstream social science discourse of globalisation. Gender analyses have involved more relational thinking (Peterson 1997) in that it has been concerned with globalisation as not only happening out there as a set of abstract practices, institutions and structures, but as also being linked to how we think (meaning, ideology) and who we are (subjectivity, agency, self and collective identity). Through its focus on localised questions of experience, culture, history and identity, feminist scholarship on globalisation provides a position for comparative and relational analysis. The concrete everyday experience of the global against the abstractions of theory is not a feminist repudiation of theory, and nor does the focus on sites mean an isolation from larger contexts in which they are located. In fact, the focus on lived experiences of globalisation in feminist scholarship helps historicise theory in both spatial and temporal senses, and recognise its limitations in dealing with differences. It gives voice to those who inhabit these sites as compared to the 'purveyors of abstractions', who claim omniscience by virtue of being outside these sites (Dirlik 2002). Leading expositions of globalisation theory have offered powerful models of circuits of movements, and social and economic changes encompassing our world. However, there is little specificity about how these are configured in particular places, for particular groups of people, and to what particular ends (Freeman 2001). The point, thus, is not one of merely noting the absence of gender in the grand renderings of globalisation, but probing into the ways in which this sets limits on our overall understanding of globalisation. However, the challenge is to move towards feminist reconceptualisations of globalisation, whereby the local and the situated underlined by feminist analyses is not merely seen as 'effects', but as constitutive ingredients of the processes of globalisation. There have been some attempts to put forth such a systemic analysis of the relations between patriarchies and global capital accumulation (Mies 1986; Ward 1991). Efforts at reconceptualisation require that the macro-picture in which the producers, consumers and those bypassed come to be situated within social and cultural processes and meanings that are central to globalisation itself. Arguing for such efforts that underscore the significance of combined conceptual forces, feminists ask—would not beginning with studies of the lives of those who provide the cheapest labour in the new technologies and clearly whose lives the technology does not permeate help to address the technological agency and inevitability that creeps into Castells' gender-sensitive and historical analysis? How would global care networks be conceptualised when the crucial networks of personal dependencies of paid and unpaid services are considered? Would not feminist perspectives bring to Bauman's conception of the division of the world into a hierarchy of owners and non-owners of means and forces of information concrete particulars of contextual difference? Does not the erasure of the power/gender dimension from Beck's frame of global inequalities of risk render it invisible and therefore vulnerable to exploitation? (Adam 2002: 10).

There have been feminist projects explicitly committed to connecting the experiential and institutional processes of globalisation. Some projects have sought to draw upon feminist theories of difference in an effort to use techniques of feminist cultural theory to understand the reconfigurations of global culture and global nature. They have provided important insights into how nature figures in the production of global products, subjects, knowledges and communities (Franklin et al. 2000). A significant contribution has been made by feminist projects that seek to address the space bias in globalisation discourse. Drawing upon feminist epistemology, the taken for granted time politics of globalisation is challenged, and time-based ontology is used to render visible the gender politics of globalisation. The time politics of globalisation is located in the four Cs—the mutually supporting processes of creation, commodification, control and colonisation of time. The gender bias associated with the four Cs, the devaluation of reproductive work while relying on this work in the shadowlands for profits, is underscored. Such analyses foreground the role of time in the legitimation of corporate imperialism, economic colonialism, and the creation of local inequalities and global socio-environmental destruction (Adam 2002). Recent works of feminists (Chang and Ling 2000; Freeman 2001; Ong 1999) have underscored the relationships between space, movement and gender in mapping globalisation. These works push us to challenge the dualism of local/global, and ethnography/theory, and to rethink macrostructural models that have limited explanatory and descriptive powers.

The contributions of feminist perspectives to social science debates on globalisation, as outlined in this chapter, make a case for combined conceptual forces. Similarly, several conceptually hazy areas in feminist globalisation studies would also further support the need for combined conceptual forces. Consider, for instance, the area of growing literature on feminist resistance to globalisation, with which this chapter has not engaged at all. Much of this work on women's resistance to globalisation either celebrates the local—meshwork or politics of place (Hartcourt and Escobar 2002), often slipping conceptually from movements to NGOs to networks as if they were one and the same. Much is being said about the impact of feminist transnational networks and organising around reproductive rights, growth of religious fundamentalism and SAP (Moghadam 1996c). Feminist analysis needs to conceptualise more clearly, drawing upon sociological analysis, the differences between the transnational networks of NGOs, social movements, issues and identity, and project coalitions.

The linkages connected to flow of resources and discourses need interrogation (Basu 2000), as do the different contexts from which optimism and opposition to transnational networks surface (Alvarez 2000). The 'success' of micro-credit networks against relatively less successful networks needs comparison. Even as the impact of NGO advocacy networks, especially post-Beijing, have been noted, several questions about the previous state-centredness of the women's movement and the engagement of its leadership with international policy-making institutions need to be explored. What decisions, choices, strategies for resistance, and identity formations do feminist subjectivities envision, especially in the context of the changing character of the nation-state? Have feminists too adopted the 'global imperative' or 'national management' (Bergeron 2001) modes of conceptualising resistance, which limit possibilities of resistance to reassertion of control over national economic space or the globalised women's movement? The implications of movement dynamics, discourses and practices remain under-theorised, suggesting that there's more to do than simply tack women on to macro-structural models of globalisation.

Acknowledgements

[1]This is a revised version of the paper presented at the Symposium on 'Globalisation, Cultural Pluralism and Identities' at the XXVIII All India Sociological Conference, IIT Kanpur, 18–20 Dec 2002. I am grateful to Maitreyi Krishnaraj and Professor Dhanagare for their comments on the paper. I am grateful to Vidyut Bhagwat and Kiran Moghe for meaningful discussions on the theme. I have benefited much from discussions with diploma students of the Krantijyoti Savitribai Phule Women's Studies Centre, Pune University.

References

Adam, Barbara. 2002. 'The Gendered Time Politics of Globalisation of Shadowlands and Elusive Justice', *Feminist Review*, 70 (1–2): 3–30.

Afshar, Haleh and Stephanie Barrientos (eds). 1999. *Women, Globalisation and Fragmentation in the Developing World*. London: Macmillan.

Afshar, Haleh and Carolyne Dennis (eds). 1991. *Women and Adjustment Policies in the Third World*. London: Macmillan.

Agarwal, Bina. 1992. 'The Gender and Environment Debate: Lessons from India', *Feminist Studies*, 18 (1): 119–58.

Alexander, Jacqui M. and Chandra Talpade Mohanty (eds). 1997. *Feminist Genealogies, Colonial Legacies, and Democratic Futures*. New York: Routledge.

Alvarez, Sonia. 2000. 'Translating the Global: Effects of Transnational Organising on Local Feminist Discourses and Practices in Latin America', *Meridians: Feminism, Race, Transnationalism*, 1 (1): 29–67.

Anderson, Bridget. 2000. *Doing the Dirty Work? The Global Politics of Domestic Labour*. London: Zed Books.

Appadurai, Arjun. 2000. 'Grass Roots Globalisation and the Research Imagination', *Public Culture*, 12 (1): 1–21.

Aslanbeigui, Nahid, Steven Pressman and Gale Summerfield (eds). 1994. *Women in the Age of Economic Transformation: Gender Impact of Reforms in Post-Socialist and Developing Countries*. London: Routledge.

Banerjee, Nirmala. 1996. 'The Structural Adjustment Programme and Women's Economic Empowerment', in N. Rao, L. Rurup and R. Sudarshan (eds), *Sites of Change: The Structural Context for Empowering Women In India*, pp. 133–46. New Delhi: Tulika.

———. 2002. 'Between the Devil and the Deep-Sea: Shrinking Options for Women in Contemporary India', in K. Kapadia (ed.), *The Violence of Development: The Politics of Identity, Gender and Social Inequalities in India*, pp. 43–69. New Delhi: Kali for Women.

Basu, Amrita. 2000. 'Globalisation of the Local/Localisation of the Global Mapping Transnational Women's Movements', *Meridians: Feminism, Race, Transnationalism*, 1 (1): 68–84.

Beck, Julia. 2000. '(Re) negotiating Selfhood and Citizenship in the Post-Communist Czech Republic: Five Women Activists Speak about Transition and Feminism', in M.H. Marchand and A.S. Runyan (eds), *Gender and Global Restructuring: Sightings, Sites and Resistances*, pp. 176–94. London and New York: Routledge.

Beneria, Lourdes. 1999. 'Globalisation, Gender and the Davos Man', *Feminist Economics*, 5 (3): pp. 61–83.

Beneria, Lourdes and Shelley Feldman. 1992. *Unequal Burden: Economic Crises, Persistent Poverty and Women's Work*. Boulder: Westview.

Bergeron, Suzanne. 2001. 'Political Economy Discourses of Globalisation and Feminist Politics', *Signs Journal of Women in Culture and Society*, 26 (4): 983–1005.

Bhattacharya, Malini. 1994. 'Women in Dark Times: Gender, Culture and Politics', *Social Scientist*, 22 (3–4): 10–16.

Biemann, Ursula. 2002. 'Remotely Sensed: A Topography of Global Sex Trade', *Feminist Review*, 70 (1–2): 75–89.

Brah, Avtar. 2002. 'Global Mobilities, Local Predicaments: Globalisation and the Critical Imagination', *Feminist Review*, 70 (1–2): 30–46.

Chakravarti, Uma and Sangari Kumkum (eds). 1999. *From Myths to Markets: Essays on Gender*. New Delhi: Manohar.

Chang, Kimberly A. and L.H.M. Ling. 2000. 'Globalisation and Its Intimate Other', in M.H. Marchand and A.S. Runyan (eds), *Gender and Global Restructuring Sightings, Sites and Resistances*. London: Routledge.

Chossudovsky, Michel. 1997. *The Globalisation of Poverty*. Zed Books, London.

Comaroff, Jean and John Comaroff. 2002. 'Millenial Capitalism: First Thoughts on a Second Coming', *Public Culture*, 12 (2): 291–344.

Dalit Intellectual Collective Report. 2002. *Vikalp/Alternatives*, 10 (2): 141–1712.

Davids, Tine and Francine Van Driel. 2001. 'Globalisation and Gender: Beyond Dichotomies', in F. Schuurman (ed), *Globalisation and Development Studies: Challenges for the 21st Century*, pp. 153–77. New Delhi: Vistaar.

Deshmukh-Ranadive, Joy. 2000. 'Introduction' in CWDS (ed.), *Shifting Sands: Women's Lives and Globalisation*, (pp. vii–xiv). Calcutta: Stree.

Dewan, Ritu. 1999. 'Gender Implications of the New Economic Policy: A Conceptual Overview', *Women's Studies International Forum*, 22 (4): 425–29.

Dietrich, Gabriele. 1996. 'Alternative Knowledge Systems and Women's Empowerment: An Organisational Perspective', in N. Rao, L. Rurup and R. Sudarshan (eds), *Sites of Change: The Structural Context for Empowering Women in India*, pp. 335–63. New Delhi: Tulika.

Dirlik, Arif. 2002. 'Women and the Politics of Place', *Development*, 45 (1): 14–18.

Duvvury, Nata. 1994. 'Gender Implications of New Economic Policies and the Health Sector', *Social Scientist*, 22 (9–12): 40–55.

Einhorn, Barbara. 1992. *Cindrella Goes to the Market*. London: Verso.

Elson, Diane. 1989. 'How is Structural Adjustment Affecting Women?', *Development*, 32 (1): 67–74.

Franklin, Sarah, Celia Lury and Stacey Jackie. 2000. *Global Nature, Global Culture*. New Delhi: Sage Publications.

Freeman, Carla. 2001. 'Is Local: Global as Feminine: Masculine? Rethinking the Gender of Globalisation', *Signs: Journal of Women in Culture and Society*, 26 (4): 1007–37.

Funk, Nanette and Magda Mueller. 1993. *Gender Politics and Post-Communism*. New York: Routledge.

Ghosh, Jayoti. 1994. 'Gender Concerns in Macroeconomic Policy', *Economic and Political Weekly*, 29 (18): WS2–WS4.

———. 2002. 'Globalisation, Export-Oriented Employment for Women and Social Policy: A Case Study of India', *Social Scientist*, 30 (11–12): 17–58.

Gothoskar, Sujata. 2000. 'Teleworking and Gender', *Economic and Political Weekly*, 35 (26): 2293–99.

Grewal, Inderpal and Caren Kaplan (eds). 2000. *Scattered Hegemonies: Postmodernity and Transnational Feminist Practices*. Minneapolis: University of Minnesota Press.

Grown Caren, Diane Elson and Nilufer Cagatay. 2000. 'Introduction', *World Development*, 28 (7): 1145–46.

Guru, Gopal. 2000. 'Dalits in Pursuit of Modernity', in R. Thappar (ed.), *India: Another Millenium*. New Delhi: Viking.

Hartcourt, Wendy and Arturo Escobar. 2002. 'Lead Article: Women and Politics of Place', *Development*, 45 (1): 7–14.

Held, David, Anthony, McGrew, David Globatt and Jonathan Perraton. 1999. *Global Transformations: Politics, Economics and Culture*. Stanford: Stanford University Press.

Hennessy, Rosemarie. 1993. *Materialist Feminism and the Politics of Discourse*. London: Routledge.

Jackson, Cecile. 1996. 'Rescuing Gender from the Poverty Trap', *World Development*, 24 (3): 489–504.

Jogdand, Prahlad. 2001. *New Economic Policy and Dalits*. Jaipur: Rawat Publications.

John, Mary E. 1996. 'Gender and Development in India: Some Reflections on the Constitutive Role of Contexts', *Economic and Political Weekly*, 31 (47): 3071–77.

Kapadia, Karin. 2002. 'Translocal Modernities and Transformations of Gender and Caste', in K. Kapadia (ed.), *The Violence of Development: The Politics of Identity, Gender and Social Inequalities in India*, pp. 142–83. New Delhi: Kali for Women.

Karlekar, Malavika. 2000. 'Women's Health—A View From the Household' in CWDS (ed.), *Shifting Sands: Women's Lives and Globalisation*, pp. 87–140. Calcutta: Stree.

Kelkar, Govind, Girija Shrestha and N. Veena. 2002. 'IT Industry and Women's Agency: Explorations in Bangalore and Delhi, India', *Gender, Technology and Development*, 6 (1): 43–63.

Krishnaraj, Maitreyi. 1988. *Women and Development: The Indian Experience*. Pune: Shubhada Saraswat.

———. 1996. *Gender Concerns in New Economic Policy*. University of Pune: Women's Studies Centre.

Leacock, Eleanor and Helen Safa (eds). 1986. *Women's Work: Development and the Division of Labour by Gender*. Massachusetts: Bergin and Garvey, Hadley.

Lechner, Frank J. and John Boli (eds). 2000. *The Globalisation Reader*. Oxford: Blackwell.

Lingam, Lakshmi, Vrinda Datta and Maveen Pereira. 2001. *Structural Adjustment Policies and the Social Sector: A Select Bibliography*. Mumbai: Tata Institute of Social Sciences.

Lutz, Helma. 2002. 'At Your Service Madam! The Globalisation of Domestic Service', *Feminist Review*, 70 (1–2): 89–105.

Marchand, Marianne H. and Anne Sisson Runyan. 2000. *Gender and Global Restructuring: Sightings, Sites and Resistances*. London and New York: Routledge.

Mies, Maria. 1986. *Patriarchy and Accumulation on a World Scale: Women in the International Division of Labour*. London: Zed Books.

Mies, Maria and Vandana Shiva. 1993. *Ecofeminism*. London: Zed Books.

Mies, Maria, Veronika Bennholdt-Thomsen and Claudia Von Werholf. 1988. *Women: The Last Colony*. London: Zed Books.

Mitter, Swasti. 1995. 'Beyond the Politics of Difference: An Introduction', in S. Mitter and S. Rowbotham (eds), *Women Encounter Technology: Changing Pattern of Employment in the Third World*, pp. 1–18. London: Routledge.

———. 2000. 'Teleworking and Teletrade in India: Combining Diverse Perspectives and Visions', *Economic and Political Weekly*, 35 (26): 2241–52.

Mitter, Swasti and Sheila Rowbotham (eds), 1995. *Women Encounter Technology: Changing Pattern of Employment in the Third World*. London: Routledge.

Moghadam, Valentine (ed.). 1996a. *Identity Politics and Women: Cultural Reassertions and Feminisms in International Perspective*. Oxford: Westview Press.

———. 1996b. 'Patriarchy and Post-Communism: Eastern Europe and the Former Soviet Union', in V. Moghadam (ed.), *Patriarchy and Development: Women's Positions at the End of the Twentieth Century*. Oxford: Clarendon Press.

———. 1996c. 'Feminist Networks North and South', *Journal of International Communication*, 3 (1): 111–26.

Mohanty, Chandra Talpade. 1984. 'Under Western Eyes: Feminist Scholarship and Colonial Discourses', *Boundary*, 2 (12): 333–58.

———. 1991. 'Introduction: Cartographies of Struggle: Third World Women and the Politics of Feminism', in C.T. Mohanty, A. Russo and L. Torres (eds), *Third World Women and the Politics of Feminism*, pp. 1–51. Indianapolis: Indiana University Press.

———. 2002. 'Under Western Eyes Revisited: Feminist Solidarity Through Anticapitalist Struggles', *Signs: Journal of Women in Culture and Society*, 28 (2): 499–535.

Molyneux, Maxine. 1994. 'Women's Rights and the International Context: Some Reflections on the Post-Communist States', *Millenium*, 23 (2): 287–313.

Moser, Caroline O.N. 1989. 'The Impact of Recession and Structural Adjustment on Women: Equador', *Development*, 32 (1): 75–83.

Narsalay, Raghav Manohar. 2002. 'A Decade of Reforms: What has it Done for the Marginalized'. *V. Kalp* 10(2).

National Federation of Dalit Women. 2001. 'NGO Declaration on Gender and Racism', World Conference Against Racism, Durban, 28 August–7 September.

Nussbaum, Martha. 1999. 'Women and Equality: The Capabilities Approach', *International Labour Review*, 138 (3): 227–45.

Ong, Aiwa. 1999. *Flexible Citizenship: The Cultural Logic of Transnationality*. Durham, NC: Duke University Press.

Patel, Vibhuti. 2002. *Women's Challenges of the New Millenium*. New Delhi: Gyan Publishers.

Peterson, Spike. 1997. 'Whose Crisis? Early and Post-Modern Masculinism', in S. Gill and J.H. Mittelman (eds), *Innovation and Transformation International Studies*, pp. 185–206. Cambridge: Cambridge University Press.

Phizacklea, Annie. 1998. 'Migration and Globalisation: A Feminist Perspective', in K. Koser and H. Lutz (eds), *The New Migration in Europe: Social Constructions and Social Realities*, pp. 21–33. London: Macmillan.

Pieterse, Jan. 2000. *Global Futures: Shaping Globalisation*. London: Zed Books.

Prabhu, Seetha K. 1994. 'The Budget and Structural Adjustment with a Human Face', *Economic and Political Weekly*, 29 (16–17): 16–23.

Rai, Shirin M. 2002. *Gender and the Political Economy of Development*. Oxford: Polity Press.

Rege, Sharmila with Pravin Chavan. 2001. 'From Satyashodhak to Ambedkarite Counterpublics: A Report Submitted to Sarai', CSDS, Delhi (unpublished).

Sassen, Saskia. 2000. 'Women's Burden: Countergeographies of Globalisation and the Feminisation of Survival', *Journal of International Affairs*, 53 (2): 503–24.

Sen, Gita and Caren Grown. 1985. *Development, Crises and Alternative Visions: Third World Women's Perspectives*. London: Earthscan.

Shah, Nandita, Sujata Gothoskar, Nandita Gandhi and Chhachi Amrita. 1994. 'Structural Adjustment, Feminisation of Labour Force and Organisational Strategies', *Economic and Political Weekly*, 39 (18): WS 39–WS48.

Shiva, Vandana. 1989. *Staying Alive: Women, Ecology and Development*. London: Zed Books.

Shiva, Vandana and Maria Mies. 1993. *Ecofeminism*. Halifax, Nova Scotia, Canada: Fernwood Publications.

Singh, Andreas M. and Anita Kelles Vitanen (eds). 1987. *Invisible Hands: Women in Home based Production*. New Delhi: Sage Publications.

Sinha, Mrinalini. 2000. 'Mapping the Imperial Social Formation: A Modest Proposal for Feminist History', *Signs Journal of Women in Culture and Society*, 25 (4): 1077–82.

Streefkerk, Hein. 2001. 'Thirty Years of Industrial Labour in South Gujarat: Trends and Significance', *Economic and Political Weekly*, 36 (26): 2398–412.

Sudbury, Julia. 2002. 'Celling Black Bodies: Black Women in the Global Industrial Complex', *Feminist Review*, 70 (1–2): 57–75.

Teltumbde, Anand. 2001. *Globalisation and Dalits*. Nagpur: Sanket Prakashan.

Tharu, Susie and Niranjana Tejaswini. 1994. 'Problems for a Contemporary Theory of Gender', *Social Scientist*, 22 (3–4): 93–117.

True, Jacqui. 2000. 'Gendering Post-Socialist Transitions', in M.H. Marchand and A.S. Runyan (eds), *Gender and Global Restructuring: Sightings, Sites and Resistances*, pp. 74–95. London and New York: Routledge.

Ward, Kathryn. 1991. *Women Workers and Global Restructuring*. Ithaca, New York: Cornell University Press.

Womenspeak. 2000. *United Voices Against Globalisation, Poverty and Violence in India*. A Report published by Six Women's Organisations. New Delhi: Progressive Printers.

FIFTEEN

Gender and Employment in the Context of Globalisation: Some Facts and Figures[*]

Rina Bhattacharya

The growth of world trade and finance hastened the spread of multinationals, who through their foreign direct investments contributed to the globalisation of the market. In keeping with these larger global processes, the Government of India in the preliminary phase of liberalisation in the mid- 1980s, followed by globalisation in the 1990s, opened up the Indian economy. As a result the structural adjustment began in India in 1991. The essentials of the new economic policy are: (*a*) privatisation; (*b*) globalisation; (*c*) modernisation, and (*d*) improving productive efficiency and growth rate. In seeking these objectives, the structural adjustment involves different processes such as (*i*) decontrol and deregulation; (*ii*) adoption of 'market friendly' fiscal exchange, trade and credit policies; (*iii*) freedom of entry to foreign goods and investment, (*iv*) cut back in public expenditure; (*v*) limitation of 'fiscal deficits' to low levels; (*vi*) adoption of up-to-date technologies; (*vii*) concentration of government investment in infrastructure, education, health and similar soft areas; (*viii*) exit policy; and (*ix*) withdrawal of subsidiaries of all kinds (Krishnaswamy 1993).

In advanced nations, globalisation has reduced the political influence and bargaining power of organised labour. Competition from low-cost producers has exerted downward pressure on wages and employment. In order to secure a competitive advantage, employers are using more technology intensive goods and services, in the process boosting recruitment of non-manual workers whose rates of unionisation tend to be lower. Similarly, in India the trade liberalisation and flow of foreign capital is expected to push the process of industrialisation.

Apart from its penetration into the industries in the Export Processing Zones (EPZs) and agriculture, the global restructuring of the capitalist economy has also created an enormous expansion of what is called the 'informal sector' in rural and urban areas. It is a characteristic of the informal sector that women are not defined as workers, but as housewives/home producers. They do not appear in labour statistics and are not protected by labour laws, and therefore are not organised (Mies 1998).

Traditional development economists and modernisation theorists have viewed economic development as a process in which economic growth and women's incorporation into the labour force go hand in hand. Others, however, argue that the process of industrialisation and economic development is accompanied by the marginalisation of women (Boserup 1970; Saffioti 1978). Further, Boserup pointed out that men's privileged access to new technologies and education lead to growing productivity differences between men and women, and hence depicts a decline of women's share in the labour force. In the agricultural sector, the growing productivity differences would cause women to withdraw, and also make them disadvantaged in the non-agricultural sector.

[*]Originally published in *Asian Women*, Vol. 8, June 1999, pp. 195–207.

The globalisation of the Indian economy would mean cheaper imported substitutes for indigenously manufactured goods, which would seriously affect the unorganised sector (Ghosh 1991). The threat posed by foreign capital as well as trade liberalisation will affect the availability of employment opportunities for women in the unorganised sector, which is a major source of employment for women. The entry of multinational corporations in agro-processing industries affects women workers, as their number is quite substantial in these industries. The import of modem technology will lead to a reduction in the low-skill jobs done by women, and will push them into taking up low-wage or more strenuous jobs for the same pay (Krishnaswamy 1993). Still, it is believed that the 'anti-globalisation' agenda makes no sense from the standpoint of women workers, especially in the Third World. It would simply deprive them of considerable employment opportunities, as also the possibility of improving employment conditions through global solidarity and coordination. A much more sensible objective would be concerted action to shape the global order in accordance with women's agenda (Hensman 2004).

There are studies (Dev 2000; Jhabvala and Sinha 2002) that have shown the impact of structural adjustment on female employment and argued that due to the structural adjustment in India, women workers have been marginalised. However, the time period for such analyses was quite short. As mentioned earlier, the process of globalisation affected the Indian economy by the mid- 1980s, though the actual adjustment began in 1991. Therefore it is appropriate to analyse the data that came in both before and after the 1991 Census. This perhaps will help in a better understanding of the changes. Many studies on this aspect have taken data from the census as well as the NSSO, while others have used only NSSO data. The NSSO data has been used more often for such analysis as it provides quality data using comparatively more probing questions, although the data is based on a sample of households, unlike the census data which is based on total enumeration. Most of these studies have explained marginalisation of women in terms of disparities in the sectoral division of work for men and women, and the differential status of employment.

The present chapter attempts to analyse the extent of female marginalisation that has taken place in India by analysing the data on employment collected by the Census of India[1] and the National Sample Survey Organisation.[2] Some suggestions to strengthen the unorganised sector, where the majority of the women workforce has been pushed into employment, in an attempt to create potential employment opportunities have been offered.

Marginalisation of Women in India

Marginalisation of women can be expressed in various forms. Some facts indicating marginalisation of females are (*i*) exclusion of women from productive employment, which can be observed either in the form of a decline in overall work participation rates of women, or a decline in their share in the wage and salaried employment; (*ii*) segregation of women workers in certain specific jobs, which are low in occupational hierarchy, payment and status; (*iii*) concentration of women workers in the informal sectors or in unpaid occupations; and (*iv*) economic inequality reflected through wage differentials and causalisation of the female labour force. However, it is not necessary that all these dimensions of female marginalisation will have to be manifest in order to prove this thesis.

It is argued that the dimensions outlined above are not different aspects of a single phenomenon. The manifestation of a particular dimension depends upon the stage of economic development. It is possible that the first dimension may manifest itself in the initial stage of industrialisation, whereas in the advanced industrial societies there may be an overall increase in participation rates of women accompanied by occupational segregation (Scott 1986). In her paper on globalisation and its impact on women, Sudarshan (2004) concluded that the success of globalisation with regard to macro-economic performance has not translated into positive benefits for large sections of the population. The public hearings conducted by the National Commission for Women (NCW) in different parts of the country clearly showed the helplessness of poor workers in the face of macro policy changes, which have led to a loss of livelihood for them.

Workforce Participation Rates (WFPR) and Female to Male Ratio of Participation by Location

Table 15.1 presents the Workforce Participation Rates of Females and Males in urban and rural locations. The results are based on NSS Employment, Unemployment Survey from 1983 to 2000. The survey takes place every five years. In the context of liberalisation and structural adjustment, it is worth analysing the trend between 1983 and 1999–2000 since this perfectly depicts the pre- and post-liberalised period.

TABLE 15.1
Gender-wise Workforce Participation Rates by Liberalisation

Year	Rural			Urban		
	Male	*Female*	*Total*	*Male*	*Female*	*Total*
1983 WFPR	54.7	34.0	44.8	51.2	15.1	35.1
1987–88 WFPR	53.9	32.3	43.3	50.6	15.2	34
1993–94 WFPR	55.3	32.8	44.4	52	15.4	34.7
1999–2000 WFPR	53.1	29.9	41.7	51.8	13.9	33.7

Ratio of Female to Male Work Participation (in %)

Location/ Rounds	38th (1983)	43rd (1987–88)	50th (1993–94)	55th (1999–2000)
Rural	62.1	59.9	59.3	56.3
Urban	29.4	30.0	29.6	26.8

Sources: NSSO, Govt of India: Sarvekshana Special Number, September 1990 and Report of the NSS, July 1993–June 1994, 50th Round, Revised Report 406, 1996.
NSS Report No. 458, *Employment and Unemployment in India, 1999–2000, Key Results.*

Note: Figures relate to usual status of individuals. Workforce covers those involved in gainful activity regularly, and those involved in gainful activity occasionally. The WFPR represent size of workforce as percent of population.

The period of liberalisation witnessed a rise in male participation rates and a near stagnation of female participation rates, resulting in the decline of percentage ratio of female to male participation in rural areas. A similar trend is seen in urban areas also. The work participation rates for urban females are much lower, roughly one-half that of the work participation rates observed for rural females. The percentage ratio of female to male participation shows a steady decline from 62.1 per cent to 56.3 per cent during 1983 to 1999–2000 in rural areas. In urban areas, there is a slight increase in female work participation from 29.4 per cent in 1983 to 30 per cent in 1987–88 (NSS 43rd round), which has declined to 26.8 per cent in 1999–2000 (NSS 55th round).

Shifts in the Pattern of Employment

The distribution of workers by industrial category shows some shift in employment from one category to another. It can be seen from Table 15.2 that there is a downward trend in male participation in the agricultural sector, while there is a slight upward trend in other sectors like construction, retail trade and community services. In the case of urban areas, the trend is almost the same, except for the fact that there is a sharp decline in the percentage of male participation in the manufacturing sector.

TABLE 15.2
Sector-wise Percentage of Workers (Principal and Subsidiary Status) by Gender

Sector	Male				Female			
	1983	*1987–88*	*1993–94*	*1993–2000*	*1983*	*1987–88*	*1993–94*	*1993–2000*
Rural areas								
Agriculture (0)	77.8	74.6	74	71.4	87.8	84.8	86.1	85.4
Mining & Quarrying (1)	0.6	0.7	0.7	0.6	0.3	0.4	0.4	0.3
Manufacturing (2&3)	7	7.4	7.0	7.3	6.4	6.9	7.1	7.6
Electricity (4)	0.2	0.3	0.3	0.2	–	–	0.1	–
Construction (5)	2.2	3.7	3.2	4.5	0.7	2.7	0.9	1.1
Wholesale/retail trade (6)	4.4	5.1	5.5	6.8	1.9	2.1	2.1	2
Transport, storage, etc. (7)	1.7	2	2.2	3.2	0.1	0.1	0.1	0.1
Community services, etc. (8)	6.1	6.2	7	6.1	2.8	3	3.4	3.7
Urban areas								
Agriculture (0)	10.3	9.1	9	6.6	32	29.4	24.7	17.7
Mining & Quarrying (1)	1.3	1.3	1.3	0.9	0.8	0.8	0.6	0.4
Manufacturing (2&3)	27	25.7	23.5	22.4	27.1	27	24.1	24
Electricity (4)	1.1	1.2	1.2	0.8	–	0.2	0.3	0.2
Construction (5)	5.2	5.8	6.9	8.7	3.3	3.7	4.1	4.8
Wholesale/retail trade, etc. (6)	20.2	22	21.9	29.4	9	9.8	10	16.9
Transport, storage, etc. (7)	9.9	9.7	9.7	10.4	1.6	0.9	1.3	1.8
Community services, etc. (8)	24.8	25.2	26.4	21	26.6	27.8	35	34.2

Source: NSS Report No. 458; *Employment and Unemployment Situation in India 1999–2000.*

As far as female participation in the rural area is concerned, there is a downward trend in the agricultural sector. However, the decline seems to be prominent (3 per cent) from 1983 to 1987–88 and again there is an upward trend between 1987–88 to 1999–2000 (2.4 per cent). On the other hand, there is an upward trend in manufacturing, construction, retail trade and the community services sector. In the urban areas, a different trend is observed, wherein there is decline in the agricultural and manufacturing sectors and a rise in community services and construction sectors. The rise in female participation in the service sector indicates that they are more involved in low-paid and low-status jobs. The fact that women are taken more into the manufacturing sector is explained by the fact that women are more ready to work for lower wages and accept appalling working conditions. As most of them come from impoverished rural or urban households, they are compelled to work. Many studies (Banerjee 1985; Baud 1992) analysing the pattern of women's employment in the manufacturing industries have shown that women are being excluded from most of the skilled jobs, and are being concentrated in lower-paid jobs and industries. Further, the concentration of women in different types of industries can be studied in more detail using the 3-Digit Industrial Classification.

Industries with High Female Employment

The National Sample Survey looks at a more detailed industrial division of workers in a 3-Digit Industrial Classification based on the 0–9 major division. Approximately 384 divisions of industry are classified by the NSSO. Table 15.3 shows that the employment of women is concentrated in only a few industrial divisions.

TABLE 15.3
Intensity of Female Employment and Number of Women Employed by NIC Code/Activity

NIC	Code & Activity	Intensity of Female Employment within Industry Groups (%)	Number of Women Employed
	Agriculture Production		
001	Growing of pulses	49	94004
002	Growing of cotton	48	1291402
006	Growing of roots & tuber	40	386196
010	Plantation of tea	45	596984
020	Cattle breeding	80	8278123
021	Goat breeding	56	579927
039	Agriculture services	42	591720
052	Production of firewood	46	187784
	Manufacturing		
202	Preservation of fruits	46	28052
213	Processing & blending of tea	46	212218
215	Processing of edible nuts	79	106413
219	Food production	48	363002
225	Raw tobacco leaf	65	30046
226	Bidi	74	2248812
230	Cotton	42	56071
231	Cotton spinning other than in mills	81	205512
232	Weaving	54	43926
233	Weaving & finishing of cotton textile handloom	44	673393
241	Wool spinning	52	64277
252	Carding & combing on coir fibre	68	49514
255	Spinning & Weaving	76	121427
261	All types of thread	50	230805
262	Embroidery raw work	66	277108
264	Floor covering	50	112365
273	Wooden & cane boxes	51	487027
277	Bamboo & cane furniture	54	61489
281	Paper box	41	47604
305	Perfume etc.	42	59328
307	Matches	75	197415
389	Miscellaneous products not classified elsewhere	49	192064
	Services		
910	Sanitation services	40	168918
941	Welfare services	49	47638
961	Laundry cleaning and dyeing	47	690479

Source: Survey of Employment Unemployment, 50th Round July 1993–June 1994, National Sample Survey Organisation, Department of Statistics, Ministry of Planning, New Delhi.

It is in only 33 types of industries that women constitute more than 40 per cent of the workers. Of these 33 industries, two industries have women employees between 80 per cent and above; seven between 60–79 per cent; seven between 50–59 per cent; and 17 between 40–49 per cent.

The industries where the percentage of females to total are 60 per cent and above include cattle and goat breeding, production of milk, cotton spinning other than in mills, manufacture of bidi, processing of edible nuts, embroidery work, zari work and making of ornamental trimmings, manufacture of matches, spinning, weaving and finishing of coir textiles, tobacco stemming, re-drying, and all other operations connected with the preparation of raw leaf tobacco, and carding and combing of coir fibres.

It is interesting to note that the industries that employ more than a million women are those involved in cattle and goat breeding, and the growing of raw cotton. The industries that employ 0.5 to 1 million women are tea plantations, agricultural services not classified elsewhere, and laundries and dyeing services.

Status of Employment

The share of rural women in self-employment has been declining since 1983 till 2000, and the same is true for males, as shown in Table 15.4. For urban males the trend shows some improvement, but for females there was a upward trend between 1983–88, which then continued declining till 2000. Regular employment for males in rural as well as urban area has been declining, whereas females have shown an increase in employment between 1983–2000. The casualisation of labour has increased among males in rural and urban areas, although between 1983–88 there was a decline among rural males. The percentage of rural males as

TABLE 15.4
Gender-wise Distribution of Total Employment by Status of Employment for Different NSS Rounds

(All-India)

Employment status and Year	Rural		Urban		Total	
	Male	Female	Male	Female	Male	Female
Self-Employed						
1983	60.5	61.9	40.9	45.8	55.9	60
1987–88	58.6	60.8	41.7	47.1	54.3	58.9
1993–94	57.9	58.5	41.7	45.4	52.9	56.6
1999–2000	55	57.3	41.5	45.3	52.8	55.6
Regular Employees						
1983	10.3	2.8	43.7	25.8	18.2	5.6
1987–88	10	3.7	43.7	27.5	18.6	6.9
1993–94	8.3	2.8	42.1	28.6	17	6.5
1999–2000	8.8	3.1	41.7	33.3	14	7.3
Casual Labour						
1983	29.2	35.3	15.4	28.4	25.9	34.4
1987–88	31.4	35.5	14.6	25.4	27.1	34.2
1993–94	33.8	38.7	16.2	26	29.3	36.9
1999–2000	36.2	39.6	16.8	21.4	33.2	37.1

Source: National Sample Survey, 38th, 43rd, 50th and 55th Rounds.
Note: Figures relate to usual status of individuals. Workforce covers those involved in gainful activity regularly and those involved in gainful activity occasionally.

casual labourers has shown a steady rise since 1983. The percentage of rural females as casual labour has increased steadily from 35.3 per cent in 1983 to 39.6 per cent in 1999–2000. The incidence of casualisation is more in the case of females as compared to males. The increased casualisation of women workers has been explained on two accounts. First, employers recruit women as casual workers in order to avoid provisions of maternity, and social, economic and other benefits. Second, with the increase in the sub-contracting of the production process, employment in general and that of women in particular is being gradually transferred from the organised to the unorganised sector (Singh 1994; Jhabvala and Sinha 2002).

Unemployment Status among Females

In order to define 'unemployed', three estimates are used using three different approaches. These are number of persons usually unemployed based on 'usual status', 'weekly status' and 'daily status' classifications. Of these three, the first estimate indicates the magnitude of persons unemployed for a relatively longer period during a reference period of 365 days, and approximates to an indicator relating to the chronically unemployed. However, the unemployed whose estimates are obtained on this time criterion could be working in a subsidiary capacity. Therefore another estimate is derived of the unemployed, excluding those employed in a subsidiary capacity during the reference period. The former is called the usually unemployed in terms of the principal status, and usually unemployed after excluding the subsidiary status workers. The latter category would be conceptually lower than the former.

The unemployment rates obtained from different quinquennial NSS rounds (38th, 43rd, 50th and 55th) indicate that the rates in 1977–78 were higher for women than men (Table 15.5). This is true according to all different concepts of unemployment in both rural and urban areas. There has, however, been a decline in the rates for both men and women during the 1970s and 1980s, barring the increase registered during 1983–87. The declining trend continued during 1987–93 as well. The decline works out to be large for rural females. As a consequence, the rural unemployment rates for women are currently at par with or slightly lower than those of men, while in urban areas the former are much above the latter.

TABLE 15.5
Gender-wise Unemployment Rates Over Various NSS Rounds

Years	Male			Female		
	us	*cws*	*cds*	*us*	*cws*	*cds*
Rural						
1983	2.1	3.7	7.5	1.4	4.3	9
1987–88	2.8	4.2	4.6	3.5	4.4	6.7
1993–94	2	3	5.6	1.4	3	5.6
1999–2000	2.1	3.9	7.2	1.5	3.7	7
Urban						
1983	5.9	6.7	9.2	5.7	7.5	11
1987–88	6.1	6.6	8.8	8.3	9.2	12
1993–94	5.4	5.2	6.7	8.5	8.4	10.5
1999–2000	4.5	5.6	7.3	6.9	7.3	9.4

Source: NSS 55th Round, Report No. 458.

Importantly, the unemployment rate has declined noticeably in rural areas by the alternate concepts (weekly status and daily status). In urban areas, however, the decline is less. As a consequence, the urban rates in 1993–94 are about twice the rural rates in 1993–94, both for males and females. Importantly, the unemployment rate for females is higher than that of males in urban areas, a fact that clearly emerges from the 55th round data of the NSS. The declining trend in the unemployment rate could mean that people are getting some kind of employment, which, however, may not necessarily be productive. Further, the unemployed status of women has gone up during 1987–88, though after that there has been a declining trend in all the categories. This could be due to the rise in short-term employment in the industrial sub-contracting sector. The multinational corporations and big companies have evolved a vendor system of sub-contracting for their production. These vendors either employ a large number of women, or give out the work to home-based workers through contractors (Jhabvala and Sinha 2002).

Female Employment in Organised and Unorganised Sectors

Employment data in India distinguished between employment in the organised and the unorganised or informal sector. The organised sector, as defined by the Directorate General of Employment and Training (DGE&T), includes all public sector establishments (including all government services at the central, state and local government levels); all public sector undertakings (public utilities/services in the fields of agriculture, industry, credit financing, etc., are categorised as a part of the organised sector); all non-agricultural private establishments (including all non-agricultural private establishments that employ 10 or more persons).

By deduction, employment outside the defined organised sector is employment in the unorganised/informal sector, including self-employment, where the relationship between the employer and employee is informal (Gopalan 1995).

Table 15.6 shows that the overall employment in the organised sector in India has been on the decline. The rate of employment in the organised sector has declined from 9.69 per cent to 6.90 per cent between 1971–2001.

TABLE 15.6

Percentage of Employment in the Organised and Unorganised Sector by Gender During 1971–2001 (in lakhs)

	Male			Female			Total		
Year	Organised Sector	Unorganised Sector	Total	Organised Sector	Unorganised Sector	Total	Organised Sector	Unorganised Sector	Total
1971	155.60	1336.16	1491.76	19.30	294.15	313.45	174.90	1630.31	1805.21
	(10.43%)	(89.57%)		(6.16%)	(93.84%)	(17.36%)	(9.69%)	(90.31%)	
1981	200.86	1625.75	1826.61	27.93	427.59	455.52	228.79	2053.34	2282.13
	(11%)	(89.0%)		(6.13%)	(93.87%)	(19.63%)	(10.03%)	(89.79%)	
1991	229.53	2014.11	2243.64	37.81	859.86	897.67	267.34	2873.97	3141.31
	(10.23%)	(89.77%)		(4.21%)	(95.79%)	(28.58%)	(8.51%)	(91.49%)	
2001	228.40	2526.23	2754.63	49.49	1220.99	1270.48	277.89	3747.22	4025.11
	(8.29%)	(91.70%)		(3.89%)	(96.10%)	(31.55%)	(6.90%)	(93.09%)	

Sources: Gopalan 1995.

Manpower Profile: The Year Book 2003; IAMR Delhi.

ECensus India, Issue No. 6, 2000.

The proportion of employment in the organised sector for males was 10.43 per cent in 1971, and has declined to 8.29 per cent in 2001. With regard to females, the proportion of employment in the organised sector has declined from 6 per cent to 4 per cent between 1971–2001.

In the unorganised sector on the other hand, employment of women has increased nearly four times between 1971 and 2001, registering a total increase in female employment from 31.3 million to 127 million. Even more significant is the fact that the rapid increase of female employment has taken place during 1981–91. The trend remains same for the period 1991–2001 in terms of increase of female employment. The fact remains, however, that men share 82.2 per cent of the employment in the organised sector, while women share only 17.8 per cent. The increase in employment for women during this period has been more in the unorganised sector than in the organised one unlike men (though at a lower rate compared to women).

Conclusion and Suggestions

It can be argued that there may be a rise in the work participation rate among women, or, in other words, that the number of women as workers has been recorded as being more in recent years. However, in reality the employment opportunities for women continue to be unsatisfactory. Due to structural reform, women are working under hazardous conditions with a lot of insecurity and low wages.

The indicators like workforce participation rate, shift in the pattern of employment in different sectors, employment status, unemployment rates and increased numbers of women in the unorganised sector point towards the marginalisation of females in India.

The workforce participation as per the (NSS) data indicates that there is an upward trend, but which declined during 1987–2000 among urban females. For rural females, the participation rate declined in 1983 and again showed an increasing trend through 1987–2000. However, the increment is not as high as in 1977–78. As far as a shift in the employment pattern is concerned, the data shows that women are pushed into the agriculture, manufacturing, and/or service sector. Employment status indicated that there is a rise in casualisation among female workers, and an alarming rate of unemployment among urban females. Regarding the unorganised sector, it can be said that more and more women are being pushed into this sector, thus making it a large one. All this indicates that the overall economic development has increasingly excluded women from productive employment, pushed them into marginal occupations, and casualised women in terms of employment. It is in this context that some suggestions are being offered so that the sector can create potential employment opportunities for women and contribute to their economic empowerment.

Home-based workers or workers in the informal sector in India produce a wealth of products ranging from baskets made of forest fibres to herbal products for which there is a large market. Since women are not operating at the market level they earn the least, and continue to be marginalised in spite of the fact that they do most of the laborious jobs of collection, sorting and processing. Women collectors of medicinal herbs earn Rs 3–6 as wage per day.[3] These women can be empowered through intervention aimed at building entrepreneurial skills. There is also a need to develop a mechanism for access to credit, design, markets, information and training.

Although there are government programmes and several organisations involved in helping these poor producers and collectors, a lot more needs to be done for providing critical marketing support, credit facilities for buying raw materials, and for ensuring better wages. Even industries with a high concentration of women workers need special attention with regard to skill upgrades, development of technology, transfer of technology development, etc., for increasing their productivity and incomes.

Notes

1. The all-India Census is conducted by the office of the Registrar General of India once every 10 years, and the latest census was conducted in 2001. Data is collected at two levels, relating primarily to individuals and then to the households to which these individuals belong.
2. The National Sample Survey Organisation (NSSO) collects data from a large, scientifically chosen sample of households using an in-depth questionnaire. This procedure ensures better quality data.
3. Based on the data collected as a part of the project titled 'Herbal Medicinal Plants: An Analysis', carried out in Himachal Pradesh, India, by the Institute of Social Studies in Delhi.

References

Banerjee, N. 1985. 'Women and Industrialization in Developing Countries', in *Occasional Paper* No. 71. Centre for Studies in Social Sciences.

Baud, Isa. 1992. 'Gender and Forms of Productions: Labour Intensive Industries in India and Maxico', in *Economic and Political Weekly*, 25 (34).

Boserup, Ester. 1970. *Women's Role in Economic Development*. New York: St Margin's Press.

Dev, S.M. 2000. 'Economic Liberalisation and Employment in South Asia-II', *Economic and Political Weekly*, 15 January.

Ghosh, Arun. 1991. 'Political Economy of Structural Adjustment', *Economic and Political Weekly*, Vol. 26 (47).

Gopalan, S. 1995. *Women and Employment in India*. New Delhi: Har-Anand Publications.

Hensman, R. 2004. 'Globalisation, Women and Work', *Economic and Political Weekly*, 6 March.

Jhabvala, R. and Sinha. 2002. 'Liberalisation and the Woman Worker', *Economic and Political Weekly*, 25 May.

Krishnaswamy, K.S. 1993. 'Notes on Issues Regarding Women and the New Economic Policy', in *The New Economic Policy and Women*. Bombay: Indian Association for Women's Studies.

Kundu, A. 1997. 'Trends and Pattern of Female Employment in India: A Case of Organized Informalization', *The Indian Journal of Labour Economics*, Vol. 40 (3).

Mies, M. 1998, 'Globalisation of the Economy and Women's Work in a Sustainable Society', *Gender, Technology and Development*, Vol. 2 (1).

Rajput, P. and Swarup, Hem Lata. 1994. *Women and Globalization Reflections, Options and Strategies*. New Delhi: Ashish Publishing House.

Saffioti, H. 1978. *Women in Class Society*. New York: Monthly Review Press.

Scott, A.M. 1986. 'Women and Industrialization: Examining the Female Marginalization Thesis', *Journal of Development Studies*, Vol. 22 (4).

Singh, G., S.P. Sharma and P. Bhardwaj. 1994. 'Structural Adjustment and Marginalization of Female Workers in India', in Pam Rajput and Hem Lata Swarup (eds), *Women and Globalization Reflections, Options and Strategies*. New Delhi: Ashish Publishing House.

Sudarshan, Ratna. 2004. 'Globalisation and its Impact on Women: Findings from the hearing conducted by the National Commission for Women'. Paper presented at the conference on 'Impact of Globalisation on Women' organised by the National Commission for Women. New Delhi, 17 September.

SIXTEEN

Globalisation and Women in India in the Nineties*

Gabriele Dietrich

It is quite difficult to speak of globalisation and women in general. How liberalisation, privatisation and globalisation (LPG) affect women depends on conditions in different countries, and gender segregated data on Structural Adjustment Policies (SAP) are not easily available. I also have to say that I am not speaking as an economist, but am trying to make sense of experiences in the women's movements, especially when working with slum dwellers, workers in the unorganised sector (e.g., construction workers, vendors, fishing communities) and environmental movements (e.g., the Narmada struggle). It is under our eyes that women are squeezed out of marketing, that vending spaces become parking spaces, that the fish dwindles, that global tenders make local labour and skills obsolete. I feel it is only through these experiences that it becomes possible to find one's way through contradictory government claims, research perspectives, NGO campaigns and movement demands. By way of introduction, I would also like to say that it is the collapse of Eastern Europe's actually existing socialism that has led to the LPG policies, which presupposes the TINA effect ('there is no alternative'). The analysis is thus always impaired by an underlying ideological deadlock. Researchers and campaigners are divided as to whether SAP can be given a more human face by building in gender awareness, (commonwealth secretariat 1989; Elson 1994; Palmer 1992) or whether building local alternatives and paralysing and quitting WTO is a better perspective, (Kocherry 2000) or whether in a contradictory situation contradictory lines of action need to be chosen.

I would like to divide this chapter into three parts:

1. A very broad brushed overview over our national economic and political-cultural situation, focusing on women in this overall picture.
2. Some of the prominent survival struggles in our country.
3. Some of the crucial conceptual (ideological) assumptions of the present market fundamentalism, and possible feminist eco-socialist alternatives.

Besides, we will have to look at social emancipation along with direct economic factors, and survival has to be seen in relation to production, food security, access to resources, health, cultural fundamentalism (like casteism and communalism), and rising levels of violence.

*This is a revised version of the paper published in *Vikalp*, Vol. IX, No. 3, 2001, pp. 77–89.

Overall Economic, Political and Cultural Trends in the Present Situation

For the purpose of brevity, let me just refer to the alternative economic survey of 1998–2000, which the Alternative Survey Group of Azadi Bachao Andolan and Lokayan has compiled. This has been pieced together by some of the leading researchers in our country. It does not have a very deep and consistent gender perspective, but it comprehensively surveys all sectors of the economy and allows for specific observations on how the present policies affect women.

To begin with, the report exposes the claimed improvement in growth rates, foreign exchange reserves and slower inflation as being more cosmetic than real (p. 11). The macro-economic progress reports leave out decisive components like the poverty ratio, employment and labour participation rate in general and that specific to gender and age, informal sector size and performance, women-headed households and their income status, changes in consumption spending and its size-class distribution. Apart from the fact that the unemployment statistics have deteriorated (4.1 crore registered job seekers as of November 1999 vis-à-vis 3.92 crores in 1997–98), the concept of wage employment itself is inadequate. Ninety-two per cent of the Indian working class work in the unorganised sector (according to NCL, 88 per cent according to the National Sample Survey; Alternative Economic Survey 2000: 125), and the proportion continues to grow as public-sector enterprise gets privatised and the trend towards the casualisation of labour goes on. This increases competition for women, as 94 per cent of working women are in the informal economy (vis-à-vis 83.3 per cent of male workers). Even within the informal sector, casualisation is on the increase and is higher for women than for men. This not only makes the economic situation more precarious, but also makes organisation of workers more and more difficult. Poverty among casual labourers is increasing, there are more women below poverty line than men, and women-headed households and girl children are in the most pathetic situation (ibid: 126). Women are concentrated in low-skilled and low-paid jobs (with lower wages than men), and state spending on education to upgrade skills has decreased. State expenditures on social sectors in proportion to the total budget are on the decrease, budgetary allocation for the Department of Women and Child Development has decreased over the past five years, and non-plan allocations to programmes for child welfare showed a negative growth in the 2000–2001 budget (ibid.: 127). These overall trends clearly outweigh some of the marginal gains of some newly-created jobs in export processing units. Generally speaking, women's employment in India during the twentieth century was concentrated only in four manufacturing industries: (*a*) food, beverages and tobacco; (*b*) textiles; (*c*) wood and wood products; and (*d*) ceramics, accounting for 30 per cent of women's employment in manufacturing over the period 1911–61. During the 1980s, employment of adult women declined, and employment of adolescent girls and child labour increased. The traditional employment went down and some new industries like chemicals, and in the metallurgical and engineering fields emerged (Banerjee 1991: 85; Krishnaraj 1991: 83). Some researchers suggested that globalisation brought in casualisation which led to the feminisation of the labour force, and thus, despite being exploitative, it had some emancipatory potential for women. This has been contested by some feminist researchers. Ela Bhat, the founder of SEWA, pointed out as early as 1992 that women would be the hardest hit by SAP (Bhat 1992). It is clear that the organised sector is disintegrating, and that therefore even the temporary gains that women workers make are not going to last. Besides, women only have access to the less skilled and underpaid jobs. A sexual division of labour in the home as well as in the labour market accounts for a continuing disadvantage, which ultimately leads to the casualisation of labour and makes organisational strategies more difficult (Shah et al. 1994).

On the one hand skill training for women will be needed, and on the other, only the organisation of the labour force in the informal sector can assert some basic rights. To enable women's participation in trade unions in the informal sector, community kitchens and *balwadi*s, which permit women greater mobility, will be needed. Such social facilities require funds, which are nowadays scrapped as wasteful social expenditure. The vicious circle closes in.

Generally speaking, the new emphasis on cost-efficiency in different fields has led to more exploitation of women's labour, for example, hospitals becoming 'more efficient' means that patients are discharged earlier, medicines are not available for free, and women's invisible family labour is compensating for this situation. As some authors have pointed out, the stretchability of this invisible labour resource has its own limits, as women's health gets ruined. Women face the lack of access to resources or outlets outside the household, inner-household markets are biased against women, and intra-household distribution of income and decision-making of expenditure is distorted (Elson 1994; Palmer 1992). Thus, the traditional social discriminations are not automatically broken down by the new development, but may be accentuated unless tackled separately. At the same time, the spaces for organising women are also narrowing.

The onslaught on Agriculture and Food Security is the most disturbing feature in the present situation. Agriculture is the traditional stronghold of women's labour, either as wage labourers or as family labour on small holdings. Agriculture accounts for about 25 per cent of Indian GDP at present—having come down from 44.5 per cent in 1970–71—but provides employment to about 70 per cent of the working population and to 84 per cent of all economically active women. While India is still self-sufficient in food production, vast stocks of the Food Corporation of India lie unused for lack of buying power, and according to the FAO, 20–34 per cent of the population was undernourished during 1995–97. The present trend to leave food distribution to the forces of the market violates two most vital aspects—food security and the insurance of employment. The neglect of both these factors is a threat to life and livelihood itself.

The effects of the opening up of the markets can be acutely felt all over the country. Since 1 April 2000, 729 new commodities can be imported unrestrictedly, among which are about 240 agricultural commodities, including rice, bone meal, meat, milk powder, and many others. On 31 March 2001 import of over 700 new commodities followed (Pillai 2000). We are all familiar with the crashing prices of cash crops like rubber, coconut, cardamom, and pepper in Kerala. The workers and owners of plantations in the Nilgiris have been fighting desperate battles against imports. Women have been brutally beaten up by the police in these struggles. Side by side, the public distribution system (PDS) is being dismantled systematically so that urban workers in the unorganised sector as well as slum dwellers and the rural poor are more in danger of starvation (Dietrich 2000).

It is therefore imperative to unleash a campaign for the protection of agriculture, agricultural labour, food security, life and livelihood. Numerous peasant organisations are fighting against the new import regimes imposed by the WTO, like the Karnataka Rashtra Raita Sangham, the Andhra Pradesh Vivasaya Viruthitharula Union, and The Tamil Nadu Peasant Movement (Narayanan Sami Naidu/Dr Shivasami) in south India. While farmers' suicides have been widely highlighted, women farmers' suicides are as a rule not even recognised or compensated for. At the same time, numerous agricultural labourers' organisations are raising the struggle for a national legislation to protect and regularise agricultural labour.

One of the most injurious developments throughout the 1990s has been the spread of intensive aquaculture along the East Coast, which has led to the rampant unemployment of agricultural labourers in the Cauvery delta, the former rice bowl of Tamil Nadu, and salinity of soils. Despite the spectacular victory of the Gram

Swaraj Movement in the Supreme Court on 11 December 1996, the judgement has not been implemented and the farms have not been closed. This has subverted not only agriculture, but also the credibility of democratic institutions.

On 13–14 September 2000, a state-wide conference of Dalit women in Madurai, attended by about 5,000 participants, raised a voice against the globalisation and communalisation of politics. The conference highlighted the deteriorating situation in the countryside, the need for alternative agriculture and food security, and the political process which communalises daily lives and aggravates caste clashes.

One important aspect in the present situation is the increasing violence against women. Two examples come to my mind. The first is the violence meted out to the whole Dalit community of Cuddalore district during the 5 September elections of 1999, which women have had to bear the brunt of. While much of this was fanned by political parties, the underlying economic competition between Vanniyars and Parayars in the struggle for survival and some minimum prosperity was very tangible in the public hearing held by the National Commission of Women in Chennai in late December 1999 (Dietrich 2001).

Another example that comes to mind is the fight against an increase in violence against women that has been waged by different women's groups in Kerala. While Kerala is the only state in India with a favourable male-female sex ratio and also has very good indicators in terms of women's health and education, the incidences of rape, molestation, dowry deaths and sex rackets has increased alarmingly. This has a clear connection with migration to Gulf countries, enhanced consumerism, cultural uprootment, penetration of the flesh trade into the bureaucracy, political parties and the police apparatus. Poverty, unemployment and lack of support are in conflict with the display of consumerism, video parlours and erosion of values, which the activist researchers dealing with such problems have clearly identified as being connected to globalisation (Vijayan and Sandya 2000).

Another form of violence is no doubt the deterioration of the health system under globalisation. It has been pointed out that investment in health has gone down in favour of investment in 'family welfare' since the 8th Plan, and it is acknowledged that communicable diseases and poverty-based morbidity are on the rise (Sagar and Qadeer 2001–2002). Malaria, tuberculosis and leprosy are again spreading. The privatisation of health services has had disastrous consequences for the availability of hospitalisation for the poor. Assistance for hospitalisation of the poor has decreased from Rs 25 crore in 1997–98 to Rs 6 crore in 2000–2001. Compared to 378 drugs under price control in 1978, only 73 drugs remained under control in 1994 (ibid.: 141). It is therefore not surprising that numerous organisations came together in December 2000 for the National Health Assembly in Calcutta and the World Health Assembly in Dhaka in order to take the governments to task on the promise of 'Health for All in the Year 2000'. While health is neglected in favour of 'Family Welfare', the item given most attention under this heading is the provision of contraceptives (30–34 per cent), while only 52–54 per cent has been made available for other services like maternal care, child survival, adolescent health, and counselling. Besides, the National Population Policy has once again re-introduced incentives and disincentives that link even the provision of continued facilities for urban slum dwellers to terminal methods of contraception. This is not only coercive, but can also have epidemiological consequences (ibid.: 142). Most disturbing is the fact that the very space to live and work has been withdrawn from the urban poor in favour of parking spaces and flyovers.

It has been claimed that globalisation, apart from causing displacement and pressure on the informal sector, has opened up new opportunities for women in the service sector, especially in tourism, electronics and communication. However, many of these jobs look insecure and have severe drawbacks for women. The tourism industry feeds into stereotypes of the sexual division of labour, which at best reinforce old patterns or, at worse, pressurise women into the flesh trade (Rao 1997). Call centres, while providing opportunities for making a fast buck, have socially dubious effects due to night shifts, and the colonisation of mind and language (Roy 2001: 181f). On the whole, the new openings do not appear to outweigh the destruction of livelihoods in the informal sector and the loss of public-sector employment for women (Mukherjee 2004).

Dams and Bombs—Militarisation and Communalisation of Development

The Home Minister's speech on 31 October 2000, at the time the height of the Sardar Sarovar Dam was being raised, following the Supreme Court judgement of 18 October significantly exposed a development trend that is technocratic and violent, and thus life-threatening. He spoke of the three great achievements of his government, namely Pokhran II, the Kargil victory, and the Supreme Court judgement on Sardar Sarovar. He also pointed out that it was no coincidence that the people against dams were also against bombs, and bracketed them as being 'against national development'.

The Supreme Court had virtually become an arena of warfare on the Indian people, especially the Adivasi population. This trend was counter-balanced in the speech of the Dalit President of the Republic during Republic Day 2001, in which he called for the protection of the Constitution as well as the rights of the Adivasi population, and for which he was attacked by the rightist press.

Arundhati Roy, in her book 'The Greater Common Good' (Roy 1999), has shown the magnitude of the displacement through big dams in India as being in the range of 50 million people, and the clash between technocratic development and the self-reliance of Adivasi life. Sanjay Sangvai (2000) has made visible the monstrosity of the whole planning process, and the tenacity of protracted struggle to protect a self-reliant economy and a unique culture of solidarity.

The Narmada struggle is an example of the destructiveness of a technocratic growth concept, which was imposed on the people with World Bank aid, and led to such levels of displacement and struggle that the bank itself had to withdraw in 1993. In November 2000, when James Wolfensohn (President of the World Bank Group) visited Delhi, he promised in front of 5,000 Adivasis to not invest in any project in the valley. The project, which comprises 30 big dams and 135 medium-sized ones, destroys the lives and livelihood of the people, and drastically alters the whole character of the river and the valley. The people of Bhargi near Jabalpur have been displaced twice and the unfinished right bank canal, which abruptly ends after two kilometres, makes a mockery of the intended irrigation by silently seeping into salinated fields.

Maheshwar Dam in the Nimad is an assault on a prosperous peasantry and threatens to destroy precious historical monuments. Built as a private dam by the S. Kumars, the struggle has left a trail of finance companies and banks who had to withdraw support. In his article 'On the Annals of the Laboratory State', Shiv Vishwanathan had pointed out the commonality between dams and bombs even before Arundhati Roy brought it to the fore (Vishwanathan 1997). He had borrowed the French concept of *triage* (selection) in order to express the selective annihilation which a laboratory-centred science brings about. This prepared-ness to dispose of whole populations shows a genocidal streak that is involved in growth at any cost. This is in painful contrast to people's tenacious struggle for their land rights (Dietrich 2000), accompanied by constructive work. The tendency of *triage* also manifests itself in the selective annihilation of communities in caste clashes and communal conflagrations. It becomes increasingly difficult to assert community rights over the resources and hold on to a self-reliant culture.

Women are affected by this violent development trend in various specific ways. As far as Narmada goes, the state governments in charge of resettlement and rehabilitation seem to be withdrawing more and more from implementing the Narmada Award and the Supreme Court judgement, and trying to escape with monetary compensation. However, while adult sons have a good chance of being recognised as having independent households, adult daughters are invariably counted as 'dependents', and thus are not entitled to any monetary compensation. Their life in the resettlement camps is confined to the house, and exposes them to an unknown life of unprecedented struggle against disease and lack of basic amenities. Kinship systems get disrupted and support structures are destroyed.

On 5 December 2004, a public hearing of the National Commission for Women (NCW), scheduled to be held in Khargone in Madhya Pradesh, was prevented by declaring Section 144 in the area. The women of Maheshwar and Maan remained undeterred, and leaving their houses under shelter of night demanded recognition of their land rights in front of the Collector's Office at Khargone anyway.

It appears to be difficult to grasp the survival rights of local communities, especially in the Adivasi areas, because the conditions are very different from what is considered 'normal' in our society.

- The land is not private but belongs to the community.
- We see an economy in which money is not at the centre, but exists only as a supplementary means of exchange.
- The Adivasis strive not to subjugate nature, but to befriend her.
- People use a different type of small-scale technology, derived from local conditions, bottom-up instead of trickle down.

Such a culture indeed preempts bombs and warfare and safeguards against communal solutions in politics. It was therefore deeply meaningful that the struggle of the Narmada Bachao Andolan (NBA) in Delhi during 11–17 November 2000 took place parallel with the Movement in India for Nuclear Disarmament (MIND) conference, which attacked nuclear weapons and was attended by 60 delegates from Pakistan as well. Participants commuted between the disarmament conference and the Adivasis camping in Rajghat.

The connection between the building of dams and the attempt to 'recuperate' Adivasis and Dalits into the Hindu fold has loomed large in the mind of the Gujarat government since long. The Morse Report, which was published in 1992, had given a scathing critique of the Sardar Sarovar Project, dismantling most of the benefit claims and stressing the loss of livelihood, especially in the Adivasis areas. The report was dismissed by then Chief Minister Chinnambhai Patel, who stated that Mr Morse and his committee had no right to tell us 'whether tribals are Hindus or not' (D'Souza 2002: Ch. 6). This politics of 'recuperation' came to the fore in Gujarat in March 2002, when concerted attempts were made to involve Dalits and Adivasis in the anti-Muslim riots in post-Godhra Gujarat. Though this did not succeed on a large scale, communal forces made significant inroads, for example in the Alirajpur area. This has contributed significantly to the destruction of social values, which were giving women relatively more space. Quite apart from this, the monstrous amount of violence against women during the Gujarat riots of 2002 has exhibited degrees of brutality that were striking and unexpected (People's Union for Civil Liberties 2002). One of the devices to distract from this spectacle of genocide was the claim to bring Narmada waters to Kutch and Sourashtra, which, of course, did not hold water in reality (*Outlook* 2003).

It is not astonishing that the atmosphere regarding the relief and rehabilitation of the dam-affected people has turned completely cynical, and that no serious attempt has been made to protect people's livelihood by giving land for land. This has to do with a serious lack of imagination regarding the development of rural lifestyles and sustainable agriculture.

The argument is not for a return to the forest, but for a re-invention of artisanal rural industries that have been destroyed under colonialism, and that can provide labour which supplements agriculture. Different eco-regions can bear different types of rural industrialisation in harmony with the natural environment. This would be a world apart from the capital intensive, labour saving hegemonic development model. However, it will only be viable if caste discrimination and untouchability is overcome. Therefore, Dalit struggles against violence are crucial.

The struggle against the WTO, which went on in Seattle in December 1999, shows clearly that trade cannot rule the world and that globalisation is not the last word. It is not an accident that women have been in the forefront of the Narmada struggle as well as in the battle at Seattle. The hegemonic development concept annihilates nature and indigenous people, while the struggle, together with constructive work, projects a lifestyle that is far removed from large-scale industrialism.

This approach rests on multi-culturalism, protecting bio-diversity and cultural diversity at the same time. It is therefore significantly different from the RSS position, which proclaims anti-colonialism in the name of Hindutva, and tries to encourage indigenous capitalists to flood the world market with competitive export articles. It is feminist in the sense that it focuses on the production of life and livelihood and is not determined by forces of the market and the primary logic of profit. It is secular and respects people's cultures and religions without ideologically appropriating them for reasons of state or of political parties. It is non-violent, yet militant. It is against caste and untouchability, and refuses to be subsumed into the logic of caste hierarchies.

Conceptualisations of Feminist Alternatives: Subsistence Approach and Production of Life and Livelihood

Feminists have been focusing on the production of life and livelihood as opposed to production for profit for the last 20 years. This approach has been consistently developed over the years in order to incorporate women's invisible labour in the household as well as in the informal sector; to make visible the labours of nature which are not often seen as a form of productivity;[1] to make visible the labour needed to sustain nature and to prevent renewable resources from becoming non-renewable; to make visible the knowledge systems of traditional and artisanal communities and the way they blend with appropriate modern technologies; and to expose the violence of the hegemonic development concept, which destroys the resource base and cultures that were trying to sustain it. Maria Mies and the Bielefeldt School have exposed the connection between patriarchy and accumulation on a world scale, and also the internal colonisation of women and indigenous communities (Mies 1986). Vandana Shiva has developed the approach further by deepening the feminist critique of Western science and technology, and attacking especially the so called gene-revolution and bio-piracy (Shiva 1988, 1998; Shiva and Mies 1993) and stating emphatically that life can neither be 'made', nor 'owned'. Chhaya Datar, Nalini Nayak and I have worked out the nurturing aspect of women's labour (Datar 1998; Dietrich 1992; Nayak and Dietrich 1989).

This perspective has been deflected to a large extent by the whole rhetoric on women and development, women in development, conceptualisation on gender, practical and strategic gender needs, and the manifold attempts at 'women's empowerment' (Datar 1995; Kabeer 1994). The gender and development debate was launched side by side with the structural adjustment programmes, and women's empowerment was deflected into 'self-help groups' comprising of small saving schemes and health groups working on 'reproductive rights'. While some of these attempts are of a certain help for women, the fundamental questions of access to land, water, food, shelter, education and right to work were often not seen in their wider context. Globalisation has given rise to market fundamentalism and speculation in finance markets. Production for profit and even profit without production has gone to extremes. In the face of this trend, subsistence production has been viewed as primitive, backward and unviable, a 'back to the trees' approach. Gail Omvedt (2001), who has taken a blatant pro-globalisation line, argues vehemently for the 'development of productive forces' along very traditional sounding Marxist lines, without either critiquing capitalism or admitting to the destructiveness of the industrialist paradigm. She glosses over the contradictions between the kulak lobby and small peasants. In a recent book on the subsistence perspective, Maria Mies and Veronika Bennholdt Thomsen (1999) have tried to envisage a new society beyond the present globalised economy, and have shown how the visible economy of capital and wage labour reflected in the GNP is only the tip of the iceberg, which consists of home workers, the informal sector, child labour, subsistence peasant work, housework, internal and external colonies, and the labours of Nature.

They sharply critique the unlimited growth concept and the 'eight articles of faith' of neo-liberalism, which equate growth and development, believe in the trickle-down effect, advocate integration into the world economy as 'progress', seek 'comparative advantage' in the international division of labour, believe that liberalisation of capital flows is leading to better allocation of means of production and view technology as being able to compensate for ecological loss, see private property as the ideal system, and expect the nation-state to be per definition less efficient than private enterprise.

Beyond these 'articles of faith', Mies and Bennholdt Thomsen raise other fundamental questions like the relationship between productive activity and consumption, and the relationship between needs and wants. They expose the contradiction between standard of living and quality of life, and propose decentralised cycles of production and consumption. They advocate people's access to land, water, forest, bio-diversity and knowledge. They critique the assumption that technological progress will compensate for ecological loss, and that physical labour will be made obsolete by machines. Even computer chips still presuppose the invisible labour of women.

They raise the question as to what an economy and nature matter, in which human beings would be like. Subsistence work needs to be at the centre of the production system as it is the base for extended production. The limits of nature need to be respected, and the economy should be just one sub-system of society, and not the dominant one. The economy would then be serving the core life systems like food, housing, clothing, shelter, health, education, transportation, communication, etc.; it would be decentralised and regional, and based on self-reliance in food production. Trade would not destroy bio-diversity, the commons would be reclaimed, and money would be a means of circulation, not of accumulation. This requires alternative marketing as well as the re-invention of the commons. As the authors are situated in Europe, the book does not focus too much on how the enormous onslaught of globalisation on the Third World can be resisted. It focuses more on re-introducing subsistence production even in societies where this has already been destroyed. This is a progress compared to earlier writings, which focused only on consumer resistance. Consumer resistance and constructive work on subsistence are indeed a necessary combination in any society; however, it is for us to envisage the struggle dimension side by side, as it is visible not only in the Narmada valley and along our coasts, but in our countryside and cities as well.

Conclusion

It is evident that the present trend of globalisation works in the opposite direction of what was envisaged as subsistence approach. Life and livelihood get uprooted and destroyed. In India, the onslaught of agriculture is about to wipe out the strenuously built up food security. The Narmada struggle has shown that dams cannot be fought in isolation, but that the battle is against the development concept itself and the international finance and marketing institutions. The forces that proclaim a second freedom struggle are on the rise. This requires indefinite mobilisation against globalisation. Women, Dalits and Adivasis are primarily affected by the destructive growth concept. Dalits lose reservations through privatisation, and lose access to the resource base on which they have been dependent. All of us are together in danger of losing the fundamental protection of democracy enshrined in our constitution. We are already losing the protection of the labour laws: the Industrial Disputes Act has been amended to render our struggles illegal (section 5/A), and the Contract Labour Act was amended to allow contract labour even in core sectors.

The struggle is not only against the economic system, but is also against the cultural dominance of the market and against the subsumption of local cultures under religious totalitarianism. Women's movements have to align with unions in the unorganised sector as well as with Dalits, peasants and ecological struggles. As globalisation also dismantles the labour laws, new alliances between workers in both unorganised and organised sectors will have to be forged. Likewise, an alliance between workers and peasants will become unavoidable. Under the onslaught on agriculture, agricultural labourers and small farmers will have to come together despite the centuries of caste conflicts. While the dominant trend is still to co-opt women as well as Dalits into globalisation under the heading of 'entering the mainstream', the volatile situation is becoming more and more visible. People are rising up in the second freedom struggle.

Note

1. Shiv Vishwanathan (1997) has drawn attention to the fact that the ignorance of the productivity of nature is closely connected with the present trend towards species extinction, *op.cit.*

References

Alternative Economic Survey 1998–2000, 2000. Alternative Survey Group. Delhi: Rainbow Publishers, *Azadi Bachao Andolan and Lokayan*.

An extensive discussion of all these trends can be found in Nandita Shah, Sujatha Gotheskar, Nandita Gandhi and Amrita Chhachi, 'Structural Adjustment, Feminisation of Labour Force and Organisational Strategies' 1994. *EPW*, Apr. 30, WS 39–WS 48.

'At the Receiving End. Women's Experiences of Violence in Vadodara'. 2002. A Report of People's Union for Civil Liberties, Vadodara and Vadodhara Shanthi Abhiyan, 31 May.

Bhat, Ela. 1992. 'Structural Reform: View from the Other Side', *The Economic Times*, Jan. 15.

Commonwealth Secretariat, *Engendering Adjustment for the 1990s*, 1989. London.

Datar, Chhaya. 1995. *In Search of Feminist Theory. Subordination of Women's Labour and Environmental Degradation*. Ph.D. Thesis, SNDT Women's University.

———. 1998. *Nurturing Nature. Women at the Centre of Natural and Social Regeneration*. Bombay: Earthcare Books.

Dietrich, Gabriele. 1992. *Reflections on the Women's Movement in India: Religion, Ecology, Development*, Horizon India Books.

———. (ed), 2000. *Perspectives on Food Security and Survival*, Madurai: AIWS and CSA, Jan. especially Utsa Patnaik, 'Globalisation, Poverty and Food Security'.

———. 2000. Dams and People: 'Adivasi Land Rights', *EPW*, 35(36): 3378–80, 16 Sep.

———. 2001. 'Violence, Dalit Feminism and the Healing of Fragmentation', presented at AIWS Biannual Conference at Hyderabad in Jan. published in Vikalp IX/3, 2001.

D'Souza, Dilip. 2002. *The Narmada Dammed. An Inquiry into the Politics of Development* (Penguin Books), especially Chapter 6.

Elson, Diane. 1994. 'Structural Adjustment with Gender Awareness?', *Indian Journal of Gender Studies*, 1(2): 145–66.

Gender and Poverty in India, A World Bank Country Study (Washington, 1991). The report quotes on p. 83 Maithreyi Krishnaraj's paper of 1985 on *Women's Position in Export Oriented Industry: The Cost of Female Preference in Employment* and Nirmala Banerjee's paper, 'Some Recent Trends in the Economic Activities of Women' on p. 85.

Kocherry, Thomas and M.G. Sanjay, 2000. 'Battle of Seattle', *NAPM Bulletin.*

Mies, Maria. 1986. *Patriarchy and Accumulation on a World Scale. Women in the International Division of Labour.* London: Zed Books.

Mies, Maria and Veronika Bennholdt Thomsen. 1999. *The Subsistence Perspective. Beyond the Global Economy.* Zed Books.

Mukherjee, Mukul. 2004. 'Women and Work in the Shadow of Globalisation', *Indian Journal of Gender Studies*, II(3): 275–90.

Nayak, Nalini and Gabriele Dietrich. 1989. *Transition on Transformation: A Study on the Mobilisation, Organisation and Emergence of Consciousness among Fish Workers*, ICSSR.

Overviews over this trend can be found in Naila Kabeer. 1994. *Revised Realities. Gender Hierarchy in Development Thought.* New Delhi: Kali for Women.

Omvedt, Gail. 2001. 'Marx and Globalisation', *The Hindu*, March 1 and 2.

Palmer, I. 1992. 'Gender Equity and Economic Efficiency in Adjustment Programmes', in H. Afshar and C. Dennis (eds). *Women and Adjustment Policies in the Third World*, pp. 69–83. London: MacMillan.

Pillai, Ajit. 2000. 'The Trade Locusts', *Outlook*, Feb. 12.

Rao, Nina. 1997. 'Women and Tourism in Kerala', Vol. 5, Iss. 3, Sep. p. 31 in *A.N. Letter* (*Equations*, Quarterly OW Third World Tourism).

'Ripples in the Rain. 2003. The Narmada Finally Gets to These Parched Pipes, the Fields are Still Some Tiem Away', *Outlook*, 2 June.

Roy, Arundhati. 1999. *The Greater Common Good.* Mumbai: India Book Distributors.

———. 2001. 'Power Politics', *The Algebra of Infinite Justice*, Viking, especially p. 181f.

Sagar, Alpana and Imrana Qadeer. 2001–2002. 'Health', in *Alternate Economic Survey 1998–2000*, Alternate Survey Group. Delhi: Rainbow, June 2000. Azadi Bachao Andolan and Lokayan, pp. 138–42.

Sangvai, Sanjay. 2000. *The River and Life.* Mumbai: Earth Care Books.

Shah, N., S. Ghotaskar, N. Gandhi and A. Chhachi. 1994. 'Structural Adjustment, Feminisation of Labour Force and Organisational Strategies', *Economic and Political Weekly*, 30 April: WS 39.

Shiva, Vandana. 1988. *Staying Alive. Women, Ecology and Survival in India.* New Delhi: Kali for Women.

Shiva, Vandana. 1998. *Bio-piracy: The Plunder of Nature and Knowledge.* London: Green Books.

Shiva, Vandana and Maria Mies. 1993. *Eco-Feminism.* New Delhi: Kali for Women.

Vijayan, Aleyama and J. Sandya, 2000. 'Violence Against Women. The Case of Kerala', *Violence Update* No. 1, April (Centre for Social Research, Delhi).

Vishwanathan, Shiv. 1997. *Carnival for Science. Essays on Science, Technology and Development*, OUP.

Section V

Information and Communication Technologies

At the Beijing World Conference, media and ICTs were codified as one of the 12 critical areas of concern for women. It is estimated that 37 per cent of the women in the world have access to a personal computer (PC) (UNIFEM Report on the Progress of World's Women, 2002). The percentage figure for female home Internet users is 23 for India, while the Asia average is 22 per cent (NASSCOM 2000). In a developing country like India, ICT issues centre on computer literacy, women's access to the Internet—information being an important resource—and, the role of new technologies in bringing economic empowerment to women. Since Indian women are over-represented among the poor, the illiterate and low-educated groups, they remain outside the pale of the information society. For those economically better-off and educated, a variety of models are in place to get on the information highway.

The urban landscape is dotted with training centres that offer different kinds and levels of computer courses/diplomas, and there is a programme underway to integrate computer courses into the school curriculum. With prices crashing, computer ownership is expected to increase. India has one of the lowest rates of computer ownership and Internet access. It is estimated that computer ownership in India is at 0.67 per cent, and it is expected to show a five-fold increase by 2010. A 2003 global survey from Nielsen/NetRatings, a media and IT research group, found that only one in every 14 Indian households with telephones had Internet access via a home PC, in contrast to 80 per cent of households in Asia and Australasia. The few fortunate ones have access to computers at the workplace. These are mostly professionals in the organised sector of work. By far the most common access for urban women is the tiered franchised business model—the cybercafes prevalent in urban centres. It is equivalent to the information kiosk in rural areas. Besides, cybercafes often double up as training centres, providing basic skills to those who need it. The enrolment figure for women in India in technology and engineering disciplines was 11.14 per cent in 1994 (IAMR 1995). This also puts them at a disadvantage, both in terms of access and in the creation of these technologies. Once access is secured, women use these technologies for a variety of purposes which are given almost equal emphasis, such as education, connectivity, entertainment, productivity, etc., unlike men, who use it predominantly to enhance work productivity.

As far as economic opportunities are concerned, women tend to be concentrated in end use, low-skilled Information Technology (IT) jobs such as data entry and word processing, and make up only a tiny percentage of managerial, maintenance and design personnel in networks, operating systems or software. However, women are making inroads into higher levels of the IT workforce, and their participation in this sector is increasing. In 1993, women comprised 10 per cent of the workforce, which increased to 18 per cent in

1998, the national average being 12 per cent. Besides software, many of the new jobs are in call centers, Business Process Outsourcing (BPO), and Geographical Information Systems (GIS) (NASSCOM-McKinsey 1999).

Unlike earlier technologies that displaced women, the new technologies offer the advantage of working from home—an option many women with work-family balance issues find attractive. It is also providing homemakers with possibilities to start business ventures from home. The idea of being empowered from e-health, e-governance, e-commerce, etc., remains in the realm of possibilities. Besides literacy, access, use and economic empowerment, the new technologies have implications for power distribution at a macro level in any society. In November 2005, before the start of the World Summit on Information Society (WSIS) in Tunis, Heike Jensen, the coordinator of the gender advocacy group, stated that 'information and communication are at the root of every society's core processes of negotiating power, norms, values and realties. Peaceful change is impossible without utilizing media and ICTs, while hegemonic powers presently utilise these for spreading their ideologies' (Jensen 2005: 10).

The theme of the fifth section in the book is **Information and Communication Technologies**, and it covers some of the issues raised above. In 'ICT and the Technological U-Turn for Women', Ashima Goyal lists the benefits that ICTs can bring to women. Unlike earlier technologies which marginalised women, ICTs offer possibilities as it compensates for women's traditional disadvantages. She outlines the various avenues for remunerative work, and argues for the need of IT education for girls and women. She concludes by challenging the earlier focus of feminists, who believed that to be equal one must mimic men. Bridging the digital divide becomes crucial if women are to be global citizens. Anikar Haseloff and Rehana Ghadially in their chapter 'Gender, Cybercafes and Internet Access: Bridging the Digital Divide?' consider the role of cybercafes in bridging the gender-based digital divide. This empirical work highlights three aspects. First, there are the reasons for not accessing the Internet and motives for future use. Second, it studies the age, income, language proficiency and place of Internet access among male and female users of the Internet. Lastly, it examines, among other things, the usage patterns of those who frequent cybercafes. In 'Empowering Women through ICT Education: Facilitating Computer Adoption', Farida Umrani and Rehana Ghadially consider computer skills as a key ingredient in women's advancement. While economic and political empowerment are much talked about in the context of ICTs, the authors look at the role psychological, social and institutional factors play in computer adoption by urban women. If computers are perceived to be useful to the women and their families, home access to the technology together with supportive training centres can give women a head start on this aspect of their education. Shoba Arun, Richard Heeks and Sharon Morgan in 'ICT Initiatives, Women and Work: Reproducing or Changing Gender Inequalities?' present findings from two ICT initiatives in South India, and scrutinise their impact on women's employment, income, social roles and relations in the workplace and community. The chapter argues that ICTs have varied implications for women in terms of employment and empowerment, and much depends on the context within which these new technologies are utilised. ICT initiatives, pursued in the context of a neo-liberal agenda, reinforce gender inequalities, whereas the gender-focused initiative involving state intervention brings positive changes for women.

References

Institute of Applied Manpower Research. 1995. *Manpower Profile India*. New Delhi: IAMR.

Jensen, Heike. 2005. 'Challenges for Gender Equality', *i4d*, Vol. III (3): 8–10.

NASSCOM. 2000. *Indian IT-Enabled Service Provider Directory 2000*. New Delhi: NASSCOM.

NASSCOM-McKinsey. 1999. *Finding on IT Industry: Projections for 1999–2007*. McKinsey Report, New Delhi.

Unauthored. 2005. 'The Tilted Balance', *i4d*, Vol. III (3): 46.

SEVENTEEN

ICT and the Technological U-Turn for Women

Ashima Goyal

Introduction

Women allocate more time[1] to the household, often at a critical period in their career. This lowers their productivity in the external labour market and, by lowering learning-by-doing in remunerative skills, lowers future earnings as well. Perceptions and power magnify these distortions. Others doubt women's ability, but women doubt themselves, and this self-doubt further harms their prospects. In these circumstances, Information and Communication Technologies (ICT) and the Internet offer many benefits to both society and women. They can reduce this waste of potential human resources since they facilitate flexi-time activity, lower location constraints, and make it feasible for women to maintain and upgrade skills.

ICT may enable a technological U-turn in more ways than one. The literature on women in development has emphasised that modernisation and the technological development that went with it initially raised the returns to work outside the home (Boserup 1970; Oldenburg 2002). Male bargaining power increased in the household and women's relative position deteriorated. Therefore the focus of the early women's movement was an ensuring that women should be able to do all that men do—they must mimic men. However, this meant a subtle devaluing of the softer values (Kabeer 1994; Steinem 1993), which are essential for a well-rounded humanity, healthy societies, and full respect for women. ICT makes it possible for women to gain economic independence and status without having to become identical to men. In economics, Kuznet's inverted U is well-known as the hypothesis that inequality first increases and then decreases with development. In the same way, technology may be able to help women more in its later stages than it did in the earlier ones, and allow them to revert to being more themselves.

Although all women share the biological constraints and historical disadvantages, there is great diversity across different categories of women, especially in India. Gender differences are compounded by those created by income inequalities, caste, religion, urban-rural divides, and cultural differences across regions. But ICT's great advantages are its own flexibility, as well as the flexibility it makes possible. Therefore it can contribute to each category.

In this chapter we explore the history that has created a resistance to technology among women and left them with many disadvantages; the thwarted development, which new technology can help resolve; the reasons why new technology can be particularly helpful for Indian women; and the impetus required from policy to push through entrenched biases and resistance.

Our hypothesis implies that participation of women in this technology should rise relative to that of others, if ICT uniquely compensates for some of women's special disadvantages. There is some evidence that this is happening. For example Morahan-Martin concluded in 1998 that:

> The Internet has been dominated by males since its inception. Although use of the Internet by females has increased dramatically in the last few years, women and girls worldwide still use the Internet less and

in different ways than males. Low Internet use by females not only gives them less access to information and services available online, but also can have negative economic and educational consequences.

UNDP (1999) noted that in that year women formed 38 per cent of US Internet users, 25 per cent in Brazil, 17 per cent in Japan, 16 per cent in Russia, 7 per cent in China, and only 4 per cent in the Arab States.

However, just two years later a survey-based study (Rickert and Sacharow 2000) recorded that in the first quarter of 2000, American women overtook men as a percentage of Internet users. In 2003, a study in the US commissioned by IBM, which compared women and men business owners with respect to ICT usage, discovered that women exceeded men both in the use of new technology, and the way it was used to assist businesses. Their lead varied from 4 to 11 per cent. Comparison was made on the use of business homepages, Internet for research, e-mail, growth opportunities, and technical inputs. Women, more than men, used ICT to respond to customers, speed up product introductions, and improve marketing efforts (Vasisht 2003). The purchasing power of women is growing. Another US study by *BizRate* reports that in January 2004 the percentage of purchases made by women was 62 per cent in the fourth quarter, while men accounted for just 38 per cent of transactions. There was a substantial rise from the year 2002 when the split was 55 per cent women and 45 per cent men. There is growing evidence to show that from the late 1990s ICT has contributed to the higher rate of growth of productivity in the American economy. The improvements come from the reorganisation ICT has made possible (Basu et al. 2004). Some of the growth must be due to the higher productivity of women, although this is yet to be tested. These studies are for America, but since this was the country where the Internet started and where it has the widest spread, it portends future trends elsewhere.

The women's movement recognises the importance of the Internet, but fears are expressed that women may be left behind and end up as have-nots. The reasons for this fear are that women may have less online access than men because they have less time, money, control, learning opportunities, and more of other commitments, and because they give priority to others' needs. The majority view is that gender bias and misperceptions stating that women can do only limited types of work and are technologically inept must first be removed for women to be able to reap the full potential benefits of the new technologies.[2] The analysis in this chapter suggests that the Internet has the potential to give women more time, educational opportunities and money, even if they continue to prioritise others' needs. However, these changes can take time and have to battle entrenched prejudices, whether those of women or their employers.

History: Power and Technology

One of the pioneers of development economics, writing in 1955, said that while it may be possible for men to debate the desirability of economic growth, it was not possible for women to do so since growth gave them the chance to 'cease to be beasts of burden' and to 'join the human race' (Lewis 1955). However, modernisation has not helped women as much as it was expected to. The women in development (WID) approach blamed development theory and practice for the under-representation of women in the modern sector. The liberal worldview expected modern man to be rational, objective and competitive, but totally neglected women or identified them only with housework and welfare. Boserup (1970) argued that differences between the sexes arose from differing work experiences, and with professional training women could be as productive as men in the external world. Instead, the development process had marginalised women, since new resources, experience and opportunities had largely gone to men.

The modernising WID perspective had, however, neglected women's own choices, biological constraints and priorities, and thus contributed inadvertently to the subtle liberal devaluing of 'women's work'. The human lifecycle has inevitable points of vulnerability in birth, death, childhood and old age, where care and nurture are essential (Kabeer 1994). True gender sensitivity requires seeing through women's eyes and respecting their other-regarding values. It is beginning to be recognised that development will be fully successful only if it is gender aware and if both sexes change—men contributing more to nurture while women become more active outside the home.

Historical processes were part of the reason modernisation and technological development did not liberate women as much as they were expected to. Across the world women's status has been better in places where they have had a productive and not merely a reproductive role. Helen Fisher (2003) collates evidence showing that the agricultural revolution made male roles more important than female ones, changing conditions that had prevailed for millions of years when women worked and brought home 60 to 80 per cent of the evening meal, and their relative position had been almost equal to that of men. Esther Boserup (1970) also argues that in the colonial period, when males were recruited for plantations, etc., women were pushed to subsistence production, which kept the supply of male labour cheap but worsened the position of women. Colonial Western culture was conservative and anti-liberal, and external jobs made available favoured men. For example, the British colonial administration co-opted Nigerian men into gender stereotypes. This destroyed the checks and balances that had maintained equality among the sexes in traditional Igbo culture, where women had been assigned separate resources in female farming systems (Nzegwu 1995). In India landed property was put exclusively in male hands. From being co-partners in pre-colonial landholding arrangements women became dependents, denied access to economic resources. In translating flexible social and customary practices into legal codes, men were made the dominant legal subject (Oldenburg 2002). This was particularly so in the patriarchal households of the northern plains, while in southern India there was less female seclusion and patrilocal residence. Women sometimes inherited property rights, and where women had land rights they had greater independence and autonomy in decision-making and household tasks. Thus, initially modernisation and technological development disadvantaged women, but a technological U-turn may now be possible.

ICT can allow both men and women the freedom to participate in care and nurture while maintaining active professional lives. Being at the technological frontier becomes compatible, for women, with more presence in the household and flexi-time. Research shows that for their position in the household to improve, women's claims to household resources must not be exercised through men (Kabeer 1994); ICT, by making remunerative activity more compatible with homework, provides such economic independence. ICT-based financial innovations allow even non-working homebound women to control and manage their financial assets, since bank accounts and financial portfolios can be operated through the Internet. Research also shows that income earnings providing access to active and purposive social networks outside the house contribute more to women's independence (Kabeer 1994). Even with home-based work, ICT makes many such networks feasible. Many task or interest-oriented websites make networking easier. It is also easier to get information about the existence of such networks.

The failure of modernisation to substantially improve women's position has contributed to a deep ambivalence in women's relations with technology. Banerjee and Mittar (1998) report that women are the first to lose jobs since they tend to do simple mechanical tasks machines can easily replace. Women have the reputation of being inflexible carriers of tradition, but this position is actually due to underlying patriarchal relations; their education is normally such that they learn only to do A and B, not why A and B. Women are regarded as technologically inept and their time is not considered valuable, they are even denied labour-saving devices such as pressure cookers in the kitchen. But Wadley (2000), in tracing four generations of women in a Brahmin household in Karimpur, a village in Uttar Pradesh, finds changes in lifestyles, incomes, education and options. Compared to their grandmothers, women running households today have much more time because foods are processed outside. For example, they no longer have to grind flour manually. However, since the time released is not continuous, and it is difficult to find productive activity matching their skills, they spend the time largely in religious rituals. ICT can make many other options available for them, such as part-time outsourcing work, entrepreneurship and marketing, or skill upgradation.

But wouldn't this imply a double burden, of home and of outside work? Women teleworkers in Mumbai work with high technology, but Gothoskar (2000) finds them clustered at the low end, doing jobs with the lowest value addition. Home work is actually a negative for them since it traps them in the power relations at home. Technology has made them non-stop workers, much like Wadley's first generation 'Amma', instead of improving their options. The key to delivering more freedoms and control over their lives to women lies either in developing a high level of skills with the superior economic status and bargaining power it gives, or in the presence of supportive organisations that improve exit options and generate awareness. Women's perceptions of possibilities are also limited and need to be changed. Chopra and Raval (2000) profiled highly successful Indian female entrepreneurs and professionals who prefer to stay single. Their lifestyles are at par with those in developed nations. Many of them are young, but they will have more options and freedoms even when and if they acquire households—no household will be able to exploit them.

ICT makes more options available, but having the ability to do more does not mean that one has to do more. It means that the choices one makes are better suited to ones skills, and therefore are more rewarding materially and mentally. The next section examines how ICT's flexibility allows it to contribute to different categories of Indian women.

Contribution Across Different Groups and Classes

For ICT to be useful, it must, first of all, be available. The digital divide is relevant, and access is lower in India compared to developed countries; and in India it is lower for backward and poor sections. Here industry structure and government ICT infrastructure and regulation policies can play an important role. India has the advantage of backwardness; it can quickly jump to best practices. Early successes should stimulate action, and since the government has allowed private-sector entry, competition should stimulate better quality. Outsourcing and other contacts with international standards will improve domestic organisation. The time required to get state of the art broadband is lower than that required to improve roads and other physical infrastructure. There are reports stating that when higher speed Internet access was introduced in the city of Birmingham, UK, it helped many single mothers make ends meet. The higher download speeds increased their efficiency, and made a whole range of new jobs requiring high-speed data access available to them. Different advantages or disadvantages flow from different kinds of access. Slower dial-up connections also add value, and may be adequate for information requirements and certain kinds of work.

Availability of supportive hardware can also be structured to suit different income classes. Relatively affluent homeworkers may have home facilities, but may have to share them. Concerns have been voiced about unequal power preventing women from getting home access, as they might have last call on the facilities. However, they might also have the freedom to adjust their tasks so that they can work when others are away, and if they have sufficient economic power they can always acquire independent access.

They also have the option of using telecentres and net-based community centres, which have become common in developed countries. These ensure availability for middle and low-income classes. They are also part answer to the charge that distance working is an isolating activity (Mitter 2000). They encourage net-working and have the potential to help with community issues. To ensure that women are included, it is important to make the place comfortable and safe. Maindiratta and Maindiratta (2004) report on a telecentre for conservative Muslim girls, which was opened in a mosque in a backward area. The location gave immediate legitimacy in the community. Local content and a local instructor made them more comfortable.

In India, cybercafes and kiosks are coming up in a big way. Ramani writes in Mitter (2000) that the growth of these kiosks has been rapid, especially in the southern Indian states where English literacy is high. They create low-cost jobs (at about $2,500 a job). Internet usage skills are also spread at low cost, thus facilitating future teleworking. A survey in eight Indian cities showed that non-working women access the net 63 per cent of the time from cybercafes, and 32 per cent from the home (*Times of India* 2000a).

Support is required for women with low resources, language and literacy barriers. UNDP launched three pilot Technology Access Community Centres (TACCs) in Egypt to make Internet facilities available to people in poor and remote areas. They initially offered free walk-in access, as well as training in skills relevant for various commercial applications. In a later stage a small fee was charged for copying and training services (UNDP 1999). Computers have begun improving life in Indian villages, and women often operate the computer centres. A knowledge centre project of the M.S. Swaminathan Research Foundation[3] connected four villages in Pondicherry with practical local information in Tamil. It proved very useful in improving agricultural practices and marketing, and access to medical facilities (Swaminathan 2000; TOI 2000b).

ITC's e-*choupal* initiative has been spreading rapidly, and by end-2004 had covered 3.1 million villagers. It aims to reach 10 million farmers by 2010 by expanding at the rate of three *choupal*s a day. Although its primary purpose is to provide various services for farmers, it has a well-designed governance structure that is likely to make it sustainable. It is run by local people and gives them commissions based on transactions through the e-*choupal*, thus motivating them to maximise use while they are made accountable to their community. The facilities are set up to be independent of local power failures, and the built-in competition lowers the cost of the services. Attracting a number of users helps to lower the costs further. Self-help NGOs that work with women have begun using the facilities, allowing them to reach large numbers of people (Saran 2004).

ICT has made it easier for NGOs to create networks and databases, especially for women. Such facilities have helped many poor and suppressed women gain independence and authority, at home and in their communities. For example, Noorjehan, a poor Muslim in Nabanna, a West Bengal village, was able to put her tailoring rates in the local e-NRICH database and receive orders from outside her neighbourhood (Ghose and Ray 2004). Organisations such as the Self-Employed Women's Association (SEWA) in Ahmedabad and Grameen Bank in Bangladesh have been able to deliver more freedom and opportunities to their low-end members. Such associations help resist the existing power centres' attempts to fight change. An instance of such an attempt was the takeover by local leaders of a successful computer-aided retail effort of Guyanese village women (TOI 2000b).

There are also spillovers in marketing and collaborations with firms and banks. Self-help groups (SHGs) of rural women formed in Andhra Pradesh have been so successful in marketing their products both at home and abroad that major consumer goods MNCs use their selling power, and outsource manufacture and packaging to them. The SHGs operate one of the biggest retail chains in the state; each district has between 10–15 of these DWACRA (Development of Women and Children in Rural Areas programme) super-markets. They have made marketing trips to trade fairs abroad and received orders from Dubai for shirts, from New Jersey and the Apec region for pickles, and for crochet caps from Malaysia and Bangladesh. About 4.5 lakh groups cover nearly 60 lakh women. They have a large turnover, make profits and are excellent debtors, having returned 98 per cent of the Rs 1,000 crore borrowed so far. As a result banks are also lining up to lend to them (Pantulu 2003). Trade organisations such as PEOPLink sell the crafts of artisans from 14 countries in Asia, Africa and Latin America. Digital reproductions of the products are displayed over the Internet (UNDP 1999). ICT makes such decentralised yet global initiatives feasible.

It also makes more organised and regular work possible. Telework, defined as work done from a distance, is becoming feasible with the new technologies. Women often do this type of work. Some see it as being easily integrated with childcare. Others see telework as a low-wage, isolating activity without pension and other benefits, where women can easily be exploited. Since these opportunities are exploding in India, the next section explores their implications for women.

Telework Opportunities in India

Over the last 10 years, the Indian software industry has grown at annual rates of over 50 per cent. Nasscom (2004) estimates that in 2001–2002, it accounted for 2.87 per cent of Indian GDP, 16.5 per cent of its exports, and 500,000 direct jobs. Every direct job created 2.5 indirect jobs through supporting service industries such as catering, transport, housing, etc. In 2008 it is expected to account for 7 per cent of India's GDP and 30 per cent of its foreign exchange inflows with exports totalling $70–80 billion, and own and indirect jobs employing four million people. IT-enabled services (ITES) is projected to reach $21–24 billion, or 12 per cent of the world market, and create 1.1 million jobs by 2008. A.T. Kearney (2003) gave India the top slot as a potential location for ITES. As software exports slowed due to the American recession in 2000, ITES export boomed at 59 per cent, with MNCs looking for cheaper outsourcing. Such captive units showed 90 per cent growth. IT software and services exports were revived in 2003–04 and exceeded expectations by growing at 30.5 per cent while ITES grew at 45 per cent. Table 17.1 shows the initial and potential projections for ITES made by Nasscom in 1999, and gives an idea of the rapid potential growth. At current rates the projections may well be exceeded.

TABLE 17.1
ITES in India

IT-Enabled Services	1998–99		2008 (projections)	
	Employed	*US $ millions*	*Can be Employed*	*US $ millions*
Back office operations/Revenue accounting/Data entry/Data conversion	9,700	97	2,60,000	4,370
Remote maintenance and support	1,600	15	1,80,000	3,105
Medical transcription/Insurance claim processing	3,800	32	1,60,000	2,530
Call centres	1,400	9	1,00,000	1,380
Database services	1,000	10	1,00,000	1,495
Content development	5,500	62	3,00,000	5,750
Total	23,000	225	11,00,000	18,630

Source: NASSCOM, India (1999) and Mitter (2000).

Although the industry is still not very large relative to total GDP or employment, the high growth rates and the industry's adaptability and dynamism are promising. When software slowed, ITES took over. It had regularly been forecast that the industry would collapse and die. First it was thought to be a fluke caused by Y2K outsourcing. However, contacts developed during such work allowed the industry to move on to other areas. These contacts also increase business in other industries and services.

A large share of these new job opportunities is coming to women. ITES and outsourcing often rely on distance work. For instance, of the 600 home-based workers employed by Datamatics, an Indian software company, 98 per cent are women. They consciously set out to tap the pool of skilled women who have left their jobs for family reasons. Call centres, finding a high attrition rate among their youthful workers, are turning to older and part-time staff. Firms such as Novell and Wipro are using telecommuting to maintain the skills of female staff with young children.

A richer menu of better-paying jobs become available for women as outsourcing centres turn to employing part-time workers, mainly women. Such work is easily integrated with childcare. An example of how technology allows women to keep working and prevents decay of human capital is the case of Praveen Mahtani, a young lawyer with a finance company who was allowed to work from home, using a computer, webcam, etc., through three years when she had to cope with a difficult pregnancy and baby care. Under similar circumstances, Purvi Datta, an investment banker for whom such facilities were not made available, quit her job after 14 months of not attending office (Shaikh 2004). The Internet helps match women and employment possibilities. It becomes possible to find high value-added work and combine it with the production function for household goods, so that women's skills do not atrophy (Goyal 2000). Employers will also be more willing to employ women since the probability that they will leave work on starting a family will decrease.

Gothoskar (2000) interviewed women teleworkers in Mumbai and got responses ranging from welcoming the freedom to fulfill family commitments to dislike of the lack of access to public and social spaces and reinforcement of the role at home. Ng and Jhin (2000) got similar responses in Malaysia, but found also that high-end workers value the freedom of working from home, while low-end workers miss going out. Employers are also reluctant to give up the physical monitoring that an office makes possible. Ng and Jhin argue that telecentres help to solve these problems by, combining homework with social spaces and organisation. Those working at the high end have much more freedom and control over their lives, and for those at the low-end, organisations and government regulations can help. The first can mitigate family pressures, and both can prevent exploitation by employers. The Internet facilitates training modules designed for different categories of workers, and can be a medium for the required skill upgradation of low-end contract workers.

The rise in ITES means an expansion in supportive services industry. This, together with outsourcing and the tradition of home handicrafts production in India, suggests a large future potential in home businesses.

Entrepreneurship, Self-employment and the Internet

The Internet can offer great aid to entrepreneurship by women. It offers databases put together by women's groups, from which women can find relevant links, connections, resources and information, and develop partnerships, not just for their services, but also for financing, mentoring and business coaching. It helps small businesses in many ways—displaying goods, checking prices, making contacts and writing contracts (UNDP 1999). Developing country and rural women, who produce goods and services, are able to sell directly without having to go through middlemen. Ghose and Ray (2004) document eNRICH, the local database that allowed women to advertise their products and made many business opportunities available, while community centres provided mentoring. The Internet can even mitigate the barrier of lack of access to capital (WIC 1997 [see note 2]). It has encouraged financial innovations, making more finance available for home-based activities. Pantulu (2003) documents the partnerships between banks and homeworkers, mediated by NGOs, in Andhra Pradesh. In America there is a boom in home businesses and marketing innovations developed by women at home, with the help of marketing support through the Internet.[4] Support groups can be formed through electronic bulletin boards.[5] These can help to organise and build solidarity with and between people working from home offices, and can break down isolation, aid job-related concerted action, or just increase information, opportunities and interaction.

A survey of 55,000 American users (Rickert and Sacharow 2000) found that women tend to make very practical use of the net, concentrating on facilities that improve their and their families' lives. The largest percentage of users are in the age group of 25–44, and one of the top 10 websites they visit has to do with developing home entrepreneurship.[6] Since web use depends on the age profile, overall travel, retail and family care are dominant for women in America and Europe. Umrani and Ghadially (2003) find a similar emphasis placed on advantage for the family. This was the primary motivation of trainees undertaking a women's special computer training course. However, a survey of 24,848 high-income Indian users found that job-related information dominated for women (Table 17.2).

TABLE 17.2
Web Use by Affluent Indian Women

Categories Generally Surfed	All Women (%)	Working Women (%)	Non-working Women (%)
Jobs/Careers	50	46	55
Chat	45	39	56
News	44	46	41
Books	28	33	19
Fashion	27	31	21
Beauty/Healthcare	38	38	37

Source: TOI 2000a.

An interesting feature of the Rickert and Sacharow (2000) survey was that it showed that although the majority of American women make non-work related use of the Internet, the fastest growing section of web users was teenage girls.[7] This familiarity with the Internet will allow them to use it for their careers in the future, much as Internet kiosks and cybercafes, which are spreading Internet skills in India, will allow an explosive growth in future use.

Devine (1994) has documented a rise in women's self-employment in the US, Canada, Mexico and Argentina. Self-employment offers real advantages for women since it allows them to fit in work from home, gives them a flexible work schedule, and is compatible with their reproductive roles. Therefore, an effective way to improve women's position is to improve the returns to self-employment. This will happen if skills and organisation rise in the latter. ICT contributes to maintaining and updating skills, and to building informal organisations.

Since corporations are downsizing and contracting out services, many men are also choosing to work from home, opening niche businesses and offering specialised services. Often couples are doing it together. This, together with more equal education, can meet the criticism that if a woman works at home, she will end up doing all the housework as well. Since ICT allows more flexible forms of working at home, child-rearing and household work can be more equally shared.

Nussbaum (2000) regards male sharing of child-rearing as very important because she is convinced by Nancy Chodorow's work that the female mothering role is responsible for the deep psychological differences between men and women. Girls grow up to value nurture and self-sacrifice, and for boys maturity means to deny need and dependence. It follows that sharing child-rearing more equally between partners would increase autonomy for women and reduce men's need to deny emotions, making both more complete human beings. Fernandez et al. (2004) present evidence that sons of working mothers are more likely to have working wives; their preferences have changed and they are more willing to help with the housework, thus encouraging their wives to invest in human capital and develop careers.

Stephen Gould (1998: 263–64) argues that behavioural differences between the sexes are not largely due to biology. Although differences in behavioural strategy have an evolutionary advantage because of the different male and female reproductive systems, similarities, because of common genetics, are much stronger. It is environmental circumstances that, together with biology, tend to elicit a particular type of behaviour. Therefore, adapting to the environment, such as technology or institutions, to compensate for biology can allow human beings to specialise in accordance with their deepest human capabilities, rather than on the basis of gender. More margins of adjustment are opened; they become free to suit their own preferences and comparative advantage. Raising a family can be more easily combined with a high-skill career. The choice set and freedoms of both sexes would expand. Specialisation according to human rather than gender-based capabilities can answer the common feminist complaint: why should women alone be responsible for harmony, beauty, nurture, while men pursue their own advantage?

Learning, Training, Education and the Internet

ICT greatly contributes to learning and to learning-by-doing on the part of women. First, they are able to find opportunities that match their skills and requirements more easily; second, they are more easily able to maintain and update their skills; third, they gain richer experience and more regular work habits, and fourth, they can become technologically adept since ICT can be customised to provide a safe learning environment. It is necessary to keep in mind the dynamic effects of learning. While it can benefit the existing generations of women and the diversity of their needs, it can ensure fundamental changes in the generations to come.

Women in developing countries often have a range of labour skills. Low-wage outsourcing provides new opportunities, and enables learning by doing for labour with lower skills. It allows their managers to interact closely with customers, and understand their requirements. Those with more entrepreneurial ability may then migrate from simple job completion to designing customised software for business processes, and finally develop their own branded products for niche markets. Some employees of large firms may set up their own start-ups. This is slowly happening in the Indian software industry, which was once written off as mere body shopping (Nasscom 2004). Thus, ICT aids the process of learning the required norms and standards and teaches regular work habits to meet deadlines even while working at home. It provides an exposure to the requirements of business, and makes it possible to speak the same language.

Apart from learning to use the Internet itself, women's access to general training also increases. IT can create a safe space for women because they appear without gender, and so escape stereotyping in perceptions. Women learn best when the material is relevant, there is time for reflection, diverse and fun-filled ways of learning are used, there are passionate teachers, good role models, and a safe environment. They can find or create such a supportive, sharing community online. The Internet aids interactivity, which is very important for effective learning. Exposure to time-management skills, essential for effective homeworking, can also be acquired. The Women's Internet Conference, held in Canada in 1997, extracted these lessons on the basis of discussions with many women's groups actively working in the area.

As Sen (1999) remarks, large observed gaps between abilities is more due to education and experience than due to a difference in natural abilities; a steady development of capabilities can lead to astonishing levels of performance.

The Internet offers time and location flexibility, support, training and opportunity. Initial technical education can help in honing the ability to seize this opportunity, make the most of it in the future, and remove the self-fulfilling belief that women and technology do not go together.

Bangalore is an IT boom town in India, and there has been a mushrooming growth in private polytechnics to supply the huge potential demand for human resources in this area. However, enrolment of women in private polytechnics is lower than in public ones (Table 17.3), and also lower in engineering as compared to other courses (Table 17.4). There is a 30 per cent reservation for girls in public polytechnics, and the fee structure is lower (Ushadevi 2000). These facts point to the necessity of policy intervention. More special women-only technical training institutes should be set up.

TABLE 17.3
Enrolment in Public and Private Polytechnics

Year	Public (Government)			Private		
	Boys	Girls	Total	Boys	Girls	Total
1993–94	12,488 (73.62)	4,474 (26.37)	16,962	26,097 (89.07)	3,200 (10.92)	29,297
1994–95	12,393 (73.78)	4,404 (26.21)	16,797	26,173 (90.21)	2,839 (9.79)	29,012
1995–96	11,795 (71.82)	4,626 (28.17)	16,421	23,788 (88.12)	3,204 (11.87)	26,992

Source: Ushadevi 2000.
Note: Brackets give percentages of the total.

TABLE 17.4
Enrolment in Polytechnics by Fields of Specialisation

Year	Total Enrolment in Polytechnics			Engineering		Non-engineering	
	Boys	Girls	Total	Boys	Girls	Boys	Girls
1993–94	38,585 (83.4)	7,674 (16.6)	46,259	83.41	16.59	10.36	89.64
1994–95	38,566 (84.2)	7,243 (15.8)	45,809	84.42	15.58	11.21	88.79
1995–96	35,583 (81.8)	7,930 (18.2)	43,513	83.49	16.51	10.74	89.26

Source: Ushadevi 2000.
Note: Brackets give percentages of the total.

Educational institutes in the field range from engineering colleges to computer training institutes to more basic training centres for ITES type jobs. Active collaboration is required from local communities, businesses and governments in setting them up. Special initiatives for backward areas and communities would be fruitful. Ghadially and Umrani (2004) point out the absence of good computer training institutes in Muslim-dominated areas in even a city like Mumbai, and the presence of only 3 per cent Muslim girls in a women's special training course at a computer institute they surveyed, while Maindiratta and Maindiratta (2004) document the success of a community-cum-training centre for girls, which was opened in a local mosque with the cooperation of the Maulana.

Muslim women are one of the more backward groups, and such support helps both them and the society. The Indian 2001 Census gives the percentage of females who are working as only 14.1 among Muslims, compared to 27.5 among Hindus. The respective female literacy figures are 50.1 and 53.2 per cent. The growth rate of the Muslim population over 1991–2001 was 36 per cent, compared to 20.4 for Hindus. It is well-established that improving female education, employment and autonomy reduces the birth rate.

The boom in ICT-related jobs in India means that there is an expansion in both the supply of education and the demand for it. Thakore (2002) documents that large firms in ICT are becoming more involved in the provision of primary education because their future depends on trained manpower. Ghadially (1996) note in their survey results that the top work aspiration of Muslim mothers for their daughters was for computer-related jobs. The rise in the returns to education means a rise in the demand for education all down the education chain. A major positive spin-off is that returns to female literacy will rise, and contribute to its spread.

One of India's great development failures is that our literacy rate is still only 65 per cent. A contributory factor is the poor state of our village schools. However, even here, involving women more is a good way of both improving the schools and empowering women. Muralidharan (2004), in a rigorous countrywide study of the absenteeism of village teachers, finds that while this is higher (at 25 per cent) in India than in most countries of the world, the male teacher is 2–4 per cent more likely to be absent than the female teacher. Absenteeism is highest in Bihar and Jharkhand, where women are less educated and respected. Mother's education makes more of a difference to school attendance than the father's education does. Finally, better infrastructure and activism of parent associations are most effective in reducing absenteeism—this activism again depends on mothers' awareness and ability. ICT can contribute to the latter, make women push for better education for their children, and train them to contribute to it as teachers. By making them more willing to send their daughters to school, over time it would strengthen these beneficial dynamic tendencies.

Leveraging Women's Values

Initially for women, status and advancement in the external world meant giving up the feminine values of care and nurture, partly because household duties were seen as taking up too much time, and partly because women's low power and economic status denigrated other regarding values associated with women. Thus, in the initial modernising WID approach, imitating men was seen as essential for the successful careers for women. However, if, with the flexi-timing ICT makes possible, economic status can be achieved without sacrificing the gentler qualities, these values may gain more respect. Technology may thus facilitate a U-curve, whereby the softer values are neglected in the initial stages of development, but there is a revival in the later stages.

Research suggests that other regarding behaviour differs with gender (Ben-Ner et al. 2003), and that women's other regarding behaviour can enhance governance. Where women's influence in public life is higher, corruption is lower. Cross-country evidence shows that a higher proportion of women compared to men believe that corrupt actions can never be justified; this is so even accounting for individual characteristics.

Women in business are less likely to pay bribes. The reason may be either that they are risk-averse or that they are more ethical. They are more likely to be altruistic and community-oriented (World Bank 2001: 93). When women control resources, more of them are used to benefit their children, compared to a situation where the male head of the household has full control over resources.

In India steps taken to empower women in political and civic activities have been very fruitful in improving urban and village surroundings. In 1992 the 73rd Amendment to the Constitution reserved one-third of village panchayat and pradhan positions for women. There are many examples of women leaders transforming the environment of their villages. Chattopadhyay and Duflo (2004) find that in villages with reservations, women spend more on public goods relevant to their needs, such as water and roads. In Mumbai there is the example of CitiSpace, an NGO that fights for the protection of public space. It was set up after its founders—three ladies—fought and won a long battle to clear the historic Oval Maidan of encroachments.

One of the reasons for the success of the American feminist movement was its decentralised structure. Women enjoy doing things together. Activism was often a by-product of local group activities. That enjoyment made possible a resolution of a potential collective action problem; each contributed to a socially valuable activity (Hardin 1982). If each women's club or group undertakes some responsibility for the provision of public goods, the potential of contributing to society is enormous. Taipei is an example of a city where this has happened. Women's narrow domestic horizon and loyalties may prevent them from being impartial and far seeing, but empathy is an essential part of good judgment, and this grows from strong personal relationships. It can be shifted to apply to larger areas of interactions as activities and horizons broaden.

Valuing women's special qualities is very important. In the Indian state of Punjab, traditional male qualities are admired. Most families want sons. Today sex-selection techniques are available. The 2001 Census shows an alarming fall in the female to male sex ratio in the 0–6 age group. It has decreased from 875 females per 1,000 males in 1991 to 793 in 2001. The all-India average is 933. Development alone is not the answer because sex-selection tendencies are more among the better-off. Only if 'female' values are respected, and women given power, responsibility and respect, will girl children be saved.

ICT has a strong potential to empower women, and with the help of ICT women can make a substantial contribution to their own development and to that of the society in which they live. Therefore, policy should focus on and leverage this new instrument that is now available.

Implications for Policy

There is increasing understanding of the importance of gender sensitivity in formulating policy. In feminist literature the modernising women in development (WID) approach has given way to the Gender and Development (GAD) approach, which is doubtful about the automatic improvement of women's position with modernisation, and argues for institution and culture-sensitive programmes. For example, as structural adjustment programmes drove women more into the informal sector, the latter's status was expected to fall. However, there is evidence that conscious policies followed for the empowerment of women in recent years have prevented this negative effect. Specific gender-sensitive policies for empowering women are effective. Improving their access to new technologies is a powerful way of empowering them. Moreover, women's willingness to use the new technologies will also improve with general empowerment.

- Since structural labour market demand and supply factors are responsible for demand and supply distortions in female labour, policies that mitigate these structural factors in order to raise female wages would be more effective compared to policies that target endowment inequalities. For example, rather than attempting to lower the reservation wage of women, it would be better to subsidise childcare. Improving female skills in, and the use of, new technology would raise female productivity and wages.

- Women are at present paid less than men and have less free time, so funding should be made available to ensure that women have access to computers and the Internet. It is necessary to ensure high bandwidth and speed. As broadband spreads, access should improve in India's smaller towns and villages.

- Special facilities should be provided to cater to low-income and rural women while maintaining respect for diversity. Self-help groups and NGOs should be encouraged to set up multipurpose networks and community centres with ICT facilities. They can form a locus for community development activities.

- Content should be developed to allow initiatives like ITC's e-*choupal*, providing Internet-based services for India's villages, to be fully used to provide marketing and home-business services for rural women.

- Special training facilities should be provided to women of backward groups and their girl children. Firms in IT services have shown an interest in education since they need skilled labour. They should be roped in to help provide such facilities.

- Formal education in these areas, and computer and technical training institutes, must have reservations for young women.

- The government should carefully think through its tax policy with respect to the IT sector. Tax holidays for IT will be coming to an end in 2010. As the industry has matured, it should begin to pay taxes, but taxes on inputs should be low, and sales taxes, especially for educational purposes, should also be low. For example, the Government of Karnataka increased sales tax on IT products from 4 to 12 per cent in 2004. This is not compatible with encouraging its widespread use.

- To enhance learning and culturally-sensitive training and information, women's-only access sites should be encouraged.

- Laws should be passed to regulate teleworking.

- Examples of women's success in Internet-related businesses could be publicised.

- A database of Indian women with technical training who are currently not active in external work should be maintained and made available to potential employers. Certified information will be more useful to the latter than personal applications, which may be of doubtful quality.

- In networks the value of the marginal user can be very high because of externalities. In broadcasting services, for example, it is more efficient to subsidise the sender of messages than the recipients. The efficiency properties of intervention to encourage web use by women should be explored on similar lines. Monitoring end-use in the home may be difficult, so subsidies should go to web services related to developing home businesses for women rather than to women users of the Internet.

Conclusion

There is evidence to support the usefulness of ICT in lowering women's presumed inherent and intial disadvantages; there is also evidence that women are aware of this and their use of such technologies is rising steadily. Its flexibility makes it possible to adapt it to the needs of the great diversity among Indian women.

Women choose more self and home employment, except when they want to escape a patriarchal household. In spite of the initial fears of being left behind, women are overtaking men in the use of the Internet. Companies are deliberately using teleworking to utilise skilled women who have left full-time work, and to maintain the skills of their young female employees.

However, existing perceptions and power trouble female employees at the low-end especially, and decrease the availability of training in the requisite skills for young women. Self-doubt and fear of technology compound these problems. The distortions imply that special policies are required to attain full benefits of the new technologies, and aid their faster adoption. The digital divide has to be addressed and fast access ensured. Women will gain, but society will gain even more from the boost to women's productivity.

This chapter puts together some pieces of evidence and suggests policies. The Internet is relatively new and its use is nowhere near its potential in India. The signs, however, are encouraging.

Notes

1. Goyal (2000) demonstrates this formally in a model of household decisions based on a specific technology of production of the household good. The arguments made here follow some evidence presented in that paper and in Goyal (2003).
2. This was the conclusion of discussions held at the Women's Internet Conference (WIC) 1997, organised by Women's Space in Canada in collaboration with a number of other women's groups. A summary of the proceedings was put up at the Conference website: www.grannyg.bc.ca/confer/, and was accessed in December 2000. Woodfield (2000) has a similar perspective.
3. The project was financed by a $1,20,000 grant from the Canadian government. It is interesting to note that the Women's Internet Conference in Canada had raised the issue of funds for connectivity of rural and remote areas. This shows that ideas can fructify into major initiatives.
4. One such innovative and very successful product was clips to prevent toddlers from unspooling toilet paper rolls.
5. The web address and newsletter of one such organisation is available at www.workingfrom home.co.uk/wfh/information zone/ newsletter/article6.htm.
6. The site is Entrepreneur.com. Another related site is hbwm.com, a national association for home-based working mothers.
7. This section grew at 126.3 per cent over 1999–2000. Teenage boys, the fastest growing section for male users, grew at only 45.4 per cent.

References

Banerjee, N. and S. Mittar. 1998. 'Women Making a Meaningful Choice: Technology and the New Economic Order', *Economic and Political Weekly*, 33 (51): 3247–56.

Basu, S., J.G. Fernald, N. Oulton and S. Srinivasan. 2004. 'The Case of the Missing Productivity Growth, or Does Information Technology Explain why Productivity Accelerated in the US but not in the UK?' Chapter 18 in M. Gertter and K. Rogoff (eds) *NBER Macroeconomics Annual 2003*, Cambridge MA: MIT Press, pp. 6–63.

Ben-Ner, A., S. Massoud and H. Wang. 2003. 'Identity and Self-Other Differentiation in Work and Giving Behaviors: Experimental Evidence', mimeo. University of Minnesota: Industrial Relation Center.

Boserup, E. 1970. *Women's Role in Economic Development*. New York: St. Martin's Press.

Chattopadhyay, R. and E. Duflo. 2004. 'Impact of Reservation in Panchayati Raj: Evidence from a Nationwide Randomised Experiment', *Economic and Political Weekly*, 39 (9): 979–85.

Chopra, A. and S. Raval. 2000. 'Work Hard, Play Harder', *India Today*, 14 August: 75–77.

Devine, T.J. 1994. 'Changes in Wage-and-Salary Returns to Skill and the Recent Rise in Female Self-Employment', *American Economic Review Papers and Proceedings*, 84 (2): 108–13.

Fernandez, R., A. Fogli and C. Olivetti. 2004. 'Mothers and Sons: Preference Formation and Female Labor Force Dynamics', *Quarterly Journal of Economics*, 479 (4): 1249–99.

Fisher, H. 2003. 'A Century for Women?', *New Scientist Magazine*, 24 May.

Ghadially, R. 1996. 'On their Own Initiative: Changing Lives of Bohra Women', *Manushi*, 96: 31–39.

Ghadially, R. and F. Umrani. 2004. 'IT Education: Initiatives among Mumbai Muslims', *Information for Development*, issue on *ICT for Poor*, 2 (February).

Ghose, J. and J.G. Ray. 2004. 'Nabanna: Empowering Women', *Information for Development*, issue on *ICT for Poor*, 2 (May): 27–31.

Gothoskar, S. 2000. 'Teleworking and Gender', *Economic and Political Weekly*, 35 (26): 2293–98.

Gould, S.J. 1998. 'The Diet of Worms and the Defenestration of Prague', Chapter 13, in S.J. Gould (ed.) *Leonardo's Mountain of Clams and the Diet of Worms: Essays on Natural History*, New York: Three Rivers Press, pp. 251–65.

Goyal, A. 2000. 'Developing Women: How Technology can Help', presented at the GDN Conference, Tokyo, 10–13 December. Available at http://www.gdnet.org/pdf/842_Ashima.pdf, and revised version http://papers.ssrn.com/sol3/papers.cfm?abstract_id=509324.

———. 2003. 'Why Women Lag and Why They May Lead', *Information for Development*, issue on *Can ICT Cross the Gender Barrier?*, 1 (3): 13–21. Available at http://www.i4donline.net/issue/sept-oct03/women.htm.

Hardin, R. 1982. *Collective Action*. Baltimore, Maryland: Johns Hopkins University Press.

Kabeer, N. 1994. *Reversed Realities: Gender Hierarchies in Development Thought*. London: Verso.

Kearney, A.T. 2003. 'Where to Locate'. Available at www.atkearney.com.

Lewis, W.A. 1955. *Theory of Economic Growth*. London: George Allen and Unwin.

Maindiratta, Y.R. and R. Maindiratta. 2004. 'ICT for Development: Does Culture Play a Role?', *Information for Development*, issue on *ICT for Poor*, 2 (May): 27–31.

Mitter, S. 2000. 'Teleworking and Teletrade in India', *Economic and Political Weekly*, 35 (26): 2241–52.

Morahan-Martin, J. 1998. 'Women and Girls Last: Females and the Internet', paper presented at the 'Internet Research and Information for Social Scientists Conference', (earlier available at http://sosig.ac.uk/iriss/papers/paper55.htm).

Muralidharan, K. 2004. 'Teacher Absence in India', presented at the NBER-NCAER Conference at Neemrana, available at http://www.ncaer.org/Upload/others/112/km.pdf

NASSCOM. 1999, 2004. Reports available at www.nasscom.org.

Ng, C. and K.K. Jhin. 2000. 'Teleworking in Malaysia', *Economic and Political Weekly*, 35 (26): 2308–13.

Nussbaum, M.C. 2000. *Women and Human Development: The Capabilities Approach*. Cambridge U.K: The Press Syndicate of the University of Cambridge.

Nzegwu, N. 1995. 'Recovering Igbo traditions: A Case for Indigenous Women's Organizations in Development', in Martha C. Nussbaum and Jonathan Glover (eds), *Women, Culture, and Development: A Study of Human Capabilities*, Oxford: Clarendon Press.

Oldenburg, V.T. 2002. *Dowry Murder: The Imperial Origins of a Cultural Crime*. New York: Oxford University Press.

Pantulu, C.C. 2003. 'Rural Women Reap Fruits of the Loom Abroad', *Economic Times* (Mumbai), 9 July.

Rickert, A. and A. Sacharow. 2000. 'It's a Woman's World Wide Web', *Media Metrix and Jupiter Communications*, August, available at www.mediametrix.com.

Saran, R. 2004. 'Rural Markets', *India Today International*, 13 December.

Sen, A. 1999. *Development as Freedom*. New Delhi: OUP.

Shaikh, J.S. 2004. 'Mum's the Word for India Inc', *Bombay Times*, 7 June.

Steinem, G. 1993. *Revolution from Within: A Book of Self-Esteem*. New York: Little, Brown and Company.

Swaminathan, M.S. 2000. 'Poverty, Agriculture and Rural Development', paper presented at the International Symposium in Honour of Professor Kirit Parikh, 12–14 July. Mumbai: IGIDR.

Thakore, D. 2002. 'Corporate Champions of Indian Education', *Education World*, November.

Times of India, The (TOI). 2000a. 'Women Courting Web Put Careers Above All: Survey', results of survey NetmonitorTM, conducted by ORG-MARG, 18 August, Mumbai.

———. 2000b. 'E-quitable Society', Editorial, 19 August, Mumbai.

Umrani, F. and R. Ghadially, R. 2003. 'Empowering Women through ICT Education: Facilitating Computer Adoption', *Gender Technology and Development*, 7 (3).

UNDP. 1999. 'Globalization with a Human Face', *Human Development Report 1999*, Ch. 2, 'New Technologies and the Global Race for Knowledge', available at http://www.undp.org/hdro/index2.html.

Ushadevi, M.D. 2000. 'Economic Reforms and Technical Education: Examining Access and Career Preparations Programmes for Women in the Emerging Careers in the New Millennium', paper presented at the International Symposium in Honour of Professor Kirit Parikh, 12–14 July. Mumbai: IGIDR.

Vasisht, D. 2003. 'Technically, it's Women on Top', *Delhi Times*, 22 July.

Wadley, S.S. 2000. 'Negotiating New Rules and Values: Four Generations of Rural North Indian Women', in 'Economic Development and the Quality of life in South Asia', Research Project of the Institute of Oriental Culture, 30 March, Tokyo.

Woodfield, R. 2000. *Women, Work and Computing*. UK: Cambridge University Press.

World Bank. 2001. *Engendering Development*. New York: OUP.

EIGHTEEN

Gender, Cybercafes and Internet Access: Bridging the Digital Divide?

Anikar Haseloff and Rehana Ghadially

Introduction

The digital divide is one of the most discussed social phenomena of our times (Warschauer 2003). It is generally referred to as the gap between those who have access to ICTs and the necessary skills to use them, and those who do not have access or don't know how to use them. The gap between the *haves* and *have-nots* can be measured along various axes like income, geographic location, gender, education, age, etc. These divides can be measured between as well as within countries. The concept of the digital divide highlights a new form of poverty—information poverty—and therefore the digital divide has become an urgent development issue over the last few years (Chopra 2005). While the existence of a digital divide in one form or the other is clearly accepted amongst scholars, the dimensions, dynamics and relevance of this phenomenon are still being widely discussed (Compaine 2001; Mossberger et al. 2003; Norris 2001).

Access to and use of ICT is considered important for development on a regional and individual level, and ICTs can be used as tools for social action and positive social change in various ways. In developing countries like India, where the overall Internet penetration rates are low and people lack the necessary income and skills to make effective use of ICTs, models of public Internet access like, for example, cybercafes, can have a strong impact on bridging the digital divide, especially for people with low income or low skills who economically cannot afford the hardware to access the Internet. In India, for example, cybercafes and village kiosks are a widespread and strongly used facility to access the Internet (Pasricha 2004).

This chapter will examine the successful and widespread model of urban cybercafes and take a closer look at the gender-related use of these public Internet facilities. What role can ICT projects based on shared use play in closing the gender gap between technology users? Do women use these centres and if so, what do they use them for? This chapter draws its conclusions from a field research that was conducted in India between November 2003 and April 2004, and in February 2005. The field research used several methods to measure the use of public Internet facilities, which will be briefly explained below.

Methodology

The data presented has been collected in two independent surveys in Bangalore and Pune. In Bangalore a street survey, covering 1,499 people, was conducted. Altogether, 769 males (51.3 per cent) and 730 females (48.7 per cent) were interviewed, with an age range from 14 to 68 years (avg. 33.32 years, standard deviation: 12.32). To do the fieldwork, trained interviewers were sent to different parts of the city using a random walk method. The survey was conducted within six days and had four interviewers in two teams, each consisting of one female and one male interviewer. Table 18.1 shows the age structure according to gender for the sample.

TABLE 18.1
Age and Gender of the Sample

	Street Survey Bangalore			Cybercafe Survey Pune		
	Total	*Male*	*Female*	*Total*	*Male*	*Female*
N	1,498	768 (51.3%)	730 (48.7%)	1,318	722 (54.7%)	596 (44.3%)
Avg. Age	33.32	33.37	33.27	26.87	26.75	26.34
Range	14–68	15–68	14–60	9–90	9–90	10–78
Standard deviation	12.328	12.466	12.191	9.133	9.435	7.882

Note: In the cybercafe survey were 154 missing cases for gender from 1,472 responses.

The survey in Bangalore was conducted in order to examine the percentage of Internet usage in the urban Indian middle and upper class. The questionnaire was designed explicitly to collect information about where people would use the net from. To get a higher concentration of Internet users in the sample, the interviewers were given quotas for socio-economic status, and were advised to interview mainly the upper and middle classes. For control, small samples from the lower and lowest class were collected (115 responses). The quotas according to socio-economic attributes will be discussed in more detail when examining the findings.

After examining the users of the Internet and where people would use the net, a second survey was conducted directly in cybercafes to learn more about using habits like frequencies and reasons for using the facility in an effort to collect data on the importance or non-importance of public access in urban India. In this second survey, a questionnaire was developed and distributed to people entering a cybercafe. They were asked to fill out the questionnaires and return it to the interviewer, who was present in case the subject had questions or could not fill out the questionnaire. The return rate was relatively high (1,800 questionnaires were printed, 1,472 were returned). This high return rate may have to do with the presence of the interviewer and the brevity of the questionnaire, which could be filled out in less than 5 minutes). One problem that occurred while using this method of distribution was that not all the returned questionnaires were filled out completely, thus reducing the samples for some questions (therefore the following discussion will provide the exact number [*N*] for each question).

The survey was conducted in eight different cybercafes in Pune. The cybercafes were located in different parts of the city, like M.G. Road, near the university, in residential areas, and one in a shopping complex. Permission of the cybercafe owner was one criteria, which was given in all eight cases (although in two case this permission was withdrawn after the first day of the survey, as the cybercafe managers felt it was too disturbing for their clients). The age of the surveyed cybercafe users ranged between nine and 90 years, the average being 26.87 years (standard deviation: 9.13) with 723 males (54.7 per cent, standard deviation: 9.44) and 598 females (45.3 per cent, standard deviation: 7.88). Table 18.1 gives an overview on the surveyed samples according to age and gender in both surveys.

Whereas in the street survey the sample is almost equally distributed among age groups and among men and women, there is a small gender divide in cybercafes, with more males having been interviewed. The samples do not differ significantly according to age, although men show a slightly broader range and higher standard deviation in the cybercafe survey. The following section will discuss the findings of these studies, first taking a look at the overall Internet usage patterns, gender and place of access, and then analysing in detail the users and use of cybercafes according to gender.

Internet Usage, Access Place and Gender

In urban areas, cybercafes are the predominant public access model. Their number is estimated at almost 50,000 in India and are used by almost 70 per cent of Internet users in urban areas (Pasricha 2004). This high amount of cybercafes may be an indicator of their relevance. Although cybercafes seem to be an important access place for a significant proportion of the population, they have not received much attention in scientific research, despite their being an interesting part of *contemporary culture* and *a distinct and dedicated use space* (Lee 1999; Stewart 2000).

In order to examine the importance of cybercafes in the urban middle and upper classes, an explorative street survey was conducted in Bangalore in February 2005. The questionnaire was designed to collect socio-economic data from respondents (age, gender, income, education and occupation), their language abilities, their knowledge of the Internet, their place of Internet access, reasons for using or not using the Internet, and future plans for Internet ownership or usage. The interviewers were given quotas and were advised to work in different areas of the town, using a random walk method covering the entire city. Interviews were conducted in a face-to-face situation by trained interviewers.

To classify respondents, the socio-economic classifications (SECs) developed by the (Indian) National Readership Survey were employed. The SEC groups urban Indian households using two factors: education, and the occupational status of the chief wage earner of the family. There are five main SECs, ranging from A (highest group) to E (lowest group). In the following survey, SEC A is considered upper class, SEC B is considered upper middle-class, SEC C is referred to as middle class, and SEC D and SEC E are considered lower class.

For the sample, the quotas for the SECs were not set according to the population statistics of Bangalore, as Internet use in the lowest SEC groups D and E is assumed to be almost non-existent. In order to get higher samples of Internet users, SEC groups D and E have been under-represented and SEC groups A and B have been over-represented in the quotas for the interviewers. In the sample SEC A has been over-represented thrice, while SEC B has been over-represented twice and SEC C is almost equal to the population statistics of Bangalore. SEC D and E have been covered just as a small control group, although in reality they represent almost half of the population of Bangalore. The findings therefore have only an exploratory character and the discussed data does not claim to be representative for India (or even Bangalore); but they do provide an interesting picture of the target group (Internet users) at the time of the survey.

Findings

Non-users of the Internet in Bangalore

The interviewers were sent to different parts of the city. They were given a randomly selected bus station where they were instructed to leave the bus. They were advised to follow the street in the driving direction, take the first road left and walk till the next road, then take a left turn and start interviewing the first person. The socio-economic data was first elicited in order to analyse the SEC group. Next the interviewer asked whether the person had heard of the Internet and if he/she used the Internet. If the person had not even heard of the Internet, the interview was ended immediately. If the person had heard of the Internet but did not use it, he/she was asked questions about the reasons for not doing so, and if he/she planned to use it in the future. If the person knew about the Internet and used it, he/she was asked about his/her places of access, and future plans regarding home ownership and access.

The data shows that knowledge and usage of the Internet differ strongly and significantly between age groups, gender, income and SEC class, as well as between English and non-English speaking communities. Before discussing the usage of the Internet and cybercafes, a brief look at the non-users of the Internet and their reason for not doing so will be discussed: asked whether people had already heard about the Internet, almost half of the surveyed population (48.3 per cent) said they had already heard about the Internet. Despite this fairly high awareness, only roughly one-third of those who knew about the Internet used it (16.5 per cent Internet users were identified in the sample). The awareness of the Internet varied strongly between different groups, for example gender: while 56.7 per cent of the male respondents had heard about the Internet, only 39.5 per cent of the female ones had heard about it (chi-square = 44.6, p < 0.01).

If the respondent had heard about the Internet but did not use it, the reasons for not using the net were asked. The question was open-ended, as the range of possible reasons was not known before. Table 18.2 shows the reasons mentioned by respondents for not using the Internet.

TABLE 18.2
Reasons for not Using the Internet

	Total	Male	Female
Don't need	33.0 (154)	33.0 (87)	33.2 (67)
Not interested	30.3 (141)	30.7 (81)	29.7 (60)
Don't know how to use	18.5 (86)	17.4 (46)	19.8 (40)
Not time	10.5 (49)	12.1 (32)	8.4 (17)
No facility near home	1.5 (7)	1.1 (3)	2.0 (4)
No money/too expensive	1.7 (8)	1.5 (4)	2.0 (4)
Don't speak English/illiterate	1.2 (6)	0.9 (3)	1.5 (3)
Other	3.2 (15)	3.0 (8)	3.5 (7)

Notes: Figures given in per cent of respondents (total cases).
N = 466.

These reasons for not using the Internet can be roughly divided into three categories: motivational reasons (*Don't need, not interested*), skill-based reasons (*Don't know how to use the Internet, don't speak English, illiterate*), and functional reasons (*No time, no money, no facility near home*). Interestingly, motivational reasons are the most mentioned ones at 63.3 per cent, whereas functional reasons are only mentioned by 13.7 per cent of the respondents. This surprising pattern may have to do with the over-representation of the upper classes, as these classes are considered to be in the financial reach of the Internet. In this context, it is also important to see that 19.6 per cent of the respondents mentioned skill-based barriers for not using the Internet.

The reasons given by men and women have been almost equal, especially the reasons *not interested* (1.8 per cent more male respondents) and *don't need* (0.2 per cent more female respondents). The biggest gender-based difference was found in *no time*, mentioned by 12.2 per cent of male but only 8.4 per cent of female respondents. A low chi-square (chi-square = 5.79, p = 0.76) shows that the reasons for not using the net did not differ significantly between the genders.

As a last question, the non-users were asked if they were planning to use the net in the future: 30.8 per cent of the people who were aware of the Internet (48.3 per cent of the total sample) planned to use it in the future. This very high figure does show that Internet usage will continue to grow strongly in the future, especially in the surveyed middle and upper classes in urban areas. Of course not all the people planning to use the Internet will do so; over the years it was seen in Germany that roughly only one-third of the people planning to use the net will de facto really use it (Gerhards and Mende 2004), which is almost the same ratio as that of the difference between people aware of the Internet and those using it in this study. Interestingly, more women (32.1 per cent) than men (29.8 per cent) planned to use the Internet in the future. The data shows, that although women use the Internet less and are less aware of it, among those who are, it is more women who plan to use the Internet in the future. This may be one sign that the gender gap could possibly close in the future, although the data also shows that it is closing at a very slow speed.

Differences between male and female respondents were further observed while asking the non-users in the study what they intended to use the Internet for. This was asked using an open-ended question, as the range of possible answers was not known before. Although respondents could have given multiple answers, all respondents gave only one reason, which may be seen as their main reason as the Internet will probably be used for more than one reason later. The main reasons for using the Internet differed strongly between the two groups. Table 18.3 shows the answers and the percentage they received according to gender.

TABLE 18.3
Motivation for Future Internet Usage

	Total	*Male*	*Female*
Education/Personal Development	40.3 (52)	31 (22)	51.7 (30)
Communication	31 (40)	35.2 (25)	25.9 (15)
Need for Business	9.3 (12)	15.5 (11)	1.7 (1)
Need for school/university	8.3 (11)	5.6 (4)	12.1 (7)
Job Search	5.4 (7)	5.6 (4)	5.2 (3)
Entertainment/Recreation	3.9 (5)	5.6 (4)	1.7 (1)
Other	1.6 (2)	1.4 (1)	1.7 (1)

Notes: All figures in percentage of respondents (total cases).
  N = 129.

Table 18.3 shows that the reasons motivating future use differed significantly between the two sexes (chi-square = 13.65, p < 0.05). Whereas more than half the female respondents mentioned *Education/ personal development* as reasons for using the Internet in the future, *communication* was the most mentioned reason by male respondents. Another interesting but not surprising pattern is seen in the answer *need for business*, which is mentioned significantly more often by male respondents. The same is the case with *entertainment/recreation*, which is mentioned more often by male respondents. Female respondents, according to this data, seem to see the Internet more as a tool for personal development and education, whereas for male respondents entertainment, communication and business-related aspects seem more driving.

After taking a brief look at non-users of the Internet and those who plan to use it, the following sections will examine the users, with special attention paid to the place of access.

The Internet Users in Bangalore

In the surveyed sample, 16.5 per cent (N = 1,496) of the respondents used the Internet. The Internet usage rate for Bangalore according to the Marketing Whitebook 2005 is 8.8 per cent (*Businessworld* 2005: p. 181), but as explained above, a higher usage rate was needed, which was obtained from over-representing the middle and upper classes.

A much higher proportion of male respondents used the Internet. While 21.3 per cent of the male respondents used the Internet, only 11.5 per cent of the female respondents did so (chi-square = 25.6, p < 0.01), which confirms the pattern described for awareness. Internet use was not only distributed unequally among male and female respondents, there were also significant differences between Internet users especially when analysing age, income, SEC and the ability to speak English, which will be briefly discussed below.

Age

When examined according to age, the data clearly showed that Internet use correlated significantly with age (chi-square $= 70.95$, $p < 0.001$). Table 18.4 shows that Internet use is strongest in the age group of respondents younger than 29 years, and then steadily declines with an increase in age. The table also provides the Internet usage according to age and gender:

TABLE 18.4
Internet Usage, Gender and Age

	Total	*Male*	*Female*
Up to 19	19.3 (47)	24.6 (32)	13.7 (15)
20–29	27.4 (116)	33.3 (70)	21.5 (46)
30–39	14.8 (50)	19.6 (35)	9.5 (15)
Above 40	6.9 (34)	10.5 (26)	3.3 (8)

Notes: All figures in per cent of respondents (cases).
      N = 1,496.

The younger sections of the urban population used the Internet much more than other age groups. While the Internet is used by substantial proportions of the society in the age group below 30, Internet usage needs to be spread, especially in the age groups above 40. The table further shows that the gender divide between male and female users is found in every age category. The gap is almost consistent between the different age groups, narrowing only in the category above 40, in which overall Internet usage is very low. This picture indicates clearly that the gender divide needs to be taken seriously, and actions aiming at reducing this divide need to be developed for different age groups.

Income

An almost similar pattern can be found when examining income and Internet usage. As expected, Internet usage increases with higher income (whereas only 4.4 per cent of respondents with an income below Rs 5,000 would use the Internet, 32.6 per cent of respondents with an income above Rs 25,000 did so). But examining this pattern controlling for gender shows an interesting pattern: although Internet usage increases with growing income for both male and female respondents, the gender gap seems to be growing in the higher income groups as 45.6 per cent of the male respondents with an income above Rs 25,000 used the Internet, while only 19.8 per cent of female respondents within the same income bracket did so.

Computing a chi-square clearly shows that with higher income, people use the Internet significantly more (chi-square $= 136.44$, $p < 0.001$). Although the same pattern can be observed for men and women, the percentage of Internet users becomes significantly higher for males than for females in the upper-income classes, reflecting the gender divide observed earlier. As income and SEC class correlate strongly with each other, an almost similar pattern was found when examining for SEC class. This data shows, that the gender divide was consistent, even controlling for other variables like age, SEC or income.

Language and Internet Usage

Another important variable that could influence Internet usage is language, more specifically the ability to speak English. An interesting case study in Slovenia observes a strong relationship between the ability to speak English and the use of the Internet. Internet use was as high as 75 per cent in the group of fluent English-speaking respondents, compared to just 1 per cent of the respondents without English language skills (Vehovar et al. 1999). The same pattern was observed in this survey, where the ability to speak English was determined as either *fluent, can understand to some extent* and *don't speak*: while 34.4 per cent of the respondents with good English language skills were using the Internet, just 3.7 per cent of those with little English language skills and just 0.4 per cent of those without English language skills were using the Internet. The pattern was almost consistent when controlling for gender, although a higher proportion of male respondents with good English language skills used the net (37.8 per cent male respondents against 29.2 per cent female ones).

Internet usage correlates significantly with the ability to speak English (chi-square = 287.84, p < 0.001). Of course, the ability to speak English depends strongly on education and the socio-economic level. For example, from the respondents in SEC A 76.6 per cent were fluent in the English language whereas in SEC C just 27.5 per cent were fluent English speakers, and in SEC E nobody could speak fluent English. However, the relation between the ability to speak English and Internet usage can also be observed by just examining SEC A: 46.7 per cent of the respondents with very good English skills were using the Internet, whereas just 2.5 per cent of the respondents with only basic English language skills used the Internet. None of the non-speakers did so. The same pattern can be observed when controlling for income. In the highest income groups, Internet usage was 46.7 per cent if the respondent had English language skills, and 1.5 per cent if the respondent had only basic skills.

This pattern was observed for male and female respondents, although it showed once again that male respondents used the Internet significantly more often (37.8 per cent male users against 29.2 per cent female users) in the group of fluent English speakers. It can be argued that in order to make use of the Internet, one needs to understand English because of the prevalence of content in English on the web. But in reality, considerable content is nowadays available in a variety of Indian languages, so the lack of content cannot explain this pattern. The relation between language and Internet use needs to be investigated further in future studies, as there could be some interesting mechanisms between language ability and Internet usage that are not limited to the relation between content and language.

Summarising Internet access, the study identified several variables that strongly influence the use of the Internet between various groups. One of the most important findings in the context of this chapter is that a strong gender divide exists. This pattern was consistent controlling for other variables like income, age or language ability. The gender divide within urban India is therefore an important topic, and one which needs to be taken seriously. The next section will examine the place of Internet access.

The Place of Internet Access

If the respondents were using the Internet, they were asked about their place of access. Respondents could choose between the following options: *home, work, friend's place, school/university, cybercafe* or *other.* The respondents could choose more than one option, as people often have access in more than one place, for example at home and in a cybercafe, at home and at work, and so on. The maximum number of access places mentioned was four, and on an average, respondents used 1.77 access places. If we look at the findings, we can see that both men and women use the Internet at more or less the same access points. Table 18.5 gives an overview on gender and access place.

TABLE 18.5
Gender and Place of Internet Access

	Total	*Male*	*Female*
Home	25 (62)	25.5 (42)	24.1 (20)
Work	43.5 (108)	46.7 (77)	37.3 (31)
At friend's place	15.7 (39)	17.0 (28)	13.3 (11)
School/University	26.6 (66)	25.5 (42)	28.9 (24)
Cybercafe	66.1 (164)	66.7 (110)	65.1 (54)

Notes: Multiple answers possible.
All figures in per cent of respondents (totals).
N = 245.

The overall pattern of access to the Internet from the different access places shows the same ranking for both groups. *Cybercafes* are the most often used access point, followed by *work* and *school*. *Home-use*, the prevalent access place in developed countries, is ranked only at fourth place. Not surprisingly, the possibility to access the net from *work* is much higher for males than for females, which may reflect the current employment patterns in which men are more likely to be working, and may perhaps be in better positions, and are therefore more likely to have access to the Internet at *work* than women. Males also use *cybercafes* and a *friend's place* more often, whereas for female respondents, besides the *cybercafe*, the access place *school/university* was more important.

A somewhat similar pattern was discovered when asking respondents about their main access place and their only access place. The main access place, mentioned by 43.8 per cent of the respondents, was *cybercafes*, followed by *work* (36.4 per cent of respondents) and *home* (10.7 per cent of respondents). Interestingly, although 25 per cent of Internet users have the facility at home, just 10.7 per cent mentioned *home* as their main access place. Women mentioned *home* as their main access place more often than men (13.6 per cent of female respondents used *home* as their main access place, against 9.3 per cent of the male respondents). While *cybercafes* are mentioned almost equally by both groups as their main access point (44.1 per cent of male respondents and 43.2 per cent of female respondents), *school* as main access point was mentioned almost twice by female respondents (11.1 per cent female respondents compared to 5.6 per cent of male ones), and *work* was mentioned more often as the main place of access by men (39.1 per cent male respondents and 30.9 per cent female respondents). Although differences between gender and main access place did exist, they are not significant (chi-square = 4.27, p = 0.37).

When analysing people who had only one access place, it was seen that *cybercafes* have been the *only* access point for 19.2 per cent of Internet users in Bangalore, with a slightly higher proportion of women (20.7 per cent) compared to men (18.4 per cent) being dependent on cybercafes as their *only* access point. This figure differs strongly controlling for other variables, like for example income—while cybercafes have been the only place of access for 28 per cent of the respondents with an income of less than Rs 5,000 only 14.3 per cent of the respondents with an income of more than Rs 10,000 mentioned cybercafes as their only access place. The difference in income groups with regard to the dependency on cybercafes was significant (chi-square = 29.80, p < 0.05). The same pattern was discovered when examining the dependency on cybercafes according to age: the younger the respondents, the more often were cybercafes the only access place they could use.

The differences between age and dependency on cybercafes as the only access place was highly significant (chi-square = 49.98; p < 0.001), indicating that cybercafes are more important for younger age groups.

In general, these findings show that cybercafes are used significantly by Internet users in Bangalore, and that cybercafes in the urban Indian context are not just an additional access point for people to access the Internet while travelling. They have to be seen as an important access point for a significant group of Internet users: 43.8 per cent of the respondents used cybercafes as their main access point, which is a remarkably different pattern when compared to most developed countries, where the prevalent access model is home access, used by more than 70 per cent as their main access place (Van Eimeren et al. 2004). Although differences between male and female respondents exist as to where one uses the net from, computing a chi-square between main access place and gender (chi-square = 4.27, p < 0.5) shows that the differences between gender and where the Internet is used from are not significant at a 5 per cent level.

Place of First Internet Experience

Quite a different pattern was discovered when respondents were asked where their first experience with the Internet was. Although cybercafes were the most mentioned places for both groups (52.8 per cent of the male respondents and 34.6 per cent of the female ones had their first Internet experience in a cybercafe), Table 18.6 shows that female respondents had their first experience significantly more often at home and at school than their male counterparts, whereas a higher proportion of the male respondents had their first Internet experience in a cybercafe.

TABLE 18.6
Place of First Internet Experience

	Total	*Male*	*Female*
Home	6.7 (26)	4.4 (15)	11.1 (11)
Work	24.6 (88)	26.4 (63)	21.0 (25)
Friend's place	2.9 (4)	1.9 (3)	4.9 (1)
School/university	17.9 (18)	14.5 (9)	24.7 (9)
Cybercafe	46.7 (106)	52.8 (71)	34.6 (35)

Notes: All figures in per cent of respondents (cases).
N = 240.

It seems that where one had his/her first experience with the Internet varies significantly when examining for gender (chi-square = 18.83, p < 0.05). Female respondents were almost three times as likely to have had their first experience at *home*, whereas male respondents were more likely to have had their first experience in a *cybercafe*. If we look at the ranking of the different places, we can see that *school/university* is the second mentioned place for female respondents, whereas for male respondents *work* is the second most important place. *Friend's place* has the same rank for both the sexes. As this data shows, patterns for the place of first experience varied significantly between male and female respondents. Whereas male respondents seem to have had their first contact mostly in cybercafes and at work (79,2 per cent of male respondents against 51.6 per cent female respondents), women seem to have had their first experience at home or at school (35.8 per cent of female respondents compared to 18.9 male respondents). This pattern could reflect the situation of women, for whom it may be more difficult to walk into a cybercafe and learn about the Internet.

It also reflects the findings that the gender divide increases with age, as school was the second most important place where female respondents had their first experience. These findings further indicate that in India the low ownership of computers at home deprives women of access to the Internet at an early age, as they have their first experience significantly less in public cybercafes than men.

Despite these differences as far as the place of first experience is concerned, the findings show that cybercafes are almost equally important for male and female users, although it seems that more males used cybercafes than female respondents. However, they still play an important role for female Internet users. Whereas the total percentage of women using the Internet was only 11.5 per cent compared to 21.5 per cent of male respondents, cybercafes played an almost equally important role for both groups as an access place (used by 69.3 per cent of male Internet users and 63.4 per cent of female ones). Future research definitely needs to focus more on this urban phenomenon, as it seems that large proportions of both men and women of the urban middle and upper classes depend on cybercafes.

It can be argued that the need for cybercafes will diminish with the steadily growing home access, but the fact is that home access will remain out of reach for substantial parts of the population. Therefore, public access points will remain necessary even in the future (Pasricha 2004; Warschauer 2003). This point was confirmed when asking respondents who used the Internet but did not have home access if they planned to have home access within the next 12 months: only 16 per cent of the Internet users (18.7 per cent of the male respondents and 10.8 per cent of the female respondents) planned to do so. This can be seen as confirmation of the fact that cybercafes will continue to play an important role, especially for females, as a smaller number of women compared to men plan to have a home computer in the near future.

After exploring the relevance of cybercafes as access place, the following section of the chapter will now take a closer look at the users in a cybercafe. What are the patterns of use, how often and what are they used for, and do the usage patterns differ between male and female users?

The Cybercafe Users

In general, the cybercafe users are young, with more than 70 per cent of the users being below the age of 30. Table 18.7 gives an overview of the age structure of the sample. As can be seen, the age of the surveyed users ranged between nine and 90 years, the average being 26.8 years (standard deviation: 9.13). The sight of elderly people using the cybercafe (often with the help of their children or even grandchildren) gives us an idea of the value this institution could have for elderly people.

The age structure of cybercafe users shows some interesting points: first, the cybercafe users are younger than the Internet users in general (cybercafe users have an average age of 26.8 years, whereas the Internet

TABLE 18.7
Age and Cybercafe Users

	Total	*Male*	*Female*
14–19	13.8 (191)	16.6 (120)	11.8 (71)
20–29	57.1 (770)	56.0 (404)	61.4 (366)
30–39	20.4 (242)	17.4 (127)	19.4 (115)
Above 40	7.3 (104)	8.7 (63)	6.0 (41)

Notes: All answers in per cent of respondents (totals).
    N = 1,307.
    Min. 9, max. 90, avg. 26.8.

users have an average age of 27.7 years). Among the cybercafe users, 70.9 per cent are below 30 years of age, and only 7.3 per cent are above the age of 40. This shows that although all age groups are found in cybercafes, young people tend to dominate.

The survey showed that no major differences existed between the users according to age and gender. While a higher proportion of male users were found in the age group of 14–19 years, the percentage of women between the ages of 20–29 using a cybercafe was higher. This finding confirms the patterns discovered above, where it was seen that males have their first Internet experience significantly more often in a cybercafe. Taking both patterns leads to the following conclusion: males access cybercafes at an earlier age and hence get a head start on both cybercafes and Internet use. This pattern could be influenced by the role of women in Indian society, and may be one of the factors causing the disparities in overall Internet usage.

Unlike the findings when examining the overall Internet usage, examining gender shows that cybercafes are not as male-dominated, with 54.7 per cent of users being males and 45.3 per cent being females. Furthermore, the gender divide within cybercafe users seems to be narrowing, as a survey conducted by the author in 2001 showed a ratio of 64.4 per cent male and 35.6 per cent female users. The shrinking gender divide in cybercafes confirms the prior finding, which showed that cybercafes have been mentioned as access points in an almost equal proportion by the two groups. The findings also show that a growing number of women are using these facilities. Cybercafes therefore seem to have an interesting potential for bridging the gender divide with respect to access to technology: while women are being strongly under-represented within the general Internet users, the ratio in cybercafes is much closer to the normal ratio, thereby showing an interesting potential in bridging this gap.

If one goes to the urban areas of India and looks at the cybercafes, one will find a variety of different cybercafes. There are big franchised outlets with more than 20 computers, offering standardised high-tech services mainly to business clientele; there are small neighbourhood cybercafes with only a few computers that mostly serve the surrounding community; there are fast-food or drinking joints that offer net access as an additional service; and there are some cybercafes that concentrate on gaming. These different models attract quite a diverse clientele, for example, young males frequent the gaming cafes whereas both groups frequent the community cybercafes to the same extent. The data presented is aggregated data from different cybercafe models, but future research could examine the use of and gender disparities for different models, as there may exist cybercafe models which are used more often by women than men.

Usage Patterns

To find out how extensively these facilities have been used, respondents were asked since when they have been using the Internet, their frequency of using a cybercafe, and the average time they spent during a session at the cybercafe. The data shows that there exists some differences between male and female respondents, and generally speaking, one could say that male respondents started using the Internet much earlier, use it more frequently, and the average time they spend during each session is longer.

While 50.7 per cent of the male respondents (N = 579) started using the net in 1998 or before, only 33.6 per cent of the women (N = 457) had done so. However, since 1998 women have caught up with Internet usage, and 1999 was the first year in which more female respondents (14.9 per cent) compared to male ones (12.3 per cent) began using the net. Altogether, 64.7 per cent of the women started using the net from 1999 onwards, whereas this group comprised of 41.3 per cent of the male respondents. This data indicates that men started to use the net much earlier than women, but as the gender distribution in cybercafes today shows, women have caught up over the last six years. If this trend continues, one can expect the gender divide in cybercafes to diminish and meet the percentages in the general population. Future research needs to examine this trend over time in order to identify the relevance of this access place according to gender.

Frequency of Cybercafe Use

The frequency of cybercafe usage differed significantly between both groups (chi-square = 28.57, $p < 0.001$). While female respondents used the cybercafe 3.54 times per week (standard deviation: 1.76), male respondents used it more often at 3.92 times per week (standard deviation: 1.94). A similar pattern can be found when examining the duration of the average session. While male respondents use the cybercafe more frequently, they also use it for longer periods per session. Table 18.8 shows the frequency and average duration of cybercafe visits according to gender.

TABLE 18.8
Frequency and Average Duration of Cybercafe Visits

| | Frequency | | Duration | | |
	1–3 Visits/week (%)	4–7 Visits/week (%)	Up to 30 min. (%)	31–60 min. (%)	Above 60 min. (%)
Total	63.1	36.9	40.3	49.2	10.5
Male	59.1	40.9	36.4	49.0	14.6
Female	69.3	30.7	42.2	51.7	6.1

As with the frequency of cybercafe use, the duration of the average session varied significantly (chi-square = 48.07, $p < 0.005$) between both groups. The average duration of a session was 46.58 minutes (standard deviation: 23.64) for female respondents and 56.12 minutes (standard deviation: 36.45) for male respondents.

These findings show that women started to use cybercafes later, used them less often, and for shorter periods per session. These differences are significant, but the data also shows that cybercafes are no longer as male-dominated as they were at the end of the 1990s. Women have been catching up especially since 1999, and a timeline comparison between 2001 and 2004 shows that the gender divide in cybercafes is shrinking. However, this divide still exists in terms of access and intensity of use.

Services and Applications Used in Cybercafes

The most frequently used service in the cybercafe was the World Wide Web (90.3 per cent), followed by email (72.3 per cent), phone calls/net phone (52.1 per cent), games (49.6 per cent) and chat (48.7 per cent). Almost half of those interviewed also used the cybercafe for educational reasons, which may be related to the high number of students. It should also be noted that many teachers use cybercafes in order to prepare their lessons. Table 18.9 gives an overview of the different services used in a cybercafe according to gender in order to examine if differences in usage exists.

The table shows that the usage patterns of male and female respondents are very similar. Both groups use the services—*Internet, Email, Chat* and *Computer-Training*—almost equally. Differences, although not significant, are found in the use of the services *Education Services* (mentioned by 4.7 per cent more female respondents) and *Job Search* (mentioned by 5 per cent more male respondents). The only significant difference on a 5 per cent level was found in the use of games: this service is used significantly more often by male respondents, a pattern that is not completely surprising. Also interesting is the fact that female respondents

TABLE 18.9
What Respondents Used in Cybercafes

	Male Respondents		Female Respondents		χ^2	P
	Per cent	N	*Per cent*	N		
Internet	90.3	653	91.6	548	0.69	0.41
Email	73	528	75.3	450	0.84	0.36
Education services	41.2	298	45.9	275	2.94	0.08
Computer training	34.1	246	32.8	196	0.25	0.62
Games	48.4	350	41.9	251	5.59	0.02
Chat	49.7	359	50.4	302	0.07	0.78
Jobsearch	35.7	102	30.7	75	1.43	0.23

Notes: Multiple answers possible.
  N = 1,319.

mentioned using the cybercafe for educational reasons more often than male respondents, confirming the previously discovered pattern that females use the Internet more often for educational reasons and as a tool for personal development.

To examine communication behaviour more deeply, respondents were asked which communication services they use. They could choose between the most common services usually offered in the cybercafes, namely *email*, *chat*, *messenger* and *newsgroup*. The service *chat* was further divided into *national* and *international* chatrooms. The data shows that cybercafes are used for a variety of communication services like *email*, *chat*, *chat national*, *chat international*, *messenger*, and *newsgroup*. Email is the most popular communication service for both groups, followed by chat and messenger. Newsgroups are used last among all the mentioned services. The communication services are used considerably by both groups, and significant differences were only found in the usage of email (chi-square = 4.47, p < 0.05) and national chatrooms (chi-square = 9.70, p < 0.005). While email was used significantly more often by female respondents, national chatrooms have been used significantly more often by male respondents. These findings show that both sexes used a variety of communication services, and that email and chat are the driving factors for cybercafe use.

Another gender-based difference was found in the respondent's opinion as to whether using the Internet would change his/her life. Respondents had the choice between *yes, very strong*; *yes, but only with small effects*; *no, the Internet has no effect*, and *don't know*. Interestingly, the two genders view the impact of computers on their lives in different ways. Altogether, 80 per cent of the respondents were of the opinion that the Internet would change their lives, and almost 60 per cent felt that it would change their lives very strongly. However, more male respondents see the Internet as changing their lives strongly than female ones (chi-square = 8.539, p < 0.05). Simultaneously, more females perceive the Internet as having no effect on their lives as compared to men.

Summary and Conclusions

The use of the Internet was distributed highly unevenly between males and females, showing a strong gender divide in the upper and middle classes of urban India. This gender divide is consistent even if controlling for other variables like age or income. Therefore, the gender divide needs to be taken as a serious pattern, and research as well as programmes are needed in order to close this divide. In this context, the research showed clearly that cybercafes could play an important role for women when it came to accessing the Internet and ICTs.

An examination of the importance of cybercafes showed that they have the potential to help bridge this divide, even without there being any special programmes in place as yet. While a strong gender divide was measured in overall Internet usage, this divide diminished when examining the users in cybercafes. Cybercafes seemed to be used only slightly more by males than by females. They have been the most used access place for both groups, and the research showed that cybercafes are a highly important institution for a substantial proportion of urban Internet users in general. Although both groups used cybercafes differences have been found, especially when examining where one had his/her first experience, or when analysing the importance of cybercafes as the additional, main or only access place. It showed that cybercafes do play different roles, and although the importance of cybercafes steadily declined with growing income or higher SEC class, it was seen that cybercafes were to some extent even used among the upper classes. Differences were further found when examining the extent to which cybercafes have been used. Male respondents started using cybercafes earlier, they use them more frequently, and they use them for longer durations per session.

When it comes to the gender divide with regard to access to technology, the role of cybercafes needs to be examined carefully over time, in different environments, and for different groups. In this context, it also needs to be considered whether special programmes for women could be offered in cybercafes to further motivate them to use or learn about ICTs, as the data showed that females already use cybercafes more often for computer training and educational purposes, while men use them more often for business-related activities, games and recreational activities.

However, in order to interpret this data, one has to bear in mind that the data collected represents only the middle and upper classes, as Internet usage was not measured among the lower classes. It is possible that the existing gender divides are much more dramatic among the lower classes, especially where Internet usage, which could require some kind of social or political action, is concerned. It is especially women of the lower classes who face multiple barriers, beginning with education, language, and their role in society. Before women of the lower classes can be seen as potential users, there need to be programmes in place to educate them, and to make them aware of the benefits. On the other hand, as the research concentrating on the upper and middle classes showed, cybercafes can be seen for these particular groups as gender-neutral places, where men and women can use ICTs equally for their personal interests.

References

Businessworld. 2005. *The Marketing Whitebook 2005: The Essential Handbook for Marketers.* New Delhi: Businessworld.

Chopra, Anand. 2005. *Bridging India's Digital Divide.* Tönning: Der Andere Verlag.

Compaine, Benjamin M. 2001. *The Digital Divide. Facing a Crisis or Creating a Myth?* Cambridge, Massachusetts: The MIT Press.

Gerhards, Maria and Annette Mende. 2004. 'Offliner 2004: Anpassungs druck steigt Zugangsbarrieren bleiben bestehen', in *Media Perspektiven 8/2004*, pp. 371–85.

Lee, Sarah. 1999. 'Private Uses in Public Spaces', *New Media & Society*, 1(3): 331–50.

Mossberger, Karen, Caroline J. Tolbert and Mary Stansbury. 2003. *Virtual Inequality. Beyond the Digital Divide.* Washington D.C.: Georgetown University Press.

Norris, Pippa. 2001. *Digital Divide. Civic Engagement, Information Poverty, and the Internet Worldwide.* Cambridge University Press.

Pasricha, Anjana. 2004. *To Get Online, Most Indians Go to Cybercafes.* VOA News Service, 15 August. Available at http://apiap.blogspot.com/2004_10_01_apiap_archive.html

Stewart, James. 2000. 'Cafematics: The Cybercafe and the Community', in Michael Gurstein (HRSG), *Community Informatics: Enabling Communities with Information and Communication Technologies*, pp. 320–39. Hershey USA: Idea Group Publishing.

Van Eimeren, Birgit, Heinz Gerhard und Beate Frees. 2004. 'ARD/ZDF-Online-Studie 2004: Internetverbreitung in Deutschland: Potential vorerst ausgeschöfft?' in *Media Perspektiven 8/2004*, pp. 350–70.

Vehovar, Vasja, Zend Batagelj and Katja Lozar. 1999. 'Language as a Barrier', Proceedings of INET 1999. www.isoc.org.inet99/proceedings/3i/3i_3.htm

Warschauer Mark. 2003. *Technology and Social Inclusion.* Massachusetts and London: The MIT Press, Cambridge.

NINETEEN

Empowering Women through ICT Education: Facilitating Computer Adoption*

Farida Umrani and Rehana Ghadially

Introduction and Review of Literature

Information and communication technologies (ICTs) are driving forces of the present century marked by globalisation and technological advancement. ICTs permit access to information and resources that encourage women to acquire education and skills, to transcend social restrictions, gain control, mainstream into development, and thus, get empowered. However, the uneven distribution of these technologies within societies as well as across the world gives rise to a new form of poverty by creating two groups—one that has an access to abundant information ('information rich') and the other, which lacks such an access ('information poor'). Such a divide occurs across race, ethnic group, class, age, religion and gender. Women in developing countries are in the deepest part of the digital divide. Lack of access to ICT thus becomes a significant factor in their marginalisation from economic, social and political participation (Huyer and Carr 2002; Mitter 1999). Access is construed not only as availability of technology per se, but also the training and social support that facilitates its adoption. Basic literacy is important in order to read and compose simple messages, navigate the Internet, and execute commands in most software application, but as women make up nearly two-thirds of the world's illiterate, and one out of every two women in developing countries is illiterate, women are more likely than men to lack basic computer skills, which would enable them to take advantage of the new global communication opportunities. Internet usage is the standard indicator of the use of information and communication technologies. Women constitute 23 per cent of Internet users in India with 0.2 per cent of the total population having Internet access. Projections indicate that by 2003, there will be nearly two million women Internet users and by 2007, it is predicted that India will have a million jobs in call centres, staffed largely by women (Hafkin and Taggart 2001).

Most of the research (Huyer 1997; Huyer and Carr 2002; Kelkar et al. 2002; Mitter 1999) in Gender Studies focuses on the empowerment potential of ICT, the digital divide, media and networking. The choice of sample is women professionals and/or NGOs. The preferred methods of Gender Studies specialists are interviews and questionnaires, and the social and economic are variables of choice in the training and use of ICT in general. On the other hand, there is a parallel body of research in Psychology, Management Studies and Information Systems, which focuses on decision-making and attitudes towards technology adoption. These researches are conducted on students and professionals. The preferred method is the use of standard tests and scales with emphasis on psychological variables. They are more specific, in that they consider particular technologies (computers, personal digital assistant, etc.) as units of study. This chapter attempts to bridge these two bodies of knowledge, and considers a psychological model of computer technology

*Originally published in *Gender, Technology and Development*, Vol. 7, No. 3, 2003, pp. 359–77.

adoption by novice urban female learners using a combination of quantitative and qualitative approaches. In the following paragraphs, a brief review of studies is presented. Henceforth, the words ICT and computers will be used interchangeably.

ICT and Gender Studies

Huyer (1997) advocated that women's access to technology and training is a basic requirement for their participation in the global information economy. It offers women useful tools for generating and transmitting their needs, priorities and knowledge globally. With these tools, women can 'virtually' gather together to share ideas and strategies, learn from each other, mobilise for action, and advocate for their equitable and democratic participation in civil society. Training women in the use of technology can empower them to maximise the use and benefits of technology, and harness its potential in ways that lead to gender equity, social justice and sustainable development. A focused and timely effort to provide women with ICT education and skills can enable them to compete successfully in the global information economy, and play a leadership role in its development. Women can master aspects of computer use and maintenance with significantly less training, as this is available outside the formal education system. They need not work for a university degree in ICT to empower themselves.

According to Huyer and Carr (2002), information and communication technologies should be considered a priority for Third World women, as these have the potential to integrate women in development. Several obstacles to access in developing countries include cost structure of the technology, lack of infrastructure, lack of technical support in repair and maintenance, and the language barrier. As a result, computer education is either unavailable or costly. Besides these barriers, women's inability to access training has been attributed to financial constraints, distance from home, paucity of time, cultural inhibitions and stereotypical attitudes. Expressing their concern for addressing women's interests in computer adoption, the researchers focus on the economic perspective for addressing these issues.

In 1996, The Association for Progressive Communication (APC) surveyed over 700 women's groups and individual women by e-mail to identify women's electronic networking needs and opportunities (Farwell et al. 1999: 53–77). Results indicated that women are less active in learning new technologies and need more initial encouragement and training. The study identified training needs, which include basic and advanced skills. Recommendations included offering women-specific free training, and deciding training methodologies and programmes in consultation with women's groups. Training techniques that encourage critical thinking and learning by doing were also emphasised.

Describing her efforts in establishing the NGO Resource Centre (NGORC) in Zanzibar, Alloo (1999: 156–61) emphasised the importance of workshops carried out to demystify information technology and enhance its use as an empowering tool. She considers such initiatives particularly crucial in places where the people tend to question the relevance of ICT.

Information Systems/Management Studies

A growing body of research in Psychology, Management Studies and Information Systems shows that attitudes play an important role in the adoption of computer technologies (Swanson 1982). Evidence supports the dependence of attitudes on the features of the system and on the conditions leading to their use (Franz and Robey 1986). Two perspectives are taken with regard to the influence of attitudes in the adoption of computer technologies: one states that attitude towards the features of the technology object stimulates action, and the other emphasises the individual's evaluations of the benefits of these technologies. The latter view forms the rationale behind the Theory of Reasoned Action (Ajzen and Fishbein 1980: 53), a model of psychological processes that mediate observed relations between attitudes, subjective norms and behavioural intention. In general, a person will hold a favourable attitude towards a given behaviour if s/he believes that performance of the behaviour will lead to a positive response from significant others. The stronger the person's intentions as shaped by favourable attitudes and norms, the greater is the likelihood of its implementation.

Davis et al. (1989) adapted the generic model of Theory of Reasoned Action to the particular domain of technology acceptance. They proposed the Technology Acceptance Model to account for the psychological factors that affect computer acceptance. The Technology Acceptance Model replaced Theory of Reasoned Action's attitudinal determinants with a set of two variables specific to the technology acceptance context, namely perceived ease of use and perceived usefulness. The former refers to the belief that using a computer will be free of cognitive effort; the latter refers to the person's belief that using it will enhance performance. Later, another variable of computer self-efficacy, which refers to the judgment of one's capability to use a computer, was added to the list (Compeau and Higgins 1995).

The Technology Acceptance Model has become well-established as a powerful and parsimonious model for predicting user acceptance. Studies (Venkatesh and Davis 1996, 2000) have found that it explains between 40 to 60 per cent of the variance in usage intention and behaviour. The first study explored perceived usefulness, perceived ease of use, and self-efficacy as antecedents of behavioural intention, and found that perceived usefulness of a technology affected intention directly whereas perceived ease of use of that technology had an indirect effect through perceived usefulness. Self-efficacy influences intention indirectly through perceived ease of use. Their second study explored the role of perceived usefulness and subjective norm to behavioural intention, and found that perceived usefulness is the most important determinant of behavioural intention. Subjective norm indirectly impacts intention through perceived usefulness via two psychological processes, internalisation (incorporating social influences into their own usefulness perceptions) and identification (performing behaviours that are consistent with group norms in order to acquire group membership and social support). Sazajna (1996) testifies that unless users perceive an information system as useful, its ease of use has no effect on the formation of intentions. In short, perceived usefulness is the factor that emerges as the most important predictor of behavioural intention to adopt computers.

Statement of the Problem

Gender Studies focuses on economic and political participation and networking as a consequence of technology adoption, and examines barriers such as financial, infrastructure and socio-cultural to women's access and use of computers and the Internet. It does not systematically address psychological factors in technology adoption, but mentions self-esteem, increased confidence, etc., as consequences of technology adoption. On the other hand, Information Systems and Management Studies consider psychological factors as causes and effective job performance as the consequence of technology adoption. Neither field champions a holistic approach, which considers psychosocial factors as causes as well as effects of technology adoption. Second, most of the researches in both the fields are conducted on students and professionals. They have consistently ignored novices and low-end users as units of study in technology adoption. Third, the methodology used in the two fields varies. Gender Studies uses the questionnaire or interview method, while Information Systems and Management Studies rely on standardised scales. The present study fills some of the gaps by considering a more holistic approach to computer adoption and use, focusing on novice users and combining the use of standard scales and questionnaires as well as informal interviews for data collection.

This study empirically validated an adapted version of the Technology Acceptance Model. The predictors of behavioural intention to adopt computers include the psychological variables of perceived usefulness, perceived ease of use, computer self-efficacy and subjective norm. In addition, the role of two social support variables was explored. One was familial support, which included encouragement to pursue computer learning, financial support for the same, the number of computer literate members, computer ownership and access. The second variable was institutional support, which included proximity of the training centre, preferred gender and personal attributes of the trainer, and trainer's perception of trainees' interaction with computers.

Method

Background

Data was collected from women trainees at a premier private computer-training institute in Mumbai, India. They were enrolled for the basic computer skills course of 18 hours duration. Eighth March being 'Women's Day', a course titled *Women's Special* was run for women computer learners. The course was offered at a subsidised rate of Rs 749 instead of the usual price of Rs 1,500. The course contents included *Introduction* (getting to know the different parts of a computer), *Windows* (familiarity with the operating system, using a mouse and using utilities like paint, calculator, etc.), *MS-office: Word* (creating simple documents, opening files and saving text, using different fonts, inserting graphics and pictures), *Excel* (creating a spreadsheet, entering data, editing, saving and printing, formulae and drawing graphs), *Power point* (creating slides, setting the slide show, saving), *Internet* (how to access and browse the Internet) and *E-mail* (sending and receiving messages).

The courseware was adapted to suit the needs of women. The programme was task-oriented and the skills were learned through the performance of specially designed tasks. Apart from English, the course was conducted in four Indian languages—Hindi, Marathi, Tamil and Gujarati. The trainees were given a copy of the language software, *Windik*, for personal use for the period of the training.

Sample

The subjects were 100 women trainees with a mean age of 36.73 (range 18–70). Fifty-four per cent were young adults (18–34 yrs), 31 per cent were middle-aged (35–52 yrs), and 15 per cent were in the older group (53–70 yrs). Forty-four per cent of them were graduates, and an equal number (28 per cent) were post-graduates and higher secondary or lower degree holders. Sixty-six per cent were married, 26 per cent were unmarried, 5 per cent were widowed and 3 per cent did not respond to the question. Sixty-three per cent belonged to the middle-income group, 18 per cent came from the upper-income group, and 19 per cent didn't respond to the question. Fifty-four per cent of the women were homemakers, 26 per cent were employed, and 20 per cent were students.

Tools

Standardised tests were used to assess the psychological variables on a 5-point Likert-type scale, and a questionnaire elicited information on support-related variables. The following tests were administered:

Behavioral Intention

This refers to the individual's decision regarding future computer use. Two statements assessed this dimension (Hill et al. 1987). In addition, one question assessed their willingness to seek an advanced course. Subjects indicated their response on a scale ranging from definitely no to definitely yes.

Perceived Ease of Use

This refers to a person's belief that using computers will be free of cognitive effort. A 7-item scale was used to assess it (Brown and Massey 2001).

Perceived Usefulness

This refers to a person's belief that using computers will result in the achievement of personally relevant goals. It was assessed by two measures—one, subjects were asked to write eight benefits they believed would result from learning to use computers in the order of importance to them (Hill et al. 1987). Following this, they were provided with a 20-item checklist of benefits prepared by the authors, wherein they rated the extent of usefulness. The 20 items were grouped under four categories: job/career, personal/family gain, entertainment and information.

Computer Self-efficacy

This refers to the individual's subjective evaluation of their cognitive competencies in dealing with computers. A 4-item scale was used to assess it (ibid. 1987).

Subjective Norm

This refers to an individual's estimation of how important others feel about one's use of computers, and motivation to comply with their feeling. It was assessed by two-items.

The questionnaire elicited information on three aspects: (*a*) demographic data, (*b*) familial support such as source of motivation to enroll in the course and sponsorship for the same, number of family members who are computer literate, computer ownership and access after the course, and (*c*) institutional support such as distance in time between home/office/college and the training centre, gender preference and qualities of trainers. In addition to this, a questionnaire was given to 17 trainers (eight females and nine males) to get an insight into their views about the women trainees. These included the learning approach of women trainees, their experience with computer interaction, their perception of women enrolled under different training schemes, and differences, if any, between men and women trainees.

Procedure

Permission was sought from the regional office of the training institute, after which the centre heads were approached for appointments to meet the trainees. Six weeks of fieldwork (February–April 2003) was conducted at eight centres located in different parts (central, south, north and northwest) of Mumbai. The scales and questionnaires were administered in person to groups of women trainees at the end of the day's learning session. The size of a group in a session varied between five to 12. Once information from the trainees was obtained, the trainers were given a questionnaire.

Results and Discussion

Technology Acceptance Model and Computer Adoption

Behavioural intention was construed as the indicator of technology acceptance. The mean score on the behavioural intention scale was high (mean = 8.50, possible range is 2–10), implying that women strongly intended to use computers in the future. This was further confirmed by the plan of half the women (50 per cent) to take up an advanced course on completion of the basic skills programme. Of the rest, one-third (37 per cent) were uncertain of their decision, and a small percentage (13 per cent) had no such plan (χ^2 = 21.14, p < 0.05). Women trainees appraised computers as moderately easy to use (mean = 23.45, possible range 7–35). The trainees reported on an average 5.34 benefits out of the possible eight they were asked to list, with 59 per cent reporting five or more benefits and 41 per cent reporting four or less. The checklist assessing the magnitude of perceived usefulness indicated that overall, women appraised computers as very useful (mean = 71.23; possible range 20–100). All four categories of benefits showed an above average rating on the magnitude dimension. The order of importance of the magnitude of usefulness was information and communication (mean = 4.06), personal/family gain (mean = 3.81), entertainment (mean = 3.56) and jobs/career (mean = 3.32). Thus, both measures of usefulness, namely the categories of benefits (to be discussed later) and the magnitude of usefulness of each category, revealed a similar pattern. The subjects perceived themselves to be highly self-efficacious (mean = 16.33; possible range 4–20), revealing a positive view of their cognitive capacities in dealing with computers. They appraised subjective norm as quite important (mean = 7.8, possible range 2–10), indicating a strong motivation to comply with the expectations of significant others to learn computers.

To explore the relationship between the psychological variables, a Pearson's product-moment correlation was computed (Table 19.1). A significant positive relationship was found between perceived ease of use and perceived usefulness to behavioural intention (r = 0.28 and 0.35 respectively, p < 0.01). In other words, the higher the evaluation of computers as being easy to use and useful, the higher the likelihood that women will adopt this technology. There was also a significant positive relationship between perceived ease of use and perceived usefulness (0.48, p < 0.01). This finding is supported by prior research (Thatcher et. al. 2002; Venkatesh and Davis 2000), which reported that evaluating computers as easy to use is associated with

TABLE 19.1
Correlation Matrix of Psychological Variables

	PEOU	PU	CSE	SN	BI
PEOU		0.48**	0.31**	0.39**	0.28**
PU			0.15	0.35**	0.35**
CSE				0.10	0.21*
SN					0.18
BI					

Notes: **p < 0.01; *p < 0.05.

their evaluation as being useful. Computer self-efficacy was significantly positively related to behavioural intention ($r = 0.21$, $p < 0.05$). This indicated that the more efficacious the women perceive themselves to be, the stronger is their intention to use computers. The relationship between computer self-efficacy and perceived ease of use was positive and significant ($r = 0.31$, $p < 0.01$). This shows that having a positive view of one's capacities to use computers is associated with evaluating the tool as easy to use. Subjective norm was not significantly co-related to behavioural intention. In other words, the opinion of significant others stating that one should learn computers has little or no impact on and of itself. However, it was found to be significantly associated with both perceived ease of use and perceived usefulness ($r = 0.39$ and 0.35 respectively, $p < 0.01$). This means that only if an individual perceives a technology to be useful and easy to use will the opinion of significant others influence his/her intention to adopt computer technology.

A regression analysis was computed to study the causal linkages among psychological variables and their contribution to behavioural intention to use computers (Table 19.2). Significant causal linkages was found for two sets of variables—first, computer self-efficacy was a significant determinant of perceived ease of use ($\beta = 0.31$; $p < 0.01$), implying that when a women views herself as competent, she also views computers as easy to handle. Second, subjective norm was a significant determinant of perceived usefulness ($\beta = 0.35$, $p < 0.01$), that is, when women feel that important people in their lives expect them to learn computes, they find the technology in question useful.

TABLE 19.2
Regression Analyses: Technology Acceptance Model

Dependent Variable	R^2	Independent Variable	B	Standard Error of b	β	T
Perceived Ease of Use	0.10	Computer Self-efficacy	0.49	2.42	0.31	3.22**
		Constant	15.82	0.15		6.53***
Perceived Usefulness	0.12	Subjective Norm	2.70	0.73	0.35	3.72**
		Constant	50.17	5.84		8.59***
Perceived Usefulness	0.27	Perceived Ease of Use	1.24	0.30	0.41	4.14***
		Computer Self-efficacy	5.00	0.42	0.00	0.01
		Subjective Norm	1.48	0.73	0.19	2.01*
		Constant	30.50	8.59		3.55***
Behavioral Intention	0.16	Perceived Ease of Use	2.01	0.03	0.09[a]	0.81
		Perceived Usefulness	2.00	0.01	0.27	2.44**
		Computer Self-efficacy	4.01	0.06	0.14	1.36
		Subjective Norm	2.00	0.03	0.04	0.38
		Constant	5.66	0.74		7.63***

Notes: ***$p < 0.001$; **$p < 0.01$; *$p < 0.05$.
[a] The overall effect of ease of use on behavioural intention was due to a direct 0.09, and an indirect (0.41 × 0.27) effect through perceived usefulness.

All the variables taken together explained 16 per cent variance in behavioural intention, the indicator of technology acceptance. Only perceived usefulness had a direct effect on behavioural intention and emerged significant (0.27, $p < 0.01$), whereas perceived ease of use, computer self-efficacy and subjective norm had no direct effect (0.09, 0.14 and 0.04 respectively). Indirect effects of these variables to behavioural intention provided further insight (Table 19.3). The overall effect of perceived usefulness increased to 0.35, with an indirect effect of 0.08 through all other psychological variables. The overall effect of perceived ease of use also had a significant effect (0.20, $p < 0.05$) when combined with the indirect effect through perceived usefulness (0.11). The overall impact of computer self-efficacy and subjective norm to behavioural intention was insignificant. These findings are illustrated in Figure 19.1.

FIGURE 19.1
Path Diagram of the Effects of Psychological Predictors on Behavioural Intention

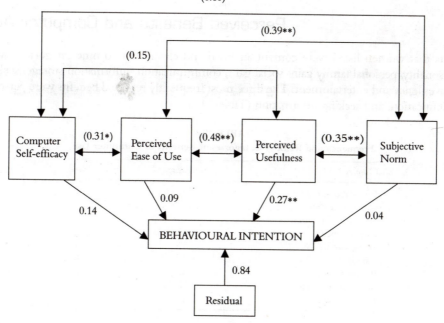

Notes: Numbers in the bracket represent correlation coefficients between the variables.
*p < 0.05.
**p < 0.01.

TABLE 19.3
Direct and Indirect Effects of Psychological Variables on Behavioural Intention

Sl No.	Variable	Direct Effect	Indirect Effect	Total Effect
1	PEOU	0.09	0.11	0.20*
2	PU	0.27	0.08	0.35**
3	CSE	0.14	0.04	0.18
4	SN	0.04	0.14	0.18

The Technology Acceptance Model is established as a powerful and parsimonious one for predicting user acceptance. A figure as high as between 40 to 60 per cent has been quoted in previous research (Davis et al. 1989; Venkatesh and Davis 1996, 2000; Venkatesh et al. 2002), which is higher than the 16 per cent variance found in the present work. This difference can be explained by way of the sample characteristics, level of technological advancement and cultural variations. These studies were conducted on students, professionals and high-end computer users. Besides, gender as a category of analysis was not considered. On the other hand, the present study was conducted on novice women users. Second, these studies were done in the technologically advanced West; in contrast, the present work was done in the technologically less sophisticated East. Perceived usefulness has been consistently found to be a strong determinant of usage intentions with variances ranging between 72–76 per cent (Sazajna 1996; Venkatesh and Davis 1996). In the current study, it accounted for 27 per cent variance in behavioural intention. Though significant, it is comparatively low.

This gap can be explained by the reasons mentioned above. In short, perceived usefulness or benefits contribute the most to computer adoption, and is discussed below in greater detail.

Perceived Benefits and Computer Adoption

The benefits that women listed were content analysed and classified into nine categories—jobs/career-related, personality, personal/family gain, social gain, communication, information storage, seeking information, convenience and entertainment. The three most frequently reported benefits were personal/family gain, communication, and seeking information (Table 19.4).

TABLE 19.4
Frequency and Rank of Categories of Benefits of Computer Use

Category	Frequency	Rank
Personal/family gain	121	1
Communication	89	2
Seeking information	75	3
Convenience	55	4
Social gain	51	5
Job/career	45	6
Personality	32	7
Information storage	28	8
Entertainment	14	9

Personal/family gain included benefits that have implications both for women and their family ('I can spend my time in a good way in my retired life'. 'I will prepare letters for my husband'). In the category of communication, responses centred around being in contact with family/kin/friends through e-mail ('I can be in touch with my children settled abroad'). Seeking information was the third most important benefit cited by women ('We get information about everything'). If seeking information and information storage are combined, information emerges as the second most important benefit for the sample (75+28 =103). Respondents were asked to list benefits in the order of priority. The women trainees reported personal and family gain (n = 77), communication (n = 59), and getting information (n = 46) as the three topmost priorities of learning to use computers, a pattern similar to that found for perceived use of computers.

It is not surprising that the major benefits of learning computers pertain to the self and family as the sample consists of women who are, predominantly homemakers. In most societies, as the responsibility of maintaining family/kin relations falls on women's shoulders, becoming computer literate meets their needs for social networking. They perceive computers as tools of empowerment as they boost their self-esteem and assist them in addressing their traditional family management roles efficiently, conveniently and quickly. This empowering feeling can best be described in their words. One woman stated, 'It makes me feel more confident.' Another lady mentioned how the Internet can help her find a groom for her daughter: 'I would want to scan her photograph and follow up the proposal on the Internet. My options increase and it assures privacy.' A few women were keen on helping their husbands in their work and teaching their children. Responses include 'I can type letters for my lawyer husband', and 'I can teach my children.' The second most important benefit women emphasise is the use of computers for communication purposes, and even here connecting with family and kin emerges as crucial. One woman stated, 'I can be in touch with my relatives abroad.' Women are aware of the empowerment potential of access to information through computers, and this was ranked the third most important benefit. They marvel at the quickness, amount and organisation of information. As shown in the case of communication, information is sought/stored for family needs. For example, 'I can store family budgets, academic records of my kids.' 'I can reserve train tickets on the Internet.'

Perception of computers as useful is strongly associated with the adoption of computers. In order to speed up the adoption process, workshops can be conducted in residential areas and places frequented by women, such as schools, health centres, markets, etc., to demystify the technology and inform women of its usefulness to them and their families. Such awareness programmes must be fine-tuned to the needs of various groups of women as differentiated by class, age, occupational status and geographic location.

Support and Computer Adoption

In addition to the psychological variables, information was sought on two sources of support—the family and the institution.

Familial Support

Familial support was assessed by questions about who encouraged them to join the course, who provided sponsorship for the same, the number of computer literate family members, computer ownership and point of access. Fifty-eight per cent were self-motivated while 42 per cent were encouraged by others to pursue the course; however, the difference between the two groups was not significant ($\chi^2 = 2.56$). In the second category, 17 per cent of husbands encouraged their wives to learn computers, and in a quarter of the cases (24 per cent) a family member other than the husband was the source of encouragement. Both self-motivation and other forms of motivation are found to be equally important in computer adoption.

As far as financial assistance is concerned, 54 per cent of the women were sponsored whereas 45 per cent paid for the course themselves. This difference was not found to be significant ($\chi^2 = 1$). In the former category, 31 per cent of the husbands funded the enrolment of their wives, family members other than the husband financed 23 per cent of them, and one was sponsored by her office. The trend is towards external financial support, though close to half the women paid for the course themselves. Despite a quarter of the sample being employed, organisations did not come forth to support their employees in their effort to become computer literate, notwithstanding the subsidy offered by the training institute. However, what seems interesting is the fact that when an educational institution offers a subsidised fee, women are willing to part with their earnings or personal savings to become literate.

Almost all (95 per cent) the women had one or more computer literate family member, while only a small percentage (5 per cent) of women had no such member ($\chi^2 = 81$, $p < 0.001$). The frequency order of the literate member was siblings ($n = 62$; brother, $n = 36$; sister, $n = 26$), children ($n = 53$; son $= 29$; daughter $= 24$), husband ($n = 36$), relatives ($n = 10$) and parents ($n = 7$). In short, the backgrounds of these women are characterised by at least one computer literate family member, who serves as a role model and inspires others in the family to become computer literate. This certainly seems to be the case with those women in the sample who had one such member. In psychological learning theories, observation or imitation of a role model is a powerful method by which persons acquire new behaviour—in this case computer adoption— by watching a role model (Matlin 1995: 194).

On the question of computer ownership it was found that 53 per cent of women did not own computers, whereas 47 per cent did ($\chi^2 = 0.36$). Although the difference was not significant, what is worth mentioning is that the figure for ownership in the sample is higher than the national norm of 6.4 personal computers per 1,000 people (Kulkarni 2003: 135). Thus, ownership plays a role in women's decision to adopt computers. On completion of the course, 54 per cent of the women was going to access a family computer. This includes the 47 per cent who own one and the 7 per cent who plan to purchase one. This was followed by cybercafes (30 per cent), friend's/relative's place (11 per cent), and office (5 per cent) ($\chi^2 = 21.16$, p < 0.01). The combination of a computer literate family member and a family computer are strong contenders in stimulating women to become computer literate. However, the combination of these two factors may also go against women. In the course of the study, it was brought into focus that even if there is a computer in the household, women may not have the time to practice/use it or a male member may dominate it. One trainee complained, 'Once we reach home, it is back to food and kids, we hardly get any time to use a computer.' Another pointed out, 'I purchased a computer for my son from my voluntary retirement funds, and he does not allow me to touch it.'

Institutional Support

Institutional support was measured by the proximity of the training centre estimated in terms of time between home/office/school and training institute, preferred gender and personal qualities of the trainer, and their role in the trainees' learning process. Almost three-fourths of the women (72 per cent) were at a distance of less than half an hour from the training centre, 18 per cent of them were at a distance of an hour, and 10 per cent over an hour ($\chi^2 = 19.36$, p < 0.01). Despite having a training centre close to home, the women who travelled an hour or more did so with the express desire of learning with their friends. Echoing the finding of Narayanan (2002), convenience in access emerged as important in facilitating computer adoption. This finding comes as no surprise as the time saved on travel enables women to balance their educational aspirations with work, family and household responsibilities. As far as gender preference of the trainer was concerned, two-thirds or 65 per cent expressed no gender preference, while one-third (35 per cent) indicated a preference ($\chi^2 = 9.00$, p < 0.01). Of these, one-fourth of the women trainees (26 per cent) said they would prefer a female trainer, while a small percentage (9 per cent) opted for a male trainer. Unlike previous research, which recommended women trainers (ibid.) to promote computer adoption by women, the gender of the trainer was not found to be important here. This can be explained by the varied sample characteristics of the two studies. Narayanan's work considered rural and semi-urban economically disadvantaged men and women trainees, whereas the present study focused on metropolitan, educated women. More than the gender of the trainer, it is his/her personal attributes that emerged as important, with the trainees emphasising patience, ability to adjust to the training needs, and knowledge of computers.

The role of trainers as a dimension of institutional support in novice women's computer adoption is a crucial one. It was assessed in terms of the trainer's observation regarding the trainees' first computer interaction, learning approach, the difference between novices and women enrolled in an advanced course, and differences, if any, between novice men and women trainees. With regard to women's first interaction with the computer, trainers were asked to classify trainees into one of three categories: eager adopters, hesitant and resisters. The trainers indicated that the majority of them were hesitant (71 per cent), a few were eager adopters (29 per cent), and none were resisters ($\chi^2 = 76.47$, p < 0.01). The trainers' perception of women's learning approach revealed a mix of positive and negative views. They reported that despite their hesitance, women are keen learners with a positive attitude. They remarked that though women trainees take longer to understand, they are quick to apply their learning in ways useful to them. For example, when taught how to e-mail, instead of typing an arbitrary message, they are systematic in the content and send a mail with a meaningful content.

Stereotypical views were revealed when trainers compared novice women trainees with advanced women users and novice male trainees. While contrasting the trainees in the basic skills programme with those enrolled in advanced schemes, the trainers remarked that women in the former group are apprehensive about their capabilities to handle and learn computers, and presume that if they make an error, they will damage the computer. Another difference highlighted was that as compared to advanced women users, novice women are not ambitious and have no plans to pursue a job or career. This view arises from the trainers' misconception that a *Women's Special* course attracts homemakers, when in fact students and working women also avail of this scheme. When asked about gender differences between novice trainees, four were stated: first, male learners have a higher initial exposure to computers than women. This view appears biased, as almost half the women in the sample had family computers. Second, male novice learners are specific in what they want to learn, whereas the women are more generalist and learn whatever is taught to them. This can be explained by two reasons, one, that women consider the benefits of computers for themselves as well as for others, and two that the training is an opportunity to revive their desire for education. Third, men have a more experimental approach and they group together, which accelerates their learning. Women, on the other hand, lack such cohesiveness, and wait for instructions. This works to the disadvantage of women who do not have the necessary peer support to facilitate their learning process. Lastly, men expect their queries to be answered immediately, while women are more patient about being attended. The last three observations of the trainers imply that men are active learners, whereas women are relatively passive. Both male and female trainers hold a traditional view of women, especially the homemakers in the sample. While this observation may be partly justified, it is equally true that a more modern role and personality of urban, educated middle-class women have emerged in India. Such old-fashioned views place extra demands on the women, adversely affecting their learning process.

Summary and Conclusion

The study provides insight into factors that need to be harnessed to promote the adoption of computers by urban women. Among the psychological variables, evaluating computers as useful plays a critical role. The benefits that women perceive revolve around performing their traditional family role efficiently and conveniently. Familial and institutional factors enable us to explain the user behaviour in a more comprehensive manner. Having a computer literate family member and a family computer can go a long way in stirring women to acquire basic skills. Proximity of the training centre to home/school/office, a subsidised fee, and a patient and adjusting trainer emerge as the key facilitators of computer learning. With regard to the role of trainers as a measure of institutional support in computer acceptance, it was found that trainers often hold gender stereotypical views.

The study suggests ways of accelerating computer adoption, access to education, and improving its quality. The empirical validation of the Technology Acceptance Model, which draws heavily from psychology, reveals that it is limited in scope in explaining the intention to adopt computers. Embracing a technology is a complex and multi-faceted process which has to be considered in a holistic way, drawing from several disciplines. Second, the study considers novice urban women learners, a population ignored by both Gender Studies and Information and Management Studies. In research, homemakers as a sub-population of urban women are neglected and deserve our scholarly attention. In order to optimise the advantages of computer learning, there is a need to educate women in the potential and versatility of this technology beyond a family agenda. This may include, among others, information technology-enabled services, which open possibilities of working from home and empowering the women economically.

To promote women's computer adoption, both long-term and short-term strategies need to be considered. This chapter has addressed select short-term strategies. Further research needs to look into other short-term strategies like technophobia in women trainees, attitudes of the trainers, schemes and policies of private computer educational institutions, etc. A comparative study between women novices and women seeking advanced courses would also provide valuable insight into the role of experience in increasing technological sophistication and reception. Courseware designed for women can be content analysed to check for stereotyped illustrations. Future research can assess the feasibility and benefits of flexible training timings. Research on urban women is required, and sub-populations like the urban poor need scholarly scrutiny. As far as policy is concerned, training institutes might do a public service by running gender-sensitive training programmes for trainers, periodically offering subsidised fees and flexible timings to attract more women, and thereby jump-start India's computer literacy programme.

References

Ajzen, I. and M. Fishbein. 1980. *Understanding Attitudes and Predicting Social Behavior*. Englewood Cliffs, New Jersey: Prentice Hall.

Alloo, F. 1999. 'Information Technology and Cyber Culture: The Case of Zanzibar', in W. Harcourt (ed.), *Women @ Internet*, pp. 156–61. London: Zed Books.

Brown, S. and A. Massey. 2001. 'An Examination of Expectation, (dis)confirmation and Information System Satisfaction'. Working paper. www.kelley.indiana.edu/ardennis/wp/tr135-1.doc

Compeau, D. and C. Higgins. 1995. 'Application of Social Cognitive Theory to Training for Computer Skills', *Information Systems Research*, 6 (2): 118–43.

Davis, F., R.P. Bagozzi and P.R. Warshaw. 1989. 'User Acceptance of Computer Technology: A Comparison of Two Theoretical Models', *Management Science*, 35 (8): 982–1003.

Farwell, E., P. Wood, M. James and K. Banks. 1999. 'Global Networking for Change: Experiences from APC Women's Programme', in W. Harcourt (ed.), *Women @ Internet*, pp. 53–77. London: Zed books.

Franz, C.R. and D. Robey. 1986. 'Organizational Context, User Involvement, and the Usefulness of Information Systems', *Decision Sciences*, 17 (4): 329–56.

Gist, M.E., C. Schwoere and B. Rosen. 1989. 'Effects of Alternative Training Methods on Self-efficacy and Performance in Computer Software Training', *Journal of Applied Psychology*, 74 (6): 884–91.

Haffkin, N. and N. Taggart. 2001. *Gender, Information Technology, and Developing Countries*. New York: Academy for Educational Development, United States Agency for International Development.

Hill, T., N.D. Smith and M.F. Mann. 1987. 'Role of Efficacy Expectations in Predicting the Decision to Use Advanced Technologies: The Case of Computers', *Journal of Applied Psychology*, 72 (2): 307–13.

Huyer, S. 1997. 'Supporting Women's Use of Information Technologies for Sustainable Development', Submitted to the Gender and Sustainable Development Unit, IDRC. *http://www.wigsat.org/it/womenicts.html*.

Huyer, S. and M. Carr. 2002. 'Information and Communication Technologies: A Priority for Women', *Gender Technology and Development*, 6 (1): 85–100.

Kelkar, G., G. Shrestha and N. Veena. 2002. 'IT Industry and Women's Agency: Explorations in Bangalore and Delhi, India', *Gender, Technology and Development*, 6 (1): 63–84.

Kulkarni, V.P. 2003. *Manorama Year Book*. Kottayam: Malayala Manorama Press.

Matlin, M.W. 1995. *Psychology*. New York: Harcourt Brace College Publishers.

Mitter, S. 1999. 'Globalization, Technological Changes and the Search for a New Paradigm for Women's Work', *Gender, Technology and Development*, 3 (1): 1–16.

Narayanan, K.N. 2002. 'Socio-Economic Impact of Subsidized Computer Education'. Submitted to Sterlite Foundation, India.

Sazajna, B. 1996. 'Empirical Evaluation of the Revised Technology Acceptance Model', *Management Sciences*, 42 (1): 85–92.

Swanson, E.B. 1982. 'Measuring User Attitudes in Management Information Systems Research: A Review', *The International Journal of Management Science*, 10 (2): 157–65.

Venkatesh, V. and F. Davis. 1996. 'A Model of the Antecedents of Perceived Ease of Use: Development and Test', *Decision Sciences*, 27 (3): 451–80.

———. 2000. 'A Theoretical Extension of the Technology Acceptance Model: Four Longitudinal Field Studies', *Management Science*, 46 (2): 186–204.

Venkatesh, V., S. Speier and M. Morris. 2002. 'User Acceptance Enablers in Individual Decision Making about Technology: Toward an Integrated Model', *Decision Sciences*, 33 (2): 297–316.

TWENTY

ICT Initiatives, Women and Work: Reproducing or Changing Gender Inequalities?

Shoba Arun, Richard Heeks and Sharon Morgan

Introduction

The development of a global 'information society' has largely been characterised by the diffusion of various information and communications technologies (ICTs). While the notion of information societies is contested, there is a clear sense of disparity between the industrialised nations with their educated populations, excellent telecommunication infrastructure and growing service sectors, and the developing countries, which mainly lack these information society components (Lim 1999). Fearful of missing out on the opportunities provided by ICTs, developing countries have therefore been adopting information society strategies, placing an emphasis on both the production side (hardware manufacture, software development, etc.) and on the consumption side (e-commerce, e-government, etc.) (Heeks 2002; Singhal and Rogers 2001).

From this growing use of ICTs in developing countries have arisen a series of studies and findings. Some have been largely optimistic and gender-neutral, seeing the contribution that ICTs can make, for example, to economic development generally or to poverty alleviation specifically (Cecchini 2002; Kenny 2002; Wakelin and Shadrach 2001). Other findings, though, have been more nuanced, seeing technology as socially contextualised and thus, for example, as gendered, with differential barriers to the access and use of ICTs by men and women (Hafkin and Taggart 2002; Huyer and Sikoska 2002; Wambui 2002). This in turn has led to the identification of a gender dimension of the 'digital divide', and to concerns that ICTs will be applied in ways that maintain or even exacerbate existing gender inequalities (Jorge 2002; Marcelle 2002).

Seeking to understand these issues in greater detail, this chapter focuses on experiences of ICT application in India. India was selected for two main reasons (Bhatnagar and Schware 2000; Singhal and Rogers 2001). First, it has for many years given a significant priority to ICTs both on the production side (as seen, for instance, in the development of its software industry) and on the consumption side (with significant investments in e-government applications, and attempts to push ICTs out into rural areas). Second, because the application of ICTs has taken place through a variety of different models; for example, from pure market to pure state, and from gender-blind to gender-focused. India therefore provides a valuable source of data for other countries seeking to journey towards the 'information society', and concerned about the gender consequences of this journey.

Because India is an entire subcontinent in itself, this chapter makes its focus even tighter and looks at the experiences of one south Indian state—Kerala—which can be viewed as a microcosm of the ICT experience in India. On the one hand Kerala has caught on to the coattails of India's 'software boom' and can be investigated to see how the demand for software labour has impacted women's paid employment in the mainstream ICT sector. On the other hand, Kerala has also played host to a number of innovative state interventions in ICTs, including *Kudumbashree*, a women-led poverty reduction programme that has made use of ICTs to enable the development of ICT-based enterprises run by cooperatives of poor women.

The study relied on a triangulation of methods. First, a survey of 110 software professionals from 20 TechnoPark software firms, each of which employed between 10 and 300 workers, conducted in 1999–2000 was used. This related to information on work practices among software professionals in IT firms in Kerala. Interviews with companies were also undertaken to understand the opportunities for young women arising from employment in software firms in India. Next, a qualitative and case-based approach was taken, involving ICT-based enterprises owned and managed by women during July 2004. These two contrasting experiences will be used in this chapter to explore differences between ICT projects that take a market-led, gender-neutral approach, and those that take an interventionist and gender-focused approach. While there may be limitations to this type of triangulation of methodology, it indeed helps throw light on the emerging issues related to the burgeoning interest in the impact of ICT production and consumption sector in India. Most importantly, it helps to compare experiences of market-led ICT opportunities for those with a higher level of human capital in terms of employment within the software firms in the private sector, and the experiences of ICT-based enterprises such as data entry, hardware assembly and IT training, which were formed and managed by women from lower socio-economic backgrounds, largely through the government strategies for poverty alleviation. During both periods, interviews were conducted at three main levels: women workers, managers (both men and women), and policy-makers (both men and women). Documentary analysis was also undertaken, ranging from government records to annual reports of enterprises. Observational periods were also in a small number of organisations.

The chapter is structured as follows: Section two examines some of the debates relating to gender, ICTs and development, and Section three proceeds to examine the ICT context in India in general, and in Kerala in particular. Section four examines survey research findings on women's employment in private-sector software production, which can be contrasted with Section five's presentation of findings from the state-led *Kudumbashree* project. Final conclusions are provided in Section six.

Gender, Work and ICT

Feminist scholarship has pointed out women's unequal relation with technology, including ICT, as gender relations often determine the use and impact of technologies. Wajcman (1991: 28), for example, argues that 'though new technologies do represent a force for change ... the outcomes are constrained by the pre-existing organization of work, of which gender is an integral part'. Likewise, Wambui (2002) notes that barriers to the effective use of ICTs in developing countries are a microcosm of existing gender relations in societies, where women are socialised towards non-technical careers and away from technical work such as software development.

Despite this gender bias in the characterisation of men's and women's work, women have not been excluded from the ICT sector. Wambui's observations, for example, refer particularly to Africa, whereas in India women have been an important part of the ICT workforce. Equally, research in industrialised countries has noted the feminisation of software production, with a higher and increasing representation of women (Wright and Jacobs 1995). Nonetheless, the contextual force of existing gender relations continues to exert a strong influence on the relation between women and technology in ICT-related work. The emergence and progressive reinforcement of a masculine culture in this field has been emphasised (Tierney 1995; Wright 1997). Studies have also found that in the software industry, women work as operators or programmers in the non-managerial group, while men are predominant in managerial positions of project leaders or departmental managers (Panteli et al. 1997).

Feminists in Western countries have explained such outcomes partly by focusing on the gendered nature of the concepts of skill and technology, which are said to be due to flexible specialisation, where flexibility is a process of economic restructuring driven by technological change, increased globalisation, and by growing marketisation that involves a drive towards a greater variability of skills, hours and contracts in the labour market and, in some sectors, a downward pressure on rights, wages and conditions (Cook 2000; Walby 2000). Two forms of flexibility have been identified in relation to employment: functional, which is the ability of firms to transfer labour between tasks and break down job demarcations; and numerical, which is the ability to adjust the number of workers they employ to correspond with the demand for labour and goods. Competitive market pressures have driven forward the growth of these flexibilities, resulting, for instance, in the creation of low-skilled and insecure jobs for women reflected in growth in the European context of practices such as home working and part-time working (ibid.).

Such findings, though, relate almost entirely to industrialised countries. Nevertheless, in general terms, relatively little has been researched or written about on the specifics of gender relations in the ICT sector in developing countries, and it is this knowledge gap that this chapter partly addresses.

If the private sector and the market produce gender concerns in relation to women, ICTs and development, what of ICT projects driven by government or NGOs? Certainly hopes that ICT projects can play an important role in reducing gender inequalities have been high (Balakrishnan 2002). Of course, there is a recognition that existing gender relations do have a strong influence—under 'normal' conditions women will find themselves facing barriers of unequal access to ICTs, and unequal access to the benefits of ICTs (Huyer and Sikoska 2002). Hence the clear guidance on good practice for ICT project interventions, from the micro-level of participatory assessment of needs to the macro-level of gender-sensitised policies on infrastructure (Jorge 2002).

However, even here there are concerns about the gender-blind nature of some interventions (Bonder 2002), and—as with market-led ICT production—the problem remains that of relatively limited work based on actual experiences in developing countries. With this in mind, we now move on to outline the context for the cases to be reported in this chapter.

The ICT Context in India and Kerala

As just noted, the context within which ICTs operate strongly influences—even determines—their impacts, including gender impacts. This section therefore sketches out some aspects of the generic context for our cases; both the general context of India and the specific context of the state of Kerala.

Shaped by economic liberalisation and privatisation, the informatisation strategy in India since 1991 has seen moves such as the de-licensing of the electronics industry and liberalisation in foreign investment and trade policies. The software and services component of the ICT sector has emerged as one of the fastest growing industrial segments, increasing from US$ 170 million worth of output in 1991–92 to US$ 8.8 billion in 2003–04 (Heeks and Nicholson 2004). Operating within a competitive business environment with successful networking with overseas entrepreneurs and supportive government policies, the software industry benefits from impressive human capital, and has gained a sustainable competitive advantage. In response, leading global software companies have set up subsidiaries and joint ventures in India, and many more local entrepreneurs have started software companies (Bajpai and Sachs 2000).

Spurred on by this, many governments in the individual Indian states have initiated micro-reforms to attract more investment in the ICT sector for their respective regions. The government of the state of Kerala (GOK) in south India is no exception, and it has developed policies emphasising ICTs as an engine for industrial growth and employment. The state's ICT policy in this domain articulates a three-fold strategy: (*i*) establishment of a vibrant ICT industry; (*ii*) building up a robust infrastructure; and (*iii*) upgradation of the quality of human resources (GOK 2003).

All three of these were brought together in the creation of the state's 'TechnoPark' at Trivandrum as an identified location for ICT-based enterprises. It was India's first technology park and remains among the largest in India, hosting over 50 IT and information technology-enabled service companies, which employ some 5,000 IT professionals (TechnoPark 2004). These firms are active in a range of software-related activities including production of business applications, Internet technologies, embedded systems, animation and Web technologies. The dominant field is software production and maintenance for large foreign and domestic clients covering a range of sectors (finance, retail, healthcare, telecommunications), innovation (from conversion of old 'legacy' systems to design of new e-commerce solutions), and skill levels (from basic programming to complete 'turnkey' projects) (Arun and Arun 2002).

The firms operating in the TechnoPark are private sector, mostly either subsidiaries or joint ventures of foreign companies, or larger domestic firms headquartered elsewhere in India. The government's policy actions in enabling the development of the TechnoPark are therefore seen as market-oriented—the government plays no direct role in the park as either customer or supplier—and also as gender-blind, since there has been no specific consideration of the role of women.

The Government of Kerala's ICT policies stretch beyond this, however, and beyond gender-blind, market-oriented initiatives to direct ICT project interventions that tap into the broader range of relations between ICTs and enhanced social and economic development. Table 20.1 shows some of these project initiatives that link ICTs with state policies on governance, poverty alleviation and public service delivery. One area of emphasis (IT@School) is on increasing IT literacy in the state by promoting the use of IT in the school curriculum: training of teachers and supply of IT hardware. In line with e-governance projects in other Indian states, initiatives such as Package for Effective Administration of Registration (PEARL) and Fast Reliable Instant Efficient Network for Disbursement of Services (FRIENDS) enable citizens to access a number of public services, such as payment of bills through computerised networking systems. *Akshaya*, a recent initiative by the Kerala state's IT Mission, aims to act holistically, by providing skills, information and services to citizens. In all of these the state has a direct ownership and/or delivery role.

TABLE 20.1
State-Intervention ICT Projects in Kerala

Name	Programme and Objectives	Location/level of Implementation	Intended Impacts
FRIENDS	Payment of bills	Capital city	Transparent administration, access to services
PEARL	Registration of land	Capital city	Transparent administration; access to services
Project *Grameen*	Education of local citizens and formulating grassroots programmes	Local council (Panchayat)	Employment, empowerment and increased local participation
Information Kerala Mission	E-governance	Local council (Panchayat)	Increased participation and empowerment
Akshaya	Providing e-services	Malappuram District	Governance, employment, participation
Kudumbashree	Poverty alleviation scheme through women's self-help groups	State-wide	Self-employment, empowerment and poverty reduction
IT@School	Learning and teaching	All Kerala government schools	Training and education

Source: Adapted from GOK (2003).

Our focus here, though, is the *Kudumbashree* initiative, selected because of the contrast it provides to the TechnoPark project. Not only does it rely strongly on government intervention, it is also strongly gender-focused. *Kudumbashree*—which means 'prosperity of the family'—is an initiative of the Kerala State Poverty Eradication Mission (SPEM), which was launched on 1 April 1999 as a women-oriented, participatory and integrated approach to fight poverty (GOK 2003). Families below the poverty line are identified by a multi-dimensional set of indicators based on non-monetary factors. Neighbourhood Help Groups (NHG) or *ayalkootam*—a type of cooperative of 10 women—are formed as the basis for each *Kudumbashree* unit, and they then operate in a multi-functional mode: partly as an enterprise aiming to increase employment and ensure a stable income for the women, but also as micro-finance organisations in the form of thrift societies, and as self-help groups for discussion and action on issues such as health and nutrition. The enterprise side of the *Kudumbashree* units can take many different forms (for example, working in clothing production or in processing of agricultural produce). However, one of *Kudumbashree*'s most innovative aspects has been its use of ICTs to form the basis for some of its enterprises. This has been innovative in its instigation—very rarely has any attempt been made to enable poor women to make direct use of ICTs—and also in its outcome: as seen below, the ICT-based enterprises have now been operating successfully for five years, despite the fact that the majority of their work is drawn from government or other public-sector sources.

Before moving on to discuss the two main cases—TechnoPark and *Kudumbashree*—some mention must be made of the more general Kerala context. Kerala rates relatively highly—as least compared with other Indian states—on various social development indicators (Franke and Chasin 1994; Parayil 2000). As per the 2001 census, the sex ratios are in favour of women, in the sense that for every 1,000 males there are 1,066 women in Kerala; women have a greater life expectancy; and there is acceptance of the small family norm. More generally, levels of education and measures of the strength of the civil society are relatively high. Some therefore talk of Kerala as having a very particular model of development based on specific institutions, interventions and historical processes (Tornquist 2000).

While certainly recognising the specificities of any particular context, we will make two points. First, the nature of the generic Kerala context does not particularly interfere with our attempt to compare the two different types of ICT-related intervention, since it is the contextual differences between the approaches that are seen as a main determinant of differences in outcome. Second, the Kerala context has not placed it outside the mainstream in many ways. For example, the economic marginalisation of women in Kerala has drawn considerable attention as a process providing an impediment to improving the status of women (Kumar 1994; Arun and Arun 2001). As one instance, while the female work participation rate in India increased from 19.7 to 22.7 per cent between 1981 and 1991, in Kerala the ratio declined from 16.6 to 15.9 per cent (GOK 2003).

Market-Oriented and Gender-Blind Approaches to ICTs and Gender: Flexibility, Insecurity and Inequality in the TechnoPark?

The survey sample[1] was classified on the basis of work experience into three groups:

- Category A: those with more than five years' software development experience.
- Category B: those with two-five years' experience.
- Category C: those with less than two years' experience.

A summary of their views on some work-related issues is presented in Table 20.2; these and other findings are discussed below.

TABLE 20.2
Perceptions of Work Practices and Prospects in Software Production in the KeralaTechnoPark

Agreement with Statements about Software Production	Category A		Category B		Category C		Total	
	Male	Female	Male	Female	Male	Female	Male	Female
Provides increased economic prospects	18 (69%)	2 (40%)	8 (73%)	27 (63%)	10 (91%)	8 (57%)	36 (75%)	37 (60%)
Appraisal systems are crucial to performance and pay	20 (77%)	2 (40%)	6 (55%)	12 (28%)	10 (91%)	9 (64%)	36 (75%)	23 (37%)
Nature of skills in the workplace are changing	24 (92%)	4 (80%)	9 (82%)	40 (93%)	9 (82%)	10 (71%)	42 (88%)	54 (87%)
Increased flexibility and skill development are offered	12 (46%)	1 (20%)	6 (55%)	12 (28%)	10 (91%)	8 (57%)	28 (58%)	21 (34%)
Work practices affect domestic responsibilities	20 (77%)	4 (80%)	9 (82%)	40 (93%)	4 (36%)	7 (50%)	33 (69%)	51 (82%)
Require more social welfare measures	23 (88%)	3 (60%)	8 (73%)	37 (86%)	6 (54%)	8 (57%)	37 (77%)	48 (77%)
Total	**26** (54%)	**5** (8%)	**11** (23%)	**43** (69%)	**11** (23%)	**14** (23%)	**48** (44%)	**62** (56%)

Source: Arun and Arun (2002).

On the positive side, employment rates for women in the surveyed software firms (40 per cent) were high relative to software industry averages in India (c.20 per cent) (Bajpai and Sachs 2000). This seems to have been driven by a relatively gender-blind high demand for software labour caused by the competitive nature of the industry, plus high participation rates for women in Kerala in relevant education. Managers in the surveyed firms thus stated that they were keen to recruit professionals irrespective of gender, with the necessary expertise or potential in engineering and computing.

Employment in software production also brought considerable economic benefits: on an average, basic monthly salaries for both women and men were up to two or even three times higher than comparable non-ICT work categories in both private and public sectors. There was thus a general perception—rising with experience in software—that the software sector provided better economic rewards than other sectors.

However, in other ways the competitive and marketised nature of work in software had facilitated the reproduction of existing environmental gender relations (Arun and Arun 2001, 2002). Work in the software firms necessitated a particular set of competencies identified by project managers: IT skills, English language skills and client sector knowledge, as well as capacities including teamwork, ability to work under pressure, and ability to work flexibly.

For some of these skills—such as those related to technology, language, or teamwork—no immediate gender differences in relation to work practices could be detected, although women were less likely to perceive skill development opportunities within their workplace than men. However, within the notions of 'working flexibly' and 'working under pressure', there were some clear differences. Discussions showed that these notions contained within them assumptions that staff in firms offering consultancy services (the majority) would travel frequently and at any time for the upgrading and maintenance of software systems. They also contained the assumptions that staff would work long—even continuous—hours in order to finish projects on time (Arun and Arun 2001).

For women, burdened still with traditional expectations of particular roles in the family and in society, meeting those expectations was harder than it was for men. All of this had a knock-on effect since these expectations were built into appraisal and promotional systems, both of which are important determinants of the impacts of work. Due to the gendered assumptions built into competency requirements and, hence, appraisal and promotion, gender differences in attitudes towards these systems were evident. Around 75 per cent of men felt the appraisal system was fair; only about half that proportion of women agreed. Women felt that performance depended on individuals and ethos rather than objective systems of appraisal. Procedures were secretive and subjective, and therefore—in an industry where senior managers are predominantly male—the potential for both a perception and a reality of gender bias crept in. Women were more likely to rate appraisal systems as stressful, and even among category C respondents (who were generally positive towards appraisal), women were significantly less likely to view appraisal positively than men, particularly in terms of its economic benefits. Thus, while the initial basic pay rates may be relatively equal and while salaries may be high for women compared to work in other sectors, appraisal systems can still have a tendency to create a divergence between the economic benefits for men and women (Arun and Arun 2001).

The same could be seen in relation to the system of promotions, which had helped create a situation in which women were significantly under-represented at the higher echelons of software firms. For instance, despite the survey being slightly skewed towards women, only two women in the survey were project leaders, compared to 18 men.

The notions of 'working flexibly' and 'working under pressure' were inbuilt in the software sector, with assumptions that employees would be able to travel or work longer hours as necessary. Women were also less likely to perceive benefits in the notion of flexibility than men, partly because this notion was translated into systems of work on contract or temporary basis, which were only renewed when firms were able to obtain further software contracts from foreign or local clients. Flexibility was also translated into particular patterns of work. Normal working time was eight hours per day for six days a week. However, employees from all categories felt they spent more time than this in the workplace, largely because of tight project deadlines and the need to put in extra hours to meet those deadlines.

Both men and women with children and with other domestic responsibilities found these market-driven work practices stressful, particularly as teams worked in an extremely competitive way to finish projects before deadlines. However, the stress of work-life balance seemed to fall disproportionately on female rather than male software staff. As one reflection, around 82 per cent of women felt that domestic responsibilities were affected by the longer working hours, whereas only 69 per cent of men felt the same way. Respondents reported that when someone was sick at home, it was women who typically took time off from work (Arun and Arun 2001). Similarly, many women discontinued software work on becoming pregnant or having children as no support was provided, and they were unable to undertake roles in both the home and the workplace without such support.

For those women who continued (or began) working in software after having children, additional support was the major factor enabling continuity of work. In many cases, other family members, who were typically themselves women, extended this support. In other cases, though, what had been seen traditionally as a family-bound role had itself been marketised: female software staff were relying on increased levels of paid domestic help (further reducing their net income, especially because domestic labour in the city was costly), and some had resorted to paid private tuition for their children as they themselves did not have time to help the children with their schoolwork.

Finally, the implications of market-based job flexibility worried women because of their concerns about long-term income security, which is generally absent in the software sector where employees were typically expected to make their own pension or provident fund provisions (Arun and Arun 2002). One can see the triad of technology, globalisation and marketisation come together in the Indian context, driving the growth in call centres and in business process outsourcing. Eulogised as the epitome of innovation and flexibility, these business activities are mirrored by the stress, insecurities and vulnerabilities of the employed workers, reflected in concerns about high attrition rates and gender implications (Ramesh 2004).

In some organisations worldwide, some of these issues can be addressed or mitigated by the presence of particular policies and practices—such as flexible office hours, working at home, adequate maternity or paternity leave, and childcare facilities—and/or by the presence of particular institutions such as workplace unions. These can often have a disproportionately greater positive impact on women than men. Their absence in the software firms studied had a correspondingly negative gender-skewed effect. Thus, 'market-friendly' ICT initiatives operating with the forces of globalisation and competition undoubtedly brings short-term benefits to women in relation to employment and income. However, these same forces—supposedly operating in gender-blind terms—have been translated into requirements for flexibility and increased vulnerability and insecurities, along with workloads that reinforce gender inequalities.

Interventionist and Gender-Focused Approaches to ICTs and Gender: Empowerment through *Kudumbashree*'s ICT-Based Enterprises

In contrast to the TechnoPark initiative, *Kudumbashree* involved significant and direct state intervention that was gender-focused. Data gathering included substantial semi-structured interviews with four state officials involved with the project. In addition, interviews and observations were conducted with 10 members of *Kudumbashree* ICT-focused units. Analysis of statistical and qualitative data provided by *Kudumbashree* ICT units was also undertaken.

In all, 1,206 *Kudumbashree* units are now operational in a range of sectors (*Kudumbashree* 2004). As noted, all are cooperative enterprises owned, managed and operated by women from poor families, and among these units there are three types of ICT-based enterprise:

- One hundred and fifty-one are IT training units (*Vidyashree*) which provide IT training to schools;
- Eighty are data entry and digitisation units which mainly create local digital content for public (and to a lesser extent private) sector organisations, but which may also do some other IT work; and
- Five are hardware assembly/maintenance units.

Some—particularly the data entry units—are attempting to move up the value chain into basic software and Web development work. A short case example of one ICT-based unit is provided in Box 1.

Box 1: Example of a *Kudumbashree* ICT Unit

Technoworld Digital Technologies (TDT) is a *Kudumbashree* ICT unit initiated in 1999 by 10 women from below-poverty-line families who provided US$ 300 of their own money, which was matched by a US$ 3,000 bank loan and a US$ 2,500 local government subsidy used to purchase a basic computing set up. Their total asset base had risen five-fold by 2004 to a system of 22 computers, plus computing peripherals worth US$ 30,000.

The unit mainly undertakes data entry work for state government departments under the government's digitisation programme. It has undertaken work such as CD rewriting and some website maintenance, and it also provides IT training to a number of government schools. Work patterns are based on two main shifts (7.30 am to 1 pm, and 1 pm to 6.30 pm), and 40 additional staff have been employed over and above the original 10 women members, including a number of men.

Source: Interviews and TDT (2003).

As in the TechnoPark, there has been a sizeable employment impact, with the ICT units creating jobs for 2,000 women so far. Initially US$ 30 per month was set as the income for each member in the ICT units contacted, but today each member earns US$ 50. In addition to this, loans for various purposes have been approved within the groups, and surplus funds are being diverted for reinvestment in the business. Therefore, women have built these small enterprises into sustainable income livelihoods. In addition, as seen in the Box 1 case study, the *Kudumbashree* units also generate jobs and enterprise-based incomes for a significant number of other community members.

One of the TDT unit members interviewed, Janu, specifically reflected on the relative merits of *Kudumbashree* vs. TechnoPark work:

Initially my family was concerned about the financial sustainability of the project, compared to a secure paid employment in related computer firm ... they preferred that I work in the TechnoPark, but with the recent slump in the IT industry and associated insecurities related to employment has changed this, most probably the thriving nature of our project has instilled confidence in self-employment as a viable livelihood.

Most of the women contacted to date—although unemployed prior to their involvement with *Kudumbashree*—do possess high levels of human capital in terms of educational qualifications and further technical training. However, this initiative has provided them with important additional competencies, because they have had to take on roles that were traditionally the preserve of men. Another TDT member, Meena, summed up this impact: 'Of course you may earn slightly more in paid employment, but we have attained increased levels of both personal and professional skills ranging from human resource management, marketing, personal skills, not to mention the flexibility that this livelihood permits.' In this case, then, flexibility is not an external factor imposing constraints on women's lives, but something inherent and controlled by the women themselves.

There is also a genuine perception on the part of the women themselves of having been empowered, and they have at least partly achieved a break from pre-existing gender relations. This is seen partly in the capacity of women to take on all of the managerial roles required in an ICT-based enterprise, and in their ability to help the enterprises grow in both employment and asset terms. It is particularly seen in the capacity of the women to hire and manage men as employees. This empowerment has already had broader impacts, with a number of women from the units having been elected as local government councillors.

It must be recognised that the development of the *Kudumbashree* IT units has required a significant degree of institutional support from government departments, banks, other financial intermediaries, and other local organisations. This is a reminder of the downsides of interventionist ICT projects—they may rely strongly on the interventions and find it difficult to sustain themselves without ongoing intervention and support. On the other hand, one should also see this as a two-way process: the institutions have helped the development of women's enterprises, and simultaneously, those institutions have themselves developed. In particular, they feel they have now developed a much better understanding of the livelihoods and needs of women in poor communities.

Conclusions

Persistent gender disparities in developing regions such as South Asia, the Middle East and sub-Saharan Africa need to be tackled. Not surprisingly, the 2000 UN Millennium Development Goals include gender equality and empowerment as one of the eight key goals, seen both as an end and means to achieving social and economic development. There is thus a growing interest in the ways in which ICTs may be used to help deliver on this goal, but there are different approaches to using ICTs in order to achieve this.

This chapter has presented two case studies from south India that reflect two of the possible approaches: a market-oriented and gender-blind approach that enables the competitive forces to exert an effect, and a state-led approach that deliberately and concertedly intervenes with a specific focus on gender. The two cases are drawn from the same geographical area, involve women with relatively similar educational qualifications (albeit drawn to some extent from different economic groups), and involve activity that falls broadly within the ICT sector. Due to their differences, they cannot provide an exact, like-for-like comparison suitable for quantitative hypothesis testing. Instead, they provide the basis for a qualitative and exploratory investigation of the ways in which the two different approaches do or do not lead to a reproduction of the existing—and unequal—gender relations that exist within the case environment.

The first case, that of Kerala's TechnoPark, shows that 'market-friendly' ICT initiatives readily draw in the forces of globalisation and competition. This undoubtedly brings short-term benefits to women in relation to employment and income. However, these same forces—supposedly gender-blind according to managers—have been translated into requirements for flexibility and workloads that reinforce gender inequalities even in a sector which is new, and which employs a large proportion of women.

This has not been the case with the highly interventionist ICT initiative, *Kudumbashree*. Intervention certainly has its disadvantages and—despite the existence of these ICT-based enterprises for five years—questions are still raised about sustainability. However, they do illustrate the capacity for a quite different approach—one that is gender-focused, locally owned and participative—and for rather different outcomes. While the incomes generated in the short term may not be as great as those in the market-oriented approach, their stability and sustainability has been greater, with flexibility seen as an internally generated virtue rather than an externally imposed vice. The range of competencies developed is considerably greater than that seen in the market-oriented approach, because women have been allowed to break out of the traditional stereotypes of inequalities of power and responsibility that exist between notions of 'women's work' and 'men's work'. They have thus been able to make at least a start at breaking down some of the social, political and even institutional bases of gender inequality.

The interventionist approach to using ICTs for women's development—as represented here by *Kudumbashree*—is by no means a panacea. It arises from a particular set of institutional arrangements and political priorities, which cannot be wholly transplanted into other contexts. Nonetheless, the contrast in gender-related impacts between this and a market-oriented approach to ICTs within the same context is notable, suggesting that lessons can be learned for other ICT projects.

Note

1. The sample was representative in terms of firm types, level of employee experience, and most other work-related factors. However, it was not completely representative in terms of gender—56 per cent of the selected sample were women, compared to an overall average of 40 per cent of the software workforce in the Technopark.

References

Arun S. and T. Arun. 2001. 'Gender at Work within the Software Industry: An Indian Perspective', *Journal of Women and Minorities in Science and Engineering*, 7 (3).

———. 2002. 'Gender, ICT's and Development: The Case of Kerala, India', *Journal of International Development*, 14 (1): 39–50.

Bajpai N. and J. Sachs. 2000. 'India's Decade of Development. Centre for International Development', CID Working Paper Number 46. Cambridge, MA: Harvard University.

Balakrishnan, R. 2002. 'Harnessing ICTs for the Advancement of Rural Women: FAO Perspectives and Strategic Action'. Paper at UN Division for the Advancement Expert Group Meeting on Information and Communication Technologies and Their Impact on and Use as an Instrument for the Advancement and Empowerment of Women, Seoul, 11–14 November.

Bhatnagar, S.C. and R. Schware. 2000. *Information and Communication Technology in Development Cases from India*. New Delhi: Sage Publications.

Bonder, Gloria. 2002. 'From Access to Appropriation: Women and ICT Policies in Latin America and the Caribbean'. Paper at UN Division for the Advancement Expert Group Meeting on Information and Communication Technologies and Their Impact on and Use as an Instrument for the Advancement and Empowerment of Women, Seoul, 11–14 November.

Cecchini, Simone. 2002. 'Can ICT Applications Contribute to Poverty Reduction? Lessons from Rural India', World Bank Working Paper. Washington D.C: World Bank.

Cook, J. 2000. 'Flexible Employment: Implications for a Gendered Political Economy of Citizenship', in J. Cook, J. Roberts and G. Waylen (eds), *Towards a Gendered Political Economy*. London: Macmillan.

Franke R. and B. Chasin. 1994. *Kerala: Radical Reform as Development in an Indian State*. Oakland and New Delhi: Food First and Promilla.

Government of Kerala. 2003. *Economic Review*. Trivandrum: State Planning Board.

Hafkin, N. and N. Taggart. 2002. 'Gender, Information Technology and Developing Countries: An Analytic Study', Academy for Educational Development (AED) for the Office of Women in Development Bureau for Global Programmes, Field Support and Research, USAID.

Heeks, R. 2002. 'i-Development not e-Development', *Journal of International Development*, 14 (1): 1–12.

Heeks, R. and B. Nicholson. 2004. 'Software Export Success Factors and Strategies in "follower" Nations', *Competition & Change*, 8 (3): 267–303.

Huyer, Sophie and Tatjana Sikoska. 2002. 'INSTRAW Virtual Seminar Series on Gender and Information and Communication Technologies'. Paper at UN Division for the Advancement Expert Group Meeting on Information and Communication Technologies and Their Impact on and Use as an Instrument for the Advancement and Empowerment of Women, Seoul, 11–14 November.

Jorge, S.N. 2002. 'The Economics of ICT: Challenges and Practical Strategies of ICT use for Women's Economic Empowerment'. Paper at UN Division for the Advancement Expert Group Meeting on Information and Communication Technologies and Their Impact on and Use as an Instrument for the Advancement and Empowerment of Women, Seoul, 11–14 November.

Kenny, C. 2002. 'ICT for Direct Poverty Alleviation: Cost and Benefit', *Development Policy Review*, 20 (2): 20–30.

Kudumbhashree. 2004. *Concept, Organisation and Activities*. Kerala: State Poverty Eradication Mission (SPEM) (see www.kudumbhashree.org).

Kumar R. 1994. 'Development and Women's Work: Interactions and Paradoxes', *Economic and Political Weekly*, 29 (51–52): 3249–53.

Lim, Edward. 1999. 'Human Resource Development for the Information Society', *Asian Libraries*, 8 (5): 143–61.

Marcelle, G.M. 2002. 'Report from the Online Conference Conducted by the Division for the Advancement of Women'. Paper at UN Division for the Advancement Expert Group Meeting on Information and Communication Technologies and Their Impact on and Use as an Instrument for the Advancement and Empowerment of Women, Seoul, 11–14 November.

Panteli, A. et al. 1997. 'Women in the UK Software Industry: How Much Do We Know', in R. Lander and A. Alison (eds), *Women in Computing*, pp. 94–101. Exeter: Intellect Books.

Parayil, G. 2000. 'Introduction: Is Kerala's Development Experience a "Model"?', in G. Parayil (ed.), *The Development Experience: Reflections on Sustainability and Replicability*, pp. 1–15. London and New York: Zed Books.

Ramesh, Babu. 2004. 'Cybercoolies in BPO: Insecurities and Vulnerabilities of the Non-Standard Work', *Economic and Political Weekly*, 9 February.

Singhal, A. and E.M. Rogers. 2001. *India's Information Revolution: From Bullock Carts to Cyber Marts*. New Delhi: Sage Publications.

Technopark. 2004. 'TechnoPark. Harmony at Work'. Available: http:// www.technopark.org/index.

TechnoWorld Digital Technologies. 2003. *Unpublished Annual Report*. Kerala: TechnoWorld Digital Technologies.

Tierney, M. 1995. 'Negotiating a Software Career; Informal Work Practices and "the Lads" in a Software Installation', in K. Grint and R. Gill (eds), *The Gender-Technology Relation: Contemporary Theory and Research*, pp. 192–209. London: Taylor and Francis.

Tornquist, O. 2000. 'The New Popular Politics of Development: Kerala's Experience', in G. Parayil (ed.), *The Development Experience: Reflections on Sustainability and Replicability*, pp. 116–38. London: Zed Books.

Wajcman, J. 1991. *Feminism Confronts Technology*. Cambridge: Polity Press.

Wakelin, O. and B. Shadrach. 2001. *Impact Assessment of Appropriate and Innovative Technologies in Enterprise Development*, July. Enterprise Development Impact Assessment Information Services (EDAIS) http://www.enterprise-impact.org.uk/pdf/ICTs.pdf

Walby, S. 2000. 'The Restructuring of the Gendered Political Economy: Transformations in Women's Employment', in J. Cook, J. Roberts and G. Waylen (eds), *Towards a Gendered Political Economy*, pp. 165–88. London: Macmillan.

Wambui, Mercy. 2002. 'Meet the Champions: DG Interview on ICT and Gender in Africa. Development Gateway', 4 October. http://topics.developmentgateway.org/ict/sdm/previewDocument.do~activeDocumentId=346156.

Wright, R. 1997. 'Women in Computing: A Cross-National Analysis' in R. Lander and A. Adam (eds), *Women in Computing*. Exeter: Intellect.

Wright, R. and J. Jacobs. 1995. 'Male Flight from Computer Work: A New Look at Occupational Resegregation and Ghettoisation', in J.A. Jacobs (ed.), *Gender Inequality at Work*. London: Sage Publuications.

Section VI

Politics and Political Participation

Politics, being a male-dominated and complicated process, represents the final frontier in the struggle for gender equality and justice. Several issues come to mind when one thinks of politics. There is political participation such as voting and campaigning; political spaces for discussing women's issues; identity politics, namely the manipulation of symbols, history and people to achieve narrow self and national interests; political representation such as leadership issues and fair share in government bodies; and political literacy such as awareness of parties, their candidates and agendas. Identity politics and political representation has received some attention from scholars and activists, whereas issues of literacy, participation and women's issues in political discourse have yet to receive any systematic attention. Economic and political participation, and safeguarding of rights enshrined in a body of laws are considered by many feminists to be the cornerstone of women's empowerment. Limited as the view may be, much attention and energy has been directed towards correcting the lopsided picture on women's political representation. Although this may refer to decision-making power in the home, at work and in their communities, representation in the nation's highest offices is the quintessential reflection of women's power in a society. Besides, women's representation in government bodies mirror the population diversity of the nation, which is perceived as a pre-condition to an authentic democracy.

The struggle from the right to vote to becoming a leader of the nation has been a long and tedious one. The justification for women's representation includes diverse ideas like: women bring special traits and qualities to leadership, women in politics facilitate sensitivity to women's issues, ensures women's public visibility in high places, provides much-needed role models for the next generation, and so on. While some of these have proved to be unfounded, the notion of democratic principles, fair play and a basic human right keeps many women activists pushing this agenda. Besides, one-third reservation for women in the *panchayats* and local bodies has been a moral booster, making them push for greater gains at the state legislatures and parliament levels. The UNFPA's report on the State of the World Population 2005 shows that women's presence in local decision-making bodies lead to a greater social sensitivity in public policies. Similar results emerge from Scandinavian countries, which, having taken the lead in establishing greater parity in their respective parliaments, also register better performance on various human development indices. This knowledge alone—that there is a relationship between women's political representation and social development—is enough for Indian women to keep pushing for quotas at higher levels of governance.

Two related issues confronting women are their own reluctance to participate in the political process due to corruption, male domination, indifference of political parties, and a lack of opportunities and role models; the other is the creation of an enabling environment that will help women perceive this participation as a worthwhile option. A beginning has been made in addressing this pressing issue. On 8 March 2004 Mr Mohammed Fazal, the governor of Maharashtra, launched a six-month course titled 'Women and Political Governance' to train women in political know-how, the study of law, the constitution and current issues, along with personality development and communication skills.

In any case, the debate around one-third reservation has been going on since 1996. If political parties are to be true to the commitments they make at the time of elections, it would be wise for the Bill to be put to vote. In the meanwhile, research and scholarship, activism, media coverage and political pressure will keep the political discourse and spaces for women's issues alive and expanding.

The sixth and last section is **Politics and Political Participation**. In her chapter 'Gender and Nationalism: The Masculinisation of Hinduism and Female Political Participation', Sikata Banarjee illustrates the culturally constructed notions of gender, and shows how these inform loyalty to a certain idea of a gendered nation and national identity among Hindu nationalist groups and right-wing political parties. The author traces the development of the emergence of an Indian notion of masculinity based on warrior characteristics with its mirror image of passive femininity, and analyses its incorporation within the rhetoric of Hindu nationalism. Despite the masculine image of the nation, women have managed to create spaces for themselves in public political life within the differing interpretations of Hindu nationalism. Leela Kasturi's chapter, 'Greater Political Representation for Women: A Brief History of Events and Debates', outlines the history of women's struggle for political participation, the state's response to it, and the debates surrounding the issue from colonial times, through independence, to contemporary times. The highlight of the chapter is its discussion of the pros and cons of reservation for women in different deliberative bodies, and the enactment of the 73rd and 74th constitutional amendments. The chapter ends with a discussion on the stalled Women's Reservation Bill 1996. In 'The Women's Question in Contemporary Politics', Vasanthi Raman addresses three issues—the Uniform Civil Code, reservations for the Other Backward Classes, and political reservation for women—that have occupied space in the political arena. These issues have thrown up a diversity of opinions among women activists, political parties, and the common man and woman. The author argues about the futility of looking at women's issues in isolation from other social and political considerations in which these are embedded, and the opportunities it opens for the democratisation of Indian society.

TWENTY ONE

Gender and Nationalism: The Masculinisation of Hinduism and Female Political Participation*

Sikata Banarjee

Introduction

The political doctrine of nationalism is based on the idea of a nation or a people, and it usually locates an 'other' who is used to reinforce ties uniting the nation. In other words, a coherent community exists because 'we' are ethnically, linguistically, religiously, and/or ideologically distinct from 'them'. It has become a truism to acknowledge that nationalism, in the oft-quoted words of Anderson (1991), is imagined. The theoretical rooting of the process of nation-building in imagination denies malicious intent to deceive or falsify, but rather highlights the creative attempts on the part of communities to build an inter-subjective identity marked by common cultural myths, symbols, heroes and heroines.

Identity draws on the grammar of everyday life. In other words, daily communication takes place because ordinary people have a shared cultural context that forms the basis for why they feel an affinity for a certain identity and for other members who share this identity. Identities are fluid and multiple. They are fluid in that over time new interpretations of an identity may emerge. For example, the meaning of the American, Canadian and Indian nations has been renegotiated in the last 100 years within a context of changing immigration patterns and emerging identity politics. Identities are multiple in that during one particular period in a specific nation-state there may be various interpretations of identity contesting for dominance, or new readings of an identity may emerge to challenge a dominant interpretation. For example, currently the categories American, Canadian and Indian are open to multiple interpretations as minority communities resist the official, mainstream view of nation within these states. Thus, the process of imagining a nation is contested as well as being historically, socially and politically constituted.

It was not till the emergence of feminist analysis that the gendered nature of imagined political identities was uncovered and deconstructed (Blom et al. 2000; Enloe 1983, 2000; Mayar 1999; McClintock 1995; McClintock et al. 1997; Yuval-Davis and Anthias 1989). But how precisely does gender play itself out within forms of nationalisms? Usually, nationalism is gendered in that it draws on socially constructed ideas of masculinity and femininity to shape female and male participation in nation-building, as well as in the manner in which the nation is embodied in the imagination of self-professed nationalists.

Women as social reproducers of cultural forms teach children rituals and myths aimed at locating them within a specific national context; in other words, by learning about brave warriors or courageous pioneers through songs, stories, or pictures, children can develop a loyalty to a certain idea of nation (Peterson 1998). Further, motherland or nation as woman to be protected by brave citizen warriors is a common metaphor

*Originally published in *Women's Studies International Forum*, Vol. 26, No. 2, March–April 2003, pp. 167–79. Reprinted with permission from Elsevier.

of nationalisms. For example, the Marseilles implicitly calls upon soldiers to protect the French nation, embodied by the beautiful young Marianne. In a similar manner, many Indian nationalists vow to protect Bharatmata or 'Mother India'. Nation as woman also intersects the nationalist discourse through socially constructed ideas of honour. In many contexts, women symbolise national honour, and thus any act (e.g., rape) that defiles and violates women's bodies becomes a political weapon aimed at destroying the enemy nation's honour. Consequently, the point of departure of an analysis of the social construction of gender and how it informs nationalism is the relationship between woman as signifier of the nation and the warriors exhorted to defend the homeland. Further, the gendered manner in which the image of the warrior is constructed within nationalist narratives as well as the notion that women embody national honour influences to a certain extent the way women participate in nationalist politics.

The above ideas shape the gendered lens I employ to analyse the narrative of Hindu nationalism as it unfolds in contemporary India. I draw upon the role and construction of masculinity within Hindutva or Hindu nationalism in the Indian context to examine the influence of the masculinisation of nationalism on female political participation. I argue that while there are multiple interpretations of Hindu nationalism, an image central to the more militant of these views is that of a male warrior. It is important to acknowledge that the notion of militancy, within the context of Hindu nationalism, is contested. Social organisations such as the Vishwa Hindu Parishad (VHP) and Rashtriya Swayamsevak Sangh (RSS), and political parties such as the Shiv Sena and Bharatiya Janata Party (BJP) all represent some aspects of 'militant' Hindu nationalism. However, there are ideological differences among them. For example, VHP members will define their nationalist mission as conserving tangible representations of the Hindu religion (i.e., temples and idols) and participating in religious rituals, while RSS activists visualise themselves as social workers who are building a strong nation with education and discipline. Although it celebrates Hindu spirituality, protecting temples, preserving idols and celebrating Hindu rituals are not the primary features of the RSS' nationalist vision. This difference is succinctly illustrated by an RSS activist in New Delhi: 'My first allegiance is to Bharatmata and not Ram (a Hindu deity revered and used by the VHP to justify many of its militant activities)' (Interview with author, February 2002).[1] However, all these organisations do have some overlap in their ideology because of close inter-personal relations. For example, Ashok Singhal, an important VHP leader, was a member of the RSS. Similarly, many activists of the Sena, BJP and the VHP have close ties with the RSS. The idea of the Hindu warrior referred to above is one of these ideological commonalities. This image rooted in a notion of masculinity defined by attributes such as decisiveness, aggression, muscular strength, and a willingness to engage in battle, as opposed to a notion of femininity that is defined by traits such as weakness, non-violence, compassion and a willingness to compromise. This image of a warrior—reflecting (as I term it) masculine Hinduism—is the culmination of a series of gendered historical and social processes that are playing themselves out in the Indian context.

Such a process of masculinisation does not necessarily have to erase women from active nation-building; after all, one of the great contributions of feminist analysis has been the separation of sex and gender. Within feminist analysis, 'sex' refers to the physical attributes that construct a biological man or woman, while gender refers to the group of culturally endorsed traits—aggression, strength, weakness—that are deemed necessary for socially accepted 'masculine' and 'feminine' behaviour. Most feminists agree that there is no biological link between sex and gender; it is possible for women to take on 'masculine' traits and for men to take on 'feminine' traits. Thus, women may simply join the project of masculine Hinduism by taking on the masculine traits approved by this interpretation of nation, and it is indeed possible that some women may do so. However, we must not forget that when women challenge societal ideas of femininity by taking on masculine traits, they are likely to face censure and sanction from the (usually male) elite leading the project of masculinisation, who, seeing their female presence as 'diluting' the resolute masculinity of the nation, may not welcome such women. Therefore, it can be argued that women as political actors may become invisible when faced with such a process of masculinisation. In reality, however, women—within the many interpretations of Hindu nationalism—have created a space within this process, delicately negotiating their way through culturally dominant ideas of masculinity and femininity in ways that are powerful and visible.

One important way in which they do so is by taking on masculine traits to become citizen warriors defending the nation. Women become warriors to defend the nation in two ways: one, by protecting national possessions (goods and land) and two by fending off attacks on their bodies. The latter act is crucial because according to the conceit of 'nation as woman', women actually embody national honour, which can be sullied if enemy soldiers rape women. Women also intersect the masculinised discourse of Hindu nationalism by playing on their roles as wife and mother, as well as on the culturally endorsed ideas of 'wifehood' and 'motherhood'. In addition, militarism has not necessarily been a masculine trait in India. Goddesses such as Kali and Durga illustrate that violence, militarism and anger have been associated with the divine figure of the feminine. The cult of the mother goddess as a symbol of martial strength and prowess inspired some nineteenth-century nationalist movements. Indeed, the existence of multiple ways of mapping gender and militarism in India has, to a certain extent, enabled female visibility in the Hindu nationalist project. However, as the discussion below will highlight, women who participate in this project are aware of and use various strategies to deal with masculinist fears that female political presence may challenge socially prescribed gender roles, and hence weaken (read feminise) the image of the powerful (read masculine) nation.

There is a body of work analysing female participation in militant Hindu nationalism (Sarkar and Butalia 1995), as well as gender and nation in India (Chowdhury 2001; Gupta 2001; Jeffery and Basu 1998; Roy 1998; Sinha 1995). The Sarkar and Butalia book offers a collection of studies on women's activism in the Hindutva movement; however, most of the authors do not draw on current feminist theorising on gender and nation for their analysis. In fact, most authors who have discussed gendered nationalism in India have predominantly focused on colonial India, have not explored some vital aspects of the historical evolution of masculinity in colonial times and its continuity within modern India, and/or have not explicitly linked feminist theorising on gender and nation to the modern Indian context. My work adds to these studies in three ways. One, while these works do allude to ideas of masculinity, I find that many of them do not provide a detailed examination of an important cultural construct: Christian manliness. This concept forms a vital party to my study, as it plays an integral role in illuminating the masculinisation of the Hindu nation. Two, although I do discuss colonial India, this is done primarily to highlight the historical evolution of masculine Hinduism. The main focus of my study is on gender and nation in modern Hindutva. Three, by explicitly locating the gendered Hindu nation within contemporary feminist theorising on nationalism, I hope to provide cultural depth to current work on gender and nation.

I will approach my argument in three parts. One, I will briefly trace the historical evolution of masculine Hinduism by emphasising the gendered impact of British colonialism on Indian society. Two, I will highlight masculine Hinduism in modern ideas of Hindu nationalism, and three, I will analyse the relationship between the masculinisation of Hindu nationalism and female participation. My argument will be based on the following organisations espousing Hindu nationalism—the BJP, the dominant party in the coalition governing India in 2003; the Shiv Sena, a political party based in the Indian state of Maharashtra; the socio-cultural organisations VHP and the RSS; and the women's wings of each organisation: the Mahila Morcha, the Mahila Agadhi, the Sadhavi Shakti Parishad, and the Rashtriya Sevika Samiti, respectively. It is important to acknowledge that although these organisations may not represent the entire spectrum of Hindu nationalist activism in India, currently they are the most visible and powerful.

Historical Evolution of Hegemonic Masculinity in India

Jeffords describes masculinity as a 'set of images, values, interests, and activities held important to the successful achievement of male adulthood' (Jeffords 1989: xiii). Femininity is the corresponding set of values and images held important for female adulthood. Although there may be many competing images and values of male and female adulthood in society, there is always a hegemonic definition of masculinity/femininity. Since the nineteenth-century, aggression and militarism have formed an integral part of British hegemonic masculinity (Connell 1995: 213). Conversely, being not aggressive and not militaristic were ideas associated with the opposing notion of hegemonic femininity. In this chapter, I use the terms hegemonic masculinity and femininity to refer to these interpretations of manhood and womanhood.

Research has linked hegemonic masculinity in Britain to the institutions of empire (Alderson 1998; Chowdhury 2001; Gilmore 1996; Gupta 2001; Hall 1994; Inden 1990; Roper and Tosh 1991; Sinha 1995; Vance 1985). Colonial administrators scoffed at Indian men for being weak and non-martial. In the words of Edward Said (1978: 207), such criticism can be related to a process of feminisation wherein the Orient (non-western colonies in South Asia and the Middle East) was created as the weak, irrational, non-martial 'other', in contrast to a rational, strong, martial European 'self'. Ronald Inden (1990: 17) alludes to the European masculine hero who would conquer and create order out of the feminised chaos that was India. Said and Inden both imply that the feminisation of the Orient encompassed a disparagement of Arab and Indian men, who were conquered because they were effeminate and seen as effeminate because they were conquered. Their conquered status constructed them as not muscular, not aggressive, and not skilled in militarism, which were values associated with hegemonic femininity. Thus, gender was a politically salient aspect of colonialism. More specifically, the idea of Christian manliness formed the bridge connecting Empire and gender, both in terms of emphasising the British need to guide Indians (who were not aware of these values) and presenting India as the ideal venue for the practice of Christian manhood.

Christian Manliness and Empire

In 1866, the Religious Tract Society of London published a monograph titled 'Christian Manliness: A Book of Examples and Principles for Young Men'. In this publication, the author outlined several characteristics necessary for constructing an ideal Christian man: faith, personal will to decide, resolve, fidelity, courage, energy, perseverance, strength, gentleness, self-mastery and prudence. The title as well as the language of the tract very clearly assumed a male audience (Religious Tract Society 1866: 95).

This text made a clear distinction between mere muscular Christianity (conceptually almost identical to the ideas underlying hegemonic masculinity) and Christian manliness, which included physical strength/martial prowess, but also went beyond mere 'muscularity' to emphasise moral dimensions. The British saw Indian men as feminised beings in need of instruction and exposure to the moral and physical dimensions of Christian manhood. Norman Vance (1985: 10) suggests that '"manliness" may relate to physical vigor and prowess ... or to patriotic and military qualities, or to the traditions of chivalry, or to a variety of moral qualities ranging from ... general benevolence to the most awe inspiring moral rigor ...'. This multifaceted definition of manhood partly constructed the gendered lens the British used to look at India and its male inhabitants. Although colonial references to Indians commonly conflated effeminacy and lack of martial prowess in the tradition of hegemonic masculinity, critical observations about Indian manhood were also based on the multi-dimensional notion of masculinity underlying Christian manliness. For example, the martial ability of some groups of Indian men may be acknowledged, yet simultaneously these same groups would be condemned for being 'unmanly' because of a lack of patriotic fervor and/or honesty.

The intersection of Christian manliness and Empire was not an isolated cultural phenomenon. The monograph published by the Religious Tract Society refers to British colonial administrators and military leaders such as Warren Hastings, Henry Lawrence and General Henry Havelock as living examples of Christian manliness. General Havelock was a favourite icon representing Christian heroism, and books such as *General Havelock and Christian Soldiership* by the Rev. Frederick S. Williams (1858) and *General Havelock or the Christian Soldier* by Lt. Col. B.D.W. Ramsay (1871) celebrated his valour. Further, adventure books written for British schoolboys incorporated the message of Christian manliness by celebrating its alliance with imperialism, while simultaneously emphasising patriotism and military courage as potent traits in this intersection (Green 1980).

In addition, well-known English intellectuals—Charles Kingsley and William Pater—debated these ideas in public fora (Hall 1994; Vance 1985), while colonial military historians classified Indian soldiers using ideas of both hegemonic masculinity (or muscular Christianity) and the multifaceted notion of Christian manliness. Sikh men were praised as being 'martial' and manly in the sense of both physical and moral rigor. However, some groups fulfilled the criteria of physical hardiness but fell short of the moral criteria of manliness. For example, Shivaji and the Marathas, who were able warriors and harassed colonial troops, occupied much of the British imagination, but even as historians spoke of their prowess in battle, these achievements were denigrated by references to the moral laxity of Maratha troops (Tone 1818; Waring 1810). Such comments are relevant to this narrative because the Hindu nationalist groups forming the basis of this analysis focus on Shivaji as a fundamental icon of Hindu martial power, and celebrate the military history of the Marathas. In other words, an aspect of the masculinising project of Hindu nationalism includes reclaiming and celebrating warriors who were dismissed as 'unmanly' by the colonial rulers.

A popular image of Indian effeminacy was the Bengali babu or clerk, who worked in the vast imperial bureaucracies (Alter 1994). Lord Macaulay, a highly placed colonial administrator, stated:

> The physical organization of the Bengalee is feeble even to effeminacy .... During many ages he has been trampled upon by men of bolder and more hardy breeds. (Lord 1931: 109–10)

Other colonial observers made similar claims:

> We do not speak of the martial races of Britain as distinct from the non-martial, nor of Germany, nor of France. But in India we speak of the martial races as a thing apart and because the mass of people have neither martial aptitude nor physical courage .... (MacMunn 1933: 2)

In British eyes, the greatest proof that Indian men could not live up to the standards embedded in ideas of Christian manhood was that 'more than one hundred and thirty million people' in a 'region of Asia equal in extent to the whole of Europe (exclusive of Russia)' was ruled by 'forty thousand British' (Duff 1840: 22).

Indian Responses to British Gendered Observations

Certain sections of the Indian elite internalised this British colonial criticism. They began to ridicule themselves for their weaknesses and inability to defend their motherland. Indian elite, including B.C. Chatterjee, Swami Vivekananda and V.D. Savarkar, called upon Indians to be men, and wrest their motherland from the British with force if necessary. *Vandemataram*—the theme song of past and present Hindu nationalism—published in Chatterjee's influential nationalist novel *Anandamath* (1882) valorised martial prowess:

Who hath said thou art weak in thy lands,
When the swords flash out in twice seventy million hands
And seventy million voices roar
Thy dreadful name from shore to shore?
With many strengths who art mighty and stored,
To thee I call, Mother and Lord. (quoted in Hingle 1999: 79)

The following speeches by Vivekananda illustrate the intense desire to create an indigenous Indian model of manhood built on ideas of hegemonic masculinity:

I will go into a thousand hells cheerfully if I can rouse my countrymen, immersed in tamas (darkness), to stand on their own feet and be men (emphasis mine) .... (Vivekananda in Rahbar 1995: 181)

What we want is muscles of iron and nerves of steel, inside which dwells a mind of the same material as that of which the thunderbolt is made. Strength, manhood, Kshatra-Virya [warrior courage] .... We have wept long enough. No more weeping, but stand on your feet and be men. It is man-making religion we want. It is man-making theories that we want. It is man-making education all around that we want ... take away my weakness, take away unmanliness, and make me a man. (Vivekananda in Jyotirmayananda 1986: 29)

This obsession with manliness carried over into an admiration for India's conquerors, the Muslims and the British. Vivekananda often proclaimed that he wanted to build an India with a Muslim body and a Vedantist brain, and maintained that no race understood as the British did 'what should be the glory of a man' (Kakar 1978: 175). The Swami called upon the Hindu men of India to assert their masculinity. To do so they must emulate the ideas of hegemonic masculinity. He implicitly placed in opposition the values of hegemonic masculinity and a femininity defined by weakness, indecisiveness and a lack of virility. In his view, those men who embodied these feminine attributes were and are Hinduism's greatest enemies. Vivekananda, it should be noted, did not always define 'manhood' as merely muscular (read physical strength and power), but also tried to create a multifaceted interpretation by combining moral values—honesty, tolerance, chivalry (also found in Christian manliness)—with Hindu spirituality. Savarkar, in his influential books *The Indian War of Independence* (1909), *Hindu Pad Padashahi* (1925, A history of the Maratha empire), and *Hindutva* (1923), expressed similar views of Hindu masculinity. Thus, Hinduism was reconfigured to embrace the ideals of hegemonic masculinity.

Note that I am not arguing for an unbroken mechanistic continuity between the nineteenth-century and contemporary Hindu nationalism. In other words, I am not assuming that the leaders of the present Hindu nationalist parties/organisations read Savarkar, Vivekananda and Chatterjee, and self-consciously apply these ideas. Rather, because these thinkers introduced such ideas of masculinity into the common cultural milieu, these ideas were available for use by Hindu nationalist organisations, regardless of whether the leaders and activists were cognisant of the origin of such thoughts. In the politics of contemporary Hindu nationalist parties and organisations, masculinity has become codified in terms of a warrior tradition; the multifaceted idea of manhood has been erased. As argued in the opening paragraph, the creation of a nationalist political doctrine usually includes the construction of an 'other' who is seen as the enemy of the citizen warriors defending the nation as woman. Before independence, this 'other', for certain proponents of a Hindu nationalism constructed with ideas of hegemonic masculinity, was the British. But now that India is independent, followers of this brand of Hindu nationalism have chosen another enemy: Islam.

As we move on to the examination of how masculine Hinduism manifests itself in contemporary Hindu nationalism, it is important to note that members of a nation constructed with ideas of hegemonic masculinity described by symbols of war and warriorhood can easily justify physical aggression against 'the other'. Indeed, this is the case in some interpretations of Hindu nationalism. Day-to-day political participation is often equated with being a warrior, and measured by involvement in violence against the enemy. If so, then how do women negotiate a space in this context of masculinisation and potential aggression? The next sections address this question by outlining the relationship between contemporary Hindu nationalism, masculine Hinduism and women.

Contemporary Hindu Nationalism and Masculinity

The RSS (founded in 1925), the VHP (1964), the Shiv Sena (1966) and the BJP (1980) constitute the four major voices of Hindu nationalism in India. These organisations do not necessarily share an identical definition of Hindutva. However, all of these groups would, with minor modifications, accept the following outlines of Hindutva. Briefly, a true India is a Hindu India and minorities (read Muslims) can live in India only if they accept Hindu cultural dominance. All who identify themselves as Indians must accept the cultural primacy of Hindu heroes such as Ram and Shivaji. Any refusal to do so will represent an act of disrespect towards India. Frequently, minority communities (mostly Muslims; Christians have recently been added to the list) are perceived as being anti-national because of their allegiance to religious prophets who are seen as being outside the context of Hindu India. More moderate proponents of Hindutva will perhaps emphasise ideas of Hindu pride and cultural dominance and downplay notions of aggression against perceived enemies of the Hindu nation, while radical followers will agitate for acts of war against the 'other' or 'enemy' of the Hindu nation, be it Islam or Christianity.

M.S. Golwalkar, an influential RSS leader, gives the following account of the organisation's mission:

Therefore, when we say that our nation should be taken to the pinnacle of glory, it also means that people should be made alert, organized, and powerful. After all, nations can stand only upon the solid foundation of their organized strength .... Then, what are the qualities required of individuals who will form the living limbs of such an organized strength? .... The first thing is invincible physical strength. We have to be so strong that none in the whole world will be able to overawe and subdue us. For that, we require strong and healthy bodies .... Swami Vivekananda used to say, 'I want men with muscles of iron and nerves of steel.' ... he would thunder, 'That is not bhakti [faith in or devotion to the divine]. That is nervous weakness. Don't sit down and weep like little girls.' What do we see today when we look at ourselves in a mirror? Do we find any sign of manliness and strength? .... The present-day fashion of our young men of decorating the skin and discarding the sinews must be given up and they should, with proper exercises and healthy habits, develop strong bodies capable of ... undergoing all the hardships of life with good cheer. (Golwalkar 1981: 66)

Golwalkar's reference to Vivekananda highlights the continuity of ideas of a reconfigured Hindu masculinity. A BJP manifesto delineates the nation that these masculine heroes are striving for:

Diversity is an inseparable part of India's past and present national tradition. The post-independence tendency to reject all ancient Indian wisdom in political life led to all pre-independence values and symbols—be it the idea of spiritual nationalism expounded by Swami Vivekananda ... or the soul stirring 'Vande Mataram' song ... as unsecular and unacceptable. The BJP rejects this attitude .... (www.bjp.org% 252Fmanifesto)

In the above excerpt from the BJP election manifesto, the reference to the 'post-independence tendency to reject all ancient Indian wisdom' reveals this party's belief that contemporary India has moved away from its Hindu cultural background (represented by Swami Vivekananda and *Vandemataram*). The manifesto goes on to interpret nationalism as being based on the idea of 'one nation, one people, and one culture'. One may ask—what will be the basis of this monolithic nation? Given the BJP's celebration of Hinduism, it may be argued that such a configuration of nationalism signifies the subordination of non-Hindu traditions to a monolithic Hindu nation constructed by the BJP.

The Sena's outline of its aims and objectives proclaims:

We are Hindustanis and therefore, Hindu is the belief of our party. We love Hindustan more than we love ourselves. Therefore, Shiv Sena's fight against anti-national forces shall be ceaseless ... it is Shivsena's [sic] belief that whatever may be our religion, whatever our form of worship, our culture is Hindu. We are a national force. Hence, we say with pride that we are Hindus. (www.shivsena.org)

These statements very clearly outline a nationalism rooted in Hinduism. The distinction that the Sena attempts to make between Hinduism as a religion and as a nationalism is not very clear, and is open to slip-page between the two. For example, it is not clear what a Hindu nation emptied of the dominance of the Hindu religion looks like, or what comprise the markers separating Hindu culture and Hindu religion. The Sena is also vague as to why people who are not Hindus by religion should pledge allegiance to a Hindu nation and say 'with pride' that they are Hindus.

The VHP also draws on a similar vision of a Hindu nation as it aggressively asserts its right to protect Hindu temples, rituals and idols. To this end, it has led the struggle to build a temple in the north Indian town of Ayodhya to celebrate the birthplace of the Hindu deity Ram. Young male VHP activists flooded this town in February and March 2002, aggressively agitating for the construction of this temple. The threat of potential violence led to heightened security and increased military presence. The VHP's militant tactics and stance in this endeavour highlights the use of a very simple and aggressive interpretation of Hindu masculinity.

The RSS, Shiv Sena, VHP and BJP use religious symbols and icons to facilitate the spread of masculine Hinduism. It is important to begin with the RSS as this is the oldest of the three, and has heavily influenced the others in their interpretation of Hindu nationalism and masculine Hinduism. Indeed, most BJP politicians and VHP activists were members of the RSS during their youth, while the Shiv Sena divides its party along the same organisational lines into shakhas or branches, a nomenclature borrowed directly from the RSS. When the RSS began its first training camps in 1927, young boys and men were encouraged to learn sword fighting, use javelins, and become proficient in the use of daggers. They saluted saffron flags (commonly believed to be associated with Hindu warriors). Their method of training and organisation was distinctly martial, and highlighted their beliefs that male Hindu warriors were being trained to defend Bharatmata. This method continues in its present training camps.

Elements of masculine Hinduism can also be found in the BJP's iconography. The BJP's reconfiguration of Ram (mythic hero, commonly believed to be the incarnation of the god Vishnu) most dramatically represents this emerging masculinist imagery. Most traditional Indian depictions of Ram are androgynous and unmuscled; his curves are definitely feminine in terms of a British gender dichotomy based on hegemonic masculinity (Kapur 1993: 86). Further, he is ethereal and unfocused, and not really engaged in the tensions of the human world (ibid.: 88). However, recently Ram has become aggressive and masculine, engaged in the process of human desires and violence (ibid.: 105). In BJP posters, Ram's muscles ripple as he towers over a Hindu temple, protecting it against aggressors. The disengaged, androgynous, divine Ram has become a masculine Hindu warrior. The BJP has seized upon the figure of the newly configured warrior Ram as an icon representing an armed masculinity, which demands that Hindu anger against national enemies should be expressed through, among other ways, aggressive action.

A male Shiv Sena leader makes the following observation during the Hindu-Muslim riots of 1992/1993:

At Radhabhai chawl they [Muslims] bolted the door from the outside and set it on fire. And all our [Hindu] children, families, they were roasted. When this hit the headlines the next day ... my wife told me, 'I should offer you bangles now. What are we? In our own country, Hindus are being burnt.' (Interview with author, January 1993)

Note that in the above quotation, the male leader describes Hindu weakness in the face of Muslim aggression with feminine images, i.e., bangles offered by his wife. The offer of bangles or jewellery worn by women is an insult to Hindu men, because it states that they have failed to protect their people. This equation of weakness with the feminine and strength with the masculine places this interpretation of masculinity squarely within the parameters of hegemonic masculinity.

Another Shiv Sena leader examines the idea of a Hindu nation:

... India is our country, whoever is against India—Hindu or Muslim—hang him. India and Pakistan play a cricket game. The Indian team loses and Pakistan wins. Firecrackers go off in Bhendi Bazaar. Bhendi Bazaar [is a] Muslim area. That means what? Their loyalty is not for India but for Pakistan. They have no right to live in India .... This country is Hindustan. It is Hindustan of the Hindus. What is wrong with calling it Hindustan? Like Pakistan which is a Muslim country. This is a country which belongs to Hindus ... riots will increase in the future. (interview with author, December 1992)

This leader begins by adopting a view of nationalism that seems to accept both Hindus and Muslims. However, by emphasising India as Hindustan or land of the Hindus and portraying Muslims as foreigners and necessarily traitors to India (read Hindustan), he clearly demonstrates his bias. The language of aggression and potential violence is implicit in his view. If one examines both these quotations, the first during Hindu-Muslim riots and the second in the absence of such violence, it is reasonable to infer that if the imagined Hindu nation is in danger, it is appropriate for Hindu warriors to defend it.

The politics of the Shiv Sena exhorts the Hindu nation to arise, and Sena activists paint the walls of cities in which they are influential with the snarling tiger emblem of the party. Statues and portraits of a muscular Shivaji holding a bow and arrow are found in their party offices. In all Shiv Sena-sponsored religious processions, the young male participants carry tridents. Their icons—the warrior Shivaji, weapons, the tiger— all represent aggressive militarism. The tiger symbol of the Sena presents a provocative cultural reading in terms of masculine Hinduism. Bhavani, the traditional patron goddess of Shivaji, is usually associated with the tiger. Notice how in the Sena's symbolic configuration the goddess (a female representation of martial prowess) has disappeared, and the tiger stands alone. Finally, the Shiv Sena activists refer to themselves as *sainik*s or warriors. The word *sena* means army. The facades of local Shiv Sena offices imitate historic Hindu forts. The saffron flag of Hindu warriors flies from the painted spires, proclaiming war on the enemies of Hinduism. The VHP's headquarters in Delhi also flies the saffron flag of Hinduism, and its activists speak passionately about the need to protect the Hindu religion. During the 1992/1993 Hindu-Muslim riots in India as well as in the recent (2002) riot in Gujarat, young VHP activists were armed, angry and aggressively projected themselves as warriors fighting for the Hindu nation.

Most of the policy-makers as well as the foot soldiers of the RSS, BJP, VHP and the Shiv Sena are men, the icons they use are resolutely masculinised, and the message they disseminate focuses on being 'masculine' warriors in politics. The position of women within this context of masculinisation and militarism becomes contested and ambiguous. Where do women fit in? Do they take on masculine traits to become 'masculinised warriors' or do they disappear completely from this political arena based on masculine Hinduism?

Masculinisation and Women in the Hindu Nation

As mentioned in the opening paragraphs, women enter the political landscape of Hindu nationalism as passive symbols of the nation as woman, as well as active participants in the roles of masculinised warrior, wife and mother.

Nation as Woman

'... Motherland is a woman's body and as such is ever in danger of violation—by "foreign" males. To defend her frontiers and her honor requires relentless vigilance and the sacrifice of countless citizen warriors ...' (Peterson 1998: 44).

In the RSS and BJP offices, it is common to see India depicted as a beautiful woman. Not only do masculine Hindus—the citizen warriors referred to above—protect the nation as woman, but they are also forever on guard, defending the honour of Hindu women who are in danger of being defiled by the enemy of the Hindu nation: the Muslims. V.D. Savarkar—discussed in the historical section and one of the early articulators of masculine Hinduism—clearly linked nation as woman, honour and rape:

> The souls of ... millions of aggrieved women might have perhaps said, 'Do not forget ... Shivaji Maharaj [the role of Shivaji as a symbol of masculine Hinduism has been discussed above] ... the unutterable atrocities committed on us by ... Muslim noblemen and thousands others, big and small .... Once they (i.e., the Muslim noblemen) are haunted with this dreadful apprehension that Muslim women, too, stand in the same predicament in case the Hindus win, the future Muslim conquerors will never dare think of such molestation of Hindu women .... It was the suicidal Hindu idea of chivalry to women which saved the Muslim women .... Their womanhood became their shield ...'. (Savarkar, quoted in Agarwal 1995: 51–52)

By adopting the voice of dishonoured Indian women, Savarkar is implicitly rebuking Hindu men for not being manly enough to protect their women and, hence, their national honour. A rather chilly implication of this rebuke is the notion of the 'suicidal Hindu idea of chivalry'—it seems Savarkar wants masculine Hindu men to rape Muslim women in order to vindicate the dishonour of Hindu womanhood. Indeed, during the 1992/1993 Hindu-Muslim riots, rape of Muslim women by a few militant proponents of Hindu nationalists was justified using this language of vindication and dishonour (Agarwal 1995), and 'rape' has also been used as a rhetorical device to call Hindu warriors to the defence of their nation. For example, the rape of Hindu women during the periods of Islamic rule in India and during Hindu-Muslim riots in the wake of the Indian subcontinent's partition into Pakistan and India are repeatedly used by the BJP and RSS in their speeches to urge masculine Hindu warriors to protect their motherland and their women (Basu 1995; Butalia 1995).

Women as Active Participants in Political Identity Struggles

But passive in the role of nation as woman, is not the only model of the intersection of female identity and masculine Hinduism within the Hindu nationalist narrative. Women themselves can become citizen warriors by adopting the traits of masculine Hinduism, but they must do so cautiously by constantly emphasising that such an action will not challenge the present gendered structure of society. The Rashtriya Sevika Samiti (literally 'Organisation of Women in Service to the Nation', and hereafter Samiti) was founded in 1936 by Lakshmibai Kelkar as the women's wing of the RSS. According to an official publication of the Samiti, Kelkar persuaded Dr Hedgewar, the founder of the RSS, that women needed to be a part of nation-building because 'Men and women are both wings of the society. Unless both were strong, the society will not progress properly' (Rai 1996: 24).

In April 1998, I attended a large meeting of the Samiti in Mumbai (formerly Bombay). The Mumbai meeting took place in a local school. At the back of the room where we met, a large poster depicted a beautiful woman embodying India, and the lion by the woman's side marked her as the goddess Durga. For an hour I watched young girls brandish wooden daggers and practice wrestling moves. The juxtaposition of India imagined as a warrior goddess and young Indian women performing martial moves eloquently illustrated the female representation of the citizen warrior. It must be noted that these young women were not really practised in martial arts; rather, their moves were stylised, almost a dance, symbolising the Samiti's emphasis on the need for Hindu women to cultivate their ability to protect themselves and their nation.

The immediate reason given for a woman's need to protect herself is the fear of rape. The Samiti's official publications (Rai 1996: 23) emphasise this rationale by re-telling a well-known story about founder Lakshmibai Kelkar. It seems that just after the founding of the Samiti, she was horrified to hear of a Hindu woman who was raped in public while her husband and other men stood by. Given the Samiti's link to the narrative of Hindu nationalism and their depiction of nation as woman, I assumed that the rapists were to be demonised as 'the other', the enemy of the Hindu nation, i.e., Muslims who dared to pollute Indian womanhood (and hence nation as woman) while cowardly Hindu men looked on. The publication does not mention the religion of the assailants but the Samiti members, in response to my question, claimed that they were actually Hindu. So the Samiti claims that women must also embody traits of hegemonic masculinity—martial prowess and physical hardiness—not only to protect Mother India, but also to prevent the Hindu sons of Mother India from attacking her daughters. If Samiti members are then questioned as to whether this means women occupy a rather ambiguous position within a masculinised Hindu nationalism, they provide evasive answers, not willing to address this potentially contentious issue. This, it seems to me, is an indication of the tensions that may arise when women claim to take on 'masculine' traits within the context of a militaristic and aggressive Hindu nationalism.

While the Samiti encourages young women to perform martial arts, the Mahila Agadhi and Mahila Morcha show their reverence for the feminine representation of martial prowess by valorising divine figures such as Durga and historical icons such as the Rani (Queen) of Jhansi, who rode to battle against the British, as role models for female behaviour, performing rituals celebrating warrior goddesses, and prominently displaying statues and portraits of these female figures in their offices. But does this celebration of feminine warriorhood actually lead to women taking up arms or participating in violence? The 1992/1993 Hindu-Muslim riots, which followed in the wake of the demolition of a Muslim religious structure, provide a response to this query.

The BJP, claiming to represent the voices of Hindu nationalism, demanded that a mosque built on the ruins of an ancient temple celebrating the birthplace of Lord Ram and occupying sacred Hindu ground should be torn down to make way for a new Hindu temple. It had been agitating around this issue throughout the 1980s and in December 1992, its political agitation culminated in the destruction of this building. This event unleashed a wave of violence that swept throughout the country, as Hindus clashed with Muslims. The politics of Hindu nationalism—i.e., the need to protect the Hindu nation from attack by the 'the other'—provided the context for these riots. The city of Mumbai—a stronghold of the Shiv Sena—was one of the most violent conflict zones. During this period of turmoil, a feminist activist commented in a daily newspaper on the feminisation of violence: According to the *Telegraph* (1993), a most disturbing aspect of the killings was that women were some of the most aggressive participants. Other scholars agreed with this assessment: '... large numbers of women have been extremely active and visible, not only in the rallies and campaigns but even in the actual episodes of violent attacks against Muslims' (Sarkar 1995: 189–91). Given the nature of such participation, it becomes reasonable to conjecture that certain women in a specific situation have indeed taken on traits of masculine Hinduism to enter into the fray as citizen warriors pro-tecting the Hindu nation. However, this feminisation of violence is of course only one model of active female participation.

Sadhavi Rithambhara,[2] a prominent female proponent of Hindu nationalism, provides another model of female participation, not a foot soldier in direct combat, but an eloquent speaker, celebrating the idea of masculine Hinduism. Although she does not take up arms or embody martial prowess, she can by no means be dismissed as a 'cheerleader' for the 'real' male warriors. The power of the sadhavi's words equals that of a Hindu warrior's weapons. The prefix 'sadhavi' refers to the female counterpart of the male sadhu, who, in the Hindu world view, has renounced a worldly life to search for personal salvation and enlight-enment. The sadhavi's message to Hindus is not one of tolerance and non-violence. Rather, it focuses on lamenting the fact that Hindu passivity has enabled Muslims to enjoy special privileges at the expense of Hindus, and eloquently arguing that the time has now come for Hindu warriors to demand their rights and protect their nation:

> I mean to say that the long-suffering Hindu is being called a religious zealot today .... The Muslims got their Pakistan. Even in a mutilated India, they have special rights .... What do we have? An India with its arms cut off. An India where restrictions are placed on our festivals, where our processions are always in danger of attack .... (Kakar 1995: 207)

It is interesting to note that even though she does not use a nation-as-woman metaphor to explicitly describe India, she very clearly embodies the nation by invoking ideas of mutilation as she refers to the partition of India by the British (supposedly in response to Muslim demands). Embodying the nation enables masculine Hindu warriors to more effectively imagine a defence of the Hindu nation, as 'what' they are protecting is no longer abstract or lifeless, but rather becomes alive. She warns the Muslims,

> Live among us like the son of a human being and we will respectfully call you 'uncle'. But if you want to behave like the son of Babar [the founder of the Mughal empire in India. The Mughals were Muslim] then the Hindu youth will deal with as Rana Pratap and Chatrapati Shivaji did with your forefathers.

[Rana Pratap, like Shivaji, is a Hindu warrior celebrated by Hindu nationalists as a popular symbol of Hindu resistance.] (Kakar 1995: 205)

Her speeches continue in this vein, skillfully invoking Ram, Shivaji, ideas of a glorious Hindu nation, casting Muslim/Islam as the 'other' of this nation, and calling upon masculine Hindu warriors to defend their nation.

Sadhavi Rithambhara, along with two other important female participants of the Hindu nationalist movement—Uma Bharati[3] and Vijayraje Scindia[4]—offer an interesting interpretation of the intersection of masculine Hinduism and female identity. All three of these women are celibate. Scindia is a widow, and Uma Bharati, like Rithambhara, is a sadhavi, a female renunciate (Basu 1995: 161). Widowhood implies celibacy because in certain interpretations of Hinduism, women who are widowed cannot marry again, and since sexual relations are allowed only within the confines of matrimony, a widow is, by definition, celibate. All three women also wear plain clothing with minimal make-up and jewellery.

Malathi de Alwis (1998: 266) describes women warriors fighting for the liberation of the Tamil nation with the Liberation Tigers of Tamil Elam (or LTTE) as 'masculinised virgin warriors', wherein '... the LTTE woman's internal body is expected to be "pure", "chaste" and "virginal"', while 'her outer body is marked as masculine; her hair is cut short and she wears a beret, combat fatigues, boots ... but no makeup or jewellery...'. Now one should not push this parallel too far. Obviously, none of the aforementioned Indian women participants are actually involved in armed combat, but a case can be made that they are indeed a part of a metaphorical battle for the Hindu nation. It seems to me that given the masculinisation of the Hindu nationalist narrative and the fact that these three prominent icons are celibate, do not have flowing locks, have eschewed traditional outer Hindu markings of the married woman (vermillion, bangles), and are reaching for prominence in a masculine political landscape, de Alwis' model does become pertinent.

This image of virgin warrior becomes even more potent with the founding in 1998 of a women's organisation affiliated with the VHP: the Sadhavi Shakti Parishad or the Organisation of Sadhavi Power (hereafter Parishad). All active members are celibate female renunciates with short hair, no jewellery, and dressed in saffron robes. Their activities include speaking in public about the need to protect the Hindu nation (many use the fiery speeches of Sadhavi Rithambhara as a model), organising gatherings where young women are trained in martial arts and taught about the ideals of Indian womanhood, and coordinating the worship of Hindu mother goddesses in public spaces. In order to enter the masculinised reality of Hindu nationalism, many women are symbolically and practically shedding outer markers of their femininity.

Women as Mother

In a nationalist narrative constructed with ideas of masculine Hinduism, women do not necessarily have to take on masculine traits or erase tangible signs of their femininity to become political actors. They can also play complementary roles which draw on their socially constructed gender roles based on ideas of hegemonic femininity, motherhood, for example. This focus on 'woman as mother' also circumvents any potential criticism of their perceived violation of societally prescribed gender roles as they enter nationalist politics. The ideals of motherhood and women's role as mother intersect with the nation-building process in three ways. One, women have the physical ability to bear children, especially sons, who will become the citizen soldiers ready to defend the nation as woman. Two, as primary caregivers of children, they socialise future warriors by passing on culture, rituals and nationalist myths to the next generation. Finally, the concept of 'motherhood' assumes that women are able to play multiple roles, and this can prove useful in shaping political rhetoric aimed at bringing women into the nationalist conflict. An official publication of the Samiti uses all three methods to legitimise the nationalist work of the Samiti:

> Even though the Sevikas [members of the Samiti] were not after power, if the occasion demanded they must have the capacity to become able administrators. It is mother who can train the children to shoulder any responsibility in life. Hence, she herself had to be an able administrator as she is the commander of her home .... 'Motherhood' has vast dimensions, it extends beyond the family to town, society, country, nation .... (Rai 1996: 45)

Here, the role of women as both cultural and biological reproducers is emphasised, as is their ability to transfer skills learned in the private sphere as mothers to the public sphere of nation-building.

The BJP draws on a similar policy: 'We can begin to see the extent to which the traditional discourse of women as matri shakti [maternal power] infuses the BJP's policies' (Kapur and Cossman 1995: 100). Evidence for the Shiv Sena women's use of ideas of maternal power is found not so much in written texts, but rather in the fact that many of the publicly performed rituals of the Shiv Sena women's wing celebrate female strength in the nation as deriving from women's role as mothers. In the narrative of Hindu nationalism, mothers of historic warriors are as celebrated as their sons. For example, Jijabai, Shivaji's mother, who encouraged her son to resist the injustice of Muslim rule and protect the Hindu nation provides a powerful model of Hindu motherhood, as does Lakshmibai, Rani of Jhansi, who fell in battle defending her infant son's kingdom. The Parishad is also eloquent in its defence of the power of motherhood. In Matrimahashakti (2000) or 'Great Maternal Power', a published collection of essays by sadhavis and other women who support the Parishad, most authors celebrate women's role as mothers, who nurture proper citizens and warriors. For example, in an essay titled 'Mothers are Divine', Sadhavi Nayasargika Giri (2000) argues that although the great Hindu warrior hero Pratap Singh's father was a coward who lost his fort and hid in the surrounding Aravalli mountains, his mother—a great and learned lady—taught her son the value of nationalism, martial prowess and courage, thus enabling Pratap Singh to become one of the greatest heroes of the Hindu nation.

However, the Parishad's relationship with motherhood is rather ambiguous. It should be noted that even though the Parishad emphasises that women's greatest contribution to the nation is her ability to nurture citizens and warriors, the sadhavis, because of their celibacy, have denied themselves this power. Consequently, through their persons and actions, sadhavis are declaring that female strength in a nation can come in forms other than that of the mother. The model of virgin warrior is central to this ambiguity; women can fight within the masculinised landscape as long as their 'femininity' is erased (this erasure is represented, for example, by the image of the sadhavi). However, if women wish to enter this space without shedding the cultural symbols that mark them as female, then they must do so in socially prescribed roles such as that of the mother. But as the Parishad and the Samiti highlight, even within such gendered limits women can become visible and effective in the Hindu nationalist struggle.

To sum up, gender is politically salient in Hindutva. As warriors and mothers women have entered its masculinist political landscape; the nation is imagined as a woman and national honour is located in women's bodies.

Conclusion

A series of gendered historical and social factors influenced the reconfiguration of Hinduism with ideas of hegemonic masculinity, and, as a result of this process, the image of a physically hardy warrior became central to some visions of the modern Hindu nation. This chapter interrogates the manner in which women and ideas of femininity intersect this process of masculinisation. Indian women have created a space for themselves within this masculinist narrative by casting themselves as warriors, utilising ideas of nation as woman, and focusing on women's role as mother as well as on culturally endorsed ideals of motherhood. Indian women have been forced to negotiate a delicate balance between seizing a space for themselves, and reassuring the male elite that activities playing out in this area will not radically retool culturally dominant ideas of masculinity and femininity in Indian society. This is demonstrated by the Samiti's unwillingness to pursue the implications of their view that Indian women face violence from all men (Hindu and Muslim), the sadhavis erasure of all outer markers of their femininity to gain access to a masculine political landscape, and the women's organisations' celebration of motherhood.

Notes

1. All interviewees have requested anonymity. These interviews were conducted during various research trips to India in the last decade.
2. Sadhavi Rithambhara is prominent as a spokesperson for the Vishwa Hindu Parishad.
3. Uma Bharati is presently a BJP Member of Parliament and a member of the cabinet.
4. Vijayraje Scindia died in 2001 after a long career in politics, most recently as a BJP Member of Parliament.

References

Agarwal, Purshottam. 1995. 'Surat, Savarkar and Draupadi: Legitimising Rape as a Political Weapon', in Tanika Sarkar and Urvashi Butalia (eds), *Women and the Hindu Right*, pp. 29–57. New Delhi: Kali for Women.

Alderson, David. 1998. *Mansex Fine: Religion, Manliness and Imperialism in Nineteenth Century British Culture*. Manchester: Manchester University Press.

Alter, Joseph. 1994. 'Celibacy, Sexuality, and the Transformation of Gender into Nationalism in North India', *Journal of Asian Studies*, 53: 45–63.

Anderson, Benedict. 1991. *Imagined Communities*. London: Verso.

Basu, Amrita. 1995. 'Feminism Inverted: The Gendered Imagery and Real Women of Hindu Nationalism', in Tanika Sarkar and Urvashi Butalia (eds), *Women and the Hindu Right*, pp. 158–80. New Delhi: Kali for Women.

Blom, Ida, Catherine Hall and Karen Hagemann. 2000. *Gendered Nation: Nationalism and Gender Order in the Nineteenth Century*. New York: New York University Press.

Butalia, Urvashi. 1995. 'Muslims and Hindus, Men and Women: Communal Stereotypes and the Partition of India', in Tanika Sarkar and Urvashi Butalia (eds), *Women and the Hindu Right*, pp. 58–81. New Delhi: Kali for Women.

Chowdhury, Indira, 2001. *The Fragile Hero and Virile History: Gender and the Politics of Culture in Colonial Bengal*. Delhi: Oxford University Press.

Connell, Robert W. 1995. *Masculinities*. Berkeley, CA: University of California Press.

de Alwis, Malathi. 1998. 'Moral Mothers and Stalwart Sons: Reading Binaries in a Time of War', in Lois Ann Lorentzen and Jennifer Turpin (eds), *The Woman and War Reader*, pp. 217–54. New York: New York University Press.

Duff, Alexander. 1840. *India and India Missions Including Sketches of the Gigantic System of Hinduism both in Theory and Practice*. Edinburgh: John Johnstone.

Enloe, Cynthia. 1983. *Does Khaki become You: The Militarisation of Women's Lives*. London: Pluto.

———. 2000. *Maneuvers: The International Politics of Militarizing Women's Lives*. Berkeley. CA: University of California Press.

Gilmore, David. 1996. *Manhood in the Making: Cultural Concepts of Masculinity*. New Haven: Yale University Press.

Giri, Sadhavi Nayasargika. 2000. 'Mothers are Divine', in *Matrimahashakti*. New Delhi: Vishwa Hindu Parishad.

Golwalkar, Madhav Sadashiv. 1981. *Bunch of Thoughts*. Bangalore: Jagarana Prakashan.

Green, Martin. 1980. *Dreams of Adventure and Deeds of Empire*. London: Routledge.

Gupta, Charu. 2001. *Sexuality, Obscenity, Community: Women, Muslims, and the Hindu Public in Colonial India*. New Delhi: Permanent Black.

Hall, Donald (ed.). 1994. *Muscular Christianity: Embodying the Victorian Age*. Cambridge: Cambridge University Press.

Hingle, G.S. 1999. *Hindutva Reawakened*. New Delhi: Vikas.

Inden, Ronald. 1990. *Imagining India*. Cambridge, MA: Basil Blackwell.

Jeffery, Patricia and Amrita Basu (eds). 1998. *Appropriating Gender: Women's Activism and Politicized Religion in South Asia*, pp. 3–14. New York: Routledge.

Jeffords, Susan. 1989. *The Remasculization of America: Gender and the Vietnam War*. Bloomington, IN: University of Indiana Press.

Jyotirmayananda. 1986. *Vivekananda: His Gospel of Man-making with a Garland of Tributes and a Chronicle of His Life and Times with Pictures*. Pondicherry: All India Press.

Kakar, Sudhir. 1978. *Inner-world: Psycho-analytic Study of Childhood and Society in India*. Delhi: Oxford University Press.

———. 1995. *The Colours of Violence*. New Delhi: Viking.

Kapur, Anuradha. 1993. 'Deity to Crusader: The Changing Iconography of Ram', in Gyanendra Pandey, (ed.), *Hindus and Others: The Question of Identity in India Today*, pp. 74–109. Delhi: Oxford University Press.

Kapur, Ratna and Brenda Cossman. 1995. 'Communalising Gender, Engendering Community: Women, Legal Discourse and the Saffron Agenda', in Tanika Sarkar and Urvashi Butalia (eds), *Women and the Hindu Right*. pp. 82–120. New Delhi: Kali for Women.

Lord, John (ed.) 1931. *Macaulay's Essays on Lord Clive and Warren Hastings*. London: Ginn and Company.

MacMunn, George. 1933. *The Martial Races of India*. London: Sampson, Low, Marston & Co.

Matrimahashakti. 2000. New Delhi: Vishwa Hindu Parishad.

Mayar, Tamar. 1999. *Gender Ironies of Nationalism: Sexing the Nation*. New York: Routledge.

McClintock, Anne. 1995. *Imperial Leather: Race, Gender, and Sexuality in the Colonial Context*. New York: Routledge.

McClintock, Anne, Amir Mufti and Ella Shohat. 1997. *Dangerous Liaisons: Gender, Nation, and Post Colonial Perspectives*. Minneapolis, MN: University of Minnesota Press.

Peterson, V. Spike. 1998. 'Gendered Nationalism: Reproducing 'Us' versus 'Them', in Lois Ann Lorentzen and Jennifer Turpin (eds), *The Woman and War Reader*, pp. 41–49. New York: New York University Press.

Rahbar, Hansraj. 1995. *Vivekananda: The Warrior Saint*. New Delhi: Farsight.

Rai, Rajani. 1996. *Life Sketch of Vandaniya Mausiji*. Nagpur: Sevika Prakashan.

Ramsay, B.D.W. 1871. *General Havelock or the Christian Soldier*. London: Halchards.

Religious Tract Society. 1866. *Christian Manliness: A Book of Examples and Principles for Young Men*. London: Religious Tract Society.

Roper, Michael and John Tosh (eds). 1991. *Manful Assertions: Masculinities in Britain since 1800*. New York: Routledge.

Roy, Parama. 1998. *Indian Traffic: Identities in Question in Colonial and Post-colonial India*. Berkeley, CA: University of California Press.

Said, Edward. 1978. *Orientalism*. New York: Pantheon.

Sarkar, Tanika. 1995. 'Heroic, Women, Mother Goddesses: Family and Organisation in Hindutva Politics', in Tanika Sarkar and Urvashi Butalia (eds), *Women and the Hindu Right*, pp. 181–215. New Delhi: Kali for Women.

Sarkar, Tanika and Urvashi Butalia. 1995. *Women and the Hindu Right*. New Delhi: Kali for Women.

Sinha, Mrinalini. 1995. *Colonial Masculinity: The 'Manly' Englishman and the 'effeminate Bengali' in the Late Nineteenth Century*. Manchester: Manchester University Press.

Tone, William Henry. 1818. *Illustrations of Some Institutions of the Mahratta People*. Calcutta: D. Lankheet Times Press.

Vance, Norman. 1985. *The Sinews of the Spirit: The Ideal of Christian Manliness in Victorian Literature and Religious Thought*. Cambridge: Cambridge University Press.

Waring, Edward Scott. 1810. *A History of the Mahrattas*. London: John Richardson.

Williams, Frederick S. 1858. *General Havelock and Christian Soldiership*. London: Judd & Glass.

Yuval-Davis, Nira and Floya Anthias (eds). 1989. *Woman–Nation–State*. London: Macmillan Press.

TWENTY TWO

Greater Political Representation for Women: A Brief History of Events and Debates*

Leela Kasturi

Introduction

The promise of complete equality for all under a democratic constitution and the demolition of formal barriers to such equality do not in themselves bring about social, political and economic change. The task is much more difficult in a stratified plural society such as India, where age-old inequalities based on gender, caste, ethnicity, entrenched privilege, and vested interests are deeply rooted. A culture that has been shaped by patriarchal values and soured by biases, particularly against women, lower castes and ethnic groups, cannot fail to reflect such prejudices in daily life and state policies. Consequently, certain sections of society, weaker or different, but anxious for a share in power, resources and political space, are marginalised. These disadvantaged groups need to be supported by affirmative action, or what in India is commonly referred to as reservation, and compensatory or protective legislation to bring them into the mainstream. The question here, however, is on whether it is relevant to introduce legislation for reservation of seats in decision-making bodies to enhance the participation of women in the public sphere.

As a means of increasing the representation of special categories, subsets, and specific communities/ groups, reservation is not necessarily associated with the principles of equality and democracy, or clothed in the pure intent of affirmative action. It is a measure that can be used for political ends, the formation of special categories itself being a political act with political consequences. Moreover, the selection of claimant groups for special empowering privileges, however justified, often draws hostility from many quarters, including pre-existing vested interests and dominant groups, unless the share of the newly categorised is negligible. In these circumstances such representatives function as mere tokens. Even as tokens, though, some outstanding leaders have been effective. With the right kind of political support the potential of even a few can be maximised. Numerical strength, however, is vital in the long run.

Reservation of seats for women in legislatures also needs to be understood in specific historical contexts and cultures. Many countries have experimented with such measures with varying degrees of success and sincerity.[1] In India, as a measure of supportive reform for women in the formal political arena, reservation of seats in all circumstances has been inextricably entwined with issues of equality, merit, equal opportunity, social and gender justice on the one hand, and the political context on the other. The issue has been debated by women's organisations for more than 70 years.

At the turn of the century, women's organisations in colonial India led by educated elite women engineered a quantum jump for Indian women: from being objects of male-directed social reform to becoming aspirants for the 'modern' principle of equality. The record of this battle is impressive by any standards (Forbes 1996). Time and again, in their struggle for political representation, the leadership of the major organisations

*Originally published in *Asian Journal of Women's Studies*, Vol. 4, No. 4, 1998, pp. 9–37.

argued against reservation as, in their view, it violated the ideal of equality. Quite obviously there were other strong voices of dissent expressed by proponents of reservation, as well as political factors which rendered choices for different sections of women far more complex than expected. After independence, assured of equal status by a forward-looking constitution, Indian women once again found themselves embroiled in this issue in the late 1980s. Their inferior political status over the last five decades compelled them to rethink their attitudes towards reservation. The debate, which is predominantly in favour of it now, is the direct result of women's experiences in independent India. In the next two sections I shall briefly describe the historical positions taken by the women's movement before and after independence. It is seen that the issue of women's rights can rarely be essentialised in terms of patriarchy alone. Gender acts as an important variable in social and political structures, movements and events. Under numerous circumstances, gender has been sought to be used as a symbol by different forces representing different philosophies at any given time. The 81st Constitution Amendment (for women's reservation) Bill (WRB) is then assessed in the light of the debate that followed its introduction in Parliament.

Women's Struggle for Political Rights 1917–47

Nineteenth-century social reform, intent on the preservation of Indian, mainly Hindu, culture, religion and identity, focused on women as symbols of the regeneration of values lost in a society debilitated under the onslaught of colonialism.[2] By the turn of the century social reform on behalf of women had all but disappeared, and it was claimed that the women's question had been 'resolved' by the nationalists. The 'domestic realm' was now viewed as a sacred space beyond the reach of the colonial state, but women continued to be seen and used as symbols of the community and nation (Chatterjee 1989; Forbes 1978; Kumar 1993: 32–95).

By the early years of the twentieth century, despite the complexity of the relation between gender, community and nation, women became activists on their own behalf and began to develop their own social and political agenda. At the same time the close connection between organised women and the freedom movement was never in doubt. Furthermore, the connection between women's oppression and imperialism, and between the struggle for women's rights and the struggle for national freedom was made by a substantial percentage of the women involved in the struggles (Agnew 1979; Chattopadhyay 1983; Forbes 1982, 1996; Jayawardena 1986; Kasturi and Mazumdar 1994; Liddle and Joshi 1986; Pearson 1979).

The public discourse on women encompassed debates on social reform, women's education, their ideal role and place, and their political and legal status. Elite and educated middle-class women of all communities, from reformist and liberal families, socially conservative rather than overtly feminist, came together in the 'extended domestic space' provided by women's associations and organisations to pursue their public activities on behalf of women and children (Minault 1981). They asked for governmental measures for better education, healthcare, protective legislation, and civil and political rights within the framework of a 'social feminist' ideology (Forbes 1996: 189).

Speaking on behalf of all Indian women, organised women articulated views and opinions on all matters, affecting their counterparts in every political arena at the time at both regional and national levels.[3] Gender difference and the ideals associated with Indian womanhood were used as arguments to support: (*a*) activities directed at the improvement of women's position; and (*b*) an enlarged role for women in public life. This stand fitted well into the discourse of nationalism, wherein women were constructed as the 'mothers of the nation' (Agnew 1979: 116, n. 5, quoting Sarojini Naidu; Chaudhuri 1993: 121–23; Everett 1979: 88, quoting Annie Besant; Kumar 1993/97: 50, n. 85, quoting Sarojini Naidu).

The three major organisations identified with the fledgling women's movement were the Women's Indian Association (WIA), founded in 1917; the All India Women's Conference (AIWC), established in 1927; and the National Council of Women in India (NCWI), organised in 1925. Their insistence on women's full and equal participation through enfranchisement and representation was *because* of the difference between men and women. Women alone were seen as best equipped to present their case for social reform (Chaudhuri 1993: 151–52; Everett 1979: 109; Forbes 1979: 5). This view appealed to all sections of the Indian elite, a factor that contributed to the entry of women into public life. It was also felt that women's franchise would ensure Hindu–Muslim unity through the solidarity of the women of India (Everett 1979: 104–5, n. 6, quoting Sarojini Naidu).

The campaigns for women's political representation went through two phases: between 1917 and 1928 the issues focused upon were women's enfranchisement per se, and their eligibility for membership in the legislatures. In 1917 the first women's franchise delegation waited upon the Montagu–Chelmsford Committee, asking for the extension of franchise to women and their right to representation. In 1919 a deputation of women also went to London to give evidence, and to argue for women's right to vote before a Joint Select Committee on the Government of India Bill. Between 1928 and 1937 the issue in focus was the liberalisation of the terms of enfranchisement and increased representation of women. By 1921 women's demand for political and civil rights had received the support of the nationalist leadership. By 1929 a limited female electorate was granted the right to vote and to sit in legislatures on the same basis as men in the British provinces, and in some enlightened Indian states (Everett 1979: 107–9).

Initially, there were no firm objections to special expedients such as nomination and reserved seats for women. Women were not often successful in direct election, and these methods of 'getting women there' were at first deemed inconsequential, women's presence in legislatures being seen as the prime necessity. Several worthy women were appointed to various positions in boards and councils. Between 1917 and 1930 women's groups did not oppose the nomination and reserved seats for women (Everett 1979: 111; Forbes 1979: 8–9, 14).

In 1930 the British nominated Radhabai Subbaroyan and Begum Shah Nawaz to the First Round Table Conference (1930), of which the WIA disapproved. These two representatives were willing to accept special franchise for women as a temporary measure, the wifehood qualification (enfranchisement, under special programmes or schemes, of women who wives of men qualified to vote) for women to vote, and reserved seats for women in legislatures, but not on a communal basis (Everett 1979: 116–17; Forbes 1979: 11). This position represented the short-term reformist approach of the women's uplift faction, composed of disparate groups of women whose proposals and compromises found favour with the numerous commissions and committees appointed to examine the question of women's franchise.[4] The other more nationalistic women's groups, whose members were important figures in the freedom struggle, persisted in asking for equal status. Around this time, when the national movement gathered momentum and the political scenario grew more complex, the three women's organisations (the WIA, AIWC and NCWI) were drawn into increasingly nationalist positions in the Indian National Congress' (or Congress) fold.[5] Thus, two distinct approaches to the women's question were now discernible.

Nineteen thirty-one was a significant year for Indian women. The role played by women in the Gandhian mass political movements won the appreciation of nationalist leaders, and inspired the Indian National Congress to pass the Fundamental Rights Resolution at the Karachi Session in April 1931. With this gesture the Congress pledged itself to universal adult franchise and women's equality in independent India.[6] In the same year the Congress party renewed its opposition to separate communal electorates (Everett 1979: 115). Joint electorates were based on the concept of democratic representation, but Muslim leaders feared marginalisation in the new constitutional scheme (Chaudhuri 1993: 168–74).

Drawing support from the Congress declarations, the three main women's organisations grew more political in the 1930s, and firmly adopted an equal rights approach—now identified with Congress nationalism—to the women's question in general, and to the issues of women's enfranchisement and representation in particular. The imposition of qualifications such as literacy, property and spousehood on voters was considered undemocratic and meaningless (AIWC 1933–34: 182). They argued steadfastly in favour of universal adult franchise, opposed the wifehood qualification, and rejected outright the devices of reservation of seats for women and separate communal electorates. Women had to be recognised as citizens and as an 'integral part of the body politic' (Asaf Ali n.d.: 357–58). In the context of increased communal tension, both wings of the women's movement appeared jointly as a very responsible political force (Everett 1979: 118). Yet, after the Communal Award[7] was announced in 1932, Muslim women supported separate (communal) electorates and disassociated themselves (Chaudhuri 1993: 155–58; Deutsch 1998; Forbes 1979: 18–19).

In 1931 the three organisations sent an official Memorandum on the Status of Indian Women in the New Constitution demanding adult franchise (direct elections), and condemned any special franchise, reservation or separate electorate (WIA Report 1931–32: 6–7 cited in Forbes 1979: 11). Along with the Memorandum, Sarojini Naidu and Begum Shah Nawaz jointly wrote a letter to the Prime Minister of Great Britain, stating that 'to seek any form of preferential treatment would be to violate the integrity of the universal demand of Indian women for "absolute" equality of political status'. They further recommended: 'there should be no sex discrimination either against or in favour of women under the new Constitution'. The AIWC protested that nomination, reservation of seats, and co-option in any sphere of activity was 'pernicious and humiliating' (AIWC 1933–34: 182).

Gandhi was pleased with the women's organisations' refusal to accept special favours and concessions (Stri Dharma XV, November 1931: 66, cited in Forbes 1979: 14). However, many women's groups felt that reserved seats for women and nomination were necessary and acceptable as it was not possible to contest otherwise, particularly at the local level (ibid.: 13–14; 17–18). They were generally critical of the equal rights wing of the women's movement (Everett 1979). This division of opinion persisted until 1947, when British rule ended.[8]

Women voters' turnout had increased over the second phase (1928–37), but women's organisations could not mobilise voters in sufficient numbers. In the 1937 elections they found they had to struggle to get elected, and realised that party support was absolutely essential and that social causes were not popular (Forbes 1979: 19–20). Fifty-six women entered the legislatures: 41 in reserved seats, 10 in unreserved seats, and five were nominated, the majority being from the Congress (Everett 1979: 138). Women were pleased with these victories, but even a staunchly equal rights organisation such as the WIA, rather than be left out, spoke at this point in favour of nomination of women to councils, boards and commissions (WIA Report 1936–38: 27, cited in Forbes 1979: 20). Yet, the shift in favour of equal rights, accompanied by a wider ideological vision for men, women and national development, continued to dominate.

In 1939 a Women's Sub-Committee, appointed under the National Planning Committee to examine the role of Indian women and make recommendations on their place in the planned economy of a free India, also rejected reserved seats for women, and endorsed the 1931 Fundamental Rights Resolution of the Congress (Women's Sub-Committee 1947: 36–38). In 1946, the AIWC announced an Indian Women's Charter of Rights, which called for gender equality as a basis of citizenship and demanded improvements in women's education, health, work, property rights, and place in the family (Chaudhuri 1993: 184–85; Krishnaraj 1995: 59–66). In the same year (1946) women's representatives sat in the Constituent Assembly, which was assigned the task of framing a constitution for the newly emerging nation-state. They did not fail to exert their influence, advise, and speak up on issues concerning women, women's rights and human rights (Parasher 1992: 222).

In the colonial context, when revivalism, nationalism and communalism were overlapping responses to British rule, the progress made by women's organisations depended on two factors—the interests of the government and support from the nationalist elites, who could not always be relied upon. The unity or disunity of women's groups was a lesser factor. While a conservative wing of the women's movement was pragmatic, the other wing upheld the long-term goal of equality, which ultimately became a principle of the Indian Constitution. Reservation was opted for by the former in the interests of women and children, and also in the belief that being left out altogether would be a worse option considering the odds against women's participation. The latter was 'ready to forego all temporary favours for obtaining a few seats in the legislatures' for the establishment of a principle, which would contribute to the general well-being of the nation (AIWC 1931–32). It is clear that over a period of 30 years the nascent women's movement had travelled from the demand for women's franchise within colonial constitutional schemes, to the assertion that women were equally entitled, and on the same basis as men, to the full rights of citizenship. Although women stood as a distinct unified political group with special interests and were largely opposed to division along communal lines, they held two conflicting positions on the key issues of reservation and special electorates.

The exchanges between the colonial power, the nationalists, and the urban women's organisations did not fully take into account the activities and potential of the masses of underprivileged, working-class, and peasant women. The issue of reservation was a far cry for them then, and it would take nearly 50 years for their needs and power to be recognised. The ordinary masses of Indian women, too, qualified for a right to political equality, as they showed a determination to struggle not only as members of organisations and in the national movement, but in the various tribal and peasant struggles that took place under the rubric of nationalism during this period (Kasturi 1991–92; Sen 1985; Sen 1990; Singha Roy 1992; Stree Shakti Sanghatana 1989).

Indian Women in Political Life: 1947–94

The women's movement in the pre-Independence period went into a decline, partly out of a sense of euphoria and confidence that gender justice would be served by the new nation-state, especially since equality had been guaranteed by the Constitution. Studies commissioned by the Committee on the Status of Women in India (CSWI) in the 1970s (Mazumdar 1979) and more recent research (Kasturi and Mazumdar 1994) have reported the withdrawal of politically active women into social work and welfare activities. The Hindu Code Bill, passed piecemeal in the late 1950s, represented their last battleground (Everett 1979: 141–89; Parasher 1992). There was no political activity of any consequence among or by women until the early 1970s, when nation-wide disillusionment with the social and economic conditions of life had definitely set in. In different contexts and classes, women had begun to express their protests in a great variety of forms, in an attempt to question the state and begin a struggle. There were protests against price rise in western India, agitation for land rights and workers' rights, agrarian struggles, tribal and ethnic movements, anti-liquor and literacy campaigns, and movements for preserving forests and the environment (Calman 1992; Everett 1981; Gandhi and Shah 1991; Kumar 1993/97; Omvedt 1975; Sen 1990; Sharma 1989). In 1972, SEWA (Self-Employed Women's Association) was formed to help unorganised women workers, who were among the most maltreated labour groups in the country. Collectives of such women are now able to deal with exploitative employers and market conditions (Rose 1992).

The Report of the CSWI, published in 1974, has documented precisely how and where the state had failed women since independence. Development and modernisation had not benefited women, except for a small percentage of elite and middle-class women, with the mass of women being left out. The government's policies and programmes contributed little to advancing women's status or protecting their fundamental rights (Government of India 1974).

By the early 1970s India was in political ferment, with swelling numbers of women voicing their nightmares and demands. In 1975, the political emergency clamped down by Indira Gandhi was preceded by and precipitated a range of popular movements including the campaign for 'Total Revolution', led by Jayaprakash Narayan in 1974 (Selbourne 1985). The need to sustain an overall struggle culminated in women's mobilisation at the grassroots and in urban centres, alongside ordinary peoples' social and political movements and struggles, which were based on caste, class, region and sector. A socially and politically violent and oppressive scenario compelled women to question not only their gendered existence, but also the basic premises of the society they were living in. The issue of democracy was easily linked to the women's question. Now it was recognised that redress required more than legal change and education, the two-pronged strategies of the earlier phase of the women's movement. The rebirth of the women's movement is linked with the failure of state policies, growing economic disparities, the deterioration of democratic institutions, and the rise of several kinds of fundamentalisms, leading to a confrontation between all classes of Indian women and the state (Agnihotri and Mazumdar 1995). In this second wave of the movement, the battles were for social, political, economic and gender equality, democracy and justice. Overall the movement has questioned the entire range of cultural, social, political and economic systems—old and new—which continue to reinforce inequalities. All these have contributed to the lowering of women's status and well-being, the main indicators of which are violence against women from birth to death, their low economic and political status, marginalisation, discrimination, exploitation and disempowerment.

Obviously women's cause is greatly disadvantaged if, in addition to all this, women's representation in decision-making bodies remains marginal. In the colonial context, forceful petition politics and the hard work of some effective women in legislatures and committees did indeed lead to limited gains for some sections of Indian women. In independent India, however, belying the expectations of women who placed faith in the Constitution, relatively few women have entered the upper echelons of power or decision-making bodies. Nor have they been allowed to contribute to lasting change in a major way. The reasons for this are well known: social attitudes towards women in mainstream politics are hostile and prejudiced; electoral processes, apart from being expensive, are unpleasant for them. Furthermore, political parties of all hues, regardless of their public stance, do not nurture women's participation.

Discriminatory patterns in women's political participation have endured for 50 years. These patterns include low numbers of women as contestants and winners in electoral processes, low representation of women in political parties, the exclusion of women from decision-making bodies of all types, and the total absence of lower-class and rural women in the political process (Government of India 1974: 283–305). Thus, although women vote in substantial numbers almost equal to that of men, in positions of power and as decision-makers they have figured at only around 8 per cent or less in the national and state legislatures. There has been a steady decline in the percentage of women in provincial and national legislatures. Even so, their presence compares favourably with that of their counterparts elsewhere, except in Scandinavia (Inter-Parliamentary Union 1997: 16). In other words, Indian women, alongside women almost everywhere, face identical problems in the public domain (Nelson and Chowdhury 1997).

It is widely acknowledged that all political parties—left, right, liberal, or class-based—are responsible for not allowing the emergence of women as candidates and leaders. There is no dearth of politically capable women, many of whom are articulate, experienced in political affairs, and knowledgeable about grassroots issues. However, they are either not selected as candidates, or many do not wish to enter politics under prevailing conditions. The few who have reached Parliament are manipulated and obstructed by party imperatives on gender issues. The solidarity of women legislators is under constant challenge. The strength of the women's movement has not been matched by the presence of a critical mass of women within the structures of power to offer resistance, or engage effectively in the struggle for women's rights.

For and Against Reservation (1974–94)

During the International Decade for Women, reservation of places for women in elective bodies and public services emerged as a major issue. The debate was kicked off by the Report of the Committee for the Status of Women in India (CSWI). Arguments in favour of reservation came from experts, scholars and many groups of women, who felt that women's dwindling presence in legislatures and councils needed improvement with the help of the law. Reservation was considered a useful supportive measure, but only for a limited period. Women legislators, however, did not agree, echoing the views of a substantial section of the earlier women's movement. In their view, reservation would be 'a retrograde step' that would contradict the equality principle enshrined in the Constitution, and would equate all women with socially backward communities, which was not entirely true. Reservation, therefore, was opposed even as a transitional measure. There were two notes of dissent, but the majority view prevailed (Government of India 1974: 303, 355–57). Recently, one of the dissenters has expressed regret about the majority view having won the day, and has stated that the CSWI 'should have paid greater heed to the issue of reservation which was necessary for the health of Indian democracy' (Mazumdar 1997: 15). There was less opposition to the idea of reservation for women in local bodies, a practice for which some precedents were already in place (ibid.). Provisions for reservation through election, co-option and nomination already existed in most state legislations governing the constitution of local bodies, and political parties tended to go along with these views.

Having weighed the matter, the CSWI rejected reservation for women in state assemblies and Parliament on several grounds, summarised as follows:

(i)   Separate constituencies would narrow women's outlook and, so far, they have served as representatives of the people;

(ii) Women's interests ought not to be viewed as separate from those of the classes, groups, and strata in society to which they belong. The minority argument cannot be applied to women, as they are not a community but a category, and they share problems with the men of their own groups, locality and community;

(iii) Reservation may lead to a similar demand from other interest groups and communities, threatening national integration; and

(iv) Once granted, it might be difficult to withdraw the privilege of reservation. (Government of India 1974: 303–4).

Nevertheless, concurring with some political parties, the CSWI felt that reservation would be useful and effective, even imperative, in representative structures at the local level (referred to as *panchayati raj* institutions or PRI).[9] For development and change in the status of rural women, more than token representation would be required. Therefore, the CSWI strongly recommended the establishment of statutory women's *panchayats* (village councils) at the village level, which were to function not as parallel structures, but as an integral part of the *panchayati raj* structure. These should have autonomy and resources for the management and administration of welfare and development programmes for women and children. Women's enhanced statutory status would then have a direct impact on their participation and general status (Government of India 1974: 304–5). The CSWI also recommended reservation for women in municipalities and in permanent committees, in order to initiate and supervise programmes for women's welfare and development. Further, it recommended that women be included in all important committees/commissions or delegations that are appointed to examine socio-economic problems (ibid.: 305). It also suggested that political parties should offer a minimum percentage of seats to women in the state assemblies and Parliament—of about 15 per cent, to begin with (ibid.).

The recommendations of the CSWI regarding the reservation of seats for women in local bodies, ignored for many years by successive governments and political parties, finally received attention in the 1980s, signifying a shift from their earlier stand. The revival of the debate is a sign of the recognition of the rising importance of women's votes; the vitality of the women's movement at regional and national levels; and the role of women in popular movements. The perception of rural women's participation as a critical instrument of rural development was acknowledged in the Sixth Five Year Plan, and in the approach paper of the Seventh Five Year Plan. One of the priorities of the women's movement is the incorporation of peasant/rural women's views and initiatives into state policy. It was felt that representation through reservation would finally break barriers to participation, as social, economic and political processes are inter-linked. Political parties introduced women's concerns in their manifestos, and began to support reservation for women from the late 1980s onwards. In response to the recommendations of the Ashok Mehta Committee (Government of India 1978) on *panchayati raj* institutions, a few states (Karnataka, West Bengal, Andhra Pradesh and Maharashtra) took the lead in rejuvenating local government and increasing the level of women's participation. Failing direct election, provision was made in most of the state enactments for the nomination or co-option of suitable women.

In 1988, the National Perspective Plan (NPP) suggested the 30 per cent formula for women's representation in government committees/commissions and local bodies. It recommended reservation in executive positions and a higher level of representation of Scheduled Castes, Scheduled Tribes, and women of weaker sections of society in all local bodies. It also called for a certain percentage of constituencies to be declared exclusively for women, and suggested that 50 per cent of all grassroots functionaries should be women (Government of India 1988: 164–65). An earlier draft of the NPP, while advocating 30 per cent reservation of seats for women in local government, had anticipated that in the initial stages these would or might have to be filled by nomination and co-option. However, in their critique of the draft NPP, national women's organisations rejected these measures as subversive of democracy (NPP 1988: 152), and emphasised direct elections to reserved seats, and not nomination. The organisations also called for an increased participation of women in the State Assemblies and Parliament, but did not demand reservation at this point. The final version of the NPP did recommend that reserved seats be filled by election, but reservation of seats for women at the two higher levels (in state and national legislatures) was not mentioned.

After the dust had settled, tangible proposals for the reservation of seats for women in PRI materialised in 1989, as a result of which the 64th Constitution Amendment Bill, providing for 30 per cent reservation for women in PRI, was introduced in Parliament. It was passed by the Lok Sabha (House of the People), but defeated in the Rajya Sabha (the Upper House) by a very narrow margin on the ground that the union government was interfering with the jurisdiction of the states on this area/subject. Realising the political potential of such a measure, the Congress Party under Rajiv Gandhi announced 30 per cent reservation of seats for women in *panchayati raj* institutions. But later, unanimous support on the part of the major political parties led to the enactment of the 73rd and 74th Constitution Amendments (1992), which ensured that 33 $\frac{1}{3}$ per cent seats in *panchayati raj* institutions and municipalities would be filled by women through direct election.

By April 1993, all the states of India had ratified the amendments and by April 1994, the states had passed the necessary legislation for amending their *Panchayat* Acts in line with the constitutional amendments. With one-third reservation for women in general constituencies as well as in constituencies reserved for Scheduled Castes and Tribes, all to be filled by election, the amendments reflected the spirit of the demand of the women's movement. The support of all parties is perhaps the most critical evidence of the impact the movement had had on the parties and the political system as a whole. It is also an acknowledgement that the empowerment of women at the grassroots is essential to the rejuvenation of Indian democracy. Currently the impact of women's participation in local government is a subject of keen interest and study for activists, researchers, political parties and bureaucrats.

The current wave of the women's movement has gone beyond the goal of gender equality—the main thrust of the equal rights wing of the women's movement in the colonial context. The women's movement now contains women of all classes, suffering from different kinds of inequality and deprivation. The emphasis now is on social transformation. The entry of a sizeable percentage of women into decision-making bodies would radically improve the empowerment of women, and enable them to affect public policy and introduce women's perspectives (CWDS 1995). As one means to achieve this, the women's movement has supported the right of women to be represented as a category by a constitutional mandate in the state assemblies and the Lok Sabha. In 1995, seven national women's organisations went on record to state that reserved seats for women in all elected bodies at all levels have to be filled through election and not nomination (*Towards Beijing* 1995).

The 81st Constitution Amendment: The Women's Reservation Bill (WRB) 1996–99

In their 1996 election manifestos, virtually every major political party promised reservation for women at state and national levels. This could be understood as lip service and political correctness on the eve of the elections, with an eye on women's votes. Be that as it may, the critical factor was the support of political parties. Members of the ruling coalition, the United Front, had committed themselves to the issue by adopting it in their Common Minimum Programme (CMP). Across the board women in Parliament united on this issue (Nath 1996: 7–16). There are many reasons for this. Women's groups and leaders feel that the criminalisation of electoral politics is responsible for women's aversion to the electoral process. The decline in the number of women contestants and representatives in legislative bodies because of this and other related reasons has led to the complete marginalisation of women in the political process. At the same time, women have been increasingly active, forceful and articulate in political movements outside the formal political arena, reflecting a paradoxical situation.

Conceding, therefore, to the pressure mounted by the women's movement and by women within political parties, the United Front coalition government introduced the 81st Constitutional Amendment (Women's Reservation) Bill 1996 in September 1996. The Bill provided for one-third reservation for women in the Lok Sabha and state legislatures. It was referred for examination to a Joint Select Committee, which recommended in December 1996 that the Bill be passed in its existing form (with some notes of dissent). Opinion polls have suggested that a wide range of men and women in the wider society supported the Bill. What followed thereafter came as a jolt.

The government had hoped for a consensus. However, the Bill has been stalled for the time being by its opponents, who have criticised the introduction of such a controversial Bill without a thorough public debate on its wide-ranging implications. It appears that the publicly 'progressive' stance of the political parties has been at variance with their true private attitudes. The ferocity of the opposition to the Bill has unambiguously revealed the dissension within parties, and the hostility felt and expressed by male politicians and members of Parliament at the very idea of losing 181 seats. The 73rd and 74th Amendments did not raise a similar furore as rural women did not, and perhaps still do not, pose a serious threat.

Briefly, the WRB proposes the reservation of one-third seats for women in the Lok Sabha and state legislatures for an indefinite period. The one-third quota for women will include women from the Scheduled Castes (SCs) and Scheduled Tribes (STs), for whom one-third of the seats will be reserved in the SC/ST category, and reserved constituencies will be rotated. The opposition has picked holes on technical, ideological and filibustering grounds. One vociferous section of the male anti-Bill lobby sees the WRB as an attempt by upper-caste 'feminists' to muscle their way into the legislatures. This group has made a counter demand on behalf of women from the Other Backward Classes (OBC) and minority groups, calling for quotas within the quota for women. The argument is that since women are not a homogeneous mass, quotas within the quota could meaningfully include the more disadvantaged among women. Opponents of this view see no need to combine the women's issue with the OBC issue. The call for 'quotas within the quota' touches upon larger questions such as who represents whom, and whether the 'politics of presence' is more conducive to better representation and a higher quality of democracy than 'the politics of ideas' (Phillips 1995: 5).

If quotas within the quota are not accepted and if the WRB becomes law, OBC-based parties would most likely field women of their own castes to increase OBC representation. It is feared that this would then encourage the formation of caste blocs within all parties, and increase the use of women as proxies. These would be both unhealthy and regrettable developments. Concomitantly, it is doubtful that OBC-based parties would genuinely encourage women in their own party structures, as the dominant male party members pay more attention to upward mobility than to gender equity (Kishwar 1996: 2871).

Another specific criticism of the Bill centres around the rotation of constituencies, which will make women candidates dependent on parties rather than on electorates, incumbency being an important factor. For men candidates, the rotation and wider spread of reserved constituencies (for SCs, STs and women) would most likely be a source of great frustration. Also, it is still not clear as to whether reservation has been contemplated as a permanent or transitory measure, and whether the percentage of reservation will be enhanced, reduced or withdrawn at some stage. In the event of the Bill's passage, it would perhaps, be wise to ask for a review after a specified period. This should be a consolation to women who are stubborn about the principle of equality.

Not surprisingly, a few women are still uncomfortable with the demand for the WRB. Since women comprise half the population, others have questioned why 50 per cent reservation cannot be given. Still others have proposed proportional representation as an alternative. A more serious suggestion, put forward by the Shetkari Sanghatana[10] in Maharashtra at a conference in 1993, was in favour of multi-member constituencies with one-third reserved seats for women, in order to do away with the limitations of the WRB in its present form (Kishwar 1996: 2873). Thus the WRB has raised many questions and points of view, which in fact are many more than can possibly be cited here (*Seminar* 1997). The variety of reactions to the WRB foretell the struggle implicit in its future journey towards enactment. The Bill was reintroduced in the Lok Sabha in December 1998, and has yet to run the gauntlet.

Conclusion

The success of and enthusiasm for reservation for women in PRI and the role played by women in some assembly elections in 1994 and 1995 convinced women's groups and women legislators that they must concertedly press for the Bill. Impatient of systemic obstacles, they are in favour of the Bill with all its flaws, loopholes and weaknesses, since it is the first step towards breaking barriers with the strength of a constitutional mandate. It is interesting that the struggles for votes and then for representation by the first wave of the women's movement and the current struggles of the women's movement have shared the same goals—the improvement of the condition of women and the achievement of a robust democratic nation-state.

On the issue of reservation, there has doubtless been a volte face more than once by the women's movement, but the value of entering mainstream legislatures is seen as important at this historical juncture, when women are not only marginalised, but are pushed to the wall by the changes in contemporary India. The forces of fundamentalism, casteism, the formation of ethnic identities, and new economic policies are among those that are particularly bent upon reinforcing inequality and strife. Political power, as well as participation in political parties, has become necessary for women's struggles. This is currently being acknowledged by women's movements everywhere, especially in democratic regimes (Nelson and Chowdhury 1997: 14).

As of now, the women's movement is wondering whether in this adversarial political climate the WRB will be passed at all and, if passed, whether it will work as it is meant to. The dangerous use of women proxies in aiding the growth of caste blocs and for party interests, the ghettoisation of women in reserved constituencies, and women's dependence on parties would subvert the intentions of the Bill. Any misuse of the proposed measure would leave women badly-off. There is a considerable body of research on women's participation in PRI that shows that these patterns have surfaced already (Kaushik 1996; Mathew 1995; Sharma 1998b). It is, however, heartening to note that there also signs of women's eager and effective participation at the local level. A recent three-state study indicates this positively (Proceedings of National Workshop on *Panchayat*s and Women, held at India International Centre, New Delhi on 1–3 January 1999). Through reservation of seats, women could form a critical mass or force, provided of course that women candidates are genuine, not proxies, and are sincerely committed to gender equality and the women's movement, rather than to individual ambition (Begin 1998).

The women's movement in India currently faces several challenges in pursuit of its aims, which are not merely gender-specific but cover a vast terrain—citizen's rights and democracy, societal values, social transformation, a more just economic order, the eradication of violence, crime, fundamentalism, identity politics, and so on (Agnihotri and Mazumdar 1995). The forces against the women's movement are too many to enumerate. Through active and critical engagement in the public world, women in formal positions could give new meaning to the concepts of democracy, development, redistribution and rights (Krishnaraj 1998).

Those against reservation per se have suggested that it poses a dilemma for democracy and the nation-state. Is reservation in itself a just measure, or will it be divisive in the event that every marginalised group/category insists on a quota? (John 1999). At best reservation is a corrective, but is only a beginning—it can never be a long-term panacea for the problems of political representation. Also, various other correctives need to be considered concurrently to make reservation work. Widespread electoral reforms are necessary to ensure violence-free and inexpensive elections. The internal reform of political parties is also vital. Inner party democracy, a commitment to fair practices in the field, a disavowal of corruption and criminalisation, and large-scale recruitment of women at all levels, including the highest party positions, are absolutely essential. It is only when politics itself is cleansed and societal attitudes change that measures such as the WRB or the 73rd and 74th Amendments can hope to fulfill their mission.

Notes

1. The Question of Affirmative Action for women has been studied carefully in recent times. For instance, according to Bacchi (1996), the addition of women to the list of discriminated categories works against them.
2. For social reform directed towards the improvement of women's status in this period, there are many good sources (Asthana 1974; Borthwick 1985; Desai 1957; Heimsath 1964; Kumar 1993; Mazumdar 1976).

3. There is a dearth of information on women's organisations in the regions. Some regional studies include Engels (1996) and Southard (1995) on Bengal; and Caplan (1985) on Madras.
4. There are several blow-by-blow accounts. Some of the best known include Agnew (1979: 104–31); Everett (1979: 101–40); Forbes (1979: 3–23); Basu and Ray (1990: 54–58); and Nair (1996: 122–44). On political developments and the dialogue between nationalists and the colonial power, refer to Sarkar (1983).
5. The Indian National Congress (or Congress) was the nationalist group that became a major political party in independent India.
6. The Congress supported women's franchise right from the start, and clarified as early as 1918 that 'women possessing the same qualifications as are laid down for men ... shall not be disqualified on account of sex' (Chaudhuri 1993: 152, n. 62).
7. The Communal Award explicitly applied communal principles to women's franchise and representation. It was a turning point for the women's movement and for Muslim women in the movement (Deutsch 1998).
8. Everett (1979: 82–100) has made a useful distinction between the 'women's uplift' and the 'liberal feminist' approaches. Earlier in origin, the former was cautious and content with reform within existing frameworks. Progressing from this stage, the demand for equal rights, developed in the 1930s, was based on the removal of barriers to equality through legal change in the status of women in economic, political and social spheres (ibid.: 82–84).
9. *Panchayat* or village council is an institution of local governance in rural India. *Panchayati Raj* refers to local self-governance.
10. An organisation of farmers of varied backward castes in Maharashtra involved in social reform, women's issues, and women's participation in *panchayats*.

References

Agnew, Vijay. 1979. *Elite Women in Indian Politics*. Delhi: Vikas Publishing House.

AIWC (All-India Women's Conference). 1931–32. *Report of the Sixth Session of the AIWC*. New Delhi: AIWC.

———. 1933–34. *Report of the Eighth Session of the AIWC*. New Delhi: AIWC.

Asaf Ali, Aruna (n.d.). 'Women's Suffrage in India', in Shyam Kumari Nehru (ed.), *Our Cause*. Allahabad: Kitabistan.

Agnihotri, I and V. Mazumdar. 1995. 'Changing Terms of Political Discourse: Women's Movement in India 1970–1990', *Economic and Political Weekly*, XXX (29).

Asthana, Pratima. 1974. *Women's Movement in India*. Delhi: Vikas Publishing House.

Bacchi, Carol Lee. 1996. *The Politics of Affirmative Action: Women, Equality and Category Politics*. London: Sage Publications.

Basu, Aparna. 1976/1990. 'The Role of Women in the Indian Struggle for Freedom', in B.R. Nanda (ed.), *Indian Women: From Purdah to Modernity*, pp. 16–40. New Delhi: Radiant Publishers.

Basu, Aparna and Bharati Ray. 1990. *Women's Struggle: A History of the AIWC 1927–1990*. New Delhi: Manohar.

Begin, Monique. 1998. *Towards a Critical Mass: Women in Politics*, The 12th J.P. Naik Memorial Lecture. New Delhi: CWDS.

Borthwick, Meredith. 1985. *The Changing Role of Women in Bengal, 1849–1905*. Princeton: Princeton University Press.

Calman, Leslie J. 1992. *Towards Empowerment: Women and Movement Politics in India*. Boulder: Westview Press.

Caplan, Patricia. 1985. *Class and Gender in India: Women and Their Organisations in a South Indian City*. London: Tavistock Publications.

Chaudhuri, Maitrayee. 1993. *Indian Women's Movement: Reform and Revival*. New Delhi: Radiant Publishers.

Chattopadhyaya, Kamaladevi. 1983. *Indian Women's Battle for Freedom*. New Delhi: Abhinav Publications.

Chatterjee, Partha. 1989. 'The Nationalist Resolution of the Women's Question', in K. Sangari and S. Vaid (eds), *Recasting Women. Essays in Social History*. New Delhi: Kali for Women, Oxford: Clarendon Press.

CWDS (Centre for Women's Development Studies). 1995. *Confronting Myriad Oppressions, The Western Regional Experience*. New Delhi.

Desai, Neera. 1957. *Women in Modern India*. Bombay: Vora and Co.

Deutsch, Karin A. 1998. *Muslim Women in Colonial North India, Circa 1920–1947: Politics, Law and Community Identity*. Unpublished Ph.D. thesis, Cambridge University.

Everett, J.M. 1979. *Women and Social Change*. New Delhi: Heritage Publishers.

———. 1981. 'Approaches to the "Woman Question in India": From Maternalism to Mobilisation', *Women's Studies International Quarterly*, 4 (2): 169–78.

Engels, Dagmar. 1996. *Beyond Purdah? Women in Bengal, 1890–1939*. Delhi: Oxford University Press.

Forbes G. 1978. 'Women's Movements in India: Traditional Symbols and New Roles', in M.S.A. Rao (ed.), *Social Movements in India*, pp. 149–65. New Delhi: Manohar Publications.

———. 1979. 'Votes for Women: The Demand for Women's Franchise in India 1917–1937', in V. Mazumdar (ed.), *Symbols of Power, Studies on the Political Status of Women in India*, pp. 3–23. New Delhi and Bombay: Allied Publishers Pvt. Ltd.

———. 1982. 'From Purdah to Politics: The Social Feminism of the All-India Women's Organisations', in Hanna Papanek and Gail Minault (eds), *Separate Worlds*, pp. 219–44. Delhi: Chanakya Publications.

———. 1996. *Women in Modern India*. Cambridge: Cambridge University Press.

Gandhi, N. and N. Shah. 1991. *The Issues at Stake, Theory and Practice in the Contemporary Women's Movement in India*. New Delhi: Kali for Women.

Government of India. 1974. *Towards Equality: Report of the Committee on the Status of Women in India*. New Delhi: Department of Social Welfare, Ministry of Education and Social Welfare.

———. 1978. *Report of the Committee on Panchayati Raj Institutions* (Ashok Mehta Committee). New Delhi: Ministry of Agriculture and Irrigation, Department of Rural Development.

———. 1988. *National Perspective Plan for Women 1988–2000*. New Delhi: Department of Women and Child Development, Ministry of Human Resource Development.

Heimsath, C.H. 1964. *Indian Nationalism and Hindu Social Reform*. Princeton: Princeton University Press.

Inter-Parliamentary Union. 1997. *Men and Women in Politics: Democracy Still in the Making, A World Comparative Study*. Inter-Parliamentary Union Series, Reports and Documents No. 28, Geneva.

Jayawardena, K. 1986. *Feminism and Nationalism in the Third World*. London: Zed Books.

John, Mary E. 1999. 'Democracy, Patriarchies and Reservations for Women: A Note', *Indian Journal of Gender Studies*, 6 (1).

Kasturi, Leela. 1991–92. 'Rural Women in Struggle in Colonial India: Some Aporiae', *Samya Shakti*, VI: 65–80.

Kasturi, L. and V. Mazumdar (eds). 1994. *Women and Indian Nationalism*. New Delhi: Vikas Publishing House Pvt. Ltd.

Kaushik, Susheela. 1996. *Panchayati Raj in Action: Challenges to Women's Role*. New Delhi: Friedrich Ebert Stiftung.

Kishwar, Madhu. 1996. 'Women and Politics: Beyond Quotas', *Economic and Political Weekly*, XXXI (43): 2867–74.

Kumar, Radha. 1993/97. *The History of Doing 1800–1990*. New Delhi: Kali for Women.

Kalima, Rose. 1992. *Where Women are Leaders: The Sewa Movement in India*. New Delhi: Vistaar Publications.

Krishnaraj, Maithreyi. 1995. *Remaking Society for Women: Visions-Past and Present*. New Delhi: Indian Association of Women's Studies.

———. 1998. 'Women and the Public Domain,' *Economic and Political Weekly*. XXXIII (8): 391–95.

Liddle, J. and Rama Joshi. 1986. *Daughters of Independence*. London: Zed Books.

Mathew, G. 1995. 'Women in Panchayati Raj', Paper presented at the National Conference on 'Women and Panchayati Raj', organised by the Institute of Social Sciences, 23–24 April, New Delhi.

Mazumdar, V. 1976. 'The Social Reform Movement in India—From Ranade to Nehru,' in B.R. Nanda (ed.), *Indian Women: From Purdah to Modernity*, pp. 41–66. New Delhi: Vikas.

——— (ed.). 1979. *Symbols of Power: Studies on the Political Status of Women in India*. New Delhi and Bombay: Allied Publishers Pvt. Ltd.

———. 1997. 'Historical Soundings', *Seminar*, 457: 14–19.

Minault, Gail. 1981. *The Extended Family: Women and Political Participation in India and Pakistan*. Delhi: Chanakya Publications.

Nair, Janaki. 1996. *Women and Law in Colonial India: A Social History*. New Delhi: Kali for Women.

NPP. 1988. *National Perspective Plan for Women 1988–2000: A Perspective from the Women's Movement*. Report of a Debate, 22–30 August, New Delhi: Centre for Women's Development Studies (mimeo).

Nath, Meenakshi. 1996. 'Cutting Across Party Lines', *Manushi*, 96 (September–October): 7–16.

Nelson C. and Najma Chowdhury (eds). 1997. *Women and Politics—Worldwide*. Delhi: Oxford University Press.

Omvedt, Gail. 1975. 'Caste, Class and Women's Liberation in India', *BCAS*, VII (1).

Parasher, Archana. 1992. *Women and Family Law Reform in India*. New Delhi: Sage Publications.

Pearson, Gail. O. 1979. Women in Public Life in Bombay City with Special Reference to the Civil Disobedience Movement. Ph.D. thesis, Jawaharlal Nehru University, New Delhi.

Phillips, Anne. 1995. *The Politics of Presence*. Oxford: Clarendon Press.

Rose, Kalima. 1992. *Where Women are Leaders: The SEWA Movement in India*. New Delhi: Vistaar Publications.

Sarkar, Sumit. 1983. *Modern India 1885–1947*. Delhi: Macmillan India Ltd.

Selbourne, David (ed.). 1985. *In Theory and in Practice: Essays on the Politics of Jaya Prakash Narayan*. Delhi: Oxford University Press.

Seminar. 1997. No. 457, New Delhi.

Sen, Sunil. 1985. *The Working Women and Popular Movements in Bengal*. Calcutta: K.P. Bagchi and Co.

Sen, Ilina. 1990. *A Space Within the Struggle: Women's Participation in People's Movements*. New Delhi: Kali for Women.

Sharma, Kumud. 1989. *Shared Aspirations: Fragmented Realities, Occasional Paper* No. 12. New Delhi: CWDS.

———. 1998a. *Power vs. Representation*, Occasional Paper No. 28. New Delhi: CWDS.

———. 1998b. 'Transformative Politics: Dimensions of Women's Participation in Panchayati Raj', *Indian Journal of Gender Studies*, 5 (1): 23–47.

Singha Roy, Debal K. 1992. *Women in Peasant Movements*. New Delhi: Manohar.

Stree Shakti Sanghatana. 1989. *We were Making History*. New Delhi: Kali for Women.

Southard, Barbara. 1995. *The Women's Movement and Colonial Politics in Bengal: The Quest for Political Rights, Education and Social Reform Legislation 1921–1936*. New Delhi: Manohar.

Towards Beijing. A Perspective from the Indian Women's Movement. 1995. New Delhi: Centre for Women's Development Studies (mimeo).

Women's Sub-Committee. 1947. *Woman's Role in Planned Economy*, National Planning Committee Series. Bombay: Vora and Co.

TWENTY THREE

The Women's Question in Contemporary Politics[*][1]

Vasanthi Raman

Introduction

The women's question in contemporary Indian politics has acquired a kind of significance that at one level seems simple enough. However, at another level the women's question bristles with complexities, and is in a sense suffused with the very contradictions arising out of the intermeshing of hierarchy and diversity, both so characteristic of the Indian social structure. All across the political spectrum is a seemingly 'commonsensical' consensus that women in Indian society have been victims of a patriarchal social order to a greater or lesser degree. And so it is high time that society acknowledges the injustices inherent in the social order and takes necessary steps so that women may take their rightful place in the society and polity. In this context, one needs to note that both hierarchy and diversity have never been static, but are continuously reconstituted and reconstructed by the operation of historical and social processes; their intermeshing has also been characterised by a similar dynamism and historicity. Thus, the women's question has never been a women's question alone. Nor are women's issues the exclusive concern of the women's movement. Perhaps the women's question, more than any other, brings to the fore both the intractability and the intransigence of structures, traditional and modern, and simultaneously opens up possibilities for addressing the question of the democratisation of the social order.

In this chapter, I propose to focus on the articulation and manifestation of the women's question in Indian politics during the last two to three decades, and the problems that have been thrown up consequently. The issues that I intend to take up to illustrate the complexity of the women's question and its embeddedness in the wider social and political matrix are those of the Uniform Civil Code,[2] the so-called Mandal[3] controversy, and the question of political reservation for women.

The Contemporary Resurgence of the Women's Movement

The 1970s saw the women's question emerge as an important focal point of mobilisation by various women's groups, and subsequently as significant even in academic discourse. Coinciding with this upsurge of interest and action, and perhaps also important in fuelling and giving direction to it, was the report of the Committee on the Status of Women in India (CSWI), *Towards Equality*, in 1974. The report also signalled the beginning of women's studies in academe. The overall framework of the report was one that emphasised the very Indian dimension of the women's question and movement. The educated middle-class women, who were the authors of the report, consciously focused on the overall and increasing marginalisation of the masses of

*Originally published in *Asian Journal of Women's Studies*, Vol. 7, No. 2, 2001, pp. 39–70.

poor and rural women in the post-independence years, and held the state responsible and accountable for their deplorable situation, despite three decades of planned development. Among the important insights offered by the report were questions about the declining sex ratio, increasing gender gaps in life expectancy, mortality and economic participation, all indicating certain policy directions and emphases. A significant contribution of the CSWI was that it drew attention to the linkages between the growing overall social and economic disparities and the marginalisation of women in the spheres of economy, education and polity.

The context of the contemporary resurgence of the women's question in Indian politics needs to be noted. It started at a time when the then ruling party, the Congress, and the state were faced with the growing crisis of legitimacy, and a whole array of social movements ranging from the traditional working-class and trade union movements led by the left, to the 'new' social movements of Dalits and tribals, which spoke the language of 'identity', had acquired a certain radical edge. Student and youth movements in the cities have been radicalised over the last three decades, both by revolutionary Marxist ideology and the civil disobedience movement led by Jayaprakash Narayan in the 1970s. In this context, the impact of the Naxalbari uprising[4] cannot be underemphasised; even though the movement failed and was brutally repressed, it contributed in no insignificant manner to a certain radicalisation of the social and political discourse. The declaration of the emergency in 1975 and the post-emergency years, which saw an upsurge in the civil liberties movement, led to a realignment of political forces. There was a consensus that civil and political freedoms had to be defended at all costs. The language of the social and political movements, whether of the left or the centre, was still an inclusive one, reminiscent of the nationalist movement consensus. Even the radical challenges spoke of the state as having failed to live up to the aspirations of the Indian people, and of its being a semi-colonial one.

The women's movement of this period shared the broad consensus of a nationalist, secular and democratic framework, even while focusing on the specific nature of women's oppression. As part of the political mobilisation during this phase, large numbers of urban, educated, middle-class women raised the issue of the specific and pervasive nature of women's oppression and marginalisation, which many felt had been ignored by the left and other centrist parties. Thus, party-affiliated national women's organisations were looked upon with suspicion among the emerging 'autonomous' women's groups, as they came to be known. There were obvious differences in emphasis and strategy between the 'autonomous' women's groups and the women's organisations of the left. The focus of the former was on uniting women as women (with the family being emphasised as an important and sometimes even the crucial site of patriarchal oppression), while the latter stressed the class nature of women's oppression and exploitation. The major issues before the emerging women's movement were those of pervasive violence against women—rape, dowry murders, amniocentesis tests, and so on. The widespread women's mobilisation on the Mathura rape case brought to the fore crucial aspects of women's situation, specifically the caste-class texture of women's oppression and the underlying deep-seated biases of the administration and even the judiciary. The issues taken up, in a sense, were unexceptionally acceptable to the leftists, the liberals and the radicals. Two important and leading participants have described one important and characteristic dimension of this phase of the women's movement in the following words:

> The women's movement in India is one of the many burgeoning efforts at reassertion of citizen's claims to participate as equals in the political and development process. This places it in a situation of direct confrontation with the forces of conservatism and reaction. (Agnihotri and Mazumdar 1995: 1869)

However, certain observations need to be made about this period: within the movement there were diversities, differences and regional specificities. For example, women's political movements in northeastern India demanding either autonomy and/or secession from the Indian union charted their own trajectories, which were determined by the larger political struggles. Thus, Naga and Manipuri women had been active in the political arena; the Nari Mukti Sanstha of Assam, a northeastern state, was formed in the struggle against the incipient chauvinism of the Assam movement and an upsurge in the peasant movement of the late 1970s led by communist revolutionaries. The Progressive Organisation of Women in Andhra Pradesh, which grew out of the radical student movement in Andhra Pradesh in southern India, had already lost a student leader in the struggle against the RSS (Rashtriya Swayamsevak Sangh), a militant Hindu chauvinist organisation. These movements and organisations can be said to have had a greater sensitivity to the regional and caste-tribe-ethnicity-class nexus, and the inextricable link between all of these and women's oppression, even though there was no special theorising on this. All in all, one can say that the dominant language of the women's movement made a universalist claim to citizenship and to equal participation in society and the polity, unsullied by particularities of caste, religion, ethnicity, and other such primordial identities.

The Watershed Years of the 1980s and the 1990s

The 1980s in a sense signalled the end of the post-colonial nation-building project, or at least it signalled the end of the consensus on the nation-building project amongst the principal political parties of the centre and the mainstream left. Three significant developments marked the 1980s: the decision to take the first World Bank-IMF loan; the Ayodhya issue,[5] which marked the shift of the forces of Hindutva (the ideology of Hindu nationhood) to the centrestage of Indian politics; and the decision to implement the recommendations of the Mandal Commission. These developments have had a far-reaching influence on Indian politics. The World Bank-IMF loan marked the beginning of India's full integration into the world capitalist system, with no holds barred. In the sphere of the economy, ideologically and politically, it was the reign of the so-called free market, which also saw the beginning of an overt communalisation of the state and a simultaneous inauguration of what has been termed 'identity politics'. The contradictions of the development paradigm, with its centralising and authoritarian thrust, became apparent and visible. As one scholar puts it, 'By the time of the Shah Bano[6] judgment, it had become increasingly clear that in every way in which the nation was being constituted by dominant discourses, the powerless and the marginal was being defined out of its boundaries' (Menon 1998: 253).

The 1980s also witnessed the manifestation of two inter-related processes. On the one hand there was an increased visibility of women in the public sphere (largely educated, upper-caste and middle-class women). On the other, there was an increased victimhood of women of the subaltern groups, i.e., Dalit (low and untouchable caste) women, tribal women, and Muslim women who were invisible, so to speak. The visibility of one lot of women was in a sense dialectically related to the invisibility of the other. The women who have been the major beneficiaries of the development process are from the upper-caste, middle-class groups. Needless to say, they have only recently penetrated a fortress that had been almost the exclusive preserve of upper-caste men, a point that even a cursory look at the educational institutions and government bureaucracy will confirm.[7] This phenomenon has to be seen in the context of the overall performance and ensconsing of the upper-caste, educated middle classes in the structures of government and administration. Conversely, women (and men) from the subaltern groups have by and large been marginalised in the development process. That these groups are Scheduled Castes (SCs), Scheduled Tribes (STs), Other Backward Classes (OBCs),[8] and minority groups (particularly Muslims) needs to be emphasised. Liberalisation policies adopted since the 1980s have only sharpened the polarising thrust of the development paradigm pursued so far, with the cushion of the welfare state finally being abandoned in the 1990s. This pursuit of the neo-liberal paradigm has heightened traditional social and economic differences of caste, class, religion, region and ethnicity. Thus, women have only *got more and not less embedded* in their groups, leading to greater differentiation among them. This also accounts for the differential political articulation among women. Public responses to the Mandal Commission and the Uniform Civil Code testify to this, as will be seen later.

The women's question has to be seen in the backdrop of this changed context of the 1980s and 1990s. It has been argued that a context is not merely a 'background' to questions and demands, but is rather the condition of possibility of certain kinds of initiatives, that is, as something constitutive (John 1996: 3071). However, it is our submission that the women's question needs to be examined not only in terms of the changed context, but also that the very vantage point of the women's movement needs to be critically reappraised from the perspective of the democratisation of Indian society. And this democratisation would have to negotiate its multi-layered and complex social structure. Such a critical reappraisal would involve engaging both intellectually and politically with issues of caste, tribe, religion, region and ethnicity, and their complex intermeshing with women's issues. However, the dominant discourse of the women's move-ment has shied away from this task, and has been either uncomfortable with or denounced such concerns as having emerged out of peripheral groups and ploys of fundamentalist or sectarian forces.

The Debate on the Uniform Civil Code

The issue of the Uniform Civil Code (UCC) is an interesting and significant one, precisely because it illus-trates the complex nature of the problem as well as the dilemmas of the women's movement. In its report, the Committee for the Status of Women in India (CSWI) had held that:

> The absence of a UCC in the last quarter of the twentieth century, twenty-seven years after independ-ence, is an incongruity that cannot be justified with all the emphasis placed on secularism, science and modernism. The continuance of various personal laws which accept discrimination between men and women violates the fundamental rights .... It is also against the spirit of national integration and secularism. (Government of India 1974: 142)

The assumption that a uniform civil code was necessary to bring about gender justice was part of the post-independence and post-partition legacy, wherein secularism (as also national integration) could be ensured by a uniform set of laws for all communities. However, given the background of the partition, the whole question of the rights of minorities was an equally important issue. A perusal of the debates and discussions of the Constituent Assembly reveals how the safeguards for minorities, which included separate representation, were abandoned, with the Constitution of India making a distinction between the *cultural rights* of minorities and *political group rights* of communities like the Scheduled Castes and Tribes. The political discourse on the nation-building project has tended to veer between two divergent viewpoints, one that advocates a uniform set of laws in the interest of national integration and a desire for an abstract notion of equality of the citizen, and the other advocating that the recognition of plurality and the rights of minorities are essential prerequisites for a democratic polity. There has always been an uneasy and unresolved tension between these two viewpoints. The existence of a plethora of personal laws was seen (and continues to be seen) as an important obstacle not only to achieving gender justice, but also to the achievement of a pure nationalism, uncontaminated by particularisms. Thus, the discomfort with the idea of plurality/diversity and difference among the dominant streams of the women's movement has to be seen in this context.

The Shah Bano judgment saw the entire mainstream women's movement speak in one voice, demanding a uniform civil code. However, by 1996 there was a sea change, and there were wide divergences of opinion on the question of a common set of laws for all women. This change was not merely confined to women's groups alone, but also encompassed the political parties (with the exception of the BJP and the Shiv Sena, professedly Hindu parties), which voiced their opposition to the UCC. This shift in position is interesting because it reveals the attempts of various groups and organisations to come to terms with the changed political scenario, characterised by the dominance of Hindu right-wing forces. The most notable change has occurred in the position of the All India Democratic Women's Association (AIDWA), which voiced its opposition to the 'fundamentalist' demand for a uniform civil code in the mid-1990s. What is significant about AIDWA's position is the recognition that gender justice and the fulfillment of constitutional guarantees of equality need not necessarily be linked to an umbrella legislation, and that such legislation, might actually be counter-productive (Karat 1995).

Other women's groups have felt the need to distance themselves from the UCC and its national integrationist thrust, and yet they uphold the goal of gender justice along with a commitment to diversity and plurality. The Working Group on Women's Rights (1996) in Delhi claimed that it attempted a conceptual shift in the way in which family laws have so far been envisaged. In doing so, it critiqued the earlier notion of the UCC on the grounds that it was mechanical, and assumed that integration of different communities could be achieved through uniform laws and would lead to national unity and integration and the strengthening of the nation-state. Moreover, the earlier notion ignored the social differentiation prevalent in India, while attempting to transcend the same in the sphere of rights. Thus, 'uniformity was attempted only in personal laws and not in social life as a whole' (Working Group on Women's Rights 1996: 1180). While rejecting the earlier notion of the UCC, the Group also considers personal laws to be 'conceptually flawed', since these deny women the rights that communities claim for themselves, i.e., the rights of self-determination, autonomy and access to resources. Besides, according to the Group,

> defense of personal laws on the grounds of defense of community is no different from the defense of the UCC on the ground of defense of the nation, it is simply that different types of particularity are being defended and the choice between them is either arbitrary or self-interested or politically motivated. (ibid.: 1181)

Thus the Working Group on Women's Rights' attempt is to:

> extract the discussion on the UCC from the framework of comparative rights of communities—between each other and between communities and the nation—and to recast this discussion in terms of the rights of women as citizens occupying the public sphere, with rights to work, to equal wages, to equality within the family in a way which does not compartmentalise the public and the private. (ibid.: 1181–82)

To enlarge the scope of democratic participation, the proposal of the Group consists of:

(*i*) A comprehensive package of legislation covering both the public and private spheres, i.e., equal rights for women within the family (property, guardianship rights, right to matrimonial home) and equal rights in the workplace; this has to be bolstered by a package of social security measures that will make the woman less vulnerable;

(*ii*) All citizens of India would come under the purview of these common laws; and

(*iii*) Citizens would have the right to choose to be governed by personal laws if they so wish.

The major problem with this position is that in attempting to steer clear of the earlier notions of the UCC—with its attendant ideas of unity and national integration, wherein gender justice is not a concern—the Group, in effect, subscribes to the view that gender justice can only be achieved through a set of common laws. The Group's vision and strategy explicitly rules out any scope for changes in personal laws by the community (including men and women). That there could be a position upholding the interests of communities (religious or tribal) along with a commitment to gender justice is not even conceived of by the Group. Thus, it commits the same error of ignoring the diversity and social differentiation of Indian society, which it had criticised in earlier notions of the UCC. Moreover, the Group equates a position of the defence of personal laws (and thereby the defence of community) with a defence of the UCC (i.e., a defence of the nation-state). It does so in a situation where communities/groups that are being marginalised are at the receiving end of an oppressive state, propelled by the hegemonistic ideology and worldview of a dominant minority. This ideology and worldview operates at many levels, and is combined with the thrust of the overall developmental model, including its most recent variants, the Structural Adjustment Programmes and globalisation. The combination leads to a situation where *communities/groups are being marginalised as collectivities*, leading to a serious survival crisis and the erosion of their self-confidence. The communities and groups that constitute the majority of the Indian population are therefore faced with the deadly combination of Hindutva and globalisation. Thus, to equate the two particularities (the community and an oppressive nation-state) is tantamount to equating the struggle for economic and socio-cultural survival of oppressed and marginalised groups with the aggressive and hegemonistic project of a dominant minority-driven state. Besides, it is important to note that *these two dimensions of the struggles for survival, the economic and the socio-cultural, are part of an integral whole*.

The option that the Group proposes is a comprehensive set of laws that would collapse the distinction between the public and the private domains, and de-link personal laws from religion. The major problem with this is that religion and personal laws are seen as occupying separate compartments, whereas the intertwining of religion, culture and personal laws is complex and historically determined. Hence the disentangling of these strands is a difficult task that cannot be effected by administrative or legal fiat, but would be possible only through a comprehensive social movement that engages politically and practically with these questions. Besides, religion is a way of life for the vast majority of men and women, comprising a worldview that shapes people's perceptions and influences their lifechoices. This is something that cannot simply be wished or legislated away. Moreover, there is a more fundamental question before us: does a democratic society presuppose a space wherein communities/groups of people can enter into a dialogue with each other and renegotiate the public/private dichotomy on their own terms, i.e., keeping in mind their specific histories, cultures, social structures and specific oppressions? Or will the manner and specificities of that negotiation be determined by some abstract notion of secularism and an equally abstract liberal notion of the rights of the individual citizen, which are rooted in the historical and cultural experience of western capitalism? These questions have to be addressed with a degree of empathy and sensitivity, particularly if one is committed to democratisation and a realistic and feasible process of ensuring gender justice.

During the high point of the demand for the UCC in the mid-1980s, there were voices from the far left that held the view that the crucial issue was not whether Muslim women have a right to maintenance, but whether the Muslims have a right to a personal law at all and that the

> ... [C]lamour for a uniform civil code is not merely the just demand of secular forces anxious to weed out the last vestiges of medievalism nor is it even a concern for the oppressive status of Muslim women; it is a manifestation of the present balance of socio-political forces of the status quo—the main thrust

of which is to suppress the religious and ethnic minorities and other oppressed castes and classes. (Communist Party of India [Marxist-Leninist] 1986)

Likewise, in 1995, in the context of the Sarla Mudgal case and the entirely uncalled for obiter dicta of the Supreme Court judgment, the same journal stated that

> Gender justice has been made a casualty precisely by posing it in terms whereby it ignores the specific *socio-cultural-historical roots of gender inequality both within and between communities*. Besides, the implicit and facile assumption that the state can steamroll problems arising out of a complex intertwining of religion, culture and personal laws is fraught with grave portents for the very social fabric of Indian society. While at a certain level it may be true to say that all women irrespective of religion are victims of a male-dominated social order, this gender oppression is mediated by religion, culture, history, social structure and politics and imparts a specificity which one can only ignore at the peril of perpetrating further injustice. These mediations have to be carefully traversed by democratic forces interested in gender justice. (ibid.: 9, emphasis added)

The above article holds that the struggle for gender justice and equality will have to be woven into the struggle for the emancipation of each of the oppressed groups and communities. Moreover, the preservation of diversity and plurality will have to be the framework within which gender justice has to be sought.

One of the important shifts among women's groups and other secularists and democrats has been with regard to the emphasis on the law. There is a greater scepticism about the importance of law when it comes to actually making a difference to the situation of women, and a greater recognition of the importance of social mobilisation. Thus, the position that reforms within the community are more consonant with democratic processes and ensures the rights of minorities has gained ground. There are examples of efforts made to mobilise opinion within the community, for instance that of groups like the *Nikahnama* Group, which drafted a model *nikahnama*, a Muslim marriage contract; the Women's Action and Research Group (WRAG); and the Joint Women's Programme (JWP), which has taken the initiative in drafting a reformed Christian law with the involvement of various church hierarchies.

On the one hand strategies for reforming outdated personal laws from within have been justified on the basis of the fact that communities do have the right to preserve their identities within the larger one of the nation-state. On the other hand, it is felt that communities ought to undertake the task of reforming those aspects of their laws that are not in keeping with the constitutional provisions of equality, or that fail to pass the tests of equity, justice and good conscience. The difficulties in the enactment of the UCC arise out of the fact that there is little clarity on what shape it will assume, and the immense legal diversities in the country, where existing laws are based on four distinct jurisprudential philosophies. Inevitably, problems of privileging one over the other would also arise. The strategy for internal reform cannot be dependent on state initiatives, since such an exercise would not only contradict the very basis of a secular state, but would also go against the principle that communities have an autonomous space. And the latter needs to be defended, particularly in a multi-ethnic society where the state is likely to become the carrier of the values of the dominant community (Ahmad 1995: 2851–52).

Our purpose in going over the terrain of the UCC, the various positions taken, and the shifts in position, is to illustrate the complexity of the women's question—that it is embedded in wider structures and processes of society, economy, history and polity, and that there are varied stakes involved in it. This issue cannot be separated from any fundamental political questions of the day. The imperative need for the women's movement to engage with issues of caste, community and religious identity, all of which are intertwined with issues of class, cannot be underemphasised. In short, issues of 'identity' need to be addressed in a serious manner. This needs to be done not merely as a concession to 'particularistic' identities in a patronising manner in contrast to the more universalistic identities of citizen or class, but as a serious political endeavour in order to understand the situation of the vast majority of women (and men) of the subaltern communities and classes. A similar point has been made by the Anveshi Law Committtee, which holds that the women's question cannot be separated from notions of 'democracy', 'equality', 'secularism' and 'modernity', all of which are being contested. Thus, the refusal to deal with issues of caste and religious community might result in an 'endorsement of existing class/caste hierarchies and the communal targeting of Muslims' (Anveshi Law Committee 1997: 453).

The Mandal Commission

The issue of the Mandal Commission recommendations, unlike the UCC or the Women's Reservation Bill, is not a 'women's issue' as such. However, I have chosen to discuss it briefly since it is linked to the controversies around the issue of women's reservation, and the question of representation for the OBCs. Besides, it illustrates the point we have been making regarding the mainstream women's movement's reluctance to deal with particularistic identities. The UCC debate during the 1980s and 1990s saw most of the major women's groups and secular-minded intellectuals retreat from a position of support in the face of political challenges posed by Hindutva forces. However, the issue of the Mandal Commission recommendations is one that is still characterised by a great deal of ambivalence, to say the least. The violence that attended the announcement of their implementation in 1990 found the women's movement strangely silent. If anything, large numbers of middle-class, educated women from urban areas (including progressive women students from universities and wives of bureaucrats) were in the forefront of the mobilisation against the recommendations of the Commission, defending 'merit'.

Niranjana (1998) discusses the social character of the anti-Mandal agitation as it unfolded in the Central University of Hyderabad, in which largely upper-caste men and women students, particularly from the English department, were active. It was one of the few agitations that received widespread support from the media, and was portrayed as a disinterested movement of idealistic youth battling to save the nation. Apart from the virulence that characterised the writings in the print media, the extraordinary consensus on the issue should have made any serious analyst pause and ponder upon the crucial significance of caste in Indian society. However, it is interesting to note that apart from a few writings of politically committed intellectuals and parties of the revolutionary left, the entire Indian upper caste, middle and upper classes spoke in one voice in defence of merit (Balagopal 1990: 2231–34). As Niranjana observed: 'In the battle for Merit, the truly patriotic (and truly secular) Indian was the one who rose above caste divisions; anyone who asked for reservations on the basis of caste was accused of a resurgent casteism' (1998: 128). What was revealing was that when issues of discrimination against women came up during the elections to the students' body, the largely upper-caste women students who had been so vociferous against Mandal found that their male upper-caste comrades were not with them. Instead, it was the Dalit students who supported their struggle. This proved to be a great learning experience for the women students, who were now impelled to look at issues of caste discrimination (ibid.: 128–29).

Prominent liberal and secular academics also lent their voice to the anti-Mandal agitation. The mainstream left tried to sidetrack the basic issue raised by referring to a so-called 'creamy layer', i.e., better-off sections within the defined backward caste groups. They were perhaps unaware that in some states where reservations for the backward classes were in operation, some differentiation had already been made between 'backward' and 'more backward' groups. In fact, the Mandal Commission has posed the issue of the democratisation of Indian society in a sharp and pointed manner. The responses to Mandal were at one level hysterical opposition on the part of the upper castes (with women playing an active role), and opportunistic support on the part of all political parties at another. These comprised significant pointers to the importance of the issue, particularly with regard to the erosion of upper-caste hegemony over the administration. After all, it should not be overlooked that it is the other backward castes (OBCs) and the Muslims—given their numerical strength and, more importantly, their social location—who can pose a real challenge to the hegemony of the upper castes, not the Scheduled Castes (SCs) and Scheduled Tribes (STs). For this reason, even the most reactionary proponents of upper-caste dominance can be very patronising about the SCs and STs, but they become hysterical in their opposition to the demands of the OBCs and the minorities, particularly the Muslims (Raman 1999).

The Question of Women's Reservation

The Women's Reservation Bill has to be viewed in the context of the violence that erupted following the presentation of the Mandal recommendations and the vicious media campaign that ensued, which was soon followed by the destruction of the Babri Masjid. As started earlier, the destruction of the mosque has been considered a watershed in the life of post-independent India, throwing into question the very framework of the secular, democratic nation-state. The social and political polarisation and the turbulence that has accompanied these two events have made the issue of women's reservation even more complicated and murky. The political innocence of the women's movement can be excused even less now compared to the period of the UCC debate of the 1980s, as social and political polarisation in the 1990s has proceeded far apace, and the forces of the Hindu right-wing have grown much stronger.

A little on the history of women's reservation may not be out of place here, and may in fact serve to put the entire issue in perspective. The issue of separate political reservation for women came up during the course of the nationalist movement in the 1920s. The principal reason for opposing the idea of reserved seats was that it deflected from the demand for universal adult franchise, and for women to stand for elections on the same terms as men. However, it would seem that women's attitudes to this question were also related to resolving the contradictions between questions of social reform and those of political rights. As John puts it,

> The public, official language of politics, especially before a colonial government, had to be a language of equality and for fundamental rights of citizenship irrespective of sex, caste, religion or creed. (John 2000: 3)

This opinion was supported by the prominent and leading women's organisations of the time, for instance the All India Women's Conference, the Women's Indian Association, and the National Council of Women in India. Groups such as the Home Rule League, the Indian National Congress, and the Muslim League also expressed this view. In 1932, a Joint Memorandum on the Status of Indian Women from the all-India women's organisations to the Franchise Committee, set up at the end of the Second Round Table Conference, expressed their demand for universal adult franchise 'irrespective of any property or literacy qualification, with no expedients such as nomination or reservation of seats'. The women's organisations also endorsed the declaration of the Fundamental Rights to Citizenship in India made by the Karachi session of the Indian National Congress in 1931, which called for equality before the law, universal adult franchise, and women's right to vote, and represent and hold public office, irrespective of religion, caste, creed or sex (*Indian Journal of Gender Studies* 1999: 129–33). However, in the face of opposition from the British, the women's organisations agreed to a compromise, which restricted the right to vote for women in urban areas. The assumption was that urban women would be in a better position to represent the women of India. However, the opposition to reservation remained, and merit was to be the only criterion.

It is important, though, to note that the opposition to the idea of reservation was not restricted to the question of women alone. The All India Women's Conference (AIWC) in their resolution expressed their opposition to the British 'Communal Award' of 1932, which sought to provide separate electorates and reserved seats for Muslims, Christians, Sikhs, Anglo-Indians, and the depressed classes. The rationale behind such opposition was that divisions along the lines of religion, caste and sect would weaken the struggle against colonial rule, and that legislatures should be filled by those who would rise above personal or communal considerations and think of the country's best interests. There were dissenting voices: Begum Sakina Mayuzada felt that desiring the good of one's community need not be at the cost of inflicting harm on others; and K.B. Firozuddin felt the comparative educational backwardness of Muslim women might put them at a disadvantage in joint electorates. Furthermore, a separate resolution calling for the abolition of untouchability was adopted (John 2000: 4).

What is relevant to our present discussion on the issue of women's reservation is that a certain definition of nationalism came to prevail. This claimed to be above the sectarian pulls of caste and religious community, and was quite different from what had been prevalent till the early twentieth century, where in fact discrete religious communities were not seen as inconsistent with an overarching national identity. The very word 'communalism' acquired a religious connotation and became synonymous with the British policy of divide and rule as of the 1920s. Inclusive nationalism, which gave legitimate space to different identities, led to a homogenising nationalism where identities based on caste, creed, and so on were seen as obstacles to the development of an Indian nationalist identity. Women's organisations, too, shared such perceptions (ibid.: 5).

The question of women's reservation came up once again in the Committee on the Status of Women in India (CSWI) in 1975. The report of the CSWI noted that in spite of equal rights and the universal adult suffrage guaranteed by the Indian Constitution, women's presence in state and national legislatures had been steadily declining over the past 25 years. While the Committee recorded arguments in favour of reservations, which were made mainly by women activists, women legislators were of the opinion that it would be a retrogressive step and would contradict the principle of equality guaranteed in the Constitution. The dominant opinion in the CSWI (1975) was against reservations, though there were two notes of dissent. However, there was agreement on the need for reservation for women in local bodies, so as to ensure the interests of rural and poor women. The 73rd and 74th Constitutional Amendments, which provide for one-third reservation of seats for women in all structures of local self-government, finally came into effect in 1994.

It would be useful at this point to dwell on the two notes of dissent in the CSWI, since they raise very fundamental questions about the manner in which political representation has functioned. Sarkar and Mazumdar note with refreshing candor that as members of the pre-independence generation, they had never been supporters of special representation, and in academic discussions had criticised the system of reservations for Scheduled Castes and Scheduled Tribes '. . . as a legacy of the colonial period which institutionalized the backwardness of certain sections of our population' (1999: 134). However, the reality has forced them to look afresh at the question. The main reasons for disagreeing with the majority opinion within the CSWI also arose out of and are consistent with the findings of the Committee. That is, despite progressive legal changes, the actual situation of the mass of Indian women has not changed significantly, and the continuing under-representation of women prevents them from participating in the decision-making process of the country. Sarkar and Mazumdar also draw attention to the narrow social base of women legislators, representing mainly the upper strata of society. The concluding paragraphs of their dissenting note merit quoting:

> When one applies the principle of democracy to a society characterised by tremendous inequalities, such special protections are only spearheads to pierce through the barriers of inequality. An unattainable goal is as meaningless as a right that cannot be exercised. Equality of opportunities cannot be achieved in the face of tremendous disabilities and obstacles which the social system imposes on all those sections whom traditional India treated as second or even third class citizens. Our investigations have proved that the application of the theoretical principle of equality in the context of unequal situations only intensifies inequalities, because equality in such situations merely means privileges for those who have them already and not for those who need them. (Sarkar and Mazumdar 136–37)

The 81st Constitutional Amendment Bill meant to provide one-third reservation of seats to women in state and central legislative bodies, and the current discussions and social turmoil surrounding it mirror the contradictions inherent in Indian society. These also reflect the contention over the access to power and resources between the traditionally deprived and excluded, and the socially and politically dominant. The Women's Reservation Bill once again throws up questions that are somewhat analogous to those raised by the UCC, insofar as it brings up the question of certain kinds of identity, specifically of caste and religion, and their articulation in the public realm, including the field of politics. These questions relate to the hierarchy of Indian society and the manner in which it operates in the field of politics and political representation. It also raises the question of the representativeness of the women's movement.

The near unanimous support for the Bill amongst the national-level women's organisations is premised on a certain understanding of the patriarchal forms of oppression and exclusion characteristic of Indian society, and the undeniable reality of the declining participation of women in political life, specifically in the legislatures. Needless to say, the suppression and exclusion of women has historically been extremely important in maintaining a Brahmianical and caste-dominated social order. Thus, affirmative action for women will undoubtedly contribute towards the democratisation of society.

The protagonists of the Bill highlight the traditionally sanctioned exclusion of women from the public sphere as crucial. An emphasis on the dimension of gender oppression at the expense of other types of domination (of caste, ethnicity, class, religion, and so on) glosses over the complex and intricate ways in which gender is embedded in these categories. Historically, women's suppression has no doubt been very important in maintaining upper-caste exclusiveness and hegemony. Affirmative action for women would certainly play a role in undermining male and upper-caste dominance. Even so, certain recent developments suggest the need for addressing gender oppression in more subtle and nuanced ways, if access to power and resources for all categories of women is to be ensured.

The continued dominance of the upper castes in education, administration and structures of government is a reality that cannot be glossed over. On the one hand this is evident in the increasing presence and visibility of women from upper castes and middle classes, and on the other, in the fact that women (and men) from the subaltern communities and classes have largely been victims of 'development'. Besides, the neo-liberal paradigm, combined with the ideology of right-wing majority Hindutva nationalism, has only exacerbated the caste, class, religious, ethnic, regional and gender divides. Thus, *women being only more and not less embedded in their groups* has led to much greater differentiation among women, which in turn has also meant a more diverse and varied political articulation.

The opponents of the present Women's Reservation Bill point out that it is likely to exclude women from the OBCs and the minorities. Almost all the political parties, except the Communist Party of India and the Communist Party of India (Marxist), are deeply divided on this issue. The ruling Bharatiya Janata Party's leadership is in favour of the Bill in its present form, even though one of its women MPs did express reservations about it on the grounds that OBC women were likely to be excluded. Needless to say, there is also strong resistance on the part of a considerable number of political leaders to what are viewed as 'encroachments' into what has traditionally been a male preserve. The media has trivialised the debate by often characterising it as a battle between 'feminists' and 'casteists'. The crux of the issue is whether the generalised oppression and exclusion of women, characteristic of Indian society, is indeed a sufficient basis for transcending the divisions of caste, religion and ethnicity, and if the women's movement is representative enough to effect a unity. Unfortunately, so far statements by the leaders of women's organisations that support the Bill have not revealed enough awareness about the complexity of the problem, nor even enough critical reflection about the variegated nature of gender relations among the OBCs and the minority communities. They have in fact tended to point to the stronger patriarchal norms prevalent among the OBCs and the Muslims, as the attitudes of the men of these communities are seen as particularly 'backward' and 'male chauvinism'. Thus, the women's organisations have focused on the family as the principal site of patriarchal control and oppression, ignoring its wider social context (John 1999: 145–49). The fact is that the women and men of these groups face the consequences of being at the lower rungs of a social hierarchy still principally dominated by upper castes. Thus, the reality and prospects of marginalisation as groups must surely affect the texture of gender relations.

Evidently there is an ongoing crisscrossing of movement of various oppressed sections in Indian society. Often, these movements pull in different and even opposite directions, thus defeating the democratisation process in the short run. It is a challenging task, both for the leaders of these movements and social analysts, to unravel the myriad oppressions that characterise Indian society. They need to draw out the major strands that will strengthen and contribute to the overall process of democratisation of society, towards which the levers of change will have to be moved. In a plural society like India, the political system has to ensure a modicum of equality between all groups and communities if history's longest oppression is to be seriously tackled. This would imply that the struggle for gender justice and equality has to be woven into the struggle for emancipation of each of the oppressed groups and communities.

Conclusion

The purpose of discussing the above issues is to highlight the complexity of the women's question in the contemporary period of India's political history. Critical issues relate to the complex inter-relationship between it and other social and political questions. These relate to the complicated nature of identities; the understanding of patriarchy and its intermeshing with a complex and highly segmented social structure; the impact of the neo-liberal paradigm; and finally and importantly, the crucial question of democracy itself.

It would seem that there is a subterranean assumption about the universality of women's identity, as though gender identity lies outside others and, in a sense, is prior to and more privileged than those of caste, religion, ethnicity, and so on. In discussing the hidden structuring of the 'humanist subject', Susie Tharu refers to the inability on the part of Marxists and feminists to '. . . critically confront inequalities of caste or community implicit in that subject or its worlds' (1996: 235). Furthermore, the imaging of the citizen-subject saw the operation of gender, caste, community, and even class only in the realm of the social, and marked these as incidental attributes of a human self. This also made invisible the historical and socio-cultural structuring of the subject of politics (ibid.: 236). Such assumptions about the universality of women's identity would often lead to a stigmatising of different and diverse articulations of Dalit, Muslim, or tribal women's identity, which were not consonant with mainstream feminism. This leads us to the complicated nature of community identity, the relationship between communities and the individual, and, of course, the nature of the relationship between the state and communities.

It is now an accepted fact that community identities are not static, and that they have been historically constituted. The fact that the colonial state played an important role in congealing identities should not lead us to a position where the colonial state becomes the principal source of identity formation, or leads us to believe that the state conjured up identities where none existed. The major contours of identity formation during the colonial period fell into shape in the second decade of the twentieth century with the move towards some form of representative government and politics. However, having said this, we are still left with the reality of caste, religious, tribal, ethnic regional, linguistic and gender identities in post-colonial Indian politics. The important point in our minds is to be able to unravel the workings of these, their intermeshing with the power structure, and the political articulation of identities, either in favour of enhancing democratisation or in attempts to shore up the status quo. This would, willy-nilly, involve differentiating between subaltern/subordinated identities and dominant ones, assessing the impact of changes that have occurred between dominant and subaltern groups, and analysing the nature of the shift from 'primordial' to more 'universalist' identities. The question of gender identity would have to be situated in this matrix.

Attempts to analyse 'multiple patriarchies' often fail to make a distinction between dominant and subaltern patriarchies, and the fact that the one most often determines and structures gender relations in the others. Besides, it would be erroneous to assume that the principal site of patriarchal oppression is the family. The nature of the state, its symbiotic relationship with the dominant groups, the manner in which its machinery functions in general, and the biases that characterise its day-to-day operations would be extremely important in determining the very parameters of the operation of that patriarchy. This would be significant among both dominant and subordinated groups. The very articulation of gender identity would vary; thus the way a Muslim woman would perceive her identity in a situation where the identity of her community is endangered would perhaps be taken to mean that the articulation of her gender identity is more ambivalent. Tharu has described the poignancy of a Muslim woman's situation, '. . . the Muslim woman is caught in zero-zero game. Either way she loses. She cannot really be woman any more than she can be Indian. As woman and Indian, she cannot really be Muslim' (1996: 252). Such a differentiated impact would also lead to varied notions of gender justice, which would even challenge accepted, dominant and mainstream notions. Indeed, the roots of oppression of a Dalit woman, a Muslim woman, a tribal woman, and an upper-caste woman would be very different, and the strategies for tackling this would also vary. A democratic movement would have to therefore allow space for plural feminisms.

What is indeed significant and disturbing today is the discourse on gender that is being promoted by international agencies in a totally de-contextualised manner. Gender is no longer about relations between men and women, nor is it about its relations to other inequities of class, caste, power and so on. It is also not accidental that gender discourse, gender empowerment and gender sensitivity are being used as devices to conceal growing inequities, both internationally and nationally. The World Bank's Report, *Gender and Poverty in India* (1991), is a good example of how the very meanings of terms such as development, the economy, empowerment, and so on have been transformed in the regime of the market. Thus, women in the informal sector who struggle under the most onerous conditions are seen as the most efficient managers of scarce resources and not as victims of exploitation. The implications of such a perspective are ominous for the vast majority of Indians. As John observes: 'Under the present dispensation (where the new economic policy is by no means at cross-purposes with an upper-caste communal culture), poor women are being feted as "good" subjects who make "sound economic sense", whereas their unruly men, seen as prone to violence, especially if they be Dalits or Muslims, become the "bad" subjects of modernity and its rationality, undeserving even of the rights of citizenship.' (1996: 3076).

The discourse of universalism tends to deflect attention from the particularistic manifestations of inequity. It is therefore important for the women's movement, now more than ever, to devise strategies that will deal skillfully and democratically with subaltern identities in the struggle for a more equitable social order. And in the course of the social movement, a more genuine universalism should emerge.

Acknowledgements

I would like to thank Mary John, Smita Tewari Jassal and Leela Kasturi from the Centre for Women's Development Studies, New Delhi, for their comments and suggestions.

Notes

1. This chapter was previously presented at a workshop organised by Lokayan in collaboration with the Society for International Development, Rome, in March 1999. The proceedings of the workshop are to be published in a forthcoming volume entitled 'In Search of Democratic Space', edited by Smitu Kothari and published by Lokayan and Rainbow Publishers, Delhi.
2. The Indian Constitution recognises and sanctions various systems of Personal Laws based on religion and customary practices. These deal with issues of inheritance, rights to property, marriage, divorce, maintenance and guardianship of minors, adoption, and so on. Such constitutional sanction to these various personal and customary laws arose out of the need to acknowledge and give recognition to the diversity and plurality of Indian society. However, the Directive Principles of State Policy in the Constitution also state that the state should endeavour to bring about a Uniform Civil Code (UCC) to govern all citizens, regardless of religion, caste and creed. But the question of the UCC has always been a somewhat knotty issue, since it invariably arouses fears about the identity and culture of minority groups who may be swamped in the name of a common code, which would be a majority Hindu code. The mainstream women's movement in India since the 1980s has raised the issue of the UCC as one that needs to be addressed if the problems of women of the minority groups are to be tackled.
3. The Mandal Commission was set up by the Government of India to look into the question of the social and educational backwardness of a whole series of groups called the Other Backward Classes (OBC). According to the Commission, these groups roughly constitute 52 per cent of Indian society, for whom it recommended 27 per cent reservation or quotas in central government jobs and in educational institutions. At the level of the different states, some of the state governments had already instituted some quotas for these groups, enabling them to overcome their marginalisation and exclusion in education and government employment. The Indian Constitution also provides for reservation in jobs, education, in the legislature, and in Parliament for the Scheduled Castes and Scheduled Tribes (as defined in the schedules of the Constitution), to overcome historically and socially-based disadvantages. The Scheduled Castes and Scheduled Tribes constitute approximately a quarter of Indian society.
4. The Naxalbari uprising was a revolutionary armed uprising of tribals and marginalised peasants led by the Communist Party of India (Marxist-Leninist) in the late 1960s. The main slogan of the movement was land and political power. It began in the eastern state of Bengal and soon spread to other eastern and southern states. Though the movement was brutally crushed, it left its mark on Indian society and politics and continues to operate, although its methods have changed.
5. Ayodhya is a town in the northern state of Uttar Pradesh where, according to Hindu mythology, Lord Rama was born. This was also the location of the Babri Masjid, a mosque constructed by the Moghul emperor Babur in the sixteenth century. Hindu chauvinist forces carried out a campaign to have a temple constructed for Lord Rama on the very spot where the mosque stood. The mosque was finally destroyed by Hindu chauvinist forces on 6 December 1992. This event has been considered a watershed in the life of post-independent India, since it dealt a serious blow to the secular and democratic character of the Indian republic. Besides, the destruction of the mosque was soon followed by the coming to power of Hindu right-wing forces at the national level.
6. Shah Bano was a Muslim woman who went to the Supreme Court of India in 1985, demanding that her husband pay her maintenance after divorce. While the Court passed a judgement giving her maintenance under the civil law of the land, the obiter dicta, calling for a uniform civil code, set off waves of protest amongst the Muslims, who stated that their rights to their personal law were under threat.

7. While there have not been many studies on the social composition of the middle classes in India, particularly in recent times, the dominance of the upper castes in administration, education and the upper echelons of the government can nonetheless be inferred. In fact, notwithstanding reservation in education and for jobs for SCs and STs, the Report of the Commissioner for Scheduled Castes and Scheduled Tribes over several years notes the backlog when it comes to fulfilling the quotas assigned for these groups in education and administration. Even now, most Class III and Class IV posts in the government are filled largely by people from the Scheduled Castes and Tribes, while their representation in the Class I and II posts is very limited. Studies by Santosh Goyal (1992a, 1992b) on the social background of the Indian Administrative Service (IAS) officers and top corporate executives in the private and public sectors reveal the dominance of upper castes in these spheres. It has thus been pointed out that the grand narrative of national development has nurtured an elite that is overwhelmingly Hindu, upper-caste, male, and Brahmin.

8. The Scheduled Castes and Scheduled Tribes comprise the lowest rungs of the Indian social hierarchy, and have been defined as such in the Constitution. They are entitled to special rights and privileges, particularly in the field of education, employment, and political representation, in order to enable them to overcome this historically rooted exclusion and deprivation. The Other Backward Classes, who are mainly agriculturists, artisans and occupied mainly in manual labour, constitute some middle rungs of Indian society, and have wrested some privileges of reservation or quotas in jobs in the state and national governments, and in educational institutions.

References

Agnihotri, Indu and Vina Mazumdar. 1995. 'Changing Terms of Political Discourse: Women's Movement in India, 1970s–1990s', *Economic and Political Weekly*, XXX (29).

Ahmad, Imtiaz. 1995. 'Personal Laws: Promoting Reform From Within', *Economic and Political Weekly*, XXX (45).

Anveshi Law Committee. 1997. 'Is Gender Justice Only a Legal Issue? Political Stakes in the UCC Debate', *Economic and Political Weekly*, XXXII (9–10).

Balagopal, K. 1990. 'This Anti-Mandal Mania', *Economic and Political Weekly*, XXV (40).

Communist Party of India (Marxist-Leninist). 1986/1995. *For a New Democracy*, Provisional Central Committee, February 1986 and January–July 1995. Calcutta: CPI (M–L).

Government of India, Department of Social Welfare. 1974. *Towards Equality, Report of the Committee of the Status of Indian Women*. New Delhi: Government of India.

Goyal, Santosh. 1992a. 'Social Background of Officers of the Indian Administrative Service', Appendix II, in Francine Frankel and M.S.A. Rao (eds), *Dominance and State Power in Modern India: Decline of a Social Order*, Vol. 1. Delhi: Oxford University Press.

———. 1992b. 'Social Background of Officers of Top Corporate Officials in the Private and Public Sectors', Appendix IV, in Francine Frankel and M.S.A. Rao (eds), *Dominance and State Power in Modern India: Decline of a Social Order*, Vol. 2. Delhi: Oxford University Press.

Indian Journal of Gender Studies. 1999. Journal of the Centre for Women's Studies, New Delhi, Vol. 6. No.1, January–June.

John, Mary. 1996. 'Gender and Development in India, 1970s–1990s', *Economic and Political Weekly*, XXXI (47).

———. 1999. 'Democracy, Patriarchies and Reservations for Women', *Indian Journal of Gender Studies*, 6 (1).

———. 2000. 'Reservation Policies and the Women's Movement', Paper presented at the Conference of the Indian Association for Women's Studies, Hyderabad.

Karat, Brinda. 1995. 'Uniformity vs. Equality: The Concept of Uniform Civil Code', *Frontline*, 12 (13).

Menon, N. 1998. 'Women and Citizenship', in P. Chatterjee (ed.), *Wages of Freedom*. Delhi: Oxford University Press.

Niranjana, T. 1998. 'Issues in Cultural Politics', in S. Tharu (ed.), *Subject to Change: Teaching Literature* in the *Nineties*. New Delhi: Orient Longman.

Raman, Vasanthi. 1999. 'The Women's Reservation Bill and Democratisation of Indian Society: An Alternate Perspective', *Economic and Political Weekly*, XXXIV (50).

Sarkar, Lotika and Vina Mazumdar. 1999. 'Note of Dissent', *Indian Journal of Gender Studies*, 6 (1).

Tharu, S. 1996. 'Towards A Contemporary Theory of Gender', in S. Amin and D. Chakrabarty (eds), *Subaltern Studies*, Vol. IX. Delhi: Oxford University Press.

The World Bank. 1991. *Gender and Poverty in India*. Washington: World Bank.

Working Group On Women's Rights. 1996. 'Reversing the Option, Civil Codes and Personal Laws', *Economic and Political Weekly*, XXXI (20).

About the Editor and Contributors

Editor

Rehana Ghadially is Professor of Psychology at the Department of Humanities and Social Sciences, Indian Institute of Technology, Mumbai. She is the author of *'Women in Indian Society: A Reader'* (Sage Publications, 1989), and has published more than a dozen papers in national and international journals on women of the Daudi Bohra sect of Indian Muslims. Her current research interest focuses on women, gender, and information and communication technologies. She is the recipient of several international fellowships.

Contributors

Shoba Arun is Senior Lecturer, Department of Sociology, Manchester Metropolitan University. Her research interests are in globalisation, gender, information and communication technologies, poverty studies and employment. She is currently engaged in a project on *Developing ICT-based Enterprises for Poor Women*, funded by the Department of International Development, UK, and the University of Manchester.

Sikata Banarjee is Associate Professor, Women's Studies, University of Victoria, Canada. She works primarily in the areas of gender, nationalism and religion, with a particular focus on Hindu nationalism in India. She is the author of *Warriors in Politics: Hinduism, Violence and the Shiv Sena in India* (2000), and *'Make Me a Man!' Masculinity, Hinduism, and Nationalism in India* (2005). She has published several articles in international journals.

Rina Bhattacharya is research co-ordinator, Institute of Social Studies Trust, New Delhi. Her research interests focus on poverty, gender and development issues.

Centre for Advocacy and Research (CFAR), a registered public trust, is committed to public interest research, capacity building, and strengthening public and policy advocacy. CFAR defines *public* as 'all sections of society marginalised and discriminated against', which includes people living with and affected by disability, women and men living with HIV/AIDS, and other circumstantial challenges. CFAR's work is shaped by the vision of constant strife to make visible the voices and experiences of the less privileged.

Mallika Das is Professor of Marketing, Department of Business Administration and Tourism and Hospitality Management, Mount Saint Vincent University, Halifax, Nova Scotia, Canada. Her research focuses on gender and cross-cultural issues in marketing.

Shamita Das Dasgupta is Clinical Adjunct Assistant Professor of Law at the New York University Law School. Her specialisation includes ethnicity, gender, immigration and violence against women. She has published several books including translations, and is completing a book titled *Body Evidence: Violence Against South Asian Women in America*. She is co-founder of *Manavi* Inc., an organisation in the United States that focuses on violence against women in the South Asian community.

Steve Derné is Professor of Sociology at the State University of New York (SUNY) at Geneseo. In 2001, he replicated a study he conducted a decade earlier to examine the effects of globalisation in India. As a Rockefeller fellow at the University of Hawaii in 2002, he completed a draft of a book that reports this research, tentatively titled *Globalization on the Ground: Culture, Class and Gender in India, 1991–2001*.

Gabriele Dietrich is Senior Professor, Centre for Social Analysis, Tamil Nadu Theological Seminary, Madurai. She is a well-known activist in the women's movement, and is a national convener of the National Alliance of Peoples Movements. She has published widely on issues of culture, communalism, feminist critique of development, and people's organisations.

Ashima Goyal is Professor, Indira Gandhi Institute of Development Research, Mumbai. Her research interests are in institutional macroeconomics, international finance, development and gender. She is the author of numerous international and national publications, and a book on *Developing Economy Macroeconomics*. She is the recipient of national and international research awards, and is also active in the Indian policy debate.

Anikar Haseloff is Researcher, University of Augsburg, Germany. After completing a Master's degree in Media and Communication, he worked for a media company, and is now completing his Ph.D. His main areas of interest and research are ICTs in developing countries, especially the role that public access models can play for marginalised communities.

Richard Heeks is Senior Lecturer in Information Systems and Development at the Institute for Development Policy and Management, University of Manchester. His publications include *India's Software Industry* (1996), *Reinventing Government in the Information Age* (1999), and *Implementing and Managing e-Government* (2006). His research interests are IT industry development, information systems and corruption, informatics in remote regions, and health information systems.

Lisa Jadwin teaches English and Cultural Studies at St. John Fisher College, and is at work on an analysis of the ritual work of detective fiction, titled *Over Her Dead Body*.

Leela Kasturi is Editor, *Indian Journal of Gender Studies*, and has researched in the areas of women and work, and women and political participation.

Rashmi Luthra is Professor in Communication at the University of Michigan. Her research interests include gender and development communication; media and women's movements; feminist pedagogies in communication; and communication and women in the South Asian diaspora. She has published widely in international journals and books.

Veronica Magar is Regional Program Advisor for Asia with CARE. Her work includes strategic planning, programme design, and strengthening the analytical, managerial and technical skills of the staff. In addition to her technical mandate, she supports advocacy initiatives, and the development and implementation of participatory action research methodologies to enhance learning and strengthen communities.

Sharon Morgan is a graduate teaching fellow at the Institute for Development Policy and Management, University of Manchester. She is researching on women in the ICT professions in the Development Informatics Group. She has taught Computer Science at universities in UK and Botswana.

Mary Beth Oliver is Professor, Department of Film/Video and Media Studies, Pennsylvania State University. Her research is on media effects with a focus on viewers' emotional responses, and on media and social cognition. She is currently co-editor of the journal *Media Psychology*.

Rupal Oza is Chair and Advisor, Women's Studies Program, Hunter College, City University of New York (CUNY). She has authored *The Making of Neo-liberal India: Nationalism, Gender, and the Paradoxes of Globalization* (forthcoming). Her current projects include organising construction workers in New York City, tracking the rise of Hindu right-wing movements in India and the United States, and a joint project with Rabab Abdulhadi on India and Palestine.

Vibhuti Patel is Professor and Head, Department of Economics, Shreemati Nathibhai Damodar Thackersey (SNDT) Women's University, Mumbai. She is the author of *Women's Challenges of the New Millennium* (2002). She is a founding member and trustee of *Anusandhan* trust and its institution, the Centre for Enquiry into Health and Allied Themes (CEHAT). She is a trustee of *Vacha*, Women's Research and Action Group (WRAG), and *Satya Vijay Seva Samaj* in Mumbai.

Vasanthi Raman is Senior Fellow and Deputy Director, Centre for Women's Development Studies, Delhi. Her areas of work include gender and communalism, childhood studies, and problems of the transition of marginalised tribes and castes in eastern India. Her current work is on Hindu-Muslim relations in Banaras.

Srividya Ramasubramanian is Assistant Professor, Department of Communication, Texas A&M University. Her research focuses on media representations and their psychological effects on audiences. Her recent projects have examined race and gender stereotypes in Indian and American media contexts.

Sharmila Rege is Professor, Department of Sociology, University of Pune, and has taught at the Women's Studies Centre, University of Pune, for over a decade. She has researched and published on gender and sociology, *Dalit* feminism, and the social history of popular cultural practices in Maharashtra. Her current research interests focus on Ambedkar, and pedagogical issues in *Dalit* cultural studies.

Jane Rudd is former associate professor in Social Work at Saint Joseph College in West Hartford, USA. For the past 20 years her research has focused on violence against women. She has contributed a study on trafficking of women in the Ukraine to *Society in Transition: Social Change in Ukraine* (2003). She is currently completing a study on the response to human trafficking in the United States.

Meenakshi Thapan is Professor, Department of Sociology, Delhi School of Economics, University of Delhi. She is the author of *Life at School. An Ethnographic Study* (1991, 2006), and has edited *Embodiment, Essays on Gender and Identity* (1997), *Anthropological Journeys. Reflections on Fieldwork* (1998), and *Transnational*

Migration and the Politics of Identity (Sage, 2005). She is the Series Editor for a five-volume series publication on *Women and Migration in Asia* (Sage Publications), and is on the editorial board of *Body and Society*. She has also published research papers and articles in professional journals in India and abroad.

Farida Umrani is a doctoral student in Psychology at the Department of Humanities and Social Sciences, Indian Institute of Technology, Mumbai. Her research interest focuses on empowering Muslim youth through information and communication technologies.

Vimochana, which means liberation, is a women's activist organisation in Bangalore. It came into existence in 1979, grew in the early 1980s, and its members are among the founders of the autonomous feminist movement in India. The group works closely with local, national and international women's groups and campaigns. Their core issue has been violence in Indian society with special focus on violence against women. *Vimochana* has several projects, *Streelekha*—a feminist bookstore—being one of these.

U. Vindhya is Associate Professor at the Department of Psychology, and Head of the Centre of Women's Studies at Andhra University, Visakhapatnam. Her research interests focus on mental health of women, domestic violence, and psychology of women's radical political activism. She has published widely in national and international journals, and has been involved in the human rights women's movement.

Index